FORENSIC INVESTIGATION

LEGISLATIVE PRINCIPLES AND INVESTIGATIVE PRACTICE

FORENSIC INVESTIGATION

LEGISLATIVE PRINCIPLES AND INVESTIGATIVE PRACTICE

RUDOLPH ZINN & SETLHOMAMARU DINTWE (Editors)

Bernadine C Benson
Trevor Budram
Antony K Cooper
Juanida Horne
Gideon Jones
Jason Jordaan
Gérard N Labuschagne
Hendrik T Lochner
Matsidinkane Solomon Manamela
Rakgetse John Mokwena
Yoginderan S Naidoo
Joe H Smith
Peter MU Schmitz
Marcel van der Watt
Johan van Graan
Teresa van Niekerk

First published 2015

ISBN: 978 0 70218 647 9

Cover design by: Drag and Drop

Project Coordinator: Deidre du Preez

Editor: Marlene Rose

Picture Researcher: Deidre Mvula

Proofreader: Sarah Johnston

Illustrator: Louwra Marais

Typesetting by: Nicole de Swardt – Fly Creative

Printed and bound by:

To our families and to those who use investigative science and practice daily in their quest for justice.

ABOUT THE CONTRIBUTORS

Bernadine C Benson
BTech: Policing (*cum laude*) (PT); MTech: Policing (*cum laude*) (TUT); DLitt et Phil: Police Science (Unisa)

Bernadine is a senior lecturer in Forensic Investigation at the Department of Police Practice at Unisa. She joined Unisa in 2007 after a career of 19 years with the South African Police Service. While employed within the SAPS Bernadine presented papers at several national and international conferences and symposia. She has presented and published locally on police corruption, crimes against cultural property and has also co-published on the handling of evidence in child rape cases.

She completed her DLitt et Phil in Police Science in 2013, with crimes against cultural heritage in South Africa as her specialist topic. She is the subeditor of the *POLSA Journal* as well as the editor-in-chief of the *South African Museums Association Bulletin (SAMAB)*. Bernadine's research interests include police corruption, integrity testing, art crime, fakes and forgeries of art, looting of archaeological sites and social media and its impact on crime.

Trevor Budhram
MTech: Forensic Investigation (Unisa)

Trevor was employed in the South African Police Service for a period of 11 years, the majority of which was spent investigating white-collar crime. Upon his resignation he joined the Special Investigating Unit (SIU) as a Forensic Investigator, where he was responsible for the investigation of corruption, fraud and maladministration. After resigning from the SIU Trevor joined retail giant Edcon, where he worked in the forensics department. He later moved to the telecommunications industry and joined iBurst, where he is the head of the forensic department.

Antony K Cooper
BSc: Information Processing (Computer Science and Cost & Management Accounting) (Rhodes); BSc Hons: Computer Science (Rhodes); MSc: Computer Science (cum laude) (UP)

Antony is a principal researcher at CSIR Built Environment in Pretoria, specialising in standards and geographical information science (GISc) theory and applications. His recent activities cover spatial data infrastructures (SDIs), crime mapping and analysis, bloodstain pattern analysis, logistics, formal concept analysis (FCA), metadata, classification, addresses, ethics, policies and programme management.

He is convenor of Working Group 7 of ISO/TC 211, *Geographic information/ Geomatics*, and chairs the Commission on Geoinformation Infrastructures and Standards of the International Cartographic Association (ICA). Antony is a registered Professional GISc Practitioner (PGP) and is currently busy with a PhD on volunteered geographical information (VGI) and SDIs.

Setlhomamaru Dintwe

B Criminal Justice (North West University); BTech: Policing (TSA [Unisa]); MTech: Forensic Investigation (Unisa); DLitt et Phil: Police Science (Unisa)

Setlhomamaru is a senior lecturer in Forensic Investigation at the Department of Police Practice at Unisa. He was a detective in the South African Police Service, stationed at Boitekong Detective Branch in Rustenburg. After being promoted to Principal Investigator, he was transferred to the Anti-Corruption Command of the Independent Complaints Directorate (ICD). He later headed the Investigation Component of ICD in Mpumalanga. In 2006 Setlhomamaru received an award from the Policing Association of Southern Africa (POLSA) for being the best student in policing matters. He also completed a certificate course in organised crime in the former Yugoslavian Republic of Macedonia.

Setlhomamaru is an accredited assessor, moderator and a certified designer and developer of learning programmes. He is a departmental representative to the International Police Executive Symposium based in the USA and has presented papers at local and international conferences. His publications and research interests include skills development, police and civilian oversight, forensic methods and techniques and monitoring in the criminal justice system.

Juanida Horne

ND: Policing (TSA [Unisa]); M-Tech: Forensic Investigations (Unisa), DLitt et Phil

Juanida is a senior lecturer in Forensic Investigation at the Department of Police Practice at Unisa. She was a member of the former South African Air Force Police (now the Military Police Agency) for 17 years. She served as Officer Commander of various police stations, gaining valuable policing experience. By the time she resigned as a Lieutenant Colonel she had a collection of certificates of appreciation and commendations. Her last posting was at SO1 System Management and Second-in-Command of the Northern Military Police Region.

Juanida completed a course in labour relations and another in advanced labour relations management, both at the University of Pretoria. She completed her doctoral studies through Unisa. Her research interests include human trafficking and organised crime.

She serves on the College of Law's Multi-Inter- and Trans-disciplinary (MIT) Research Committee and was awarded Unisa's Developing Researcher Award in 2011. She has presented at local and international conferences and has published on crime information analysis within a public service organisation.

Gideon Jones

Gideon is the CEO of Jonbeck Skills Consultants (JSC), a South African company that provides professional investigation and training services to the private and public sectors. He has been in the law enforcement and investigation environment for the past 30 years. He was a police officer in the South African Police Service for 19 years and attained the rank of Colonel. During his tenure with the SAPS he attended a wide range of courses at institutions such as the FBI, among others. Over the years he received numerous commendations from regional, divisional and national commissioners and government departments.

For the past 14 years Gideon has been a forensic investigator and trainer in the state, corporate and private environments. In 2013 he received the Association of Certified Fraud Examiners (ACFE) award as Trainer of the Year. He is also a member of the Institute of Commercial Forensic Practitioners (ICFP).

Jason Jordaan

BTech: Policing (Unisa); BCom Hons: Information Systems (UCT); BSc: Criminal Justice Computer Science (summa cum laude) (Grantham University, USA); MTech: Forensic Investigation (Unisa); MSc: Computer Science (cum laude) (Rhodes)

Jason is a professional forensic scientist (digital and multimedia evidence) and a specialist in the prevention and investigation of cybercrime. He is the founder of DFIRLABS, an independent digital forensics laboratory, where he is currently the principal forensic scientist. He was previously the head of the Cyber Forensic Laboratory of the Special Investigating Unit of South African. Prior to this he was a detective with the SAPS Commercial Branch. He has 23 years forensic investigation experience. He spent the last 16 years specialising in the field of digital forensic science and cybercrime investigation.

Jason is a Certified Forensic Computer Examiner (CFCE), a Certified Fraud Examiner (CFE), a Professional Member of the Chartered Society of Forensic Sciences (MCSFS), and a Professional Member of the Institute of Information Technology Professionals of South Africa (PMIITPSA).

Jason is also an academic and researcher in the field of digital forensics and is currently an adjunct instructor at the University of Pretoria on the Cybercrime Investigation certificate. He also teaches at Rhodes University. He is an internationally published author in the field of digital forensics and is a regular public speaker on the topics of digital forensics and cybercrime. Jason regularly testifies as an expert witness in South African high and lower courts.

Gérard N Labuschagne
BA: Psychology (UP); BA Hons: Psychology (UP); MA: Clinical Psychology (UP); MA: Criminology (UP); PhD: Psychology (UP)

Gérard is Professor *Extraordinarius* at the Department of Police Practice at Unisa. He has the rank of Brigadier in the South African Police Service and is the section head of the Investigative Psychology Section (IPS) in the Forensic Services Division of the SAPS. He is registered as a clinical psychologist with the Health Professions Council of South Africa and as a criminologist with the Criminological Society of Southern Africa. Gérard is also a trained hostage negotiator and homicide investigator, having attended the Los Angeles Sheriff's Department Homicide and Death Investigation Course.

He is on the editorial board of the *Journal of Investigative Psychology and Offender Profiling* and the *Journal of Threat Assessment and Management*, and a fellow of the International Academy of Investigative Psychology. He is a member of the British Psychological Society and of the International Homicide Investigators Association. He is an adjunct faculty member of the California School of Forensic Studies and also holds an Honorary Associate Professorship in the Division of Forensic Medicine and Pathology at Wits University.

Hendrik T Lochner
ND: Police Administration (DEC); ND: Security Management (TSA [Unisa]); BTech: Policing (TSA [Unisa]); BTech: Security Risk Management (Unisa); MTech: Forensic Investigation (Unisa)

Hennie is a senior lecturer in Forensic Investigation at the Department of Police Practice at Unisa. He was a police official for 30 years where he amassed extensive experience in taxi violence, farm attacks and murders and bank and cash-in-transit robberies. He was the commander of the Serious and Violent Crimes unit in Limpopo Province from 1995 until 2000. At the time of his retirement from the South African Police Service he was responsible for the coordination of intelligence and investigation of cash-in-transit robberies in Gauteng.

Hennie was trained as a detective to investigate serial killings and rape cases. In the course of his career, he received numerous commendations for his detective work and innovations, among others a commendation from Smit J for the excellent detective work which resulted in the conviction of six suspects in three farm murders.

Hennie has registered a trademark known as the 'Lochner principle', which makes use of cellphone mapping to link criminals to crime scenes. He has published widely in the field of crime scene investigation.

Matsidinkane Solomon Manamela

ND: Policing (TSA [Unisa]); MTech: Policing (TUT); BTech: Policing (Pretoria Technikon)

Matsidinkane is a senior lecturer in Forensic Investigation at the Department of Police Practice at Unisa. He was a member of South African Police Force for 16 years, during which he gained valuable policing experience. He worked at a community service centre, at a detective branch and at the Firearm Registration Centre. While working at the Pretoria North Local Criminal Centre as fingerprint expert and photographer, he was recognised as best candidate in the photography and video course.

His last posting was at the SAPS National Head Office Career Management Division where he was responsible for compiling generic competency profiles and performance assessment instruments for various jobs in the SAPS. Matsidinkane has completed courses in fingerprints, photography and video and human resource assessment. His research interests include criminal and forensic investigation and the policing of domestic violence. He is currently registered for a doctorate in Policing at Unisa.

Rakgetse John Mokwena

ND: Police Administration (TSA [Unisa]); BTech: Policing (Unisa); MTech: Forensic Investigation (Unisa)

Rakgetse is a lecturer in Forensic Investigation at the Department of Police Practice at Unisa. He was a member of the South African Police Service from 1990 until 2009, working as a detective, researcher and developer of detective courses. At the Pretoria North Local Criminal Record Centre he specialised as a fingerprint expert and photographer. He was recognised as the best relief commander in 1998 while working in Mamelodi. On being promoted to the rank of Captain at the SAPS National Head Office Training Division he coordinated detective, criminal record centre and forensic science laboratory courses.

Among the short courses Rakgetse developed are the SARPCCO Code of Conduct and Human Rights and the Law Enforcement Executive Development programmes, both of which were held in Botswana. He is a SASSETA registered assessor for Resolving of Crime and Crime Investigation related unit standards and is currently registered for a doctorate in Forensic Investigation at Unisa.

Yoginderan S Naidoo

BTech Degree: Forensic Investigations (Unisa) ND: Policing (TSA [Unisa]); Diploma: Criminal Justice & Forensic Investigations (University of Johannesburg)

Yoginderan is a forensic specialist for First National Bank. He was a member of the South African Police Service for 21 years and attained the rank of Detective

Captain. In addition to basic police training, branch commander training and SWAT training, he also completed training in fraud, street survival, detective work and computer crimes. He also successfully completed specialist training in criminal investigation and technology in China and training in money laundering and anti-terrorism presented by the FBI.

Joe H Smith

MTech: Business Practice

Joe is a Brigadier in the South African Police Service and the section head of Forensic Database Management at the Division Forensic Services of the SAPS. He has more than 27 years' experience in the field of forensic science and quality management and has constructively contributed to setting standards for forensic training, forensic DNA examinations and forensic DNA database management.

Joe was also previously chairman of the Standard Technical Committee for Forensic Science in the South African National Accreditation System (SANAS) and also a member of the South African Qualification Authority (SAQA) Standard Generating Body for forensic qualification. He played an instrumental role in providing a legislative framework for the National Forensic DNA Database of South Africa. At present his primary focus is on ensuring that the Criminal Law (Forensic Procedures) Amendment Act 37 of 2014 is effectively implemented. His duties include, among other things, ensuring that the forensic investigative leads identified by the database are followed up by the detectives.

Peter MU Schmitz

BSc: Education (Rand Afrikaans University); BSc Hons: Geography (Rand Afrikaans University); BSc Hons: Geoinformatics (University of Pretoria); MSc: Geography (cum laude) (University of Durban-Westville); PhD: Geography (University of Johannesburg)

Peter is a registered professional Geographic Information Science practitioner in South Africa and works as principal researcher at CSIR Built Environment in Pretoria. His activities include the fields of geospatial analysis, forensic geography, logistics (specialising in supply chains for the military) and forensic geosciences (looking at cellphone usage when crimes have been committed). He supervises research on the effects of leached explosives on plants and the use of sand grains and chemical properties to link poachers to poaching sites.

Peter has received several awards for his work in geospatial analysis and regularly presents papers at local and international conferences. He is part of the CSIR team that has been doing the election-night forecasting at national and local municipal elections since 1999. He publishes in peer-reviewed journals and is a member of the Royal Society of South Africa.

Marcel van der Watt

Higher Certificate: Business Management (Damelin); ND: Policing (cum laude) (Unisa); BTech: Policing (cum laude) (Unisa); M-Tech: Forensic Investigation (Unisa)

Marcel is a lecturer in Forensic Investigation at the Department of Police Practice at Unisa. He was a member of the South African Police Service for 10 years where he worked at various units including Family Violence, Child Protection and Sexual Offences (FCS) and the Hawks (DPCI). He was an active hostage negotiator and received specialised training in the investigation of psychologically motivated crimes, ie serial rape and murder.

He gained international recognition for his work in counter-human trafficking and has received numerous awards and commendations for the investigation of crime. These include awards from the National Police Commissioner, Rotary International, ADT Security and a nomination as a finalist in the Police Star of the Year competition. For his contribution in the field of counter-human trafficking, Marcel received an unreserved endorsement from E Benjamin Skinner, fellow at the Harvard Kennedy School CARR CENTER for Human Rights Policy (Massachusetts, USA) and author of *A Crime So Monstrous*.

Marcel is a member of the Gauteng Rapid Response Task Team for Human Trafficking and acts as case manager for the National Freedom Network. He is currently enrolled for a doctorate in Police Science at Unisa.

Johan van Graan

ND: Policing (TSA [Unisa]); BTech: Policing (Unisa); MTech: Policing (Unisa); DLitt et Phil: Police Science (Unisa)

Johan is an Associate Professor at the Department of Police Practice at Unisa. He was a member of the South African Police Service for 17 years before joining the ranks of academia in 2011. He resigned from the police as a Warrant Officer with a collection of commendations for his involvement in the covert investigation of various high-profile national and international crime investigations.

He has successfully completed courses in specialised and unconventional methods and techniques in the gathering of covert crime intelligence, among other things. He is also actively involved in community policing.

Johan is the project leader for Unisa's Community Engagement flagship project. The primary aim of this project is to develop an instrument for measuring the vulnerability (risk) of households to crime.

Johan's research interests include the dynamic field of community policing, the prevention and investigation of crime against women and children, police management and intelligence-led policing. He has published locally and internationally in these fields.

Teresa van Niekerk
ND: Police Administration (TSA [Unisa]); BTech: Policing (Unisa)

Teresa is a lecturer in Forensic Investigation at Unisa after joining the Department of Police Practice in 2011. Before joining UNISA she was a part time marker at the Department of Police Practice since 1994. She was a member of the South African Police Service for 21 years and worked in several units, among others Internal Investigation, Family Violence, Child Protection and Sexual Offences (FCS), Area Detectives as well as at detective units at station level. She was the Detective Commander at Brixton SAPS for five years. Her last posting before she resigned as a Lieutenant Colonel was as a group leader and investigator of drug-related cases in the Sophiatown precinct, where she attained great success.

Teresa completed several courses while she was a member of the SAPS. She studied through Technikon SA and Unisa and is currently busy with her Master's degree in Policing at Unisa. Her research interests include crimes against women and children.

Rudolph J Zinn
ND: Police Administration (DEC); National Higher Diploma: Policing (TSA [Unisa]); MTech: Correctional Services Management (TSA [Unisa]); DLitt et Phil: Police Science (Unisa)

Rudolph is currently Professor of Policing and Forensic Investigation at Unisa's College of Law at the School of Criminal Justice. Prior to entering academia, he worked in various capacities in the South African Police Service, at Radio Control Brixton (Flying Squad) and a specialised investigation unit. He also received training in conducting fingerprint classification and analysis. After eight years he resigned with a collection of high court commendations for crime investigation.

Rudolph has undertaken extensive research into violent crime in South Africa, with special emphasis on motor vehicle hijackings, house robberies (home invasions) and community safety networks. He has initiated and organised a series of world conferences on Modern Criminal Investigation, Organised Crime and Human Rights and was co-founder of postgraduate qualifications in Forensic Investigation and Policing. He also served as an adviser in the training of the Scorpions, the Malawian Anti-Corruption Unit and other law enforcement units.

Rudolph is a member of the editorial board of various accredited journals. Over the last 24 years he has published widely on crime investigation.

FOREWORD

In the 30 years that I have been a prosecutor there have been significant changes in our country. Among other things, we have created one of the most advanced constitutions in the world and now live in a democratic, open society. Many of these changes have impacted on the policing and prosecution of criminal cases.

Policing, specifically crime investigation, has become an increasingly multifaceted and technological process. Keeping abreast of these changes is a challenge for investigators and prosecutors alike. A textbook like this is long overdue. It covers aspects from the start of the investigation such as the constitutional underpinning of policing and the characteristics of a good investigator. It highlights the basic concepts of investigation and moves on to more sophisticated specialised services such as medico-legal evidence, DNA and policing in a cyber world.

What is also unique is its inclusion of more recent concepts such as analysing the behaviour of the offender and the choices he or she makes during the crime event. These aspects are dealt with in relation to forensic geography and offender profiling or, as it is more correctly known, Criminal Investigative Analysis. The book takes the reader from crime scene to courtroom, from investigation to prosecution, the nexus of which is essential to successfully combat crime. More importantly, the authors themselves are experts in their respective fields, thus making this book real and applicable to the reader.

Because a case in court is only as good as the investigation that has been conducted by the police, this book is set to play a significant role in ensuring that current and future generations of investigators remain in tune with the challenges and changes in policing and the prosecution of crime.

I often quote my favourite barrister, the fictional Rumpole of the Bailey, who states: 'With all due respect to Your Ladyship, I was thinking that a criminal trial is a very blunt implement for digging out the truth.' I believe that this book will do much to turn this implement into a finely honed blade that can help to dig out the truth more efficiently.

Adv Gerrie Nel

PREFACE

Forensic Investigation: Legislative principles and Investigative practice is a fundamental and deliberate work produced by a collective of experts in the field of forensic investigation. The book is intended to demystify the meaning and practice of forensic investigation and to provide academic guidance in the field.

The main intention of the editors and authors was to position forensic investigation as a comprehensive subject field and a subdiscipline of the social sciences rather than a branch of forensic science as practised in forensic laboratories and during forensic auditing. This book is therefore not about forensic analysis; it is a combination of the natural, social and human sciences and management skills pertaining to the investigation of crimes, incidents and transgressions. As such, it focuses on forensic investigation as undertaken by an investigating officer or detective. Forensic investigation in this sense is broadly defined as an in-depth, meticulous search for the truth through the use of specialised skills and expert knowledge and the application of scientific investigation methods and techniques, with the aim to lawfully discover, collect, prepare, identify and present evidence in a court of law or to a disciplinary council, instructing client or company.

The structure of the book coincides with the consecutive phases followed during an investigation. It ranges from the first phase, when a crime, incident or transgression is suspected to have happened or reported, to the last, when the case is concluded or resolved in a criminal or civil court or a quasi-judicial forum. The book is structured chronologically to include the preliminary phase, the further investigation phase, the judicial phase and the rounding-off phase of an investigation. It also includes other specialised aspects of forensic investigation, namely:

- medico-legal evidence
- serological evidence
- imprint evidence and related specialities
- criminal investigative analysis, which includes profiling, forensic geography, digital forensics and cyber forensics.

In the final chapter recent developments in forensic technology are discussed.

One of the primary aims with *Forensic Investigation: Legislative principles and Investigative practice* has been to address the knowledge deficiencies hampering the forensic investigation milieu in South Africa. The editors' and authors' wide experience – based on their own postgraduate studies; practical experience in forensic investigation as practitioners; and teaching and supervising research in forensic investigation – has led them to recognise the inadequacies of forensic investigation material as understood and practised in South Africa and Africa.

In addition, the Africanisation agenda of knowledge, especially in higher education in South Africa, has been the primary motivation for contextualising forensic investigation in South Africa. While the universality of science in practices such as dactyloscopy, deoxyribonucleic acid (DNA) analysis and forensic geography, among others, compelled the editors and authors to retain existing concepts unchanged, the accompanying processes of searching for the truth to resolve disputes remain contingent to the prescripts, regulations and legislation of the South African jurisdiction. Although it was envisaged that the book should be suitable for world-wide use, South African experiences are explicitly shared because we believe much can be learnt from how forensic investigation is applied in the South African context.

The editors and authors of *Forensic Investigation: Legislative principles and Investigative practice* are sincerely grateful to a multitude of stakeholders without whom this book would not have been possible. We thank all our colleagues at the University of South Africa (Unisa) and from the forensic investigation milieu in general, the management of the Unisa, the South African Police Service (SAPS), the statutory investigative agencies, the Council for Scientific and Industrial Research (CSIR), Juta Law Publishers and many other participants.

It is our belief and hope that this book will contribute towards increasing knowledge, which empowers and forms the premise of progress.

'Knowledge is power. Information is liberating. Education is the premise of progress, in every society, in every family.' – **Kofi Annan: *Where On Earth Are We Going***

Editors
June 2015

TABLE OF CASES

TABLE OF STATUTES

NATIONAL LEGISLATION

Year	No	Title	Page
1997	75	Basic Conditions of Employment Act	9–10
1965	25	Civil Proceedings Evidence Act	
		s 22	234
1996		Constitution of the Republic of South Africa	2, 10–11, 14, 179, 204, 259
		Chapter 2: Bill of Rights	166, 178, 254, 412
		s 1	14
		s 6(1)	236
		s 9	412
		s 12(1)	259
		s 12(2)*(b)*	412
		s 10	412
		s 14	410, 412
		s 23(1)	10
		s 28	413
		s 35	232, 413
		s 35(1)	176, 203
		s 35(1)*(f)*	259
		s 35(2)	176, 203
		s 35(3)	176
		s 35(5)	178
		s 36	178, 413–414, 417
		s 165	253
		s 199	15
		s 205	15
		s 205(3)	15
2010	6	Criminal Law (Forensic Procedures) Amendment Act	
		s 37(1)*(c)*	410
2013	37	Criminal Law (Forensic Procedures) Amendment Act	410–411, 414–415, 418
		s 5N(2)	416

Year	No	Title	Page
		s 15H–M	415
		s 15S	416
		s 15V	416
		s 36D(1)	410–411
		s 36D(2)	411
2007	38	Criminal Law (Sentencing) Amendment Act	253
1977	51	Criminal Procedure Act	10–11, 18–19, 23, 174, 258–259, 410–411, 437, 441
		Schedule 1	264
		Schedule 2	260
		Schedule 5	264
		Schedule 6	261, 264
		Schedule 7	260
		s 22	221
		s 36E(2)	411
		s 37	243
		s 37(2)*(a)*	411
		s 37(3)*(b)*	411
		s 39	202
		s 40	203
		s 42	203
		s 42(1)*(c)*	203
		s 42(2)–(3)	203
		s 47	204
		s 50(1)*(b)*	259
		s 50(6)*(c)–(d)*	261
		s 58	259
		s 59	260
		s 59A	260
		s 60	259, 261
		s 60(4)	262
		s 60(4)*(a)–(e)*	262
		s 60(5)–(10)	262
		s 189	223–224
		s 205	46, 222–223, 231, 328, 429
		s 212	231, 234, 240, 252, 454–457

FOREIGN LEGISLATION

Canada

CONVENTIONS AND TREATIES

REGULATIONS

RULES

CONTENTS

ACRONYMS AND ABBREVIATIONS

ACFE	Association of Certified Fraud Examiners
AFIS	Automated Fingerprint Identification System
aGPS	assisted-GPS
BBM	BlackBerry Messenger
BMC	Border Movement Control System
CAS	Crime Administration System
CBD	Central business district
CCD	Charged-coupled device
CCMA	Commission for Conciliation, Mediation and Arbitration
CCTV	Closed-circuit television
CD	Compact disc
CF	Call forward
CGT algorithm	Criminal Geographic Targeting algorithm
CIA	Criminal Investigative Analysis
CODIS	Combined DNA Index System
CPA	Criminal Procedure Act 51 of 1977
CPI	Combined Paternity Index
CRC	Criminal Record Centre
CSM	Crime scene manager
DEM	Digital elevation model
DNA	Deoxyribonucleic acid
DPCI	Directorate for Priority Crime Investigations
DPP	Director of Public Prosecutions
DVD	Digital Video Disk
EMI	Environmental Management Inspectorate
ESDA	Electrostatic Detection Apparatus
FBI	Federal Bureau of Investigation
FBO	Faith-based Organisation
FIC	First information of crime

FSL	Forensic Science Laboratory
GIS	Geographical Information System
GNSS	Global Navigation Satellite System
GOVNET	Government Network System
GPR	Ground-penetrating radar
GPRS	General Packet Radio System
GPS	Global Positioning System
HITS	Homicide Investigation and Tracking System
IBIS	Integrated Ballistic Identification System
ICFP	Institute of Commercial Forensic Practitioners
ICIAF	International Criminal Investigative Analysis Fellowship
IPS	Investigative Psychology Section
IRDA	Infrared Detection Apparatus
LEIU	Law Enforcement Intelligence Unit
MMS	Multimedia messaging service
MOC	Mobile originating call
MOSMS	Mobile originating SMS
MTC	Mobile terminating call
MTSMS	Mobile terminating SMS
NATIS	National Traffic Information System
NGO	Non-government organisation
NPA	National Prosecuting Authority
NPO	Non-profit organisation
NTFS	New Technology File System
NYPD	New York Police Department
OLEA	Office of Law Enforcement Assistance
PAC	Pan Africanist Congress
PC	Personal computer
PCR	Polymerase Chain Reaction
PI	Paternity Index
PIN	Personal identification number
PM	Project manager

POCA	Prevention of Organised Crime Act 121 of 1998
pr test	Primer residue test
PSD	Particle size distribution
PSIRA	Private Security Industry Regulatory Authority
RICA	Regulation of Interception of Communications and Provision of Communication-related Information Act 70 of 2002
SABRIC	South African Banking Risk and Information Centre
SAPS	South African Police Service
SARB	South African Reserve Bank
SARS	South African Revenue Service
SCA	Supreme Court of Appeal
SD	Secure digital (memory card)
SIU	Special Investigations Unit
SMS	Short message service
SOP	Standing operating procedure
STR	Short Tandem Repeat (used in DNA analysis)
SWOT	Strengths, weaknesses, opportunities and threats
Unisa	University of South Africa
ViCLAS	Violent Crime Linkage System
VLCC	Very large crude carrier
VSC	Video spectral comparator
W×5; H principle	Who, what, where, when, why and how
XDS	Expert decision system

FORENSIC INVESTIGATION OF CRIME, IRREGULARITIES AND TRANSGRESSIONS

Chapter 1

B C Benson • G Jones • J S Horne

1.1 INTRODUCTION

The forensic investigation of a crime or an incident involves more than mere investigation. Forensic investigation is first of all a recognised science in its own right. During the course of an investigation the natural sciences may play a pivotal role in solving the crime or incident, for example through DNA analysis, but the human sciences also play a role. The human sciences include the science of policing, which in turn includes the scientific processes followed by an investigator in investigating a crime or an incident, irregularity or transgression. For example, a scientific process is followed to analyse the scene of incident (natural sciences), and then the investigator selects the most effective interviewing technique that suits the personality of the suspect, witness or complainant (human sciences).

To investigate something or someone is an immense responsibility which investigators must undertake to the best of their ability. This demands dedication and a commitment to a road of continuous learning because daily changes occur in the fields of technology, legislation, policy and science. However, the field of investigation is not the only one in which the investigator needs to grow.

The investigation of a crime or an incident necessarily also incorporates aspects and elements from the management discipline. If investigators do not know how to manage themselves, their resources or their time, and if they do not know how to identify a strategy and develop a plan to implement that strategy, they are going to be walking a very rocky road. In the many decades spanning their careers in law enforcement (predominantly in crime investigation), the authors of this chapter have learnt how important it is to plan and have a vision.

1.2 CONTENT OVERVIEW

This first chapter lays the foundation for what the book is about, namely investigation (of crimes, or incidents that are not classified as crimes but rather as transgressions) in the South African context. The authors will discuss issues that are creating confusion and will try to clarify the roles and mandates of the various stakeholders and role-players in an investigation. In the context of society and its rules, various legal options are available to a victim when an incident or crime occurs, namely criminal recourse, civil recourse or restorative justice. Investigation has its foundation in the Constitution of the Republic of South Africa, 1996 and as such should have a clear purpose and objectives.

Utilising empirical research spanning seven years, which was undertaken by students doing the Master's degree in Forensic Investigation at the University of South Africa (Unisa), the authors discuss and clarify the concepts of criminal investigation and forensic investigation in modern-day society with reference to current literature. The investigation process is explained with specific reference to the flow of an investigation, the investigator's task and mandate and the difference between a police and a private investigation. Seven techniques that can be applied in an investigation are mentioned.

The authors examine and contextualise the most crucial role-player in this entire process, the one who is more often than not ignored but is blamed when things go wrong: the investigator. Who is this person? What skills, attitudes and characteristics do they need to be successful at what they do? Why are some investigators successful and others not? The importance of ethics and moral actions on the part of the investigator is highlighted.

Finally, the modern-day investigation cycle and the value of intelligence-led investigation are discussed. The chapter is concluded with a self-evaluation checklist for investigators.

The remainder of the book consists of 11 chapters that cover crucial aspects within the investigative field, namely:

- the principles of investigation (chapter 2)
- medico-legal evidence (chapter 3)
- serological evidence and DNA analysis (chapter 4)
- imprint evidence and other specialities (chapter 5)
- the preliminary investigation phase (chapter 6)
- the further investigation phase (chapter 7)
- the judicial phase of investigation (chapter 8)
- an applied perspective on Criminal Investigative Analysis (chapter 9)
- forensic geography (chapter 10)
- digital forensics and cybercrime (chapter 11)
- developments in forensic technology (chapter 12).

1.3 CONTEXT AND TERMINOLOGY

The high crime rate is a reality and a major problem in South African society. The investigation of crime is part of the answer to this problem. However, within the arena of crime investigation in South Africa there is some confusion, double-talk and jargon which, instead of adding value and clarifying issues, are creating misunderstandings and bewilderment. It is the purpose of this first chapter to demystify and clarify some issues and concepts related to investigation, crime investigation and forensic investigation. For the purposes of this chapter, we will primarily make use of the descriptor 'forensic investigation'. However, we will alert the reader should we at any stage only want to refer to the concept of 'crime investigation' or the more general concept of 'investigation'. 'Investigation' is meant to include 'the investigation of a crime, a transgression or an incident'. When we refer to an 'incident' it may also include a crime or a transgression. However, when reference is made only to a 'crime' then that is what is meant: a crime as defined in law.

When we refer to a 'scene of incident' it is meant to include a crime scene and the scene where the incident (which does not necessarily constitute a criminal act) took place. When we refer to an 'investigator' we mean not only the South African Police Service (SAPS) investigator (detective) but also the statutory and corporate/private investigator as discussed later in this chapter. Police, for the purposes of clarity, implies the 'organised civil force of a state, concerned with the maintenance of law and order', which in the case of South Africa is the SAPS. In relation to this, 'policing' will imply '... the policies, techniques and practice of a police force in keeping order, preventing crime ...' which the SAPS is constitutionally mandated to do.[1]

1.4 SOCIETY AND THE RULES THAT GOVERN SOCIETY

Before one can discuss the principles relating to investigation, one first needs to understand the context and environment within which an investigation is conducted. This environment is the South African society, which is governed by certain rules.

Bearing in mind that while there are many citizens whose conduct does not require 'policing', some elements in society just do not seem able to conform to what is required by law or policy and thus need policing in some or other form. Policing is therefore a direct result of the fact that society is not able to police itself and requires an external mechanism for social control. For this reason the police force is the primary role-player responsible for social control and, as a result, to a greater extent responsible for guiding the conduct and activities of the citizenry than any other government department.[2] Burger[3] argues that the idea that the police alone can prevent crime is basically flawed and an 'impossible mandate'. The same author goes on to write that many people have started to realise in modern times that it is not so much an inability as an impossibility for the police to prevent crime.[4] The police can at most only contribute towards preventing crime by serving as a deterrent against crime through their proactive and reactive actions (law enforcement, crime investigation, the maintenance of order and visible policing).[5]

1 Burger (2007) 27.
2 Lyman (1999) 31, 33.
3 Burger (2007) 41–42.
4 Burger (2007) 42.
5 Burger (2007) 111.

The private security industry has expanded greatly in recent times and currently makes an extensive contribution in the areas of preventing and combating crime (which include investigation). The extent of this industry's growth can be seen in the Private Security Industry Regulatory Authority (PSIRA) annual report as tabled in Parliament in 2011.[6] According to this report, PSIRA at the time had 411 109 registered security officers and 8 828 registered security companies compared to approximately 160 000 police officers in South Africa. Since 2001 the number of registered companies has increased by 61% and the number of registered security officers by 111%.[7]

Additionally, forensic investigators provide the private security industry with the investigation capacity and capability to investigate incidents that occur within a private entity and that are not necessarily the subject of an official police investigation.

1.5 UNDERSTANDING CRIME INVESTIGATION

Before one can fully embark on a meaningful discussion of crime investigation, it is necessary to consider the concept of crime or, as some authors refer to it, an 'offence'. The well-known concept of crime was described in the early 1900s by an array of authors as an intentional act or omission in violation of criminal law, whether statutory or common law, committed without defence or justification and sanctioned by the state as a crime or misconduct.[8] Seminal authors emphasise the legality component in their discussion of crime and define it as 'a phenomenon that includes an act or omission, which is prohibited and punishable by law'.[9] This understanding is in line with the thinking of Joubert[10] who defines an offence as '[u]nlawful and blameworthy conduct which is defined by law as a crime and for which punishment is prescribed'. Hence, before an act or omission can be deemed to be a crime or an offence, there must be a law that says it is a crime and the law must prescribe a penalty. Crimes or criminal offences are made explicit in criminal codes or statutes as a result of customary or common law. These descriptions are important in criminal investigations because they provide the basis for each offence that needs to be proved in order to secure a successful conviction.[11]

Investigators in the private environment deal not only with unlawful and blameworthy conduct but also with conduct that is not defined by law as a crime. Investigators often investigate incidents where transgressions have taken place. A transgression may, for example, be a violation of duty, commands, instructions

6 Fourie (2011) 2.
7 Fourie (2011) 2.
8 Tappen (1960) 10.
9 Berning et al. (2004) 74.
10 Joubert (2010) 33-44.
11 United Nations (2006) 5.

or procedures, or disobedience. Such investigations usually lead to disciplinary processes and hearings, dismissals and/or litigation.

The investigation of a crime or an incident is not a game or exercise in probability, or a twist of fate as depicted in television series or crime novels. Investigators therefore cannot rely on chance or accidental success to conduct successful investigations. The investigation of a crime or an incident requires an individual who conducts a systematic search for the truth in accordance with embedded scientific principles. One such principle is known as the Locard principle[12] (this principle is discussed in chapter 2). Various well-known authors on criminal investigation are of the opinion that the criminal investigation process also requires a positive attitude towards the search for evidence at a crime scene or scene of incident and that experience plays a crucial role during this process.[13] These aspects will be discussed in section 1.12 when we examine the skills and characteristics an investigator should possess.

1.5.1 Criminal versus civil recourse

It is not the intention of the authors to present a legal discussion in this chapter, but merely to highlight in clear, simple language the different routes a case may take.

It is safe to say that when a crime is perpetrated, it is usually not only the rights of the aggrieved party that are affected but also those of society or the community as a whole. When this happens, the state may institute criminal proceedings against the perpetrator even if the victim does not want to do so. When the state follows this route, the case more often than not is more difficult to prove because the victim does not voluntarily want to testify.

However, an aggrieved person may also follow a civil route, as illustrated in the scenario below.

Scenario 1.1: Criminal or civil recourse?

Mrs X is arrested by the police. During the arrest she is assaulted by some of the police officers. After the arrest she is detained at the local police station and then released without being charged. It later turns out that the arrest was wrongful. The identity of the officer who carried out the arrest is known but unfortunately Mrs X is not able to identify the officers who assaulted her. Based on legal advice, Mrs X decides not to lay any criminal charges but to institute civil litigation against the police. As a result, the wrongful behaviour of the police officers involved in the incident may be internally investigated by the police. They may even decide to open a criminal case as a result of the incident.

12 Gilbert (2007) 23.

13 Callanan (1992) 8; Lee et al. (2003) 69; Horswell (2004) 4.

In the scenario above both a criminal and a civil recourse can be followed. Mrs X may lay a criminal charge against the arresting officer for the alleged assault. In addition, she may also institute civil proceedings against the SAPS and/or the arresting official for wrongful arrest.

In the event where the Director of Public Prosecutions (DPP) declines to prosecute (for whatever reason), a private person may, through their legal counsel, apply to the DPP for private criminal prosecution. In such an event the DPP will request the case docket for perusal and make a decision at the hand of that particular case. The decision may be to 'refer back to the police for further investigation', or to instruct the prosecutor to institute a prosecution on behalf of the state, or to issue a certificate indicating that the DPP declines to prosecute, which entitles the private person to institute criminal prosecution via their own legal counsel.

The type of recourse will determine what the burden of proof will be. 'Burden of proof' means the obligation to prove an assertion. For criminal cases the prosecution will have to prove the case beyond reasonable doubt. This implies that, if the defendant is able to create doubt regarding their liability, then the state must acquit them. However, for a civil or 'administrative' case, the burden of proof required is based on a 'preponderance of probabilities', which implies that what the claimant alleges must be more probable than what the defendant alleges, thus whose version of events seems more likely.[14]

A disciplinary hearing is a civil process and therefore the burden of proof is based on a 'preponderance of probabilities', as mentioned above. The following scenario illustrates an investigation into an incident.

Scenario 1.2: Investigating an incident

A security guard, who is tasked with the guarding of a building or premises, deserts his post. During that time a break-in and theft occurs at the premises.

The police conduct a criminal investigation into the break-in and theft.

At the same time a private investigator is also mandated to investigate the incident, which includes the criminal act as well as any transgression that might have taken place. The private investigator will also look into the violation of duty by the guard, disciplinary procedures and the possible civil liability of the security company.

The owner of the premises that were broken into may have suffered a substantial loss. That loss may be recovered through civil litigation or other processes.

The police will attend to the criminal investigation regarding the break-in and theft. This will be done from the criminal investigation perspective, which implies that the burden of proof is 'beyond reasonable doubt'. →

14 Joubert (2010) 33–34.

→
The private investigator may also be involved with some of the aspects relating to the break-in and theft. He will hand over his findings to the police for inclusion in the criminal case docket. In addition, the private investigator might also be tasked with investigating the disciplinary and civil liability aspects. Disciplinary procedures and litigation are civil processes and therefore the burden of proof is on a 'preponderance of probabilities', as explained above.

Having addressed both a crime and an incident and the recourse (criminal or civil) available to the victim, there remains another alternative which is not always well understood by investigators, namely the alternative route of restorative justice.

1.5.2 Restorative justice

To understand the term 'restorative justice', explanations offered from two very different sources are included, namely the article 'Restorative justice as world view' by Van Ness[15] and an article by Bekker and Van der Merwe on a decided court case (*S v Maluleke* 2008 1 SACR 49 (T)),[16] where the court made use of restorative justice as part of the sentencing. Both these articles can be sourced electronically.

In the first article, Van Ness highlights the difficulties associated with drafting a definition for restorative justice. He indicates that the drafting committee (during the development of the UN Basic Principles on the Use of Restorative Justice Programmes in Criminal Matters) therefore decided to not define the concept *per se* but rather to focus on the guidelines that restorative justice programmes should follow. From this approach three distinct concepts emerged, namely 'the encounter', 'reparation' and 'transformation'.[17]

The first concept, the encounter, implies that the people affected by the crime/incident come together to discuss what happened and how they were affected. This is followed by a step where restitution must be made for harm caused, either through community service, public apology, financial payment or the like (the reparation). The last step is the transformation step. This is where the behaviour and perspectives of not only the offender are challenged and transformed (for the good) but also those of the victim, the family members and, where relevant, the community. In the end the entire group thinks more in terms of relations and how what we do impacts on those around us.[18]

By contrast, Bekker and Van der Merwe define restorative justice as:

> ... an approach to justice that focuses on repairing the harm caused by crime while holding the offender responsible for his or her actions, by providing an opportunity for the parties directly affected by the crime – victim(s), offender

15 Van Ness (2005).
16 Bekker & Van der Merwe (2009) 239-250.
17 Van Ness (2005).
18 Van Ness (2005).

> and community – to identify and address their needs in the aftermath of the crime, and seek a resolution that affords healing, reparation and reintegration, and prevents further harm.[19]

When compared to the aforementioned concepts set out by Van Ness, this definition clearly also contains the three concepts of encounter, reparation and transformation.

In addition, three basic principles lie at the core of restorative justice:

- Justice requires that we work to restore those who have been injured.
- Those most directly involved and affected by the crime should have the opportunity to participate fully in the response, if they wish.
- The government's role is to preserve a just public order, and the community's is to build and maintain a just peace.[20]

Restorative justice occurs when a criminal case is made but the courts feel that more harm than good would come from a long, drawn-out criminal court case. Depending on the seriousness of the crime, the parties involved may enter into negotiations about the most suitable course of action and then, if all the parties are satisfied, proceed on the restorative justice route.

If handled professionally and with the correct level of empathy, restorative justice is a very powerful tool that can not only bring healing but also deal with less serious crimes that would have taken months and perhaps years to settle through the normal court process.

It is important to note that for this route to be followed, the parties involved must be willing to place all the facts on the table. This not only ensures that the resultant reparation is in line with the offending act, but also that this route is indeed the best one to follow. This approach follows a similar process as a normal criminal case except for the court proceedings. The entire case must be investigated in the normal fashion as for a criminal case. The decision to go the route of restorative justice is only made once the case is ready for trial. Then, and only then – after consultation between all the affected parties (the prosecutor, victim, suspect and the defence) – may this route be decided on. Finally, restorative justice is about guilt that is *admitted*, not proved.

1.5.3 Other transgressions and incidents

In addition to the aforementioned, also bear in mind that not all 'bad' acts are necessarily crimes. Most companies and businesses in South Africa have a set of rules that governs and guides conduct in the workplace. This also includes legislative prescriptions. One of the most important legislative frameworks that governs employer/employee relations and interaction in the workplace is the Basic

19 Bekker & Van der Merwe (2009) 245.
20 Claassen (1996); Van Ness (2005).

Conditions of Employment Act 75 of 1997. This legislation was developed to give effect to s 23(1) of the Constitution, which addresses fair labour practices. Section 23(1) sets out rules and regulations with which employers and employees must comply. Transgression by either side will have consequences and may result in an investigation (not necessarily a criminal one).

Company policy is another form of rules that govern the conduct of employers and employees. These policies contain guidelines and prescriptions about, among other things, working hours, conduct at work and the use of company property such as vehicles and equipment. When staff misuse company property or misappropriate company resources the company can institute an investigation into the matter. An investigation into transgressions at work has multiple facets. The investigator needs to determine whether a transgression has indeed taken place, who is responsible for the transgression and how to close the 'loophole' to prevent further losses or recurrences of the transgression. When a company suffers a loss as a result of employee conduct, it may institute civil litigation against the responsible employee to recover the loss. In the majority of these incidents, proceedings against the relevant employee are instituted in terms of the Labour Relations Act 66 of 1995. Depending on the seriousness of the offence or transgression, the law provides for a variety of recourses, ranging from a warning to a dismissal.

1.6 CONSTITUTIONAL FOUNDATION FOR INVESTIGATIONS

In modern-day South Africa law enforcement, specifically the investigation of crime, has become an enormously complicated matter. While the various role-players in official investigations derive their powers and functions from different pieces of legislation, government policy or organisational/institutional policy, it is crucial to bear in mind that, irrespective of the investigator's authorisation or mandate, there are two primary pieces of legislation with which all investigators need to comply. These are the Constitution and the Criminal Procedure Act 51 of 1977.

Figure 1.1 gives a schematic representation of the various investigators in the investigative arena. The sequence, shape and size of the diagram is not intended to portray the importance or precedence of one over the other, but rather the relationship within this context.

The very moment the investigator steps onto the playing field (the investigative arena) they must abide by the rules of the game. No one is exempt from this. It is therefore in the best interests of investigators and the institutions they represent to familiarise themselves with this legislation and, if they are not sure of an aspect, to ask before acting.

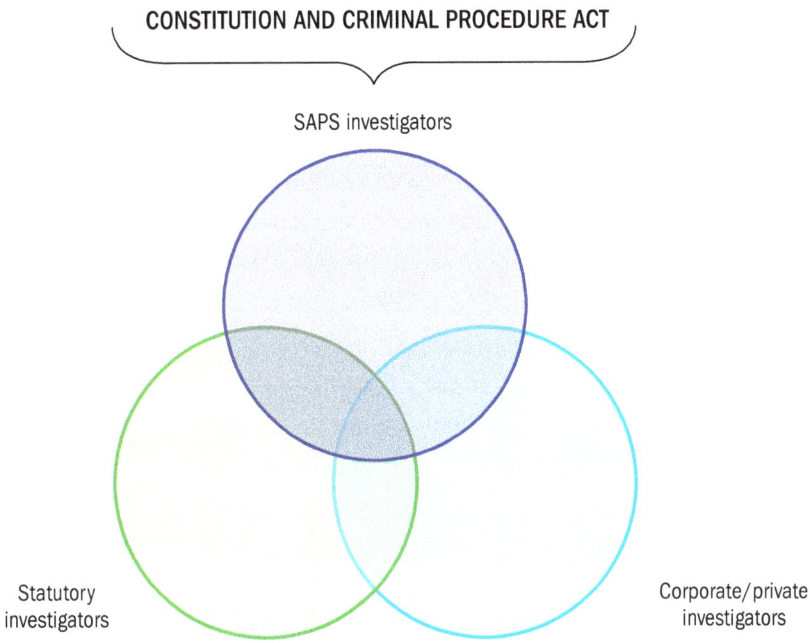

Figure 1.1: The interrelationship between the SAPS, statutory investigators and corporate/private investigators within the ambit of the primary bodies of legislation in South Africa.

1.7 PURPOSE AND OBJECTIVES OF AN INVESTIGATION/ INQUIRY

It is important to clarify the terms 'purpose', 'goals', 'aims' and 'objectives' with reference to an investigation. In prominent (and even less prominent) literature these concepts are often used interchangeably. For the purposes of this discussion, we will make use of the terms 'purpose' and 'objectives'.

1.7.1 Purpose

The intention of any investigation/inquiry is to establish what actually happened. Investigators should therefore not rely on presumptions but need to prove the crime/incident by means of evidence.[21]

The purpose of forensic investigation is thus to investigate evidence in a scientific manner and to determine how this evidence can be utilised to ultimately bring the perpetrator(s) to book.[22] During the investigation different methods and techniques are used to gather evidence that will stand the scrutiny of the court. Investigators play a vital role in this process – it is their duty to gather the evidence

21 Adams et al. (2004) 4; Lee & Harris (2000) 3.

22 Kempen (2007) 37.

by using a variety of techniques that will be admissible in court, to liaise with the prosecutor, to testify and to assist the prosecutor in presenting the evidence.

The main purpose of investigation is therefore to trace offenders by using scientific techniques or approaches, or to detect alleged offenders by furnishing scientific proof of their involvement in the crime. As summarised by Ogle,[23] the ultimate purpose in these investigations is to reconstruct the event of the crime in order to answer the questions: What happened? Who was responsible for each action? What was the sequence of actions?

So, what is the purpose of an investigation? The authors concur that, as in all crime situations, investigation should be approached scientifically and objectively to link the perpetrator to the crime scene. A crime is seen as a scientific problem that requires a solution.

As the investigator, you must be clear on what you understand 'purpose' to mean. Find reliable literature that you can use and lay your foundation on that. This will ensure that **you** know what you mean when you use the word 'purpose', and that you can clearly convey this to your client.

In practice, we suggest that you select only one central purpose (hence the use of the singular), for example 'to solve the crime successfully'. Clarifying the purpose of the investigation in your own mind is meant to help you focus on a single aspect; how you get there, however, is another matter altogether.

1.7.2 Objectives

Once the purpose has been established, the investigator should set the objectives that will achieve the purpose. It stands to reason that each investigation must have a purpose and a set of objectives. This is true for police investigations and for investigations conducted by detectives outside the SAPS. The purpose and objectives should preferably be communicated to a client before an investigation mandate is concluded.

The terms 'goals' and 'objectives' are often used interchangeably. From a project management perspective a 'goal' is a declaration of intent while 'objectives' are the measurable milestones on the investigation road. These milestones depend on the predetermined mandate for which the private investigator was contracted, which sets clear outcomes within the agreed parameters. This is a crucial process because the milestones serve as a yardstick to determine whether the investigator has successfully investigated the case or not.

Note that the term 'objectives' is used in the plural, thereby implying that, unlike a purpose, there should be more than one objective. Objectives may be likened to

23 Ogle (2004) 2.

steps that are climbed to reach the top of a ladder; if steps are skipped or missing then the outcome may be less than desirable.

In practice, a private investigator may be contracted to conduct an investigation and to achieve certain negotiated deliverables. The successful achievement of the predetermined objectives is usually linked to remuneration for the project (in this case, the investigation).

The objectives of an investigation are described as follows by Swanson et al.:[24] to establish that a crime had actually been committed, to identify and apprehend the suspect(s), to recover stolen property and to assist in the prosecution of the person(s) charged with the crime.

The following central themes are presented as the objectives of a criminal investigation:

- a systematic, organised search for the truth
- detecting crime
- identifying the crime
- locating and identifying suspects
- locating, recording and processing evidence while observing all constitutional considerations
- gathering objective and subjective evidence about an alleged crime or incident
- discovering certain facts, or ascertaining the existence of such facts
- arresting the perpetrator while observing all constitutional considerations
- recovering property
- preparing for trial, which would include the completion of accurate documentation
- getting the accused convicted by testifying and assisting in the presentation of legally obtained evidence and documents.[25]

Similarly, various other seminal authors[26] added the following points:

- individualisation of the crime
- evaluation of and involvement in the prosecution process.

From the preceding sections the objectives can very simply be reinterpreted to include an incident which is not a crime, such as non-compliance with company policy.

24 Swanson et al. (2003) 28.
25 Becker (2009) 12; Osterburg & Ward (2010) 5.
26 Becker (2009) 12; Van der Westhuizen (1996) 4; Van Rooyen (2008) 13.

Example 1.1: Setting the purpose and objectives of an investigation

You are an independent investigator. A well-known recruitment agency approaches you to investigate an advertisement offering employment at their company. They did not place the advertisement and their reputation is being tarnished as a result of the fraudulent activity. They are also very concerned about the potential prejudice which they might suffer as a result. The advertisement reads as follows:

Wanted: Office managers at Floris Recruitment

We are a renowned recruitment agency and have several positions available for office managers. R21 000.00 p/m neg. Please deposit R500.00 into XYZ bank account and fax proof of payment to 0860 125 4637 to enable us to commence with the administration of your application. Provide us with your email address for further correspondence. On receipt of proof of payment we will, within 14 days, email you the contract of employment for your perusal and acceptance. Contact person: Deon at 079 785 XXXX.

Purpose:
- to investigate the fraudulent advertisement on behalf of the client (Floris Recruitment).

Objectives:
- to determine the origin of the false advertisement
- to identify who the responsible persons are
- to obtain evidence of possible fraud
- to report the matter to the SAPS for further investigation.

Investigators may have the most profound skills set and all the technology in the world at their fingertips but if the purpose and objectives of the investigation are not clear from the outset, they might end up like Alice in Wonderland, not knowing where they're going.

1.8 TYPES OF INVESTIGATORS

1.8.1 The SAPS as primary role-player in criminal investigations

The Constitution is the supreme law of the country. This means all laws enacted in South Africa must be consistent with the Constitution for them to be considered 'lawful' or constitutional. Section 1 of the Constitution confirms the importance of the law as legal order by emphasising the supremacy of the Constitution and the rule of law. This implies that, if any law or section/subsection of the law is found to be in conflict with the Constitution, that law or section/subsection would be deemed invalid. The term 'rule of law' simply means that nobody is above the law and every person, including an investigator, is equal before the law.[27] Thus all investigations and laws in terms of which investigations are conducted should conform to the provisions of the Constitution.

27 Nel & Joubert (2004) 26.

Section 199 of the Constitution provides for the establishment of various security services which are to be responsible for the national security of the country. As a result, the SAPS was constitutionally mandated in terms of s 205 of the Constitution as the only national police service that would be responsible for upholding and enforcing the law.

In addition, s 205(3) of the Constitution states that the objectives of the national police service created in terms of s 199 of the Constitution are to:

- prevent, combat and investigate crime
- maintain public order
- protect and secure the inhabitants of the Republic and their property
- uphold and enforce the law.[28]

As one of the core functions of the SAPS, the effective investigation of crime is viewed by many as playing a crucial role in combating crime.[29] Effective crime investigation would by implication mean that a perpetrator is apprehended after committing a crime, is processed successfully through the court system and receives a sentence suited to the crime and other relevant factors. The SAPS is considered to be a primary role-player in this process.

It is clear that the responsibility for crime investigation is a constitutional one. The role and mandate of the police investigator or detective are well defined and regulated. For police investigators to undertake this task in a responsible manner, they have to be familiar with the powers and duties as prescribed by the law.[30] The investigative powers afforded to police officials are extensive, well defined and regulated and their mandate is broad, encompassing the investigation of all forms of crime. However, they are not the only role-players in the field of investigation.

1.8.2 Non-SAPS investigators

It has become common practice to establish investigative capacity within state departments, government agencies and private companies, but the categories, roles and functions of these investigators are not as well known, defined or regulated as those of their SAPS counterparts. The focus of the following discussion will therefore be on the investigator or detective who plies his trade outside the scope of the South African Police Service Act 68 of 1995. These investigators are not SAPS members.

In civil society, specifically in the business environment, in-house investigators deal with a wide variety of investigations. These investigations often include criminal acts such as shoplifting and theft by employees. These cases are not necessarily always referred to the SAPS.

28 Nel & Joubert (2004) 27.
29 Burger (2007) 14.
30 Nel & Joubert (2004) 26.

For the purposes of our discussion we have named the two remaining role-players in the investigation arena, namely statutory investigators and corporate/private investigators. The reader must remember that the principle of a broad mandate as it applies to SAPS investigators does not apply to these two groups.

1.8.2.1 Statutory investigators

The category or term 'statutory investigator' refers primarily to an investigator who has been formally appointed in terms of a specific law or statute to investigate specific matters spelled out in that law or statute.

Statutory investigators usually have limited powers as prescribed in that law or statute. Their mandate and powers are usually limited to a specific field of law enforcement and investigation. These investigators would, for example, have a mandate to investigate a specific corruption incident including the right to search, seize exhibits and arrest suspects. However, they will not have any 'policing powers' should they for instance witness a shoplifting incident. In such circumstances their powers would be limited to those of a civilian person.

A statutory investigator is usually found in a government department or public agency and often conducts specialised investigations. The following are examples of statutory investigators:

- investigators of the Special Investigating Unit (SIU)
- investigators of the South African Revenue Services (SARS)
- investigators of the Environmental Management Inspectorate (EMI)
- investigators at the South African Reserve Bank (SARB).

1.8.2.2 Corporate/private investigators

In the context of this section a corporate/private investigator is a person who operates in a private capacity and for the benefit of another party such as a company, private person or a foundation, for example.

Example 1.2: Using private/corporate investigators

An example of a private investigation is where an investigator is appointed by the family of a murdered person to investigate the case independently from the police. During such an investigation the private investigator normally works closely with the police and will hand over any evidence they find. It often happens that private investigators uncover evidence that leads to the successful solving of a case.

Another example may be where an investigator in a corporate environment is tasked with investigating an incident where important company information was leaked to a competitor company. During this investigation the investigator may uncover evidence that may lead to disciplinary hearings, civil litigation or administrative penalties. Certain evidence could also lead to criminal cases being opened and investigated.

The information and evidence gathered by a corporate/private investigator becomes the property of the party on whose instruction the investigation was conducted and who financed the investigation. Upon completion of the investigation the investigator submits the results to the client or employer. The decision of what to do next lies with the client or employer, except in cases where the investigator is legally obliged to hand over the investigation to another party, such as the SAPS. Where an investigator uncovers evidence that is material to a criminal case and finds the murder weapon, for example, they are obliged to hand over the case to the police.

The Private Security Industry Regulation Act 56 of 2001 similarly defines a private investigator as a person who, in a private capacity and for the benefit of a third party, investigates the identity, actions, character, background or property of another person, without the consent of that person.

This legislation has a specific focus, but unfortunately excludes certain investigation activities. As such, it does not reflect the reality of the private investigation environment in South Africa today, where private investigators are often contracted to carry out internal investigations or investigations on behalf of companies relating to the security and strategic and operational business interests of those companies. Investigation activities that are not covered by the legislation include the following:

- investigators conducting internal investigations into employee misconduct in a company or organisation
- internal investigators in a company or organisation conducting investigations which a business, other than an investigation business, may undertake in the course and scope of its normal and reasonable endeavours to safeguard its security, strategic, operational or business interests.

This Act goes further and determines that no person is excluded from the definition of a private investigator if they conduct any investigation that does not fall within the exclusive functions of the state. This basically means that any private person who conducts an investigation falls within the ambit of the Act and is obliged to register with the Private Security Industry Regulatory Authority (PSIRA).

Although there is currently no formal code of conduct for private investigators, a number of organisations are attempting to introduce professional standards, the two most notable being the Association of Certified Fraud Examiners (ACFE) and the Institute of Commercial Forensic Practitioners (ICFP).

In the modern-day environment there are numerous instances where an investigation is required to solve specific problems that do not necessarily require police involvement. Examples of such investigations are:

- background checks (this is confirmation of aspects such as previous employment history, verification of academic qualifications and consumer history)
- insurance claims
- stock shrinkage
- employee misconduct.

It has also become common practice for private investigators to be appointed and mandated by interested parties, clients and victims of crime to conduct criminal investigations into matters such as a fraud scams, kidnapping and murder separately from the police (ie running concurrently with the police investigation).

In most of these cases the private investigator works independently from the police but gathers information and evidence in exactly the same way. This information is shared with the police and often plays an important role in solving a particular case.

Private companies, private persons and even government departments frequently obtain the services of private investigators to conduct investigations into alleged illegal activities or misconduct by employees. For various reasons a large number of private institutions employ their own investigators to do this. It has become quite common to see private or corporate investigators interview witnesses and take down statements for later use in criminal and/or civil cases.

In a private or corporate environment an investigation is conducted within a specific framework or mandate. An investigator's approach is usually very specifically focused and targeted. Any investigation must be conducted within the boundaries of the law, the applicable disciplinary codes and the mandate of the client. At the same time human rights must be respected and the rules of evidence, specifically with reference to the Criminal Procedure Act 51 of 1977, must be adhered to.

This implies that corporate/private investigators, just like police investigators, have to adhere to strict requirements when conducting investigations. Non-compliance may lead to a flawed investigation process and the possible loss of a case. It might also expose an investigator to criminal prosecution, civil litigation and refusal of payment by the client.

1.9 CRIMINAL VERSUS FORENSIC INVESTIGATION

The proper and true meaning of the term 'forensic investigation' is cause for much confusion and debate in the investigation industry. As a result of the vast increase in investigations in the corporate and private sectors, the term 'forensic investigation' has become synonymous with 'investigation', hence departments and sections dealing with investigations in the corporate and private sectors were accordingly called forensic investigation departments.

In the sections below the authors attempt to demystify the concepts 'criminal investigation' and 'forensic investigation', which are often used interchangeably, by referring to researched literature and presenting a working definition in a table format.

Based on the information from reviewed studies, there is no clear distinction between the concepts 'criminal investigation' and 'forensic investigation'. The concept 'criminal investigation', however, only covers investigations of a criminal nature, while forensic investigations can also include civil or administrative investigations.[31]

Criminal and forensic investigations share the following common features:

- They commence after a crime has been committed or irregular conduct is reported or detected.
- They result in a systematic and organised investigation process in order to search for the truth.
- They focus on discovering, collecting, preparing, identifying and presenting information and evidence in order to resolve or find a solution to a reported crime or incident.
- They involve the application and use of different investigation methods and techniques during the investigation process.
- They result in the presentation of the results of the investigation, whether in a court of law for criminal, civil or administrative proceedings, or at a disciplinary hearing.

Criminal and forensic investigation can be compared in a table format, as follows:

Table 1.1: A comparison of criminal and forensic investigation

Criminal investigation	Forensic investigation
In the light of the discussion in literature and research data, the following working definition for the concept 'criminal investigation' is presented: **Definition:** Criminal investigation can be defined as a systematic, organised, thinking, reasoning, examination and analysis process designed to search for the truth, during which an inquiry and thorough analysis is conducted of all types of crimes or unlawful acts. The purpose is to legally gather information and evidence involving traditional methods guided by the Criminal Procedure Act in order to:	In the light of the discussion in literature and research data, the following working definition for the concept 'forensic investigation' is presented: **Definition:** Forensic investigation can be defined as an in-depth, meticulous investigation, searching for the truth through the use of specialised skills and expert knowledge and the application of scientific investigation methods and techniques, in order to lawfully discover, collect, prepare, identify and present evidence which can be presented to a court of law, disciplinary council, instructing client or company. The primary purpose is finding a positive solution to a crime or transgression in order to: →

31 Lambrechts (2001) 93.

→

• reconstruct a crime scene • identify the perpetrator • discover, identify and collect objective and subjective information and evidence • establish whether a crime has been committed • determine what happened and who is responsible • find a positive solution to the crime • prepare a case for prosecution • bring a case before a court of law • ensure a successful prosecution.[32]	• reconstruct a scene of incident • identify the perpetrator • discover, identify and collect objective and subjective information and evidence • establish whether a crime and/or irregular conduct has been committed; and/or confirm an allegation • determine what happened and who is responsible • find a positive solution to the crime or incident • prepare a case for prosecution • bring a case before a court of law or presiding authority • ensure a successful prosecution • institute criminal, civil, administrative or disciplinary proceedings • apply scientific knowledge to a legal problem • methodically and systematically analyse evidence for the purpose of finding proof of and establishing financial transactions • identify motive and intent • examine and analyse documentation and financial records • prepare evidence that will stand the scrutiny of the presiding authority • trace and recover stolen property or misappropriated assets.[33]

1.10 THE INVESTIGATION PROCESS

In a private or corporate environment the investigation approach may differ from the approach followed by the police. The type of investigation which an investigator conducts, as well as their mandate, will usually determine the approach.

Investigations traditionally follow a set path, as illustrated in Figure 1.2.

32 Bennett & Hess (2004) 4, 7; Brown (2001) 3; Gilbert (2007) 46; Marais (1992) 1; Palmiotto (2004) 6; Sennewald & Tsukayama (2001) 3; Van der Westhuizen (1996) 1, 3, 54; Van Rooyen (2008) 13.

33 Kennedy (n.d.) 1; Lambrechts (2001); Shah (2002) 10; Van Rooyen (2008) 7; Zysman (n.d.) 4.

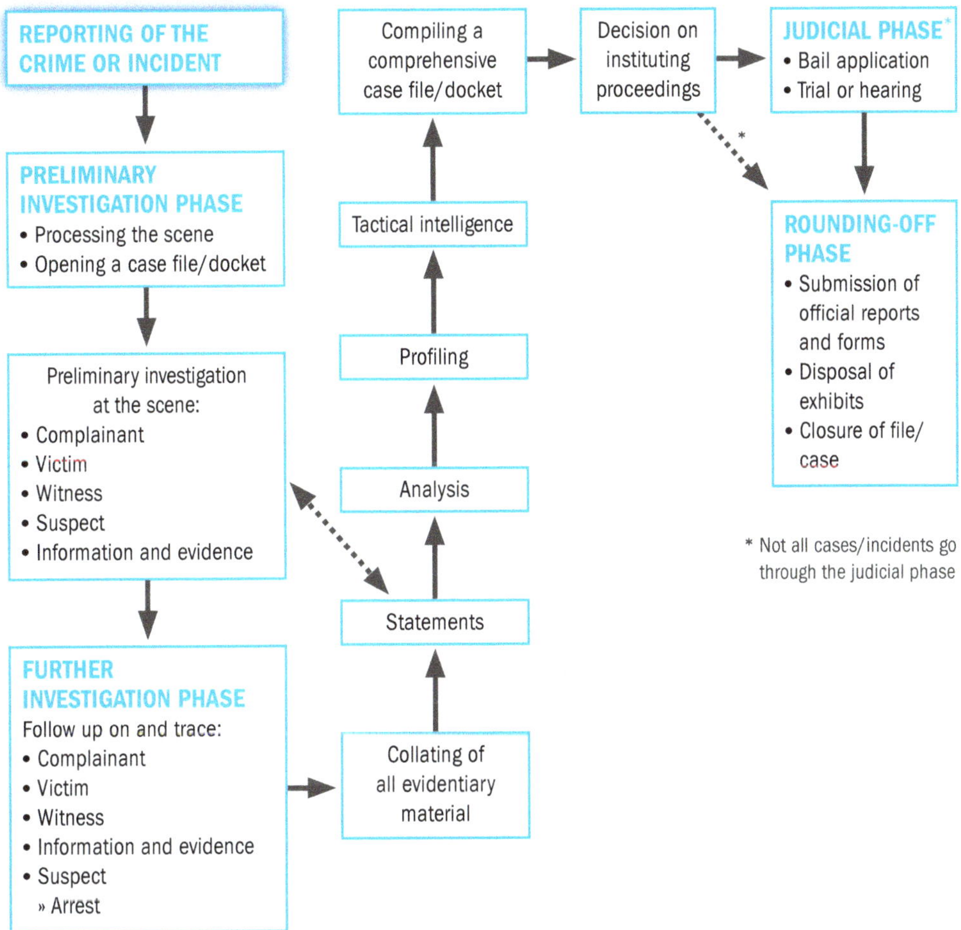

Figure 1.2: The crime investigation process

However, it is important to note that not all investigations follow this exact path. In this illustration the process commences when a crime is committed and reported and ends with the closure of the file or case. The investigation goes through various phases, namely the preliminary investigation phase, the further investigation phase, the judicial phase and the rounding-off phase.

Although the following discussion is specifically from the point of view of a criminal investigation, it can be adapted to other types of investigation such as forensic investigation. The important thing to remember, similar to building a house, is not to skip phases during the investigation.

1.10.1 Flow of an investigation/inquiry

During any investigation it is imperative that the investigation be accurately documented and communicated. In order to be effective, the investigation must be incrementally and progressively done in distinct phases:

- reporting the crime
- analysing the information
- identifying and arresting the suspect
- charging the accused
- preparing the evidence for court.[34]

These phases are interlinked through the flow of information and can be illustrated as follows:

Table 1.2: The flow of an investigation/inquiry

<table>
<tr>
<td>Reporting the crime
Upon receiving a crime report, the information should be thoroughly assessed to find an appropriate way of dealing with it. The understanding of a crime report is of the utmost importance in order to gather the right resources that will be useful at the crime scene. →</td>
<td>Analysing the information
Information is the lifeblood of any investigation. All information gathered from investigations should be properly coordinated. When all the comprehensive information of the investigation has been gathered by investigators, possible links can be determined for effective and efficient investigation of the crime or irregular conduct. →</td>
<td>Identifying and arresting the suspect
Once all the relevant information has been gathered and the suspect has been individualised or identified, the investigator can effect the arrest of the suspect.
↓</td>
</tr>
<tr>
<td colspan="2">Preparing the evidence for court
Investigation is a systematic process, whereby all evidence should be gathered in an orderly and methodical manner. In reality, the prosecutor is accountable for the interpretation and presentation of evidence during the trial. Investigators must gather and prepare reliable and admissible evidence that must be accessible in court.</td>
<td>← Charging the accused
The moment the offender is detained in custody and there are reasonable grounds to believe that the offender has indeed committed the crime, the investigator must charge the offender in accordance with the requirements of the law.</td>
</tr>
</table>

Whatever the crime or incident that forms the basis of an investigation, and by whatever means an investigator gets involved, when an investigator is tasked or mandated with conducting an investigation, the logical point of departure

34 Bennett & Hess (2004) 5-6.

will be where the crime or incident has taken place. Irrespective of the nature of the investigation, the starting point will always be the reporting of the crime or incident. In certain cases this may not be as obvious or clear-cut (the scene of incident might, for example, be a document on which information has been falsified). Not every investigation requires all the steps or actions to be followed, but investigations generally follow the same steps irrespective of the type of crime or incident that is being investigated.

Every investigation has a victim (or complainant), and usually also witnesses and possible suspects. Apart from the crime scene and the evidence gathered at the scene, these persons often provide valuable information and evidence that can be used to solve a case.

During an investigation, from first visiting the crime scene to individuals being interviewed and interrogated, the objective of an investigator is to gather evidence that will lead to solving the case. This evidence will be in the form of physical evidence and verbal accounts by witnesses recorded in the form of statements. All the information gathered during an investigation is reflected in a case docket or case file (see examples 1.7 and 1.8). The docket or case file serves as the management instrument and vehicle by which a prosecutor presents the accumulated evidence to a court or hearing or, in the case of corporate/private investigators, to the presiding authority or their client.

The investigation process ends when the evidence is presented to a court or hearing as documentary or oral testimony and it is accepted or rejected as such. Any items seized in the course of an investigation and brought before the court will be disposed of by order of that court in terms of the Criminal Procedure Act 51 of 1977. A court may, for example, order that a weapon be destroyed or specific property be handed to its original owner or the person from whom it was seized. The court is also entitled to award compensation for damage incurred or property lost by a victim through the actions of the perpetrator whose case is being heard by the court.

However, the outcome of an investigation may also result in a process of restorative justice (see section 1.5.2). Research has shown that restorative justice programmes are used more among juveniles than among adults and for minor offences rather than serious crimes.[35] The goal with restorative justice programmes is to restore harmony between the victim and the offender. For the victim this means restitution of losses (tangible and emotional) and for the offender it means taking responsibility, confronting the shame for the misconduct and then ultimately regaining dignity.[36]

35 Hagan (2010) 188.
36 Hagan (2010) 187.

1.10.2 Investigator's task

The word 'investigate' is derived from the Latin word *vestigare*, meaning 'to track or trace', a derivation easily related to police investigation.[37] The investigation of crime or irregular conduct is deemed to be a patient, systematic, step-by-step examination, inquiry or observation. It is a careful examination, a recording of evidence or legal inquiry, and forms the basis of any investigation.

In conducting an investigation, investigators must:

- apply scientific knowledge acquired through study and experience
- use skills acquired through the artful application of learnt techniques
- expand their ability to see relationships between essentially unrelated facts
- question the incontestable.[38]

The investigator has to conduct a systematic search for the truth with the primary purpose of finding a positive solution to a crime with the help of objective or subjective clues.[39]

The final measure of an investigator's skill lies in the acceptance of the investigator's testimony at a court or other hearing, or by the client. Professional investigators must be able to present the information they have collected at a hearing. Investigators are usually considered professional witnesses and as such are expected to deliver testimony of a high standard. The quality of the investigator's work is revealed when it is presented in an open forum such as a court, and is accepted, rejected, praised or criticised.

1.10.3 Mandate

The investigator searches for the truth using methods that are legal and ethical. In order to do this, the investigator must receive a specific mandate for the investigation. Once there is clarity about the mandate, the investigator can employ the relevant set of skills required for the investigation.

When the private investigation process is compared to the traditional investigation process, important differences are highlighted. The first difference lies in the start or mandate of the investigation. The police must investigate every case reported to them and must investigate a crime if it is brought to their attention. For example, if a murder is committed, the police have no choice but to investigate the matter. On the other hand, private investigators can only get involved in an investigation if they have a mandate or legal standing in the matter.

For corporate/private investigators the mandate impacts directly on the skills set they need in order to function effectively within that specific environment. The mandate may differ from case to case, and the measured result will differ accordingly.

---

37 Bennett & Hess (2004) 3.

38 Bennett & Hess (2004) 6.

39 Van der Westhuizen (1996) 1.

1.10.4 Differences between a police investigation and a private investigation

An example of a typical private investigation process is as follows:

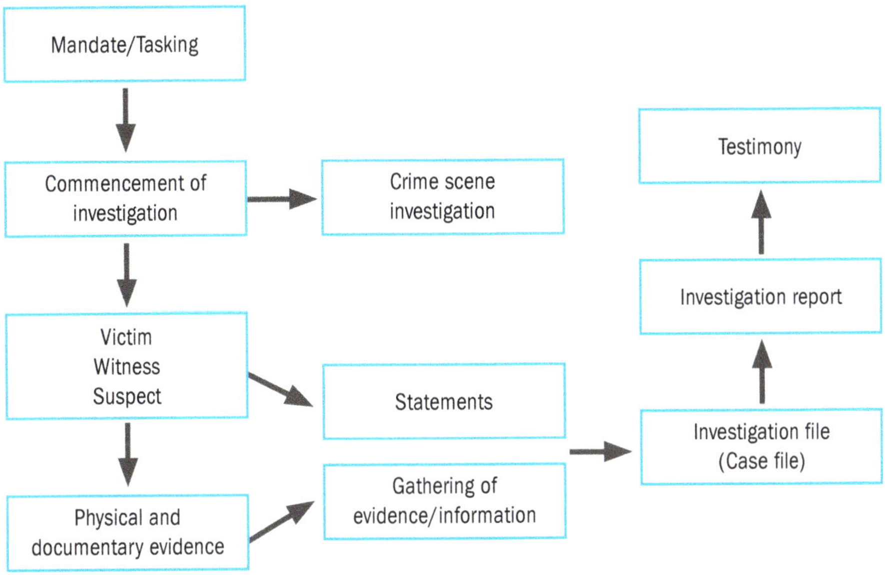

Figure 1.3: Typical private investigation process

One of the main differences between a police investigation and a corporate/private investigation is the way the investigation is recorded and presented. The police have to follow strict guidelines, while private investigators operate according to client instructions or personal preference.

The police will also investigate only criminal cases while the private investigator will investigate criminal cases and other kinds of incidents.

In a corporate or private environment the success of investigators is usually measured by the report they submit at the end of their investigation. Private investigations are not always aimed at or do not always end in the presentation of evidence at a hearing or court case, but they should be conducted as if they would. When a case does end up in court or at a hearing, the quality of an investigator's work is judged by the quality of the evidence gathered and the statements taken or submitted.

1.11 INVESTIGATION TECHNIQUES

Investigators have at their disposal various tried and tested investigation techniques that they may employ in their search for the truth. In order to identify the specific knowledge and skills required by a modern-day investigator, the investigation techniques that are most often used must first be identified.

Nossen[40] identified six major investigation techniques, namely:

- collecting and analysing information and evidence
- interviewing and interrogation
- surveillance
- electronic interception and monitoring
- undercover operations
- undercover agents and informers.

Apart from the six major investigative techniques listed above, there is a seventh approach to investigation which Nossen,[41] a recognised expert in the detection, investigation and prosecution of financial crimes, introduced in 1975. This approach is focused on the investigation of organised crime and white-collar crime through:

- asset-related investigations.

It can be argued that most of these techniques belong in the domain of the SAPS. For example, electronic interception and monitoring, undercover agents and undercover operations are used predominantly by the SAPS, and then only under very strict guidelines set down by legislation and the office of the Director of Public Prosecutions (DPP). Although some of these techniques are more generally used than others in the corporate/private investigation environment, all of them are important and will be discussed briefly.

1.11.1 Collecting and analysing information and evidence

The collection and analysis of information and evidence are commonly done by all investigators and form the basis of nearly every investigation. As mentioned before, every investigation has a logical starting point. For police investigators this point is usually the reporting of a crime; for corporate/private investigators it is the mandate they receive (see section 1.10.3).

When starting on an assigned case, investigators have to establish what happened and who is responsible. They should apply the W×5; H principle: who, what, where, when, why and how (see also section 1.12.6). All information and evidence collected are gathered in a file (electronically and/or in a case docket or case file). The investigator then analyses the information and evidence and compiles a report.

40 Nossen (n.d.).
41 Nossen (n.d.).

1.11.2 Interviewing and interrogation

In almost all investigations human interaction and communication takes place as part of the process of collecting information. A key skill for investigators is the ability to interview witnesses and suspects, obtain relevant information from them, and convert that information into evidence in the form of statements. The interrogation of suspects is similarly a key skill: investigation efforts often reach their peak with the interrogation of an identified suspect. Even if a suspect does not confess, the information legally obtained from him or her during an interrogation usually forms the cornerstone of a case.

1.11.3 Surveillance

Surveillance has long been associated with the intelligence world and the world of the private investigator who follows a cheating spouse, for example, to obtain evidence for the wronged party. In modern society, surveillance (whether by vehicle, on foot, static or electronic) has become a very important part of investigations. The information and evidence gathered in this way often means the difference between success and failure. Surveillance is a highly specialised skill, usually far removed from how it is popularly portrayed on television and in crime novels.

1.11.4 Electronic interception and monitoring

Electronic interception and monitoring refers mainly to the monitoring of communication by a third party. A typical example will be where an investigator intercepts the private telephone conversations of a person they are investigating when the investigator is not part of the actual conversation. Obviously information obtained in this way can be extremely valuable in an investigation, especially if the suspect is not aware that their conversations are being monitored. In South Africa, an investigator needs an order from a judge of the Supreme Court who has been specifically appointed to deal with the granting of authority in such matters. However, only on rare occasions will this authority be granted. Third-party monitoring of conversations without a court order is illegal in South Africa and evidence so obtained will not be acceptable as evidence in a court of law. Investigators who conduct electronic monitoring and interception outside the law expose themselves to legal action.

1.11.5 Undercover operations

Undercover operations as an investigation technique is almost exclusively conducted by the SAPS. In an undercover operation an investigation is carried out in secret against a target, the target usually being a high-profile crime figure. As part of the investigation, an undercover police officer is infiltrated into the organisation or crime group to which the crime figure belongs. The police officer strives to obtain evidence against the target. The whole operation is carried out in secret, but the idea is to obtain evidence for use in a later court case. During the court case the whole investigation is exposed, including the existence of the undercover agent. Informants may also be infiltrated or recruited in such an operation. Only highly skilled investigators should utilise this technique.

1.11.6 Undercover agents and informers

The term 'undercover agent' normally refers to a police officer who, for a period of time, assumes a made-up identity and infiltrates into a crime group or syndicate to obtain information and evidence about the activities of that group for court purposes. This process is highly regulated and managed in terms of s 252A of the Criminal Procedure Act 51 of 1977.

Informers are persons who provide information, usually for remuneration, to the police or other organisations about the illegal activities of a person or group. Informers are widely used by the police and by private investigators, as they provide an investigator with direct information about a target they are investigating. They enable an investigator to directly home in on key aspects of the investigation and to obtain evidence for use in a later hearing.

The value of informers lies in their anonymity, therefore informers as a rule are never exposed. There are a number of reasons why the identity of informers is kept secret, for instance they have to be protected from retribution from those on whom they have provided information, and they could be utilised again to provide information.

1.11.7 Asset-related investigations

Asset-related investigations came to prominence in the late 1970s and early 1980s in the USA in the fight against organised crime, specifically the Mafia. Asset forfeiture is a civil process involving the recovery of assets from organised and high-profile crime figures. It is aimed at recovering the monetary value these people accumulated through their criminal activities. In the South African context this type of investigation stems from the Prevention of Organised Crime Act 121 of 1998 (POCA). Moreover, it is only official investigation bodies such as the Directorate for Priority Crime Investigations (DPCI) and the Special Investigations Unit (SIU) that would utilise this legislation when investigating criminal networks and organised crime groups.

1.12 SPECIFIC CHARACTERISTICS OF AN INVESTIGATOR

A professional investigator is a person who possesses certain characteristics, has acquired specific knowledge and is able to apply specialised skills in the investigative arena. The following characteristics are vital for an effective investigator:

- intellectual and emotional intelligence
- sound moral and ethical character
- the ability to operate independently and as part of a team
- the ability to improvise and adapt to challenging situations
- the ability to interact effectively with other people
- being an analytical and critical thinker
- following an organised and systematic approach
- being well versed in new technology
- perseverance.

Each of these characteristics is briefly discussed below.

1.12.1 Intellectual and emotional intelligence

An investigator must be a person of substantial intellectual and emotional intelligence. In today's complex operational environment the investigator will have to deal with a wide variety of investigation problems, different types of investigations, and people from different backgrounds and with different personalities. Investigators must have the intellectual and emotional intelligence and capacity to deal with a wide variety of problems and people, as illustrated by the following example:

Example 1.3: Dealing sensitively with sensitive cases

An investigator is tasked with investigating a case of alleged child sexual assault. The complaint was made against the child's parents by a grandparent of the child. If the investigator is either still very inexperienced or emotionally not stable or mature enough to handle such a volatile situation, more harm than good will be done. Relationships in the family could irrevocably be damaged if the investigator does not first establish the facts of the case before confronting the parents. Using the incorrect interviewing techniques could result in the child being traumatised (again) and the witnesses deciding not to testify in court.

1.12.2 Sound moral and ethical character

Investigators must have a sound moral and ethical character – they are the opposite of people who commit crimes. The conduct of the investigator must always be legal, ethical and above reproach. The investigator must be a believable and credible witness and person.

Example 1.4: Acting ethically

Investigators are not the most highly paid professionals in the workforce. It is tempting when the investigator is offered a large sum of money to turn a blind eye to crime, especially when no one will know that they had taken an envelope stuffed with cash. Investigators are human beings and form part of a society that does not necessarily consider such actions as wrong. However, if they succumb to this conduct it will undermine the concept of justice.

1.12.3 Ability to operate independently and as part of a team

An investigator must be able to operate independently and as part of a team, although this statement may appear to be contradictory. Investigators are often required to operate individually – in these instances they must be able to plan, execute and conclude an investigation or task without any outside help. This means they must have the self-discipline to successfully operate on their own.

On the other hand, the investigator may be required to conduct an investigation or task as part of a team. In a modern environment, large or intricate investigations are almost always tackled using a team approach. Thus investigators will have to be good team players if they want to be successful.

1.12.4 Ability to improvise and adapt to challenging situations

An investigator should be able to improvise and adapt to challenging situations. Experience is a vital commodity in the world of an investigator. It can only be acquired over an extended period of time while plying the craft. However, in our fast-changing world investigators are often confronted with new challenges and situations. This means they must be able to adapt in a proactive manner, conduct research on new solutions in the sphere of investigation, and improvise to meet new challenges. This can be illustrated by the following example:

Example 1.5: Adapting to new circumstances

A fraud investigator specialises in cheque fraud. Suddenly he is confronted with an investigation environment where cheques are seldom or no longer used. He now has to investigate electronic banking fraud schemes conducted on the internet by perpetrators operating from offices situated in far-off, unknown states. This investigator must be able to adapt to the continually developing world and jargon of electronics and the applicable legislation in this regard.

1.12.5 Ability to interact effectively with other people

An investigator must be able to communicate and interact effectively with people from different walks of life under different circumstances to obtain the required information and evidence needed to solve the crime. Crimes and offences are committed by people; the investigator works with people, such as victims and witnesses, and will end up facing a suspect, the focus of the investigation.

The investigator will therefore not use the same approach for interviewing a victim who has been severely traumatised and for interrogating an aggressive suspect.

One of an investigator's most important skills is the ability to get a suspect to cooperate with the investigation, subject to the requirements of the law and best practices. It might even be argued by some that the ultimate test of any investigator's skill is the ability to get a suspect to cooperate, talk and confess. However, obtaining a confession or admission should not be the investigator's primary focus. The emphasis of an investigation is usually to uncover, collect and be able to provide sound, objective evidence to a presiding officer to decide on the guilt or innocence of the suspect. If a confession is obtained during the investigation it should be considered a bonus.

1.12.6 Being an analytical and critical thinker

An investigator must be an analytical and critical thinker. The majority of investigations present a problem that has to be solved, usually by answering the following questions – who, what, where, when, why and how (the W×5; H principle). As such the investigator has to identify and focus on the essence of the matter and critically analyse relevant information to get to the truth. The following example illustrates this point:

Example 1.6: The value of critical, analytical thinking

An investigator is tasked with investigating an elaborate fraud scheme. He starts off his investigation by examining thousands of documents. Only about 5% of these documents are relevant to the case, and even fewer have evidential value. He quickly feels that he is getting lost in the chaos but then remembers the W×5; H principle.

By applying this principle he starts analysing the information contained in the documents. It provides him with a formula to extract all the relevant information and helps him to direct the inquiry. As he works, he becomes increasingly confident of his success.

1.12.7 Following an organised and systematic approach

An investigation usually ends up in court or at a hearing. The work done by the investigator is open to scrutiny and sometimes also to cross-examination. This means the investigator needs to be thorough in obtaining, recording and presenting the information pertaining to the case and pay meticulous attention to detail. A mistake can effectively mean a lost case and subsequent failure.

The same example of the fraud investigator mentioned above (Example 1.6) can be used. When confronted with thousands of documents at the start of the investigation, it is imperative that the investigator goes about the task in a systematic and organised manner. The investigator's filing and administration systems must be in order; everything they have done must be explained and defended in court. If vital documents cannot be found or produced or the chain of evidence related to the document cannot be proven, it may lead to failure in court.

In this regard, the case docket or case file is of the utmost importance.

Example 1.7: What does a case docket consist of?

A case docket is the formal management structure and tool (file) used by the SAPS to facilitate and conduct the investigation process. It is captured in an officially numbered file and consists of six pages. These are divided into the following sections:

Page	Section	Contents
Page 1	Cover page	This page contains the following, among other things: • name of the station at which the criminal case has been registered • name and contact details of the investigating officer • details related to the crime • case details as registered on the national computerised Crime Administration System (CAS) • details of the complainant(s) • record of court proceedings and the results (if applicable) • information about the exhibits • information about the disposal of the docket • decisions made about the case docket itself and brought forward dates, if relevant.
Page 2	Section A Also known as the A clip	This page contains the following: • all the documents that have evidential value to the case • statements • the First Information of Crime (FIC) • particulars of the deceased (if relevant) • photo album (if relevant) • sketch of crime scene (if relevant) • documents (SAP 69) about the fingerprints of the suspect (if relevant).
Page 3	Section B Also known as the B clip	This page contains the following: • all correspondence and documents not forming part of sections A or C • certifications in relation to the CAS checklist, 24-hour inspection, closure of the docket, disposal of exhibits and certification by the Archive clerk.

→

→

Page	Section	Contents

Page 4	Section C Also known as the C clip	This page is used for the following:
		• recording progress with the investigation that was conducted on an SAP 5 (A4 lined page divided into three columns). The columns are used as follows:
		  ◦ *Left-hand column*: date and time
		  ◦ *Centre column*: progress details
		  ◦ *Right-hand column*: full signature (includes initials and surname, rank and service number if it is a police official) of the person making the entry.
		Correspondence between the prosecutor and the investigating officer is also recorded on SAP 5.
		• recording information relevant to the prosecutor for possible bail applications
		• recording the outcome of the court case
		• recording the exhibit disposal instructions issued by the commanding officer.
		
		The docket is submitted for monthly inspection to the commander who will write further instructions/give guidance to the investigator/indicate that the docket is ready for court.
		
		If there is no progress in the case, the commanding officer may decide to close the case with a brought forward date indicated.

Page 5	The page behind Section C	This page contains: • particulars of the accused • the relevant SAPS document numbers relating to the accused • right front thumbprint of the accused.
Page 6		This page provides additional space: • for the capturing of court dates, list of exhibits, date/time that evidence was sent to Forensics (elsewhere) for analysis • for instructions regarding the disposal of exhibits.

Example 1.8: What should a case file contain?

A case file is the formal management structure and tool used by investigators external to the SAPS to facilitate and conduct inquiries and investigations.

There is no statutory or other formal prescribed format for keeping a case file. The manner in which the file is compiled differs from investigation to investigation and also from investigator to investigator. The format of a police case docket is often used as a guideline to compile an investigation file.

We suggest that a case file should include at least the following sections:

1. mandate of the investigation
2. correspondence
3. statements
4. documents relevant to the case
5. investigation diary.

1.12.8 Being well versed in new technology

Technology plays an increasingly important role in every aspect of an investigator's professional life. Technology changes on a daily basis and will most probably keep on developing and changing in this manner. The availability of technology provides the investigator with more resources to conduct an investigation but obviously also works to the advantage of the modern-day criminal. Criminals utilise and sometimes even create new technology to beat the system. How an investigator uses these resources is essentially a matter of skill, ingenuity, personal contacts, creativity and tenacity.

Investigators must keep up with, and actually be at the forefront of, technological developments in the field to be better than their opponents, which in this case are the offenders.

It is not strange to see an investigator interviewing a witness using only his iPad. The interview is recorded on the device and notes are typed and automatically linked to the recorded interview. At the conclusion of the interview, it is immediately emailed to the witness and to the office of the investigator and possibly the client.

1.12.9 Perseverance

An investigator must be a person who perseveres. Continuing and persevering in the face of adversity is the only way to beat an opponent during a forensic investigation. The tenacious investigator does not give up easily, but tracks the suspect and gathers the required evidence until success is attained.

There are numerous examples of investigations that lasted years, such as the Krion pyramid scheme investigation which took nearly 10 years to conclude. In most of these cases only the perseverance of the investigator prevented the case from falling by the wayside.

1.12.10 Other important characteristics

Adding to what has already been discussed, an investigator should also have a keen understanding of what motivates human behaviour. This is closely linked to a thorough understanding of the field of Criminology, which will help the investigator to answer the question *why* people act as they do.

Being streetwise, an attribute which is difficult to define, measure or train, is a must. An investigator must know *how* as well as *where* to look for and find information. For example, being streetwise would include knowing where to look for stolen property within a specific community; knowing who could be potential informers (for example shebeen owners); knowing what modes of transport would have been available in the area for suspects to use, and which places suspects might frequent.

Investigators should critically evaluate their own skills set and characteristics and ask themselves honestly: Do I have the necessary skills, knowledge and attributes to be a good investigator? If there are some gaps in their skills, the good news is that the majority of skills an investigator needs can be learnt.

1.13 THE MODERN-DAY INVESTIGATION CYCLE

The world of a professional investigator is a complex one. The modern investigation environment presents many challenges unknown to investigators of a few decades ago. New technology and new emerging crime trends are constantly posing new challenges. As humankind evolves, its collective knowledge develops at an ever-increasing pace. Crime evolves in a similar way, but unfortunately the combating thereof remains reactive and slow. Ironically, private investigators often find themselves at the forefront of this fight as state institutions and corporate entities are slow to embrace new and innovative initiatives in the field of investigation.

In the traditional investigation cycle, an investigation usually commenced only when a complainant laid a complaint at a police station. As such, police investigators were mainly reactive. If no crimes were reported, the detectives at a specific police station did not have much work to do. The exceptions were detectives who investigated offences such as diamond and gold offences and drug- and vice-related crimes. These detectives had to continuously and proactively obtain information about illegal activities and then arrest the perpetrators. Smugglers and participants in these crimes kept their activities secret and investigators had to expose and investigate them.

In the modern-day environment, phenomena such as organised crime, cross-border crime (transnational crime) and cybercrime have altered the crime investigation arena to a large extent. Crime has become an organised business and syndicated and criminal activities are often managed as business enterprises. Similarly, police no longer follow a mere reactive approach; they also concentrate on proactive investigation, especially of individuals who operate behind the scenes as 'crime bosses', and of structures used in organised crime syndicates. Proactive and disruptive policing now form an important part of any investigation strategy.

In the private sector the same approach is also followed by corporate/private investigators. They no longer just wait for a crime to take place; they plan and implement strategies and investigations proactively. An example is the cash-in-transit environment. Private companies that transport assets (cash) implement intelligence investigations and disruption strategies as part of an overall investigation strategy.

Linked to these phenomena (and one could argue that this perhaps was the causational factor) is the rapid development of human knowledge and associated social and technological development.

Proactive investigations have become important to obtain information on syndicates, organised crime structures and the activities of groups that are planning to commit crime, and to determine projected crime trends and patterns. This is done to prevent crime from taking place or from continuing to be orchestrated even if the 'field workers' are arrested. There is general consensus that investigations should focus on the relatively small number of crime bosses, organisers, masterminds or initiators who are responsible for a large number of crimes. These individuals are seldom brought to book. They corrupt good government in order to carry out their activities, destroy countless lives by drawing people into crime and contribute very little to society. An example is the drug bosses who are responsible for the importation of narcotics into South Africa. Street sellers and users are often arrested and prosecuted, but the people making the profit do not even reside in the country where their product is sold.

To be able to counter sophisticated and complex crimes, an investigation unit consisting of investigators needs to collect proper crime information through a process of proactive crime intelligence initiatives.

The importance of integrated forensic databases in proactive policing is discussed in section 12.11.1 in chapter 12.

A proactive investigation cycle, according to Jones,[42] may look as follows:

42 Jones (2012).

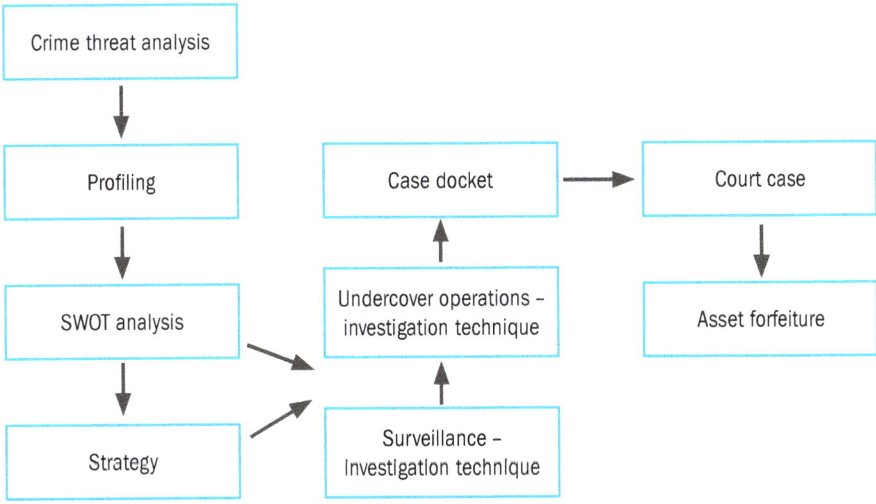

Figure 1.4: A proactive crime investigation cycle

In this cycle the focus is on the compilation of a crime threat analysis. Such an analysis focuses on individuals responsible for crime and prioritises the most important ones by using set criteria.

Once these individuals have been identified and it is discovered whether they are part of a crime structure or operate individually, the investigator gathers intelligence on them.

The investigator will then compile a profile on the identified individual(s). Such a profile will contain standard background information, for example name, surname, identity number, address(es) and contact numbers. The profile will also contain more elaborate information such as possible criminal contacts, methods of communication, security awareness and forensic lifestyle, among other things.

To be able to compile a profile of the individual, the investigator must access information from all possible sources. These would include official sources (limited to police detectives) and so-called open sources.

The most common official sources that are usually accessed by police detectives in South Africa are the Criminal Record Centre (CRC) and Forensic Science Laboratory (FSL). The type of information that can be obtained from the CRC and the FSL is discussed in chapters 3, 4 and 5.

Confidential and personal information can usually not be sourced from the SAPS by investigators in the private sector. In practice it means that this type of information can only be accessed by investigators in the private sector if they obtain a court order or permission from the person whose details are being investigated. Examples of personal and confidential information include information about financial records, communication (cellphones), medical records, DNA information and HIV status.

Open-source information is information that is readily available in the public domain such as social media profiles (eg Facebook and Twitter), company registration records, deeds, directory information and vehicle registration information. No court order or consent from the suspect is required to obtain information from an open source.

All the information is used for building a profile of the possible offender. Based on this profile a SWOT analysis is usually compiled. Such an analysis focuses on the **s**trengths, **w**eaknesses, **o**pportunities and **t**hreats posed by the individual. The most useful areas to the investigator are the strengths and weaknesses.

Example 1.9: Capitalising on strengths and weaknesses

An example of an area of strength may be that the targeted individual always observes his immediate surroundings before engaging in any incriminating activities. Armed with that knowledge the investigator will be careful to use an investigation technique such as surveillance.

An example of an area of weakness may be that the targeted individual constantly communicates with associates via his cellphone. The investigator can exploit this knowledge by using an investigation technique such as electronic interception and monitoring.

As a practical example, we can do a SWOT analysis for 'Deon', the suspect mentioned in Example 1.1.

Example 1.10: Practical example of a SWOT analysis

You are an independent investigator. A well-known recruitment agency approaches you to investigate an advertisement offering employment at their company. They did not place the advertisement and their reputation is being tarnished as a result of the fraudulent activity. They are also very concerned about the potential prejudice which they might suffer as a result. The advertisement reads as follows:

Wanted: Office managers at Floris Recruitment

We are a renowned recruitment agency and have several positions available for office managers. R21 000.00 p/m neg. Please deposit R500.00 into XYZ bank account and fax proof of payment to 0860 125 4637 to enable us to commence with the administration of your application. Provide us with your email address for further correspondence. On receipt of proof of payment we will, within 14 days, email you the contract of employment for your perusal and acceptance. Contact person: Deon at 079 785 XXXX.

→

→

SWOT analysis		
	Perpetrator	**Investigator**
Strengths	Perpetrator is unknown and has probably used a false and/or an assumed identity	Perpetrator is unaware of the investigation against him and will most likely continue with his crime. We have the fax number, cellphone number and a bank account number of the perpetrator.
Weaknesses	Perpetrator is unaware of the investigation against him and will most likely continue with his crime. Perpetrator had to place an advertisement and open a bank account, thereby leaving a paper trail.	Perpetrator is unknown and has probably used a false and/or assumed identity. Details of person placing the advertisement are probably false. Fax number is probably untraceable.
Opportunities	Perpetrator continues to conduct a lucrative fraudulent scheme without the fear of being exposed and prosecuted.	Tracing of the cellphone to establish the physical whereabouts of the perpetrator. Bank account details are known therefore it is possible to monitor when and where funds are withdrawn from the account.
Threats	Being exposed, arrested and prosecuted.	The difficulties associated with legally obtaining the required information to successfully trace, identify, apprehend and prosecute the perpetrator.

For modern-day policing to be effective, proactive, intelligence-driven investigations are a requirement. In this fast-moving and ever-changing world criminals can cause massive damage if they are not stopped early or, even better, prevented from committing their crimes in the first place.

Example 1.11: The importance of proactive policing

A few years ago a gang of foreign nationals entered the country and began placing card-skimming devices in ATM machines. In this way they obtained the banking details of hundreds of victims and were able to withdraw large amounts of money before the scheme was detected. By the time the police became involved the suspects had already left the country. These suspects were linked to a local gang whose members were known to the police.

Imagine how much damage could have been prevented had the authorities (or the banking institution) been privy to the information of the impending scheme and able to apprehend the criminals before they concluded their deeds. Unfortunately this was not the case and the criminals came, saw, conquered and left with the spoils.

1.14 SELF-EVALUATION CHECKLIST FOR INVESTIGATORS

Investigators should be able to place themselves within the investigation arena and apply the knowledge contained in this chapter. Answering the following questions will clarify your personal vision, mandate and investigation approach.

✓ **CHECKLIST**

- ❑ How would the proactive crime investigation cycle contribute to the successful investigation of a crime or incident within my working environment?
- ❑ Can I apply the flow of an investigation or inquiry within my working environment?
- ❑ Can I identify with the characteristics of an investigator portrayed in my specific working environment?
- ❑ Where do I as investigator fit into this environment?
- ❑ Do I know and understand what my mandate is?
- ❑ How do the ethics fit into my skills development plan?
- ❑ Can I formulate a purpose and objectives for my investigation?
- ❑ Am I able to complete a SWOT analysis for targeted individuals suspected of criminal activities?

1.15 SUMMARY

The content of this chapter is broadly divided into three sections. In the first section terminology used in the chapter was defined to ensure that the reader understands what the authors are referring to. This was followed by a brief discussion of the rules that govern society, what crime is and the criminal and civil recourse available when crime is committed. Restorative justice was highlighted as one of these options. Other transgressions and incidents not necessarily belonging to the criminal or civil categories were also considered.

In the second section the constitutional foundation of investigation was addressed. The purpose and objectives of an investigation were explained. In South Africa investigations are generally carried out by SAPS investigators, statutory investigators and corporate/private investigators. These investigators function in an investigative arena and must adhere to specific legislation. 'Criminal investigations' and 'forensic investigations' have features in common but also differ in some respects.

In the third and final section the authors examined the investigation process. Every investigation or inquiry flows along specific lines. Police investigations and investigations by private investigators differ in certain respects. Investigators generally use seven investigation techniques. The task of an investigator is a multidimensional one and to cope in this environment investigators need specific skills and characteristics because the modern-day investigative cycle differs from the traditional one. The chapter concludes with a self-evaluation checklist for investigators.

REFERENCES

TF Adams, AG Caddell & JL Krutsinger *Crime Scene Investigation* 2 ed (Pearson Education 2004)

RF Becker *Criminal Investigation* 3 ed (Jones & Bartlett Publishers 2009)

JC Bekker & A van der Merwe 'Indigenous legal systems and sentencing: *S v Maluleke* 2008 1 SACR 49 (T)' *De Jure* 2009 at 239–250. Available at http://repository.up.ac.za/bitstream/handle/2263/14243/Bekker_Indigenous%282009%29.pdf?sequence=1, accessed 19 November 2013

WW Bennett & KM Hess *Criminal Investigation* 7 ed (Wadsworth/Thomson Learning 2004)

J Berning, D Mistry & S Tait 'Crime prevention and partnership policing' in J Smit, A Minnaar & J Schnetler (eds) *Smart Policing for Law-Enforcement Officials* (New Africa Education 2004)

MF Brown *Criminal Investigation, Law and Practice* (Butterworth-Heinemann 2001)

J Burger *Strategic Perspectives on Crime and Policing in South Africa* (Van Schaik 2007)

T Callanan 'Principles of crime investigation: Training manual for investigation' (Pretoria, SAPS 1992)

R Claassen 'Restorative justice: Fundamental principles' (1996). Available at http://www.peace.fresno.edu/rjprince.html, accessed 24 April 2012

H Fourie 'Platsak reguleerder trek na "glaskasteel"' *Beeld*, 26 October 2011 at 2

JN Gilbert *Criminal Investigation* 7 ed (Pearson/Prentice Hall 2007)

FE Hagan *Introduction to Criminology, Theories, Methods and Criminal Behaviour* 7 ed (SAGE Publications 2010)

J Horswell *The Practice of Crime Scene Investigation* (CRC 2004)

G Jones Unpublished document with diagram as designed by and in possession of author (2012)

C Joubert *Applied Law for Police Officials* (Juta 2010)

A Kempen 'Forensics: an unbiased scientific tool in fighting crime' (2007) 100(3) *Servamus* 37

RB Kennedy *International Association for Identification* (n.d.). Available at http://www.theiai.org, accessed 12 March 2008

D Lambrechts 'Forensic investigation' (2001) 94(10) *Servamus*

HC Lee & HA Harris *Physical Evidence in Forensic Science* (Lawyers & Judges Publishing 2000)

HC Lee, T Palmbach & MT Miller *Crime Scene Handbook* (Academic Press 2003)

MD Lyman *The Police: An Introduction* (Prentice Hall 1999)

CW Marais *Physical Evidence in Crime Investigation* (Henmar Publications 1992)

F Nel & C Joubert 'Legal aspects' in J Smit, A Minnaar & J Schnetler (eds) *Smart Policing for Law-Enforcement Officials* (New Africa Education 2004)

RA Nossen 'Advanced investigative techniques for private financial records' (n.d.). Available at http://www.scribd.com/doc/63864394/Advanced-Investigative-Techniques-for-Private-Financial-Records, accessed 24 April 2012

RR Ogle *Crime Scene Investigation and Reconstruction, with Guidelines for Crime Scene Search and Physical Evidence Collection* (Pearson Education 2004)

JW Osterburg & RH Ward *Criminal Investigation: A Method for Reconstructing the Past* 6 ed (LexisNexis & Ward 2010)

MJ Palmiotto *Criminal Investigation: Methods and Procedures* 3 ed (University Press of America 2004)

CA Sennewald & JK Tsukayama *The Process of Investigation: Concepts and Strategies for Investigators in the Private Sector* 2 ed (Butterworth-Heinemann 2001)

G Shah *Investigation of Crime and Criminals* (Anmol Publications 2002)

CR Swanson, NC Chamelin & L Territo *Criminal Investigation* 8 ed (McGraw-Hill 2003)

PW Tappen *Crime, Justice, and Correction* (McGraw-Hill 1960)

United Nations Office on Drugs and Crime *Policing, Crime Investigation: Criminal Justice Assessment Toolkit* (UN 2006)

J van der Westhuizen *Forensic Criminalistics* 2 ed (Heinemann 1996)

DW van Ness 'Restorative justice as world view' (2005). Available at http://www.educ.cam.ac.uk/research/projects/restorativeapproaches/DanielWVanNess.pdf, accessed 24 April 2012

HJN van Rooyen *The Practitioner's Guide to Forensic Investigation in South Africa* (Henmar Publications 2008)

A Zysman 'Forensic accounting demystified' (n.d.). Available at http://www.forensicaccounting.com/one.htm#start, accessed 13 October 2007

PRINCIPLES OF INVESTIGATION

2

J van Graan • T Budhram

Chapter

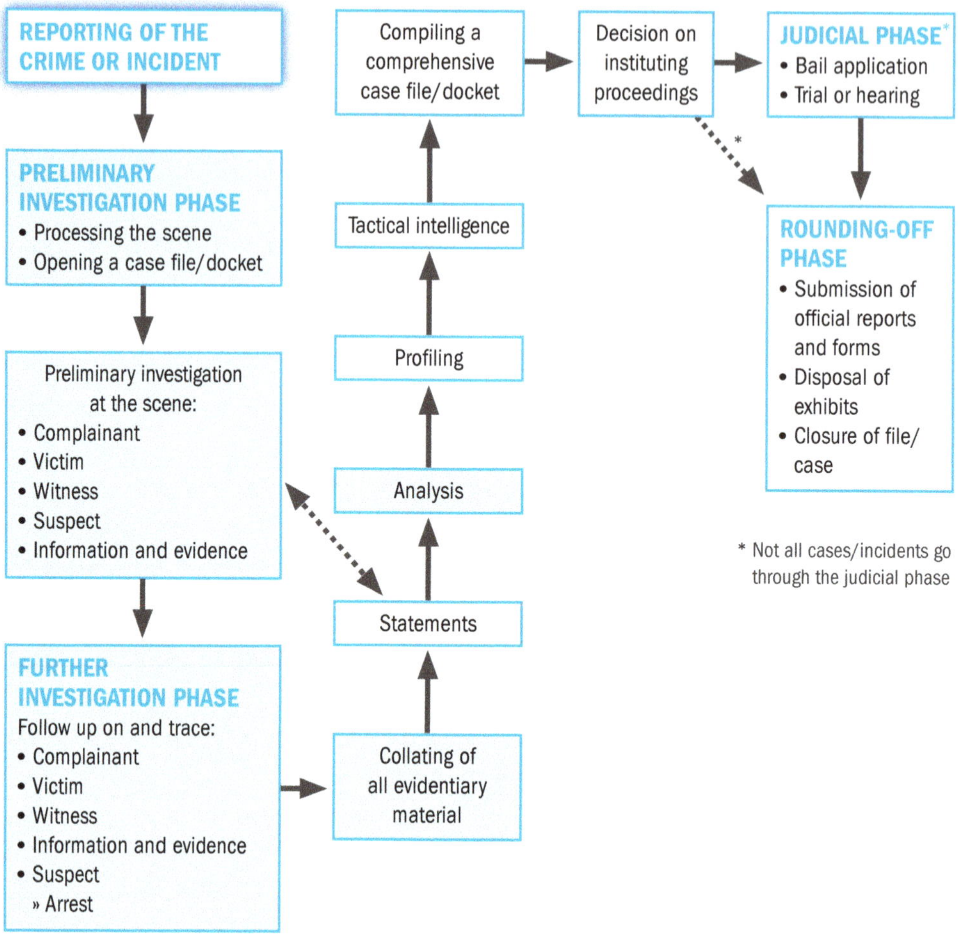

Figure 2.1: Areas of the crime investigation process covered in this chapter shown in shaded area

2.1 INTRODUCTION

The investigation of a crime, incident or transgression is a science. It is therefore important that an investigator should apply scientific methods, up-to-date techniques and logical reasoning during the investigation process. In order for the investigator to ensure that a scientific approach is adopted during an investigation, the investigator must be familiar with the principles of investigation.

There is no single definition that describes or explains the principles of investigation. However, in this context, these principles include identification, individualisation, the Locard exchange principle, examination and the gathering of factual information that answers questions or solves problems. It is therefore important to acknowledge that the principles of investigation include three main categories, namely:

- identification
- individualisation
- the Locard exchange principle (also see section 11.2.2 in chapter 11).

The purpose of identification in forensic investigation is to identify physical evidence, which can then be analysed to help the investigator pursue a productive path based on the clues provided by the specific characteristics of the physical evidence. The Locard exchange principle is known as the foundation on which identification is based, while individualisation can be seen as a more specific and later facet of identification.

Figure 2.1 illustrates the aspects of the crime investigation process that are covered in this chapter.

2.2 THE LOCARD EXCHANGE PRINCIPLE

One of the most significant and influential concepts in the history of forensic investigation and any other investigation is known as the Locard exchange principle.

The Locard exchange principle was theorised by forensic scientist Edmond Locard. He was the director of the earliest crime laboratory in existence, situated in France. The hypothesis of the Locard exchange principle is that some form of evidence is usually left behind when two objects or people come into contact with each other. Locard's hypothesis has been noted in the annals as follows:

> Wherever he steps, whatever he touches, whatever he leaves, even unconsciously, will serve as a silent witness against him. Not only his fingerprints or his footprints, but his hair, the fibres from his clothes, the glass he breaks, the tool mark he leaves, the paint he scratches, the blood or semen he deposits or collects. All of these and more, bear mute witness against him. This is evidence that does not forget. It is not confused by the excitement of the moment. It is not absent because human witnesses are. It is factual evidence. Physical evidence cannot be wrong, it cannot perjure itself, it cannot be wholly absent. Only human failure to find it, study and understand it, can diminish its value.[1]

This principle is fundamentally applied to a scene of incident (traditionally referred to as a 'crime scene') where the perpetrator comes into contact with the scene. In other words, Locard's hypothesis assumes that the perpetrator will bring something into the scene, leave something at the scene, and leave with something from the scene, be it physical or electronic. Locard based his argument on the fact that it is impossible for an individual to act without leaving traces of their presence.

1 Kirk (1953).

When a crime, a transgression or an incident is committed, some or other clue is usually left behind because, on the basis of the Locard exchange principle or contact theory, a mutual transfer of 'tracks' takes place when two objects or persons come into contact with each other. For example, when a suspect touches a glass window, they leave traces on it in the form of fingerprints. Reciprocal traces from the windowpane, such as dust or glass splinters, are transferred to the suspect's hand. The 'tracks' at the scene of incident can be used to reconstruct or recreate the scene of incident and individualise the perpetrator.[2] For this reason preventative measures should be taken to eliminate contamination of evidential material.

The Locard exchange principle is the scientific theory that all investigators must subscribe to if they want to successfully analyse and investigate the scene of incident. Modern-day technology has presented scenarios in which perpetrators can be identified without two objects or persons physically coming into contact with one another in order to transfer 'tracks'. This argument can be substantiated by looking at cellphone technology.

Electronic signals, for example cellphone signals, can help to identify the whereabouts of a perpetrator. A cellphone receives and sends invisible radio signals. This invisibility of the 'tracks' poses a challenge to investigators because they must learn how to identify invisible clues of this nature. It is therefore important that an investigator has a sound knowledge of the Criminal Procedure Act 51 of 1977 (CPA) and, more specifically, of s 205 of that Act. In terms of s 205 of the CPA an investigator may apply to a court for authorisation to subpoena cellphone service providers to make available the invisible information in the form of documentary evidence so that the investigator can identify and individualise the perpetrator. The identification process by means of this technology makes it possible to physically identify the owner of the instrument and the type of instrument used, and links the perpetrator to the scene of incident and the contact persons. Identification by means of these invisible 'tracks' is illustrated in *S v Moodley* [2006] JOL 18074 (W).

2.3 IDENTIFICATION: A CONCEPTUAL CLARIFICATION

Identification, in its most basic explanation, entails the act of identifying a person or object. This poses a challenge to an investigator who has to ensure that an innocent person is not held liable for an incident they have not committed and equally to ensure that the perpetrator is identified. It is therefore essential that the investigative process provides for the successful and positive identification of a person who has committed a crime, transgressed a company policy or procedure, or has been involved in an incident or irregularity. As a result, the identification process plays a vital role in the criminal and forensic investigation

2 Van Rooyen (2004).

process which, in a modern context, may include criminal investigations, civil investigations, departmental investigations and tribunals.

In broad terms, all forensic science concerns identification of some sort. In the more focused context of forensic investigation, identification entails the positive identification and linking of a person, object, substance and culpability to a crime or incident. Identification can therefore be considered as a point of departure in the investigation process and the foundation of any investigation.

The term 'identification' is explained as a classification system when objects with similar characteristics are classified into one category (class) and a name is given to each category. Identification concerns the identification of something or somebody as belonging to a specific category.[3]

Identification can thus be defined as a process that utilises the class characteristics of an object or known substances to compare to evidence collected from a scene of incident.

For investigators to fully appreciate the potential value of physical evidence, they need to understand what class characteristics are. Simply put, class characteristics are characteristics of physical evidence that are common to a group of objects or persons.[4] Class characteristics are described as the features that place an item in a specific category. For example, the size and shape of a tool mark may indicate that the tool used was a screwdriver rather than a pry bar.[5]

Identification can thus be described as a process of identifying, collecting and classifying evidentiary material from a person or object (which is usually visible but in certain cases not visible to the naked eye) into a specific category that will allow for proving or disproving a fact in contention.

In forensic investigation the successful identification of evidence is paramount if one wants to continue with the investigation. When an incident has taken place, an investigator is faced with the challenge of collecting evidence at the scene of incident. The scene of incident is of great importance to the investigator because it allows for the identification of evidentiary material and clues, and gives the investigator an overall picture of what happened. An investigator visiting the scene of incident should be familiar with the theory of the Locard exchange principle. As mentioned above, this principle provides that an investigator can with certainty accept that there will always be evidence at a scene of incident. However, the detection and identification of that evidence is not always a simple task because of the complexities of the evidence, for example disputed documents, digital evidence, hair, blood or saliva.

---

3 Van Rooyen (2001).
4 Swanson et al. (2003).
5 Bennett & Hess (2004).

2.4 ORIGINS OF IDENTIFICATION

The Frenchman Alphonse Bertillon is known as the founder of identification. In 1888 Bertillon developed his method of identification, called anthropometry, based on the uniqueness of the human frame. This revolutionary method of identification was surprisingly logical, simple and easy to use. Bertillon's theory was based on the effective and consistent method of identification using rigid physical characteristics that are not susceptible to change. By this method, the human body was measured in 11 key places. These measurements were then recorded with characteristics such as the colour of the eyes, hair and skin. This led to a method of identification based on scientific principles. Bertillon continued to forge ahead in the field of police science and identification and can also be credited with the development of police photography, methods of preserving plaster casts and utilising ultraviolet photography to examine disputed documents. Bertillon was also instrumental in developing the science of fingerprinting. Although he did not invent the fingerprinting technique, Bertillon valued its potential and continued to become the first identification expert in Europe to solve a murder case solely by means of fingerprint evidence and identification.[6]

2.5 CLASSIFICATION OF IDENTIFICATION

The cumulative nature of identification is clearly reflected in the fact that a series of identifications is sometimes required to establish the guilt or innocence of an individual. Identification is classified into various categories in order to assist in individualising an individual. The investigator will select a specific identification category based on the specific crime, transgression or incident being investigated. The various categories of identification include:

- situation identification
- witness identification
- victim identification
- imprint identification
- origin identification
- action identification
- perpetrator identification
- cumulative identification.

These categories are discussed below and substantiated with South African case law and examples.

2.5.1 Situation identification

Situation identification (ie identification of the situation) specifically relates to the circumstances of the incident. To be more specific, the initial task of the in-

6 Gilbert (2004).

vestigator should be to establish whether an incident, a crime or a transgression has indeed taken place, and to identify the specific incident. To confirm that an incident has indeed been committed, the investigator should determine the type of incident and immediately evaluate the situation in order to formulate an investigative hypothesis that takes account of the situation of the incident. This implies that investigators should draw on investigative knowledge and expertise to familiarise themselves with the facts of the incident so that they can isolate the facts that can shed light on the situation of that particular incident.

Situation identification can further be explained as a psychological reconstruction of the situation of the incident. By reconstructing the events the investigator strives to form a realistic hypothesis about what happened. The reconstruction can be based on a deductive or an inductive approach. If the deductive approach is used, the investigator reconstructs the events by considering the general appearance and circumstances at the scene in order to find possible explanations for the events. The inductive approach requires the logical generalisation of events at the scene to reach a conclusion based on observation. The adopted hypotheses should then be evaluated and analysed against the evidence on hand to reach a conclusion about the situation of the incident.

However, due to the limitations of human observation, situation identification must be approached with caution. If the situation is not correctly identified, the incident may be incorrectly approached and/or investigated. Valuable evidence can be lost and it is highly probable that the investigative hypothesis will remain unsubstantiated. In forensic investigations, particularly in private companies, this can be a costly exercise as resources may be wasted in the investigation of false alarms.

2.5.2 Witness identification

Evidence collection always starts at the scene of incident. Whereas evidence relates to people and objects, witness identification deals with people rather than objects and documents. Every scene of incident has a victim and/or a complainant, therefore people are essential sources of information about an incident. Witnesses can be directly involved in an incident, for example the victim of a sexual harassment case, or they can simply be an eyewitness to the commission of an incident, for example an eyewitness to a robbery. Witnesses may also be involved in an event but not present during its execution, for example an expert witness who has analysed a fraudulent document.

In other instances, persons can merely act as a source of information despite not being directly or indirectly involved in the crime, transgression or incident, for example a media reporter.

Witness identification (ie identification of the perpetrator by a witness or witnesses) can thus be described as the process of linking an individual perpetrator to a specific incident on account of statements by witnesses and complainants.

> **Example 2.1:** *S v Zwayi* and *Ketani and Another v S*
>
> An example of witness identification from case law is found in the case of *S v Zwayi* [1998] 1 All SA 569 (Ck) where the accused had committed various counts of murder, kidnapping, robbery and attempted robbery. The court found that there had been sufficient opportunity for the witnesses to observe the features of the perpetrator and found each of the witnesses to be credible and their evidence reliable.
>
> Witness identification is further substantiated in *Ketani and Another v S* [2002] 3 All SA 15 (C), which deals with an appeal against the conviction and sentence on charges of robbery with aggravating circumstances. Much of the court's emphasis was directed at the identification of the accused by the witnesses. It was common cause that the accused were identified by their features and had not been known to the identifying witnesses prior to the robbery. The accused were identified individually by the witnesses by means of a photo album. The court was satisfied that the witnesses had corroborated each other in material respects as to what had transpired. The accused were found guilty.

2.5.3 Victim identification

The identity of the victim forms a significant part of the investigation process. Identification of the victim mainly relates to, but is not limited to, deceased victims. This type of identification is often the most important and sometimes the only starting point to solving an incident.

> **Example 2.2:** Victims of financial crime
>
> In an incident of credit card fraud the lawful owners of credit cards are in most cases the victims. However, the victims are always traceable due to the fact that the financial institutions have their personal details. Victim identification is becoming increasingly significant in economic crimes and in forensic investigation in general.

Victim identification can furthermore be illustrated in the exponential growth of the internet that has given rise to advanced forms of cybercrime, for example identity theft. This crime occurs when criminals use your personal information without your knowledge or consent to commit crimes such as fraud, deception or theft. Identity thieves steal or obtain key pieces of personal information and use that information to impersonate the victim and to commit crimes using the victim's name and identity profile. The crime of identity theft is difficult to police or monitor because it can range from the simple unauthorised use of a credit card to a complete takeover of a person's identity.

However, in cases where victims are deceased and not identifiable by those known to them, the investigator has to rely on available information found at the scene of incident. This could include an identity document, a driver's licence, personal belongings such as distinctively engraved jewellery and clothing, or photographs of family, relatives and colleagues. Should the incident be murder or if the victim is unconscious, the identification process may take more time to complete.

2.5.4 Imprint identification

The identification of imprints is the process of comparing two instances of friction ridge skin impressions from human fingers, the palm of the hand, footprints or even toes to determine whether these impressions could have come from the same individual (see chapter 5 for more details). Imprint identification is, however, not limited to friction ridge skin impressions and could also include impressions such as bite marks, tyre marks and tool marks.

The fundamental principle of imprint identification is that the distinctive characteristics of an object are transferred to the surfaces with which they come into contact. The value of identification in this case depends on the nature of the object and the surface upon which the imprint was made. In most cases of documentary fraud, for example credit card and cheque fraud, the fingerprints of suspects are always left on the document.

Imprint identification is also known as individualisation. Individualisation means to ascribe something to a specific individual, be it a person or an object. With reference to imprint identification, it confirms whether two friction ridge impressions are likely to have originated from the same finger, palm, toe, footprint, tyre mark or bite mark. In other words, a disputed imprint is compared to a control imprint in order to effect individualisation.

Imprint identification is used in the investigation process to identify the victims of an incident, a crime or a transgression and to place suspects at a scene of incident. As such it is often of critical importance. The uniqueness of imprints makes it possible to use prints from a scene of incident to either link a suspect to the scene or eliminate a suspect from consideration. However, before imprints can be identified, the investigator must be able to detect them. Imprint identification techniques continue to evolve in tandem with the development of modern technology.

Example 2.3: ***Pongola v S***

In *Pongola v S* [2006] JOL 26512 (E) the appellant was convicted of the theft of a motor vehicle. A fingerprint taken from the stolen vehicle was matched to that of the appellant. The appellant could not give an explanation for his fingerprint being found in the motor vehicle. He was found guilty and sentenced.

2.5.5 Origin identification

The identification of the origin of evidence is the process that seeks to determine, trace or identify evidence in dispute that have a common origin. This type of identification allows for the analysis of organic and inorganic solids and fluids in order to determine whether a common origin exists.

Origin identification, therefore, relates to the investigation of death, poisoning, the use of prohibited substances, fraud, maladministration and non-compliance with company policy and procedure. The process includes the analysis of various kinds of samples, such as disputed documents, company policy and procedure, urine, blood, hair and saliva, in order to determine a link between the disputed samples.

In cases where disputed documents are used to commit a crime, a transgression or an incident, the investigator must pay particular attention to the origin of these documents.

In investigating the possible use of prohibited substances, the investigator should pay particular attention to the physical symptoms of the person, for example bodily injuries, fatigue, an inability to focus or concentrate, profuse sweating, uncontrollable trembling, tense muscles and nausea, as well as evidence at the scene of incident that may assist in the investigation, for example pill bottles, used needles, powders, trace residue and any other chemicals.

2.5.6 Action identification

The identification of an action relates to human behaviour that directly constitutes all the elements of a crime, a transgression or an incident. In forensic investigation this type of identification is relevant to incidents such as fraud, forgery and uttering or any other crime or incident where a disputed document is either directly involved in its commission or could be an important revealing clue. Action identification must be further substantiated by a process known as individualisation. For example, in a forgery case it must be established whether the disputed handwriting is the work of a particular individual. Examples of disputed documents can include business contracts, identity documents, cheques and credit cards.

Documents are part of a person's everyday existence. The importance of documents and the probability that a document can be forged in almost any type of business transaction have made business people, attorneys, law officials and the general public much more aware of the fact that documents should be safeguarded. Experts in the field of disputed documents have also become important in analysing and providing scientific findings. The document expert is as reliant on comparison standards as other forensic experts. A document expert can make an inference by comparing disputed documents (which include handwriting, typewriting, paper and ink) with comparison standards coming from or found in the possession of the suspect. A comparison standard can for instance be a handwriting sample which is offered as a standard and against which a disputed handwriting sample may be tested. It can serve as proof of being the original handwriting of the person with whom the disputed document or signature is linked. Example 2.4 illustrates an authentic signature, S, followed by a forged signature, Q.

Example 2.4: Illustration of an authentic signature (S) and a forged signature (Q)

(S)

(Q)

The basic principle in the investigation of disputed documents is to obtain all the facts that are relevant to the document. Every piece of information regarding the origin and possible authenticity of the document and its author is important. The exact nature of what is being disputed must also be clarified, for example handwriting, a signature, authorship, additions, alterations or erasures, or the identification of inks or papers.

Example 2.5: *NDPP v Pelser and Others*

In *NDPP v Pelser and Others* [2006] JOL 18094 (T) the defendant was a businessman who entered into a joint venture with another businessman. The two were joint signatories to the joint venture's bank account. When the second signatory discovered that the defendant had issued cheques drawn on the bank account to himself and his other companies by forging the second signatory's signature, the defendant was charged with fraud, forgery and theft. Based on the facts before the court, there were reasonable grounds that the defendant could be convicted of forgery or theft.

There was no dispute that the defendant's company, or companies in which he was the sole shareholder, had benefited from the money withdrawn from the bank accounts of the joint venture. As a result, the likelihood of a confiscation was more than real.

2.5.7 Perpetrator identification

The identification of a perpetrator specifically relates to the positive identification of the suspect in person, rather than the identification of the illegal act. In forensic investigation, determining the identity of the perpetrator or suspected perpetrator of an unlawful act is of decisive importance because the detection and, by implication, the clarification of the incident situation are hardly possible without it. The collection of information and facts to determine the identity of the offender and their part in the incident remains the crux of any investigation.

The most common direct method of perpetrator identification involves identification parades. In *S v Nkomo* 1990 (1) SACR 682 (ZS) the question was whether it was the appellant who had committed the murder. The witness to this murder identified the appellant at an identification parade. The court was satisfied with the witness's identification. The appellant was convicted of murder and sentenced to death.

Perpetrator identification was further highlighted in *Charzen and Another v S* 2006 (2) SACR 143 (SCA) in which an armed robbery at the home of the complainant resulted in certain suspects being arrested for the crime. The complainant identified the appellants at an identification parade. The appellants were then charged, convicted and sentenced on charges of, inter alia, robbery and attempted murder.

Example 2.6: Indirect identification

Identification can also be in the form of indirect identification. In *S v Sothalaza* [2005] JOL 14266 (Tk) the accused was charged with raping a 16-year-old girl. The only issue to be decided was the identity of the rapist. The accused had pleaded not guilty to the charge. Blood samples had been drawn from the accused for testing to prove his guilt. A report from the forensic scientist who tested the specimens taken from the complainant and the accused found that rape could not be excluded. Consequently, the accused was found guilty of rape.

2.5.8 Cumulative identification

Cumulative identification is where contributions of different specialists are collectively considered within the framework of the history and relevant circumstances of the situation as a whole.[7] With the exception of omission, a person cannot commit an incident, a crime or a transgression without performing some act. Irrespective of the nature of the act, be it violent or taciturn, the possibility remains that the perpetrator will leave or remove something from the scene (the Locard exchange principle), which could connect them to the unlawful act.

7 Du Preez (1996).

One form of evidence in cumulative identification includes verbal evidence. This form of evidence is quite often not available, for example when the victim is dead or when witnesses were not present. In these situations, reliance must be placed on the evidential value of physical evidence.

The best-known example of physical evidence is fingerprints, which can only be left by contact with certain objects.[8]

Physical evidence includes a large variety of objects. Almost any object, substance, trace or impression could constitute physical evidence. Here it is a matter of objects rather than people. Anything that could indicate that an incident has been committed, or which could point to the identification, detection or association of an individual, such as weapons, fingerprints and other prints, handwriting, hair, blood, semen, containers, tool pieces, fingernail scrapings, soil, grass and documents, may be termed evidence. In a murder case it could be a weapon or the victim's corpse, and in a burglary it could be a piece of fabric on a broken window pane or a screwdriver at the burglary scene.

Example 2.7: Cumulative evidence

In *Seyisi v S* [2006] JOL 16703 (Ck) the appellant was convicted on 1 025 counts of fraud. The appellant was granted leave to appeal against the conviction. The state's evidence was based on the testimony of a fingerprint expert. The expert evidence was properly placed before the court, which in turn was entitled to rely on this evidence. The appeal was dismissed.

Cumulative identification is further highlighted in *Ntsele v S* [1998] 3 ALL SA 517 (A). The appellant had been convicted of robbery with aggravating circumstances, three counts of murder and five counts of attempted murder. It was the cumulative impression that had to be weighed up in making the decision whether the guilt of the accused had been proved beyond reasonable doubt. On the facts, the court found that it had correctly found the appellant guilty beyond a reasonable doubt and the appeal was accordingly dismissed.

Cumulative identification is further illustrated in *Gobe v S* (2008) SA 188 (E).

2.6 TYPES OF IDENTIFICATION

In addition to the abovementioned classification, the investigator can make use of two types of identification during the investigation process, namely direct identification and indirect identification.

2.6.1 Direct identification

The direct method of identification refers especially to techniques to identify perpetrators, such as personal descriptions, sketches, identification parades,

8 Marais (1992).

incidental identification, photo identification, voice identification, identification by means of closed-circuit television and the perpetrator's *modus operandi*. These direct methods lead to the identification of a specific individual on the grounds of direct experiences of the incident.

2.6.1.1 Personal descriptions

Every person has distinctive features that clearly distinguish one person from another based on their physical appearance. Physical features, such as the eyes, nose and mouth, contribute to a person's distinct character and are therefore significant in the identification process and in descriptions that could lead to identification. A description of a person should be as accurate as possible, with limited possibility for inaccuracy, to allow individuals reading or listening to the description to form a clear picture of the person being described. This will increase the probability of the person being identified. Regardless of the development of modern-day technology, such as digital photographic equipment, the accurate description of a person continues to play a vital role in identification.

A word picture of a person, also known as *portrait parle*, is normally used to describe the general features of a person for identification purposes. The physical description starts at the head, but if the person has an unusual or eye-catching characteristic, such as a prominent mouth, a facial scar, other markings such as tattoos, a speech defect, jewellery or a beard or moustache, that characteristic will be described first.

Universal terms used to describe the general features of a person are illustrated in the following checklist:

Table 2.1: Checklist for a physical description

Gender	Male	Female			
Race	Black	Brown	White	Indian/ Asian	Other
Height	Estimate if exact height is not known				
Build	Large	Average	Small		
Posture	Upright	Normal	Bent or stooping	Leaning forward	
Weight	Obese	Average	Slender		
Age	Estimate if exact age is not known				
Complexion	Black	Brown	White	Dark	Fair

After the general features have been described, the *portrait parle* starts with a description of the person's head. The features of the head include the forehead, hairline, hair, colour, eyebrows, colour of the irises, prominence of the eyeballs and whether the person wears glasses. Other features of the head include a description of the nose, mouth, lips, teeth, chin, ears and cheeks. Thereafter features of the neck, shoulders, arms, hands, fingers, chest, hips, legs and feet are described. Distinguishing features, such as scars or other markings (tattoos, etc) speech defects, jewellery or a beard or moustache should also be described.

The description should be as comprehensive as possible to enable others to effortlessly create a clear mental picture of the person's features. Figure 2.2 and Figure 2.3 illustrate the distinctive characteristics of individual features that clearly distinguish one individual from another.

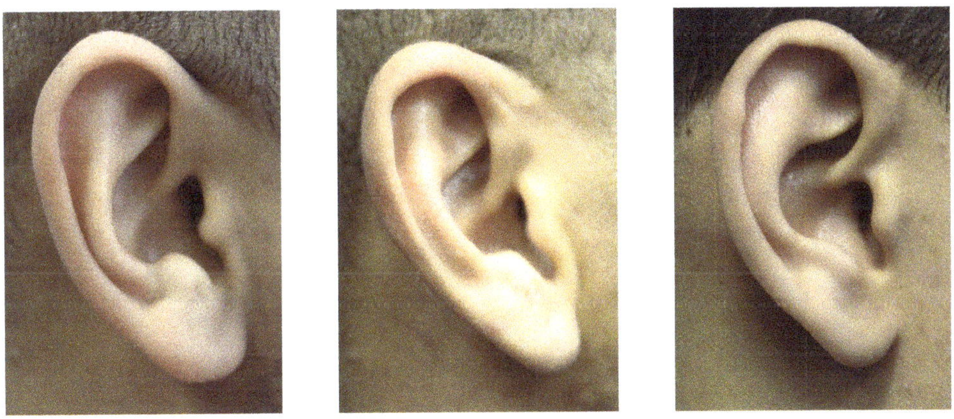

Figure 2.2: Distinctive characteristics of individuals' ears

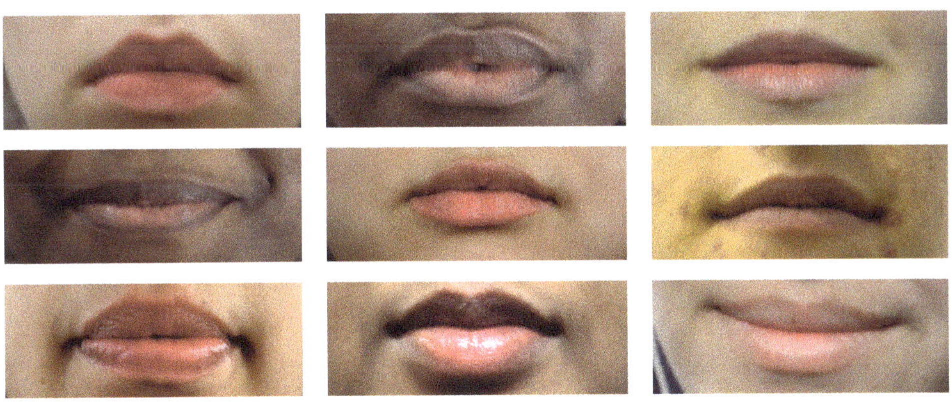

Figure 2.3: Distinctive characteristics of individuals' lips

2.6.1.2 Identification parades

An identification parade is when a group of persons of more or less similar stature, height, age, weight, appearance, clothing, gender and race, including the suspect, are gathered together for the purpose of establishing if a victim or witness can directly and personally identify the suspected individual. If a person is positively identified in an identification parade, it can be used as evidence in court.

It must be noted that the accused is entitled to legal representation during the identification parade so as to guard against the rights of the accused being violated. However, the purpose of an identification parade is merely to confirm or disprove the identification of an individual.

An identification parade is usually conducted through a one-way mirror to protect the identity of the victim or witness. However, in recent years the advancement of technology has made video identification parades possible. This method allows a witness to identify an individual without viewing the suspect in person. The video identification parade is a pre-recorded image of a physically conducted parade and is digitally played back to a victim or witness at any location on a monitor such as a television screen or a laptop. Figure 2.4 illustrates a typical identification parade.

© iStock.com/ RichLegg

Figure 2.4: Identification parade

2.6.1.3 Photo identification

Photographic images are an effective method of identification. However, the effectiveness of photographs as identification method relies on the quality of the photograph and on how recently the photograph was taken. Modern-day digitally captured photographs provide a clearer picture quality, thus enhancing the possibility of identification by means of a photograph. Figure 2.5 illustrates a photo that can be used to identify an individual.

If a photograph is not available, the investigator can rely on the assistance of experts to construct an identikit of the facial features of an individual based on the descriptions provided by witnesses, family members or acquaintances. An identikit is normally compiled from a composite of various principal facial characteristics such as the eyes, mouth, nose, chin, forehead and hairline. The people providing the description of the individual to be identified choose those principal features that most closely resemble the face of the person that needs to be reconstructed. Identikits can be circulated in the printed and electronic media or among victims or witnesses of incidents to enhance the possibility of a person being identified. Figure 2.6 illustrates an identikit of the facial features of an individual.

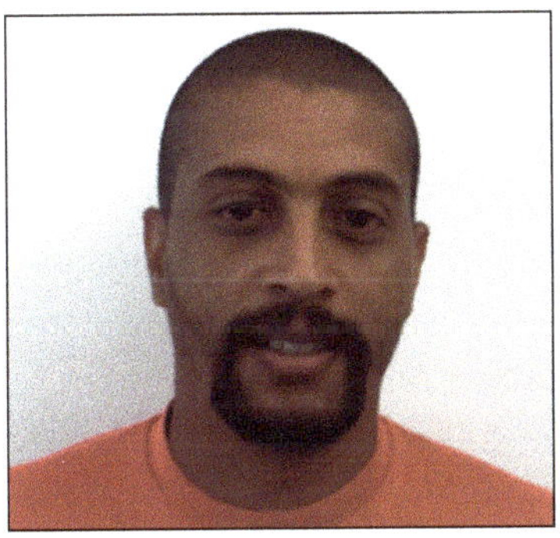

Figure 2.5. Identification by photograph

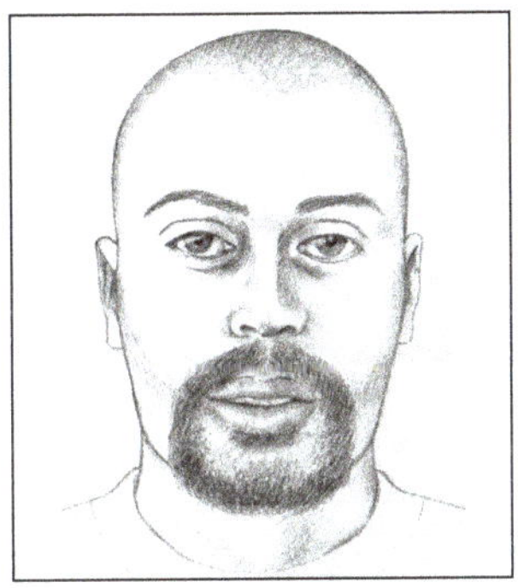

Figure 2.6: Identification by identikit

2.6.1.4 Voice identification

During an incident or normal communication between persons, an exchange of words could take place between the perpetrator and the victim, witnesses, client or service provider. This communication can help those involved in or who witnessed the incident or transaction to identify an individual's voice. Every person's voice is unique and has many distinctive characteristics, making it possible for people to identify voices they have heard before. However, a distinction should be made between voice recognition by the human ear and voice identification. Voice identification does not rely on the human ear, but utilises technology to electronically illustrate the identifying characteristics of an individual's voice. It follows that voice prints from an individual can be generated and compared to reach a conclusion on the identifiability of an individual. Voice recognition by the human ear is not reliable because there is always a possibility of error. The unreliability and scope for error in voice identification can thus be challenged in a court of law.

In the past, voice identification played a more significant role as a means of eliminating a suspicious person than of positively identifying someone.

Voice identification has developed into a sophisticated identification technique, using the latest technology science has to offer. One of the latest advances in voice identification technology introduced in South Africa is voice biometric identification. Voice biometrics, also known as speaker recognition, verifies whether you are who you say you are by comparing the speaker's voice print with the voice print registered for the owner. This voice identification technique enables secure voice-based self-service transactions and replaces authentication questions from call centre agents such as personal identification numbers (PINs) or passwords. This identification technique could thus prove to be a useful tool to prevent fraudsters from gaining access to the personal information of a company's clients from call centres. South African companies are continuously searching for ways to improve their security measures and voice biometric identification could play a significant role as a preventative measure for identity theft-related fraud, such as credit card fraud.

Voice identification is only permissible in a court of law if an existing voice impression can be compared with the voice of an offender. The admissibility of voice identification in South African courts rests on the principle of the witness having to identify the voice of an offender among other voices.

Example 2.8: Admissibility of voice identification

The admissibility of voice identification is illustrated in *Nnasolu and Another v S* [2009] SACR 561 (KZP) where the magistrate convicted the first appellant partly on the basis that the witness had given evidence that the person he had spoken to on the telephone on previous occasions was the same person as the first appellant because he had recognised the voice on each occasion.

2.6.1.5 Identification by means of closed-circuit television

The application of closed-circuit television (CCTV) for identification purposes is mainly threefold:

- CCTV is used for the prevention of incidents
- CCTV is used as a monitoring method
- CCTV is used to obtain information that can be used as evidence after an incident has occurred.

Monitoring by means of CCTV surveillance of public and private areas, such as financial institutions, mining premises, gambling houses and freeways, has become common practice. These public and private CCTV systems are implemented for a number of reasons:

- real-time monitoring of areas to detect incidents and identify individuals, for example the identification of a bank robber
- recording of events to use as evidence in investigations, for example the identification of offenders during a mass protest.

The development of technology has replaced the analogue CCTV system with an advanced digital generation CCTV system. The intelligent digital CCTV system has significant value for identification, for example automatic face recognition, automatic number plate recognition and the tracking and identification of a suspicious individual.

The use of CCTV surveillance systems in the larger South African central business districts (CBDs) as an urban crime management system has escalated over recent years. One of the significant functions of this CCTV initiative is to help identify people and vehicles involved in incidents. CCTV as an identification technique is used in the corporate, industrial and retail sectors and footage can be used as evidence in a court of law. *Mdlongwa v S* [2010] ZASCA 82 illustrates how the state relied on CCTV footage as evidence in a bank robbery to sufficiently establish the identification of the appellant. Figure 2.7 illustrates CCTV footage during a bank robbery while Figure 2.8 illustrates the identification of vehicles by means of automatic number plate recognition.

Figure 2.7: CCTV footage of a bank robbery

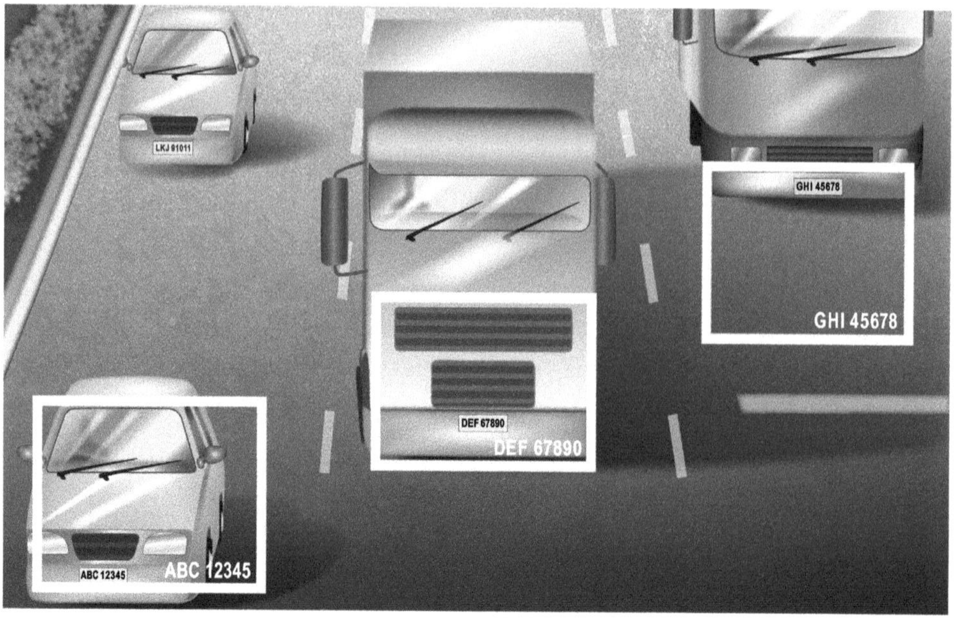

Figure 2.8: Automatic number plate recognition

2.6.1.6 *Modus operandi*

Identification by means of *modus operandi* is based on the theory that an offender is likely to use the same method consistently in the execution of similar incidents. The recordkeeping and analysis of these methods can help the investigator to identify the perpetrator in a particular incident(s). In other words, *modus operandi* is a learnt behaviour which the offender applies and refines over time. As a result, the investigator can reach a fairly accurate conclusion to determine whether the perpetrator is the same repeat offender or a new offender. Although the *modus operandi* of a transgressor can slightly change over time, an experienced investigator would be in a position to link an offender to a specific incident based on the fundamental characteristics of the *modus operandi*. *Modus operandi* is discussed in more detail in chapter 9.

Example 2.9: The Sunday rapist

The Sunday rapist, who raped a series of girls in Gauteng and North West between November 2008 and October 2011, consistently used the same method in each incident. The *modus operandi* of the perpetrator provided the investigator with an accurate conclusion that these incidents were executed by the same repeat offender. After the perpetrator's arrest he was identified as the 'Sunday rapist' based on the elementary characteristics of his *modus operandi*.

2.6.2 Indirect identification

The method of indirect identification concerns physical evidence and phenomena by which the identity of the offender and their part in the incident may be determined. Examples include physical evidence left behind at the scene of incident by the offender (eg fingerprints, footprints, handwriting, tool impressions) and physical evidence connecting the offender with the victim or the scene of incident (eg blood, semen, hair, fibres).

2.6.2.1 Physical evidence

The investigator usually collects and examines physical evidence for the purposes of identification and comparison. The purpose of identification is to determine the physical or chemical identity of an object or substance beyond any doubt. Physical evidence includes any object or substance that can confirm whether an incident has been committed or that can link an incident to the victim or the perpetrator. Physical evidence includes, inter alia, fingerprints, footprints, tool impressions, organic and physiological fluids, paint, petroleum products, plastic bags, blood, semen, soil, serial numbers, fibres, hair, saliva, documents and firearms.

Example 2.10: Microdotting

The introduction of microdotting for the identification of motor vehicles in South Africa is an illustration of new advances in motor vehicle identification. Microdotting is a process whereby vehicle manufacturers spray a number of about 10 000 minute dots, each comprising a unique identification number, in at least 88 different places on a vehicle. This process leaves a lasting imprint of the original identity of the motor vehicle and its associated parts. The microdots can easily be detected with an ultraviolet light and magnifier.

Figure 2.9 illustrates a magnified image of a microdot used to physically identify the original identity of a motor vehicle.

Figure 2.9: Magnified image of a microdot

2.7 INDIVIDUALISATION

The overall aim of individualisation is to individualise the incident as the act of a particular person or persons. Individualisation can be described as a process that starts with identification, progresses to classification and leads, if possible, to assigning a unique source to a given piece of physical evidence. It refers to the demonstration that a particular sample is unique even among members of the same class. Individualisation can further be explained as the process of linking physical evidence to a common source.

Individualisation involves the identification and comparison of disputed objects found at a scene of incident in order to adequately link each object to the incident and/or to a person. These identifications and comparisons have a twofold aim:

- to positively individualise the various objects in dispute
- to conclusively determine the involvement of the object or person by providing the standard of comparison.

However, the mere identification of an object does not have much evidential merit unless it is positively linked to a specific individual. When an object such as handwriting is positively compared to that of a specific individual, it increases the value of the object for the investigator and the subsequent trial or other quasi-judicial processes. This comparison allows the investigator to determine the individuality of an object. In other words, the object has been 'individualised'. This explanation clearly demonstrates that identification and individualisation are interconnected processes. Investigators cannot apply them separately. Identification paves the way for individualisation, and individualisation cannot take place without a cycle of identifications.

Individual characteristics form an integral part of the individualisation process. These characteristics can be described as features that distinguish one item from another of the same type, for example chips and wear patterns on the blade of a screwdriver may leave marks that can be distinguished from those of any other screwdriver. Palm prints, fingerprints, footprints and DNA (deoxyribonucleic acid) are examples of evidence with individual characteristics and can be identified with a high degree of probability as originating from a particular person or source. South African courts have long accepted fingerprints as evidence of identification, although statistics regarding the significance of the match are generally not provided. The use of DNA to identify individuals has been highly scrutinised and the forensic laboratory must provide statistics demonstrating the significance of genetic profiling results. By examining a number of genetic locations, the frequency of occurrence of a genetic profile will become so small that the examiner may conclude that the evidence came from a particular individual.

As a process, individualisation begins at a scene of incident and ends with giving evidence in a court of law, at a disciplinary enquiry or at a special tribunal.

2.8 DIFFERENCES BETWEEN IDENTIFICATION AND INDIVIDUALISATION

The term 'individualisation' is often mistaken for 'identification'. However, it is evident from literature that there are distinct differences between these two concepts. These differences are important when it comes to investigation. In any forensic investigation, evidence must first be identified before the investigation can continue. It follows that the investigator should identify evidence by asking questions such as: Is this a disputed document? Is this a blood stain? Is this an imprint?

Identification and individualisation in forensic investigation are two inalienable and complementary concepts. Identification without individualisation has no evidential value; it merely gives direction to the investigation of an incident, victim or perpetrator. Identification is merely concerned with the identification of something or somebody belonging to a specific category. It does not allow comparisons to be drawn, for example A is simply A, and a hair is simply a hair.

Individualisation, on the other hand, involves comparison, usually of the disputed object found at the scene of incident with an object of known origin obtained from the suspected person, for example the fingerprint of a known perpetrator (fingerprints of known origin). A comparison is made to determine whether the print in dispute that was found at the scene of incident is that of the known perpetrator whose fingerprints are on record due to their previous convictions.

To add value to the investigation process, it is important that identification and individualisation satisfy certain requirements, namely:

- uniqueness
- individuality
- invariability
- reproducibility
- classifiability.

These five requirements will ensure that evidential material collected during the investigation process allows for the positive linking of suspected persons to an incident. Evidence with individual characteristics can be used to identify a specific suspect and link that suspect to a particular incident, crime or transgression.

Evidence is classified into two characteristic groups by means of individual characteristics or class characteristics. Class characteristics are common to a group or class of objects.

Example 2.11: The difference between individual and class characteristics

Evidence with individual characteristics: fingerprints, palm prints and footprints.

Evidence with class characteristics: fibres and other items that can be placed in a general category, such as oil found at a scene that had leaked from an engine, and soil transferred to or from a scene.

DNA evidence is still described as evidence with class characteristics, with the decision about identity being based on statistical probability.

2.9 SUMMARY

The process of investigation is a scientific one. It requires sound knowledge, ethical principles and a thorough understanding of the principles of investigation, namely the Locard exchange principle, identification and individualisation. If every investigator visiting a scene of incident considers the basic principles of investigation, it will result in cases being investigated professionally and honestly and, most importantly, help trace and identify perpetrators and resolve cases.

REFERENCES

WW Bennett & KM Hess *Identification and Arresting Suspects: Criminal Investigation* (Wadsworth/Thomson Learning 2004)

G du Preez 'Criminal investigation' in J van der Westhuizen (ed) *Forensic Criminalistics* 2 ed (Heinemann 1996)

JN Gilbert *Criminal Investigation* 6 ed (Prentice Hall 2004)

PL Kirk *Crime Investigation: Physical Evidence and the Police Laboratory* (Interscience Publishers, NY 1953)

CW Marais *Physical Evidence in Crime Investigation* (Henmar Publications 1992)

CR Swanson, NC Chamelin & L Territo *Criminal Investigation* (McGraw-Hill Higher Education 2003)

J van der Westhuizen *Forensic Criminalistics* (Heinemann 1996)

HJN van Rooyen *Investigation: The A–Z Guide for Forensic, Private and Corporate Investigators* (Henmar Publications 2004)

HJN van Rooyen *Practical Guide for Private Investigators* (Henmar Publications 2001)

Chapter 3

MEDICO-LEGAL EVIDENCE

J H Smith • R J Mokwena

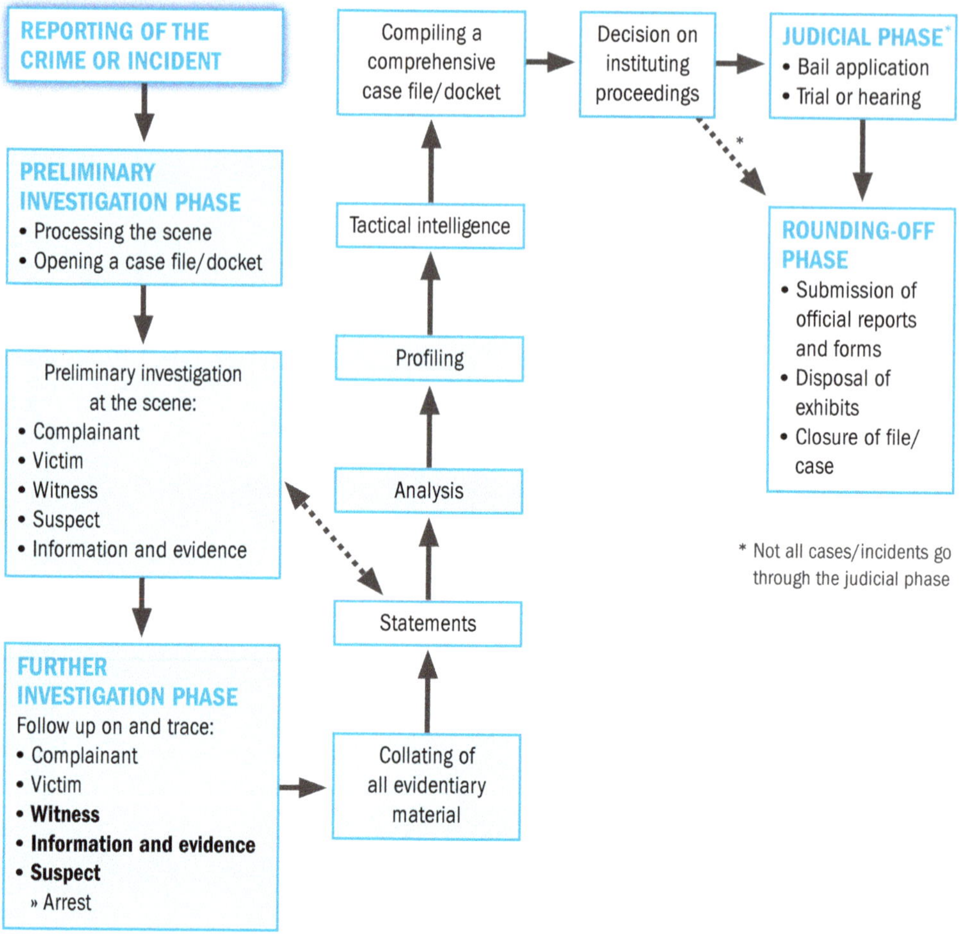

Figure 3.1: Areas of the crime investigation process covered in this chapter shown in shaded area

3.1 INTRODUCTION

As part of the progressive world, it has become necessary to intensify the approach in the fight against crime and criminality in general. Successful investigation, the resolving of incidents and the prosecution of perpetrators are increasingly relying on physical evidence. According to Locard's exchange principle (see chapter 2) every contact leaves a trace. During the commission of a crime, a transgression or an incident, the perpetrator may scratch, touch, remove or lift certain items or objects. In theory, every scene of incident should therefore have physical evidence that can be lifted for investigative purposes. This physical evidence may exonerate an innocent person, could be used to prosecute a perpetrator or may enable the investigator to make a finding as to the cause of the incident.

Physical evidence is also called associative evidence. In forensic investigation, associative evidence is one of the clues that can lead the investigator to solve a particular incident. The scientific analysis of this evidence can not only prove that the perpetrator was at the scene, but in certain cases can also prove beyond reasonable doubt that the perpetrator has committed an incident or was responsible for the incident, for example the dumping of hazardous chemicals. Therefore, it is important for the forensic investigator to correctly identify, develop, collect and process the physical evidence from the scene of incident.

The investigator needs to have a good understanding of the types and investigative value of physical evidence. This chapter focuses on the medico-legal evidence pertaining to forensic investigation. For the purposes of this book, medico-legal evidence means the physical evidence gathered by investigators under the direction of a medical examiner. This evidence cannot be obtained and analysed by investigators; they have to rely on someone who is qualified in medical sciences – such as a medical doctor – to do so. Medico-legal evidence includes pathological evidence, hair analysis, toxicology and odontology.

3.2 FORENSIC PATHOLOGY EVIDENCE

Forensic pathology is defined as the study of medicine related to diseases and trauma,[1] while a forensic pathologist is defined as 'a person who studied the changes in body tissues as a result of disease or death and the impact of such evidence on legal cases, typically homicides'.[2] The second definition is particularly relevant to forensic investigation, as the pathologist performs duties that are more in line with the duties of an investigator, but within the discipline of medicine. Any death considered to be unnatural due to injuries or possibly poison is investigated to determine the cause either in the form of homicide, negligence or intention.[3]

The functions of a forensic pathologist include, among other things:

- determining the cause of death
- determining the manner of death
- gathering physical evidence from the scene of incident
- identifying the deceased
- conducting an autopsy
- writing comprehensive reports on the findings
- testifying in court on the findings.

1 Osterburg & Ward (2010).
2 Gilbert (2004).
3 James & Nordby (2005).

3.2.1 Determining the cause of death

Only unnatural deaths are usually the focus of a legal enquiry because natural deaths are not associated with criminal acts or acts of negligence. An 'unnatural death' means there are some doubts as to the cause of death. These doubts need to be clarified through forensic investigation. Since death can have many causes, there are many factors that one should investigate in order to scientifically determine the cause of death. This is where forensic pathologists come into the picture: they apply medical science in the field of law in order to detect the actual cause of death. Death may be caused by:

- *strangulation*, when a rope or wire is put around the neck of the victim and tightened to cut off respiration
- *hanging*, when a rope or cord is placed around the neck of the victim to hang the person; this could occur accidentally or deliberately (murder or suicide)
- *drowning*, by water accessing the body through the mouth and nose, causing insufficient oxygen to reach the lungs, blood and brain
- *electric current* or *lightning*, when the person is electrocuted by an electrical current or lightning causing visible exit points and burn marks where the current exits the body; death by electric current could occur due to an accident, suicide or murder
- *fire*, when a victim is burnt and dies due to injuries, suffocation or carbon monoxide inhalation; if the victim was still alive during the fire, particles of smoke that were inhaled will have left residue in the lungs
- *freezing* as a result of suicide, an accident (trapped in a walk-in fridge) or drunkenness (falling asleep outside in the cold)
- *poisoning*, either accidentally or deliberately (suicide or murder)
- *gunshot*, when a bullet causes fatal injuries
- *industrial accidents*
- *wounds* from the following causes:
  - blunt objects: abrasions, bruises, lacerated wounds
  - sharp objects: incised wounds, stab wounds
  - penetrating wounds
  - general injuries
  - bite wounds
  - self-inflicted wounds.

Forensic experts can be distinguished in terms of training and expertise. A clinical pathologist, for example, generally works in hospitals and is concerned with determining the cause of death. These experts are usually qualified medical doctors. Other experts might be qualified pyrotechnicians, chemical analysts or ballistics experts.

3.2.2 Determining the time of death

It is very easy to estimate the time of death if the time of death is close to the time when the investigation or examination is conducted. The investigator may find the body still warm, which indicates that death has occurred very recently.

3.2.2.1 Time pieces

In general, a watch on the person of the victim or assailant or clocks at the scene of incident could be important in determining the time of death. Most watches display the date and if the watch stops during a struggle or is damaged by force, it will give an accurate indication of the time and date of the incident that might be correlated with the time of death. In addition, cellphones and office phones (land lines) can be useful in determining the time of death if their data is properly analysed.

3.2.2.2 Food consumption analysis

Forensic pathologists have the expertise to determine the time of death through the proper analysis and interpretation of various factors. The last food consumed by the victim is of the utmost importance – the state of digestion may provide a clue to determine time of death. If the death is due to alleged poisoning, the remains of the food in the alimentary canal will be used as samples for analysis.

3.2.2.3 Body temperature

Forensic pathologists are also trained to determine the time of death and establish the interval since the time of death (the death interval) by other means than analysing the contents of the stomach. After death, specific internal and external processes take place in the body. One of these is a change in the body's internal temperature. The deceased body will automatically take on the temperature at the scene after a set period of time. The normal body temperature is 37 °C. This decreases after death and synchronises with the ambient temperature as time passes until the body temperature is the same as the ambient temperature at the scene. However, it is important to exclude hypothermia as the cause of death.

3.2.2.4 Cooling-down period

It is imperative for the investigator to have a clear knowledge of temperature changes after death. The cooling-down period of the body is primarily the decline of the internal body temperature after death. The cooling-down period is affected by conditions at the scene of incident and the individual's body reactions. Factors that play a role in the cooling of the body include body fat, age, size and medical conditions (eg kidney failure will cause slower heat loss), among other things.

The following factors are crucial when determining the time of death:[4]

- the environment where the body lies
- whether the body is covered or uncovered
- the weather conditions and seasons (winter or summer?)
- the cause of death.

As the body starts cooling down, the limbs become less flexible and a condition called rigor mortis sets in.

3.2.2.5 Rigor mortis

Rigor mortis is caused by a chemical change in the muscles after death. Initially, the limbs of the corpse become stiff, making it hard to move them or change their position. In humans, rigor mortis sets in three to four hours after death. Maximum stiffness is reached after 12 hours, whereupon it gradually dissipates until approximately 48 to 60 hours (three days) after death. Warm conditions and physically strenuous activity on the part of the victim before death can speed up the process of rigor mortis because it accelerates the metabolic processes and thus the decomposition process.[5] Rigor mortis differs from situation to situation and as a result of the exposure of body parts to the surrounding environment (with or without clothing), whether the body was submerged in water and other factors such as heat, moisture and rain.[6]

Another scientific method that is used during the investigation of an unnatural death is hypostasis.

3.2.2.6 Hypostasis

Hypostasis refers to the blood that flows through vessels and veins to the lower part of the body after death due to gravity.[7] This collection of blood in the lowest parts of the body causes a visible discoloration in these parts. If a person was hanged, for example, this would be the lower arms, the calves and feet, the lower part of the face and the lower part of the pelvis. If a person drowned and was found floating face down in the water, the lower part of the face, the abdomen, forearms and hands and the lower legs and feet will be discoloured. This discoloration becomes fixated as the blood cools down and clots. If the body is moved after death, the blood will not flow again and the discoloration will remain. Hypostasis is fixed and cannot be manipulated or changed.

---

4 Horswell (2004).

5 Rigor Mortis as defined online at http://www.deathreference.com/Py-Se/Rigor-Mortis-and-Other-Postmortem-Changes.html#ixzz3Y1m6VhKQ accessed 20 April 2015.

6 Marais (1992).

7 Marais (1992).

Hypostasis will help forensic experts to determine whether the body was moved after death.[8] It can occur as soon as 20 to 30 minutes after death, with the maximum period being 6 to 10 hours after death. If a body is found after hypostasis has already occurred, the discoloration will tell the forensic investigator whether the person died in that position or whether the body was moved after death (and hypostasis occurred).

Another factor to consider is the colour of the discoloration. A living person's blood is red and changes to a darker colour after death. The usual colour of hypostasis is dark blue due to the fact that the blood is no longer circulating in the body and the decomposition cycle has commenced.

3.2.2.7 Changes in the eyes

After death the cornea dehydrates and becomes dull, causing a film to appear on the eyes.[9] The eyes of the deceased change within about 10 minutes after death. This can be a reliable yardstick to determine the time of a recent death. Forensic pathologists can withdraw fluid from the eyeball to determine potassium levels, which can help to determine the death interval. The level of dehydration in the eyes may also be affected by the temperature and humidity of the surroundings, where the body is located and whether the eyes were closed or open at the time of death.

3.2.2.8 Decomposition

The body's decomposition starts immediately after death. However, this process, also known as putrefaction, is not immediately noticeable. In normal circumstances decomposition only becomes visible 48 to 72 hours after death.[10] The complete process of decomposition is when the skeleton is the only remainder of the human body. The decomposition process of the skeleton is a longer and much slower process than the ordinary decomposition stages of the soft tissue of the body. Putrefaction is the natural transition of the body from organic to inorganic material.

The rate at which this transition takes place is very important in forensic investigation. The forensic investigator should take careful note of the climatic conditions and other possible factors that might affect the estimation of the time of death and the determination of the cause of death when the body is discovered. This information will assist pathologists in their later examination of the body.

8 Jackson & Jackson (2004).
9 Fisher (2004).
10 Fisher (2004).

The degree of putrefaction when the body is discovered will help the investigator to estimate the time of death more accurately. Arsenic poisoning, for example, will normally significantly slow down putrefaction. Factors that affect the rate of putrefaction include the presence of bacteria, fungi, injuries, insects, larvae, micro-organisms in the body (especially the stomach), temperature and atmospheric changes. If the deceased suffered from a disease and/or infection at the time of death, it might escalate the putrefaction process.

During the decomposition stages of an exposed corpse, insects would feed off the body. The investigator should therefore also take note of the presence of different types of insects during the examination of an exposed putrefying body as specific insects are associated with the various stages of putrefaction. The presence of specific insects could provide a clue as to the time of death.

The principle is that the sooner the examination is conducted after death, the more accurately the time of death can be determined since various variables will then have relatively less influence on the rate of putrefaction. This will eliminate unknown or complex variables such as the difference in decomposition rates due to temperature, atmospheric changes, the deceased's medical history, the presence of fungi, etc, and will enable a more accurate estimate of the cause and time of death. It is therefore essential that a forensic pathologist attends the scene of incident as soon as possible after discovery of the body.

3.2.3 Scene or incident of death

Forensic pathologists should also visit scenes of incident in order to personally observe additional factors that might help them to compile a comprehensive report about the situation. This includes information on environmental and general conditions at the scene of incident. If possible, pathologists who will perform an autopsy should visit the scene of incident in order to know where to look for more information and what to focus on during the post-mortem process. Some of the reasons why pathologists should visit the scene of incident are to:

- ascertain the position of the body at the scene and photograph the scene (this information should be correlated with hypostasis information)
- take detailed and accurate notes at the scene, following the correct procedure
- confirm death at the scene
- identify wounds, scrapings and injuries (to differentiate from injuries that were sustained when the body was transported to the mortuary)
- establish any signs of struggle
- observe the clothes of the deceased and the condition of the furniture (overturned, smashed, etc)
- trace any notes or information on paper at the scene
- trace any instruments and objects that might reveal more information

- trace blood patterns at the scene
- identify the area from which the body was removed, for more information.

3.2.4 Post-mortem

A post-mortem (also called an autopsy) can be defined as a surgical examination conducted by a medical doctor or a pathologist to determine the cause of death. This examination may also be useful in determining the circumstances and the time of death (the death interval). Pathologists will conduct an external examination as well as internal examination.[11]

It is recommended that investigators who attended the scene of incident should also attend the autopsy. Photographs of the exterior of the body should be taken before the autopsy. These photographs should preferably be taken from a general orientation, followed by mid-close-up and lastly close-up depictions of the following lesions:[12]

- blunt injuries (abrasions, bruises, lacerated wounds)
- sharp injuries (incised wounds, stab wounds)
- penetrating wounds
- heat, cold and electrical injuries
- general injuries
- injuries to the scalp
- injuries to the orbital area
- injuries to the mouth area
- injuries to the genital area
- bite wounds
- self-inflicted wounds
- scars, tattoos, birthmarks
- nails and hair
- skin conditions.

By law, an autopsy can only be conducted by a qualified pathologist in the presence of role-players sharing the common objectives, such as the investigator, the next-of-kin and a photographer.

After the pathologist has conducted the external examination of the body, the internal examination will continue. In this process the body is opened up.

The entire procedure is done under the strict control of a well-trained pathologist. Generally speaking, an autopsy consists of:

- a complete external examination
- opening up all important parts of the body
- removing the internal organs
- selecting parts and samples to be forwarded to the laboratory for analysis.

11 Gilbert (2004).
12 Schwär et al. (1988) 81-97.

3.3 HAIR

During an investigation, hair is recovered from different places and objects. Hair can mostly be found in contact crimes but may also be recovered in other crimes or incidences such as theft and robbery. Because the victim and the perpetrator have had physical contact, the transfer of hair during contact is highly probable. A balaclava and masks that are sometimes used by suspects are examples of objects on which hair will most probably be present. The investigator should also consider clothes and bedding when searching for hair at the scene of incident.

Hair is physical evidence and can be used to associate the suspect with the scene of incident. Due to its micronature, the presence of hair is usually neglected by both suspects and investigators at the scene of incident.

3.3.1 Composition of hair

Hair is a bundle of fibres of hardened keratin which is formed in the root.[13] Hair consists of the scale, cuticle, cortex and medulla. Keratin is a very strong protein that is resistant to chemical decomposition and can retain its structural features for a long time.[14] Hair has been found on the body of a deceased hundreds of years after the time of death. Therefore, because it stays intact even if the rest of the body has decomposed, hair plays an important role in identifying victims whose bodies are only discovered long after death.

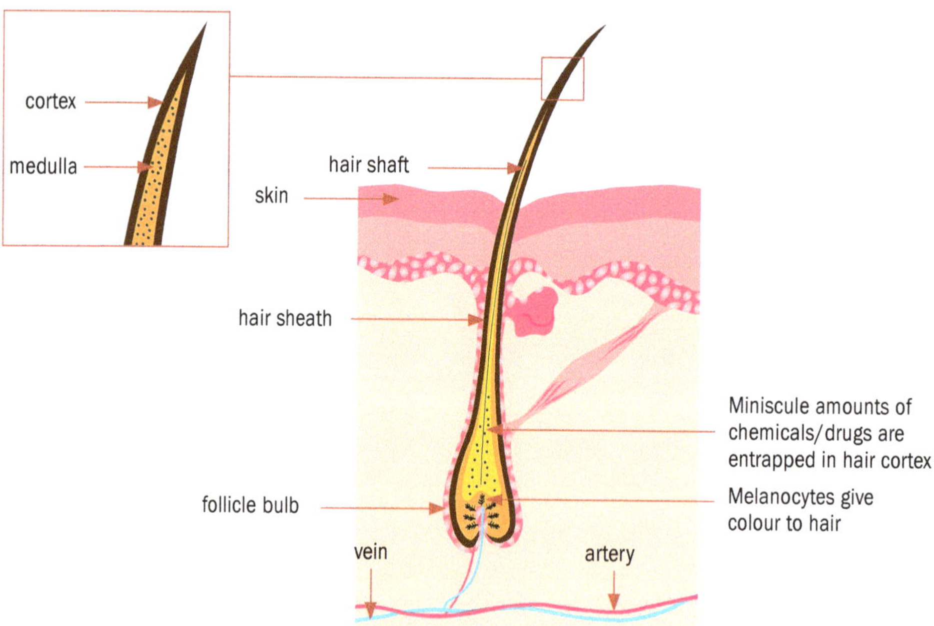

Figure 3.2: The composition of hair

13 Van der Westhuizen (1996).
14 Girard (2008) 90.

3.3.2 Value of hair in forensic investigation

Hair can play a significant role in the investigation process. It is noteworthy, though, that hair must always have a root if it is to be used for individualisation through nuclear DNA (deoxyribonucleic acid) analysis. This is because the hair shaft does not contain DNA; living tissue is only found in the bulb. However, there are laboratories that can do mitochondrial DNA testing on the hair shaft.

Furthermore, hair can be removed by burning, it may be shed during chronic heavy-metal poisoning, or it may be abraded away by a blunt force.[15]

Besides identification of hair as human or animal hair, hair might be used to identify the body of origin (of the victim or the suspect). Hair can also be used to identify the race and ethnic group of a person, and plays a role in the gender classification of human beings.

3.3.2.1 Determining race

Hair exhibits microscopic characteristics that distinguish one racial group from another. Head hair is most reliable for the determination of race.[16] Race determination is based on only three types, namely Caucasoid (European ancestry), Negroid (African ancestry) and Mongoloid (Asian ancestry).[17] Caucasian hair is fine to medium, straight or wavy and comes in various colours ranging from blonde to black.[18] African hair is black and curly or kinky and it has a coarser texture. Mongoloid hair is coarse and straight and is usually black, often with a reddish appearance.

3.3.2.2 Origin of hair

It is essential to categorise the origin of hair from the human body as hair from the head, eyebrows, eyelashes, pubic area or underarms because hair from various parts of the body differ. Hair from the eyebrows is rough, short and curved with a pointed end, while hair from a beard is coarse, straight and triangular in shape. Pubic and underarm hairs are similar and are coarse and curly.

3.3.2.3 Determining sex

The structure of the hair can reveal whether the hair is from a male or a female. A man's hair has an X and a Y chromosome element, whereas a woman's hair has two X chromosomes. Men's eyebrows are thin and stronger while hairs from women's eyebrows are thicker.

3.3.2.4 Determining age

The colour of hair in certain instances may be helpful to establish the age of the deceased. Old people have grey hair without pigment. However, relatively

15 Schwär et al. (1988) 97.
16 Marais (1992).
17 Gardner (2005).
18 Van der Westhuizen (1996).

young people may also have grey hair, therefore hair should not be used as the absolute criterion for determining the age of individuals during the investigation process.

3.3.3 Collecting and packaging hair at the scene of incident

The collection of hair from the scene of incident might be done with tweezers, tape lift, combing or brushing. Vacuuming is another method, but is not popular due to fact that it collects all dust and not only exhibits.

The person who collects hair at the scene of incident should keep an accurate record of where and when it was found, ie the specific place, time and the reason why it was collected should be recorded.

A hair sample is the hair collected from the suspect or victim for comparison with the hair that was found as evidence at the scene of incident. Hair samples should be labelled as such and the origin of that hair should be specified by the investigator.

A sample collection from the suspect or victim should be at least 20 to 40 hairs. This is to ensure that there is a hair sample of sufficient size for analysis.

The different types of hair evidence must be placed on a clean sheet of paper and sealed in an envelope and labelled as such. Samples can also be collected in a clean, dry glass or plastic container. Pubic hair must be collected in a separate container.

3.4 FORENSIC TOXICOLOGY

For the purposes of criminal or civil investigation, forensic toxicology is the study of poisonous, toxic or hazardous chemical substances and their effect on a particular subject. Forensic toxicology deals with the metabolic reaction to poisonous substances, ie how the toxins in the substance act in the human body, when the harmful effects of the toxin may occur and the symptoms of and treatment for poisoning.[19]

The forensic toxicologist works closely with the pathologist to establish what role a particular poisonous substance played in the cause of death. The following matters should be considered during an autopsy or medical examination of the victim, especially when poisoning is suspected:

- the physical symptoms displayed by the victim
- related evidence such as pills, plant material or chemicals left and collected at the scene of incident that may be helpful in focusing the toxicology examination process.

---

19 Available at http://www.forensictoxicology.net.

The forensic toxicologist then embarks on a process of determining which substances are present in what concentrations and what effect they may have had on the victim. Forensic toxicologists have a wide variety of analytical instruments and methods at their disposal for this investigation. Analytical instrumentation has become very sensitive and specific so that toxic exposures of all kinds in very small quantities can be identified and similar compounds can be excluded.[20] To develop an optimal analytical examination strategy, the forensic toxicologist needs to rely on information about the history of the incident and observations made by the investigator and the pathologist. These observations may include any suspicious objects (such as medication, herbs or substances originating from plants) lying near the body or found at the scene of incident, objects that have been removed from the scene of incident, or anything that appears to be out of the ordinary. This includes information about the behaviour of the victim prior to the incident.

3.4.1 Types of poison

A poison can be considered as any substance which, if taken in sufficient quantities, may lead to death. The venoms found in certain snakes, spiders and insects are poisonous to humans. Other poisons may be considered as substances that are absorbed through epithelial linings such as the skin or gut. Certain chemicals found in the home or garage can be poisonous. Poisons can be categorised into the following three broad groups:

- drugs and health-care substances
- biological poisons originating from animals, fish and plants
- industrial and agricultural chemicals.

Forensic toxicologists commonly group poisons according to the method used to isolate the substance from the specimens provided:

- *gases*: some gases may be isolated from the blood or lung tissue by aeration processes
- *steam volatile poisons*: the specimen is made acidic or basic and is isolated by steam distillation (cyanide, alcohol, nitrobenzenes and chloroform can be distilled from an acidic medium, while amphetamines and meperidine can be distilled from a basic medium)
- *non-volatile organic poisons*: most of the drugs of interest to the police are grouped here
- *metallic poisons*: all organic material is chemically removed from the tissue to leave the metallic toxin in the ash
- *other types* of poisons excluded from the above groups, eg inorganic anions, water-soluble organic ions, organic compounds insoluble in water or alcohol. A vast array of modern methods is available to identify these poisons.

20 Fenton (2002) 6.

3.4.2 Detecting toxins in the body

The forensic pathologist may provide the forensic toxicologist with the post-mortem report (a report about the observations made during the autopsy and the cause of death) and various specimens of organ parts, hair, stomach contents and body fluids in cases where fatal poisoning is suspected. In cases where the victim survives poisoning, blood samples must be taken as soon as possible after the suspicion is raised and submitted for toxicological analysis. In some instances hair samples may also be requested several weeks after the incident. The investigator must liaise with the toxicologist and establish if and when hair samples must be collected from the victim.

The specimens received are divided into acidic and basic fractions for toxin extraction. Once the acid-base procedures have been performed, screening tests and confirmation testing may follow. Screening tests are useful to identify a wide range of toxins for further confirmation tests.

Table 3.1 presents a list of substances and their adverse effects on the human body.[21]

Table 3.1: Substances that adversely affect the human body

List of substances	Adverse effects on the body
Acids (nitric, hydrochloric, sulphuric)	Burns around mouth, lips, nose
Aniline (hypnotics, nitrobenzene)	Skin of face and neck is quite dark
Arsenic (metals, mercury, copper, etc)	Severe, unexplained diarrhoea
Atropine (belladonna/deadly nightshade), scopolamine	Pupils of eyes are dilated
Bases (lye, potash, hydroxides)	Burns around mouth, lips, nose
Carbolic acid (or other phenol)	Odour of disinfectant
Carbon monoxide	Skin is bright cherry red
Cyanide	Quick death, red skin, odour of peach
Food poisoning	Vomiting, abdominal pain
Metallic compounds	Diarrhoea, vomiting, abdominal pain
Nicotine	Convulsions
Opiates	Pupils of eyes are contracted
Oxalic acid (phosphorous)	Odour of garlic
Sodium fluoride	Convulsions
Strychnine	Convulsions, dark face and neck

21 O'Connor (n.d.).

The following most likely causes of death by poisoning were observed in an international study:[22]

- household cleaning supplies
- analgesics (aspirin, acetaminophen)
- cosmetics
- cough and cold remedies
- plant scrapes and insect bites
- pesticides
- topical creams and lotions
- hydrocarbons (gasoline, kerosene)
- anti-microbacterial soaps
- sedatives/hypnotics/antipsychotics
- food poisoning
- alcohol.

A study on toxicology casework in South Africa by the Forensic Chemistry Laboratory of the Department of Health during the period 1991–1996 indicated that agricultural chemicals are a major cause of mortality. It was reported that, among drugs of abuse, combinations of methaqualone/diphenhydramine and cyclizine/dipipanone contribute a disproportionately high percentage of cases examined by this laboratory. Metal poisoning is common, as are cases of poisoning attributed to remedies prescribed by traditional healers.[23] Anecdotal evidence indicates that this is still much the trend today.

In a retrospective study, the post-mortem records of 153 cases of suspected fatal poisoning or overdose during the period January 2000 to December 2001 at the Pretoria Medico-Legal Laboratory were analysed. Toxicology results were conclusively positive in only 53 (34,64%) cases. Anecdotal evidence indicates that the percentage of conclusive positive toxicology results has only improved slightly since this study was conducted.

Some of these cases tested positive for more than one type or class of 'poison'. The fatal 'poisons' identified in these 53 cases were as follows:

- pharmaceuticals (47,17%)
- illicit drugs (41,51%)
- agricultural poisons (20,75%)
- alcohol (13,21%)
- traditional medicines (3,77%)
- heavy metals (3,77%).[24]

Due to the lack of available published data it could not be confirmed if trends

22 O'Connor (n.d.) 1.
23 Stewart et al. (1999).
24 Bhana & Visser (2004).

observed in the aforementioned study differ significantly from those observed in other countries.

3.4.3 Role of the investigator

The investigator should critically observe and take note of anything at the scene of incident that may indicate that the victim had been exposed to a toxin. Toxins or containers indicating possible toxins or plant material at the scene must be collected and given to the forensic toxicologist for examination. The investigator must be attentive to note any out-of-the-ordinary conditions, such as a transitory peculiar smell at the scene of incident.

The investigator should interview any person who may have been in contact with the victim during the last few weeks to ascertain any strange behavioural patterns the victim may have displayed immediately before or in the weeks leading up to their death. In many cases of poisoning the victim was exposed to the poison over several weeks. In these instances, they would have come into contact with people who may have observed some unusual behaviour or symptoms.

Good communication is essential in solving a case where it is suspected that the subject was poisoned. Investigators must share with the pathologist and forensic toxicologist their observations at the scene of incident or information they have elicited. The pathologist or forensic toxicologist may also provide some information that could be useful during the investigation of the case.

The investigator must ensure that the necessary specimens (blood, stomach contents and tissue samples) obtained from the pathologist are correctly packaged and preserved, and transported timeously to the Forensic Chemistry Laboratory of the Department of Health for examination. Any other substance, container, plant material, chemical or pill found at the scene of incident or on the suspect or victim that is required for toxicology examination must be submitted to the Forensic Science Laboratory of the South African Police Service (SAPS). Once the case is ready for prosecution, the investigator will brief the state prosecutor on the investigation and the findings made.

3.4.4 Exhumation of a body

Due to the advent of new toxicology methods, it is now possible to identify the toxin with which a victim was poisoned. This was previously not possible. It may be necessary to exhume a body from a known grave or burial site if further testing is required to prove poisoning. Bodies buried for a number of years may still prove useful and their bones may yield forensic evidence to prove whether the victim had been poisoned or not.

The perpetrator may have buried a victim who was poisoned at a clandestine or unknown site. Knowledge of plant succession can help investigators locate these hidden graves. In searching for a burial site in a specific location, the investigator must take note of any disturbance in the vegetation pattern. When soil is disturbed for a burial, it does not remain bare for long; pioneer species soon colonise the site, followed by later-succession species and finally, the climax assemblage of species. For some geographical locations and habitat types the change in a site's plant species composition can be predicted to some extent. If a certain localised site shows a different successional stage than the surrounding area, it is an indication of a potential burial site. Disturbances in vegetation can be identified more than 20 years after the event.

Exhumation of a deceased person must be based on archaeological principles to ensure that the maximum amount of information and material is retrieved. It is always best to put an experienced archaeologist in charge of the exhumation, otherwise forensic evidence may easily be overlooked. The investigator may approach the Archaeology departments at universities, such as the one at the University of Pretoria, to assist with exhumations.

3.4.5 Collecting toxicology specimens

When blood, urine and tissue specimens are required to be submitted for toxicology analysis, it is best practice for the investigator to first liaise with the laboratory and confirm the latest requirements with respect to the specimen quantity, appropriate containers and packing requirements. General requirements for exhibits, such as the labelling of containers and envelopes and the maintenance of the chain of custody, must be adhered to. It is critical to keep tissue samples in cold storage at all times and during transport. The toxicology specimens should be submitted to the testing laboratory within 48 hours after collection to ensure optimal test results.

Typical sources of fluid and tissue specimens include:

- blood
- urine
- bile
- eyes (vitreous humour)
- liver
- brain
- kidneys
- lungs
- gastric tract.

Other exhibits which may be collected for toxicology analysis from a scene of incident and that may have evidential value include any type of medication or ethno-medicinal (natural medicine) plant or tissue material. Natural medicine is typically prescribed by traditional healers or ethno-medical practitioners.

3.5 FORENSIC ODONTOLOGY

Forensic odontology is the identification, examination and evaluation of odontological (dental) make-up for criminal and civil investigation and prosecution purposes. Identification of a donor is based on the study of dental records and photographs that were collected before. Forensic odontology plays a major role in the identification of those individuals who cannot be identified visually or by other means, when the body has been exposed to extreme forces and/or temperatures,[25] or many years after death.

Forensic odontology assists in:

- linking bite marks left on objects to the donor through physical comparison
- identifying the person to whom the teeth belong
- identifying victims in mass disasters
- identifying unknown human remains
- identifying the age of subjects
- performing an injury analysis to determine the presence and extent of dental injuries or physical neglect in cases where an adult, child or elderly person has been abused.[26, 27]

3.5.1 History and status of forensic odontology

Although it is not known when forensic odontology was first applied, Dr Oscar Amoedo is credited with being the father of forensic odontology. He published the first treatise on forensic odontology in 1898.[28] As far back as AD 49, in the time of Nero, Agrippina identified Lollia Paulina by using visual recognition of her distinctive coloured teeth as proof that she had indeed been killed by her soldiers. Some other examples in history where teeth were used to identify people include the following:

- 1477: Charles the Bold, from a missing upper tooth
- 1776: General Joseph Warren, by Dr Paul Revere via a fixed wire silver and ivory bridge
- 1849: Dr Parkman, by Nathan Keep from the fit of dentures on study models
- 1869: Two incinerated females by M'Grath, who described the use of dental characteristics to differentiate between them
- 1945: Adolf Hitler at the end of World War II
- 2001: Victims in the New York City World Trade Centre bombing
- 2004: Victims of the tsunami in the Indian Ocean.

---

25 Sweet 'Forensic dental identification' (2010).
26 Leung (2008).
27 Lewis & Senn (2010).
28 Taylor (2009).

3.5.2 Dental anatomy

Dental anatomy is the study of the development, appearance and classification of teeth. Normally a person starts with 20 primary teeth in their early life and ends up with 28 to 32 permanent teeth (incisor, canine, premolar, molar teeth) by adolescence. Ten of the primary teeth are found in the upper jaw (maxilla) and the other 10 in the lower jaw (mandible). Sixteen permanent teeth are found in the upper jaw and 16 in the lower jaw.

3.5.3 Computer-aided forensic odontology

Computer-aided forensic odontology is applied by using the ante-mortem (before death) and post-mortem (after death) dental charting records of the victim captured on electronic dental record systems, ie software applications specifically developed to capture dental observations of patients and victims. The software is used to compare the records in an attempt to match unknown with known dental records.

Software may also be used by the forensic odontologist to simulate control bite marks by using the ante-mortem dental records of a suspect. These are then compared to the image of the bite marks on the victim's body.

Some law enforcement and military agencies are capturing the dental charting records of soldiers and police officials on a database that may be used for identification purposes later should one of their staff be killed and forensic odontology be required to identify the body. The Federal Bureau of Investigation (FBI), for example, is not only capturing the ante-mortem dental charting records of missing persons but also those of unidentified corpses. This data is then made available to law enforcement agencies for comparison purposes.

3.5.4 Individual identification

The forensic odontologist is commonly confronted with the problem of disfigured bodies that cannot be identified by a family member. Although forensic DNA analysis may be performed and compared with samples known to originate from the deceased, traditional identification methods such as fingerprinting and forensic odontology are usually first attempted because they are cheaper and can be done relatively quickly.

The forensic odontologist compares the remains of the subject's teeth and jaw (post-mortem records) with ante-mortem dental records to determine the identity of the body. These records include written notes, study casts and radiographs kept by the dentist of the deceased before death. Congenital and acquired dental characteristics are compared between ante- and post-mortem records.[29, 30, 31]

29 Sweet 'Forensic dental identification' (2010).
30 Hill, Hewson & Lain (2011).
31 Hill, Lain & Hewson (2011).

3.5.5 Mass-disaster identification

A forensic pathologist normally coordinates the investigation of mass disasters during which many victims are mutilated, fragmented, burnt or even decomposed, for example during an aircraft crash or train accident. In these investigations, the forensic pathologist works closely with civil authorities such as the police, the military and local government, and other forensic experts such as forensic odontologists, fingerprint experts, forensic ballistic examiners and forensic DNA examiners. It is crucial that law enforcement, civil institutions and scientific personnel collaborate and cooperate when they respond to mass disasters. The International Criminal Police Organisation has established working groups in forensic odontology to help develop agreed standards for the collection of dental data.[32]

The following main categories of activities relevant to the investigation of mass disasters can be identified:

- identification and documentation of the site, which will include aerial photographs and sketches depicting the geographical location of the incident
- deployment of experts with specialised equipment and collection kits to the scene of incident
- detailed photographic capturing and recording of observations made at the scene of incident
- identification of the bodies recovered.

When a body is recovered, investigators must make meticulous notes and take photographs to facilitate identification. The gender, race, stature, hair colour, clothes worn, jewellery found on the body, contents of the wallet or anything found in pockets, any unique birthmarks, tattoos or scars and any deformities must be recorded. Forensic odontologists will focus on the teeth and record the observations made during their examination.

During the investigation of the tsunami mass disaster in Thailand in 2004, forensic odontologists followed the Interpol protocols. Meticulous records were made of the dentures. These records described sound, pathological, restored and missing (ante-mortem or post-mortem) teeth, attrition and oral anatomical abnormalities. The forensic experts furthermore developed a technique to gain access to both the maxillary (upper) and the mandibular (lower) teeth by making a semicircular incision, from ear to ear, behind each mandibular angle and passing through the anterior cervical region (front of the neck), below the submental area (chin).[33] This technique proved to be much faster than existing approaches and gave quick access to the required dental areas.

32 Sweet 'INTERPOL DVI best-practice standards – An overview' (2010).
33 Beauthier et al. (2009).

3.5.6 Bite-mark analysis

A bite mark is a bruise, with or without a laceration of the skin and caused by teeth. It has a specific pattern, ie the imprint of the teeth that caused it.[34]

Bite-mark analysis is the detection, recognition, description and comparison of bite marks that occur in living or inanimate objects (such as butter or cheese) caused by humans and animals.[35] Teeth differ from one person to another due to natural formation, malformations, wear and fractures that form over time. Due to these differences, bite marks differ from person to person. However, the differences become significant in forensic investigation when they are evident as well-defined bite marks and have been adequately recorded.

Due to some questionable interpretations and lack of experience on the part of some odontologists, the legal fraternity has become sceptical about the validity of bite-mark interpretation.[36, 37] Bite-mark interpretation should therefore only be made by the most experienced experts in the field and then with extreme caution.[38] It is highly recommended that any interpretation made should be independently peer reviewed by another forensic odontologist before the findings are released. Furthermore, the bite-mark evidence should preferably be substantiated with other physical evidence.

Bite-mark evidence can be divided into two groups, namely:

- bite marks on the victim's body
- bite marks on other objects at the scene.

Bite marks are usually seen in cases of sexual assault, murder and child abuse. The perpetrator may also leave bite marks on the victim as part of exerting animalistic dominance over the victim or subduing the victim during an incident of rape. Biting is seen as a sign that the perpetrator wanted to degrade the victim. Bite marks can be on any area of the victim's body. Soft areas like the stomach, breasts and genital area are frequently targeted. The bite may leave a distinct bite mark pattern on the bitten object. However, the victim may also leave bite marks on the perpetrator's body during a struggle to defend themselves.

Bite marks can also occur on various objects at the scene of incident, namely hard food like cheese, chewing gum or packaging material. The perpetrator may have taken a bite of or have left half-eaten food at the scene of incident.

Bite-mark analysis in crimes related to assault, sexual assault and/or murder may prove helpful as supporting evidence. It may also exclude possible perpetrators of the offence when the bite mark does not match that of the suspect.

34 Schwär et al. (1988) 448.
35 Pretty & Sweet (2010).
36 Clement (2010).
37 Barsley (2010).
38 Pretty & Sweet (2010).

During bite-mark analysis, the forensic odontologist may also collect trace salivary evidence for later DNA analysis matching.

Medical practitioners must ensure that they make an accurate and precise recording or take impressions of any bite marks on a person. If they wait, the forensic significance of the bite mark may be reduced over time. It is also important to take a swab (preferable by using dacron or polyester) of the bite mark to determine if foreign DNA from the perpetrator is present. As a control, also take a swab from another area of the victim's skin.

Regarding the taking of impressions of bite marks from the victim's body, it is advisable that this be done by an odontologist who will have the necessary consumables such as vinyl polysolxane and polyether to make an accurate impression of the bite mark left on the skin. Dental acrylic or plaster may be used as a support for the impression material in order to ensure an accurate record of the curvature of the skin.

Notes must be made describing the injury, including its physical appearance, colour, size and orientation. These notes must not be restricted to the bite mark but must include detailed descriptions of any bruises or cuts observed. There may be a need to place a reference scale or ruler next to the bite mark(s) and take detailed close-up photographs. The long axis of the lens should be perpendicular to the bitten skin to reduce perspective distortion in the photographs.

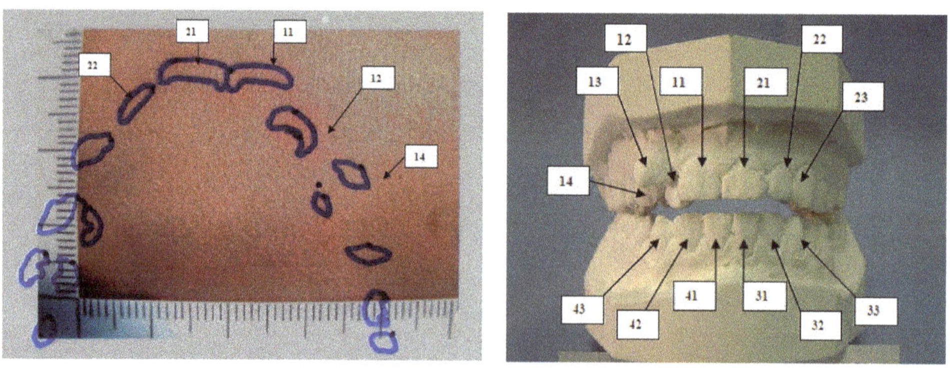

Figure 3.3: Left - Bite mark on hand

Right - Dental cast of perpetrator's teeth[39]

Because the bite mark may deteriorate over time, it is very important that it is photographed as soon as possible. Close-up photographs, with scale of reference, must be taken of all bite marks. Close-up photographs should also be taken of the perpetrator's teeth for comparison purposes.

39 Golden (2011).

The general guidelines to photograph bite-mark evidence are as follows:

- take the photograph perpendicular to the surface
- include a scale device (such as a ruler) with two axes in the photograph
- apply oblique lighting from different angles to highlight the 3D-features of the bite mark
- place an identifier in the photograph, especially in cases with more than one bite mark on the victim or object
- apply the chain of custody principle.

3.5.7 Exhibit collection and packaging of bite marks

DNA swabs should be taken from the skin of the bite mark. A swab should also be taken from another area of the victim's skin to act as a control sample. It is important to make castings of the bite mark. The suspect should be taken to a forensic odontologist, who will make a dental cast of the suspect's teeth in cases where the suspect has bitten the victim. A cast must be made of the entire mouth, upper and lower jaws. Dentists use water and powder (dental stone) to create a medium that can assume a particular shape and dry off in that position. It is important to mark these casts properly with the case reference, the suspect's name and which cast is of the upper and which of the lower jaw, and to deliver them to the laboratory within 24 hours. Dental casts must be wrapped in a wet paper towel and kept in cold storage until delivered to the Forensic Laboratory for examination.

Similarly, if a suspect who was bitten by the victim is apprehended soon after the incident, DNA swabs may also be taken of the bite mark for DNA comparison purposes. If the suspect is apprehended and there is reason to believe that there is no genetic material of the victim in the bite mark, then the bite mark should be analysed by the forensic odontologist. Bite marks may only be removed from a corpse by the pathologist performing the post-mortem examination. The tissue sample must be preserved by putting it into a mixture of formalin, alcohol and glacial acetic acid.

Exhibits such as food into which the suspect has bitten at the scene of incident should be sealed in a plastic container or plastic bag and stored in a refrigerator at 2–8 °C. They must not be frozen as this will cause damage and changes to the shape of the bite mark. This means that all exhibits of this nature must be delivered to the laboratory within 24 hours.[40]

In the case of a deceased person or a victim, the control samples will normally be in the form of dental records consisting of X-rays, scans, photographs and written notes, ie ante-mortem records obtained by the investigator from the person's dentist(s). This implies that the investigator must have a possible lead on who the unidentified corpse is and must have managed to trace his or her dentist(s).

40 SAPS (2008).

Dental evidence is best handled and collected by the forensic odontologist because special techniques are required. It is the task of the scene of incident examiner to thoroughly check the scene of incident as well as the bodies of the victim and the perpetrator for bite-mark evidence, and to document where and on what or whom it was found. The investigating officer must be guided to obtain the services of a forensic odontologist to document and analyse the evidence to the fullest extent.

3.5.8 Obligatory keeping of dental records by dentists

A dentist is required by the National Health Act 61 of 2003 to maintain accurate records of all patients examined. Health records, including dental records, should be stored for a period of not less than six years from the date on which they become dormant. Health-care practitioners should enter, inter alia, the following information for each patient consulted:

- personal (identifying) particulars of the patient
- the bio-psychosocial history of the patient, including allergies and idiosyncrasies
- the time, date and place of every consultation
- the assessment of the patient's condition
- details of referrals to specialists, if any
- test results
- imaging investigation results.[41]

In terms of the Occupational Health and Safety Act 85 of 1993, health records must be kept for a period of 20 years after treatment.

These records can also be used in the event of a malpractice insurance claim against the dentist. The dental records may be used in a court of law to establish the diagnostic information that was obtained and the treatment that was rendered to the patient. It can also be used in defence of allegations of malpractice and to determine whether the diagnosis and treatment conformed to acceptable standards. Moreover, these records serve as a valuable database for investigators in cases where the ante-mortem dental records of a deceased are required for forensic comparison. Orthodontic restorations and extractions add to the forensic significance of the teeth and assist in the identification of the body.

3.5.9 Dental restorations

Dental restoration involves different techniques that the dentist uses to restore flaws in the teeth or to replace a missing tooth or part of a tooth. The following are examples of dental restorations:

41 Medical and Dental Professions Board (2007).

- *Sealants* are used as a temporary preventative measure and commonly applied to fill the decay-susceptible grooves on the molars (back teeth) in children.
- *Fillings* in various forms, such as silver amalgam, gold or composite resin fillings, are placed directly into the prepared tooth.
- *Crowns*, tooth-shaped 'caps', are placed over the entire tooth to provide structure to hold a bridge in place or cover a dental implant.
- *Bridges* are false teeth that are designed to 'bridge' the gap created by one or more missing teeth.
- *Implants* consist of a small post made of metal that is placed into the bone socket where teeth are missing to replace the root of the tooth. The implant is covered with a replacement tooth called a crown.
- *Veneers* are thin porcelain facings that cover the front side of teeth. This is often a cosmetic procedure to change the appearance of teeth.
- *Dentures* are a removable replacement for missing teeth and surrounding tissues. Partial dentures can be made of a metal or acrylic base. Removable full dentures are used when no teeth remain.

3.5.10 Root canal

The root canal is the natural space within a tooth and consists of the pulp chamber. Root canal treatment is needed when the root becomes infected or inflamed due to an injury or a large cavity in the tooth's root. The infected dental pulp and debris are removed with dental files and irrigation. The reshaped canals are then subsequently filled with material.

3.5.11 Extractions

Extractions involve the removal of a tooth or teeth and may be performed for various reasons such as tooth decay, making space for other teeth, and cosmetic reasons for orthodontic treatment or restorations.

3.6 SUMMARY

Forensic medical evidence is crucial for the successful investigation or prosecution of a case. A medical examiner may provide valuable information that was gathered during the examination of the victim.

However, such evidence is often badly taken or incomplete. During investigations investigators may be required to liaise with medical practitioners to ascertain what medical records exist and what observations were made during previous medical examinations or what evidence should be collected during an existing medico-legal examination in the context of the case. The sharing of information about the scene of incident, the evidence collected or to be collected from the victim and/or the alleged offender, the injuries sustained during the attack, or advice given on other possible evidence that could be collected may prove to be critical later on in the investigation or prosecution of a case.

It is evident that medico-legal evidence, such as forensic odontology, forensic toxicology and forensic pathology, is vital during any investigation. Evidence is only of value if the examination is properly conducted and all the specimens for forensic analysis are properly collected and preserved.

REFERENCES

RE Barsley 'Odontology as a forensic science, the North American experience' (2010) 201 *Forensic Science International* 507

J-P Beauthier, E de Valck, P Lefevre & J de Winne 'Mass Disaster Victim Identification: The Tsunami Experience' (2009) 2 *The Open Forensic Science Journal* 54–62

BD Bhana & JM Visser 'Medico-legal investigation of suspected fatal poisonings in Pretoria: 2000–2001' (2004) 23(4) *Med Law* 859–873

JG Clement 'Is current bitemark analysis a misnomer?' (2010) 201 *Forensic Science International* 33–37

JJ Fenton *Toxicology: A Case-Oriented Approach* (CRC Press 2002)

BAJ Fisher *Techniques of Crime Scene Investigation* 7 ed (CRC Press 2004)

Forensictoxicology.net. Available at http://www.forensictoxicology.net, accessed 30 December 2011

RM Gardner *Practical Crime Scene Processing and Investigation* (CRC Press 2005)

JN Gilbert *Criminal Investigation* 6 ed (Pearson Prentice Hall 2004)

JE Girard *Criminalistics: Forensic Science and Crime* (Jones & Bartlett 2008)

GS Golden 'Standards and practices for bite mark photography' (2011) 29(2) *J Forensic Odontostomatol* 29–37

AJ Hill, I Hewson & R Lain 'The role of the forensic odontologist in disaster victim identification: Lessons for management' (2011) 205 *Forensic Science International* 44–47

AJ Hill, R Lain & I Hewson 'Preservation of dental evidence following exposure to high temperatures' (2011) 205 *Forensic Science International* 40–43

J Horswell *The Practice of Crime Scene Investigation* (CRC Press 2004)

ARW Jackson & JM Jackson *Forensic Science* (Pearson Prentice Hall 2004)

SH James & JJ Nordby *Forensic Science* (CRC Press 2005)

KK Leung 'Forensic odontology' (2008) 13(11) *Dental Bulletin* 16–18

JM Lewis & DR Senn 'Dental age estimation utilizing third molar development: A review of principles, methods, and population studies in the United States' (2010) 201 *Forensic Science International* 79–83

CW Marais *Physical Evidence in Crime Investigation* (Promedia 1992)

Medical and Dental Professions Board 'Guidelines for Good Practice in the Health Care Professions, Booklet 15: Guidelines on the Keeping of Patient Records' 2 ed (29 May 2007)

T O'Connor 'Forensic Toxicology' (n.d.). Available at http://www.drtomoconnor.com/3210/3210lect04.htm, accessed 9 November 2011 at 1

JW Osterburg & RH Ward *Criminal Investigation: A Method for Reconstructing the Past* 6 ed (Anderson Publishing 2010)

IA Pretty & D Sweet 'A paradigm shift in the analysis of bitemarks' (2010) 201 *Forensic Science International* 38–44

SAPS. South African Police Service 'Forensic Fact File' No 11 of 2008

TG Schwär, JD Loubser & JA Olivier *The Forensic ABC in Medical Practice: A Practical Guide* (HAUM 1988)

MJ Stewart, JJ Moar, J Mwesigwa & M Kokot 'Forensic toxicology in urban South Africa' (1999) 101(3) *Forensic Science International* 177–178

D Sweet 'Forensic dental identification' (2010) 201 *Forensic Science International* 3–4

D Sweet 'INTERPOL DVI best-practice standards – An overview' (2010) 201 *Forensic Science International* 18–21

J Taylor 'A brief history of forensic odontology and disaster victim identification practices in Australia' (2009) *J Forensic Odontostomatol.* Available at http://www.iofos.eu/Journals/JFOS%20Dec09/TaylorHistory64-78.pdf, accessed 30 December 2011

J van der Westhuizen *Forensic Criminalistics* 2 ed (Heinemann 1996)

SEROLOGICAL EVIDENCE AND DNA ANALYSIS

Chapter 4

M S Manamela • J H Smith • R J Mokwena

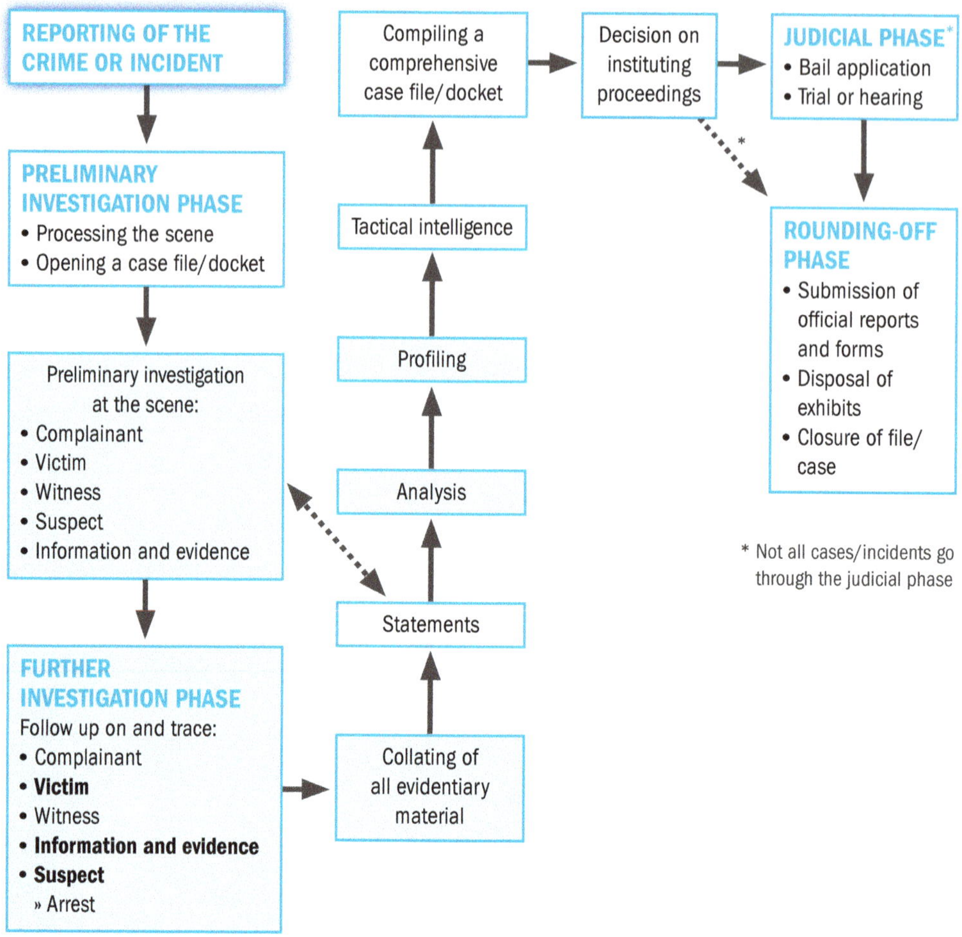

Figure 4.1: Areas of the crime investigation process covered in this chapter shown in shaded area

4.1 INTRODUCTION

Visual or chemical testing of serological evidence is a critical element of crime scene processing and laboratory examinations. Classical serology testing refers to using presumptive testing to indicate that it is indeed a body fluid, and confirmatory tests to identify the type of body fluid deposited at the crime scene or on a stain of evidence. The presumptive test is normally a colour test which is used as a screening tool to indicate the possible type of body fluid such as (but not limited to) blood or semen, but it does not indicate what kind of blood or semen (human or non-human) has been deposited. Confirmatory tests are tests that are positive for the substance in question and only for that substance. Generally, confirmatory tests are performed at a laboratory and may consume large portions of a stain. Presumptive and confirmatory tests provide laboratories with a structure to prioritise or determine which stains will be submitted for DNA (deoxyribonucleic acid) analysis. Serology testing has value if it is necessary for the investigation to determine what type of body fluid it is.

Many laboratories do not conduct serology testing on serology evidence and will submit certain evidence directly for DNA testing. This is mostly done when the sample or stain is limited in size. Because post-coital samples taken from sexual assault victims are limited in size, most laboratories do not perform any serology testing but submit these samples directly for DNA analysis. There is also no serology test for detecting 'skin cells' (epithelial cells or touch-DNA) and these samples are also submitted directly for DNA analysis. In many court proceedings the fact that there is DNA from the perpetrator to accompany the visual identification is adequate in the context of the case and the type of body fluid does not need to be determined. The linking of the perpetrator to the crime through DNA typing is normally adequate.

4.2 SEROLOGICAL EVIDENCE

4.2.1 The meaning of serological evidence

Serology is the scientific study of blood serum and other bodily fluids. Serological evidence means that bodily substances such as blood, semen and sweat can be used as evidence to identify the perpetrator(s) during criminal and civil investigation and prosecution.[1]

The evidential value that can be derived from serological evidence varies depending on the types of tests that are performed. Developments in DNA analysis have greatly enhanced the evidential value of serological evidence. Before the advent of technology that permitted the use of DNA for identification, forensic examiners had to rely on less distinguishing features such as the blood group or enzyme group in the bodily substance to establish identity. All forensic marker serology-based tests, such as ABO blood grouping and enzyme marker systems, have been replaced with DNA-based markers. However, despite the role of DNA analysis, the presence of serological evidence still has evidential value even though it will not carry the same degree of decisiveness as DNA analysis.

4.2.2 Circumstances under which serological evidence will have evidential value

Serological evidence will have evidential value when:

- found at the scene of incident:
    - where the victim's bodily substances are at a location associated with the suspect

1 Houck & Siegel (2010) 230.

  - where the suspect's bodily substances are at a location associated with the victim or not associated with the suspect
- the bodily substances of the victim are found on the suspect or on items originating from or used by the perpetrator
- the bodily substances of the suspect are found on the victim or on items associated with the victim.

Thus the serological evidence will be of value when, for example, the victim's blood is found in the car of the suspect, or the victim's blood is found on a weapon in possession of the perpetrator, or the victim's saliva is left on a bite mark on the suspect, or the suspect's semen is found on the victim's body or clothes.

It is important, however, that the investigator be well trained to distinguish serological evidence from stains that are often confused with serological evidence. There is a range of substances that create stains that will appear visually similar to body fluid stains. To document and collect these stains blindly will lead to the following:
- a false sense that evidence has been found
- a waste of resources to process non-evidence
- false expectations in the legal process with regard to evidence that does not exist.

Presumptive test reagents may be used by scene of incident examiners to verify whether the identified stains are body fluid stains. These tests are called presumptive tests based on the outcome of the results they deliver. A positive result does not indicate the absolute presence of a specific body fluid but rather gives a strong indication that a body fluid is present. The test methods used are **sensitive** and **specific** and therefore much more reliable than a visual inspection of a suspected stain.

Example 4.1: Detecting blood stains

In some cases it is important to determine whether blood was washed from surfaces at the scene of incident.

Luminol is a popular blood enhancement reagent used to detect invisible blood stains. Luminol is sprayed onto the suspected stain and if it is blood, the reagent will glow. The effect is not lasting and must be photographed while the blood or bloody prints are luminescent.

A blood enhancement reagent such as Amido Black is recommended if a permanent visualisation of invisible blood is required, as in the case of bloody shoeprints.

After performing these tests the stain can still be subjected to DNA analysis.

Evidence recovery and presumptive testing are normally also the first steps in the laboratory where exhibits are analysed after being received. Forensic examiners will:

- document the chain of custody of the exhibit material by documenting the condition of the packaging material. This includes the unique seal number and unique inscriptions on the packaging material.
- document the appearance and description of the exhibit. Photographs and/or sketches are used for documentation purposes.
- perform screening analyses on the exhibits with the aid of presumptive test methods in order to determine whether any possible blood or semen is present on the exhibits. Exhibits which have been tested by the scene of incident examiner may not be required to be retested.
- determine the evidential value of biological evidence identified on exhibit material.
- remove biological evidence from exhibits for forensic DNA analysis.

In the past, forensic science laboratories routinely employed serological screening tests, based on biochemical and immunological assays, to confirm the presence of biological fluids in order to identify possible sources of DNA. These tests require multiple serial testing to be performed, consume much of the stain and are also time consuming. Moreover, the presence of multiple biological fluids such as saliva, vaginal secretions and menstrual blood cannot be conclusively identified using current tests. Many forensic laboratories have elected to bypass the serological tests and proceed directly to forensic DNA analysis.[2] This approach is increasingly becoming more popular since it provides laboratory results in a shorter time and more of the stain is preserved for DNA testing. Identifying foreign DNA or the source of the DNA that cannot be explained on an object or person has much more evidential value than merely identifying the type of body fluid.

4.2.3 Other body fluids of significant value

Body fluids not only refer to typical body liquids such as blood or semen but also to any trace evidence with a biological origin, including hair, bone, teeth, faeces and skin or muscle tissue. Forensic analysis can also be done on blood, saliva and urine to identify substance-specific metabolites derived from the physiologic transformation of medications, illicit drugs, poisons or alcohol. Thus body fluids, tissues and organs may be used to detect drugs or other harmful chemicals present in the body. This type of examination is conducted not only on the

2 Hanson & Ballantyne (2010).

victim but also on the suspected perpetrator of the crime. It may be valuable to determine if the suspect was under the influence of a substance or had used an illegal substance.

4.2.4 Selecting for collection an exhibit with evidential value

The evidential value of exhibits to be collected is the key to examining a scene of incident effectively. Some jurisdictions refer to this as probative evidence, which is evidence that will provide the investigator with probable cause to make an arrest. This evidence may be collected if it is believed that, at a later date, it would prove significant to the investigation. However, this evidence should be well documented in the exhibit logs and the case docket. The exhibits should be stored in an adequate facility for exhibits until such time as they are required for forensic examination.[3]

The evidential value of physical evidence refers to evidence that is sufficiently useful to prove something important in the criminal/civil investigation by linking a perpetrator to the scene of incident, providing evidence to eliminate a person from the criminal investigation of an offence, or proving the innocence or guilt of a person.

Evidential value is used by investigators or forensic fieldworkers to determine which exhibits to select. After the evidential value of physical evidence has been determined, the investigator needs to consider whether there is an opportunity to construct a forensic DNA profile. If there is, the examiner needs to decide which exhibit material needs to be collected for DNA analysis. Similarly, the evidential value of other types of forensic evidence must also be considered.

Exhibits are selected that will make the greatest contribution to putting the pieces of the puzzle together. Three key questions play a role in this selection:

- What type of exhibit is it?
- Where was the exhibit found? (Location/place where it was found and/or the position of the exhibit material and/or a stain of the exhibit material)
- To whom does the exhibit belong? (Ownership)

Thus the usefulness and evidential value of forensic analyses of any exhibit material are determined by the type of exhibit, the location (place where and/or position in which it was found) and the ownership of the exhibit material and/or stain.

The scene of incident does not remain there indefinitely, so once the samples are collected the investigator may not necessarily be able to go back to collect more.

3 Blozis (2010).

This becomes especially tricky during the collection of skin cells for DNA analysis in property crimes. The scene of incident examiner needs to make a logical decision as to which samples will be used.

Example 4.2: Skin cells must be collected as soon as possible

Say, for example, a factory is burgled. To collect skin cells from the handle of the main entrance door would not be of any value because everyone entering the building has to touch the handle to open the door. The scene of incident must be evaluated to determine which other objects the perpetrator could have touched or come into contact with that could yield good single-source DNA and have evidential value. Normally the points of entry, such as windows and doors, are good sources of skin cells because there is a strong possibility that the perpetrator had touched the surfaces.

The scene of incident examiner must collect and observe the clues and information (including information from eyewitnesses and/or other persons who were at the scene during or after the incident) to contextualise the events and reconstruct how the offence was committed. Physical evidence is considered to be of little use without an interpretation of the significance of its presence and/or the information that can be obtained for criminal investigation. The value of physical evidence can be measured either in generic terms, which may ultimately be subjective, or in contextual terms.

The scene of incident examiner must also consider the different types of physical evidence and the different types of forensic examinations (for example trace analysis such as paint and fibre; ballistic examinations; disputed document examinations; chemical analyses; etc) that may be performed on physical evidence.

The samples collected from a scene of incident will be sent to the respective forensic disciplines in the Forensic Science Laboratory. The main aim of the forensic biologist will be to use the techniques available, including DNA analysis, to either include or exclude the alleged suspect(s) from being present at the scene of incident. It should be noted that if a forensic DNA profile cannot be obtained, it does not imply that the person was not involved in the crime. The courts will then make use of all the investigation angles, for example the use of witnesses, circumstantial evidence and so forth to reach a conclusion based on facts. The serological analysis, which includes DNA evidence, is just one of the tools law enforcement agents use to bring criminals to book.

Example 4.3: Which exhibits might have evidential value and should be collected?

The following scenarios illustrate when serological evidence or other forensic evidence may have evidential value and should be collected by the forensic fieldworker at the scene of incident.

SCENARIO 1

A woman is attacked and raped in her own apartment by an unknown person.

Analysis of Scenario 1

The residence of the victim is considered to be the 'victim's scene of incident environment'. This implies that the scene of incident will contain evidence related to the crime but also serological items that are not related to the rape.

The victim's own DNA deposited on her own clothing or property in her apartment will have no evidential value and should not routinely be collected.

The perpetrator's DNA on any item found in the victim's apartment will, however, have evidential value. It will place him on the scene to which he had no previous legal access. Any object or location on the scene containing the perpetrator's DNA or linking the perpetrator to the scene will have evidential value and need to be evaluated for collection. If the perpetrator was injured and left semen or his blood (stains) on the linen of the victim's bed, the blood and semen stains will have evidential value and will provide an excellent opportunity to obtain a forensic DNA profile.

SCENARIO 2

A man enters the house through the window of the victim's property and steals some items from inside the property.

Analysis of Scenario 2

The victim's own DNA found on any item on the property will have no evidential value and should not normally be collected.

The perpetrator's DNA found on any item on the victim's property will, however, have evidential value. It will place him on the scene to which he had no previous legal access. Any object or surface on the scene containing the perpetrator's DNA or linking the perpetrator to the scene may have evidential value and needs to be evaluated for collection.

There is a good indication that the perpetrator had left smudged prints or skin cells on the window sill. He also left a cigarette butt in the ashtray (nobody in the victim's household smokes or they smoke a different brand). The smudged prints cannot be used for fingerprint analysis, but the skin cells they contain are a good source of touch-DNA. Thus both the cigarette butt and the skin cells have evidential value and provide a good opportunity to obtain a forensic DNA profile.

4.2.5 Collecting and packaging serological samples

If possible, collect the most fragile forensic evidence first. The evidential value of an exhibit must be established before collection. It is useless to collect evidence with no evidential value. The context of the items (exhibits) found on the scene of incident must be kept in mind. For example, cigarette butts in a dedicated smoking area of a public place have very little evidential value in normal circumstances.

Forensic scene of incident examiners processing a scene of incident must collect, store and transport body fluids in accordance with prescripts that will not compromise the exhibit material. Exhibits may be compromised by contamination or by not maintaining the chain of custody. The location of the exhibits at the scene must be well documented and photographed.

Where appropriate, exhibits removed from the scene of incident should be packaged in evidence sealing bags or appropriate containers, sealed and properly labelled. It is advisable to package the exhibits in paper or an envelope or cardboard box before placing them in the evidence sealing bag so that the exhibits do not 'sweat' and so cause the DNA to degrade. The paper or cardboard will absorb the moisture during 'sweating'.

Dedicated evidence collection kits have been developed by law enforcement agencies to facilitate the taking of samples and the packaging and storage of different exhibit material. These evidence collection kits ensure that samples are taken appropriately, that exhibit material is not contaminated during storage and that the chain of custody is maintained. A primer residue kit ensures that the sample is taken in the correct manner and preserved. A DNA swabbing kit ensures that skin cells are collected using the correct type of swab to ensure a DNA result.

Evidence collection kits are made available by the SAPS to facilitate the packaging of exhibits. Typical evidence collection kits normally available for use by investigating officers or scene of incident examiners may include:

- sexual assault evidence collection kits to be used by a medical practitioner in the examination and collection of samples from the victim
- paediatric assault evidence collection kits to be used by a medical practitioner in the examination and collection of samples from children
- blood alcohol kits to collect blood from the suspect for blood alcohol analysis
- DNA reference collection kits to collect DNA samples from the suspect or victim
- DNA tissue evidence collection kits to collect tissue samples from corpses for DNA analysis
- clothing evidence collection kits to package the clothing from victims or suspects for DNA analysis
- DNA swabbing evidence collection kits to collect DNA such as blood, semen or skin cells (touch-DNA) from a scene of incident

- toxicology tissue kits to collect tissue from corpses for toxicology analysis by a pathologist
- primer residue evidence collection kits to collect samples from the suspect for primer residue analysis.

Tamper-evident collection bags (evidence sealing bags) should be used to package exhibits. By using tamper-evident collection bags it is possible to demonstrate that the contents were not accessed or tampered with, thus maintaining the chain of custody. Where DNA swabbing evidence collection kits are not available, Dacron swabs may be used to collect DNA evidence at a scene of incident.

The use of the correct and clean packaging material can prevent contamination of exhibit material by:

- providing a clean storage environment
- removing the exhibit from the scene of incident environment
- providing a favourable environment for the preservation of biological material
- allowing laboratory personnel to keep evidence separated for storage and examination.

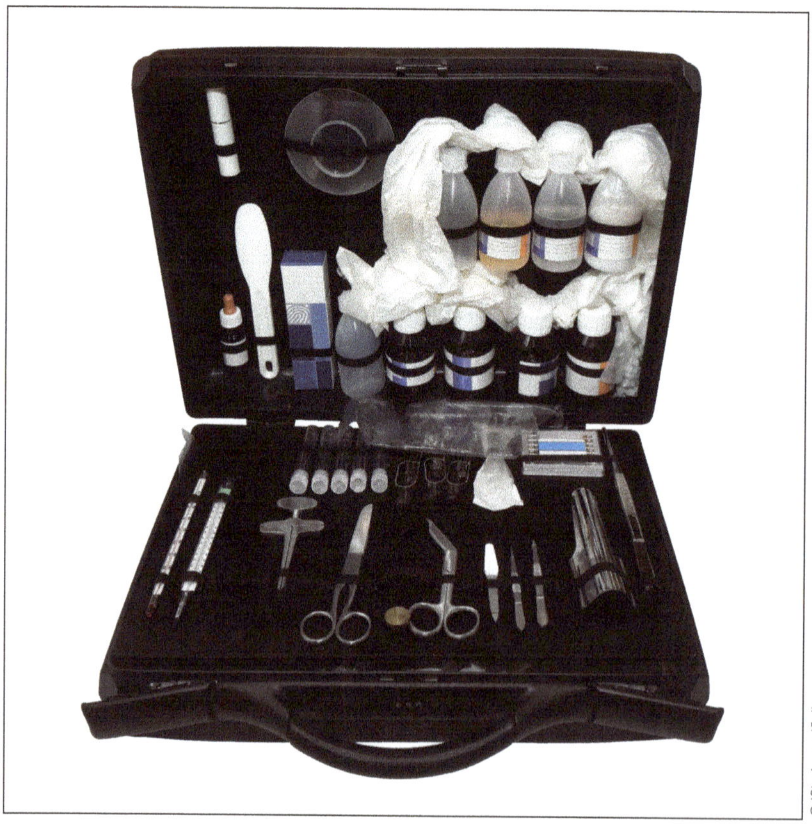

Figure 4.2: Typical evidence collection kits used for the collection of exhibits[4]

4 SAPS (2013).

The packaging material itself may contain substances that could act as contaminants. For example, if unused, open containers or bags are kept in the trunk of a vehicle, contaminants may accumulate in them. This can be avoided by ensuring that any items used to package the evidence are kept clean and stored in a sealed and uncontaminated manner.

Wet or moist exhibits should be air-dried and not be placed in direct sunlight before packaging. Exhibits should be packaged separately to prevent cross-contamination.

An exhibit log of exhibit material removed from the scene of incident should be maintained. The validity and acceptability of the evidence may be questioned in court if this procedure is not properly followed and reported.

4.2.6 Guidelines for preparing exhibit material for DNA analysis

The table below illustrates some guidelines for collecting and packaging exhibit material for DNA analysis at the scene of the incident.[5, 6, 7]

Table 4.1: Guidelines for collecting and packaging exhibit material for DNA analysis

Exhibit	Comments
Chewing gum	• Wrap the chewing gum in wax paper and place it in an envelope with drying agent. • Then place it in an evidence sealing bag.
Cigarette butts	Gather information from occupants of the premises to assess which cigarette brands they smoke. Identify cigarette butts that could have been left by the perpetrator. • Collect the cigarette butts from the top, middle and bottom of the ashtray if the ashtray is full. Package the butts from each layer separately. • Collect cigarette butts lying at the scene of incident. • Send the butts for DNA analysis.
Straws	• If the straw is inside the drinking vessel, cut the exposed part of the straw at an angle (45 degrees) and place it in an envelope. • Then place it in an evidence sealing bag.
Ice cream sticks	• Air-dry the ice cream stick and put it into an envelope. • Then place it in an evidence sealing bag.
Abandoned clothing	• Photograph the abandoned clothing in context at the scene of incident. • Also photograph labels or unique identifiers on the clothing. • Place the clothing in a paper bag with a drying agent. • Then place it in an evidence bag or package it in the clothing evidence collection kit. →

5 Kock (2010) 1.
6 Smith (2009) 1–2.
7 Blozis (2010).

→ Exhibit	Comments
Cellphone	• Examine the cellphone for fingerprints first by using the cynoacrylate fuming (superglue) method. • Then swab the cellphone for DNA. • The DNA swabbing evidence collection kit may be used.
Tools used during a burglary or commission of an offence	• Assess the surface of the tool and decide if fingerprints could have been left or not. • If the cynoacrylate fuming (superglue) method is used, the tools should be swabbed for DNA. • The DNA swabbing evidence collection kit may be used. • It is advisable to rather submit the tools to the laboratory for examination.
Food	• Only food that shows possible bite marks such as a half-eaten apple, cheese, etc should be swabbed for skin cells. • Swab the areas surrounding bite marks or lip marks. • The DNA swabbing evidence collection kit may be used.
String/rope	• Package any string or rope with evidential value found on the scene of incident, eg shoelaces, in an envelope or box. • Then place it in an evidence sealing bag and send it for DNA analysis.
Ligatures (any item used to bind the victim; it may include rope, duct tape, electric cords, belts, scarves, bandanas and wire ties)	Ligatures are usually attached to the dead body or victim. • Knots in the ligature on a dead body must be swabbed at the scene of incident. The rest of the ligature will be removed during the post-mortem. • Package the ligature in an envelope or box with the knots intact. Then place it in an evidence sealing bag and send it for DNA analysis. An analysis of the knot might indicate whether the victim could have tied the knot him-/herself (suicide) or not (murder). • A reference DNA sample of the victim must also be submitted for control purposes.
Cable ties	• Place the cable tie in an envelope. • Then place it in an evidence sealing bag and send it for DNA analysis.
Duct tape	• Examine the duct tape for fingerprints. • Consider the ends for a physical match (cuts may be linked to the instrument used for cutting). • DNA analysis may also be considered. →

→ Exhibit	Comments
Wires, cables, cords and plugs	These include car radio wires, ignition wires that have been damaged/tampered/interfered with. There should be an indication of disturbance during crime. Those handled frequently by the occupants should be disregarded. • Swab the item for DNA. • The DNA swabbing evidence collection kit may be used.
Toilet paper/ tissues/paper and envelopes	Paper items analysed for skin cells have demonstrated low success rates for DNA. They should rather be examined for fingerprints and visually inspected for hair, blood, semen or saliva/mucous. • If present, collect; if not, do not collect. • Package the item into an envelope or box. • Then place it in an evidence sealing bag and send for DNA analysis.
Knives	• Assess the surface of the knife and decide if fingerprints have possibly been left on it or not. Use the cynoacrylate fuming (superglue) method. • If there is visible blood, perform a presumptive test for blood. If the test is positive, swab the blood. • If there are fingerprints in the blood, photograph the fingerprints. Perform a presumptive test for blood. If the test is positive, swab the blood. • Thereafter swab the knife for DNA (the DNA swabbing evidence collection kit may be used) or submit as is for DNA examination. • Package the knife in an evidence sealing bag and send for DNA examination. The Sharp & Dangerous Items Collection Kit may also be used to package the exhibits.
Firearms and cartridges	Most of the firearm is not conducive to fingerprinting because of its uneven surface. • Examine the firearm and magazine first for fingerprints by using the cynoacrylate fuming (superglue) method. • Then swab the firearm, magazine (including the lip area where cartridges are inserted and the bottom of the magazine) for DNA. • Swab the cocking mechanism/slide, the grip and the front surface of the trigger with different swabs. The head stamps or ends of discharged shells and cartridges may be sources of skin cells. • The DNA swabbing evidence collection kit may be used to collect the DNA and package the evidence. →

→ Exhibit	Comments
Drinking vessels (cans, bottles, cups, drinking glasses, etc used for soft drinks or alcoholic drinks)	• Examine the drinking vessel for fingerprints first by using the cynoacrylate fuming (superglue) method. • Then swab the drinking vessel for DNA. The rim should always be swabbed first. If the cap is still in place, the cap must be swabbed. • The swabbing evidence collection kit may be used to collect and package the evidence. • Then place it in an evidence sealing bag and send for DNA analysis.
Windows, window sills/panes/handles	• Assess the surface for fingerprints or other body prints, for example of the forehead, ear, etc. • Swab the item for DNA. • Body prints must be swabbed inside the contact area. • The DNA swabbing evidence collection kit may be used to collect DNA and package the evidence.
Door handles	The handles of doors with damage associated with breaking and entering are normally a good source of the perpetrator's DNA. Door handles that are frequently used by various individuals normally do not provide a good source of interpretable DNA. • Swab the handle for DNA. • The DNA swabbing evidence collection kit may be used to collect DNA and package the evidence.
Household appliances	Consider those household appliances that show signs of having been disturbed. • The DNA swabbing evidence collection kit may be used to swab and package the evidence.
Damaging (breaking) and entering or theft from a vehicle or abandoned vehicle	• Examine vehicles for fingerprints and foreign hair: the areas that show signs of damage (breaking) and entering; wires that show signs of disturbance; the gear leaver and the rear windows. • The DNA swabbing evidence collection kit may be used to collect DNA and package the evidence.
Clothing items	• Send clothing items that have evidential value to the laboratory for examination. • Each piece of clothing can be placed in a paper bag. • Then place it in an evidence sealing bag and send for DNA analysis.

4.2.7 Information required in covering letters

Investigators should always ensure that a covering letter accompanies any physical evidence that is sent for forensic analysis.

The covering letter should contain the following information:

- the name of the police station/institution and the CAS/reference
- the postal address of the station or institution from which the exhibits originated
- the investigator's particulars, such as the rank, initials, surname, telephone number (office and cellphone numbers are required), postal address, fax number and email address (if available)
- the charge or offence.
- a short description of the case and the date the incident happened. The following should be adequately addressed:
  - **what** happened?
  - **when** did it happen?
  - **what** physical evidence was collected?
  - **where** was the physical evidence collected?
  - **when** was the physical evidence collected?
  - **why** was the physical evidence collected; in other words, what is expected from the Forensic Science Laboratory?
- a list of all the physical evidence that was submitted, how it was packed, labelled and sealed
- the following additional information is required on the insert in the evidence collection kit, for cases where DNA typing is requested:
  - names of suspects and victims
  - identity number or passport number of suspect(s) and victim(s)
- whether the victim is a minor
- for rape cases, whether the victim had sexual intercourse within five days prior to the incident or after the incident. If the answer is affirmative, a reference DNA sample must be included from the relevant individual with whom the victim had intercourse, for exclusion purposes.

4.2.8 Sexual assault evidence

The victims of sexual assault should be taken to a medical practitioner as soon as possible for a medico-legal examination. In order to prevent cross-contamination, the victim and the suspect must not be transported in the same vehicle or come into contact with each other before the medico-legal examination has been completed and the evidence collected. Any such contact may bring into dispute the exact time that foreign trace evidence found on the victim or the suspect was deposited. The investigator must provide the medical examiner with a sexual assault evidence or paediatric kit for this examination. The medical practitioner will interview the victim and collect the appropriate samples.

Investigators must not only focus on ensuring that physical evidence is collected from the victim but must also consider that physical evidence from the victim may have been left on the perpetrator.

4.3 DNA

4.3.1 What does DNA refer to?

The human organism is composed of multiple organs. Each organ consists of tissue, which in turn consists of cells. Cells consist of molecules and molecules consist of atoms bonded together. The cell is the basic unit of life. It is a miniature factory that produces raw materials, with energy and waste material generation capabilities that are necessary to sustain life.

The genetic material known as DNA (deoxyribonucleic acid) is the genetic blueprint of life and carries information for the expression of genes in the tissue and genetic attributes in each individual. An organism consists of a large number of cells. As the smallest functional unit in an organism, most cells contain a nucleus. The DNA molecule has a unique double helix structure and is found in the nucleus of the cell. The human genome contains, in total, approximately six billion nucleotides per diploid genome. These nucleotides are distributed between 23 pairs of chromosomes.

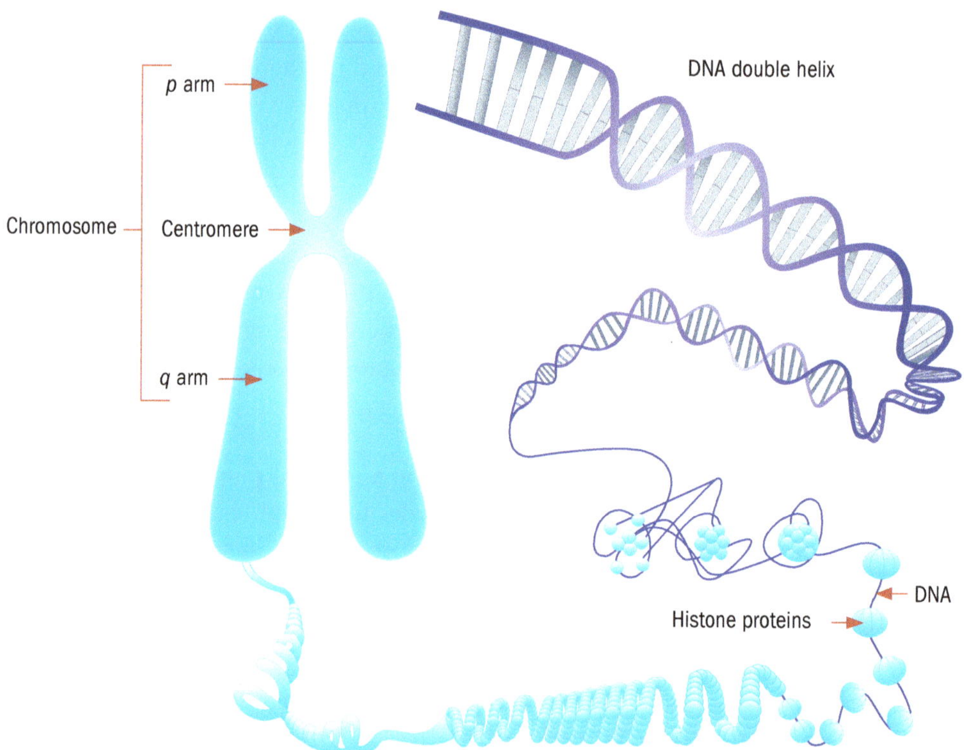

Figure 4.3: DNA in the chromosome[8]

8 Adapted; source available at http://www.nlm.nih.gov.

A chromosome is an organised structure of DNA and protein that is found in the cells. It is a single piece of coiled DNA containing many genes, regulatory elements and other nucleotide sequences. Chromosomes have different regions based (very broadly) on known functional properties. The so-called 'coding regions' contain DNA sequences (genes) which primarily determine the amino acid sequences of the proteins which they code for. They also determine the degree of expression of the gene in any tissue at any time.

'Non-coding' DNA generally contains DNA sequences for which no function has yet been established or, possibly, for which no function exists. Forensic DNA analysis has developed chemistry that focuses on testing the variance between individuals in these non-coding areas. Other than information about the sex of the person, the forensic DNA profile contains no personal information or information about the person's health status, physical characteristics or behaviour.

The DNA in all the cells in the body of one person is the same. Any part of the human body or material originating from the human body which contains cells with nuclei can be used as a source of DNA. For this reason forensic DNA analysis is a powerful tool to link individuals to a scene of incident.

Major sources of DNA (genetic material) are the following:[9]

- blood
- semen
- saliva
- soft tissue (muscle)
- bone
- skin cells (epithelial cells).

Objects from which skin cells (touch-DNA) of the perpetrator can be obtained include the following:[10, 11]

- cigarette butts
- chewing gum
- breasts and genitalia of sexual assault victims
- postal stamps
- envelope flaps
- sides and rims of drinking vessels (bottles/cans/cups)
- friction surfaces.

---

9 Stray & Shewale (2010).
10 Blozis (2010).
11 Kock (2010) 1.

4.3.2 Identification by DNA characteristics (DNA typing)

The application of forensic DNA analysis in the solving of crimes is a powerful tool. In 1985 Alex Jeffrey was the first to describe how DNA could be used to identify humans. The identity of the donor of genetic material (DNA) can be determined by forensic DNA analysis. A person can therefore be linked to a scene of incident through bodily (evidence) material that is found at the scene.[12, 13] Forensic DNA analysis is performed to determine the various forensic DNA profiles of evidence material (crime samples) and to compare these profiles with control samples of the persons allegedly involved.

Figure 4.4 illustrates a simplified example of the comparison between a crime scene sample (E) and two suspects (S1 and S2 respectively):

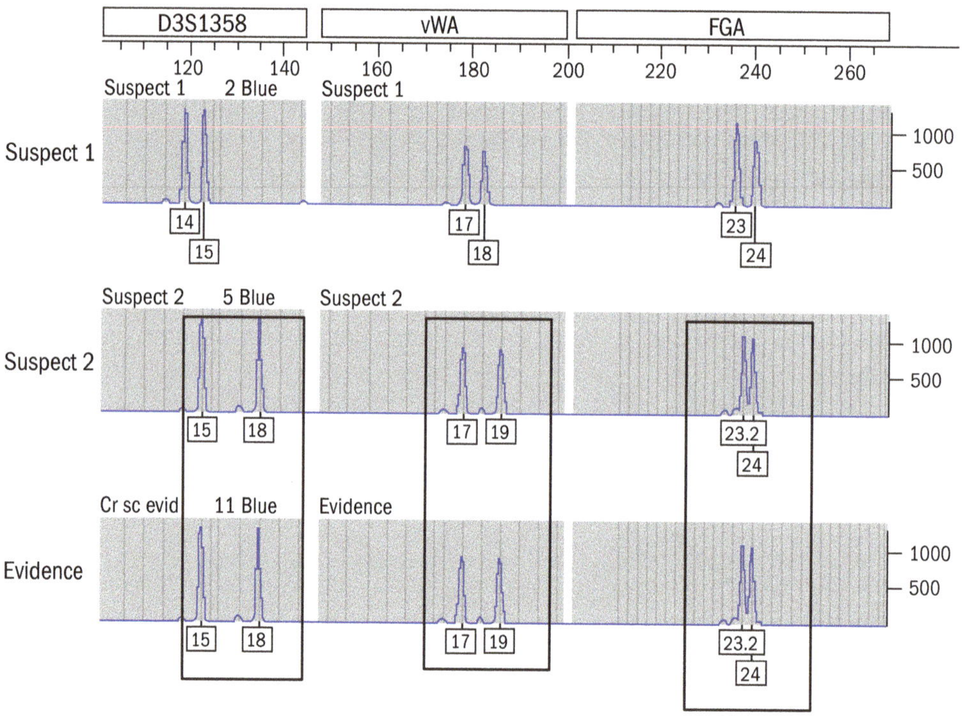

	D3	vWA	FGA
(S1)	14, 15	17,18	23,24
(S2)	15, 18	17,19	23.2,24
(E)	15, 18	17,19	23.2,24

Figure 4.4: Example of DNA comparison

12 Jeffreys et al. 'Hypervariable "minisatellite" regions in human DNA' (1985).
13 Jeffreys et al. 'Individual-specific "fingerprints" of human DNA' (1985).

The designations D3, vWA and FGA in the above figure represent three different chromosomal locations under DNA analysis. The forensic DNA is:

- Suspect 1 (S1): D3:14,15; vWA:17,18; FGA:23,24
- Suspect 2 (S2): D3:15,18; vWA:17,19; FGA:23.2,24
- The crime sample (E): D3:15,18; vWA:17,19; FGA:23.2,24

It is evident that the DNA profile of Suspect 2 is the same profile as that of the crime scene sample. This means the profile of the evidence material (the crime scene sample) is a *match* for the profile of Suspect 2 (S2). The difference between the forensic profiles of Suspect 1 (S1) and Suspect 2 (S2) lies at the FGA chromosomal locations (ie although both suspects share the 24 allele, Suspect 1 has a 23 allele and Suspect 2 a 23.2 allele).

A forensic DNA profile that is used in criminal investigations is a string of alphanumeric characters that denotes identity. This sequence of alphanumeric numbers is nothing more than biometric information of a purely objective and irrefutable character. Thus the forensic DNA profile contains on purpose no medical information, or information of the person's predisposition to any medical conditions, or any physical characteristics (for example, the colour of the person's eyes or hair or how tall or short they are).

Sources of genetic material (DNA) with evidential value (samples or exhibits) need to be identified, documented, collected and preserved at the scene of incident in such a way that it is possible to use them for forensic DNA analysis. Reference samples (non-intimate buccal samples or fingerprints) of the persons involved in the alleged crime, such as the victim(s), suspect(s) or other parties who need to be excluded, need to be collected for comparison with the crime samples. The identification subject only has value when comparing it with another forensic DNA profile.

Forensic DNA profiling techniques have undergone rapid development and become more sensitive to allow degraded and limited samples to be analysed. Presently the technique used in forensic DNA analysis is called Short Tandem Repeat (STR) Forensic DNA analysis.[14, 15, 16]

Short tandem repeats are repeating sequences of two to six base pairs of DNA. They are very useful as tools in forensic DNA typing because of their abundance and small size. These traits are valuable when working with forensic samples, as the DNA of these samples tends to be degraded and/or is present in very small amounts.

14 Kimpton et al. (1993).

15 Lygo et al. (1994).

16 Mulero et al. (2008) 838.

Within a specific STR locus (the position of the gene on a chromosome; plural: loci) the number of times a repeat unit is repeated varies, leading to a large amount of polymorphisms within a given population because there is such a large number of possible allele variations. Polymorphism means when two or more clearly different observable characteristics or traits such as the colour of eyes, for example, exist in the same population of a species. These characteristics are called phenotypes. This makes it possible to use allele designation in forensic investigations to match the forensic DNA profile obtained from the crime sample to that of the reference sample of the suspect.[17]

A forensic science laboratory performs forensic DNA analysis typically on given loci (DNA regions) that have repeat units, for example on four base pairs in length (tetranucleotide repeat units) with a size range of 75 to 400 base pairs. Base pair here refers to one of the pairs of chemical bases joined by hydrogen bonds that connect the complementary strands of a DNA molecule, which has two strands.

Forensic DNA analysis consists of the following steps:[18, 19, 20]

1. The DNA within the cells of the exhibit material is released during the DNA isolation step.
2. The amount of DNA isolated needs to be quantified. An aliquot (the exact factor of a quantity) of isolated DNA is then normalised so that the required DNA can be used for amplification.
3. The target area of interest in the DNA is amplified by a process called polymerase chain reaction (PCR). Amplification is done in order to multiply the targeted area of the genome so that it can be detected and visualised during the fragment separation step or electrophoresis step (to enhance the visualisation of the resultant DNA segments (alleles)).
4. The DNA segments (alleles) are then separated according to size by a process called electrophoresis.
5. The separated DNA segments (alleles) are interpreted by examiners using expert software systems to provide a forensic DNA profile.
6. The forensic DNA profiles are contextualised in a report (for example a suspect is excluded or included or no finding is made).
7. Computer-generated results are interpreted by the DNA reporting officers to make a finding on whether a suspect is excluded or included as the donor of the DNA.

Forensic DNA analysis has a proven record of success in the South African courts, as Table 4.2 illustrates.

17 Butler et al. (2003) 1054.
18 Barbisin & Shewale (2010) 199.
19 Stray et al. (2010).
20 Shewale (2010).

Table 4.2: The success of forensic DNA in some recent prominent casework

Case	Suspects	Sentencing details
Avahatakali Netshisaulu, the son of City Press Editor, Mathatha Tsedu, who was murdered	Three suspects were identified through forensic DNA analysis.	Life sentences for all three accused
Orange Farm serial murders	David Nocela was identified and linked to the crimes through the forensic DNA database.	Three life sentences
West-End serial killer	Jack Mogale was linked through forensic DNA to 11 murders and other cases.	Twenty life sentences
Westonaria serial rapist	Uria Molefe was linked to 13 sexual assault cases through the forensic DNA database.	Suspect pleaded guilty
Muldersdrift serial rapist	Shavhani Phophi was linked to sexual assault cases, including sexual assault of a 10-year-old girl, through the forensic DNA database.	Found guilty on six counts of rape, two counts of theft and three counts of robbery with aggravating circumstances. Two life sentences.

4.3.3 Kinship identification

In the case of people who are close relatives, such as parents and offspring, full siblings, half siblings and cousins, scientist can use the model of Mendelian segregation to calculate the amount of shared genetic information. Mendelian inheritance (or Mendelian genetics) is a scientific description of how hereditary characteristics are passed on from parents to their offspring. Once the expected conditional probabilities between two relatives are established, one can more precisely calculate either an exclusion probability or a likelihood ratio. The likelihood ratio expresses how much more likely it is that the DNA evidence came from people with a specific relationship as opposed to two ostensibly unrelated people.

Kinship analysis is usually done when known DNA reference samples or the forensic DNA profile is not available for a reported missing person and remains (the body of a victim) are found that could possibly be those of the missing person. In this case DNA reference samples are requested from close relatives. The forensic DNA profiles from the remains are then compared to the forensic DNA profiles of the close relatives. The relatedness of the remains to the family is made by kinship analysis and expressed as relative likelihood ratios. This procedure also allows families to be excluded as possibly being related to the remains.

It is not always possible to identify remains through kinship analysis because a significant level of statistical confidence cannot be provided, especially if close relatives are not available to provide reference DNA samples. Close relatives are at times also victims of the same disaster, for example a fatal aircraft crash when the whole family was travelling together. It may also prove difficult to distinguish same-sex siblings who were victims of the same disaster from each other, especially if the remains are fragmented, because same-sex siblings share a large quantity of similar genetic information.

Immigration cases also involve kinship testing to determine if an individual could have a proposed relationship to the providers of reference samples. A person who is applying for citizenship may allege that he or she is related to an alleged grandparent who has citizenship and was born in the country for which an application is being made. Kinship identification will then be used to establish the truth.

4.3.4 Paternity testing

Paternity testing in kinship analysis is usually used to establish paternity (ie who is the father?) and to identify missing persons in mass-disaster investigations that involve reverse parentage analysis (ie could these sets of remains have come from a child of these reference samples?). These cases typically involve the mother, the child, and one or more alleged fathers.

The most common form of paternity testing uses forensic DNA profiles from a mother and a child to answer the question whether the alleged father rather than a random man (untested alternative father) could have fathered the child. With a reverse paternity test, forensic DNA type from one or both parents is used to determine if an observed type could have resulted from a child of the alleged father and mother.

This approach has a long-standing precedent in paternity determination where an exclusion probability can be calculated to express how rare it would be to find a random man who could not be excluded as the biological father of the child. The calculation thus provides information that can be used to make an assessment whether a parent is the father or mother of a child.

The determination of paternity is made based on whether or not alleles (alternative forms of a gene) are shared between the child and the alleged father when a number of genetic markers are examined. The outcome of paternity testing is simply a likelihood of inclusion or exclusion of a subject. In other words, the results would for example say that the alleged father is not the biological father of the child, or that there is a 98% likelihood that the alleged father is the biological father of the child.

Paternity testing laboratories often utilise the same forensic DNA profiling methods as those used in criminal casework testing laboratories.

A child has two alleles for each autosomal (non-sex chromosome) marker (one from the mother and one from the father). A child (son or daughter) will have his or her mother's haploid mitochondrial DNA (barring mutation) and a son will have his father's Y-chromosome haplotype (barring mutation). Mitochondrial DNA is found in the mitochondria of the cell (which is found outside the cell nucleus) and is inherited from the mother. A haploid cell is a cell nucleus that contains one of each type of chromosome (the threadlike linear strand of DNA containing the genes and hereditary information of a person). A cell mutates if the DNA changes permanently. This could involve a physical change in the chromosome relations or a biochemical change in the make-up of genes. An example of a haplotype is a sperm cell which may have either an X or a Y chromosome.

If the man tested cannot be excluded as the biological father of the child in question, statistical calculations are performed to indicate the strength of the match. The most commonly applied test in this regard is the paternity index.

The paternity index (PI) is the ratio of two conditional probabilities where the numerator assumes paternity and the denominator assumes that a random man of similar ethnic background was the father. The numerator is the probability of observed genotypes, given that the tested man is the father, while the denominator is the probability of the observed genotypes, given that a random man is the father.

The paternity index is therefore a likelihood ratio of two probabilities conditional upon different competing hypotheses. This likelihood ratio reflects how many times more likely it is to see the evidence (for example a particular set of alleles) under the first hypothesis compared to the second hypothesis. The first hypothesis could be, for example, that the DNA evidence came from a man related to the child. The second hypothesis could be that the DNA evidence came from a man not related to the child.

The paternity index is calculated for each locus. Individual PI values are multiplied to obtain the combined paternity index (CPI) for the entire set of genetic loci examined. The generally accepted minimum standard for an inclusion of paternity is a PI of 100 or greater.[21]

21 Coleman & Swanson (1994).

A PI of 100 correlates to the probability that, compared to a random man, the alleged father has a 99 to 1 chance of being the father of that particular child.

Another statistical test performed in paternity testing is the exclusion probability. This is the combined frequency of all genotypes that would be excluded if the pedigree relationships were true assuming the Hardy-Weinberg equilibrium. The Hardy-Weinberg principle states that both allele and genotype frequencies in a population remain constant – that is, they are in equilibrium – from generation to generation, unless specific disturbing influences are introduced. Those disturbing influences include non-random mating.[22] This is relevant to forensics in the sense that the alleles in a forensic profile can be considered as independent and a product rule can be applied. The frequency of occurrence in the population of each of the alleles in the forensic DNA profile can be multiplied to give the overall frequency of occurrence.

Computer software programs used for statistical calculations in paternity testing include DNA View,[23] Familias[24] and EasyDNA.[25]

4.4 SUMMARY

Although serology testing on serological evidence may be useful to determine the type of body fluid at a scene of incident, it is mainly used as a screening tool in most forensic science laboratories to identify which stains should be submitted for DNA analysis. If it is critical in a case to know the type of body fluid, the investigator must communicate this to the testing laboratory. A match between the DNA found at a crime scene and that of a suspect (or other person of interest), is essentially a positive identification, except in the case of identical twins.

DNA evidence is well accepted in the courts of law. It provides the investigator with a means of linking a suspect to a scene, excluding a person from further investigation, establishing a paternity relationship or assisting in determining the identity of a missing person.

The investigator must always consider the DNA evidence in the context of a case. In order to prosecute a case, the DNA evidence must be supported by other evidence. DNA analysis techniques are becoming increasingly sensitive and less labour intensive to perform. It may not be long before DNA analysis is no longer restricted to a laboratory but can be performed in close proximity of the scene of incident, and on the same day.

---

22 Hardy-Weinberg principle available at http://anthro.palomar.edu/synthetic/synth_2.htm accessed 20 April 2015.

23 Available at http://www.dna-view.com/dnaview.htm.

24 Available at http://www.math.chalmers.se/~mostad/familias.

25 Fung et al. (2004).

REFERENCES

M Barbisin & JG Shewale 'Assessment of DNA extracted from forensic samples prior to genotyping' (2010) 22 *Forensic Science Review* 199–214

J Blozis 'Forensic DNA evidence collection at a scene of incident: An investigator's commentary' (2010) 22 *Forensic Science Review* 121–130

JM Butler, Y Shen & B McCord 'The development of reduced size STR amplicons as tools for analysis of degraded DNA' (2003) 48 *Journal of Forensic Sciences* 1054–1064

HC Coleman & ED Swanson *DNA in the Courtroom: A Trial Watcher's Guide* (Genelex Press 1994)

WK Fung, CT Yang & W Guo 'EasyDNA: User-friendly paternity and kinship testing programs' (2004) 1261 *Progress in Forensic Genetics 10 (International Congress Series)* 628–630

EK Hanson & J Ballantyne 'RNA profiling for the identification of the tissue origin of dried stains in forensic biology' (2010) 22 *Forensic Science Review* 145–157

MM Houck & JA Siegel *Fundamentals of Forensic Science* (Elsevier 2010)

AJ Jeffreys, V Wilson & SL Thein 'Hypervariable "minisatellite" regions in human DNA' (1985) 314 *Nature* 67–73

AJ Jeffreys, V Wilson & SL Thein 'Individual-specific "fingerprints" of human DNA' (1985) 314 *Nature* 76–79

CP Kimpton, P Gill, A Walton, A Urquhart, ES Millican & M Adams 'Automated DNA Profiling employing multiplex amplification of short tandem repeat loci' (1993) 3 *Methods Application* 13–22

J Kock *Learner Guide for Forensic Biological Crime Scene Examination* (2010)

JE Lygo, PE Johnson, D Holdaway, JP Woodroffe, TM Whitaker, CP Clayton, P Kimpton & P Gill 'The validation of short tandem repeat (STR) loci for use in forensic casework' (1994) 107 *International Journal of Legal Medicine* 77–89

JJ Mulero, CW Chang, LM Calandro, RL Green, Y Li, CL Johnson & LK Hennessy 'Development and validation of the AmpFlSTR® MiniFiler™ PCR amplification kit: A MiniSTR multiplex for the analysis of degraded and/or PCR inhibited DNA' (2008) 53 *Journal of Forensic Science* 838–852

SAPS Evidence Collection Kits, 'Forensic Fact File' No 5 of 2013. Available at http://intranet.saps.gov.za/about/downloads/forensics/fact_5_2013_crime_kits.pdf. Accessed 5 August 2013.

JG Shewale 'Importance of pre-genotyping workflow in forensic DNA analysis' (2010) 22 *Forensic Science Review*

JH Smith 'Guidance on collecting and packaging of exhibit material from crime scenes for DNA analysis' (2009) Internal SAPS communication 1–2

JE Stray, JY Liu, MG Brevnov & JG Shewale 'Extraction of DNA from forensic biological samples for genotyping' (2010) 22 *Forensic Science Review* 159–175

JE Stray & JG Shewale 'Extraction of DNA from Human Remains' (2010) 22 *Forensic Science Review* 177–185

Chapter 5

IMPRINT EVIDENCE AND OTHER SPECIALITIES

M S Manamela • R J Mokwena

- Introduction
- Disputed documents
- Forensic photography
- Polygraphy
- Imprints
- Footwear and tyre imprints
- Tool marks
- Firearms
- Summary

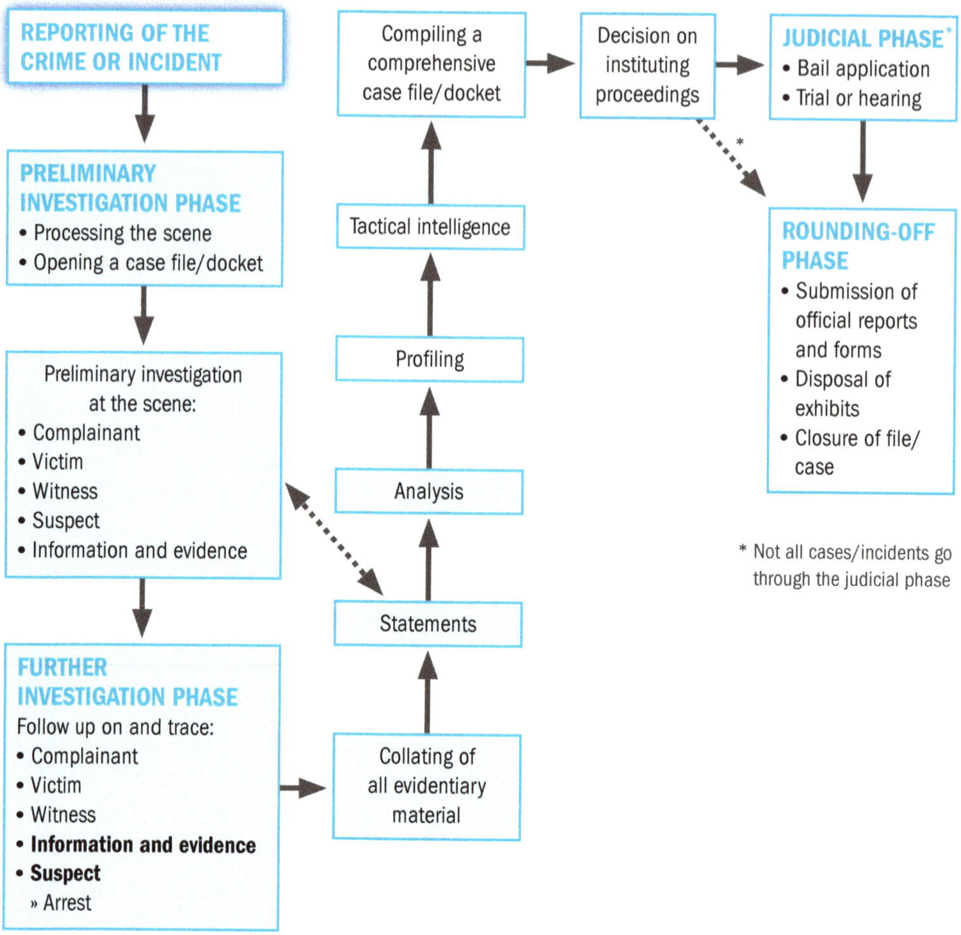

Figure 5.1: Areas of the crime investigation process covered in this chapter shown in shaded area

5.1 INTRODUCTION

Imprint evidence can be understood as physical evidence that results from the contact between two objects or surfaces. Imprint evidence is also referred to as 'impression evidence' or 'markings' and as a group represents one of the largest classes of forensic evidence. Examples of imprint evidence include markings made on cartridge cases and bullets, bite marks, tool marks, fabric impressions, shoe prints, tyre prints and, in many cases, fingerprints. Different names are given to different classes of impressions depending on how they came into being. For instance, scraping produces impressions called striations.

> **Example 5.1:** Striations
>
> Striations include bullet markings and many tool marks.
>
> When a screwdriver scrapes across a metal surface, the scratching that results contains striations. In many cases, striation patterns must be studied under a microscope. For bullet comparisons a comparison microscope is used.

Impressions can also be made by compression of one surface under the weight of another, such as when shoe impressions are made in mud or a fabric impression is transferred to a bullet passing through clothing.

In general, an imprint is considered to be a flat impression (thin, as a fingerprint on glass), whereas an indentation also has depth, for example a muddy shoe print. In other words, imprints are two-dimensional, while indentations are three-dimensional. Because the original is preferred for laboratory analysis, the impression and the substrate should be transported to the laboratory intact, if possible.

Although the description of imprint evidence by certain authors may sometimes be narrow, for the purposes of this book the description is as wide as any physical evidence resulting from a contact of two or more objects or surfaces. In addition to the traditionally known imprint evidence such as fingerprints, palm prints, footprints, tyre imprints, firearms and tool marks, this chapter also deals with disputed documents and how they are handled in forensic investigations. Photography and polygraphy are two of the instruments generally used in the study of imprint evidence in forensic investigations.

5.2 DISPUTED DOCUMENTS

Disputed documents are any type of document requiring detailed scientific examination of its physical features in offences such as fraud and forgery, or where a person needs to be included or excluded as the author of handwriting. Through examining the document, the examiners will discover and prove the facts pertaining to that particular type of document, bank note or legal document and the related material, such as the ink, paper and toner from a fax machine or photocopier.

5.2.1 Composition of a document and its investigative value

A document may be considered as anything bearing marks, signs or symbols that carry meaning or convey a message to the recipient. In forensic investigation a 'document' is considered any item which may require detailed scientific examination of its physical features, as would be done for a disputed document. Thus a 'document' in this sense may even include writing on a wall or in the sand.

The following are typical issues that need to be resolved by the document examiner:[1, 2, 3]

- determine who is the author of the handwriting or document content
- establish the validity of the signature
- observe and decipher any alterations, erasures, deletions, additions and substitutions by using instruments such as a Video Spectral Comparator (VSC) to examine the document through infrared illumination using an infrared-sensitive CCD (charged-coupled device) camera as a detector
- identify and decipher indented writing (an imprint that appears on the page underneath the original page on which the actual writing was done) or marks, including machine indentations, by using instruments such as the Electrostatic Detection Apparatus (ESDA) and the Infrared Detection Apparatus (IRDA) to produce a visual image of the indented writing on transparency film
- establish the source of the instrument or pen used
- establish the origin of the substrate or paper.

5.2.2 Concealment of handwriting characteristics or disguised writing

A person will attempt to suppress or disguise their own writing style when forging someone else's handwriting or signature. However, the longer the document that is being written, the more difficult it becomes for the person to conceal their own writing style.

Common methods used to forge documents are:

- the forger attempts to imitate the signature or writing
- the signature or writing is traced
- the forger makes a simulation of the signature or writing from a specimen
- the document and the purported signer are fictitious
- a 'cut and paste' job is done where a genuine signature, or copy thereof, is transferred from some authentic source to a fraudulent document
- the signature or writing is genuine, but is obtained in such a manner that the author later denies that he or she could have signed or written that document.

5.2.3 Variation in writing

No two individuals have the same handwriting. Distinct differences can be observed in the combination of characteristics in the handwriting of each individual. It needs to be mentioned that natural variation also occurs in the handwriting of individuals (ie the person's handwriting may vary slightly from day to day) and this needs to be examined and understood by the examiner. However, despite this range of variation, every person's handwriting develops from the classic forms

1 Berty (2009).
2 Giles (2010).
3 Parkinson et al. (2010).

taught in childhood into an individual and identifiable form of written expression.

Handwriting may be categorised according to the following characteristics:

- *Class characteristics*, which include characteristics common to a group such as a particular writing system or a foreign language system. Different cultures and countries have different writing styles, which will be exhibited as class characteristics in the individual's writing. When writing is initially learnt, persons may learn to write in the same way. In time, individual characteristics develop but class characteristics are very often retained.
- *Individual characteristics*, which include those combined characteristics or letters which are particular to an individual. Each person develops a peculiar way of expression in writing certain letters and symbols.

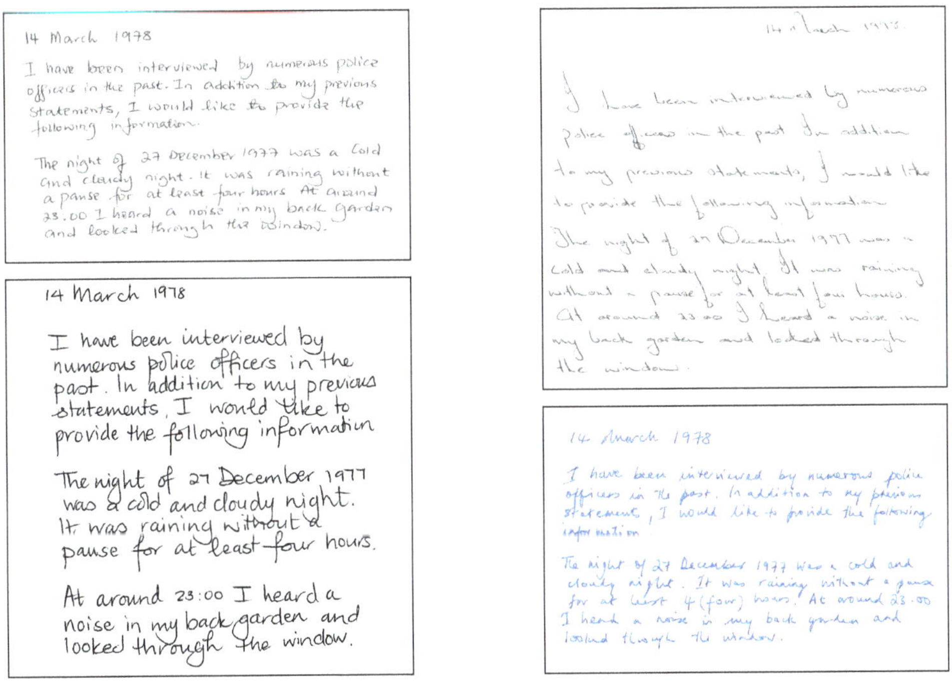

Figure 5.2: Images illustrating class and individual characteristics of handwriting

The ability to distinguish class characteristics from individual characteristics is widely accepted as being one of the fundamental principles an examiner needs to distinguish between original and forged documents.[4]

5.2.4 Forged signatures

The examination of forged signatures involves the comparison of a known reference specimen signature with the disputed signature. A representative sample of specimens containing all the natural variations that exist in the handwriting of

4 Turnbull et al. (2010).

individuals must be obtained. Signature forging may be done either by tracing or freehand. It is very difficult for a fraudster to achieve accuracy in the shape and proportions of a signature and simultaneously achieve the correct smoothness of the pen line. Normally a copy is made either by writing slowly to achieve accuracy (and in the process losing fluency) or by writing rapidly so that more fluency is obtained (and in the process losing the shape).

5.2.5 Typescript: obtaining comparative standards

The examiner needs to ascertain the manner in which the disputed document was produced. This includes determining if a dot matrix printer, an ink-jet or a laser printer, or a manual or electric typewriter was used. Class characteristics identified from the letter spacing and the typeface will provide information on the particular make and model of a machine. The expert will determine which type of machine was used, and the investigator can then focus on finding that particular machine. This will make it easier for the investigator to obtain specimens for comparisons.

The individual characteristics of the typescript are the unique characteristics of a particular machine which develop over time due to wear and tear of the mechanical parts.[5] If it is suspected that a document may have been recently altered or added by using a typewriter, the ribbon should be obtained.

5.2.6 Handling and collecting evidence

The following are general guidelines for dealing with disputed documents that have been submitted for forensic examination:[6]

- All exhibits and reference specimens should be clearly labelled with the name of the institution or station, and the reference number, description and alphanumeric designation of the exhibits. Do not mix together different exhibits from different institutions or stations, or exhibits with different reference numbers.
- No direct markings must be made on any exhibit or specimen. Attach a label.
- Keep a copy of the documents and reference specimens in the investigation file.
- Obtain quality reference specimens which are similar to the disputed document. The following aspects are important in this regard:
  - The subject must never be given or permitted to see the disputed document when asked to produce the reference specimen.
  - The subject must be warned that the reference specimen may be used in the investigation.
  - The subject must be made comfortable and be allowed to write with ease. First encourage the subject to write a few sentences before instructing them as to what to write.

5 Dogaroiu (2011).

6 SAPS, 'Forensic Fact File' No 3 of 2009, 35. Available at http:www//intranet.saps/gov.za/about/downloads/FFF_03.2009_Questioned_Documents.pdf.

  - Vary the speed of dictation – be mindful not to give the impression that the subject has to write in a specific way so as to correspond to the forgery.
  - Give the subject different sheets of paper and remove the previous written page or document so that the subject cannot refer to it again.
- Package each disputed document and/or reference specimen separately.
- Package reference specimens from each individual separately.
- Do not package different exhibits that need to be submitted for forensic examination together.
- The exhibits and alphanumeric designation used to identify the exhibits should correspond with the covering letter.
- Evidence sealing bags with unique numbers and that have been approved by the specific laboratory should be used. Only use other packaging material if the exhibit is too large for the evidence sealing bag.

5.2.7 Forensic handwriting examination

Original

Digital cut and paste

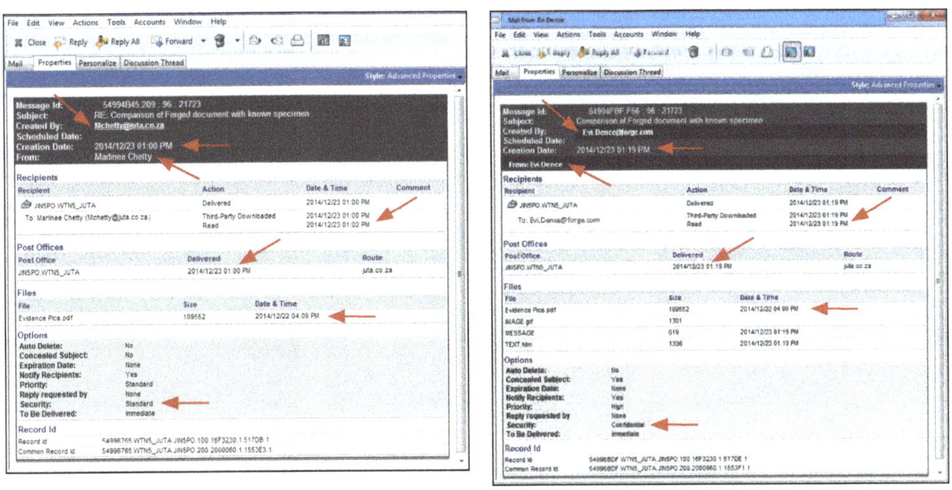

Figure 5.3: Comparison of forged document (right) with known specimen (left)

Forensic handwriting examination uses the scientific principles of observation and deduction, applies appropriate tests and compares the disputed document to known reference specimens.[7] The lack of any natural variation in handwriting is often the single most telling sign that the handwriting in question has been forged. Forgers spend much of their energy ensuring that each character looks the same as that of the known writing. Thus no natural variation is observed, which becomes very obvious in extended writing (ie writing longer documents) when the forger attempts to write exactly like someone else by copying the handwriting.

When handwriting examination is conducted, the known reference specimens must be similar to the disputed document. For example, when a disputed signature on a cheque needs to be compared, it should be compared to authentic signatures of the suspect on cleared cheques which they signed before the incident.

The Video Spectral Comparator (VSC) is an important instrument used by examiners to make visible hidden features in the comparison of printed documents. This instrument is used to examine features such as security characteristics, for example the tracking dots left by some laser printers; images that are only visible in ultraviolet or infrared light, or inks or paper with luminescence. Various chemical tests may also be used during the examination of disputed documents.

5.3 FORENSIC PHOTOGRAPHY

Figure 5.4: Image of a motor vehicle interior for forensic evidence, with sticks (left) indicating bullet entry

The word 'photography' is derived from the Greek word *photos*- meaning 'light', and -*graphos* meaning 'drawing'. Literally, photography therefore means 'drawing

7 Dogaroiu (2011).

with light'. Photography can be described as 'the art, science and practice of creating durable images by recording light or other electromagnetic radiation, either chemically by means of a light-sensitive material such as photographic film or electronically by means of an image sensor'.[8]

In simple terms one may say photography is the taking of pictures with a camera, although other devices may also be used for this purpose.[9] Basically, photographs taken by a private person are equally admissible as evidence as long as the photographs meet the admissibility requirements in court and are relevant to the facts. The rules of authenticity and reliability apply equally to still and digital photography.

5.3.1 Investigative value of photography

There are various types of photography, each of which has a particular value in the investigation process. The fields of scientific research and forensic investigation apply photography for both the micro- and macrorecording of physical evidence. Photography plays a vital role in the analysis of physical evidence in forensic laboratories, and in court. Besides refreshing the memory of witnesses and investigators, photographs convey an image of the scene of incident and the circumstances of the incident to the court or tribunal.[10]

In forensic investigation photography:

- documents the scene of incident and individual pieces of evidence
- provides investigative leads through identification parades, victim/suspect interviews, identifying people and objects and reconstructing the scene of incident
- refreshes people's memories, confirms the testimony of witnesses, clarifies uncertainty and verifies whether a witness or suspect is telling the truth
- can be presented as evidence in court
- helps the investigator to prepare for court proceedings
- can be used to corroborate or refute the statements of suspects and witnesses
- can be used to complement plans, sketches and notes of the scene of incident
- may be used as a substitute for fragile or transient physical evidence, eg swabs, rain, mist and ice
- supports and enhances understanding of the scene of incident
- assists the investigator when writing the investigation report
- can illustrate the location of and conditions at the scene of incident and relate certain activities of the suspect at the scene of incident to the incident under investigation.

Forensic photography can also be applied in more advanced methods. It is, for example, possible to use reflective ultraviolet photography to photograph injuries to the body up to nine months after the injuries were sustained. Long-wave

8 Wikipedia online '*Photography*'. Available at http://en.wikipedia.org/wiki/Photography, accessed 21 October 2013.
9 Robinson (2010) 19.
10 Fisher (2004) 82.

ultraviolet rays penetrate deeper into the skin to pick up bruises or bite marks that cannot be seen using visible light.[11] This gives an investigator an opportunity to analyse the nature and extent of the injury even if images of the injuries were not taken immediately after they were sustained.

5.3.2 Presenting the photographs

The person who took the photograph must be available in court in order to testify about the accuracy of the images. The photographer will be asked to explain how the photographs were taken, in which sequence, and what their relationship is in terms of scale, form and distance. If the photographs were taken with cameras still using film, all negatives should be available for the court to view, should the need arise. This is sometimes needed in order to demonstrate that the photographs have not been altered in any way. The other purpose of keeping negatives is for enlargement of any object if the court needs further clarity.

In the case of digital photography, the digital image memory card should also be handled in such a way as to ensure its continuity of possession (ie chain of custody) until the matter is presented in court and the digital images are needed for their evidential value.

The investigator should bear in mind that photographs should be relevant and should form a substantive part of the case presented before the court.

5.4 POLYGRAPHY

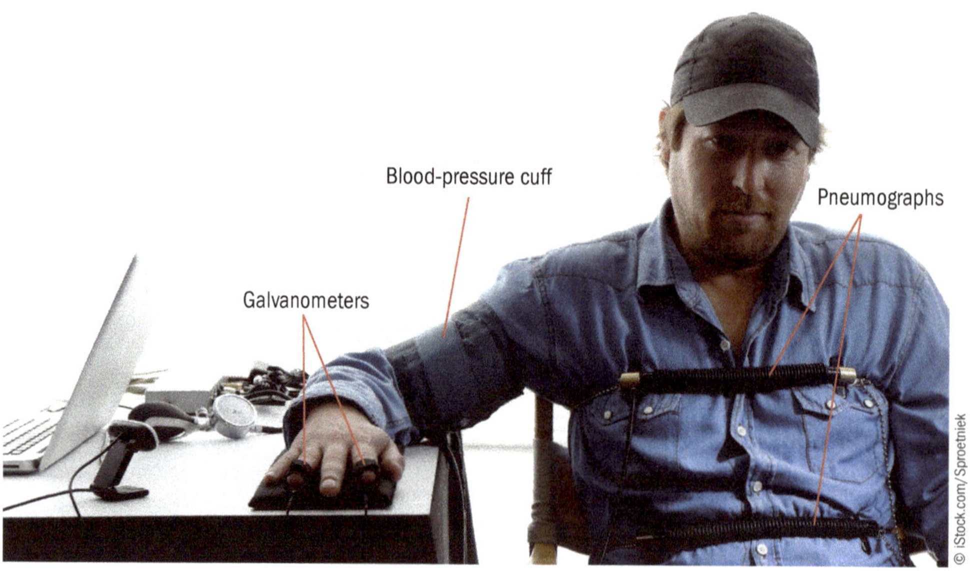

Figure 5.5: Diagram illustrating the items used during a polygraph test

11 Available at http://www.crime-scene-investigator.net/uvchildphoto.html, accessed 21 October 2013.

The word 'polygraph' refers to a device that simultaneously measures and records selected physiological activities and electro-physiological activities. A polygraph is defined as an instrument that measures certain physiological changes in the body (heart rate, blood pressure, respiration rate) triggered by emotional responses to specific verbal questions. It is generally used as a lie detector to determine deception.[12] The results of a polygraph test are not 100% exact scientific evidence and are open to interpretation by the polygraphist. According to South African law, these results are therefore not admissible as evidence in a court of law.

However, the results of a polygraph test are admissible in labour courts and other civil courts in South Africa. There are several cases on record where this technique was used, but it was not used to prove that the person had committed a particular incident. In the case of *Amalgamated Pharmaceuticals Ltd v Grobler NO and Others* (2004) 25 ILJ 523 (LC); (2004) 6 BLLR 537 (LC) it was concluded that the court would admit polygraph test results in civil cases only if there was relevant corroborating evidence.

Although the results of a polygraph test does not prove that someone is guilty, they provide an indication of the person's responses and reactions. To prove the allegation, polygraphy findings must be corroborated with other evidence. Polygraph evidence will not pass muster before a criminal court without corroborating evidence.

5.4.1 Requirements of conducting a polygraph

Just like any other instrument used in forensic investigation, a polygraph must also be conducted within boundaries laid down by the relevant legislation. The following requirements must therefore be satisfied before a polygraph test can be conducted:

- *Consent*: The participants must give their consent after being briefed about the intended test. They must indicate that they clearly understand how it works.
- *Pre-test information*: The polygraphist should explain the entire process and procedure to the participants before conducting the test.
- *Privacy*: The test should be done in private and the rights of the participants should be protected.
- *Freedom of choice*: The participants must be informed of their right not to participate in the test.
- *Professional standing*: Polygraphists must be available to testify as experts in the civil court or at a hearing and must provide proof of their qualifications. Polygraphists have been accepted as expert witness in South Africa by the Commission for Conciliation, Mediation and Arbitration (CCMA).

12 Gilbert (2004) 602.

5.5 IMPRINTS

Imprints are the most common – and often the most valuable – form of impression evidence that relate directly to the objective of investigation and the identification of offenders. Finger-, palm and footprints, shoe or footwear imprints, tyre imprints, tool marks, fired cartridge cases and bullets are different types of imprint evidence.

An imprint or an impression occurs when objects or the friction ridges of skin touch, impress or push against one another, allowing the material on the objects or on the friction ridges, such as ink, oil, grease or perspiration, to be transferred and/or retained by other objects.[13] In most cases victims and investigators share unrealistic expectations in that they believe that every incident or crime must be investigated by an expert for imprints despite the fact that imprints cannot be traced and found at every incident.

Imprint evidence can show class and individual characteristics. Class characteristics include overall patterns such as finger-, palm and footprints; the sole prints of shoes or footwear; the number of ribs and grooves in a tyre track, and the number of lands (raised areas between two grooves) and grooves of a firearm. Individual characteristics are unique accidental marks which occur on friction ridges or objects, such as scars on fingertips; cuts in shoe soles; stones attached to tyre treads, and the mark direction of the twist of the rifling on cartridges, cartridge cases and bullets.

Firearm identification falls under the discipline of imprint evidence. It is of interest to the forensic investigator to determine whether cartridges, cartridge cases, bullets and primer residue (gunshot residue consisting of burnt and unburnt particles from the explosive primer) were discharged from the investigated firearm.

5.5.1 Finger-, palm and footprints

Finger-, palm and footprints are the impressions of friction ridges characteristic of the inner part of the hand and the bottom of the feet. These prints are unique to every individual. Finger-, palm and footprints are the result of friction ridges on the surface of the hands and feet. These ridges facilitate the gripping of an object and the sense of touch, which is developed from birth.[14] In most cases, these prints found at the scene of incident are considered to be the first (and the most commonly used and most successful) method of identifying a person. Investigators should therefore not overlook the possibility of the suspect's imprints having been left at the scene of incident or on objects handled by the suspect. The assigned forensic investigator must be able to

13 Ogle (2004) 172.

14 Osterburg & Ward (2010) 48.

identify surfaces, objects and items from which prints could be traced and lifted for comparison purposes.

Finger-, palm and footprints are regarded as definite or real evidence in an investigation and cannot be easily disputed in court. The most universal features of finger-, palm and footprints in the identification process are the following:

- prints are unique to an individual
- prints do not change throughout a person's lifetime, except if the epidermal and dermal layers of the skin have been damaged
- if damage has occurred, the scars that remain are also unique and can be used for individualisation.[15]

5.5.2 Types of fingerprint impressions

Fingerprint experts must be able to identify the different types of fingerprint impressions left at the scene of incident.[16] These fingerprints can be classified into the following categories:

- plastic fingerprints
- visible fingerprints
- latent fingerprints.

Plastic prints are those prints impressed into some substance such as wax, soap or putty. These types of prints require no enhancement to be viewed as they are immediately identifiable because the friction ridges of skin can be seen on the substance. For instance, in a burglary case where a suspect has gained entrance through a window, prints may be found in soft window putty, whereas in a house robbery where the victims were tied up with duct tape or other adhesive tape these prints may be found on the sticky part of the tape.[17]

Visible prints are impressed prints that have been coated with some colour substance such as blood, grease, paint, dust, mud or ink.[18] These types of prints can be seen with the naked eye and are usually easily noticeable.

Latent fingerprints are those impressed prints that are not visible to the naked eye and need some form of development process to be visible.[19] The prints are usually developed with chemical reagents and powders, but certain objects might be photographed with special photographic techniques to reveal the prints. Latent prints result from the oily substance in sweat which is deposited on an object when the person touches a smooth surface during the commission of an incident. This is the most common type of print found in forensic investigations.[20]

15 White (2004).
16 White (2004).
17 Osterburg & Ward (2010) 50.
18 James & Nordby (2005) 349.
19 James & Nordby (2005) 349.
20 Bennet & Hess (2004) 97.

5.5.3 Basic patterns and classification of fingerprints

Fingerprints are impressions of friction ridges of skin found on the inside and tips of the fingers and thumb of the hand. The impression consists of ridges and valleys. When a fingerprint is taken, the ridges are the dark lines on the fingerprint whereas the valleys are the white lines between the ridges. The ridges and valleys on finger-, palm and footprints form a number of basic patterns.[21] There are three main fingerprint patterns:

- arch patterns
- loop patterns
- whorl patterns.

To identify these three basic patterns, the fingerprint investigator or expert should determine the delta. The delta is the point where lines from three directions come together. The whorl has two deltas whereas the loop has one delta and the arch has no delta.

These basic patterns may be further divided into eight subgroups of classification that can provide useful information during identification. Fingerprint classification is important because it significantly reduces the time needed to identify fingerprints, especially where accuracy and speed are required. It can also be very helpful in reducing the cost of searching large fingerprint databases.[22] For example, the suspect's fingerprints on the SAPS 76 form are classified using a magnifying glass. The fingerprints are separated from one to 10. Then the fingerprint investigator or expert places fingerprint cards in the specific file in order of their classification order. During a manual search of a fingerprint database this quickly yields results.

As mentioned above, prints and their related patterns are divided into three general pattern groups, namely arches, loops and whorls.[23]

5.5.3.1 Arches

Arches are mainly described by the fact that they do not have deltas and no significant core (see Figure 5.6).[24] In arches, the ridges of the finger run continuously from one side of the finger to the other with no recurving. There are two subgroups that further define the arch pattern:

- *Plain arch*: The plain arch is the simplest of the fingerprint patterns. It has a consistency of flow to it, which means it flows through the fingerprint with no significant change.[25] The ridge starts on one side of the finger and cascades upward slightly, almost resembling a wave on the ocean. The plain arch then continues its journey along the finger to the other side.

21 Bennet & Hess (2004) 342.
22 Rajanna et al. (2009) 1.
23 Girard (2011) 139.
24 Horswell (2004) 164.
25 Van der Westhuizen (1996) 247.

- *Tented arch*: The pattern of the tented arch does not have the same 'easy' flow as that of the plain arch.[26] Like the plain arch, the ridge pattern starts on one side of the finger and flows to the opposite side. However, in the tented arch the ridges in the centre are not continuous. They join each other in the centre, converge and thrust upward, giving the impression of a pitched tent.

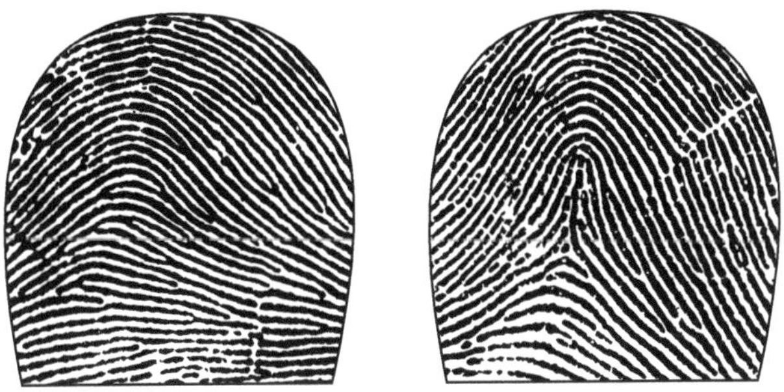

Figure 5.6: Diagram illustrating a plain arch and a tented arch

5.5.3.2 Loops

A loop is a fingerprint pattern with ridges entering on one side of the print, forming a wave, and flowing out on the same side (see Figure 5.7).[27] In other words, the ridges start on the same side and double back in the direction from where they started. This backwards turn, or loop, is differentiated by how the loop flows on the hand and not how it flows on the card on which the fingerprint is taken. The impression on the fingerprint card is a mirror image.

There are two subgroups identified in this category:

- *Radial loop*: This is the loop pattern ridge which flows in the direction of the thumb (see Figure 5.7).[28] The ridges flow towards the radius (the bone in the forearm that runs on the thumb side of the arm). In other words, the downward slope of the loop runs from the direction of the little finger in the direction of the thumb.
- *Ulnar loop*: This is the loop pattern ridge which flows in the direction of the little finger (see Figure 5.7).[29] The ridges flow towards the ulna (the bone in the forearm that runs on the little-finger side of the arm). In other words, the downward slope of the loop runs from the direction of the thumb in the direction of the little finger.

26 Girard (2011) 140.
27 BCSO Identification - arches online (2012) Finger print patterns - arches, accessed 20 May 2012.
28 Available at ridgesandfurrows.homestead.com/landmark.html.
29 Available at ridgesandfurrows.homestead.com/landmark.html.

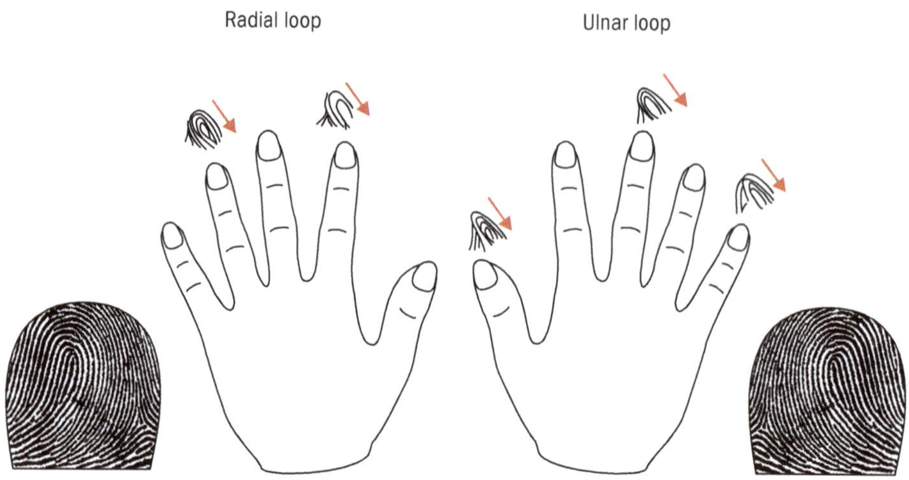

Figure 5.7: Illustration of radial and ulnar loops

5.5.3.3 Whorls

Whorls refer to the ridge patterns that form concentric circles in the centre of the finger pad (see Figure 5.8).[30] Whorls contain patterns with two or more deltas and a recurve precedes each delta. There are four subgroups of whorls:

- *Plain loop whorl*: In these whorls the ridge pattern turns a complete circuit, forming a circular or spiral shape. The plain whorl is the simplest and the most common form of whorl. There are at least two deltas and a ridge whose circuit may be shaped like a spiral, an oval or a circle.
- *Double loop whorl*: These whorls contain two separate loop formations, each of which contain, in turn, two entirely separate and distinct sets of cores and deltas.
- *Central pocket loop whorl*: In these whorls, one or more simple recurves, as found in the plain whorl, recurves a second time.
- *Accidental whorl*: In these whorls, the composition of the pattern is derived from two distinct types of patterns with at least two deltas. Whorls containing ridges that match the characteristics of one of the whorl subgroupings are classified as accidental whorls.

30 Available at ridgesandfurrows.homestead.com/landmark.html.

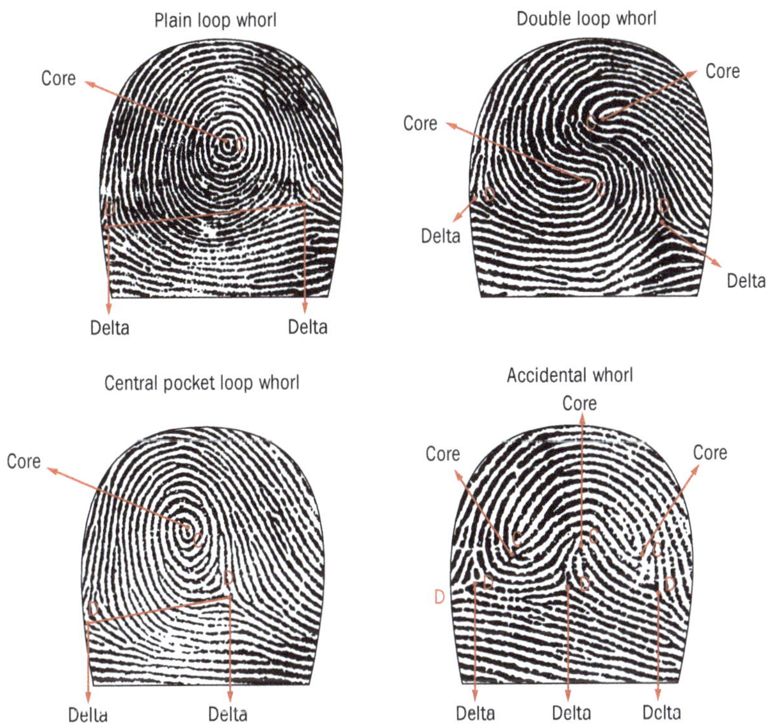

Figure 5.8: Different types of whorls

5.5.4 Processing prints

Immediately after arrival on the scene of incident, the imprint expert must identify non-porous and porous surfaces for the examination of prints. On non-porous surfaces such as glass, paint or varnish and hard plastic moulding, fingerprints can be developed using a brush and powders. Chemical reagents and alternate light sources are used to trace and develop prints on porous surfaces such as rough or grainy hard plastic moulding.

After tracing and developing the prints on non-porous surfaces, the fingerprint experts must use lifters such as adhesive tape (folien) or scotch tape to lift the prints. On porous surfaces fingerprint experts will use a camera to photograph the prints because they will not be able to lift the prints from these surfaces.

Before lifting prints, regardless of the surface, fingerprint investigators or experts must first record the following information on the lifter report form or incident report form:

- the name of the station and the case number
- the full description of the place and position from which prints were lifted
- a sketch of where prints were found and lifted.

Once the information is recorded on the lifter or incident report form, the fingerprint expert may lift the print from the surface, record the date and time, and sign the form. The complainant should also sign the form as proof that the expert had lifted the prints at the scene of incident. The fingerprint expert will then photograph the prints in the laboratory and prepare photos to be searched in the search room or scanned into the Automatic Fingerprint Identification System (AFIS). These facilities are available at any local Criminal Record Centre office for the purpose of comparison and identification.

5.5.5 Preserving and analysing prints

In the past, a number of methods were used to search, identify and process prints. In South Africa police currently file prints in two places, namely a search room and an electronic database on the SAPS computerised system called the Automatic Fingerprint Identification System (AFIS). In the search room prints are filed according to types, patterns and ridge count characteristics. AFIS is a computer software package that allows the police to store and search fingerprints. Prints are scanned onto a computer to create an electronic database.

These two storage facilities are used by fingerprint experts to search, compare and identify individuals by fingerprints, either manually or electronically. In a manual search, prints filed in the search room in filing cabinets are manually compared to prints on the inquiry form (in South Africa this form is normally referred to as SAPS 91) to identify suspects. AFIS compares the scanned fingerprints lifted from the scene of incident to fingerprints already on the database.

Investigators use an inquiry form to take a suspect's fingerprints for enquiry. The same form is then used by the fingerprint expert to verify and confirm the identification of the fingerprints.

There are several points (minutiae) that can be identified and confirmed by fingerprint experts. This identification is done manually on a single print:

- *ridge ending*: where a friction ridge ends or starts; these ridges run through the pattern without interruption, while others may discontinue to form an ending[31]
- *bifurcation*: a line breaks into two separate ridges to form a shape like a fork in the road[32]
- *trifurcation*: the point at which one friction ridge divides into three friction ridges

31 Available at ridgesandfurrows.homestead.com/landmark.html.

32 Available at www.rcs.k12.va.us/wbms/library/fingerprintcharacteristics.doc, accessed 20 May 2013.

- *short ridge islands*: the ridge starts, travels a short distance and then ends
- *lakes or enclosures*: a single ridge that bifurcates and reunites shortly afterwards to continue as a single ridge
- *dots*: an isolated ridge of approximately the same length and width
- *spurs (hooks)*: a bifurcation with a short ridge branching off a longer ridge
- *pores*: openings of subcutaneous eccrine sweat glands located in the fingertip's epidermis
- *crossovers:* a short ridge that runs between two parallel ridges.[33]

In terms of South African standards, fingerprint experts must match at least seven points before concluding that prints are identical.

Minutiae	Example	Minutiae	Example
ridge ending		bridge	
bifurcation		double bifurcation	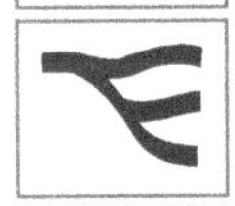
dot		trifurcation	
island (short ridge)		opposed bifurcations	
lake (enclosure)		ridge crossing	
hook (spur)		opposed bifurcation/ ridge ending	

Figure 5.9: Basic and composite ridge characteristics (minutiae) that can be identified on fingerprints[34]

Once the print has been compared and identified by an expert, two prints, which consist of one from the scene of incident and another from the suspect, are sent to the laboratory for enlargement. The expert will then compile a court chart that will illustrate all the points marked from both identified prints (see Figure 5.10). The court chart will be used as an exhibit in court.

33 Available at www.rcs.k12.va.us/wbms/library/fingerprintcharacteristics.doc, accessed 20 May 2013.

34 Fingerprint Comparison Guide. Available at flash.lakeheadu.ca/~lubiotec/Fingerprints%20Comparison%20Guide.pdf, accessed 20 May 2013.

Figure 5.10: Points that can be identified on fingerprints for use in court[35]

During court proceedings, a fingerprint expert may be requested to present evidence regarding the fingerprints. This will include explaining the procedure of how the fingerprints were analysed as well as how the results were determined and interpreted. The fingerprint expert will illustrate the abovementioned points on the court chart, which will be used as an exhibit during the trial.

5.5.6 Value of prints in forensic investigations

The mere fact that prints found at a scene of incident have been identified does not prove a suspect's guilt. An imprint expert has to investigate the legitimacy of the prints and prove beyond reasonable doubt that the prints are linked to a person suspected of an alleged crime. Prints found at the scene of incident will help the investigator to do the following during the investigation:

- *Locate* the person who allegedly committed an incident by comparing and identifying the suspect's or the scene prints (prints collected from the scene of incident) manually or electronically via an AFIS search. Once a suspect has been identified, the fingerprint expert will forward the suspect's name and address to the investigating officer so that they can locate and arrest the suspect.
- *Eliminate* the person from the alleged incident by taking prints of victims or the complainant and comparing them to prints gathered from the scene of incident. After comparison and identification, the victim or complainant's prints will be eliminated from the ones found at the scene of incident.

35 Fingerprint Comparison Guide. Available at flash.lakeheadu.ca/~lubiotec/Fingerprints%20Comparison%20Guide.pdf, accessed 20 May 2013.

- *Identify* human remains, especially when other methods of forensic investigation cannot be used.

In court, the prints may corroborate the evidence provided by the investigator to place the person at, or associate them with the incident, especially when suspected persons deny their involvement in the alleged offence and their presence at the scene. It is noteworthy that in certain instances the imprint evidence may serve as sufficient proof to convict the accused person.

The absence of a fingerprint of a specific person can also be used to prove that that person was not at the scene of incident at that time, thereby proving an alibi, as well as the fact that that person had never been at the scene or had not handled a specific object.

Example 5.2: Absence of prints

A person who is responsible for the signing of legal documents usually leaves their finger- or palm prints on these documents. The absence of fingerprints or palm prints will be proof that the person did not touch or handle the said documents or that they were wearing something like rubber gloves to avoid leaving any evidence of having handled the documents.

5.5.7 Capturing legible fingerprints

The clear and legible capturing of fingerprints forms the foundation of the fingerprint database. Forensic investigators routinely collect both rolled and plain fingerprints of all 10 fingers of suspects. Rolled impressions are the upper 10 impressions captured individually, which are the thumb, index, middle, ring and little fingers of each hand. Plain impression are impressions of the four fingers on the left and the right hand which are captured simultaneously at a 45-degree angle on the fingerprint form (SAPS 76).

The basic equipment required to capture rolled and plain fingerprint impressions are an ink pad or a print pad, a roller, printer's ink and rubber gloves.

5.5.8 Steps for capturing rolled and plain fingerprints

Before capturing rolled or plain fingerprints on the SAPS 76 form, the fingerprint investigator or expert must first record the following information:

- name of the suspect
- name of the station and the case number
- charge or committed offence
- suspect's identity number
- name of the suspect's next of kin.

After recording this information, the forensic investigator or expert should adhere to the following steps:

1. Encourage the individual being fingerprinted to relax.
2. Grasp or hold the fingers of the right hand, starting either with the base of the little finger or the thumb.
3. Touch the tip of each finger to keep it extended, then roll the extended finger through the ink and make sure that the ink covers the whole print.
4. Roll the inked finger onto the fingerprint form, capturing the fingerprint impression in a single movement.
5. Repeat the movement until you have finished all 10 fingers.

5.5.9 Avoiding common errors

It is of the utmost importance to capture legible fingerprints. In this regard the fingerprint investigator or expert may encounter the following challenges:

Table 5.1: Common problems in taking fingerprints and how to overcome them

Common problem	Solution
Sweaty hands	An individual whose hands are sweaty should be asked to wipe them on a dry cloth.
White lines/cracks/worn ridges in the fingerprint area	An individual's fingerprint ridges may be improved by massaging the fingertips to force the blood to circulate, or by applying Corn Huskers Lotion or aloe vera lotion.
Not rolling fingerprints widely enough	An individual fingerprint should be rolled continuously from nail edge to nail edge. Make sure that that the entire first joint is in contact with the sensor or fingerprint form.
Incomplete fingerprint patterns	A little pressure should be applied to an individual fingertip in order to capture the complete fingerprint pattern.
Smudges/non-discernable fingerprints	No excessive ink and pressure should be applied to individual fingertips. Fingerprints should be captured by applying enough ink and exerting the correct pressure to ensure a clear image.
Capturing multiple fingerprints in one space	Only one fingerprint should be captured in a required space.

5.6 FOOTWEAR AND TYRE IMPRINTS

The examination of footwear and tyre impressions is a study of marks or imperfections in the soles of footwear and tyres for the purpose of comparison and identifying similarities between similar footwear and tyre imprints. Footwear imprints are also referred to as shoe imprints, but for the purposes of this discussion the term 'footwear' will be used.

During the commission of an incident, the person committing the incident could leave footwear tracks at the scene or drive their vehicle through the scene of incident. Vehicles and footwear leave tracks on hard and soft surfaces in the form of indented impressions or transferred prints. Indented or transferred impressions are created when footwear or tyres are pressed or bumped against a surface such as a floor or furniture and the characteristics of the footwear or tyres are transferred to the surface or substrate.[36]

Small particles of material from the scene of incident might also cling to or get embedded in the thread of the suspect's footwear or car tyres when they leave the scene of incident. These particles can be scientifically examined and may be linked to a specific location.

For many reasons, footwear and tyre tracks are overlooked by investigators at scenes of incident. Investigators may not be aware of the value of this evidence in the forensic investigation. If such evidence is not immediately recognised and protected by the investigator, it can be easily destroyed. This will diminish the possibility of providing an investigative lead to identify the culprit.

5.6.1 Types of footwear and tyre marks

Although the types of footwear and tyre impressions have been described differently by different authors,[37] they all agree that there are two types of evidence that can be deposited at the scene of incident by footwear and tyres, namely:

- two-dimensional impressions or transfer prints
- three-dimensional impressions, also known as indented impression or compression marks.

Two-dimensional impressions or transfer prints are prints transferred from a soft surface to a hard surface. These prints are usually found indoors on surfaces such as counter tops, drinking glasses, paper, cardboard, ceramic tiles and waxed floors.

Example 5.3: Transferred footprints

In case of a burglary, the perpetrator could have stepped into a patch of mud or dust outside and could carry it to a hard surface, such as a counter top, when he climbs through the window.

Another form of transferred footprints would be when a suspect steps in blood at the scene of incident and then walks around other parts of the scene. These blood-stained footprints not only serve to match the suspect's footwear prints but also provide a clue as to the suspect's actions at the scene of incident after stepping into the blood.

36 Srihari (2011) 40.
37 Srihari (2011) 40.

Three-dimensional impressions, or indented impression or compression marks, are prints transferred to a softer surface. These impressions or compression marks are usually discovered outdoors in a surface like dirt, sand, clay, mud, tar or snow.

5.6.2 Processing footwear and tyre impressions at the scene of incident

The investigator needs patience and common sense to identify and process footwear and tyre impressions. But before processing these impressions, a footwear or tyre impressions examiner must record the following valuable information on the lifter report or incident report form:

- name of the station and the case number
- full description of the place and position from which impressions were lifted
- a rough sketch of where the impressions were found.

Various procedures are followed to preserve and process impressions at the scene of incident.

- The entire impression can be lifted or scooped up by, for example, lifting the section of dried mud which contains the imprint.
- A cast is made of the three-dimensional impression. A good example of casting is when a dentist uses water and powder to create a medium (dental stone) that can assume a particular shape and dry off in that position. Imprint casts are usually made by an expert field worker, although forensic investigators are expected to have a basic knowledge of how this can be done. Dental stone or plaster of Paris can be used.

Example 5.4: Making a cast of a footprint impression

When the investigator has to make a cast of footprint impression evidence, it is recommended to use a casting frame and casting material recommended by their unit or section.

Various disposable casting frames have been developed by different companies for use in the field to collect footprint impressions as evidence.

Each frame consists of two strips of heavy-duty, moisture-resistant, corrugated Correx board, which can be assembled in seconds using the adhesive tabs. The size of the frame can be adjusted to accommodate different types of impressions.

Then pour the plaster of Paris, dental stone or other casting medium into the frame. When the casting medium is dry, remove the frame.

5.6.3 Identifying footwear prints

The examination of footwear prints involves the comparison of the investigated footwear impressions found at the scene of incident to the known footwear of suspects. This is done by visual inspection and the use of a magnifier such as a microscope.

In order for the footwear examiner to conclude that the investigated footwear imprints and those found on the suspect's footwear are identical, the examiner should examine and compare the following:

- class characteristics, ie characteristics which are not unique, but are typical of that range of footwear:
  - design or pattern on the sole of the footwear
  - physical size and shape
- individual characteristics, ie characteristics which are unique and individual to the suspect's particular footwear to the exclusion of all others:
  - wear patterns and characteristics (footwear worn at the toe, pronation, etc)
  - random marks or imperfection (cuts, tears, nails, etc).

5.6.4 Identifying tyre marks

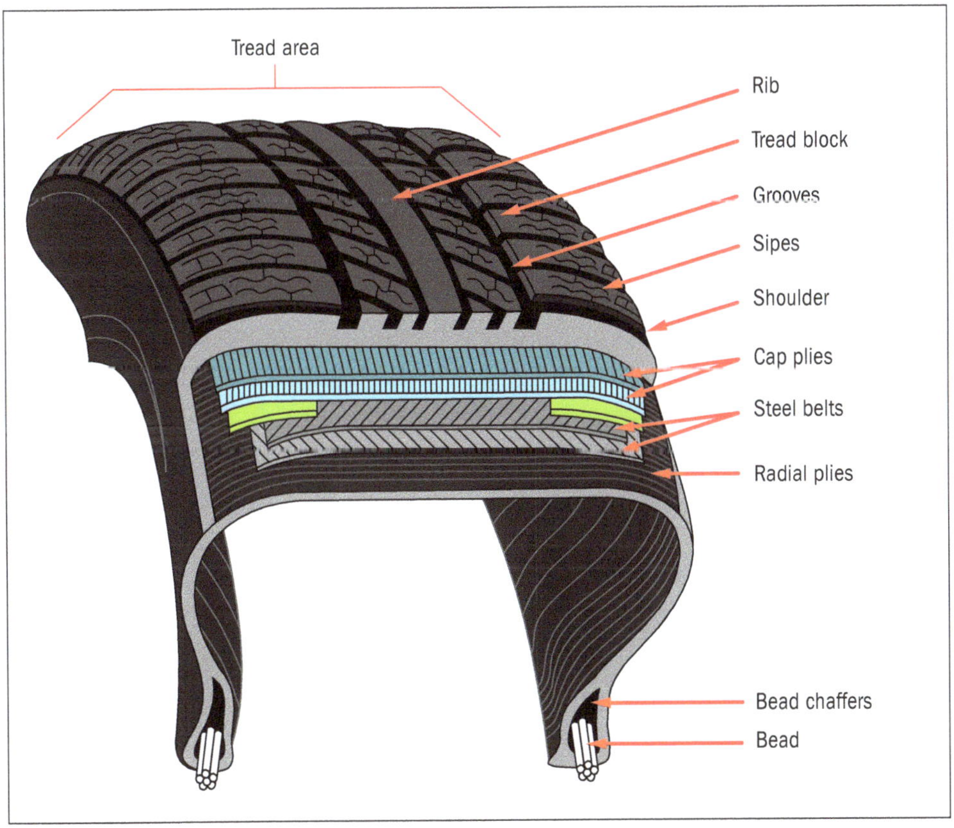

Figure 5.11: Illustration of tyre points[38]

38 Srihari (2011).

When an attempt is made to analyse and identify tyre prints to establish that the prints found at the scene of incident and those of a tyre belonging to the suspected vehicle are identical, the experts will take the following into consideration:[39]

- *brand of the tyre*: the preserved tyre impression from the scene of incident will be compared to the tyre(s) belonging to the suspected vehicle
- *number of segment shapes*: the part of the rubber portion that forms the tread of the tyre
- *ribs*: lines or rubber elements of the tyre treads
- *grooves*: large void areas adjacent to the ribs
- *sipes*: narrow slots moulded into the ribs of the tread design to improve the traction ability of the tyre on wet surfaces such as mud
- *slots*: narrow grooves connecting major grooves to improve traction
- *lugs*: a varied arrangement of holes to accommodate studs for maximum winter effectiveness, found in some snow tyres.

5.6.5 Value of imprint evidence

After the scene of incident has been processed, it is the responsibility of the investigator to try to find the footwear or vehicle from which the imprints originated so the imprints can be sent to the laboratory for microscopic comparison. The reason for this is to see whether the imprints match those found at the scene of incident, or whether there are any traces of material that still cling to the footwear or tyres.

Footwear or tyre impressions found at the scene of incident may help the investigator to solve a particular incident by:

- identifying tyre and footwear impressions, which can be done through their ridge characteristics
- differentiating between tracks of vehicles that have no legal authority to be in a particular place, such as a government parking garage, and then eliminating those that have authorisation to be there
- determining the footwear brand and size, and the number of suspects
- establishing the presence of a vehicle at a particular scene
- determining the tyre tread pattern and brand, and the direction of tracks
- tracking and tracing the suspects using the direction of footwear or tyre impressions
- using police dogs (K9) to track and trace the suspect(s) by following the scent of the suspect(s).

39 McDonald (1993).

5.7 TOOL MARKS

A tool mark refers to impression marks created during the commission of an incident when an instrument or object comes into contact with another object. This typically occurs when a suspect uses a screwdriver or a crowbar to force open a door at a scene of incident.

Tool marks are unique and may be classified to identify the type of instrument that was used during the commission of an incident. It is important for the investigator to examine a variety of surfaces during the investigation of an incident to trace possible impression marks. Forensic investigators must also be able to recognise different types of tool marks typically left by particular tools, such as crowbars, knives or screwdrivers.

Tools are designed differently by different manufacturers who use a variety of materials. Tools therefore leave very specific microscopic marks or indentations on the surface with which they come into contact.[40] The wear and tear on tools also cause damage on the working surfaces of the tool and might then create specific individualising characteristics for that particular tool.

Tool marks can be found on different surfaces and objects at the entire scene of incident, not only at the place of entry. It is important that the investigator should closely examine any point of impact where a tool could possibly have been used in order to identify marks left on a surface or an object.

Although one may think that crime scene technicians should gather evidence at every scene of incident for the purpose of investigation, there is a limited number of these technicians in South Africa. This means that technicians will only attend to the most serious incidents. Investigators therefore need to have extensive knowledge and experience to process tool marks at the scene of incident. In cases of residential burglary, for example, most of the investigated tools and tool marks will be processed by investigators because of the limited number of crime scene technicians.

5.7.1 Types of tool marks

Tool marks found at the scene of incident are usually in the form of impressed, striated, 'drag' or 'shear' marks created by the movement of the tool during the contact with an object or a combination of objects.

- *Shear* impression tool marks are a little deeper than the dent marks created by a tool such as a crowbar or screwdriver.

40 Adams et al. (2004) 153.

- *Striated* tool marks are left by a tool that scrapes, abrades or slips over an object or surface softer than itself. When a crowbar slips during the application of force it creates striated tool marks.[41]

After identifying the tool mark, the investigator should follow certain steps to collect the tool mark.

5.7.2 Collecting and processing tool marks

Once the tool mark has been identified at the scene of incident, the investigator should document the place and height where it occurs and draw a rough sketch to illustrate the position of the mark. Then the investigator will need to decide on the method to recover the identified tool mark. The investigator will either photograph the tool mark with a camera or apply a special rubber material such as silicone to make a cast of the tool mark.

In criminal cases the tool mark together with the instrument (tool), if available, must be forwarded to the metallurgy section at the SAPS Forensic Science Laboratory for examination. In other cases the examination will have to be conducted by private forensic experts. The metallurgist will carefully conduct a microscopic examination of the disputed tool mark and tool submitted for examination.

After the examination, the metallurgist will provide the investigator with one of the following statements:

- The tool mark matched the class characteristics of the submitted tool.
- The tool mark does not match the class characteristics of the submitted tool.
- The decision cannot be taken as the class characteristics are insufficient to match the tool mark and the tool.

5.7.3 Value of tool marks in forensic investigation

The impression marks created by a tool may leave a valuable clue to identify a tool used to commit an incident. In some cases physical objects found in possession of the suspect could be linked with the tool found at the scene of incident and marks could be compared to prove that the same tool (or part thereof) was used at different scenes of incident. The tool marks can help the investigator to do the following:

- link separate incidents with the same *modus operandi*
- find new investigative leads as evidence
- indicate the size and the shape of the tool used to commit an incident
- identify tool characteristics which may link the tool to certain objects or may reveal that that item belongs to another class of objects
- match the tool with the tool mark(s).

41 Adams et al. (2004) 301.

5.8 FIREARMS

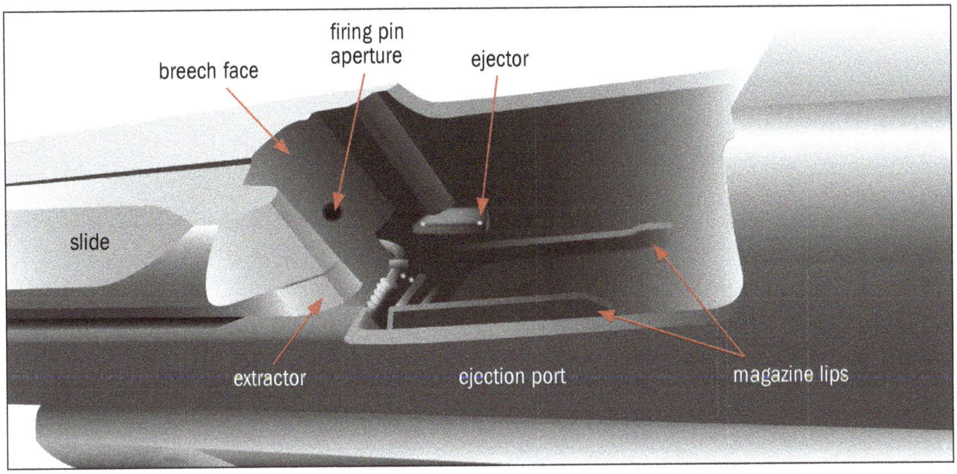

Figure 5.12: Mechanical parts of a firearm

Impressions left by the grooves inside the barrel, the firing pin, extractor and other parts of a firearm are also classified under imprint identification. A large number of incidents reported to the SAPS annually are committed by perpetrators using firearms. Firearms are designed to discharge bullets from a distance to kill or at least incapacitate the target.[42] Therefore, when investigating a scene of incident where a firearm was used, it is important for the investigator to detect and collect items such as firearms, cartridges (shells) and bullets that could serve as physical evidence in forensic investigation. A cartridge is ammunition enclosed in a cylindrical casing containing an explosive charge and a bullet that is fired from a rifle or handgun.[43] A bullet is a projectile fired one at a time from the barrel of a gun.[44]

In South Africa, the most commonly found firearms at the scene of incident are pistols, shotguns, rifles and submachine guns. Pistols, rifles and submachine guns are firearms designed to fire cartridges without reloading after each shot. Their mechanisms automatically unload each fired cartridge case from the chamber and reload another cartridge from the magazine. The inside of the barrels of pistols, rifles and submachine guns are cut with spiral grooves called rifling, which cause the bullet to turn inside the barrel.[45] A shotgun's cartridges are manually loaded and unloaded after firing and its barrel is smooth. Unlike other classes of firearms, which discharge bullets, a shotgun is designed to discharge pellets.[46]

42 Adams et al. (2004) 269.
43 Adams et al. (2004) 479.
44 Jackson & Jackson (2004) 240.
45 Jackson & Jackson (2004) 271.
46 Jackson & Jackson (2004) 273.

5.8.1 Preserving and processing firearms and ammunition

The preservation, processing and collection of physical evidence at the scene of incident have been discussed in detail in the previous chapters. Firearm and ammunition form part of the physical evidence which the forensic investigator should identify, preserve, collect, interpret and reconstruct during investigation. It is the responsibility of the forensic investigator to provide clear information on how firearm and ammunition evidence from the scene of incident was processed.

At the scene of incident where a firearm was involved, the forensic investigator should properly record, sketch (by making a scene sketch), mark and measure the location where the firearm, cartridges, bullet holes and bullets were identified, found or collected. The firearm found at the scene should be made safe before being packaged for forensic examination. If more than two firearms are recovered at the scene of incident, they should be packaged separately to prevent cross-contamination. The ammunition from the firearms should also be packaged separately and forwarded to the ballistic section of the Forensic Science Laboratory for forensic examination.

5.8.2 Identifying firearms and ammunition

Once the firearm(s) and ammunition have been identified at the scene of incident, an experienced forensic investigator or crime scene expert may be able to determine the following:

- type and calibre of the firearm, by checking the ammunition (cartridge cases or spent bullets) found at the scene of incident, which may indicate whether a pistol or a rifle was used
- the make and serial number of the firearm, unless these have been removed.

5.8.3 Laboratory examination of firearms and ammunition

It is a scientific fact that no two firearms ever leave precisely the same marks on a cartridge, cartridge case or bullet. Therefore it is possible to link the bullet to the weapon in virtually every instance. Firearm examination may be properly described as both an art and a science.[47] Before examination can be conducted on disputed firearms, a ballistic expert should understand the firing mechanisms by testing those firearms. A disputed firearm and ammunition are a firearm and ammunition collected at the scene of incident or from the suspect for forensic laboratory examination. Control sample ammunition is ammunition fired by forensic experts to test the firing mechanisms of the disputed firearm(s). It is also used to compare with ammunition found at the scene.

The ballistic expert will first measure the accuracy of trigger pressure and the firing mechanism by cocking the weapon, putting the safety catch on fire and then pressing the trigger. Then the firearm will be loaded with ammunition to test the effectiveness of the mechanism. Ammunition will be fired into a water

47 Jackson & Jackson (2004) 285.

tank or other device so that the cartridge cases and bullets can be recovered for the purpose of comparison.

5.8.4 Identifying cartridges

Firearm identification is a specialised subspecialty of tool mark identification, specifically related to the firearm mechanism's working surface.[48] When the firearm is fired, cartridges are marked with firearm impressions. Therefore, the examination of cartridge cases can reveal both the class characteristics and the individual characteristics based on unique cartridge impressions, which are produced during the normal functioning of the firearm. During the microscopic examination of cartridges or cartridge cases it is possible for ballistic expert to identify:

- *firing pin marks on the primer cup*: when firearms discharge a cartridge case, the firing pin strikes the primer cup and impresses the firing pin's mark into the soft metal of the primer cup
- *ejector marks*: the ejector creates marks on the base of the cartridge case when it ejects the cartridge case
- *extractor marks*: the extractor creates marks inside the rim of the cartridge case when it removes the cartridge case from the chamber
- *breech face marks*: the breech face creates marks on the base of the cartridge case[49]
- any significant marks on the case wall made during chambering, discharge or extraction.[50]

The abovementioned impression marks on the surfaces of cartridge cases are called striated marks or impressions as the cartridge cases are fired in or cycled through the firearm, as shown in Figure 5.13. Striated marks are described as scratch marks, abrasion marks or friction marks.[51]

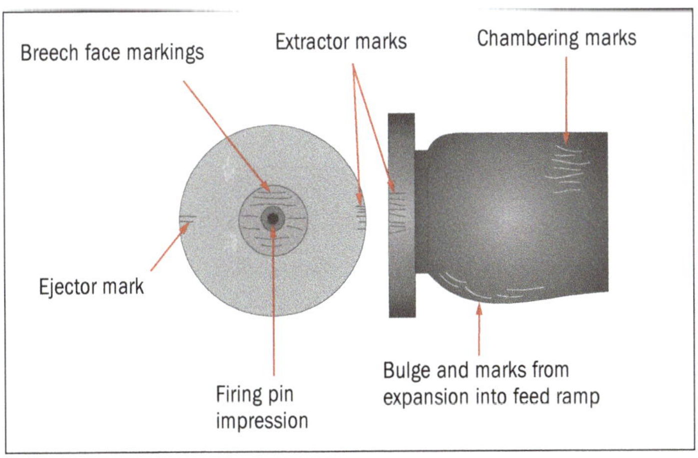

Figure 5.13: Marks on a cartridge casing

48 Thompson (2010) 8.
49 Jackson & Jackson (2004) 283.
50 Jackson & Jackson (2004) 283.
51 Thompson (2010) 9.

5.8.5 Identifying bullets

When bullets are discharged from a firearm, they are marked with firearm impressions. In order to compare bullets or wads fired from the same weapon, the ballistic expert will discharge the disputed firearm loaded with control sample ammunition into a water tank or other device to recover the bullet points or wads. Most firearms, except shotguns, have rifled bores, as shown in Figure 5.14. A rifled bore features a series of spiral grooves and lands along the length of the interior surface.[52] The grooves put a spiral spin on the bullet for greater accuracy. Spiral grooves are lines cut in the inner surface of the bore whereas lands are the spaces between the grooves. The direction, width and depth of the grooves and lands vary from one manufacturer to the next. When a firearm is discharged, the spiral grooves and lands make impressions on the fired bullets. The diagram indicates the interior section of a rifle, handgun and shotgun. The bore of a shotgun is smooth because rifling would spread the shot pattern too soon.

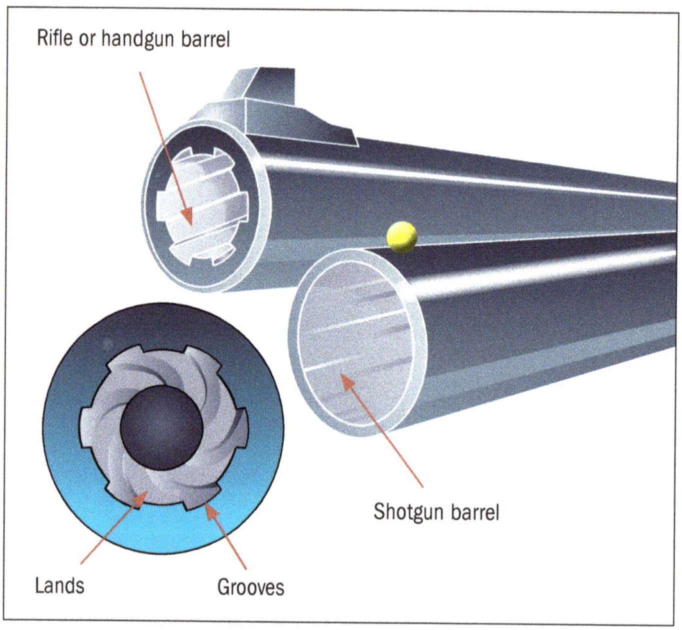

Figure 5.14: Firearm barrels with and without spiral grooves and lands

The recovered bullets from the laboratory test will enable the ballistic expert to compare the impressions created by a rifled bore to bullets gathered from the scene of incident. This will indicate whether the same firearm was used to fire the bullets or wads found at the scene of incident.

52 Jackson & Jackson (2004) 242.

Figure 5.15: Firearm tool marks and impressions

5.8.6 Value of firearm and ammunition evidence in forensic investigation

Once the firearm and ammunition have been identified at the scene of incident, the evidential value of these items may help the investigation by providing the following information:

- the type, calibre and manufacturer of the firearm, by identifying the type of firearm and ammunition used during the commission of an incident
- the person who discharged the firearm, by conducting primer residue tests and metal object tests to make sure that the culprit had used that particular weapon
- the direction from which the shot was fired, by measuring the angle of bullet holes at the scene of incident
- the distance of the firearm from the victim, by identifying carbon marks on the bullet wound or clothing of the victim, a muzzle impression on the skin, or powder fragments at the entrance area or around the wound
- whether the firearm is in working order or not, by testing the trigger pressure of the firearm found at the scene of incident.

The forensic investigator must also compare the following:

- impressions on cartridges and cartridge cases, by microscopically identifying class and individual characteristics during laboratory examination to match the mark of the firing pin on the primer cup, the ejector mark on the base of the case, the extractor mark inside the rim, breech face marks on the base and any significant marks on the case wall which were made during chambering, discharge or extraction (see Figure 5.13)
- impressions on the bullets, by microscopically identifying class and individual characteristics during laboratory examination. This is done by identifying the identical number of marks left by spiral grooves and lands, the direction of twist, the degree of rifling and the widths and depths of lands and grooves.

5.8.7 Primer residue test (pr test)

When the firearm is discharged, the firing pin strikes the back of the primer cup, creating the shock that ignites the gunpowder. This explosion provides the required pressure to force the bullet down the barrel. The ignited gunpowder forms heat and gases, which propel the projectile. Frequently not all the powder burns and primer residue is forced out through all the openings of the firearm, namely the cylinder gap and the ejection port or muzzle.

Primer residue samples can be recovered from the hands of the person who fired the gun, from someone who was in close proximity to the discharged weapon, from a surface in close proximity to the discharged firearm and from a wound site. Primer residue sprays onto the hands and any object or piece of clothing within an approximate radius of three metres from the shooter. However, this may vary according to the type of firearm, the type of ammunition, the number of shots fired and the environment.[53]

To avoid the loss of primer residue evidence, the forensic investigator should take samples within two-and-a-half hours from the time of shooting because primer residue is easily removed from surfaces. Suspects should not be allowed to wash or rub their hands prior to sampling. Often activities such as putting one's hands in one's pockets, rubbing the hands together or handling items can wipe primer residue away. In this case, primer residue should be collected from the suspect's trouser pockets and hands. Washing of hands can remove most, if not all the primer residue particles. The particles can also be transferred from a surface or person to another individual's hands or clothing. The suspect should not be fingerprinted prior to sampling.

In suicide or murder cases where a firearm was used, samples should be collected from both the hands and the clothes of the dead body before being preserved and forwarded for further analysis at the Forensic Science Laboratory. At the scene of incident, the hands of the deceased must be enclosed in plastic bags and the clothes may not be removed before having been examined by the person performing the post-mortem.[54]

5.8.8 Restoring serial numbers

In many instances criminals will obliterate serial numbers from objects so that ownership cannot be traced. Firearms, motor vehicles, bicycles and motorcycles are commonly recovered with identification numbers removed or altered in an attempt to prevent the identification of the original owner. Over the years, several methods have been used successfully to restore these numbers on different items.

---

53 Trimple (2011) 26.
54 Schwär et al. (1988) 231.

The most commonly used methods are magnaflux and acid etching. The magnaflux method is a process whereby a magnet is attached on opposite sides of the iron or steel surface and a mixture of fine iron filings and light oil is applied on the obliterated area to reveal the numbers removed from the item.

There are two types of acid etching methods, namely Fry's reagent and Vilella's reagent. Fry's reagent, a mixture of hydrochloric acid, copper (II) chloride and ethyl alcohol, is applied to the obliterated area on the iron or steel surface to reveal the removed numbers. Vilella's reagent, a mixture of glycerol, hydrofluoric acid and nitric acid, is applied to aluminium surfaces to reveal the removed numbers.

5.8.9 Value of restoring numbers on metal objects

By restoring an obliterated or altered serial number, the number can be used to individualise the object. The serial number can be compared to registration records, such as information captured on the firearm registration database, which will reveal the owner's name and address. The investigator can easily trace the owner of the object and gather more information that can be positively used in the investigation process. After investigation the object may be returned to its original owner.

5.9 SUMMARY

In this chapter a variety of issues pertaining to imprint evidence was addressed. Although photography and polygraphy are often not seen as part of imprint evidence, these related specialties were also included. The examiner of disputed documents is involved in the scientific examination of handwriting, typewriting, printing, photocopying or other mechanical ways of producing written material. This specialist may also analyse the ink, paper and other components of documents, which could include wills, letters and ransom notes. Other examinations include identifying the source or writer of the document, deciphering obliterated or erased text, detecting alterations and deletions, and examining indented writing and burnt or charred documents.

On the other hand, criminalists who specialise in impression evidence are concerned with various types of two- or three-dimensional markings, such as fingerprints, palm prints, footprints, footwear impressions and tyre impressions. Evidence impression marks are compared with known impression markings made by the person or object suspected of causing the imprint or impression. Some types of impression evidence, such as fingerprints and tool marks, fall within the ambit of subspecialties. The chapter also touched on fingerprint examination as currently used in South Africa, firearm examination for investigation purposes and the analysis of tool mark impressions with the intention of solving a variety of incidents.

REFERENCES

TF Adams, AG Caddell & JL Krutsinger *Crime Investigation* 2 ed (Pearson Education 2004)

WW Bennet & KM Hess *Criminal Investigation* 7 ed (Thomson 2004)

RE Berty 'A new IR-based technique for examination of writing strokes: IRDA – Infrared Detection Apparatus' (2009) 42 *Canadian Society of Forensic Science Journal* 117–134

BCSO Identification – arches online (2012) Finger print patterns – arches. Available at http://wwwbarzoria-county.com/sherrif/idfingerprint/id-arches.htm, accessed May 2012

C Dogaroiu 'Forensic examination of typewritten and office printed documents' (2011) 1(1) *International Journal of Criminal Investigation* 11–16

BAJ Fisher *Techniques of Crime Scene Investigation* 7 ed (CRC Press 2004)

JN Gilbert *Criminal Investigation* 6 ed (Pearson Prentice Hall 2004)

A Giles 'Forensic document examination – the science today' (2010) 1-4 *STEP Journal*. Available at http://www.step.org/forensic-document-examination-science-today

JE Girard *Criminalistics: Forensic Science, Crime and Terrorism* 2 ed (Jones & Bartlett 2011)

Hernandez, GA 'Overview of analyzing firearm, tool mark and impression evidence at the Miami-Dade Police Department' (2011) Available at http://www.dtic.mil/ndia/2011ballistics/Keynote_Hernandez.pdf, accessed 14 May 2013

J Horswell *The Practice of Crime Scene Investigation* (CRC Press 2004)

AR Jackson & JM Jackson *Forensic Science* (Pearson Prentice Hall 2004)

SH James & JJ Nordby *Forensic Science* (CRC Press 2005)

B Leonard (ed) *The Science of Fingerprints: Classification and Uses* (US Department of Justice: Federal Bureau of Investigation 1988)

P McDonald *Tire Imprint Evidence* (CRC Press 1993)

RR Ogle *Crime Scene Investigation and Reconstruction* (Pearson Education 2004)

JW Osterburg & RH Ward *Criminal Investigation: A Method for Reconstructing the Past* 6 ed (Anderson Publishing 2010)

A Parkinson, M Colella & T Evans 'The development and evaluation of radiological decontamination procedures for documents, document inks, and latent fingerprints on porous surfaces' (2010) 55(3) *Journal of Forensic Science* 731–734

U Rajanna, A Erol & G Bebis 'Comparative study on feature extraction for fingerprint classification and performance improvements using rank-level fusion' (Springer-Verlag London 2009) Available at http://www.cse.unr.edu/~bebis/UdayFingerprint.pdf, accessed 20 November 2013

EM Robinson *Crime Scene Photography* 2 ed (Elsevier 2010)

TG Schwär, JD Loubser & JA Olivier *The Forensic ABC in Medical Practice: A Practical Guide* (HAUM 1988)

SN Srihari 'Analysis of footwear impression evidence' (2011) Final technical report, Research Foundation of the State University of New York

RM Thompson *Firearm Identification in the Forensic Science Laboratory* (National District Attorneys Association 2010)

M Trimple 'The current status of GSR examination' (May 2011) *FBI Law Enforcement Bulletin*

SJ Turnbull, AE Jones & M Allen 'Identification of the class characteristics in the handwriting of Polish people writing in English' (2010) 55(5) *Journal of Forensic Science* 1296–1303

J van der Westhuizen *Forensic Criminalistics* 2 ed (Heinemann 1996)

PC White *Crime Scene to Court: The Essentials of Forensic Science* 2 ed (Royal Society of Chemistry Cambridge 2004)

Chapter 6

THE PRELIMINARY INVESTIGATION PHASE

M van der Watt

- Introduction
- The scene of incident
- Approaching and assessing the scene of incident
- Aids and experts
- Potential risks, obstacles and considerations
- Processing the scene of incident
- Collection and preservation of evidence and the chain of custody
- Evaluation and debriefing
- Arrest, detention and use of force
- Practical handy hints
- Summary

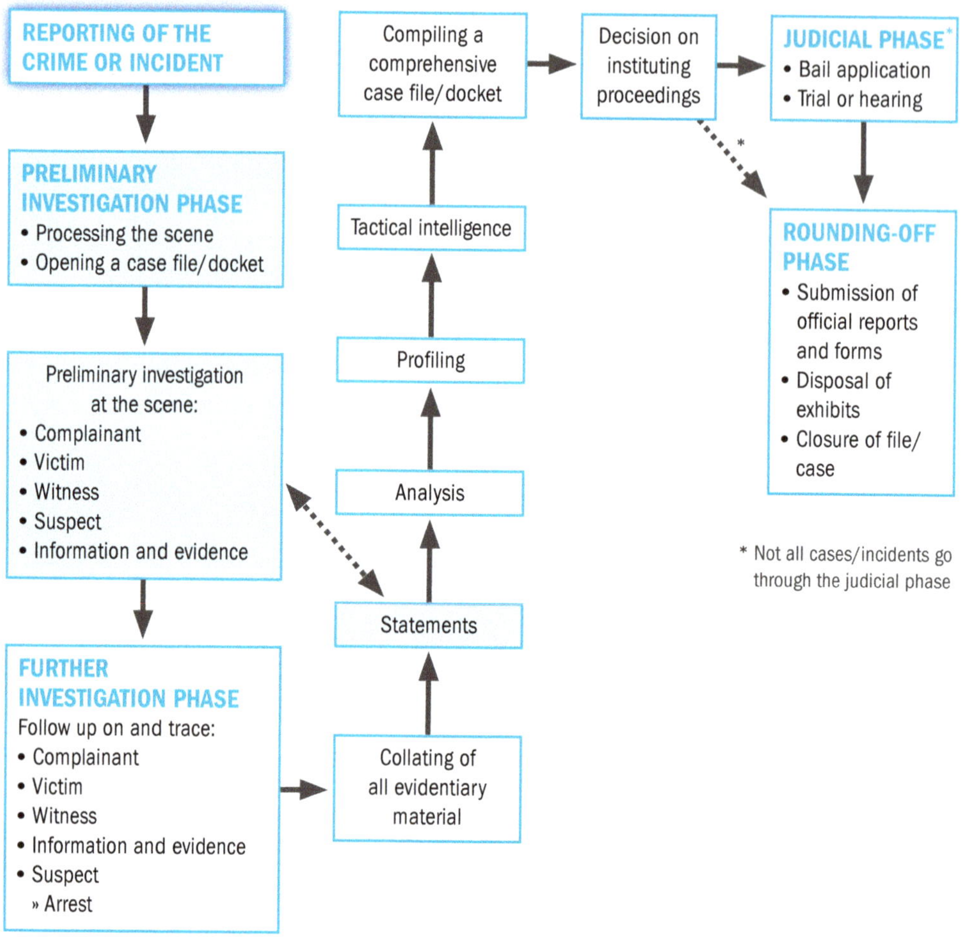

Figure 6.1: Areas of the crime investigation process covered in this chapter shown in shaded area

6.1 INTRODUCTION

The actual investigation conducted at a scene of incident (crime scene) is probably one of the most complex undertakings in the entire scope of activities related to forensic investigation. In addition to the initial state of disarray and confusion that may reign at the first response to a scene of incident, the work of those involved at the scene is usually scrutinised by the media, the general public and role-players involved in the events that lead up to the trial. The criminal trial is the sum total of all efforts by the prosecution to prove the guilt of the accused beyond reasonable doubt, whereas the accused will either attempt to refute charges brought against them or try to capitalise on technicalities surfacing as a result of questionable practices by those involved in the investigation. This statement also applies to civil cases and other tribunals, although in those cases the test is normally based on the balance of probabilities.

The investigator will ultimately have to account for every phase of the investigation process. All actions taken, decisions made and methods used to gather evidence will be laid bare during the trial or other quasi-judicial process. The evidence-gathering process is usually initiated during the preliminary investigation phase with the scene of incident as a fundamental source of information. A concerted effort will therefore be made by the defence to highlight unprofessional conduct of those involved at the scene of incident in order to render any subsequent evidence inadmissible. Evidence at the scene of incident that is gathered in a systematic and lawful manner will not only assist the investigator in answering important questions such as 'what happened?' and 'who was responsible?' but will also contribute to securing a conviction.

In this chapter the focus is the preliminary investigation phase. This phase of the investigation originates when a crime or incident is reported and continues until the scene of incident is processed and cleared. The preliminary investigation serves as the foundation of the case.[1] It should therefore be accurate or it may jeopardise the entire investigation if not carried out properly.

Although no hard-and-fast rules can be laid down for how each scene of incident should be approached and processed, the fundamental principles remain the same and should be adhered to at all times. Investigators attending to a scene of incident can use forensic investigation as a systemic and scientific tool to deal with the complexities at the scene of incident and understand the procedures that should be followed. It is beyond the scope of this chapter to discuss specific methods for specific crimes or incidents. Instead, a generic overview of the preliminary investigation phase is given.

6.2 THE SCENE OF INCIDENT

For the purposes of this book, the words 'scene of incident' are used to replace the traditionally used concept of 'crime scene'. In forensic investigation an enquiry may relate not only to criminal cases but also to civil cases, corporate investigations and disciplinary cases. By means of the media and popular television shows such as *CSI*, the terms 'crime scene', 'forensics' and 'DNA' have become buzzwords that have increasingly made their way into many living rooms over the past decade. A scene of incident has become synonymous with a body being found in a room covered in blood or a bank robbery where the closed-circuit television footage is the most vital piece of evidence in existence. However, in certain instances the scene of incident may be synonymous with a document used in the commission of fraud or even an online 'chat room' used by employees and which bears evidence of collusion, racial slurs, threats or sexual harassment.

1 Gilbert (2004) 63.

Statements obtained from complainants, victims, witnesses and suspects could culminate in a scene of incident when it is found that the deponent had perjured or used the statement to deceive or obstruct an investigation.[2] The inappropriate use of a word by a suspect could indicate who had committed the harassment, murder or other crime and whether fraud was involved.[3]

Experienced investigators will agree that the scene of incident, often misconstrued as a physical location only, can be more complex than most people – including law enforcement officials – may imagine. A cellphone found at a scene of incident is increasingly being viewed not only as an object that constitutes physical evidence but as an 'untapped wellspring' of information within the larger scene of incident. Aspects such as social networking and technology (which are increasingly being used by perpetrators to commit crimes), civil delicts and corporate illegitimacies are all contributing factors to our rapidly changing society.

These factors not only increase the challenges faced by investigators, but may have a bearing on how investigators view or define a scene of incident in a specific case. In addition to a physical location where an incident has occurred, the scene of incident now increasingly includes visible and implicit scenes that may contain physical, non-physical, direct or indirect information and evidence. The scene of incident goes beyond the actual location where the incident occurred to include the staging and planning areas, the routes used by the perpetrator to and from the primary scene and the routes between the primary and secondary scenes. Thus a scene of incident could span across various countries and include dozens of physical locations and individuals, thousands of exhibits and nearly as many witness statements.[4]

A distinction can be made between a primary and a secondary scene of incident. The primary scene of incident is the area where the most actions occurred or where the highest concentration of physical evidence is located, for example the shooting scene. The secondary scene is where preliminary or further actions occurred that contain physical evidence, such as the getaway vehicle.[5]

In its physical form, a scene of incident may include a person, a place or premises (including vehicles, boats or aircrafts) where some physical action occurred and evidential material could have been transferred.[6] Implicit or hidden scenes of incident are synonymous with crimes such as money laundering, extortion, certain types of fraud and especially computer-related crimes.

2 Brown (2005) 167–168.
3 Brown (2005) 168.
4 Genge (2004) 3.
5 P Bekker, forensic expert attached to the Eastern Cape Provincial Criminal Record and Crime Scene Management Centre. Statement to author, 31 October 2011, Port Elizabeth.
6 Trueman (2009) 28.

Scenes of incident associated with computers are complicated by the transient nature of electronic evidence, the speed of information transit, the possibility of sophisticated encryption and the anonymity available to users.[7]

Irrespective of how a scene of incident presents itself, information must be gathered for the purpose of analysis, interpretation and individualisation. The primary task of the investigator at the scene of incident begins with a thorough understanding of the incident that has taken place. If a crime was committed, the elements of the crime will have to be proven by means of objective evidence found at the scene. Corporate investigative assignments usually involve incidents related to personnel, products, intellectual property, physical facilities and professional and business reputations.[8] In addition to an understanding of criminal law, criminal procedure and relevant pieces of legislation, corporate scenes of incident may require the investigator to have an operational understanding of, among other things, organisational and departmental policies, procedures and directives. These will serve as decision-making tools when approaching a scene of incident for the purpose of identifying wrongful conduct and collecting relevant evidence to substantiate charges.

6.3 APPROACHING AND ASSESSING THE SCENE OF INCIDENT

It is of utmost importance that investigators are well acquainted with the powers afforded to them by relevant legislation and the limitations applying to those powers. Legislation and regulations (see chapter 1) empower investigators from different agencies to conduct investigations. Disregarding legislation and regulations will adversely affect the admissibility of evidence and the outcome of an investigation. It may even expose an investigator to criminal or civil action.

The existence of a scene of incident usually comes to the attention of an investigator through some form of reporting. The reporting process may be initiated by a complainant or victim, a member of the public who either witnessed the incident or came across the scene, an employee or whistle-blower in a corporate environment, a public or private investigative agency which reports the crime to the police, or police officials who, during their official duties, report the crime by opening a case. Irrespective of who initiates the reporting process, the following information should be obtained concisely and accurately from the person who reports the incident. This information will serve to inform first responders to the scene of incident what they could expect to find upon arrival:

- name, address, contact details and capacity of the person who has reported the incident
- description of the incident

7 Genge (2004) 201-202.
8 Montgomery & Majeski (2005) xxviii.

- time dynamics, ie has the incident already occurred?
- is it in progress or is it being planned?
- the location of the incident and the type of premises
- are the suspects still at the scene?
- how many?
- description?
- how and in which direction did the suspects flee?
- description of vehicles
- are there any threats or hazards to responding personnel, ie weapons, fire or hazardous material?
- are there any injured persons at the scene of incident?
- if so, how many?
- type and severity of injuries
- are there any persons who might be in danger?
- which emergency services need to be dispatched?

Another important aspect to establish during the initial reporting process is whether the complainant or victim has access to specific technology that may help first responders to the scene or investigators to track stolen items in real time and rapidly apprehend the perpetrators. Such technology may vary from a tracking system activated in a stolen motor vehicle to more sophisticated satellite technology that can be registered as applications on iPads, iPhones and smartphones. Recent media reports have highlighted success stories of numerous incidents where suspects have been apprehended within hours after first responders were alerted to the location-tracking potential of stolen technological devices.[9]

When the reporting of an incident commences, it is of the utmost importance that the 'documentation journey' commences simultaneously. Proper documentation of all aspects relating to the incident is of fundamental importance because it will influence decision making about the approach and assessment of the scene of incident.

In most law enforcement and policing agencies the uniformed member is usually the first responder on the scene. In the corporate environment the first responder may be an administrative clerk, a line manager or an internal auditor. A rapid response time is often fundamental to the success or failure of the entire investigation[10] because an unattended scene of incident is unprotected, making it more vulnerable to contamination. Contamination occurs when evidence at the scene is altered, removed or destroyed. Contamination at the scene of incident may adversely affect the integrity of evidence and so render that evidence inadmissible during the subsequent trial or tribunal.

9 Ajam (2012) 1.
10 Gilbert (2004) 93.

6.3.1 Responsibilities of a first responder

First responders to the scene of incident should have an operational understanding of what will happen when they hand over the scene of incident to the investigation team. The initial decisions and actions by the first responder have a fundamental bearing on how the investigation process will unfold. It is therefore important for the first responder to act in an organised and systematic manner. An understanding of the investigation process will help and guide first responders to execute their duties more effectively when arriving at the scene. These may include:

- securing the scene of incident (cordoning-off)
- doing a threat analysis, ie establishing any immediate dangers and arranging medical assistance and support services (dog unit, traffic, fire brigade, air wing)
- establishing what incident has occurred
- identifying and securing all information sources (witnesses, documents, files, video footage)
- identifying and securing possible suspects
- identifying and safeguarding any possible physical evidence
- making detailed notes and establishing a safe and dedicated route to and from the scene to avoid contamination
- summoning aids and experts (forensic science laboratory, local Criminal Record Centre).

6.3.2 Cordoning-off

Cordoning off the scene of incident is fundamental to the forensic investigation process and, more specifically, the continuum of evidence preservation. A well cordoned-off scene creates the impression of professionalism and competency. Conversely, a scene of incident that is not cordoned off usually displays a lack of control and proficiency on the part of investigators and responding personnel.

Large scenes of incident may require first responders to erect an inner and an outer cordon. First responders will also have to use their discretion in determining the parameters for the cordons and may have to rely on input from the public or witnesses regarding what transpired at the scene. The inner cordon is usually erected around the entire scene of incident while the outer cordon is erected around the inner cordon. The outer cordon will serve as an undisturbed buffer area from which the investigation team can view the unprocessed scene and plan and initiate the scene-processing activities.

Scenes of incident in built-up areas like central business districts (CBDs) may require the first responder to arrange for the evacuation of buildings and the closure of roads. Safe and dedicated access routes to and from the scene of incident should be clearly marked. These will serve as the only gateways for emergency services that may have to attend to injured persons and dangers such as fires or other safety hazards. Corporate scenes of incident in an office block may be cordoned off by evacuating the relevant section of the building or merely limiting access by closing an office door. Prevailing circumstances and the merits of each case will determine how these activities should be managed.

© Phillip Bekker, South African Police Service

Figure 6.2: Scene of a cash-in-transit heist cordoned off at a busy intersection

6.3.3 Active scenes of incident

Active scenes of incident are those scenes where the commission of the incident is still in progress. Active scenes of incident usually require investigators to work at an increased pace due to the real-time recording of events and the concurrent management of a wide range of tasks. These incidents may include hostage situations or public violence resulting from mass protests. For active scenes of incident a command centre must be established from which all administration can be managed and activities coordinated.

Another form of an active scene of incident is where investigators or agents monitor the commission of an incident or crime through the use of unconventional or covert investigative techniques. However, in terms of the Bill of Rights, the use of covert investigative techniques 'will only be justifiable if the evil that one seeks to combat is a greater evil than the use of such techniques'.[11] These techniques include the setting up of police traps and undercover operations authorised by s 252A of the Criminal Procedure Act 51 of 1977 (CPA) and the interception of communication authorised by the Regulation of Interception of Communications and Provision of Communication-related Information Act 70 of 2002 (RICA).

11 Geldenhuys (2002) 352.

Active scenes of incident where covert techniques are used may include the controlled delivery of stolen vehicles to a storage facility or an agent who purchases a rhino horn hidden in the suspect's garage. These techniques are most often used in the investigation of organised crime. These scenes of incident are usually monitored and recorded by means of electronic equipment or devices such as micro video recorders, wiretaps and bugging devices.

Investigators should bear in mind that, if these techniques are employed in circumstances other than those authorised by the relevant sections in the Acts, evidence thus obtained would most probably be deemed inadmissible in a court of law. Organisational policies usually include precursory administrative procedures that have to be followed before the use of such methods is approved within the relevant legislative framework.

Example 6.1: Active scenes in a corporate environment

Active scenes of incident in the corporate environment where undercover operations are likely to be used successfully could include the following:[12]

- where there is consistent and reliable information suggesting employee misconduct or criminal activity, but insufficient details to permit appropriate corrective action or identification of those involved
- when misconduct or losses are known to occur in a specific area, but there is no information as to how they occurred or who is involved
- when there is a strong suspicion or actual indicators of on-the-job alcohol or illegal drug abuse or drug dealing in the workplace.

6.4 AIDS AND EXPERTS

The prospect of successfully investigating and solving an incident is severely hampered when available experts and aids are not utilised at the scene of incident. The underutilisation of experts was identified as a contributing factor in a 2012 study by the author into unsolved stranger rape cases in Port Elizabeth in the Eastern Cape. A content analysis of 184 stranger rape dockets closed as 'undetected' revealed that only five of the 184 dockets contained proof that a photographer had been used, eight of the 184 dockets contained proof that a fingerprint expert had been used and none of the 184 dockets contained evidence that a sketch artist had been used to compile an identikit. The underutilisation of experts at the scene of incident severely hampers any prospects of an arrest being made, especially when the perpetrator of the incident is unknown (ie a 'stranger').[13]

The use of relevant aids and experts is therefore fundamental to a team or multidisciplinary approach to investigation. Referring mainly to corporate

12 Ferraro (2006) 159.
13 Van der Watt (2012) 85.

investigations, Montgomery states the following:

> Investigators use experts as tools to document evidence and provide consulting for direction and advice with regard to given situations. Investigators and security specialists have an obligation to themselves and to their clients to understand the limits of their ability.[14]

Investigators will ultimately have to account for the decisions they made at the scene of incident and the methods they used to record or document the scene, and present the tribunal with a true reflection of what transpired at the scene of incident.

Although the list of aids and experts that can be used during the preliminary investigation phase is inexhaustible, some of them are mentioned in Tables 6.1 and 6.2.

Table 6.1: Experts in the multidisciplinary approach to scene of incident investigation

→ Expert(s)	Purpose
Accident reconstructionist	• Can assist with investigating the causes, circumstances and events related to a motor vehicle accident. • These experts rely on the principles of physics and engineering and also make use of computer software for calculations and the reconstruction of events.
Arson/fire investigator	• Has an operational understanding of the chemistry and dynamics of fire. • They can add value to criminal investigations by establishing whether a fire was set intentionally (arson), or in civil cases to establish the liability for a fire.
Cybercrime investigator/ digital forensic expert	• Can provide assistance in evidence and data recovery from computers, cellphones and other software/internet applications. • Also provides expertise in the collection procedures of computer-related evidence at scenes of incident.
District surgeon or pathologist	• Can provide assistance with medical examinations and autopsies.
Draughtsman	• Can compile a proper plan or sketch of the scene of incident.
Experts attached to the different components of the Forensic Science Laboratory	• *Biology unit:* Trichological (hair) analysis; biochemical and microscopic tests; DNA analysis. • *Ballistic unit:* Internal ballistics; external ballistics; terminal ballistics; intermediate ballistics. • *Disputed document unit:* Handwriting analysis; determination of the origin, authenticity and age of documents. • *Chemistry unit:* Analysis of prohibited substances, eg drugs and medicine; toxicology, ie insecticides, weed killers and traditional medicines. →

14 Montgomery (2005) 235-236.

→ Expert(s)	Purpose
Fingerprint expert	• Can identify, collect and process latent and patent prints (finger-, hand, palm, foot- and shoeprints).
Forensic accountant	• Usually has specific areas of expertise which may include accounting, auditing, commercial law, fraud examination and the collection, analysis and evaluation of financial information as evidence. • They use financial and quantitative skills to calculate damages.
Forensic anthropologist/ facial reconstructionist	• Can assist with the identification of deceased individuals whose remains are decomposed or unrecognisable. • Facial reconstruction entails the recreation of the face of a deceased person from their skeletal remains. • The deceased person's identity is usually unknown, and reconstruction serves as an attempt to identify the person.
Forensic archaeologist	• Can assist with the location and excavation of evidence that has been buried. • Evidence may include human remains or any item of physical evidence, such as money or a cellphone that was buried.
Forensic botanist	• Through the study of plants a forensic botanist can make valuable deductions from leaves, seeds or pollen found either on a body or at a scene of incident. • They can provide valuable input on the timelines of an incident and say whether the body or object was moved between two or more different locations.
Forensic engineer	• Can assist with an investigation of mechanical processes and failure of machinery or vehicles which subsequently led to injury or death. • They are most often used in civil suits or compensation claims.
Forensic entomologist	• Through the study of insects a forensic entomologist can make deductions and help to establish the approximate time that lapsed after a person has died, based on the lifecycle and types of insects found in a decomposed body.
Forensic odontologist/ forensic dentist	• Can assist with the examination and evaluation of dental evidence. • This may include age estimation in children, bite marks left on a victim, perpetrator or objects found at the scene of incident, or the identification of an unknown individual to whom the teeth belong.
Forensic osteologist	• Can assist with determining the cause and circumstances of death by studying the bones or skeletal remains of a deceased person. • These experts are usually used in the investigation of genocide-related cases. →

→ Expert(s)	Purpose
Investigative psychologist	• Can provide guidance in the investigation of psychologically motivated crimes, serial murders and serial rapes, based on the offender's behaviour at the crime scene. • Can also help to compile a linkage analysis between crimes that display a similar *modus operandi*.
Photographer	• Can photograph all aspects at the scene of incident that may have evidential value, eg overall features and condition of the scene, exhibits, injuries to the victim or suspect.
Police sketch artist	• Can compile a sketch which resembles the facial features and appearance of a suspect, victim, missing or deceased person for the purpose of identification or rendering evidence. • The information for compiling the sketch may be provided by a witness or by a family member when a recent photograph is not available. Stolen valuables may also be sketched for identification purposes.
Video operator	• Can make a video recording of the overall appearance of the scene of incident, exhibits and bystanders. • A video operator is also important during identification parades and the subsequent pointing out of a suspect.

Table 6.2: Aids in the multidisciplinary approach to scene of incident investigation

Aid(s)	Purpose
Air wing	• Can assist with a rapid response to a scene of incident or when a fleeing suspect or vehicle is being pursued. • They also provide assistance to photographers when aerial photography is used to record scenes of incident.
Cellular network providers	• An application can be made for cellphone records and itemised billing for a suspect's phone. This information can be used to chart a suspect's movements, identify contacts and accomplices and link the suspect to the scene of incident. • The Regulation of Interception of Communications and Provision of Communication-related Information Act 70 of 2002 (RICA) was implemented on 1 July 2009. This effectively means that, by law, everyone who has an active cellphone number or who purchases a new prepaid starter pack has to register their SIM card and show a valid identity document.
Corporate and private investigators	• Usually function within a corporate environment, in a private capacity or on behalf of another party that may be a private person or a business. • Their focus may include criminal, civil or disciplinary investigations. • Their skills set may range from statement analysis, electronic countermeasures, competitive intelligence gathering, audio- and videotape enhancements, to computer analysis and surveillance.
Credit bureaus	• Can supply information on people who have a credit record. →

→ Aid(s)	Purpose
Customs and border authorities	• Can provide information on the movement of people through South African borders and the import and export of restricted and prohibited goods.
Deeds office	• Can provide information relevant to the acquisition of property (ownership and property details).
Dog handlers	• Can assist with tracking and rescue, and the identification of drugs, perlemoen, biological fluids and explosives. • Some dog handlers are also trained in the use of dental stone for the collection of foot- and tyre imprints.
Films and Publications Board	• Can provide assistance with the classification of pornography and child pornography and the monitoring of compliance with the Films and Publications Act 65 of 1996, as amended.
Financial institutions	• Bank records (account details, transactions history, investment records, etc) can be obtained from banks and other financial service providers if a subpoena is obtained.
Department of Home Affairs	• Can provide assistance with identifying different types of documents, establishing the status of documentation and investigating undocumented persons. • Can also provide access to birth records, residential details, fingerprints and family records.
Hostage/suicide negotiators	• Can provide assistance at active scenes of incident such as kidnappings or hostage situations originating from a failed robbery attempt. • Can also provide crisis negotiations with suicidal persons or during incidents of volatile conflict.
Informers	• Can be tasked by the investigator to search for and gather information.
Internal media liaison officers	• Can provide assistance with formulating communication strategies relating to sensitive situations or investigations. • Can also act as a communication link with the media, community, clients and employees within an organisation.
Interpol	• Can provide assistance to police agencies in cross-border investigations and access to an international police database.
Media (print, radio and television)	• Can provide assistance with the communication of important information to the community, eg crime threats or alternative routes as a result of an investigation at a scene of incident. • Can also assist with the tracing of suspects, stolen property and witnesses. →

→ Aid(s)	Purpose
Municipalities	• Most municipalities have a database of, among other things, building plans, aerial photographs and ownership details of properties and business premises. • Every adult who rents or owns a house has to be registered/on record. Almost no credit or financial transaction can be conducted without a copy of a municipal account to verify a person's residential address.
Non-government organisations (NGOs); faith-based organisations (FBOs) and non-profit organisations (NPOs)	• Each of these organisations has a different focus and a diverse range of expertise and information sources. • Are usually well informed about different societal problems and understand the dynamics within their communities.
Police divers	• Can provide assistance with underwater scenes of incident and the collection of evidence, recovery of bodies and rescue operations.
Prosecutors	• Can provide valuable advice and guidance relating to the legality of search and seizure and the expeditious preparation of search warrants. • Can also add value to investigative decision making.
Registrar of Companies	• Can provide information on registered companies as well as the persons involved in those companies.
SAPS Special Task Force	• Can assist with high-risk operations at active scenes of incident, eg hostage release or suspect apprehension.
Social workers	• Can provide valuable assistance at scenes of incident involving children or abused women. • Can also assist with the preliminary psychosocial assessment of a victim and thereby provide advice to the investigator.
Statutory investigators attached to government departments or other public agencies	• Statutory investigators can come from a variety of agencies including the Special Investigating Unit (SIU), the South African Revenue Services (SARS), the Environmental Management Inspectorate (EMI), the South African Reserve Bank (SARB). • Can provide guidance or advice on department- or agency-specific procedures, policies or regulations. • Can also be included in a project team focusing on multifaceted investigations.
Telkom	• Can provide names and addresses of people who have telephone and internet connections. • Wanted persons may be traced through the telephone directory.
Vehicle registration office	• Can provide information on the ownership and registration documents of vehicles.

6.5 POTENTIAL RISKS, OBSTACLES AND CONSIDERATIONS

Numerous factors, including a wide range of risks and potential obstacles, may be present before, during or immediately after the investigation at the scene of incident. If not properly considered and managed by either or both the first responder and the investigator, these factors may adversely affect the proper management and investigation at the scene. Due to the unpredictable nature of scenes of incident and circumstances in general, the list of factors and potential risks and obstacles are inexhaustible. In this chapter the focus is on the following:

- weather and light conditions
- witnesses
- victims
- suspects
- legal practitioners
- media
- bystanders and police officials
- corporate considerations
- legal risks and considerations
- extraordinary challenges.

6.5.1 Weather and light conditions

Weather conditions as a determining factor should be considered, especially when processing outdoor scenes. Evidence may be altered, concealed and even destroyed by rain or wind. Another factor that needs to be considered is the deterioration of natural light. The detection of fragile pieces of evidence may be complicated during the search of indoor and outdoor scenes at night time and when artificial light sources are being used. Based on the nature of the scene of incident and the types of evidence being searched for, the investigator will have to make a decision as to whether the scene should rather be protected and preserved until daylight. Shoe impressions are an example of evidence that is particularly vulnerable to weather conditions and deteriorating light sources and should therefore be prioritised during the processing of the scene of incident. However, it is noteworthy that with the current developments in technology, most of the scenes can be handled at any time of the day or night.

6.5.2 Witnesses

Investigators obtain evidential information from people who know the facts. Witnesses are people who have firsthand knowledge of an incident or, in the criminal justice system, information about a particular crime, which they have gathered through their senses (seeing, hearing, smelling or touching). Witnesses can help to clarify important aspects about the crime or incident.

A witness who has seen the event firsthand is known as an eyewitness. A witness who has special knowledge and experience in their field of expertise is called an expert witness (see section 5 in chapter 8 for more details). Witnesses and complainants may be juristic persons or big corporate companies.

Witnesses at the scene of incident should be dealt with tactfully. They should be removed from the scene of incident to prevent contaminating the scene and be separated as soon as possible in order to ensure that they do not influence one another's version of events. If this was not done by the first responder, the investigator should do so immediately. A brief synopsis of each witness's version should be obtained. This may contribute towards decision making at the scene regarding what evidence to search for or deciding what immediate action to take. The investigator may not always be in the position to immediately interview a witness and therefore may have to assign a colleague to manage this process.

Care should be taken in so-called 'whistle-blowing' cases where a witness summons police or investigators to a scene where a corporate theft or fraud case is in progress. Negligent exposure of such a witness's identity could cause severe harm or even loss of life. There have also been instances where suspects identified themselves as witnesses in an effort to derail the investigation. It may therefore be a worthwhile exercise to request a video operator, if present, to make a recording of bystanders and witnesses at the scene. This could also assist with the identification of witnesses at a later stage.

The investigator must also look ahead and consider the value of witnesses in a court case. In order to act as a witness, a person must be competent to testify. Factors that might influence the competence and compellability of witnesses are mental illness or 'imbecility of mind', deafness, muteness and being a child, an officer of the court, a spouse, the accused or the co-accused. These persons may be called upon to testify, but there are cautionary rules in the Criminal Procedure Act 51 of 1977 which govern the admissibility of their testimony. For example, it is established judicial practice for trial courts to apply cautionary rules to the testimony of young children and single witnesses and also to adopt a cautionary approach to complaints in sexual cases. The purpose of the cautionary rules is to assist the court in deciding whether or not guilt has been proven beyond reasonable doubt.

6.5.3 Victims

A victim is a person who suffers due to some adverse circumstance. In criminal matters, a victim's first contact with the criminal justice process is when they report the crime to the first police official.

In forensic investigations a victim may also be a juristic person, for example a big corporate company that had just lost a large amount of money due to fraud.

When attending to any scene of incident, the investigator's first priority should be those victims in need of medical attention. Depending on the circumstances, this could imply that the first responder or the investigator may not be able to immediately interview and obtain information from the victims. The investigator may therefore have to brief medical personnel on issues regarding evidence collection and the recording of important information.

Victims of any incident should always be treated with the necessary care and dignity. Despite the challenges faced by personnel attending to a scene of incident, the interaction with a victim should be professional and empathic. It is also important that victims are removed from the scene in order to prevent secondary trauma or possible contamination of the scene. In cases of rape and sexual assault, the victim should be given the same priority as the scene of incident and be managed accordingly. The SAPS 'National Instruction 22 of 1998: Sexual Offences: Support to victims and crucial aspects of the investigation'[15] is a valuable source to consult when dealing with victims of sexual offences.

South Africa's new comprehensive Prevention and Combating of Trafficking in Persons Act 7 of 2013 gives credence to a victim-centred approach, which is consistent with international best practice. Therefore, when investigators or frontline responders are confronted with the subversive crime of human trafficking, their priority should be to identify possible victims. These people often find themselves veiled as persons in prostitution, street beggars, petty thieves and undocumented migrant workers.

6.5.4 Suspects

The identification and arrest of a suspect are fundamental to any investigation. However, when a suspect is identified and arrested at the scene of incident, great care should be taken to prevent contamination of evidence. Once again, the circumstances in which first responders or investigators find themselves may vary, as may their immediate actions towards the suspect according to the incident being investigated. For example, it is more likely that a suspect arrested and detained at the scene of a murder or rape could contaminate evidence than a suspect arrested and detained for shoplifting in a mall. The basic principle is: the risk of contamination increases the longer the suspect remains at the scene of incident because the suspect may alter the scene of incident by removing evidence or by changing the position or adding additional objects to the scene. Intimidation of victims or witnesses is another reason for removing suspects from the scene of incident as soon as possible.

As soon as suspects have been identified at the scene of incident, they should be removed from the scene and searched. Any evidence found in possession

15 SAPS (1998).

of the suspects or on their clothing should be photographed and collected. Photographs taken of the physical condition and appearance of the suspect may later prove valuable in refuting allegations of assault or abuse by those who had effected the arrest. These photographs should ideally be taken prior to the suspect being booked out of the cell for investigation purposes or for a medical examination by a doctor. Photographs should again be taken on the suspect's return to the cell. The suspect should never be transported away from the scene in the same vehicle as the victim as this could adversely affect the integrity of evidence.

6.5.5 Legal practitioners

Experienced police officials and investigators can provide interesting accounts of how the presence of the suspect's legal practitioner can complicate efforts at the scene of incident. Notwithstanding the right of suspects to consult their legal representatives, the scene of incident is not the platform for this discussion. Legal practitioners often manage to identify the 'weak link' in the investigation team or among those personnel who respond to a scene of incident. This individual is then pressurised to provide sensitive information regarding the investigation or to compromise crucial procedures. This may include influencing a police member to hand over personal possessions of the suspect, eg a cellphone, wallet or apparent valuables, without considering that these items may be part of the evidence. Every member at the scene of incident must be assertive when called for and portray an image of uncompromising professionalism. The legal representatives must remain outside the cordoned-off scene of incident and may be supplied with the name of the investigator who will contact them after the scene of incident and the suspect have been processed. Every member who interacts with suspects and their legal representatives should have an operational understanding of s 35(1), (2) and (3) of the Constitution of the Republic of South Africa, 1996, as discussed in chapter 1.

6.5.6 Media

In many ways the media can be equated to a 'double-edged sword'. The media can be a valuable tool in distributing information regarding a fleeing suspect or vehicle, or sensitising the community to aspects concerning personal safety. However, scenes of incident are probably some of the most sensational topics covered by the media and journalists may use every possible opportunity to photograph a dead body or expose malpractice by investigators or responding personnel. An internal media liaison officer should be used as far as possible when communicating with journalists about any aspect of the incident under investigation. It is sometimes necessary to educate journalists and media liaison officers on the sensitivity of a particular investigation and the fact that irresponsible reporting may complicate the investigation or, even worse, cause further injury or loss of life.

Example 6.2: The media often complicates investigations

A police raid was conducted on a building where a human trafficking syndicate detained female victims who were used as prostitutes. The media arrived at the crime scene and photographed the building as the victims were being rescued. After publishing the articles and photographs, a member of the same syndicate who was detaining victims in another city identified the crime scene and some of the rescued victims and immediately relocated to an unknown location.

The publicity by the media derailed the police investigation and attempts to trace the suspect and rescue the victims in the other city were in vain.

Similarly, serial rapists or murderers may alter or change their *modus operandi* based on how their crimes are being depicted or reported in the media.

6.5.7 Bystanders and police officials

Bystanders at the scene of incident and police officials who have not been assigned to any tasks should remain outside the cordoned-off area. Contamination as a result of these persons usually occur because they smoke and/or eat at the scene of incident. Cigarette butts, chewing gum and empty cool-drink containers are among the many items that are sometimes discarded at the scene of incident or in close proximity thereof. This may lead to confusion among officials processing the scene and could derail an important investigation. During the processing of large and newsworthy scenes of incident, scattered objects at the scene are vulnerable to being removed by police officials or bystanders who would then boast that 'they were there'.

© Tiro Ramathatse

Figure 6.3: The photograph published with the article entitled 'Robber lies dead in driveway of home' on the front page of *The Star* on Tuesday 10 January 2012.

In the picture in Figure 6.3 one notices the disorganised appearance of activities at the scene. The photograph shows the covered body of a fatally wounded suspect lying in a driveway. No police tape is visible. The cones on the scene (possibly) indicate exhibits. An emotional member of the public is standing in close proximity to the body while police members are standing around aimlessly. Furthermore, the photographer managed to take the picture from within the crime scene. One wonders how he or she got access to do so.

The member of the public and the journalist/photographer may unintentionally destroy the integrity of exhibits. They could also cause cross-contamination and transfer additional items (hair, fingerprints, etc) to the scene. All in all, this is an example of a particularly poorly managed scene where the presence of bystanders, among other things, was not properly controlled.

6.5.8 Corporate considerations

The discovery of a scene of incident during the course of business hours could present some challenges for investigative decision making. The saying 'time is money' is something that is well understood by corporate managers whose performance is measured in terms of their productivity. Therefore, the cordoning off of a scene of incident in the corporate environment, and the removal of employees from an office block for the purpose of evidence collection and scene processing may not be viable. A mere two hours' delay in business caused by a preliminary investigation at the scene of incident can have numerous negative effects on the business. These may include despondent clients, impediments to a variety of production systems, neglected deadlines and ultimately the loss of capital. Some incidents require third-party investigators to be contracted due to the lack of skills of in-house investigators,[16] or even the selection of an entire investigation or project team.[17]

6.5.9 Legal risks and considerations

The constitutional framework should always be borne in mind during every aspect of forensic investigation and should guide investigative decision making. The Bill of Rights (Chapter 2 of the Constitution) is viewed as the cornerstone of democracy in South Africa and affords every person the right to equality, human dignity, life and freedom and security of the person, among other things. However, s 36 of the Constitution ('Limitation of Rights', also referred to as the 'limitation clause') provides for the limitation of these rights to the extent that the limitation is reasonable and justifiable. Actions by investigators at the scene of incident that violate these rights or misconstrue the provision of s 36 will be judged harshly. Section 35(5) of the Constitution clearly indicates that evidence obtained in a manner that violates any right in the Bill of Rights will be deemed

16 Hulme (2005) 25.
17 Ferraro (2006) 209.

inadmissible. The following questions should be considered by every investigator before, during and after the investigation at the scene of incident:

- Am I acting within the mandate and legislative framework of my profession?
- Are my actions reasonable and justifiable as required by the Constitution?
- Am I following the prescribed procedures for search and seizure, arrest and obtaining evidence?
- Do I have the prescribed legislative and/or organisational authority for using covert techniques to gather intelligence and evidence? If not, how will the use of covert techniques impact on the admissibility of evidence gathered?

Ignorance and disregard of legal considerations can have adverse consequences for investigators. A corporate or private investigator who acts beyond the scope of the boundaries created by legislation such as the Private Security Industry Regulation Act 56 of 2001 (PSIRA) could be held liable during subsequent criminal or civil action.

Example 6.3: The consequences of ignorance and the disregard of legal considerations

A private investigator receives information from an informer about a corporate theft in progress. The private investigator is the first to arrive at the scene of incident where the stolen merchandise is being loaded onto a truck. Instead of securing the scene and alerting the police, the private investigator confronts the suspects. The private investigator takes photographs of the suspects, whereupon they flee. The private investigator then calls a colleague who helps him to drive the truck and the stolen merchandise to the nearest police station, where they open a criminal case.

In this case, the scene of incident was contaminated and not recorded or processed. Consequently the private investigator and his colleague can be charged with defeating the ends of justice.

Similarly, investigators who act without a warrant on undocumented hearsay evidence and use excessive force to enter a residence at midnight to search for a stolen cellphone inevitably expose themselves to civil action.

6.5.10 Extraordinary challenges

Here the term 'extraordinary' is used to refer to pioneering challenges experienced by investigators attending to 'extraordinary' scenes of incident where conventional and even modern-day approaches to investigation at the scene of incident are challenged beyond expectation.

18 Genge (2004) 3.

Example 6.4: 9/11

The so-called 9/11 terrorist attack on the World Trade Center in New York on 11 September 2001 bears evidence of the multilayered complexities experienced by responding emergency workers and investigators attending to such scenes of incident. The initial reports by the Federal Bureau of Investigation (FBI) on the preliminary investigation into the attacks were astounding. It was reported that nearly 7 000 investigators and support personnel were following up '35 000+ leads' and looking into 'numerous international possibilities'.

Secondary scenes of incident related to the 9/11 attacks included vehicles at several airports, apartments and hotels spread across several locations in the USA that had to be secured.[18]

Example 6.5: A maritime scene of incident

The April 2011 investigation on board a Very Large Crude Carrier (VLCC) at sea off Durban in KwaZulu-Natal is an example of a scene of incident that presented extraordinary challenges due to the entire vessel being the scene of incident and situated in the maritime domain. The VLCC was the largest oil tanker ever hijacked. It was held hostage by Somali pirates for 58 days prior to the scene being processed by a team of forensic experts and investigators.

As the VLCC was too large to enter the Port of Durban, the scene of incident was located approximately five nautical miles offshore and presented numerous challenges, some of which included the following:[19]

- access to equipment and the availability thereof were hampered due to the location of the scene of incident at sea
- increased moisture and humidity at sea level adversely affected some of the forensic equipment used to process the scene of incident
- the performance of the investigation team members on board the VLCC was adversely affected by some instances of motion sickness
- communication between members of the investigation team was hampered by poor cellphone signal strength off the coast and handheld radios were not available for communication between team members
- the VLCC's crew members could not be removed from the scene of incident during interviews and scene-processing activities as would normally be the procedure at a terrestrial scene of incident
- there were no standing operating procedures (SOPs) in place for scenes of incident of this nature.

Figure 6.4: The VLCC lying five nautical miles off the coast of Durban

19 Fouché & Meyer (2012) 1-18.

6.6 PROCESSING THE SCENE OF INCIDENT

Once investigators arrive at a scene of incident they should immediately be briefed by the first responder regarding everything that had transpired prior to their arrival. This information is crucial and will help investigators to get an initial sense of the situation and a preliminary idea of the type of evidence that should be searched for at the scene of incident. Investigators should never approach a scene of incident haphazardly. Before initiating the actual investigation, they can only benefit from reminding themselves of some basic principles regarding the scene of incident:

- No investigator has the luxury of processing the same scene of incident twice. The investigator should therefore use every opportunity to solve the incident.
- Evidence or information not gathered on the first visit to the scene of incident may significantly derail the investigation.
- Neglected evidence at the scene of incident will inevitably lose its integrity due to contamination and may even result in the wrongful arrest of an innocent person.

Investigators should bear in mind that the principles pertaining to the scene of incident remain the same regardless of the type of scene of incident and despite the fact that the scene of incident could be extraordinary and extremely unapproachable due to the unique circumstances of that particular case.[20]

The processing of the scene of incident should not be regarded as a one-off or isolated task. Instead, similar to the systematic nature of forensic investigation, the processing of the scene of incident consists of numerous subactivities that should as far as possible be conducted systematically and in a sequential manner. The prevailing circumstances (type of incident, scale of the scene of incident, weather conditions, availability of experts and resources, etc) will dictate which strategies should be followed when processing the scene.

In workplace (corporate) investigations an investigation team must be constituted irrespective of the complexity of the investigation. This team usually consists of fact-finders or investigators, the project manager and a legal counsel or an attorney.[21]

It is at this point that a decision will have to be made whether a crime scene manager (CSM) should be appointed at the scene of incident. In the corporate environment this person is usually referred to as the project manager (PM). The main responsibility of the CSM will be to manage all the role-players at the scene (investigators, forensic experts and technicians, uniformed police officials, medical personnel) as one team. The CSM is also responsible for 'protecting' the role-players at the scene of incident from unnecessary interferences, acting as

20 Prinsloo (1996) 20.
21 Ferraro (2006) 209.

a communication liaison person and alleviating any unforeseen burdens that might be experienced by role-players.[22] The CSM should as far as possible be a senior member of the investigation team with a wealth of investigation experience, should possess excellent communication skills and have the ability to coordinate a multifaceted investigative approach at the scene of incident.

The following are some of the functions of the project manager in corporate investigations:[23]

- day-to-day fact-finder supervision
- periodic preparation and dissemination of reports
- timekeeping and record administration
- law enforcement liaison
- expense and budget management
- team communication
- project coordination
- mission achievement.

What follows are numerous activities pertinent to the processing of the scene of incident.

6.6.1 First walk-through

A small team, usually consisting of the investigator (who will be responsible for the case docket/evidence file), the CSM/PM and a forensic fieldworker, also referred to as the crime scene technician, will conduct an initial walk-through at the scene of incident. The team should take brief notes and make observations while taking great care not to disturb any evidence because the scene will be processed later. The walk-through provides the investigator with an opportunity to generate an initial hypothesis of what had transpired and, in conjunction with the CSM/PM and the crime scene technician, stimulate ideas for processing the scene.

The first walk-through can be divided into two phases:

- The first phase will entail the investigator, the CSM/PM and the crime scene technician obtaining a holistic view of the scene of incident and making brief notes on the different types and locations of evidence. This will generate an initial idea of the anticipated workload that will have to be divided among members who will process the scene. With due consideration to prevent contamination, a witness could be used to accompany members during the first walk-through in order to point out key aspects such as where a suspect could have left fingerprints, or to point out concealed evidence.

22 R Swanepoel, detective attached to the Directorate for Priority Crimes Investigation (Hawks). Statement to author, 31 October 2011, Port Elizabeth.

23 Ferraro (2006) 211-212.

- The second phase will consist of generating specific enquiries as to the nature and origin of each key aspect observed during the first phase.[24]

Example 6.6: Brief notes, observations and enquiries generated during the first walk-through

Aspect/Evidence	Position (Phase 1)	Enquiry (Phase 2)
Brown leather wallet containing money (notes)	Kitchen floor, next to silver rubbish bin	Who is the owner? If property of the victim, why was it not stolen?
Disconnected computer cables	Lounge, behind desk	What is missing? Desktop? Laptop? Is there internet connectivity?
Cellphone	Kitchen, on top of breakfast nook counter	Ownership? Last known calls? To whom? When? Link?

On completing the first walk-through, the investigator, the CSM/PM and the crime scene technician now have an initial sense of the crime situation based on the overall appearance and condition of the scene of incident. The sum total of this information will now have to be considered by the investigator, the CSM/PM and the crime scene technician to develop a systemic plan to process the scene of incident.

6.6.2 Planning

Preparation and a clear division of roles is of the utmost importance. The different skills and experience of experts and aids at the scene of incident are among the factors that should be considered when assigning individuals to specific roles.

A general distribution list can be used by the investigation team as part of a response plan to scenes of incident. The distribution list will stipulate who should assume responsibility as the chief investigator at the next scene of incident. The chief investigator will then also be responsible for the subsequent investigation of the case. The responsibilities assumed by members of the investigation team will then change on a rotational basis from one scene of incident to another. This will build capacity and skills among members of the investigation team and will prevent overload.[25]

24 R Swanepoel, detective attached to the Directorate for Priority Crimes Investigation (Hawks). Statement to author, 31 October 2011, Port Elizabeth.

25 R Swanepoel, detective attached to the Directorate for Priority Crimes Investigation (Hawks). Statement to author, 31 October 2011, Port Elizabeth.

When a scene of incident has to be investigated, a planning session takes place to brief all role-players on the observations and notes made during the first walk-through at the scene of incident:

- The crime scene technician will be responsible for coordinating and managing the activities of the different experts who will be processing the scene. He or she will be in constant communication with the CSM/PM and the chief investigator.
- Experts will be briefed on the key aspects and physical evidence at the scene of incident, and will agree on investigation methods and processing activities.
- The evidence recorder will be responsible for maintaining the exhibit log. This is an important role.
- The chief investigator will brief the investigation team on different roles, which may include gathering intelligence, interviewing witnesses and taking statements, participating in the search and securing evidence such as CCTV footage.

Enquiries linked to specific aspects or physical evidence noted during the first walk-through will furthermore guide investigators to make use of different sources of information by involving various experts (see tables 6.1 and 6.2). It should be borne in mind that prevailing circumstances and the scale of the scene of incident will ultimately determine the level of planning and the different roles that will be assumed. At many small-scale scenes of incident the investigator and one expert (a fingerprint expert or a photographer) are more than sufficient to process the scene.

6.6.3 Recording of evidence

The continuum of evidence recording starts when the incident has been reported and ends when the proceedings are finalised at the relevant tribunal. The recording of evidence is intertwined with every decision and activity that takes place at the scene of incident. No incident, crime scene or any piece of information from an informer or member of the public can be overdocumented. It is investigators' responsibility to ensure that every resource at their disposal is used optimally at the scene of incident in order to reconstruct the scene and understand what transpired before, during and after the commission of the incident. Accurately maintained records of the scene and evidential items recovered serve to prove the integrity and ensure the chain of custody of each item.[26] These records should bear evidence that each item collected was kept intact, remained undisturbed and is presented in court in the same condition as when collected at the scene of incident.

26 Trueman (2009) 51.

The size of the scene of incident and the volume of potential evidence are two of the factors that are considered when the crime scene technician and the processing team decide on a specific numbering convention. An exhibit found during the search is allocated a unique alphanumerical indicator according to the numbering convention used at that particular scene of incident. This is normally done by zoning the scene, for example 'A1' is a cartridge case in Zone A, the kitchen. The exhibit is then marked with a visual scaled alphanumerical marker (showing distance and the size relationships of objects) and documented *in situ* by means of a video recording and photographs. It is further plotted on a sketch and recorded on a scene report.[27] The marking of evidence occurs during the search phase as each item of evidence is located and collected. The type of mark placed on the object depends on the following factors:[28]

- the size of the object
- the physical nature of the object (ie solid or liquid)
- the value of the object
- the number of like objects.

© Phillip Bekker, South African Police Service

Figure 6.5: Marking of exhibits at a scene of incident

Methods of recording include investigation notes, video recordings, photos, sketches and tape recordings.

27 P Bekker, forensic expert attached to the Eastern Cape Provincial Criminal Record and Crime Scene Management Centre. Statement to author, 31 October 2011, Port Elizabeth.

28 Gilbert (2004) 107.

6.6.3.1 Investigation notes and pocketbooks

Taking complete and accurate investigation notes is probably one of the most important responsibilities of any investigator attending to a scene of incident that needs to be reported on during criminal, civil or disciplinary action. Testimony during the relevant tribunal is often required months or even years after such a scene of incident has been attended to by the investigator, and a single undocumented fact or observation may just be the difference between a conviction and an acquittal. Everything discovered at the scene of incident should be recorded sequentially as it happened. The location and description of objects at the scene should also be meticulously recorded. Basic visual depictions of objects in the form of a sketch can complement these recordings in investigation notes. It is of the utmost importance that investigation notes are clear and understandable because it may cause additional challenges and delays at a later stage if notes are illegible. The extent of notes is more or less proportionate to the seriousness of the incident. For example, a housebreaking investigation may not merit as many detailed notes as a murder investigation.[29]

Investigators should use a pocketbook, which should be kept up to date at all times. Practical advice on the completion of a pocketbook includes the following:[30]

- Make entries without delay about investigations carried out, statements taken and exhibits seized, with details of the exact place, time and reference numbers.
- Document answers to the questions who? what? when? where? why? and how? (the W×5; H principle).
- Record complete details and descriptions of observations relating to the deceased, the victim and the suspect.
- Record detailed information and contact details of all role-players at the scene of incident.
- If investigators write down what a person says to them, they should do so in direct speech and make sure that they record the conversation verbatim, ie word for word.

Due to the fact that investigation notes may later be used by their author (ie the investigator, first responder or forensic fieldworker) to refresh their memory during judicial and quasi-judicial proceedings, the admissibility requirements should already be kept in mind as investigation notes are made. When witnesses want to refresh their memory by using notes or documents, the state must lay the grounds for admissibility by proving that such notes are:[31]

- *authentic*: witnesses wrote the notes themselves or they were written on their instruction

---

29 Fisher (2004) 53.

30 Grobler & Naicker (2008) 59-64.

31 Joubert (2010) 348.

- *contemporaneous*: witnesses must have made the notes during or immediately after the events
- *disclosed*: the other party is entitled to inspect the notes or documents and the court may also view them
- *the original document*: or true copies, even if the originals still exist.

Example 6.7: Documentation used to process scenes of incident

The following are some examples of reports and logs that are used in practice when scenes of incident are processed. They serve to ensure the recording of complete and detailed information, some of which may also be used to prove the chain of custody:

- report by the first member (first responder) attending the crime scene
- record of access to the scene of incident
- casualty log
- exhibit log
- witness log
- report by the CSM/PM
- report by the crime scene technician.

6.6.3.2 Video recordings

A video recording of the scene basically gives a general overview of the scene of incident. It may later prove to be valuable, especially when other role-players who were not present at the scene of incident have to come on board. They can then start by viewing the recording in order to better understand the dynamics of the scene. Similar to photography at the scene, the video recording should start from general to specific elements of importance at the scene. The investigator should guide the video operator through the scene of incident and provide the narrative for visuals being recorded. No sweeping statements or unequivocal conclusions should be made by the narrator, eg '*Here we have the murder weapon containing the blood of the victim*'. Statements such as these can point towards prejudice when facts have not yet been established and evidence has not yet been scientifically analysed. Similarly, when a video recording is made of a scene of incident in the corporate environment, the narrator should refrain from using the names of the perpetrators even if these are known. Should it be necessary to refer to the perpetrator to indicate important aspects, it should be done without any indication of prejudice, eg '*This is the office of the financial manager, Mr RG Edwards ...*'.

Narration should include the details of the speaker (narrator), the date and time of the video recording, the location or address of the scene and the case number (if available). Important aspects or information should be included by the narrator as the scene is recorded.

6.6.3.3 Photographs

The scene of incident should be photographed as soon as possible after the investigation team has arrived on the scene so as to serve as a representation of the scene in its pristine state. Photography of the scene of incident is an ongoing process and will continue until every piece of potential evidence has been identified and recovered.[32] Forensic photography is discussed in chapter 5.

6.6.3.4 Sketches

Photographs alone are not sufficient for the adequate recording of a scene of incident. Sketches, however, clarify the appearance of the scene of incident, making it easier for prosecutors and the court to comprehend what has transpired.[33] Sketches drawn of the scene of incident will complement the photographs to establish a permanent record of objects found at the scene.

Aspects such as the condition of objects and their size in relation to one another are of the utmost importance. Distances between different objects, physical evidence, furniture, bodies, persons as well as the entrances and exits to and from a scene should be included in the sketch.

Non-movable objects should be used as a fixed point when indicating the location of different items in relation to one another. At least two measurements from a fixed point should be used to indicate each object at the scene of incident.

Fixed points at interior scenes may include walls, doors, a toilet or basin or any other fixed structure. At exterior scenes fixed points may include lampposts, an electricity substation or the pavement at the corner of a street.

It is important for investigators to understand the utility of sketches and develop their skills pertaining to the drawing of sketches. The following information should accompany a sketch:

- the details of the official who drafted the sketch
- the location of the scene
- the date and time that the sketch was drafted
- weather and lighting conditions
- any other factor that could prove to be important at a later stage.

6.6.3.5 Tape recordings

A tape recorder could serve as a valuable aid to the investigator. It should, however, never substitute or replace other methods of recording, ie investigation notes, video recordings, photographs and sketches. Audio recordings could be used if the circumstances at a scene of incident are of such a nature that note

32 Trueman (2009) 51.
33 Fisher (2004) 86.

taking is severely hampered by, among other things, weather conditions, lighting or dangers associated with active scenes, such as fire. In such instances the investigator could use a tape recorder by speaking clearly and describing aspects such as weather conditions and the date, time and location of each important observation. Making an audio recording is usually less tedious than note taking and a useful tool when the investigator faces time constraints. Furthermore, it serves as a reference for the investigator and complements other recordings with richer data.

6.6.4 Searching the scene of incident

Those involved in the search of the scene of incident should discard any assumptions or preconceived ideas about what they might find. By 'jumping to conclusions' those involved in the search unconsciously limit the effectiveness of the investigation.[34] For example, investigators may be searching an office block for evidence in a fraud case and then come across an office filled with stolen electronic merchandise. Flexibility in investigative strategies is an important buffer against unforeseen challenges. Those involved in the search should remain focused on the search area to which they are assigned in accordance with the search method decided on during the planning phase (see section 6.6.5).

Physical evidence is likely to be found during the search, but should not be handled immediately. It should first be photographed, recorded on the sketch of the crime scene and then be described according to the following criteria:[35]

- time and date that the evidence was found
- the location at which it was found
- the name of the investigator who located the evidence
- a description of the item
- identifying marks, if any, to further distinguish or individualise the item
- the names of officers who witnessed the discovery in order to add credibility to the investigator's statements during the trial.

The following are important aspects to consider during the search of the scene of incident:

6.6.4.1 Collateral evidence

Scenes of incident with a sexual theme, such as rape, child pornography, sexual assault and harassment, may result in the discovery of a diverse range of collateral evidence. Collateral evidence in sexual offences refers to any item that will not directly associate the offenders with the offence, but provides information about their sexual preferences, fantasies, interests and habits. It has value as

34 Gilbert (2004) 104.
35 Gilbert (2004) 104.

proof of intent and as a source of information. The finding and presentation of collateral evidence may influence bail, a guilty plea, sentencing or conviction. Collateral evidence in sex crimes involving children may include children's clothing or underwear, a variety of toys, or albums containing magazine pictures or drawings of children.[36]

6.6.4.2 Vehicles

Vehicles at the scene of incident are another valuable source of information. When searching a vehicle, it is important to keep the Locard exchange principle in mind, namely 'every contact leaves a trace'. Depending on the type of incident being investigated, the variety of evidence that can be found inside a vehicle is almost inexhaustible. Cigarette butts, chewing gum, food particles, beverage containers, clothing, fingerprints, receipts and other documents, soil particles and hair (both animal and human) are some of the pieces of evidence that may be found. The track of a vehicle tyre could also be compared with a disputed cast.

Another valuable source of information that should never be overlooked is a Global Positioning System (GPS). It can provide valuable information in organised crime investigations where patterns, communication and relationships between the targets of an enterprise need to be established. Personal contacts and places that are regularly visited are but a small fraction of possible intelligence offered by a GPS.

An increasing security issue is the illegal smuggling of people across borders. Long-distance drivers involved in this crime are very skilled at creating hidden compartments in a vehicle. These spaces are used for, among other things, transporting people or illegal immigrants, drugs, merchandise or any other item for the purpose of creating an additional or 'illicit' income.

6.6.4.3 Buildings, offices and residences

Those involved in the search of the scene of incident should exercise great caution because evidence may be found anywhere. Contrary to evidence at the scene that is clearly identifiable due to its size or visibility, such as a firearm, broken glass or a muddy footprint on a white surface, other evidence might be more difficult to locate. The most prominent types of minute evidence found at a scene include hair, fibres, soil particles, pieces of glass, liquids, bodily fluids, latent fingerprints and shoe impressions. Areas that are often undervalued during searches include rubbish bins, the inside of a stove or washing machine, toilets and hand basins, fireplaces, air-conditioning systems and air vents, the interior of a ceiling, drainage systems and areas underneath loose tiles or carpets. Small items such as a key or USB thumb drive can easily be hidden inside or underneath a computer tower. Adhesive materials are also used to affix items underneath drawers or office desks.

36 SAPS (2009) 193.

6.6.4.4 Complementary evidence

During the search of the scene of incident the investigator should remain open-minded by considering the subsequent interview and bail application in the event of a suspect being arrested. The value of a passport or visa found at the scene of incident or at the residence of a suspect implicated in a seemingly minor case such as theft or housebreaking may be viewed as insignificant, but could be a determining factor in a bail application. Complementary evidence may provide valuable insight into the habits and lifestyle – and thus the character – of the suspect. Family photographs, sporting equipment and pets may not be identified and collected as evidence, but can serve as a vehicle for establishing common ground and building a rapport with suspects when interviewing them. This principle is also used by hostage and suicide negotiators at active scenes of incident where rapport building with the 'subject' is viewed as a fundamental success in the journey towards stabilising a volatile situation.

6.6.5 Search methods

Available literature usually refers to the spiral, strip, grid and zone search methods.[37, 38, 39]

6.6.5.1 Spiral search method

The spiral search method is useful for both indoor and outdoor scenes. This method entails those involved in the search starting at the outer boundaries of the scene of incident and moving in a circular (spiral) fashion towards the centre of the scene. This method can be put to good use by a single searcher in a small indoor scene such as a room. By using this method, the chances of locating information outside the scene of incident and associating it with the scene itself are strengthened.[40]

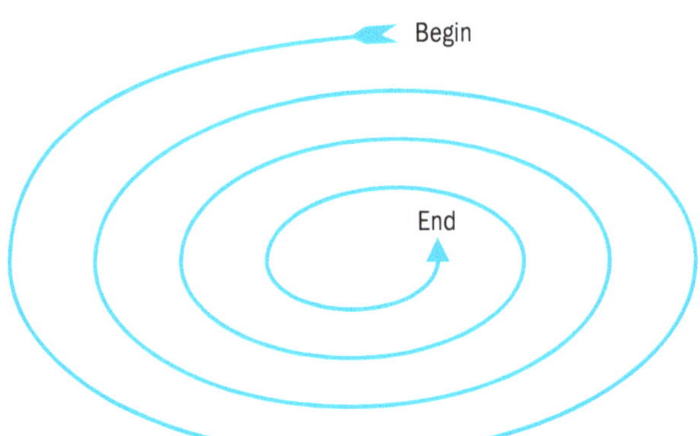

Figure 6.6: Spiral search method

37 Prinsloo (1996).
38 Gilbert (2004).
39 Fisher (2004).
40 Prinsloo (1996) 26.

Table 6.3: Advantages and disadvantages of the spiral search method

Advantages	Disadvantages
• Effective in small spaces. • The search can be executed by a single investigator. • Contamination of the scene is minimised when only one investigator is used.	• Value decreases as the search area expands. • Important evidence may be overlooked if only one investigator is involved. • It may be time consuming, especially at large outdoor scenes.

6.6.5.2 Strip search method

This method requires the searcher to start at one end of the scene while walking across, from left to right, to the other end. The searcher will then return to the starting point, not searching the same area as previously, but moving parallel to the original path, from right to left. The scene is therefore divided horizontally into small strips or lanes, each approximately one metre wide.

Figure 6.7: Strip search method

Table 6.4: Advantages and disadvantages of the strip search method

Advantages	Disadvantages
• Can be used indoors and outdoors. • Can be conducted by two or more investigators. • It is an uncomplicated but thorough search method.	• Dense or uneven outdoor scenes could be problematic to search. • It may require a number of investigators for effective use.

6.6.5.3 Grid search method

This method is based on the same principle as the strip search method. However, for the purpose of increased thoroughness the scene is divided into cross-sections. After searching the initial lanes from side to side (as for the strip search method) the investigators will continue to search across the original lanes, from top to bottom.

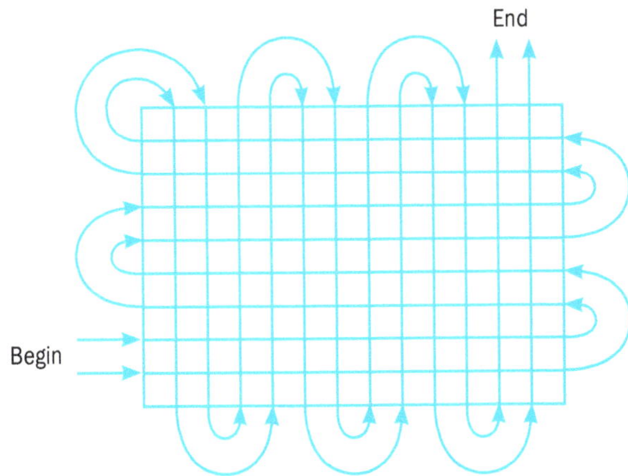

Figure 6.8: Grid search method

Table 6.5: Advantages and disadvantages of the grid search method

Advantages	Disadvantages
• Can be put to effective use indoors and outdoors. • Useful when searching large and open areas. • Valuable when searching for small items of evidence. • One or more investigators can carry out the search. • Each section is searched several times.	• It may require a number of investigators to perform the search effectively. • Dense or uneven outdoor scenes could be problematic to search. • Could be time consuming if only one investigator searches a large area.

6.6.5.4 Zone search method

The zone search method is also known as the sector search method. The scene of incident is divided into equal-sized sections. One searcher is usually assigned to each section. After completing a section, the searchers can be rotated (clockwise) to the next section and continue until all sections have been searched by different searchers.

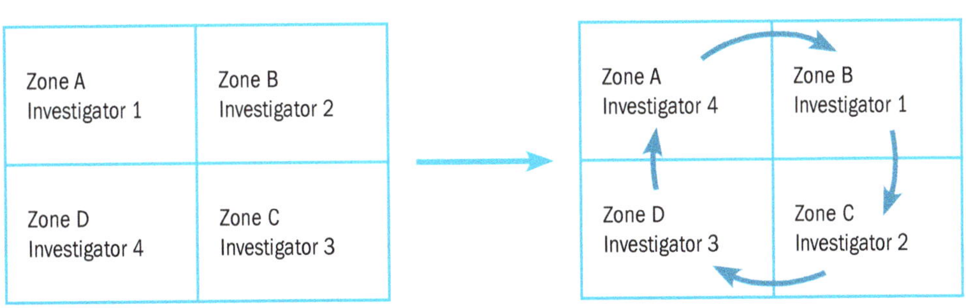

Figure 6.9: Zone search method using clockwise rotation

Table 6.6: Advantages and disadvantages of the zone search method

Advantages	Disadvantages
• Most effectively employed at outdoor scenes or indoors for very spacious rooms. • Thoroughness can be increased by rotating investigators to search each section.	• It may require a number of investigators to perform effectively.

6.7 COLLECTION AND PRESERVATION OF EVIDENCE AND THE CHAIN OF CUSTODY

Activities aimed at the collection and preservation of evidence and the chain of custody are interdependent and take place concurrently. Consider a major scene of incident where hundreds of evidential items are present. It may take many hours to collect evidence and to complete the different investigative activities. Each piece of evidence will have to be collected. From the moment of collection every effort should be made to preserve evidence and to prevent contamination until its presentation at the relevant tribunal. The chain of custody should also be initiated from the moment of collection. Each event and person who comes into contact with the collected evidence should be properly documented and recorded. This process should be followed for every item of evidence that is collected.

6.7.1 Collecting evidence

Those involved in investigations at the scene of incident should at all times be prepared by having the necessary tools or at least some of the basic equipment readily available. Scenes of incident are very similar to circumstances – both can be unpredictable! For example, a forensic fieldworker may not always be readily available or weather conditions at an outdoor scene may demand immediate action by the first responder or investigator. Similarly, an investigator busy with a corporate security enquiry may come across documentation which could later be essential in proving a criminal case of fraud. Documentary evidence is a 'mainstay' of fraud investigations[41] and probably one of the most frequently collected pieces of evidence at any scene of incident.

Some general rules for the collection and handling of documentary evidence include the following:

- examine documents for fingerprints
- place documents in a clean container such as an envelope or plastic bag
- handle documents with tweezers or rubber gloves
- make copies of the documents and only use the copies when interviewing complainants, witnesses or suspects

41 Hopwood et al. (2012) 226.

- do not damage the documents by using pins or punching holes in them for filing purposes
- do not write the case reference number or anything else on the documents
- keep detailed records of the documents, describe them and list the date, place and from whom they were received or where they were found
- issue receipts to the complainant, witnesses and the suspect.

Some of the fundamental equipment used by experts includes forceps or tweezers, latex gloves and an assortment of containers, namely envelopes, paper bags, forensic bags and glass jars. With a basic understanding of evidence integrity and preservation, these tools can be used by the investigator or first responder if a forensic fieldworker is not available. If gloves are not available at the scene of incident, a creative solution could be the use of a clean, flexible material which may be wrapped around the investigator's hand to function as a glove,[42] such as a clear plastic bag or a clean plastic shopping bag. Every effort should be made to handle evidence as little as possible.

The main collection techniques are:[43]

- *Removal of the whole object*: This is the preferred method to collect evidence. The complete object with no alterations or minimal damage is collected for processing in a controlled laboratory environment to maximise the number of sequential forensic processes. A single exhibit such as a firearm collected in the correct manner will yield not only ballistic evidence but possibly also fingerprints, touch-DNA, skin cells, blood, hair, fibres and contaminants.
- *Handpicking (tweezers or gloved hand)*: Single loose objects visible to the eye are collected from a larger object or surface, eg hair on a shirt or glass fragments embedded in skin. Disposable tools should be used to prevent cross-contamination.
- *Pipetting*: A sample of fluids is collected by means of a disposable pipette, eg petrol, vomit or liquid poisons.
- *Tape/gel lifting*: Adhesive gel lifters or strips of tape are applied to a surface to lift trace evidence, eg hair, fibres, botanical specimens, microscopic glass or plastic fragments and dust/stone particles. Adhesive stubs are used to lift microscopic evidence such as gunshot residue.
- *Sweeping*: Large amounts of trace evidence are collected with a disposable brush and pan from an area of interest.
- *Vacuuming*: Large amounts of trace evidence are collected with a hand-held vacuum cleaner from an area of interest, eg the boot of a vehicle. A removable sterile nozzle and filter attachment is used for each area.

42 Gilbert (2004) 107.

43 P Bekker, forensic expert attached to the Eastern Cape Provincial Criminal Record and Crime Scene Management Centre. Statement to author, 31 October 2011, Port Elizabeth.

- *Swabbing*: An area of interest is swabbed with dry or wet cotton- or polyester-tipped swabs. Microscopic material, eg blood or explosive residue, is collected due to the fibrous quality of the swab. This is the most effective method for collecting minute quantities of forensic evidence. A relatively large area can also be 'blind swabbed' for evidence, such as skin cells on a steering wheel.
- *Scraping*: A sample is collected by scraping a surface with a disposable scalpel blade or scraper, eg dried blood or foreign paint on a vehicle.
- *Cutting*: An area of interest is cut out of an object with a disposable scalpel blade to collect the sample, eg a bed sheet saturated with blood or semen.
- *Casting*: A casting medium such as forensic putty/silicone is used to replicate bite marks on skin and tool marks on a variety of surfaces. Impression evidence such as shoe prints in soil is cast by means of dental stone. This creates a removable three-dimensional physical copy of the evidence for macro- and microscopic comparisons.
- *High-resolution capturing*: Evidence such as fingerprints or spattered blood is digitally captured with a macrolens camera at a high-quality colour resolution for comparison or analysis. Microscopic digital images of trace evidence are captured for computerised tonal and spatial recognition.

The exhibit is lifted with an appropriate technique and packaged separately in a suitable container or bag (see Figure 6.10 and also section 4.2.5 in chapter 4). The container or bag is marked with a corresponding incident scene-specific alphanumerical indicator, initialled, dated and sealed with a unique tamper-evident seal. The case number or address is written on the package and documented with photographs. The process is recorded on the scene report and exhibit log.[44] It is of the utmost importance that the most delicate evidence or those items particularly vulnerable to changing weather conditions be collected first. Examples of these may include footprints and fingerprints. Evidence containing DNA such as blood, chewing gum, empty beverage containers and cigarette butts should then follow.

6.7.1.1 Reference samples

Reference samples with which disputed samples can be compared should as far as possible be obtained at the scene of incident. The reference sample is a sample of known origin, which will then be used in an attempt to identify the origin of the disputed sample. Hair found at a murder scene will be collected as evidence (disputed sample), which will then be compared to the hair of the victim, another known person or animal (reference sample) that had some relationship or

44 P Bekker, forensic expert attached to the Eastern Cape Provincial Criminal Record and Crime Scene Management Centre. Statement to author, 31 October 2011, Port Elizabeth.

link to the scene of incident. The same principle can apply to corporate investigations involving documents that contain evidence of sexual harassment, or to anonymous threats among employees within an organisation. The notes or letters written by the unknown suspect (disputed sample) can be compared to diary entries or written notes of known employees (reference samples) within the organisation in an attempt to identify and individualise the specific handwriting (see section 2.7 in chapter 2 for a discussion of individualisation).

6.7.1.2 Evidence or exhibit logs

Complex scenes of incident are usually synonymous with an increased volume and variety of evidence, which means that a greater number of investigators and experts will be involved in evidence collection. The person or investigator assigned as evidence recorder will be responsible for maintaining the evidence/exhibit log. At crime scenes this person will usually be an expert attached to the local Criminal Record Centre. The exhibit log will contain the details of the evidence recorder/exhibits official and, among others things, the description of exhibits, packaging type, seal and reference numbers, place where found and by whom, reason for collection and the details and signature of the member to whom the exhibits were handed over.

6.7.2 Preserving evidence

Preservation basically implies that evidence has to be maintained without altering, tampering, contamination, loss or injury.[45] Proper collection and packaging techniques for a specific type of evidence are also fundamental to preserving the condition of evidence.[46] Should some form of contamination or alteration to evidence occur, it should be noted and recorded immediately.

In an effort to promote the preservation of exhibits, the following steps are proposed when dealing with exhibits:[47]

- Collect and package different exhibits separately.
- Keep exhibits separate during safekeeping and keep the chain of custody intact.
- Prevent contamination or the introduction of foreign material to an exhibit. Use disposable sterile equipment (eg tweezers) and personal protection gear (eg a surgical mask and a full-body suit). Change gloves regularly.
- Collect transient exhibits such as shoe impressions and blood stains in outdoor scenes before environmental or accidental damage can occur.
- Collect and package fragile, volatile and small exhibits by using appropriate techniques and packaging, eg use sterile, airtight paint tins for arson-related exhibits to contain the volatile gases.

---

45 Marais (1992) 13.

46 Ogle (2012) 25.

47 P Bekker, forensic expert attached to the Eastern Cape Provincial Criminal Record and Crime Scene Management Centre. Statement to author, 31 October 2011, Port Elizabeth.

- Prevent the deterioration of biological exhibits by using drying processes and packaging the exhibits in porous paper-based containers. Wet bloody swabs should be mounted in breathable swab guard boxes before sealing them in plastic evidence bags.
- Prevent damage by stabilising exhibits inside the packaging, eg secure a firearm with cable ties in a cardboard box to protect fingerprints and the firing pin.

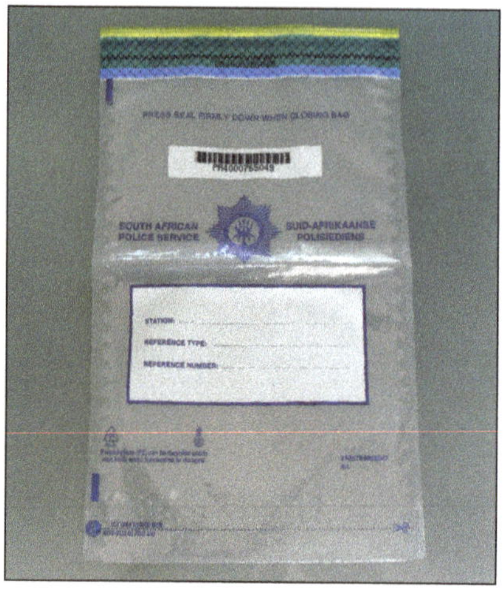

Figure 6.10: Evidence bags

In workplace investigations, the evidence file is a favoured tool used to catalogue and preserve evidence. The evidence file is a basic folder in which evidentiary documents are placed for safekeeping. A variety of 'tools' can be used in the corporate environment for the purpose of storing and preserving evidence. These may include accordion folders, corrugated boxes, filing cabinets, safes or evidence lockers.[48]

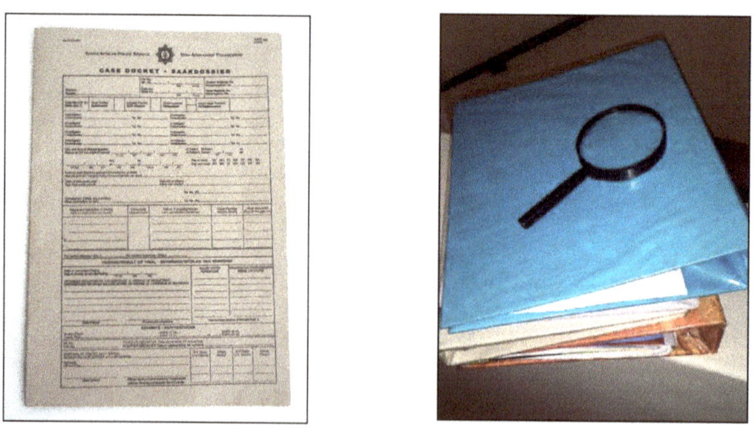

Figure 6.11: Examples of evidence files

48 Ferraro (2006) 92.

Subsequent to the collection of evidence at the scene of incident, the separately sealed exhibits are placed in a container or bag and kept under personal control at all times. The exhibits are then transported to the Exhibit Control Room as soon as possible and booked into safekeeping with the corresponding exhibit log. The exhibits are then placed in an access-controlled walk-in safe. This process and any subsequent movement or actions are recorded in a register and diary of the case docket to establish a chain of custody.[49]

6.7.3 Chain of custody

Also referred to as the 'chain of evidence' or the 'chain of possession', this fundamental principle in forensic investigation is intertwined with just about every phase of the investigation process. The chain of custody must be demonstrated in order to prove that the integrity of the physical evidence has been maintained.[50] The chain of custody will indicate who had contact with the evidence, at what time, under what circumstances and if changes were made to the evidence. In the event of any changes being made to the evidence, such changes must be fully disclosed. Similar to the SAP 13 storage facilities used by the police, access to evidence compounds or storage facilities in the corporate environment should be strictly managed to allow access to authorised personnel only, namely the private or in-house investigator, security or loss-prevention personnel.

The generic principles and sequential actions of personnel who come into contact with evidence are fundamental to maintaining the chain of custody, as the case study below illustrates.

Case study 6.1: Maintaining the chain of custody

A uniformed police official responds to information regarding the illegal possession of drugs on a street corner and arrests a suspect who is found in possession of two Mandrax tablets. The police official takes precautionary measures against the contamination of evidence and uses a gloved hand to confiscate the Mandrax tablets as evidence.

The police official then packages the evidence in a small forensic bag, seals and marks it with the corresponding case reference and SAP 13 register number. The evidence is then photographed, whereupon it is kept in safe custody in the SAP 13 storage facility. The case docket is assigned to an investigator who will be responsible for booking out the forensic bag from the SAP 13 storage facility, whereupon it will be submitted for analysis to the chemistry unit of the Forensic Science Laboratory.

The chain of custody and proper preservation will have to be proven by means of thorough documentation by each member who had contact with the evidence until it is received by the analyst. Corresponding and sequential details of time and reference numbers are of the utmost importance.

49 P Bekker, forensic expert attached to the Eastern Cape Provincial Criminal Record and Crime Scene Management Centre. Statement to author, 31 October 2011, Port Elizabeth.

50 Fisher (2004) 10.

Case study 6.2: A breach in the chain of custody – *S v Kaptein*

In the case of *S v Kaptein* 1984 (3) SA 316 (CPD) the court held that the chain of custody had been compromised after the pharmacist who gave expert testimony had measured the weight of dagga to 738 g instead of the original recorded mass of 745,5 g. The case presented further evidence of confusion caused by the improper marking of exhibits and the lack of accountability by members of the SAPS.

The following are some of the lessons learnt from the case of *S v Kaptein*:[51]

- All exhibits should be handled with care.
- Accurate records should be made each time exhibits are moved, handled or exchanged between one person and another.
- Exhibits should be properly marked and have sufficient and accurate records of measurements of quantity and weight.
- The handling of any exhibit should be minimised to the lowest number of people possible.

The proper management and filing of pocketbooks and notebooks should be viewed as an integral part of the preservation process. Once a pocketbook or notebook is full, it should be kept in safe custody. The reference number of each pocketbook or notebook should be recorded sequentially in an official register which meticulously accounts for the receipt and handing out of pocketbooks and notebooks to investigators. A lost pocketbook or notebook can cause a serious dilemma as it may effectively jeopardise the entire chain of custody.

The preservation process involves the forwarding of evidence to the laboratory for examination and analysis, obtaining it from the laboratory and keeping it safe under lock and key where it cannot be tampered with until it is presented in court.[52]

6.8 EVALUATION AND DEBRIEFING

It is important to reiterate that a scene of incident will never have the same value and potential for evidence collection once it has been cleared by the investigation team. If something was initially overlooked, the odds are great that it will be permanently lost. Maintaining control over the scene of incident is crucial for those involved in the investigation to retrace their steps and to 'double-check' the thoroughness of their work. This process is usually referred to as the evaluation phase. Role-players involved in this phase should ideally include the investigators and their teams, the duty officer from visible policing, the CSM/PM (if one was appointed), the crime scene technician, the various experts who fulfilled a role at the scene and a media liaison officer.

51 Dintwe (2009) 63.
52 Marais (1992) 13.

Aspects that are usually discussed during the evaluation of the scene of incident are the following:

- How comprehensively was the work conducted?
- What is outstanding and who is responsible for outstanding aspects?
- Have the necessary reports and documentation of exhibits been completed? If not, does the person responsible for completing reports and documentation have access to the relevant information?
- What are the do's and don'ts regarding the media? Will a press release be issued, and by whom? In the corporate environment this may relate to internal communications to management, clients and employees. Investments, sales and production are but some of the aspects that may be adversely affected by a corporate incident. Tactful internal communications are therefore fundamental to ensuring that rumours, exaggerations and fears are contained.
- Can the scene of incident be cleared up? If so, who will be responsible for the further investigation and to whom must progress in the investigation be reported?

A debriefing session after the evaluation of the scene of incident presents a platform for role-players to communicate what they consider to be the successes achieved, mistakes made, obstacles encountered and general shortcomings found in the approach and management of the scene of incident. Those present are given an opportunity to make suggestions for corrective actions, which could then be incorporated in the response plan for the next scene of incident that will inevitably come about. In this sense, the combination of an evaluation and debriefing of actions at the scene of incident can serve as a valuable quality management tool. It may further add value to the credibility of those officials who will give testimony about procedures followed at the scene of incident. Even though evaluation and debriefing are fundamentally an internal mechanism implemented by the role-players involved in processing the scene of incident, credibility may be promoted due to the iterative nature of evaluation and debriefing. These two steps reflect professionalism and competency and should be viewed as the final act of quality assurance at the scene of incident.

6.9 ARREST, DETENTION AND USE OF FORCE

Although it is beyond the scope of this chapter to exhaustively discuss arrest, detention and the use of force, it is the responsibility of every first responder and investigator who may engage with these actions at the scene of incident or during the further investigation phase to be informed and knowledgeable about their execution.

Arrest of a suspect was briefly referred to in section 6.5.4. The drastic and far-reaching consequences of ignorant and wrongful actions regarding arrest, detention and the use of force have a compounding effect on society as a whole. These consequences can range from an individual's rights to human dignity, privacy and even the right to life being compromised, to the subjugation of a country's economy and moral fibre. A recent revelation by the *Mail & Guardian* newspaper highlighted that civil claims against the police nationally have exceeded the R14 billion mark.[53] Notwithstanding the chaotic circumstances that may be present at the scene of incident, first responders and investigators should guard against acting with compulsion or responding to a speculative or emotional call by the public to make an arrest.

An arrest is effected when a person is taken into custody and is thereby deprived of freedom of movement. It should be noted that all arrested persons become detainees once they have been arrested. The continuation of a person's deprivation of freedom after an arrest hinges on numerous factors. These may include whether further investigation is required before the person is actually charged with the crime or whether that person may be released on bail, a warning or a written notice to appear in court.

Example 6.8: Arrest cannot be used to guarantee a person's presence in court

In the case of *Louw and Another v Minister of Safety and Security and Others* 2006 (2) SACR 178 (T) the court held that the decision to arrest is not an appropriate option for ensuring the suspect's presence in court if such a person:[54]

- does not represent a danger to society
- will in all probability attend his/her trial without the arrest
- will not abscond
- will not harm him-/herself and is not in danger of being harmed by others; and
- may be able and be keen to disprove the allegations against him/her.

Should the opposite of these factors be present, the police may have a legal duty to arrest a suspect in the interest of justice. The power to arrest is a fundamental tool in the quest for justice and the unfolding of due process in the criminal justice system.

The option to arrest should never be an arbitrary mechanism for exploitation and punishment. Section 39 of the Criminal Procedure Act 51 of 1977 (CPA) explains the manner in which an arrest should be effected and highlights that an arrest can be effected with or without a warrant. Prevailing circumstances during an arrest will dictate whether the use of force is justified or not. The use of force will obviously be excessive and unjustified if the person to be arrested submits to custody or if a mere touch to the body is sufficient.

53 Evans (2013).

Investigators and first responders to scenes of incident should consider the following five requirements of a lawful arrest:[54]

- The arrest must be authorised. The arresting official must either be in possession of an arrest warrant, or rely on the provisions of s 40 of the CPA.
- The person being arrested must be taken into custody physically and his or her freedom of movement must be restricted.
- The arrested person must be informed of the reason for the arrest as soon as possible during or immediately after the arrest has been made.
- The arrested person must be taken to a police station or prescribed authority as soon as possible.
- The arrested person who is subsequently detained must be informed of the rights of arrested and detained persons as contained in s 35(1) and (2) of the Constitution.

It may also happen that a member of the public is the first to arrive at the scene of incident and accost the suspect while the commission of a crime is in progress. In such instances s 42 of the Criminal Procedure Act 51 of 1977 authorises a private person to arrest, without a warrant, any person:[55]

> (1) *(a)* who commits or attempts to commit in his presence or whom he reasonably suspects of having committed an offence referred to in Schedule 1;
>
> *(b)* whom he reasonably believes to have committed any offence and to be escaping from and to be freshly pursued by a person whom such private person reasonably believes to have authority to arrest that person for that offence;
>
> *(c)* whom he is by any law authorized to arrest without warrant in respect of any offence specified in that law;
>
> *(d)* whom he sees engaged in an affray.

An example of an arrest carried out in terms of s 42(1)*(c)* can be found in s 9(1) of the Stock Theft Act 57 of 1959, where a private person may, upon reasonable suspicion that the other person has committed an offence mentioned in the Act, effect an arrest without a warrant.

The private person is furthermore authorised in terms of s 42(2) to:

> … forthwith pursue that person, and any other private person to whom the purpose of the pursuit has been made known, may join and assist therein.

Section 42(3) of the Criminal Procedure Act authorises the owner, lawful occupier or person in charge of a property to arrest any person who is found committing any offence, and any person authorised thereto by the owner, occupier or person

54 Joubert (2010) 242.
55 Joubert (2011) 130–131.

in charge, may without a warrant arrest the person committing the offence. Every male inhabitant of the country between the ages of 16 and 60 years is furthermore obligated in terms of s 47 of the Criminal Procedure Act 51 of 1977 to assist any police official who calls upon him to assist in the arrest and detention of a person.

Detention is interpreted as the most basic deprivation of a person's freedom. It therefore means that a person who has not yet been arrested can be detained prior to being arrested. Arrest in itself is therefore not necessarily a precursor to detention, for example where a motorist is stopped during a roadblock, where a person is taken to a police station for questioning or when a person is stopped and searched. However, it is important to inform that person that they are being detained and that the detention does not constitute an arrest. It should also be explained to a person being detained in such circumstances that they are under no obligation to accompany the police, but are free to go should that be preferred. However, the police may then have to arrest that person.[56] There is a fine line between the legal and the temporary detention of a person, for example at a road block, and illegally depriving a person of their freedom.

The use of force during the execution of duties relating to law enforcement and investigation should always be carefully considered within the ambit of the Constitution and relevant legislative instruments. In many instances the use of force becomes a necessity in activities relating to arrest, entering premises to search for persons or to seize articles, the protection of self and others, the prevention of crime or the escape of someone who poses a serious threat to the life of another person. First responders and investigators at the scene of incident should consider whether the use of force is necessary, justifiable and reasonable in the circumstances that prevail and must be able to account for the degree of force they use to reach a specific objective.

The principle of subsidiarity should always be considered as a yardstick despite the use of force being justified in certain circumstances. This principle suggests that if there is a reasonable alternative way of achieving the objective without the use of force, that alternative must be used.[57]

6.10 PRACTICAL HANDY HINTS

Recent times have seen an increase in the complexity of tasks managed by investigators. This calls for higher levels of professional competence if investigators are to perform their role effectively.[58] Many of the skills required in forensic investigation take a lifetime to develop. General knowledge, intuition and proficiency in specific investigative tasks, methods and techniques are not things that can be

56 Venter (2002) 182.
57 Geldenhuys (2002) 194.
58 Stelfox (2009) 2.

acquired in their totality by enrolling for a forensic investigation course or completing a detective learning programme. These skills and virtues develop parallel to the investigator's exposure to each and every scene of incident and its subsequent investigation.

Investigators are bound to make mistakes. However, the key is to view mistakes as a component of progress and learning while guarding against their repetition. Every investigator should take time to reflect on lessons learnt after completing an investigation at a scene of incident. Use a journal and record any uncertainties or hypothetical questions arising from your experience at the scene of incident and discuss them with experienced colleagues, experts or prosecutors. Such a journal could serve as a reference guide for future scenes of incident. Investigators should furthermore nurture a habit of reading and aspire to be up-to-date with answers to questions such as 'what are the latest developments in my specific field of forensic investigation?', 'what are the latest technology, methods or techniques that I can use?' and 'what is contained in recent case law relating to investigation and procedures at a scene of incident?' Academic journals and textbooks are valuable sources of information.

When attending a scene of incident, always be prepared and ensure that you have the following:

- sufficient stationery, such as your notebook, the relevant documentation, paper and pens
- sufficient resources and equipment, such as forensic bags and packaging material, gloves and protective gear, handcuffs, a torch, additional battery capacity for cellular and radio communication, a GPS or map book
- standby lists and the contact details of relevant experts and aids.

Consider the following handy hints when attending to the preliminary investigation at a scene of incident:

C-R-I-M-E S-C-E-N-E

C: CAUTION! YOU ONLY GET TO DO THIS ONCE!
R: Record everything by using available resources, aids and experts
I: Integrity of evidence at the scene must be maintained
M: *Modus operandi*: Who? What? When? Where? Why? and How?
E: Eliminate preconceived ideas and focus on facts

S: Systematic process and procedures
C: Chain of custody and preservation
E: Extensive notes on all aspects of the investigation
N: Never assume
E: Evaluate the process by retracing your steps

6.11 SUMMARY

The past decade has brought about a change in the role and responsibilities of the investigator as a specialist who is educated and trained to be knowledgeable about complex systems, societal differences and organisational theory.[59] The multifaceted activities involved in the preliminary investigation phase and the globalised world as the context within which modern-day forensic investigation takes place require investigators to respond appropriately. On a cognitive level investigators should think both holistically and critically about the incidents they investigate. Investigators should consider that every decision they make represents a piece fitted into the larger puzzle created by the incident under investigation. On a practical level, their decisions should be translated into actions characterised by the scientific method of forensic investigation. A systematic, planned and organised approach to the investigation at the scene of incident is well documented as the most effective defence against evidence contamination and the most viable in facilitating a solution to the incident puzzle.

REFERENCES

K Ajam 'APP-REHENDED! Bryanston family uses iPad to find assailants' *Saturday Star*, 30 June 2012

GR Brown 'The statement as a crime scene: Low-tech tools for corporate investigations' in RJ Montgomery & WJ Majeski (eds) *Corporate Investigations* 2 ed (Lawyers and Judges Publishing Company 2005)

WJ Chisum & BE Turvey *Crime Reconstruction* 2 ed (Academic Press 2011)

SI Dintwe 'The significance of biological exhibits in investigation of rape cases' (unpublished M Tech dissertation, University of South Africa, 2009)

S Evans 'Public claims against police exceed R14bn' *Mail & Guardian*, 24 April 2013

EF Ferraro *Investigations in the Workplace* (Auerbach Publications 2006)

BAJ Fisher *Techniques of Crime Scene Investigation* 7 ed (CRC Press 2004)

H Fouché & J Meyer 'Investigating sea piracy: crime scene challenges' 2 March 2012. *WMU Journal of Maritime Affairs*. Available at http://link.springer.com/article/10.1007%2Fs13437-012-0020-7, accessed 4 December 2013

T Geldenhuys 'Alternative techniques of investigation' in F Nel & J Bezuidenhout (eds) *Policing and Human Rights* (Juta 2002a)

T Geldenhuys 'The use of force' in F Nel & J Bezuidenhout (eds) *Policing and Human Rights* (Juta 2002b)

---

59 Osterburg & Ward (2010) 5.

NE Genge *The Forensic Casebook: The Science of Crime Scene Investigation* (Edbury Press 2004)

JN Gilbert *Criminal Investigation* 6 ed (Pearson Education 2004)

S Grobler & S Naicker *Investigative Principles for Policing 1: Study Guide for OVM1502* (University of South Africa 2008)

WS Hopwood, JJ Leiner & GR Young *Forensic Accounting and Fraud Examination* 2 ed (McGraw-Hill 2012)

BH Hulme 'The FCRA and corporate investigations' in RJ Montgomery & WJ Majeski (eds) *Corporate Investigations* 2 ed (Lawyers & Judges Publishing Company 2005)

C Joubert *Applied Law for Police Officials* 3 ed (Juta 2010)

JJ Joubert (ed) *Strafprosesreghandboek* 10 ed (Juta 2011)

CW Marais *Physical Evidence in Crime Investigation* (Henmar Publications 1992)

RJ Montgomery 'Doing business with your experts' in RJ Montgomery & WJ Majeski (eds) *Corporate Investigations* 2 ed (Lawyers & Judges Publishing Company 2005)

RJ Montgomery & WJ Majeski (eds) *Corporate Investigations* 2 ed (Lawyers & Judges Publishing Company 2005)

RR Ogle *Crime Scene Investigation and Reconstruction* 3 ed (Prentice Hall 2012)

JW Osterburg & RH Ward *Criminal Investigation: A Method for Reconstructing the Past* 6 ed (Anderson 2010)

J Prinsloo 'The scene of the crime as a source of information' in J van der Westhuizen (ed) *Forensic Criminalistics* (Heinemann 1996)

SAPS. South African Police Service 'National Instruction 22 of 1998: Sexual Offences: Support to victims and crucial aspects of the investigation' (Commissioner of the SAPS, Pretoria 1998)

SAPS. South African Police Service *Psychologically Motivated Crimes Course Learner Guide* (Government Printer, Pretoria 2009)

P Stelfox *Criminal Investigation: An Introduction to Principles and Practice* (Willan Publishing 2009)

K Trueman 'First officer attending' in R Sutton & K Trueman (eds) *Crime Scene Management: Scene Specific Methods* (John Wiley & Sons 2009)

M van der Watt 'The value of docket analysis in stranger rape investigations: A case study in Port Elizabeth' (unpublished M Tech dissertation, University of South Africa, 2012)

M van der Watt, S Grobler, G Jones & J Mokwena *Investigative Principles for Policing 1: Study guide for OVM1501* (University of South Africa 2012)

E Venter 'Arrest and detention – Part 2' in F Nel & J Bezuidenhout (eds) *Policing and Human Rights* (Juta 2002)

THE FURTHER INVESTIGATION PHASE

Chapter 7

T van Niekerk • H Lochner • Y Naidoo • RJ Zinn

Introduction
↓
Witnesses, victims and suspects
↓
Registering and opening a case docket or case file
↓
Tracing a known suspect
↓
Arrest of the suspect
↓
Follow-up investigation after arrest of suspect
↓
Search warrant
↓
Interviewing and interrogation
↓
Statements
↓
Alternative methods of obtaining information and evidence
↓
Motive
↓
Charging or releasing the suspect
↓
Statement and summary by investigator
↓
Case management
↓
Continuing victim support
↓
Summary

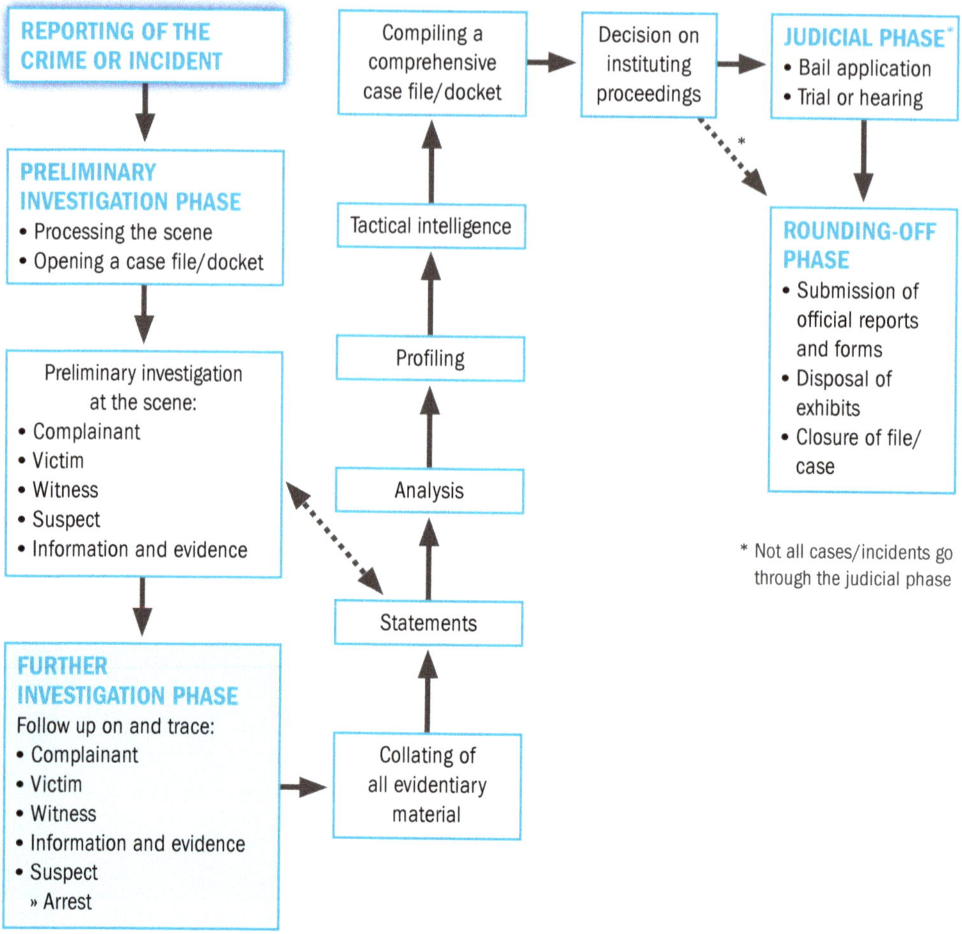

Figure 7.1: Areas of the crime investigation process covered in this chapter shown in shaded area

7.1 INTRODUCTION

After the preliminary investigation phase, the investigator embarks on the second phase of the investigation process, namely the further investigation phase. This phase starts immediately after the scene of incident has been completely processed. It must be noted, though, that certain things such as the arrest and the taking of statements may happen during the preliminary investigation phase. This mostly occurs when the suspect was found on the scene of incident and when other people such as victims, complainants and witnesses are still at the scene. However, more often than not, investigators focus on processing the scene of incident and then begin with other activities at a later stage. In that instance, these activities are seen collectively as the further investigation phase.

The three phases of the investigation (the preliminary investigation phase, the further investigation phase and the judicial phase) can be represented as follows in a diagram, with specific reference to the elements of the further investigation phase:

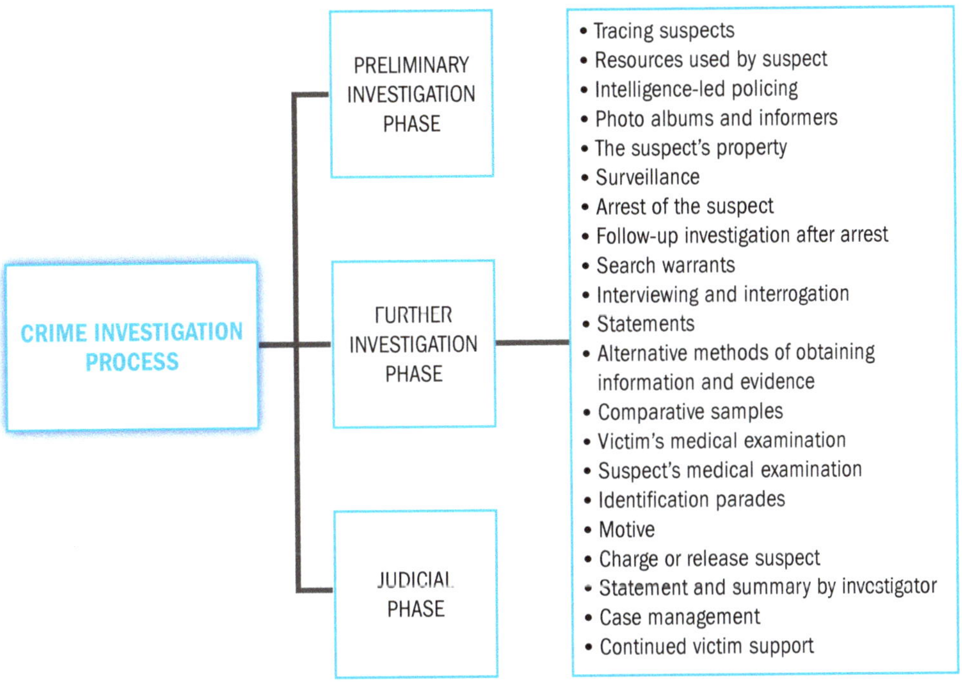

Figure 7.2: The three phases in the crime investigation process

The further investigation phase therefore starts after the completion of the processing of the scene of incident and continues until the case is handed over to the relevant tribunal, or closed. This means that all evidence, information and leads or clues are followed up to the point where the investigation is finalised.

The investigation can only proceed formally when it has been formally registered as a case or, in the case of a private investigation, after a mandate has been received. It is necessary to do all possible investigation in order to substantiate that a crime or other defined transgression has been committed. Registration of a case or a mandate is known as the situational identification. When *prima facie* evidence of such a crime or transgression has been established, the offender has to be identified and traced.

The case docket (in criminal cases) or the case file is then presented for final inspection before being forwarded to the prosecutor for criminal prosecution, or to the civil court, case manager or other quasi-judicial tribunal such as a disciplinary committee. During the course of this process, witnesses, victims and complainants are interviewed, suspects are interrogated and statements are obtained.

7.2 WITNESSES, VICTIMS AND SUSPECTS

Obtaining information is an essential procedure in the investigative phase of case preparation. As mentioned in chapter 6 (see sections 6.5.2 to 6.5.4), during the investigation process an investigator will encounter a variety of witnesses, such as eyewitnesses, expert witnesses, victims, spouses, children and others. Witnesses are often called before a court of law or other quasi-judicial tribunal to testify in trials. The oral testimony or evidence of a knowledgeable witness is often the investigator's primary source of information.

7.3 REGISTERING AND OPENING A CASE DOCKET OR CASE FILE

Unless this has already been done during the preliminary investigation phase, the investigating officer must obtain statements from the complainant and witnesses and open a case docket or case file.

A case docket (see Example 1.7 in chapter 1) is the official dossier that a police agency uses to file and permanently record the evidence it has gathered during the investigation of an offence. It helps to manage the investigation. This evidence also includes evidence that might be declared inadmissible in court.

A case file (see Example 1.8 in chapter 1) is the equivalent of the police dossier, but is used in private-sector institutions to permanently record the evidence that was gathered about an offence, transgression or irregularity.

When the witness, victim or complainant has been interviewed, the official assisting the witness, victim or complainant will determine whether a crime, an irregularity or a transgression has indeed been committed and whether there is any criminal or civil liability. In other words, the officer will determine whether all the elements of the crime, irregularity or transgression (which will differ from case to case) are present to necessitate investigations. The law defines a 'crime' as the unlawful and blameworthy conduct for which punishment is prescribed. The general elements of a crime can thus be identified as:[1]

- legality – the conduct is of criminal nature
- conduct – an actual physical act or omission must take place
- unlawfulness – the conduct is unjustified
- culpability, which includes capacity – the accused must have been criminally accountable (this includes intention or negligence).

The complainant must provide the official with information and particulars of the incident which allegedly has been or is likely to be committed. If witnesses are present, their statements must also be obtained. If the complainant was injured they must be requested to visit a doctor for an injury report (J88). Based on

1 Joubert (2010).

the seriousness of the matter and the availability of the perpetrator, an arrest may be effected. The investigator must stay abreast of the facts in issue, including the elements of the crime or incident, and must ensure that evidence is obtained to prove these elements.

The prosecutor relies on the information in the case docket to decide whether or not to prosecute. This also applies to transgressions that may not be criminal in nature. The case docket or case file must contain all the facts and evidence relevant to the case. These include documents such as photographs, sketches and medical and forensic reports. It sometimes happens that different cases and files are combined and that the master file, key dossier or key file contains all the relevant information and evidence.

In some instances, corporate companies such as banks and mining companies open their own case files. They investigate the case fully before either handing over the case file to the police or referring the case to an internal disciplinary committee. These corporates have forensic investigation departments that do all the investigations and gather all the evidence.

7.4 TRACING A KNOWN SUSPECT

Methods and techniques of tracing the suspect will vary according to the circumstances.

The basic steps include the following:

- following up on any possible leads or information which the investigator may have
- making use of informers to establish who committed the crime or incident and where the suspect can be found
- circulating the suspect's information in the media
- offering a reward if it is applicable
- if the suspect is on record for a previous conviction, obtaining his or her last known address and particulars from the Criminal Record Centre
- having fingerprints and palm prints compared with those of known suspects and other individuals found at the crime scene.

7.4.1 Using the suspect's ID number to obtain personal particulars

Obtaining the suspect's identification (ID) number provides a number of ways for the investigator to try to trace the suspect:

- *Vehicles:* Vehicles registered in a suspect's name can be traced by police using the vehicle registration computer (eNatis). This is done by checking the individual's ID number and/or names and their residential and work addresses.

All the addresses that were provided when the vehicle was registered should be checked as well. More than one address might be registered, such as the residential address, the postal address and the business address of the owner. The investigating officer should visit and monitor these places when trying to trace the suspect.

- *Telephone and cellphone companies*: The investigator should contact the local telephone company and cellphone companies for possible accounts, contact details, possible addresses and references given by the suspect. Cellphones can be traced through the South African RICA (Regulation of Interception of Communications) Agency. The Regulation of Interception of Communications and Provision of Communication-related Information (RICA) Act 48 of 2008 makes it compulsory for all cellphone owners to register their details. The following information is recorded during a RICA registration:
  - cellphone number
  - SIM card to be registered
  - full names and surname
  - proof of identity: green bar-coded ID document OR new Smart ID Card OR temporary ID certificate OR passport
  - the cellphone owner's home address on a document such as a bank statement, municipal bill, cellphone or retail account (not older than three months), existing lease, rental or credit agreement, insurance policy, current TV or motor vehicle licence document that includes their name and residential address OR if the applicant lives in an informal settlement they could submit a letter and/or affidavit from a school, church or retail store where they receive their mail (this letter must be on an official letterhead or bear the stamp of the school, church or retail store).
- *SAPS Criminal Record Centre (CRC)*: The investigator can contact the SAPS Criminal Record Centre to trace the suspect's last known address. If the suspect is found to be involved in a criminal investigation, the investigator should immediately circulate the suspect's particulars on the official police database.
- *Banking institutions*: Banking institutions can be contacted to establish whether the suspect has banking accounts. The South African Banking Risk and Information Centre (SABRIC) is a private initiative supported by various banks, security companies and other stakeholders in South Africa. SABRIC provides information and risk analyses to the banking and cash-in-transit industries to combat organised crime. It is therefore also a valuable source of information on crime risk information, possible suspects and their *modi operandi*. SABRIC also renders operational support to their clients with regard to intelligence, investigations and prosecutions, both criminal and civil. The investigating officer must follow up on these records and addresses and on references given by the suspect to banks (personal and other business accounts).

Electronic tabs can be placed on a suspect's accounts so that the bank can record where the suspect draws money and keep the investigator informed of the suspect's whereabouts. However, it is necessary to understand that all the abovementioned information has to be obtained legally.

- *Retail and other businesses*: The investigator should contact businesses or organisations where the suspect has been granted credit accounts, hire purchases, life insurance policies, short-term insurance policies, asset insurance and pension funds shares, etc. Information should also be obtained from companies and organisations such as the deeds office, courts (court records), professional bodies, the Department of Home Affairs, the voters' roll, time share on vacation properties, clubs, casinos, previous employers and car rental companies. These companies and organisations can be interviewed for more information on the suspect, for possible leads and for the personal and business references provided by the suspect.
- *'Blacklisting' companies*: Financial 'blacklisting' companies can also be contacted to find out whether they have any information on the suspect and their latest whereabouts.
- *Department of Home Affairs*: The Department of Home Affairs is a valuable source of information. The investigator can request any records of the suspect's last known addresses, records of the birth of children and marriage records. The suspect's spouse or former spouse(s) can be contacted and interviewed to ascertain the suspect's whereabouts. If the suspect is from a rural area, a local chief or elder might be a valuable contact in tracing the suspect or the suspect's relatives. Police officials can also check on passports issued or being issued.
- *XDS database*: Additional resources exist in the private domain, for example the private credit bureau Expert Decision Systems (XDS).[2] XDS retains information on an individual or company's vetting and screening, credit reports, biometric information, credit-related information, information on authentication, commercial reports, bank verifications, bank codes and other related or specifically selected information. All the information on the XDS database can be used to obtain more information on the activities of a suspect.

7.4.2 Using personal particulars to locate the suspect

Once the investigator has managed to obtain the suspect's full personal particulars such as ID number, address(es) and contact details, this information can be used for further actions to locate the suspect. These actions include obtaining a warrant for the suspect's arrest, personal interviews to establish the suspect's whereabouts and following various other avenues.

- *Warrant of arrest*: Once the suspect's personal particulars are known and the investigator knows where the suspect is, the investigator can obtain a warrant

2 http://www.xds.co.za, accessed 4 November 2013.

of arrest, if applicable. The investigator should apply for a warrant of arrest if the identity of the suspect is known and the circumstances justify an arrest. This is done by submitting a detailed affidavit containing all the details of the crime and the investigation, the particulars of the suspect, the grounds on which it is suspected that this particular person was involved in committing the crime and substantiating evidence, if any. The affidavit and the case docket are then taken to the state prosecutor. If the state prosecutor agrees, they will arrange for such a warrant of arrest to be issued by the court. Also see section 7.5.

- *Personal contacts*: The investigator can visit and interview the suspect's friends, family and workplace to determine the suspect's possible hiding places or favourite places of entertainment such as clubs or discos. The homes of the suspect's family and friends can also be visited, either regularly or at different times, to try to find the suspect. Studies of motor vehicle hijackers and house robbers have shown that suspects in the majority of cases kept in contact with especially their girlfriends and other friends while they were being sought by the police. If necessary, the suspect's contact persons can be kept under surveillance in case the suspect makes contact with them.
- *Business and personal references*: The investigator can follow up and interview business and personal references listed at retail and other institutions to establish whether these persons have any knowledge of the whereabouts of the suspect or any further possible leads. These persons should be encouraged to notify the investigator if they become aware of the suspect's whereabouts at any point in the future.
- *Medical scheme records*: A suspect's medical scheme records could also be used to trace their whereabouts.
- *Internet and social media*: The internet is a valuable tool for finding information on a suspect. An internet search for Facebook pages, emails, professional networks – such as LinkedIn – and alumni pages of universities and schools may provide valuable leads on the suspect's connections and where the suspect could be. Some of these pages might even contain photographs of the suspect. Other valuable sources are social media facilities such as Twitter, MXit, WhatsApp and BBM, all of which may provide information on the suspect.
- *Interpol*: If the suspect is suspected of having left the country, arrangements must be made through the SAPS head office for the monitoring of airports, border posts and harbours. Interpol can be alerted through the local Interpol offices to inform foreign police services to be on the lookout for the suspect.
- *Dealers in stolen goods*: It could be useful to visit pawnshops or known dealers in stolen goods to try to locate any property that was stolen or removed by the suspect. This could include the suspect's own belongings, which might have been pawned or sold to obtain cash.

7.4.3 Tracing resources that could have been used by the suspect

When a vehicle has been used in committing the crime or stolen, the investigator should first establish whether the vehicle has been fitted with a tracking device or an anti-hijacking system. In the case of a tracker system, the service provider should be notified immediately so that they may try to trace the vehicle.

If an anti-hijacking device has been fitted, the immediate radius around the crime scene should be searched as the anti-hijacking device will cause the engine of the vehicle to stall and prevent the vehicle from driving any further. Devices of this sort are usually set to cut the engine within a few minutes after the device has been activated.

The investigator should obtain the registration particulars of the vehicle and the insurance details if the vehicle was insured. In the case of a criminal investigation, the vehicle's details can be circulated on the SAPS computer system. The investigator can also visit known places or suspected dealers in stolen vehicles or parts.

If the vehicle is found, fingerprints must be lifted from the vehicle and from objects within it, and the vehicle must be cancelled on the SAPS computer system before it is returned to the owner. Once the vehicle or other stolen property (eg cellphones) is recovered, it must be identified by the owner.

7.4.4 Intelligence-led policing

The investigator should use intelligence-driven tactics by obtaining all possible intelligence on the crime and the suspects, the *modus operandi* information available at the Criminal Record Centre, the names of possible dealers or syndicates and places where stolen goods and vehicles are sold, and follow up all possible leads.

Investigators should:

- communicate to their colleagues as much information as possible that can lead to the tracing of the suspect
- communicate the relevant information to relevant police stations and police structures
- study the *modi operandi* of known criminals because these could reveal similarities among crimes
- try to identify possible accomplices of the suspect
- try to identify other crimes in which the suspect might have been involved
- if the suspect was possibly involved in other crimes, follow up on those investigations to determine whether there are possible additional leads on the whereabouts of the suspect.

7.4.5 Using crime photo albums and informers as resources

Crime photo albums are useful resources to investigators who are trying to identify suspects. An identikit of the suspect can be composed and circulated in the public media.

Informers are one of the most valuable resources in crime information. Investigators can task their informers with trying to trace the suspect. Depending on the merit of the case and the contribution made by the informer to solve the case (ie a conviction), the investigator should apply for a reward for the informer. Always be wary, however, of the ulterior motives an informer might have as they are usually involved in crime themselves. This is how informers usually get their information on other criminals.

7.4.6 Suspect's property

The possessions of possible suspects must be searched. The investigator should establish if there are reasonable grounds to do so and apply for a search warrant (see section 7.7 for more details). If the premises of a suspect are searched it might be of value first to keep the premises under surveillance to determine at which times the suspect is present.

7.4.7 Surveillance

There could be possible accomplices who might visit the suspect. All people entering and leaving the suspect's premises should be observed, including their vehicles. The investigator can run ownership traces for the further investigation and possible identification of accomplices.

The investigator could also apply for permission to intercept and monitor the communication of the suspect via mail, telephone, cellphone and the internet. This permission is granted in accordance with the Interception and Monitoring Prohibition Act 127 of 1992.

7.5 ARREST OF THE SUSPECT

Depending on the circumstances, a warrant of arrest may have been issued for the arrest of the suspect. If the identity of the suspect is not known, it will obviously not be possible to obtain a warrant and the person, when found, will have to be arrested without a warrant.

See section 6.9 in chapter 6 for the requirements of a lawful arrest. For a discussion on the legal aspects see *Applied Law for Police Officials*.[3]

When suspects are arrested, investigators must ensure that arrested persons are informed of their rights, ie their constitutional rights as well as the Judges' Rules,

3 Joubert (2010).

immediately after arrest. Arrested persons must be taken to a police station for detention and be made to appear before a lower court within 48 hours of arrest. Unless a warrant of arrest specifies that the arrested person must be taken elsewhere, they must be taken to a police station as soon as possible. If the person is not released sooner because no charge is to be brought, they may be detained for up to 48 hours.

7.5.1 J175 summons

As an arrest constitutes a serious infringement of the fundamental rights of the individual, an arrest cannot always be used to secure the attendance of an accused person in court. In cases where an incident was committed and the seriousness of that incident did not justify the immediate arrest of the person involved, a J175 summons may be issued. This means that in criminal matters a peace officer may under strict conditions issue a J175 summons for a suspect to appear in court.

In practice it is sometimes found that a fully investigated case docket with all evidential material will be handed to the prosecutor. An investigator or any person authorised by the higher authority may discuss the docket with the prosecutor. Based on whether there is *prima facie* evidence in the case docket the prosecutor will then decide whether to prosecute that individual or not. If the suspect will be prosecuted, a J175 summons will be issued for the suspected person to attend court and be formally charged for the offence brought against them.

7.5.2 Indictment

An indictment can be used in a case that serves before a high court. In such cases a document can be prepared containing detailed information of the charge. This document can then be served on the suspect, with the effect of having the suspect appear before the court on a specified date.

7.6 FOLLOW-UP INVESTIGATION AFTER ARREST OF SUSPECT

Research has shown that the investigator's first contact with the suspect after arrest can be decisive because this is the most likely time that the investigator will get cooperation from the suspect. It is important to keep a proper and detailed record of the suspect's initial reaction and what they said or did when first confronted and arrested.

- The investigator should note the suspect's immediate reaction because it may be relevant during the trial, eg attempting to destroy exhibits by trying to burn them or flushing them down the toilet.

- Any comments or denials made by the suspect after being informed of their rights might also constitute confessions or admissions. The investigator should record in detail any statements, admissions or confessions made by the suspect.
- After arrest the investigator must obtain the suspect's fingerprints and forward them to the Criminal Record Centre (CRC) for comparison with those found at the crime scene. The suspect's previous convictions must be obtained from the CRC on form SAPS 69.
- After the suspect has been arrested, the investigator must search for relevant exhibits in the suspect's possession, such as shoes that fit the footprints found at the scene.
- If a suspect wants to make a confession, the investigator should arrange that the suspect can be taken to a magistrate for the taking down of the confession and/or for a police officer (a commissioned rank officer or a Justice of the Peace) to take the suspect for the pointing out of the crime scene and/or exhibits.
- When a firearm is found at the scene or in possession of the suspect, the investigator can use the serial number of the firearm to trace the owner. If the firearm has been reported stolen, the reference number and a statement to that effect should be obtained from the owner.
- An identification parade must be held.
- The investigator should search the arrested person's residence and workplace. On the basis of reasonable grounds, the suspect can be charged and their warning statement obtained.
- If a cellphone has been stolen or used by the suspects, it should be reported as stolen to the service provider (eg MTN, Vodacom or Cell C). The cellphone can be traced by monitoring the service provider's network.
- The investigator should check the alibis of possible suspects. This is necessary to be able to either refute or substantiate their alibis in court. The investigator should also visit the places that form part of the suspect's alibi, and/or persons who form part of the alibi. A suspect's alibi can be either refuted or supported by proper interviewing and following up supporting evidence, such as recorded images of closed-circuit cameras (CCTV) in city centres and at petrol stations, in public places and at places of entertainment.

7.7 SEARCH WARRANT

When premises have to be searched for exhibits, it is always advisable to apply for a search warrant in advance. In certain cases the lawful occupant will give the investigator permission to conduct a search without a warrant. If, however, the investigator first goes to the premises without a search warrant only to be turned away, this may alert the occupants and risk exhibits being destroyed in the time it takes the investigator to apply for a warrant.

A search warrant is usually only obtained once a detailed statement under oath or affirmation has been submitted by the investigator, justifying the search and describing what is to be searched for.

The search warrant must authorise an investigator to seize the specific object mentioned in the search warrant. While s 22 of the Criminal Procedure Act 51 of 1977 makes provision for an officer to search and seize without a warrant, this is only permitted in exceptional circumstances. An officer may search and seize without a warrant where there is an immediate threat to a person or property, or where there is reasonable ground to believe that a search warrant will be issued if they applied for it and that a delay will defeat the object.

For a discussion of the legal aspects, see *Applied Law for Police Officials* by Joubert.[4]

7.8 INTERVIEWING AND INTERROGATION

While the comparative value of physical evidence is strongly emphasised, verbal evidence obtained through interviewing and interrogation plays an important role in obtaining all possible information on a crime or an incident under investigation. The investigator obtains this verbal information by interviewing the witness and interrogating the suspect. Interviewing and interrogation refer to the 'unlocking' of a person's thoughts during the process of gathering information. While information may be obtained by asking questions, it may also be given voluntarily, such as when a person reveals all the facts without being prompted with questions.

7.8.1 Interviewing

Interviewing can be described as the process of communication between an interviewer and an interviewed person (the interviewee). The principles of freedom and privacy apply during this process. In the criminal investigation context the person being interviewed is a witness, a victim or a complainant. This person is not suspected of committing a crime and is therefore neither detained nor the subject of legal prosecution. The purpose of such an interview is to obtain information concerning the interviewee's knowledge of a specific incident or any other information they may have that could lead to determining the truth to resolve the matter and trace the suspect or exhibits.

7.8.2 Interrogation

Interrogation, as distinct from interviewing, entails communication between the interrogator and the interrogated person. In the criminal investigation context this person is either a suspect or an uncooperative witness (also known as a

4 Joubert (2010).

hostile witness – see section 7.8.3). The suspect under interrogation maintains their constitutional rights, such as the right to remain silent and the right to not provide evidence against themselves (in other words not to provide incriminating evidence). Nevertheless, by means of s 205 of the Criminal Procedure Act 51 of 1977, a hostile witness can be forced to appear before a magistrate to provide information on a criminal incident which they refuse to reveal to the police.

Interrogation thus refers to the formal questioning of a suspect in order to establish their identity and whether the suspect wants to offer an alibi or other facts to exonerate themselves from the crime or incident. It also includes questioning to find out whether the suspect wants to disclose facts willingly about the crime or incident or provide a written statement (a warning statement, for example); or to find out whether the suspect is willing to point out a crime scene or exhibits.

In this book not all the possible judicial restrictions on interrogation are discussed and the list here is not exhaustive. The reader should therefore consult books on law and policing for more information on this topic. Here only concise legal information with practical implications for the investigation process is provided.

Investigators should be fully aware of the judicial aspects that guide the interrogation process. This is necessary to ensure that the information they obtain is admissible as evidence in court or at a hearing and to protect themselves from civil claims against them for illegal or unconstitutional conduct. It is important to thoroughly analyse every aspect of the interrogation so that the information thus obtained will meet the requirements of admissibility for confessions, admissions and pointing out. Investigators will be assured of success if they adhere to all the legal prescriptions for obtaining evidence. For example, following the guidelines set out in the Judges' Rules will assure the admissibility of the evidence and success in court. Read more about these aspects in *Applied Law for Police Officials*.[5]

Interrogation is an art that requires careful study and lots of practice. Interrogators must learn how to approach different people and how to use different techniques, among other things. They must be able to assess the suspect or witness in a short period of time and then decide which approach or technique to use. The interrogator must bear in mind that an incorrect approach may antagonise the witness or suspect.

The investigator will find that interrogation is a complex and demanding task. Interrogations require proper planning on how they should be done and what interrogation technique should be used. The interrogator must be able to understand and be understandable to the specific suspects, and to read, understand and react appropriately to the personality of the suspect. The investigator should

5 Joubert (2010).

study the details of the case before embarking on the interrogation and the interrogation must be timed for the most opportune moment during the investigation.

Interrogation should not be confused with 'extraction'. Extraction is an approach in which investigators force suspects to reveal information that they are not prepared to offer voluntarily. As the rights of the individual are ignored in this method of gathering information, extraction is almost always illegal.

7.8.3 Uncooperative witnesses

Certain witnesses may not be willing to cooperate with the investigation. Typical of these are corporate institutions such as banks, medical institutions and businesses, or professional people such as doctors. They will quite likely not be willing to provide the investigator with information on their records concerning the suspect. The reason will be their ethical considerations, and sometimes legal considerations that govern their relationship with their clients.

If the investigator encounters a witness who can be legally compelled to make a statement during the investigation of a crime but refuses to do so or to make the information available to the police, the police can then apply for a subpoena in terms of s 205 of the Criminal Procedure Act 51 of 1977 to force that person to make the information available. The application of s 205 of the Criminal Procedure Act is discussed in section 7.8.4.

It is often not necessary to actually apply and serve institutions such as banks with a section 205 subpoena because banks may provide the investigator with the information on the basis of a letter from the investigator's investigation unit. In this letter it should be stated that the investigating officer requires the information for a specific criminal investigation and that they will apply for a section 205 subpoena should the specified information not be forthcoming. This will enable the institution to justify why they agreed to provide the information to the investigator should their cooperation be questioned at some point. Excellent results and cooperation can be achieved by proper and professional communication with such institutions.

7.8.4 Section 205 subpoena

A section 205 subpoena is directed to the person who holds information that may be relevant to the commission of a crime or incident, or who has access to specific information.

A judicial officer may subpoena any person to give evidence or provide documents needed as evidence in the investigation of a particular case. This is provided for in s 205 of the Criminal Procedure Act 51 of 1977 (CPA). Section 205, read with s 189 of the CPA, makes it a criminal offence for a person to refuse to supply information that may be relevant to the commission of an alleged incident. Unless the person is deemed to have a 'just excuse', in terms of s 189, for failing or refusing to furnish the required information, they may be rendered liable to a prison sentence of up to five years without an option of a fine.

The investigator should maintain the highest degree of integrity and professionalism in conducting the investigation. A good investigator gains the confidence of a witness and is thus more likely to obtain all the relevant information for the investigation from the witness.

7.9 STATEMENTS

It is of paramount importance that the semantic explanation of the word 'statement' be investigated and explained because of the different meanings that are attached and attributed to this word. In criminal research literature a 'statement' is defined as a verbal account of events and evidence that relates to the crime committed.[6] One of the purposes of criminal and forensic investigation is to gather evidence. A statement is seen as the vehicle whereby the investigator transfers evidence to the courts and other quasi-judicial tribunals on or before the hearing.[7] Therefore it can be safely argued that the principal purpose of a statement in the criminal justice system or in the process of uncovering the truth is to record evidence.

Although attorneys may draw a slight difference between an affidavit and a statement, the concepts are used interchangeably for the purposes of this book. What is noteworthy is that, legally speaking, affidavits are notarised whereas statements are not. However, in the context of forensic investigation and this book, an affidavit is synonymous with a statement in that the description of an affidavit is provided as a written statement sworn on oath or affirmed to be true.

Investigators obtain statements for the following reasons:

- from victims, witnesses and complainants to establish if a crime was committed, what transpired, how it transpired and who was responsible for the crime, transgression or irregularity
- from victims, witnesses and complainants to confirm other people's versions of what happened
- from suspects to give the suspect the opportunity to give their version of the events.

Nowadays it is not only investigators from state agencies who investigate crimes or incidents, therefore it is imperative that the definition of a statement

6 Brown (2001).
7 Van Rooyen (2004).

also includes the word 'incidents' to accommodate those investigators who investigate in-house incidents or aspects that are not crime related.

Taking statements cannot be pinpointed to a specific phase in the investigation process, nor can it be limited to a specific type of investigation. Any form of investigation, whether private or criminal, relies on written statements. Statements can also be taken at any point of the investigation: during the preliminary phase, the further investigation phase, the judicial phase, and even after the court case.

Example 7.1: Statements can be taken at any point

Statements are an integral part of every investigation phase.

In the preliminary phase witness statements can be taken when the crime is reported at the police station's community centre. Statements can also be taken at a crime scene or scene of incident by the police officer who attends the scene.

During the further investigation phase information is obtained and filed in the form of a written statement in the case docket or case file. In the investigation environment this is referred to as the building phase of the investigation.

It sometimes happens that witness statements need to be taken while a court case is still in progress (during the judicial or third phase) because the existence of a witness only becomes known during the trial.

Witness statements are also obtained after the completion of a court case during the rounding-off phase, especially if the presiding officer still needs to make a decision on exhibits of value.

When new information emerges or comes to light that justifies the reopening of a closed investigation, new and additional statements are taken.

7.9.1 Characteristics of a good statement

A good statement is one which is free from any contradiction as these can destroy the credibility of the deponent.[8] A deponent is a person who makes a statement under oath. In order to avoid contradictions in statements, the person taking the statement needs to prepare for taking and writing down a statement. These preparations normally entail interviewing the witness or complainant and making notes of important facts and aspects before starting to formulate the statement itself. This helps to create a better picture of what happened and how the statement is going to be structured. Writing a good statement is an art and to develop this skill takes time and experience. It cannot be emphasised enough that time and effort should be spent on preparing for taking the statement.

8 Weston et al. (2000) 145.

Example 7.2: A well-planned statement

BIANCA BOTHA states u o English:

1.

I am an adult female, 25 years old, with id number 870205 3121 021, residing at 1223 Lange Avenue, Quellerina, tel. no. (011) 245-6789 and cellphone 075 075 1234. I am a pharmacist at Discpro, 25 DF Malan Road, tel. no. (011) 345-1234.

2.

Sunday, 2012-03-03, ± 14:00
1223 Lange Avenue, Quellerina
Doors locked, windows closed, alarm, electric fencing → shopping

3.

Returned 17:00, gate opened. Front door open. Entering - disorder.

4.

A white man, dressed → blue jeans, red t-shirt JEEP in blue, white takkies → blue eyes, blond hair, scar right cheek came running out. Hand - knife. Stabbed me - right arm. Serious → blood. Screamed → he ran away.

5.

Neighbour Ronnie Ferreira → assisted, called ambulance.
Flora Clinic → 15 stitches → J88

6.

List → stolen prop. → attached.
Injuries → J88
Witness R Ferreira → address + tel. no.

7.

No permission.
Further investigation.

Page 1 of 1 Botha

The investigator should consider the following aspects when preparing to take a statement:

- *Place*: Where is the statement going to be taken?
- *Language*: In which language is the statement going to be obtained?
- *Draft*: This deals with the preliminary formulation, logic, organisation and presentation of the statement.

- *Obtaining all the facts*: All the important facts and information should be included.
- *Proper interviewing*: Witnesses must be interviewed to determine what happened and to prepare a good, coherent statement that will cover all the elements of the crime or incident.

In addition, a good statement should have a dual accuracy, namely:

- The statement must reflect what the deponent said and what happened.
- The statement should contain the essential facts of what the deponent is prepared to testify about in a court of law or at other tribunals.

Example 7.3 gives an example of an investigator's notes in planning the statement.

Example 7.3: An investigator's notes in planning the statement

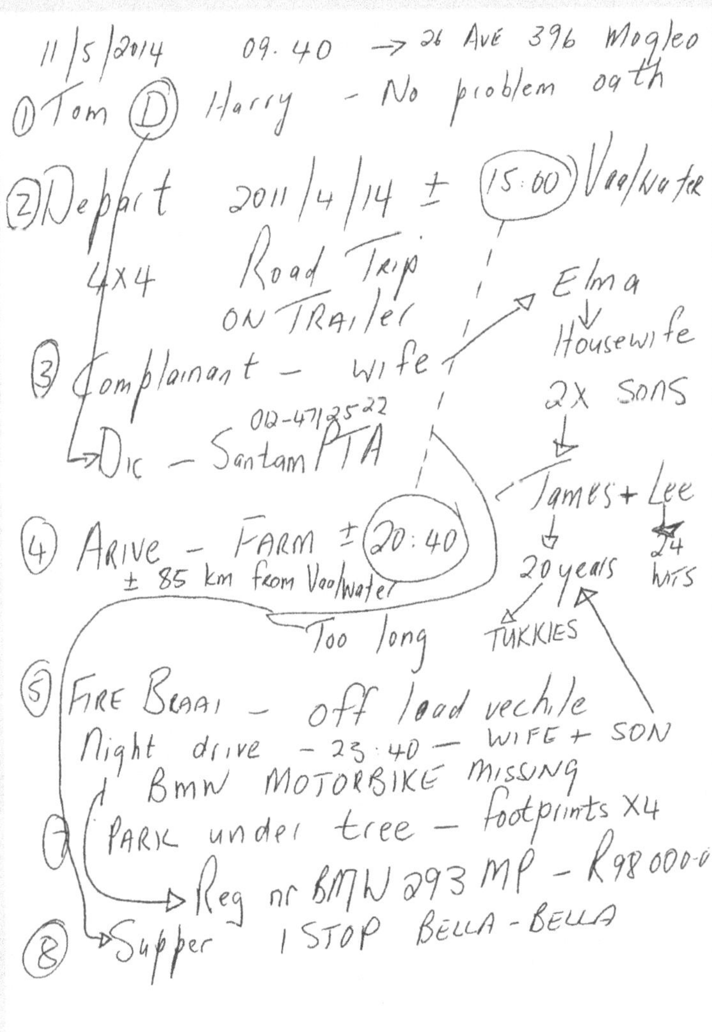

7.9.2 Requirements of a statement

Although there are many requirements that are pertinent to a good statement, the following are chosen for the purposes of this book:

- *Accuracy*: The statement must be a correct and true account of what happened. The deponent must know and understand everything that is written in the statement. Accuracy manifests in a number of ways and includes the proper spelling of names and titles. Carelessness in writing a statement can cause many problems such as the conviction of an innocent person or the exoneration of a guilty person.
- *Completeness*: The relevant facts must be mentioned in the statement. The what, when, where, why, who and how (Wx5; H principle) can be used to make sure that all the facts are mentioned and explained in the statement. Important facts should never be withheld.
- *Clarity*: The statement should be clear, ie it should tell the reader what the deponent meant to say.[9] The person who reads the statement must understand everything written in the statement, ie there must be no room for guesswork or deductions.
- *Conciseness*: When the statement is brief, understandable and complete, it meets the requirement of conciseness. Although there is a need to include all the facts, a statement should not carry information that may not be of substantial importance in proving the matter under investigation. Conciseness therefore means that the statement must be short and to the point.
- *Objectivity*: The emotions of the person who made the statement or the official responsible for obtaining a statement can distort the contents of the statement. This means that emotions must not play a role when a statement is taken. The essence of the statement is to record the exact words and expressions of the deponent, free from any emotional influence. A statement's function is as much to implicate the guilty person as to protect the innocent. If the statement therefore reveals information about the innocence of a suspect, that information should be included in the statement.
- *Comprehensiveness*: All the relevant issues should be covered in the statement. The admissibility of the evidence recorded in the statement should be left to the court or other tribunals that are tasked with making decisions of this nature.[10]
- *Truthfulness*: Everything in the statement should be the truth, and the meaning of facts and words should never be changed. This requirement relates to objectivity. The person obtaining a statement must bear in mind that not each and every statement will prove the guilt of the suspected person. The facts as provided by the deponent should therefore not be changed to strengthen the case under investigation.

9 Scott (1978).
10 Van Rooyen (2004).

7.9.3 Amendments to statements, supplementary statements and annexures

If mistakes or inaccuracies are found in the statement that need to be changed or if anything needs to be added, both the deponent and the person who takes down the statement must sign or initial next to every correction or change. The date on which these changes were made should also be added. Under no circumstances must words be deleted using a correction pen or an erasing rubber. This will compromise the trustworthiness of the statement in the eyes of the court or the presiding officer. Rather, simply draw a line through the text under correction. The following is an example of how the statement can be rectified.

Example 7.4: Making changes on a statement

Northcliff 2012-01-15

I left the premises at 8 Jennifer Avenue, ~~North Riding~~ at 08:00 and I personally locked all the doors and closed the window. I also activated the alarm before I left. I was away until approximately 16:00 before I returned. When I came back I found the iron gate leading to the garages was open.

2012-01-15

In addition, supplementary statements can be taken should a victim or complainant want to reveal additional information after the first statement was taken.

Example 7.5: A supplementary statement

David Marlo van der Wall further states under oath:

1

In addition to my previous statement made on 30 April 2011, I have discovered on 1 May 2011 that the keys to the stores were also taken from the top drawer of my desk. The keys are marked: 'Stores'.

2

I gave nobody permission to take the keys. I request further investigation into and prosecution of this matter.

3

I know and understand the contents of this declaration.

I have no objections to taking the prescribed oath.
I consider the prescribed oath to be binding on my conscience.

____

[Signature of complainant]

I certify that the statement was taken down by me and that the deponent has no objection to taking the prescribed oath and that he acknowledged that he knows and understands the content of this statement. This statement was sworn before me and the deponent's signature was placed thereon in my presence in Pretoria on 2 May 2011 at 09:00.

____

[Signature of person taking the statements]

Commissioner of Oaths: Full names and surname
Address: 20 Tower Avenue, Pretoria West.
Rank:

Page 1 of 1

Annexures can also be appended to statements in order to clarify or prove certain aspects.

7.9.4 Purposes of statements

Before a statement is obtained, the investigator interviews the witness to obtain the relevant information to prove all or certain elements of the crime. A statement is then obtained from the witness, which means the investigator writes down the details and information disclosed by the witness during the interview. This prevents the deponent from changing their version of events later on and reduces the possibility of altering and manufacturing evidence during a hearing or trial.[11] A statement also prevents a deponent from becoming corrupt or from being bribed with the intention of changing the description of what actually happened. The ultimate purpose of a statement is also to provide a written record for a case file or case docket.

The use of a statement during a civil or a criminal hearing is well understood, but statements also have value in union arbitrations, company hearings, unemployment compensation claim hearings, investigations and determination of claims hearings. In private companies the management may also use statements as a loss-prevention tool. By analysing and studying the statements, effective measures can be identified and implemented to prevent financial losses and damages. Statements are also an excellent tool that can help insurance companies to establish loss: a statement can be used to determine if employees have breached their fiduciary duty to the company, determine the dishonesty of an employee or determine if the same *modus operandi* was used by an employee during losses.

In general, statements can be used for court purposes or investigation purposes.

7.9.4.1 Court purposes

Statements are used by the prosecution at the trial or by disciplinary officers during the disciplinary process to refresh the relevant persons' memory of incidents, to impeach witnesses and in general to monitor testimony to some extent.

- Since the hearing may take place long after an incident has occurred, statements can be utilised by witnesses, victims or complainants to refresh their memory.
- The availability of a statement is likely to discourage a witness from wrongfully changing the testimony during a hearing.
- In order to reduce the element of surprise normally associated with unforeseen testimony, statements can be used by the prosecution and officers in various tribunals to plan their presentations.
- Statements are used by the prosecution or a person responsible for instituting departmental hearings to evaluate the information and evidence in the

11 O'Hara & O'Hara (2003) 165.

statement before making a decision to prosecute or withdraw a case.

- Statements are the foundation for a better courtroom testimony. Deponents can review their statements before testifying and that in itself helps the deponent to give better and more accurate testimony about the facts pertinent to a crime or incident.
- Statements are used by the defence to prepare a client's defence and can corroborate the testimony of other witnesses and evidence. This means that statements can support other types of evidence before the court of law or other tribunals.
- The statement also provides the attorney with an understanding of what a witness might testify on, which can be very useful in the early stages of a lawsuit.
- A statement can also act as evidence should the deponent die prior to the hearing or trial.[12]

7.9.4.2 Investigation purposes

Apart from playing an important role in courts of law and other quasi-judicial processes, statements are also important in the investigation process.

- Just as in the courts, having made a statement can discourage a witness from wrongfully changing their testimony at any stage of the investigation.
- The information provided in statements is used as leads by the investigator or by a person responsible for investigating internal transgressions to find more information or locate other witnesses.
- Statements facilitate the writing of reports. Reports are sometimes compiled after the conclusion of the investigation, hearing or court case and statements serve as an excellent source of information from which an accurate report can be compiled.
- Statements can also provide background information for interviews with witnesses or complainants. Statements previously made by other witnesses or complainants are used by skilful investigators as a source of information when witnesses or accused persons are interviewed.
- Sworn statements (see section 7.9.5.2) are also used during the investigation process to apply for a search warrant and a warrant of arrest, to investigate unnatural deaths under the Inquest Act 58 of 1959, and to apply for information in terms of s 205 of the Criminal Procedure Act 51 of 1977.[13]

7.9.5 Types of statements

Statements can be classified by their purpose or by the type of a deponent making the statement. The latter categorisation includes ordinary unsworn statements, warning statements, a statement made under oath or affirmation, section 212 or 213 statements and dying declarations.

---

12 O'Hara (1976) 140.
13 SAPS (1990).

7.9.5.1 Unsworn statements

(a) Ordinary unsworn statements

An ordinary unsworn statement is a statement that is not sworn to by the deponent. Although it is a general rule that statements should be sworn or affirmed to be the truth, there are exceptions to this rule.

Example 7.6: Unsworn statements

In 1990, the railway officials at Hoedspruit hunted game by placing traps next to the railway line. This is against the law. One of the officials used the railway's official vehicle to remove the wild animals from the traps and then gave his senior official some of the meat as compensation for the 'official use of the vehicle'. This senior official was approached to make a statement. However, on the day that he was supposed to make the statement, the official tried to belittle the investigating officer in the presence of his worker. He wrote on a cigarette box: 'My workers won't steal. I don't always know where they are and they don't eat meat'. He then crumpled up the cigarette box and threw it into the dustbin. Later that day the investigating officer returned to the site to seize the cigarette box.

During the hearing of the workers on a charge of illegal hunting, the senior official tried to claim in his testimony on behalf of the accused that he was always in control of his workers and of the railway's vehicles. However, the cigarette box was then submitted as evidence (this was before the *Chabalala* decision). The prosecutor successfully argued that the senior official had made two contradictory statements.

(b) Warning statements

A warning statement is the most common unsworn statement. It is made by a person who is under arrest, or suspected of or charged with an offence. This statement is taken after the suspect has been arrested or informed (warned) of the suspicion and after their rights have been explained to them in terms s 35 of the Constitution of the Republic of South Africa, 1996. The charges are put to the suspect and they are given the opportunity to give their version in response to the charges. A warning statement is usually taken down on a pre-defined document on which appear the various constitutional rights in terms of s 35 of the Constitution. These constitutional rights are explained to the suspect. The suspect's response is then recorded word for word.

The signature and right thumbprint of the suspect should appear on every page of the warning statement. In addition, the warning statement must be signed by the official present at the time that the warning statement is made. In cases where the suspects are minors, their parents or guardians must be present when a warning statement is obtained. The legal representative can also be present and their particulars must also be recorded on the warning statement. The warning statement should be taken down in private.

It is desirable that warning statements should not be made under oath. The fact that a warning statement should not be made under oath was decided in the case

S v Makiwa 1970 (4) SA 151 (E). Eksteen J mentioned that it is undesirable that suspects should be asked to swear to the truth of statements made by them following the warning given. A written record of the warning statement is normally kept in the case file.

7.9.5.2 Sworn statements (statements under oath) or affirmations

A sworn statement is an affidavit or a statement taken under oath or affirmation. The term 'affidavit' encompasses both a sworn statement and an affirmation. These are permanent written or typed documents that are signed. They contain important facts to provide courts with relevant information of the investigation that was done following the commission of a crime, incident or transgression.

As far as the contents of the statement are concerned, there is no difference between a statement under oath or an affirmation. The only difference is the taking of the oath. The court does not differentiate between a sworn statement and a statement that has been affirmed. There is also no difference between the evidential value of these statements.

The most important fact is that a deponent, in making a statement under oath or affirmation, must consider the oath or affirmation to be binding on their conscience. If the deponent has an objection to taking the prescribed oath and does not consider the oath to be binding on their conscience, the statement is affirmed. This means that, instead of taking the oath, the deponent declares that the contents of the statement are true by saying the words: 'I truly affirm that the contents of this declaration are true'.

In a sworn statement the deponent considers the oath to be binding on their conscience and has no objection to taking the prescribed oath. When the statement is sworn to, the deponent will utter the words: 'I swear that the contents of this declaration are true, so help me God'.

A sworn statement is a written declaration that is sworn to or affirmed by a commissioner of oaths. A commissioner of oaths is appointed in terms of the Justices of the Peace and Commissioners of Oaths Act 16 of 1963. The way and manner in which a statement is taken is not prescribed. Statements are taken according to the regulations of the respective institutions and departments (government or private). The current view held by the courts is that the regulations are not mandatory but rather regulatory. In effect this means that a person making the statement can do so in their own way and/or manner, as long as the statement is sworn to and signed by the deponent.

What is indeed mandatory is the fact that the statement should be sworn to (hence a 'sworn statement') and that it should be signed. Legislation prohibits the taking of a sworn statement by a commissioner of oaths who has an interest in the matter.

Contrary to belief, investigators are also witnesses. The investigator is therefore at all times responsible for recording information and factual aspects in their statement. Although a statement by the investigator is not compulsory, the absence of a sworn statement by the investigator (called 'the investigator's statement' or 'the investigator's affidavit') in the case docket or case file should be treated with suspicion.

7.9.5.3 Section 212 and 213 statements

There is no reason why formal and reliable evidence should be presented orally. The growth in s 212 of the Criminal Procedure Act 51 of 1977 made it possible for a variety of evidence to be presented in the form of a sworn or affirmed statement and this section covers a wide spectrum of aspects. Statements made in accordance with ss 212 and 213 of the Criminal Procedure Act are in general made by experts such as handwriting analysts, ballistic experts, pathologists, vehicle accident reconstruction experts or experts who analyse blood for different purposes and reasons. The statements of experts are either made under oath or are affirmed by the deponent. Section 212 also makes provision for statements to be made by people who can testify about a transaction, action or event that did or did not occur in a state department or a subdepartment of the state or provincial administration. In addition, s 212 makes provision for a state or provincial official to state that particular information or a document was provided or not furnished to him or her.

The civil equivalent of s 212 is s 22 of the Civil Proceedings Evidence Act 25 of 1965. This section makes provision for evidence by a competent person by means of a sworn statement about any fact that was determined through a process requiring skills in bacteriology, biology, chemistry, physics, astronomy, anatomy or pathology. Except for these broad instructions there are, however, other regulations that permit and regulate the use of sworn statements in civil proceedings.

Statements in terms of ss 212 or 213 of the Criminal Procedure Act or in terms of s 22 of the Civil Proceedings Evidence Act are usually made to reduce court time. The deponent does not have to go to court to testify on the content of the statement unless there is a dispute over the findings and the procedure used in the analysis leading to the findings. Such statements will to a large extent consist of the findings of experts and are made and compiled by the experts themselves.

7.9.5.4 Dying declarations or deathbed statements

A dying declaration or a deathbed statement is made by a person who is dying or who is thought to be about to die. Dying declarations are accepted as evidence because it is believed by assumption that a person would not lie at the moment of death. This type of statement will almost certainly not be signed because the deponent will be dying. For a court to accept a dying declaration, certain requirements must have been met. When taking down a dying declaration, investigators should keep these requirements in mind:

- The deponent must have realised that death was about to happen.
- The deponent must have given up all hope of recovery.
- The deponent must have died after making the statement.[14]

7.9.6 Format of the statement

An oral statement can be put into writing in a variety of different formats. These formats consist of a narrative statement, question-and-answer format, formal statements as well as audio and video recordings of statements.

7.9.6.1 Narrative statements

A narrative statement is the most common form of a written statement. It is usually a handwritten statement of accounts in which the deponent tells a story in the first person to explain what happened during the incident.

7.9.6.2 Questions and answers

The interviewer identifies a series of questions and writes them out by hand or types them. The deponent then needs to answer these questions in writing. This is done to clarify important issues. One advantage of this format is that it allows the interviewer to ask open-ended questions which seek specific answers from the deponent. Investigators often use this format in complex investigations. A disadvantage is that it takes time to draw up and complete statements of this nature.

7.9.6.3 Formal statements

A formal sworn witness statement is presented in a prescribed manner and usually contains complex scientific, mathematical and accounting facts or an explanation of the operations and systems of an organisation or business.

A formal statement is normally of a prescribed and official nature because of its gravity and possible financial implications. This category of statements is used when a senior employee of a company is asked to testify on behalf of the company, especially in lawsuits in which the company's liability is at risk. In serious criminal cases or where the financial impact or cost to the company is significant, a formal statement should be obtained. Unlike question-and-answer statements, formal statements can be completed in a fairly short time.

These statements are characterised by the use of specialised terminology, abstract content and complex concepts that may not make sense to the ordinary reader.

14 Brown (2001).

The intention of formal statements is to prevent deponents from omitting valuable information. Formal statements are made to prevent spelling and writing errors, which can have a detrimental impact on the meaning of critical aspects.

7.9.6.4 Statements recorded on audio- or videotape

The availability of technology makes it possible for statements to be recorded on audio- or videotape. There are legal considerations that must be taken into account when a statement is recorded in this way but if correctly used, a video recording, for example, is a powerful aid because it shows the deponent at the time of making a statement. However, the recorded statement must still be transcribed and filed in the case file. It is also advisable that the investigator who uses this technique of statement taking should obtain written permission from the deponent in which they give consent for the conversation to be recorded.

7.9.7 Language usage in statements

Section 6(1) of the Constitution provides for the language in which a statement can be made. In South Africa, English and Afrikaans are currently the dominant languages, although a deponent can make a statement in the language of their preference. An interpreter can be used if the investigator is not familiar with the language that was chosen by a deponent. A statement should be made in plain and understandable language. The language of an ordinary, uneducated manual worker will differ from the language used by an educated chief executive officer of a financial company. Using sophisticated language to illiterate deponents can lead to the argument by the lawyers of the accused that the deponent could not understand the words and was therefore possibly influenced by the official who obtained the statement. The use of swear words, jargon and obscene language is not acceptable, except where these words form part of the crime or incident under investigation, for example *crimen iniuria*. If the deponent uses these words when making the statement, they should not be included in the statement and acceptable alternatives should be used. However, the witness should agree to and approve the replacements and must understand the meaning of the alternative word. In cases of *crimen iniuria* the language or the words used to insult the complainant must be used *verbatim* to prove the crime.

7.9.8 Structure of the statement

A statement needs to follow a specific structure so that facts can be stated in a logical manner (see Annexure 3). If the investigator or person obtaining the statement follows a logical sequence, the statement will include all the elements of the crime or any other aspects that need to be included in the statement. The structure of the statement can be divided into the preamble, the contents, the conclusion and the oath or affirmation.

7.9.8.1 Preamble

The preamble is the introduction to the statement. It normally contains information that identifies the person who makes the statement (deponent) and their address(es) and telephone number(s), which can be used to locate the deponent, if necessary. The information should be explicit enough so that the reader of the statement will be able to identify the deponent. These identification particulars form part of the evidence and must therefore be true. The following must appear in the preamble: the full names and surname, age, sex, race, identity number, occupation, complete residential address, home telephone number, complete work address and work telephone number, cellphone number, email address and home language of the deponent.[15]

If the statement is to be sworn or affirmed after completion, the deponent must be informed in advance so that they cannot at a later stage allege that they were not informed. In fact, the deponent will also need to indicate in the preamble whether they will be making a statement under oath or affirmation.

Some institutions in the criminal justice system, investigators and other law enforcement agencies prefer to add information in the preamble indicating that the statement was made free from any pressure, promise or leniency, which is quite acceptable. However, experience has shown that the inclusion of this information creates suspicion and normally leads to rigorous cross-examination in court.

Some investigators are of the opinion that the way in which the statement was derived should also be recorded as the last sentence in the preamble because it places the statement in context, for example 'The information in this statement is to the best of my knowledge true because I have full access to all the documentation of the company'.

7.9.8.2 Body

The body is the most important part of the statement. It is the heartbeat of any investigation because it carries the information that is often needed to solve a particular crime or incident. Everything done or to be done in the investigation derives from the content in the body of the statement.

A lengthy interview with the deponent will elicit the necessary information that will be recorded in the statement. Interviewing a witness is a delicate psychological task that should be performed by someone who is well qualified, trained and experienced.

There is a misconception by the public that only suspects or accused persons are interviewed. This is not the case. Witnesses are also interviewed to obtain

15 Sennewald & Tsukayama (2001) 157.

information that could further the investigation. The success of a good statement depends on the content and the interview preceding the statement.

Before doing the interview, the investigating officer should do their homework about the witness. First, they should obtain information about the witness, the witness's availability and the information the witness could possibly provide. Secondly, the investigating officer should determine what information is needed to prove the case in court. It is recommended that the investigating officer draws up a list of questions that need to be answered and explained by the witness during the interview, if necessary.

It is also recommended that the interview should be done in private and that detailed notes be kept to clarify misconceptions and other relevant facts. When the investigator is satisfied that all the aspects have been covered during the interview, they can proceed with taking down the statement. It is not a prerequisite that a statement should be taken immediately after the interview. Aspects such as time limits and the emotional state of the witness should be taken into account. The notes taken during the interview can therefore serve as a reference point.

The content of the statement will be determined by the crime or incident and the circumstances. The information in this part of the statement identifies the crime or incident that was committed. It gives direction to the investigation process and helps the prosecutor or person responsible for prosecuting in hearings to identify the appropriate criminal charge or misconduct. The following information is recorded in the content of the statement:

- What happened, when did it happen, who did that, where did it happen, why did it happen and how did it happen? (Wx5; H principle)
- Regarding the answer to the question 'where did it happen?', if there was more than one place, it must be stated. This will help the prosecutor to formulate the correct charge sheet.
- The answer to the question 'when did it happen?' will indicate the date and time of the week that the incident took place. It is advisable to give only the approximate time because time is often disputed during hearings.
- The property that is involved in the investigation needs to be described and the monetary value of the property must be mentioned. The deponents must declare whether they will be able to identify the property or the suspect.
- A description of the suspect or witnesses should be included in the contents of the statement. It is important that the information and description should be correct because incorrect information will steer the investigation in the wrong direction.

7.9.8.3 Conclusion

The information in the conclusion of the statement sometimes helps to record certain elements that are important to decide whether a prohibited act was really committed or a prescribed act really omitted. The following information may be included in the conclusion of the statement:

- that the perpetrator did not have the right to perform the act or omit the prescribed act
- that the deponent desires prosecution
- that the deponent is willing or not willing to testify.

7.9.8.4 Administering the oath or affirmation

Administering the oath or affirmation forms an integral part of taking the statement and can be likened to closing the lid of a jar. Without the oath or affirmation the statement cannot be complete and cannot serve the purposes mentioned earlier (see section 7.9.4). After the statement has been completed and read by (or to) the deponent and before the oath is taken, the deponent is asked the following questions and their responses are recorded in the statement:

- Do you know and understand the contents of the declaration?
- Do you have any objection to taking the prescribed oath?
- Do you consider the prescribed oath to be binding on your conscience?

The answers are recorded using full sentences, without repeating the questions. Depending on what the deponent answers, the oath or affirmation will contain the following:

- I know and understand the content of this declaration.
- I have no **objection/object*** to taking the prescribed oath.
- I consider the prescribed oath **to be binding on my conscience/not to be binding on my conscience.***

  * Delete what is not applicable

If the deponent objects to taking the prescribed oath, the affirmation will be administered (see section 7.9.5.2).

After taking the oath or affirmation, the deponent signs the statement in the presence of the commissioner of oaths. Below the signature or the thumbprint of the deponent, the commissioner of oaths will then declare as follows:

> *I certify that the above statement was taken by me and that the deponent has acknowledged that he/she knows and understands the content of this declaration. This statement was sworn to or affirmed before me and the deponent's signature or thumbprint was placed thereon in my presence at .... [place] on .... [date] at .... [time].*

The commissioner of oaths then signs the certificate and states the following below their signature:

____

[Signature]
Commissioner of Oaths.

Full names and surname in BLOCK LETTERS:	*eg OMPHILE LEKOMANYANE*
Business address:	*eg 21 Igumbo Street, Rangeview*
Position or rank in the SAPS:	*eg Brigadier, SAPS*

7.9.9 Examples of statements

Statements are very important in the investigation fraternity in general. Research has shown that badly obtained or poorly written statements are usually the cause of cases being withdrawn in courts of law and at quasi-judicial tribunals.

The following aspects were illustrated in examples in this chapter:
Example 7.2: A well-planned statement
Example 7.3: An investigator's notes in planning a statement
Example 7.5: A supplementary statement

The following examples are contained in the annexures:
Annexure 1: Example of a section 212 statement (drugs)
Annexure 2: Example of a section 212 statement (ballistics)
Annexure 3: Example of the structure of a statement
Annexure 4: Example of a detailed statement with annexures

7.10 ALTERNATIVE METHODS OF OBTAINING INFORMATION AND EVIDENCE

7.10.1 Admissions and confessions

Sections 219 and 220 of the Criminal Procedure Act 51 of 1977 deal with admissions and confessions. Both admissions and confessions are distinct sources of evidence. A confession is a complete acknowledgement of guilt in criminal proceedings, while an admission is a statement of fact in either a civil or a criminal case. A confession can be defined as an out-of-court statement, voluntarily, knowingly and intelligently made by a suspect, which acknowledges that they have committed or participated in the commission of an incident. Also, a confession makes it clear that there is no defence in law that would make their conduct lawful.

An admission, on the other hand, represents a statement that tends toward proving the suspect's guilt. The content of an admission must be incriminating. This is its most important characteristic. Thus an admission can be defined as the acceptance by the suspect (orally, in writing or by conduct) of any fact that is prejudicial to that person. Another form of admission is when an accused person admits a fact which is relevant to the main issue in dispute, thereby placing it beyond dispute.

7.10.2 Pointing out

A pointing out is an extra-curial admission and must therefore be compliant with the requirements of the admissibility of admissions. As it is an action, pointing out can amount to an admission by conduct. The evidence may be admitted at criminal proceedings when anything that was pointed out by an accused who is appearing at those proceedings, or any fact or thing that was discovered in the consequence of information given by the accused, is compliant. Note that pointing out made under duress is not admissible even if a discovery was made.

7.10.3 Comparison samples

Comparison samples must also be obtained from the suspect during the investigation. Examples of these are medico-legal comparison samples, such as blood, hair and buccal swabs for DNA, and samples for ballistic comparisons. All these samples must be obtained by an appropriately qualified and designated expert. If the handwriting of the suspect appears on disputed documents, the investigator must obtain handwriting samples of the suspect.

7.10.4 Exhibits found in possession of the suspect

The investigator should always confiscate, record, label and handle all exhibits found in the possession of the suspect in such a way that continuity of possession is maintained. The clothing of the accused should be searched for hair, blood and semen stains. The investigator should also seize any property that has been reported missing by the complainant and which is found in possession of the accused.

7.10.5 Medical examination of the victim

Generally, in the case of sexual and violent crimes, at least two crime scenes are found. These consist of (1) the place where the incident took place and (2) the body of the victim. Exhibits are often found only on the body of the victim. Examples include pubic hair and semen from the suspect in the case of rape, or blood in the case of other types of violent crime.

It is most important that, during the initial questioning, the investigator convinces the victim that a medical examination is essential. The investigator must explain to the victim why the exhibits are needed. As clothing will be seized as exhibits, the investigator should also ask the victim to take a clean change of clothing to the hospital or to the registered forensic practitioner's consulting rooms. Inform the victim that the original clothing will be sent for forensic analysis and that during this process it might be damaged.

The victim must be examined by a registered forensic practitioner or a registered forensic nurse as soon as possible after the incident. The investigator must accompany the victim to the forensic practitioner's consulting rooms. Note that a male investigator may not be present during the examination of a female victim, nor a female investigator during the examination of a male victim. The investigator must complete all the appropriate documentation and hand it over to the forensic practitioner along with form J88 and the 'crime kit' applicable.

In the case of an underaged victim, the investigator must get permission for a medical examination from the victim's parent(s) or guardian. Adults can give permission themselves by signing form SAP 308. Under certain circumstances, however, a magistrate or even a police official may grant permission for a medical examination to be performed. This is in terms of s 335B of the Criminal Procedure Act 51 of 1977.

The investigator should tactfully inform the complainant or victim about the examination and what it will entail so that they can be prepared. In cases of a sexual nature especially, these examinations can be stressful for the complainant or victim.

When the investigator arrives at the hospital or consulting rooms, they must briefly inform the attending registered forensic practitioner or forensic nurse about the circumstances and the exhibits that are required. The purpose is to let the forensic practitioner know what type of evidence to look for. While interviewing the victim, the forensic practitioner must also obtain general particulars about their medical history.

The aim of the medical examination is to obtain physical evidence on the victim's body and to evaluate their psychological state. Obtaining the physical evidence is necessary for the following reasons:

- *Determining the suspect's identity*: Hairs, fibres, blood and other bodily fluids on the victim's body and clothing can help to determine the suspect's identity.
- *Determining assault or duress*: Evidence such as torn and stained clothing, bruises, cuts or hair that has been pulled out can indicate that the victim acted under duress or was assaulted.

For a complete medical examination, the following aspects are usually included:

- *Appearance*: Observe and describe in detail the victim's general appearance and the condition of their clothes and underwear.
- *Emotion*: Observe and describe the victim's emotional state.
- *Signs of injury*: Make a detailed and localised description of marks, wounds and external injuries to the body (localised means specifying the place where

these appear). The examiner can call in a photographer for this purpose.

- *Medical samples*: In the case of rape, conduct a complete gynaecological examination of the victim and take vaginal samples (smears) and semen samples. These smears must be forwarded to the Forensic Science Laboratory as soon as possible to prevent deterioration of their quality.
- *Genital examination*: In cases of a sexual nature and when relevant, conduct a detailed examination of the external genitals and remove any hair belonging to another person.
- *Clothing*: Examine the clothes for blood, urine and semen stains, as well as hair and other physical evidence.
- *Nail scrapings*: Where applicable, take fingernail scrapings.

Investigators are responsible for the receipt and continuity of possession of evidence received from the forensic practitioner. They must pack, label and record any exhibits found. All seized clothing should be kept in a paper packet. It is crucial that continuity of possession is maintained.

The investigator should inform the complainant or victim of all the support and medical services available to them. The complainant or victim should also be given the case number and the contact details of the investigating officer.

7.10.6 Medical examination of the suspect

The investigator must ensure that the investigation remains focused on court proceedings. When the suspect is arrested, all the possible physical evidence must be obtained, such as exhibits in the suspect's possession and all physical evidence on his or her body. These could include blood samples, hair, fingernail scrapings, injuries and identification marks such as tattoos and scars.

The suspect will have to go for a medical examination depending on the circumstances of the case. Provision is made for the police to obtain samples from the suspect in s 37 of the Criminal Procedure Act 51 of 1977.

The investigator should take the suspect to the forensic practitioner or forensic nurse for a medical examination, if this is required. A medical examination could reveal marks, injuries and bruises inflicted on, or described by, the victim or complainant. It is also the way to obtain hair, blood and other samples for comparison with the exhibits found at the crime scene.

If the same investigator is dealing with the victim and the suspect, neither this investigator nor any other person should come into contact with both the victim and the suspect. This is to prevent possible contamination of exhibits until both the accused and the victim have been examined. The victim or suspect should also not be interviewed or interrogated if the accused is arrested shortly after a violent crime during which the victim or suspect was injured or raped.

To prevent the contamination of exhibits, for example, the accused should not be transported to the forensic practitioner in the same car as the victim. The same investigator should also not touch, handle or package the exhibits of both the victim and the accused. An exception would be when the examinations take place on different occasions. If the examinations are done on the same occasion or shortly after each other, the clothing of the suspect and the victim should also not be packaged or placed on the same table and their physical examinations should also not be done in the same room or on the same surface. These precautions are to prevent the accused alleging in court that they both became contaminated during the examinations.

The suspect's body must be examined by the forensic practitioner for any scratch marks or other wounds that they could have obtained according to the complainant. This can provide evidence that the suspect had committed the crime or at least link the suspect to the crime scene. All injuries must be photographed.

Form J88 must be completed by the forensic practitioner, who must make particular reference in this form to any injuries on the accused's body and to any other observations made during the examination. Fingernail scrapings must be taken from the accused if the complainant has been scratched. This will obviously depend on how long after the incident the accused is arrested.

7.11 MOTIVE

It is important that the investigator tries to establish the motive for the crime because in many cases it will help to identify the suspect and will serve as evidence against the suspect in court. A motive will also serve as a very good indicator of who might have committed the crime. This is usually highly important evidence that can determine the outcome of a trial.

7.12 CHARGING OR RELEASING THE SUSPECT

Note that a person can only be detained as a suspect for a maximum of 48 hours. On the basis of the facts of the case, the investigator must decide before the 48-hour period has expired whether to release or formally charge the suspect. If the suspect is to be charged, the actual charge is put to the suspect, for example 'the murder of Mr X on date, time and place'. The investigator should then ask the suspect whether they wish to say something in response to the charge. The suspect must be informed that they are not compelled to do so, but that what they say will be taken down in writing and might be used as evidence against them in court. (For more on this, see rule 8 of the Judges' Rules). The investigator then usually takes a warning statement from the suspect (see section 7.9.5.1).

See section 8.4 in chapter 8 for a discussion of the bail application process.

7.13 STATEMENT AND SUMMARY BY INVESTIGATOR

The investigator must submit a detailed affidavit of all investigations conducted and file it with a summary of the case in the case docket. This is called the investigator's statement. The prosecutor will need this summary to make sure all the facts of the case are taken into consideration when they decide whether prosecution will be instituted, and to ensure that all evidence is taken into consideration during the actual trial. The investigator should take the docket to the prosecutor for a decision.

7.14 CASE MANAGEMENT

In some cases it becomes clear that the suspect can be linked to other crimes. This information is usually supplied by the Criminal Record Centre (for fingerprints and *modus operandi*), the Forensic Science Laboratory (for ballistics and DNA), the Criminal Investigative Analysis (as discussed in chapter 9) and forensic and other exhibits that match those found at other crime scenes. Links to other crimes may also sometimes be found through information received from informers and other sources. In such cases the investigation can usually be done more effectively if the case dockets are all centralised and investigated by one investigator or team of investigators.

This is especially important in the investigation of serial crimes. The investigator(s) should read all the information in the case dockets from scratch, including the investigation diary. Experience has shown that this is worth the effort in cases where case dockets are taken over from previous investigators. It is the only way in which the investigator(s) will become acquainted with all the information and evidence. In this way, they will be able to identify all similarities, omissions, peculiar aspects and contradictions. The investigator(s) will also be able to recall important information and identify possible links as the investigation unfolds.

7.14.1 Preparing the case

The docket must be carefully prepared with all relevant statements including those from analysts and experts, as well as detailed reports on all the physical exhibits.

If stolen property is recovered, the investigator should:

- obtain a recovery statement from the person who found the property
- have the recovered property identified and then obtain a statement to that effect from the complainant
- take photographs of the recovered exhibits.

The investigator should also put together all outstanding photographs and reports, etc and file them in the docket. All the relevant statements should be obtained.

These would include statements by supporting witnesses who are linked to the case but who were not present at the scene. Examples of supporting witnesses are the accountants at a bank who can provide information on the suspect's financial matters in a fraud investigation.

Computer software can be very useful in serial cases or cases of a great magnitude. When the information is captured on a database, the computer can identify possible similarities. Examples of these are names, places, telephone numbers and vehicle registration numbers and descriptions. The right software for this can also draw flow charts to illustrate a sequence of events and visual graphics of links between numbers, persons and events, for example.

Information in a case needs to be contextualised. Investigators should properly organise the information to create a context – it will help the prosecutor to decide who to charge for which crime on the basis of the available evidence. The prosecutor can also use this information during the trial as a summary of all the relevant evidence and it will help to ensure that the witnesses and suspects are cross-examined on all the facts available.

7.15 CONTINUING VICTIM SUPPORT

The investigator should keep the complainant informed of the progress with the investigation. This includes regular updates, such as date of arrest, bail applications, court dates and any negative news concerning progress with the investigation. The complainant should also be advised on possible security or personal safety measures to prevent them from becoming a victim of crime again.

Certain non-government organisations offer support services for victims, such as rape victims, for example. With the support of their commander or station commander, investigators must put the victim in touch with these organisations, or with a local church, for example, if such an organisation does not exist in the area.

The court proceedings must be explained to the victim, as well as the likelihood of the case being remanded more than once.

In cases of a serious nature the investigator must obtain a second statement from the victim before the court case begins. This is sometimes also called an impact statement. The purpose of this statement is to alert the prosecutor and hence the court to the impact of the crime on the victim and his or her life. The impact statement can, for example, include facts about the victim's personal life, career, family life, sense of security or any other changes that occurred in their life or lifestyle as a result of the crime.

7.16 SUMMARY

The further investigation phase of forensic investigation carries the majority of the steps that need to be followed when investigating a particular incident. This phase starts immediately after the scene of incident has been handled. Most of the time spent on investigation is spent on this phase. This is not surprising, given the number of events included in the further investigation phase.

This is the phase where the case docket or the investigation files are initiated. It must be borne in mind that at this stage, no or very few statements may have been obtained. Some of the outstanding statements or those that could not be obtained during the preliminary investigation phase will be obtained during the further investigation phase. Apart from the statements, different warrants for searches and arrests will be obtained, arrests will be effected and the perpetrators will be brought to court. It is not by mistake that some of the cases are only sent to court or other quasi-judicial tribunals years after the investigation process started. It is only after the mammoth task of investigating the case has been accomplished that the next phase of investigation, known as the judicial phase, begins.

The successful prosecution of cases mainly depends on the quality, accuracy and thoroughness of the criminal investigation. Thus the level of investigation has become the single most important factor in determining the image of a police service. A standard of excellence in this regard will restore justice and the confidence of victims, witnesses and the public in the police.

REFERENCES

V Basdeo *Investigative Principles for Policing III: Study Guide for OVM30701* (University of South Africa 2010)

CM Bozza *Criminal Investigation* (Nelson-Hall 1978)

MF Brown *Criminal Investigation* (Butterworth-Heinemann 2001)

G du Preez 'Criminal investigation' in J van der Westhuizen (ed) *Forensic Investigation* 2 ed (Heinemann 1996)

JN Gilbert *Criminal Investigation* 3 ed (Macmillan 1993)

JM Hawkins (ed) *The Oxford School Dictionary* (Oxford University Press 1994)

C Joubert *Applied Law for Police Officials* 3 ed (Juta 2010)

JP Kenney & HW More *Principles of Investigation* (West Publishing 1994)

CW Marais 'Die krimineel-taktiese metodes by die insameling van inligting tydens die voor-arrestasiefase in misdaadondersoek' (unpublished MA dissertation, University of South Africa, 1988)

CW Marais *Fisiese Getuienis in Misdaadondersoek* (Henmar Publications 1992)

CW Marais & HJN van Rooyen *Misdaadondersoek* (Promedia 1990)

Merriam Webster New Collegiate Dictionary (Merriam Webster Inc. 1981)

Merriam Webster Thesaurus (Merriam Webster Inc. 1989)

CE O'Hara *Fundamentals of Criminal Investigations* (Charles C Thomas Publishers 1976)

CE O'Hara & GL O'Hara *Fundamentals of Criminal Investigations* (Charles C Thomas Publishers 2003)

RF Patterson & J Dougall *Virtue's English Dictionary* (Virtue 1953)

IA Pepper *Crime Scene Investigation* (Open University, New York 2005)

K Ramsland *The Forensic Science of SCI* (Berkley Trade 2001)

SAPS. Suid-Afrikaanse Polisie: Afdeling vir Gevorderde Opleiding *Verklarings* (Staatsdrukker 1990)

JD Scott *Investigative Methods* (Reston Publishing 1978)

CA Sennewald *The Process of Investigation* (Butterworth-Heinemann 1981)

CA Sennewald & JK Tsukayama *The Process of Investigation* (Butterworth-Heinemann 2001)

J Stein & L Urdang *The Random House Dictionary of the English Language* (Random House 1967)

Technikon SA *Investigation of Crime II: Study guide for OVM241ZE* (Technikon SA 2001)

TJ van Heerden *Kriminalistiek* (University of South Africa 1985)

TJ van Heerden *Inleiding tot die Polisiekunde* (University of South Africa 1986)

HJN van Rooyen *Investigation: The A–Z Guide* (Crime Solve 2004)

M Victor-Zietsman *Criminal Investigation: A Study Guide for SEP131CE* (Technikon SA 2002)

PB Weston, C Lushbaugh & KM Wells *Criminal Investigation* (Prentice Hall 2000)

RJ Zinn 'An evaluation of sentenced motor vehicle hijackers in Gauteng as a source of crime information' (unpublished M Tech Dissertation, Technikon SA, 2001)

DE Zulawski & DE Wicklander *Practical Aspects of Interviewing and Interrogation* (CRC Press 2002)

Chapter 8

THE JUDICIAL PHASE OF INVESTIGATION

J Jordaan • S Dintwe

Introduction

↓

Relationship between investigators and legal practitioners

↓

Role of the courts in relation to forensic investigations

↓

Bail

↓

Testifying

↓

Expert witnesses

↓

Summary

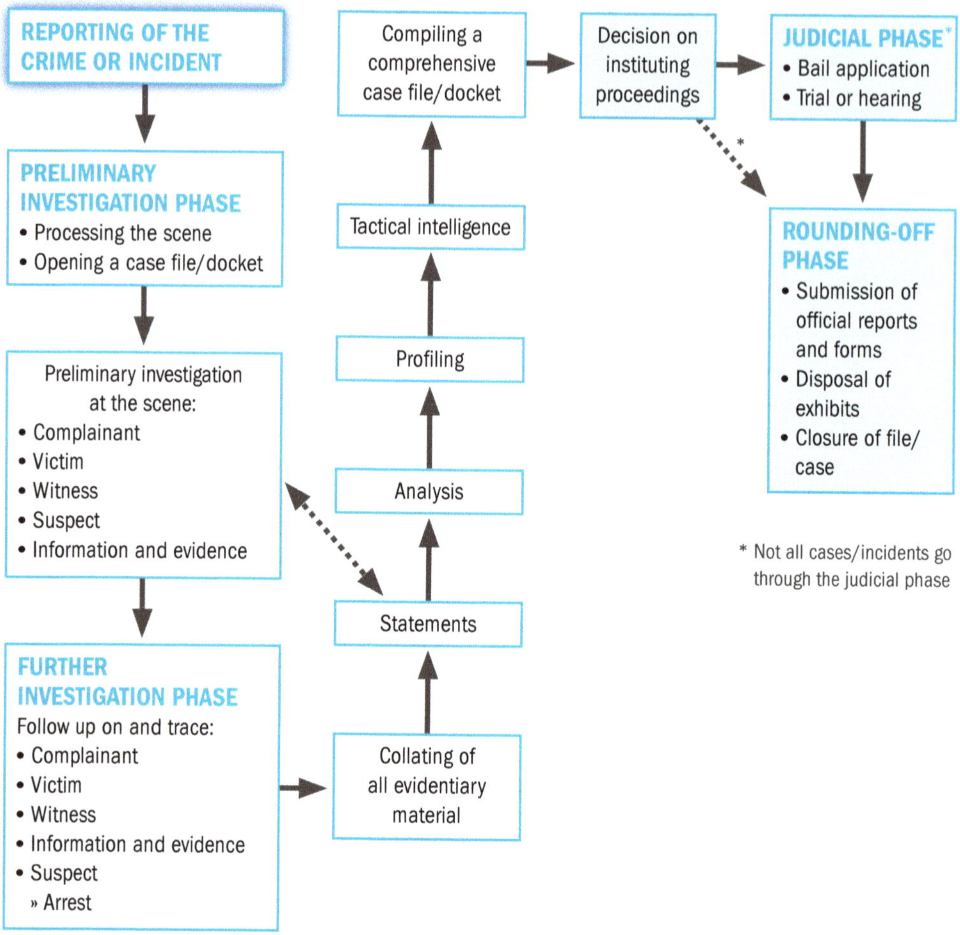

Figure 8.1: Areas of the crime investigation process covered in this chapter shown in shaded area

8.1 INTRODUCTION

The purpose of any forensic investigation is to collect evidence to either prove or disprove an incident under investigation, whether that incident is the commission of a criminal act, the breach of some civil liability or contract, or even violating a policy within an organisation. However, the purpose of an investigation is merely to collect the evidence, not to make judgments.

The judicial phase of a forensic investigation is thus the final stage of an investigation where the evidence that has been obtained during the preliminary and further investigation phases is presented and tested in court or other quasi-judicial tribunals. While the principal role-players in the judicial phase of an investigation are the legal practitioners and the presiding officers in court, investigators still have a crucial role to play.

8.2 RELATIONSHIP BETWEEN INVESTIGATORS AND LEGAL PRACTITIONERS

The role of investigators during the investigation of an incident is to identify and obtain all the evidence they can realistically obtain to prove or disprove the incident they are investigating. The role of legal practitioners (attorneys and advocates) is to place cases before the court, present this evidence before a court of law and argue the case before the presiding officer (a magistrate or judge). It is noteworthy that, although reference is made to courts of law, the principles discussed are also relevant to other quasi-judicial processes such as disciplinary hearings. Investigators and legal practitioners, while having distinct roles and functions, complement one another and in effect have a symbiotic relationship. Investigators are dependent on legal practitioners to get their cases to court and to argue these cases, and without investigators, legal practitioners may be limited in terms of the cases and evidence they may bring before a court. To ensure an efficient working relationship, it is crucial that investigators and legal practitioners maintain a professional relationship. A key to this professional relationship is to provide effective support to legal practitioners.

8.2.1 Importance of an investigation report

A key to building a professional working relationship with a legal practitioner is to provide the legal practitioner with a comprehensive and well-written investigation report. This report should detail the incident under investigation and the evidence that has been obtained, and should show how the evidence proves or disproves the investigated incident.

The investigation report helps to prepare and inform legal practitioners, providing a logical framework for them to work with. Just as a professional and well-written report strengthens the investigator's relationship with the legal practitioner, so a poorly written report will have a negative impact on this relationship.

8.2.2 Importance of affidavits

Whether the trial is a criminal prosecution or civil litigation, affidavits (sworn statements and affirmations – see discussion in section 7.9 of chapter 7 for more details) will be required. These affidavits will generally form the basis of the evidence presented in court. In the event of a criminal prosecution, the affidavits of all witnesses are generally made available to the defence well before the trial. In civil litigation, the affidavits from the plaintiff and defence witnesses are generally made available to the opposing parties during the discovery processes before the trial.

Affidavits are a crucial means of recording the observations and recollections of witnesses who may have to testify in court. Affidavits should be written in the language of the witness's choice using the witness's own words as it is often these words that the witness will use when testifying. Doing this gives the legal practitioners who will lead their evidence in court an understanding of the witness, and allows them to adapt their strategy and linguistic register accordingly. Investigators are often tempted to paraphrase what a witness has said in their affidavits to make the evidence more focused or technical. However, this can create a false impression of the witness's linguistic competence and lead to legal practitioners misjudging how to address or question witnesses.

Another aspect with regard to affidavits is that, although many investigators may write their affidavits by hand, legal practitioners prefer witness affidavits to be typed out, as it makes them easier to read.

The findings or observations of an investigator should be documented by way of a sworn or affirmed investigator's statement before the case even gets to court. This statement must document the entire scope of the evidence which the investigator will give in court, and must only present the facts and factual findings. The only time that an opinion may be given in an affidavit is if the investigator will be testifying as an expert witness.

If the investigator is testifying as an expert witness, and if the investigator is employed by the state, the investigator's statement should be made in terms of s 212 of the Criminal Procedure Act 51 of 1977 (CPA) unless there is any objection from the opposing party in court or the presiding officer, the affidavit can be tendered as evidence in court, this is only applicable to criminal trials. These statements can simply be admitted into evidence (see Annexures 1 and 2 for examples of section 212 statements).

8.2.3 Importance of real, documentary and digital evidence

If the case before a court is going to make use of physical, documentary or digital evidence, the investigator must ensure that this evidence is available in court when the legal practitioner requires it. The investigator must also safeguard the evidence until such time as it has been formally handed into safe custody of the court.

This evidence may or may not be contained in the case docket or case file, depending on the nature of the evidence presented. For example, documentary evidence may be filed in the docket or case file itself, but physical evidence, such as a firearm used in a crime, would not be.

8.2.4 Responsiveness to the legal practitioner's requests

The legal practitioner in a case may require further investigation to be done by an investigator. Investigators should be responsive to these requests. Often legal practitioners will consider an issue important enough to be followed up, even though the investigator may not have done so. However, investigators need to take heed of these requests and trust the legal practitioner's experience, knowledge and skills concerning the legal aspects of the case. In the interest of a comprehensive investigation, it is important that investigators perform this follow-up investigation for the legal practitioner.

8.3 ROLE OF THE COURTS IN RELATION TO FORENSIC INVESTIGATIONS

The role of the courts – whether criminal or civil courts – in South Africa is to receive evidence for consideration in connection with an incident. A presiding officer will consider the evidence presented by legal practitioners, hear their arguments and render a judgment based on these arguments. Just as it is the role of the investigator to collect evidence, so it is the role of the legal practitioner to present the evidence in court. The role of the court is to reach decisions with regard to the evidence before it and pronounce a judgment accordingly.

8.3.1 The South African court system

The South African court system is independent and is the judicial authority of the Republic of South Africa as set out in s 165 of the Constitution of the Republic of South Africa, 1996. The courts have a hierarchy: the Constitutional Court has the highest judicial authority, followed by the Supreme Court of Appeal, then the high courts and then the lower courts.[1]

8.3.1.1 Lower courts

The lower courts deal with less serious criminal and civil cases. These courts can be divided into two groups:

- regional magistrates' courts
- ordinary magistrates' courts (also called district courts).

District courts try less serious cases. They cannot try cases of murder, treason, rape, terrorism or sabotage, for example. They can sentence a person to a maximum of three years in prison or a maximum fine of R100 000. Ordinary magistrates' courts can hear civil cases when the claims are for less than R100 000. They cannot deal with certain matters, such as:

- divorce
- arguments about a person's will
- matters determining whether a person is mentally sane or not.

Regional magistrates' courts try cases that are more serious (but not serious enough to warrant being tried by a high court). In terms of the Criminal Law (Sentencing) Amendment Act 38 of 2007 a regional magistrates' court can sen-

1 Joubert (2001) 38.

tence a person who has been found guilty of offences that include murder or rape, to imprisonment for life. The court can also sentence people found guilty of certain offences such as armed robbery or stealing a motor vehicle, to imprisonment for a period of up to 20 years. A regional magistrates' court can impose a maximum fine of R300 000.

8.3.1.2 High courts

The high courts of South Africa used to be called 'Supreme Courts'. The high court divisions have 'jurisdiction' (the right to hear a case) over defined provincial areas in which they are situated. High court decisions are binding on magistrates' courts within their areas of jurisdiction. They usually only hear civil matters involving cases of more than R100 000 and serious criminal cases. They also hear any appeals or reviews from lower courts (magistrates' courts) which fall in their geographical jurisdiction. The high court usually hears any matters involving a person's status (adoption, insolvency, etc).

High court cases are heard by one judge, ie a legal practitioner with many years of practical experience. However, if it is a case on appeal, then at least two judges must hear the case.

If the case is about a very serious crime, a judge and two experienced legal practitioners, usually retired advocates or magistrates, will sit on the bench with the judge. These legal practitioners are called 'assessors'. Although the judge is not obliged to take their legal opinion into account, assessors usually help the judge to make a decision.

8.3.1.3 Supreme Court of Appeal

The Supreme Court of Appeal (SCA) rules on all appeals from a high court, other than those involving constitutional issues (which are heard by the Constitutional Court). Before an appeal can be heard in the SCA, leave to appeal must first be obtained from the high court that made the judgment.[2] The decisions of the SCA are binding on all high and lower courts.

8.3.1.4 Constitutional Court

The Constitutional Court is the highest court in the Republic of South Africa and deals with the interpretation, protection and enforcement of the Constitution. This court may only decide on constitutional matters, such as those contained in the Bill of Rights.[3] In essence the Constitutional Court is a court of appeal, but only in relation to constitutional matters. The judgments of the Constitutional Court are binding on all other courts.

---

2 Joubert (2001) 40.
3 Joubert (2001) 41.

8.3.1.5 Specialised courts

There are also a number of specialised courts in South Africa that hear various matters within a limited scope. However, these courts still ultimately fall into the category of either a local court or a high court. Investigators should be aware of the various specialised courts. Some of the specialised courts used in South Africa include, but are not limited to:

- Child Justice courts
- Sexual Offences courts
- Specialised Commercial Crime Court
- Competition Appeal Court
- Labour courts
- Land Claim courts
- Equality courts.

8.3.2 Differences between criminal and civil courts

Investigators collect evidence that can be used in criminal prosecution, in civil litigation, or in both in certain instances. Investigators should therefor be familiar with the differences between criminal courts and civil courts.

8.3.2.1 Principles of civil law

Civil law generally falls within the sphere of private law and in essence regulates the relationships and interests between two or more parties. These interests are generally private interests dealing with either the law of family, the law of family relations, the law of succession, the law of contract, the law of delict or labour law. Each party in the relationship brings their case before the court, where each presents their case so that the court can adjudicate on the dispute or issues at hand.

The purpose of taking a case before a civil court for adjudication is not to punish any party. The purpose of civil law is to deal with disputes between parties. Its primary purpose is to restore the situation between the two parties to what it was before the incident or incidents that led to the dispute. Although this may appear to be a punishment, it is not, as the person who is determined to be at fault in the dispute is merely being made responsible for their actions.

(a) Plaintiff and respondent

The party or parties seeking redress against another party or parties through civil action is known as the plaintiff. The plaintiff brings the matter before the court, seeking a judgment against another party or parties to restore the situation in principle to the way things were before the dispute or damages arose. The party or parties against whom the civil case is instituted is known as the respondent. Any of these parties can be a natural person or a juristic person (such as an organisation, the state or a state department). It is not uncommon to have multiple plaintiffs or respondents in civil litigation. Thus, in a civil case the plaintiff holds the respondent liable for restoring the situation to the way it was before the dispute.

(b) Balance of probabilities

In civil litigation, the burden of proof is on the plaintiff to prove their case against the respondent on a balance of probabilities. What this means is that the presiding officers will consider all the facts brought before them by the plaintiff, and weigh them up against the facts brought by the respodent in response to the claim instituted by the plaintiff. Fundamentally, whoever presents the most convincing evidence and arguments is most likely to win. If we had to express this context in numerical terms, if the plaintiff only obtained evidence to prove their case with a 50% certainty, and the respondent could only prove their case with a 40% certainty, then the plaintiff would win the case. If, on the other hand, the respondent proved their case at about 51% certainty, they would win and the plaintiff would lose.

(c) Burden of proof

Many investigators view civil cases as easier cases to investigate due to the burden of proof being a balance of probablities. There is a misconception that you do not need the same amount of evidence in civil cases as you would need in criminal prosecutions. However, this approach will limit the chances of success in a civil investigation. If the other party's investigator does a more comprehensive investigation and has a better prepared case, then in all likelihood they will win. Even though the burden of proof is lower than in criminal courts, it is still important to prove your case to the best of your ability to reduce the chances of the other side winning. In fact, if investigators applied the standards for a criminal investigation, ie to provide sufficient evidence to prove the case beyond a reasonable doubt, they would most likely ensure a winning case in civil litigation.

(d) Quantum

Quantum is an important concept in civil law. It refers to the amount of money that is deemed to be legally payable to the plaintiff by the respondent for damages as a result of the respondent's actions or conduct. As the purpose of civil law is not to punish the respondent, it is important that quantum be correctly calculated so that the correct liability for damages can be claimed. The concept of quantum also becomes important when there is more that one respondent, as different respondents may be held liable for different amounts of the total value, depending on the different levels of liability they have. It is critical in investigations for civil litigation that quantum be determined as accurately as possible.

(e) Liability

A concept that goes hand in hand with the determination of quantum is the determination of liability. Liability is defined as 'being legally answerable for'.

In other words, before you can act against a respondent in civil litigation, you must determine exactly how the respondent is responsible, and for what. After all, if the respondent were not responsible for the action which is now being addressed through civil action, how can you attempt to hold them liable? In cases where there is more than one respondent, it is important that investigators determine the extent to which each party is liable. Respondents can also be held jointly and severally liable. This means a group of respondents is held equally liable for the actions, with the result that quantum is applied to the group, and not to individuals. It does not matter who pays the damages from that group, as long as the damages are paid.

(f) Prescription

Another important concept in civil law is that of prescription. This is basically the period within which the plaintiff must institute civil action against the respondent, or else lose all claims to civil remedy against the respondent. Prescription is an important concept for investigators because in civil matters, if a matter is considered to have prescribed, then generally you cannot institute civil action in the matter. However, prescription can be argued in court within reason and, if successful, a court may condone a civil action that is lodged after a matter has prescribed. Prescription is governed by the Prescription Act 68 of 1969. The Act itself can seem complex, but from an investigative perspective, investigators should be aware of certain fundamental issues regarding prescription.

Prescription begins to run as soon as the potential plaintiff is aware of the events for which they can institute a civil claim. However, knowledge of the event is not enough. The potential plaintiff must also know who the potential respondents are and have sufficient knowledge of the facts of the case to be able to institute appropriate civil action. A number of different prescription periods are prescribed in s 11 of the Prescription Act, but in general the prescription period is three years.

8.3.2.2 Principles of criminal law

Criminal law generally falls within the sphere of public law and determines which act or conduct is considered a crime. It includes crimes defined in statutory law and crimes defined in the common law. The purpose of taking criminal action is ultimately to punish those individuals who, through their actions or inactions (omissions), have transgressed the laws of the land.

(a) Prosecution

All prosecutions of criminal acts are instituted on behalf of the state, which is represented by the National Prosecuting Authority (NPA). The person bringing the case before a criminal court is a public prosecutor, who is an employee of the NPA, or a legal practitioner who has received a delegation to prosecute a matter from a Director of Public Prosecutions (DPP). It is sometimes possible to bring a private prosecution before a court in terms of the Criminal Procedure Act 51 of 1977, but this is the exception rather than the rule and a compelling case needs to be made before this can be done.

(b) Perpetrator

No criminal offence can be brought before a court without there actually being a perpetrator of the crime, who has been identified and brought before the court in one of several ways. Before this person is brought before the court, they are known as a suspect. As soon as they have been brought before a court and charged, they are known as an accused. In general, an accused can be either a real person or a juristic person. The accused can be represented by a legal practitioner should they so choose.

(c) Complainant

There is generally one additional party in a criminal matter, namely the complainant. Although it is the public prosecutor who decides to institute criminal action, they cannot make these decisions without some evidence of a crime, and as such a party must bring the offence to the attention of the NPA. The complainant is generally the party who has been the victim of a crime. However, if the victim is not capable of laying a complaint (eg a murder victim) or the victim is a principle (eg the integrity of the financial system), then a representative of the state generally acts as the complainant.

(d) Beyond reasonable doubt

In criminal prosecutions the onus is on the state to prove its case against the accused beyond reasonable doubt. In short, the state must remove any reasonable doubt that the accused is in fact the party that could have committed the criminal offence in question. The reason why the burden of proof in criminal cases is so high is because criminal law is intended to punish offenders who have transgressed the law. It would certainly not be conducive to a free and just civil society governed by the rule of law to have anything less. This burden of proof arises from the philosophical legal statement that it is better for a hundred guilty people to walk free than to punish a single innocent one.

(e) Statute of limitations

The majority of criminal offences have a statute of limitations. This is the maximum amount of time the state has to institute a criminal prosecution against an accused from the time that the accused has commited the crime. If this time limit is exceeded, no criminal prosecution can be brought against the perpetrator of the crime. In South Africa, the statute of limitations is 20 years for all crimes, except for murder, which has no statute of limitations.

8.4 BAIL

In a criminal investigation the gathered facts may necessitate the arrest and detention of an individual. However, this may take place way before a trial is set. In the interest of presumption of innocence as well as the constitutional rights of those suspected, arrested or detained, it may not always be in the interest of justice to keep such an individual in detention. In this instance, the court may grant an individual bail while they are awaiting trial. There are also certain instances where it may not be in the interest of justice to release a person on bail, hence the investigator may be required to gather information and provide it to the prosecution so as to oppose application for bail by the individual in question.

It is therefore crucial that investigators are familiar with the guidelines on what information or evidence will be required by the court before a bail application can be opposed. A failure by the investigator to collect sufficient and relevant information to oppose bail can be detrimental to the entire case under investigation. For instance, the accused may, after release on bail, cause further harm to the victims, intimidate or harm witnesses, or even be a danger to themselves or society in general.

8.4.1 Legislative framework pertinent to bail

Release on bail mitigates the infringement of s 12(1) of the Constitution, which provides that every person has the right to freedom. The moment an individual is arrested or detained, this constitutional right is affected. In addition, s 35(1)*(f)* of the Constitution makes provision for the release of arrested persons from detention, subject to the reasonable condition and if the interests of justice permits. Although legislation such as the Criminal Procedure Act 51 of 1977 refers to the 'accused person', the correct term is actually 'arrested person', as advocated in s 35(1)*(f)* of the Constitution and s 50(1)*(b)* of the Criminal Procedure Act.[4] In the spirit of the Constitution, the investigator may not keep a person in detention with the intention of furthering the investigation and then deny such a person the opportunity to apply for bail. Such a denial of the opportunity to apply for bail is unlawful and a direct contradiction of the Constitution.

The second main piece of legislation that regulates bail is the Criminal Procedure Act. Section 60 of this Act, which has been amended by the Criminal Procedure Second Amendment Act 75 of 1995, provides that every person has the right to be released on bail before conviction, provided it is in the interest of justice. Section 58 of the Criminal Procedure Act refers to a payment or the furnishing of a guarantee to pay, which must be made by the arrested person before they can

4 In this discussion the term 'arrested person' is used unless there is a specific reference to legislation which uses the term 'accused person'.

be released on bail. Accompanying the conditions and the release on bail is the fact that an arrested person will be required to appear in a particular court on a specific date and at a specific time.

The legislation discussed thus far clarifies the fact that bail is non-penal in character. This means that neither the amount determined for bail nor the refusal of bail may be influenced by punitive notions, for example, to punish the alleged offender or to deter other possible offences.[5] The amount determined in the recent case of Oscar Pistorius, which is discussed in Example 8.1 and Case study 8.2, was influenced by a number of factors and not necessarily as a deterrent to the prospective offender.

8.4.2 Different authorities granting bail

Different authorities may grant bail to the arrested person. The general rule is that bail is essentially a judicial decision, which means that it must be determined by a court of law. However, bail can be granted by police officials, prosecutors and the courts. These authorities are mandated to grant bail through different legislative provisions, as explained in Table 8.1. The requirements that pertain to the granting of such bail are also mentioned.

Table 8.1: Authorities authorised to grant bail

Authority	Legislation	Requirements
Police	Section 59 of the Criminal Procedure Act	This is also referred to as 'police bail' and relates only to trivial cases not listed in Part II or III of Schedule 2. The following requirements must be met: • It must be granted by a police official of sufficient rank. • It must be granted in consultation with the investigator. • It relates to offences not listed in Part II or III of Schedule 2 of the Act.
The prosecutor	Section 59A of the Criminal Procedure Act	This bail may be granted by the Director of Public Prosecutions (DPP) or a prosecutor authorised thereto without the intervention of the court. The following requirements must be met: • It must be granted by an authorised prosecutor. • It must be granted in consultation with the investigator. • It relates to offences listed in Schedule 7 of the Act.

5 Joubert (2009) 149.

The court	Section 60 of the Criminal Procedure Act	This bail is commonly granted during the first court appearance of the arrested person. It falls squarely at the discretion of the court. The other stakeholders, such as the investigator, the prosecutor and the legal representative, are merely aids in the process. The following requirements must be met: • It must be proven that it is in the interest of justice to grant bail. • The onus of proof may be: ▸ on the state to prove that it is not in the interest of justice to grant bail, or ▸ on the arrested person to convince the court that they should be released on bail.

While bail may be granted by the police and prosecutors before the first court appearance of the arrested person, bail granted by the courts may happen within 48 hours in a court with the proper jurisdiction. However, the decisions in *Minister van Wet en Orde en Andere v Dipper* (1993) (3) SACR 221 (A) and *S v Du Preez* (1991) (2) SACR 372 (CK) imply that the arrested person may arrange an earlier appearance and that investigators must assist rather than obstruct them in doing so. Similarly, based on the testimony of the investigator, a prosecutor may ask the court to postpone the bail hearing for up to seven days in accordance with s 50(6)*(d)* of the Criminal Procedure Act. As far as jurisdiction is concerned, it is worth noting s 50(6)*(c)* of the Act, which states that an arrested person charged with a Schedule 6 offence may make a bail application only in a regional court unless it is unavailable in a particular town or place, in which case an alternative court may hear the bail application.

8.4.3 Grounds to be considered in a bail hearing

The court will usually weigh the interest of the arrested person against the interest of justice when deciding whether to grant bail or not. In the context of forensic investigation, the focus is on those factors that may lead to a refusal of bail. Knowledge of these factors is crucial as it will enable the court to arrive at a proper decision. Investigators are required to be fully conversant with these factors so that they can bring them to the attention of the prosecutor or mention them when giving evidence in court. Factors which may lead to the refusal of bail are the following:

- where there is likelihood that the accused person will attempt to evade the trial
- where there is likelihood that the accused person will attempt to influence or intimidate witnesses, or conceal or destroy evidence

- where there is likelihood that the accused person will undermine or jeopardise the investigation or the proper functioning of the criminal justice system, including the bail system
- where there is likelihood that the public order will be disturbed or that the public peace or security will be undermined.

The decision of the court on whether to grant bail or not will be based on the abovementioned considerations, as set out in s 60 (4)*(a)* to *(e)* of the Criminal Procedure Act. Additional factors are set out in s 60(5) to (10) of the Act.

8.4.4 Bail conditions and remedial measures

When granting bail to the arrested person, a court may set specific conditions. These conditions include factors such as attendance of the court hearing on the specified date and time. Investigators must know the conditions attached to each and every bail application that is granted because if the conditions are not met, it will have an adverse effect on the case under investigation. For instance, the investigator may be required to retrace and rearrest the person released on bail, depending on what the court may order. It is also important to know what the conditions are so that the investigator can monitor whether the arrested person is adhering to these conditions.

The bail conditions should always be clear and unambiguous but can be altered at any time, even after the bail has been granted.

Example 8.1: Bail conditions for Oscar Pistorius

The amendment of bail conditions was illustrated clearly in the bail of the internationally renowned Paralympic athlete, 'blade runner' Oscar Pistorius.

Pistorius was charged with the premeditated murder of his model girlfriend, Reeva Steenkamp. He returned to court to successfully apply for the amendment of his bail conditions. At that stage the bail had already been granted, but his defence team argued that the conditions were ambiguous and unreasonably strict in certain instances.

By their nature, bail conditions are envisaged as a tool used to exclude the risks mentioned earlier, such as the evasion of trial (see s 60(4) of the Criminal Procedure Act). The following are examples of bail conditions that may be imposed on accused people released on bail:

- They must hand in their travelling documents to the investigator.
- They must inform the investigating officers of their intended overseas travel or visits to other parts of South Africa.
- They may not consume alcohol or use any narcotics.
- They may not contact any witnesses or complainants.

- They must move out from the identified or shared household or property.
- They must report at their local police station at specific times.

Bail conditions are not in all cases observed and satisfied. If bail conditions are breached, the investigator must approach the court where bail was granted and make a statement either under oath or affirmation that the bail conditions had been breached. Commonly, if the court is satisfied, a warrant of arrest may be issued. This means that the accused person released on bail will be arrested again, but will also be given an opportunity to give evidence to the effect that bail conditions were not breached intentionally or by negligence. If the person released on bail does not succeed in proving that the conditions were not intentionally or negligently breached, the bail may be withdrawn and the money paid will be forfeited to the state.

The two case studies below illustrate bail as a method of release by referring to two prominent bail hearings. The first involves the nine police officials accused of murdering a Mozambican taxi driver, Mido Macia, and the second involves Paralympic athlete, Oscar Pistorius.

Case study 8.1: The Daveyton Nine

Mido Macia, originally from Mozambique and working as a taxi driver in South Africa, was allegedly involved in a conflict with police officials. It was alleged that the police officials had handcuffed him to the back of a police van and dragged him down a street to the police station at Daveyton. He later died in police custody and nine police officials were charged with his murder. During the subsequent bail application, the magistrate denied the nine police officials bail and cited the following reasons:

- It was not in the interest of justice to grant them bail.
- The public order may be disturbed as there were potential risks that Daveyton residents could try to seek revenge.
- Some of the witnesses were the accused's colleagues in the police and it would be easy to get hold of them.
- Some evidence was already missing and the prosecutor argued that the accused had tried to 'cover their tracks'.[6]

Although the accused in this case appealed, the high court confirmed the decision of the court *a quo*.

The advantage of thorough investigation came to the fore during this bail hearing. Sufficient evidence had already been gathered by the investigators. The cause of death of the deceased was revealed to the court, as was the fact that some items belonging to the deceased, such as a shoe, were missing. To the court this meant that the police officials could have tried to conceal evidence or even destroy it. The investigators were swift in proving that the accused had not been honest about what had transpired on the day in question.

It is worth noting that the accused police officials were subsequently released on bail after approaching a court again.

6 www.timeslive.co.za/local/2013/03/12, accessed 14 March 2013.

Case study 8.2: Oscar Pistorius

In this case, the double-amputee Paralympic athlete, Oscar Pistorius, was charged with the premeditated murder of his model girlfriend Reeva Steenkamp. The prosecution argued that the murder of Reeva Steenkamp was premeditated and rejected the earlier inputs that the deceased had been mistaken for a burglar when she was shot three times through the bathroom door.[7]

The fact that the charge was premeditated murder changed the burden of proof and Pistorius's defence council decided to submit an affidavit on behalf of the applicant. These circumstances led to information being revealed by the applicant during the bail application which cannot be easily retracted during the trail. On the basis of this information and the testimony led by the state prosecutor, the court was able to make a ruling on the bail application.

Pistorius was granted bail and the court set a number of conditions. Among other things, Pistorius had to:

- hand over his passport
- avoid his home in Pretoria and all witnesses in the case
- report to the police station twice a week
- abstain from drinking alcohol.

He later appealed to the high court and requested that his bail conditions be eased. As a result, the judge relaxed some of the conditions and described the decision not to allow Pistorius to travel as wrong. Among the amendments to his original bail conditions were the following:

- Pistorius could travel and compete in international competitions before his trial.
- He no longer had to be regularly supervised by a probation officer.
- The ban against him drinking alcohol was lifted.

In this case, the court was not satisfied with the investigation that had been carried out. This even led to the National Commissioner removing the investigating officer from the case. This case proved that it is very important to gather evidence for bail applications as accurately as would have been done for the main trial. The investigation carried out at the scene of incident in this case played a major role in assisting the court to reach a conclusion.

8.4.5 Lessons for investigators

It is clear from both case studies that the court will still need to consider evidence to decide whether or not to grant bail to an arrested person. This evidence may relate to numerous factors, including whether the investigators and the prosecutors have reason to oppose bail. The general lesson is therefore that investigators must collect evidence procedurally and within the ambit of the law. Such evidence, including information on whether the arrested person has any previous convictions or previous convictions for an offence referred to in Schedule 1, 5 or 6 of the Criminal Procedure Act, must be presented to the court hearing a bail application. In some cases, and in the case of Oscar Pistorius, the

7 www.iol.co.za/gallery-Oscar-Pistorius-bail-application, accessed 14 March 2013.

prosecution may rely on the investigator to either testify in person or to submit any relevant and admissible evidence in court.

Other lessons that can be learnt from the case studies and the preceding discussion are:

- The investigator may be required to assist the prosecutor in identifying those matters that are not in dispute.
- The investigator may be required to assist the prosecutor in gathering evidence pertinent to matters that are in dispute.
- If the bail is not to be opposed, the investigator may provide the prosecutor with acceptable reasons for not opposing bail.
- The investigator must monitor the accused person after they are released on bail.
- The investigator must bring to the attention of the court any information about the breaching of the bail conditions or any circumstances warranting the cancellation or withdrawal of bail.
- The investigator may approach and request the prosecutor to apply to the court for the addition of bail conditions.
- The investigator may request that an appeal be lodged by the Director of Public Prosecutions if he or she is totally dissatisfied with the granting of the bail.

8.5 TESTIFYING

An investigator must understand how to testify effectively, as poor testimony can ultimately lead to losing a case and, even more importantly, losing credibility as a witness in court. Criminal or civil court trials are formal events, while disciplinary hearings are less formal. The focus of this section is to address testifying in a criminal or civil court trial, but many of the aspects relating to testifying effectively will be just as applicable to disciplinary hearings or other quasi-judicial procedures.

8.5.1 Preparing to testify as an investigator

For the purposes of this section, an investigator includes any person who is a specialist forensic practitioner, such as a forensic scientist or a criminalist.

Prior to the trial, it is important that investigators should meet with the legal practitioner who will be leading the evidence so that they are clear about the evidence that the investigator will be providing to the court, and to ensure that the legal practitioner clearly understands the investigator's evidence. Legal practitioners may not brief investigators or tell them how to testify and about what. If the legal practitioner attempts to do so, it is professional for the investigator to ask the legal practitioner to stop and to end the meeting.

If the investigator is testifying for the prosecution in a criminal trial, they may actually have to initiate this meeting (especially if the case will be heard in a magistrates' court). If the investigator is testifying for the plaintiff or the defendant in a civil trial, or as a defence witness in a criminal trial, the legal practitioner leading the investigator's evidence will most likely initiate this meeting.

A few days before testifying, it is prudent for investigators to review their statements to refresh their memory. If the evidence they will be presenting is of a highly technical or specialised nature that may not be easily understood, investigators should practise presenting their evidence using plain language and simple descriptions that are easy to understand, without losing the integrity of the evidence they will be presenting. If the investigator is going to use visual aids in court when testifying, such as illustrations, photographs or diagrams, these must be prepared before the time. Similarly any technological aids, such as a digital projector to display illustrations, photographs, diagrams or any other information, must be arranged and/or tested before testifying. Investigators must ensure that they have made a copy for themselves of their statements and any reports or other information they plan to use in court. Copies must also be made for the legal practitioners on both sides and for the presiding officer.

The evening before testifying, the investigator should get an early night's sleep to be well rested in the morning. On the day that they will be testifying they should ensure that they have had a well-balanced but not heavy meal to ensure that their blood sugar levels are optimal. Eating a balanced meal will certainly help the body to withstand the stress of testifying. The investigator should ensure that they are hydrated but should not drink too much water.

Impressions count in court. When preparing to testify, investigators must ensure that they are well groomed. They must dress conservatively and professionally. Male investigators are advised to dress in a dark suit with appropriate shirt and tie and polished comfortable, formal shoes. They are discouraged from wearing any jewellery other than a smart watch, cufflinks, tiepin and wedding band. Female investigators should dress conservatively in a dark woman's suit and smart blouse, or smart dark skirt and matching jacket with blouse. Under no circumstances should the blouse be low-cut or the skirt be too short. They should wear formal but comfortable shoes. Discreet earrings may be worn with a smart watch and wedding or engagement band if appropriate, and maybe a discreet necklace. Under no circumstances should flashy or excessive jewellery be worn.

Investigators are urged to be as relaxed as possible. The court will be a stressful environment over which they have no control. By being well prepared, the investigator will be better equipped to deal with the stresses associated with giving testimony.

✓ CHECKLIST

The investigator's checklist before testimony

- ❑ Visual aids – compiled and organised?
- ❑ Hardware/equipment arranged and checked?
- ❑ Four copies of affidavit (for self, prosecution, defence, presiding officer)
- ❑ Outfit chosen, clean and ready?
- ❑ Transport arranged?

8.5.2 The court environment

Court trials are formal events with formalised practices. It is expected from all parties, including witnesses and especially investigators, to observe these practices. While courts may allow some leeway for lay witnesses, an investigator is considered a professional and will be held to the same standards that apply to someone who knows and understands the court environment and its rules.

Before testifying, investigators will not be allowed into the court room and will have to wait outside the court until called. It is important not to discuss the case or their testimony with anyone else who might be in the waiting area with them. When it is their turn to testify, they will be called into the court by a court official.

When entering the court, the investigator must do so quietly, close the door behind them, turn and face the presiding officer and bow towards him or her as a sign of respect. The investigator must then enter the witness box and stand at ease. They will have to stand the entire time while testifying. Investigators should stand still and not fidget or move about while in the witness box. If the investigator has a medical reason that does not allow them to stand for long periods of time, they need to tell the presiding officer and request permission to be seated during their testimony.

All evidence given in court must either be under oath or affirmation. The investigator will be asked to take an oath or affirmation, and once done, they are considered sworn in or affirmed and are bound to tell the truth. The investigator must remain in the witness box until excused by the presiding officer.

The investigator must accept that the presiding officer is the main authority in court, is in total control of the court and is able to immediately sanction any misconduct or breaking of the rules, procedures and conduct in court.

When addressing the presiding officer in court, the correct terms of address must be used. In a high court, the presiding officer, who is a judge, is addressed as 'Milord' or 'Milady'; in a regional or magistrates' court, the presiding officer, who is a magistrate, is addressed as 'Your worship'.

When investigators are excused from the witness box by the presiding officer, they may leave the court. If the court is still in session, they should walk quietly to the exit, turn and face the presiding officer and bow towards him or her, and then quietly exit the court.

8.5.3 The testifying process

Court trials are adversarial, with witnesses being called to testify by the prosecution and the defence. The formal process of testifying consists of three phases, namely examination in chief, cross-examination and re-examination.

8.5.3.1 Examination in chief

The legal practitioner who has requested the investigator to appear as a witness in court will lead the investigator's evidence. The investigator will be asked to identify themselves and give their credentials, experience and so on. Once this is done, they will present their evidence to the court and answer any questions posed to them by the legal practitioner leading their evidence.

The investigator's statement or affidavit will form the basis of their testimony and as such their testimony should not deviate from their affidavit, unless they have a valid reason for doing so. The evidence provided must be factual and, unless qualified as an expert witness, the investigator may not give an opinion during their testimony.

When the investigator has provided all their evidence in chief, the legal practitioner who requested them as a witness in court will inform the presiding officer that they have no further questions for the investigator. The legal practitioner will then hand the investigator over to the legal practitioner representing the opposing party in the trial, for them to challenge the investigator and their testimony.

8.5.3.2 Cross-examination

The legal practitioner representing the opposing party in the trial will now question the investigator in an attempt to challenge their evidence and discredit either the investigator or the evidence. It is probable, especially in high-profile cases, that the legal practitioner representing the opposing party in the trial will have researched the investigator and attempt to discredit them personally. In this regard, investigators should be very careful how they use social media on the internet and mobile networks, such as Facebook, LinkedIn, WhatsApp, BBM and Twitter, because what they post on these platforms is often easy to find. Anything negative about the investigator will very likely be used against them by a resourceful and well-prepared legal practitioner.

During cross-examination the legal practitioner representing the opposing party in the trial will often attempt to identify any contradictions in the investigator's evidence in chief, and attempt to use these against the investigator.

In addition, the legal practitioner will use a variety of other tactics during their cross-examination, such as:

- *Asking a series of rapid-fire questions* and allowing no time to answer properly between questions. To overcome this, simply continue to answer the previous question, stating that you have not completed your answer yet and would like to do so for the court's benefit before answering the next question.
- *Asking leading questions* such as 'is it not true that ...' or 'is it not possible that ...'.
- *Repeating the testimony of the investigator* back to them, but with a twist that changes the meaning. To overcome this, simply correct the statement.
- *Pretending to be friendly* towards the investigator, and then suddenly becoming antagonistic. To overcome this, simply remain neutral and do not react emotionally to the lawyer or advocate questioning you.
- *Pretending to be shocked, outraged or even bewildered* at statements made by the investigator. To overcome this, simply ignore the feigned emotion and continue with the testimony.
- *Remaining silent for a long time* after the investigator has answered a question, so as to cause discomfort in the hope that the investigator will repeat what they said in simpler words (and in doing so contradict themselves) to fill the silence. To overcome this, simply wait for the next question.

These are not the only tactics that will be used, but they are among the most common ones.

Investigators should expect anything and be prepared for a very uncomfortable experience that could place them under significant stress and pressure. The key is to remain calm and simply state the facts as you know them, no more and no less. Above all, it is important for the investigator not to take anything personally during the cross-examination phase.

8.5.3.3 Re-examination

Once the legal practitioner representing the opposing party in the trial has finished cross-examining the investigator, the legal practitioner who had asked the investigator to testify in court will be afforded the opportunity to ask them additional questions. The questions asked during re-examination are limited only to clarifying issues raised during cross-examination. No new questions may be asked.

Once the re-examination is completed and if the presiding officer has no follow-up questions, the investigator will be excused from the witness box and may leave the courtroom.

8.5.4 Perjury

All witnesses testifying in court are bound to tell the truth, and nothing but the truth. Generally the truth consists in facts and not opinions (unless testifying as an expert witness). Investigators should therefore limit themselves to the facts of the case.

It is common for investigators to sometimes forget something due to the length of time that has elapsed between the completion of an investigation and the trial. In this case the investigator can simply say that they cannot remember, but under no circumstances should they try to fabricate facts or speculate on what may have happened. It is for this reason that an investigator may need to refresh their memory by consulting their working notes (although if they do so, these notes will have to be provided to the legal practitioners in court as well).

If the investigator is ever caught out being deceitful in court, there is every possibility that they will be charged with perjury, which is a criminal offence. If convicted, it could result in their imprisonment at worst or a fine at best. However, regardless of the penalty imposed, the fact of the matter is that an investigator who has perjured themselves has effectively ended their career, as no court is likely to ever consider their testimony credible again.

8.5.5 Enhancing your credibility as a witness

As professionals that at some stage in their careers will testify as witnesses in court, investigators can develop skills and attitudes that will enhance their credibility. Investigators should not appear nervous. An investigator who is uncomfortable with public speaking and fidgets or moves around in the witness box appears nervous, and this will be exploited during questioning. Investigators should stand with their feet shoulder-width apart, back straight and shoulders back. They should keep their head up so that they will be able to speak clearly. Hands should be clasped behind the back, or in front of them to stop nervous hand movements. Investigators should use their hands only if necessary in presenting evidence.

When testifying, the investigator should not rush their testimony and should answer slowly and clearly, especially as the presiding officer will likely be making notes of their testimony. They should note the speed at which the presiding officer is taking notes and pause in their testimony if necessary so that the presiding officer can keep up.

The investigator should speak clearly and confidently when testifying. It is important that they consider the questions carefully before answering and not be tempted to always answer immediately. A pause before answering is a good technique to learn. When applicable, the investigator should answer questions with a simple 'yes' or 'no'. It is also important that they should not try to memorise their answers as it may cause undue stress to try to recall specifically memorised answers. It is also not advisable to volunteer any additional information when being questioned, especially during cross-examination.

Investigators must remember that, although they are asked questions by the legal practitioners from both sides in the trial, they ultimately answer those questions to the court, and thus to the presiding officer. Their answers should therefore be directed to the presiding officer. If the investigator is talking and the presiding officer or any of the legal practitioners start talking, immediately stop talking and listen to what is being said before continuing or responding.

No matter what happens during testifying, the investigator must always remain calm and not get emotional in their testimony or responses. Under no circumstances should they ever become angry. The key to being a credible witness is simply to remain totally impartial and speak only of the facts. It is not the responsibility of the investigator to ensure a successful prosecution or litigation but merely to present honest evidence before the court for the presiding officer to consider and reach a decision.

8.6 EXPERT WITNESSES

While many investigators are considered professionals, and possibly even experts in their own field, from a legal perspective they may not always be considered experts. In a court of law, an expert witness is a witness who is allowed to give opinion evidence. The role of the expert witness is to provide expert guidance to the court to help the court appreciate or interpret the evidence from a particular field of expertise. In other words, the court simply cannot make a decision about a particular matter without the use of expert guidance.[8]

There is no defined list of fields of expertise that the courts rely on in terms of expert witnesses. However, courts have readily accepted the following fields as being suitable fields for expert witnesses:

- Accounting and auditing
- Anatomy
- Astronomy
- Ballistics
- Biochemistry
- Biology
- Chemistry
- Computer science
- Criminology
- Dactyloscopy (fingerprints)

8 Schwikkard & Van der Merwe (2002) 89.

- Engineering
- Geography
- Geology
- Mathematics or applied mathematics
- Metallurgy
- Microscopy
- Pathology
- Physics
- Psychology
- Questioned documents and handwriting
- Sociology
- Statistics or the analysis of statistics
- Toxicology.

When a person testifies as an expert witness, it is necessary that they lay a foundation for the court to make a determination as to whether or not it accepts their expertise.[9]

- The expert witness must prove that they have specialist knowledge, training, skills and experience, which place them in a position to assist the court in deciding the issues before it.
- The expert witness must indeed be an expert for the purpose of the issues they will be testifying about and on which they will be giving an opinion.
- The expert witness must not express any opinion on hypothetical facts. They must limit themselves to those facts that are relevant in the case and which can be reconciled with the other evidence presented in the case.

It is critical that a prospective expert witness establishes all these criteria when testifying.

It must always be remembered that the court has the ultimate discretion on whether or not it legally recognises a prospective expert witness as such.[10] While an expert witness is allowed to provide opinion evidence, it is important to always remember that the opinions given need to be based on the evidence and that the expert witness needs to be able to prove the basis of their opinion. The application of the scientific method often comes into play here, especially when the expert witness is testifying in relation to a scientific or applied scientific field. It is crucial that an expert witness substantiates their evidence at all times.

---

9 Schwikkard & Van der Merwe (2002) 92.
10 Schwikkard & Van der Merwe (2002) 92-93.

8.7 SUMMARY

Taking a case before court at the conclusion of an investigation is the ultimate test of the quality of an investigation, and an investigator is often evaluated based on the success or failure of an investigation in court. The judicial phase of an investigation is perhaps the most critical phase, as it is here that a judgment is made.

While an investigator is not able to control the judicial phase of the investigation, their actions in relation to the legal practitioners and presiding officer involved, how they prepare their cases and witnesses, and ultimately how they testify, can all have a significant impact on the outcome of the case in court.

REFERENCES

C Joubert *Applied Law for Police Officials* 2 ed (Juta 2001)

JJ Joubert *Criminal Procedure Handbook* (Juta 2009)

PJ Schwikkard & SE van der Merwe *Principles of Evidence* (Juta 2002)

Chapter 9

CRIMINAL INVESTIGATIVE ANALYSIS: AN APPLIED PERSPECTIVE

G Labuschagne

Introduction

↓

Modus operandi

↓

Criminal Investigative Analysis

↓

Summary

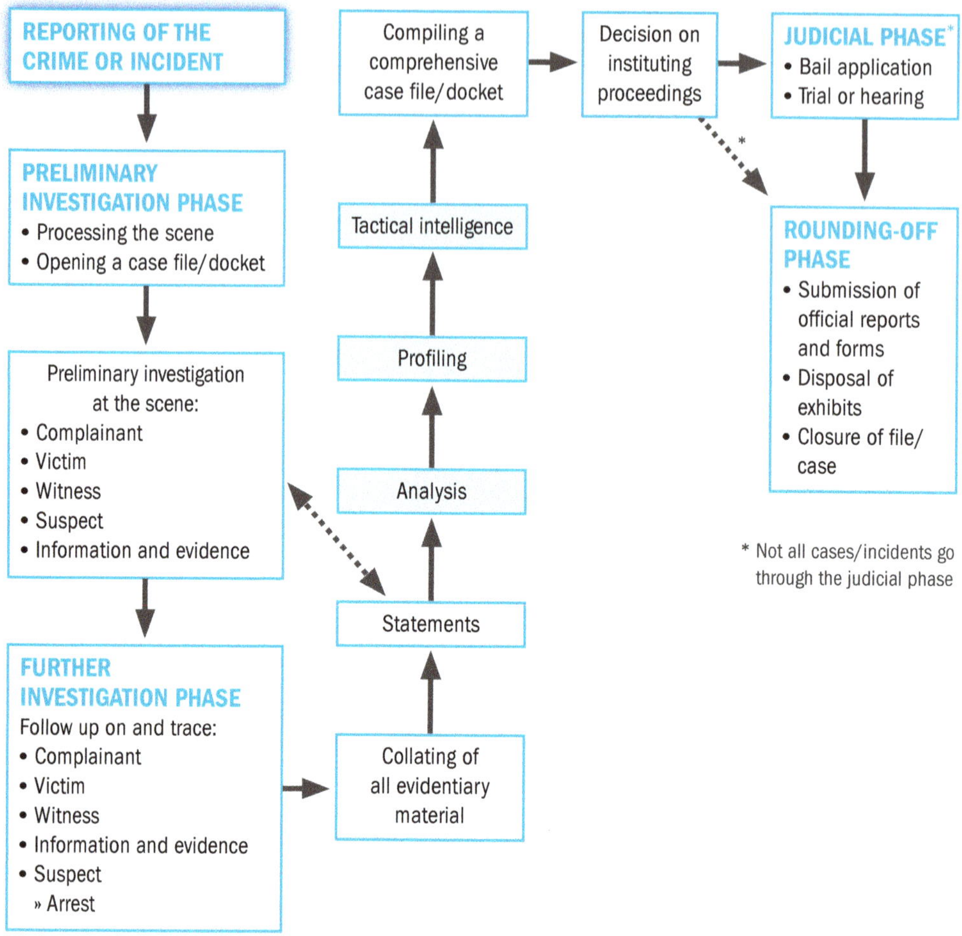

Figure 9.1: Areas of the crime investigation process covered in this chapter shown in shaded area

9.1 INTRODUCTION

Crime information gathering and crime intelligence have become important processes in investigating crimes or incidents. Crime information is all the raw data that is available on crime while crime intelligence is processed crime information. However, the collection and processing of crime intelligence comprise a range of processes or steps that could deliver a variety of intelligence products. These processes would include, for example, spatial analysis of where a crime took place, crime trend analysis, crime threat analysis and various forms of profiling. These include profiling of the yet unknown suspect, the arrested suspect, and the convicted and sentenced perpetrator. Crime information and crime intelligence have also evolved and become subdivided into specialised and specific subactivities. One of these specialist subactivities is Criminal Investigative Analysis (CIA).

Criminal Investigative Analysis is a specialised field in obtaining crime information and is usually performed by specialists who assist an investigator during an investigation. There is also a lot of confusion as to what the field of Criminal Investigative Analysis comprises, which is compounded by a still developing science and various experts contesting each other's interpretations and methods. Intense scrutiny is a normal and healthy way for a scientific subfield to develop until it reaches a universally accepted standard. This chapter relays the practical experience of the author, who is at the time of writing the head of the South African Police Service's Investigative Psychology Section (IPS), on aspects associated with Criminal Investigative Analysis. The SAPS Investigative Psychology Section is not located within the crime intelligence division of the SAPS, but is part of the SAPS Forensic Services Division.

In this chapter you will be introduced to concepts like *modus operandi*, signature, fantasy and Criminal Investigative Analysis with its various subactivities. While many of us have heard of the term *modus operandi* from literature and television, 'signature', 'fantasy' and Criminal Investigative Analysis of the suspect may be new concepts. *Modus operandi*, signature and fantasy are often the building blocks for the activities that encompass Criminal Investigative Analysis.

Criminal Investigative Analysis is an umbrella term, sometimes referred to as criminal behaviour analysis or profiling, which includes activities such as offender profiling, geographic profiling (also discussed in section 10.4 in Chapter 10), equivocal death analysis, psychological autopsies and linkage analysis, to name but a few. These concepts are all described below, even though some of them are also described in other chapters of the book. In this chapter the discussion of these concepts focuses on how they interlink with Criminal Investigative Analysis.

9.2 *MODUS OPERANDI*

Modus operandi is a term of Latin origin meaning 'method of operating'. The starting point in any Criminal Investigative Analysis activity is often to examine the *modus operandi* of the offender. *Modus operandi* often plays an important role when investigators attempt to link different offences to one offender. However, *modus operandi* must be distinguished from an offender's signature, as will be discussed shortly.

Modus operandi analysis can enable law enforcement agencies to better allocate resources. If it is clear that the most popular time of the day for housebreaking in a certain area is between 02:00 and 04:00 in the morning on a Wednesday, then visible policing could be allocated to that time and area to more effectively deter or catch housebreakers. Typically this type of analysis would be conducted by a Crime Intelligence Analysis Centre at a local police station. Thus *modus operandi* not only has a linkage aspect (identifying and linking multiple crimes by the same offender) but can also be used as a resource management tool for multiple offenders (by identifying popular times and areas in which criminals operate). Finally, *modus operandi* can be used to warn members of the public to prevent them from becoming victims of crime (for example, by informing the public of a certain con-story used by offenders to gain access to private homes).

9.2.1 Definitions of *modus operandi*

As mentioned above, the term *modus operandi* (MO) is a Latin term meaning 'method of operating' and refers to the manner in which the crime has been committed.[1] Douglas & Munn state that MO can be described as 'the offender's actions while committing the crime'.[2] Bartol & Bartol indicate that MO refers to the actions and procedures in which the offender engages to successfully commit the crime. It is a behavioural pattern which offenders learn as they gain experience by repeatedly committing the offence.[3] According to Hickey, the MO includes techniques used in committing the crime and may evolve as the offender becomes more skilful and confident.[4] Hazelwood & Warren argue that the MO has three primary functions: protecting the identity of the offender, ensuring success and facilitating escape and evasion of prosecution.[5]

Hazelwood & Warren state that *modus operandi* is a term used to encapsulate the entire range of behaviour required to successfully complete a particular offence.[6] This includes all the behaviours initiated by the offender in order to acquire a victim and complete the criminal acts without being apprehended or identified. Among other things this can include time and day of offence, place, tools used, method of gaining access to and controlling a victim, and method of escape. The MO can be very simplistic or extremely complex, with various levels of sophistication that reflect the experience, motivation and intelligence of the offender. The MO is learnt behaviour that develops and changes over time. It is also dynamic and malleable. The MO can also be influenced by the behaviour of the victims: if a specific course of action is unsuccessful, the offender will adapt accordingly.[7]

1 Turvey (2003).
2 Douglas & Munn (1992).
3 Bartol & Bartol (2005).
4 Hickey (2006).
5 Hazelwood & Warren (2001).
6 Hazelwood & Warren (2003).
7 Douglas, Burgess, et al. (1992).

9.2.2 Distinction between *modus operandi*, signature and fantasy

To recap, *modus operandi* is the behaviour that allows an offender to successfully commit a crime and avoid identification. If a person was asked to plan a bank robbery on paper, everything written down would relate to the *modus operandi*. Therefore every crime will have a *modus operandi*.

Fantasy, on the other hand, is often regarded as the underlying blueprint for psychologically motivated crimes. Where most crimes are driven by an underlying gain or profit motive with the crime being a stepping stone to obtaining items of value, in a psychologically motivated crime the crime itself is the offender's reward. For example, serial rapists or serial murderers do not have a profit motive but an inner desire to rape and/or murder their victims. A paedophile molests children because he has a sexual interest in children, not because he will benefit financially from doing so. Fantasy also explains why, when offenders repeat their crime, it will have certain similarities to the previous ones. With a psychologically motivated crime there is thus a further 'layer' which influences the *modus operandi* – the fantasy. Another way of saying this is that the fantasy causes the offender to use a certain *modus operandi* in an attempt to fulfil that fantasy. Both *modus operandi* and fantasy can give rise to the third element, a signature.

Signature is regarded as the offender's unique 'calling card'. The signature can be verbal, as in the case of a serial rapist who repeats certain phrases, or behavioural, such as posing the body in a degrading position in a homicide or using a particular method of gaining access to premises. A signature can stem from the *modus operandi* or from the offender's fantasy.

A *modus operandi* is not always unique enough to be regarded as an offender's signature. Because a signature is regarded as an offender's 'calling card', when investigators see the same unique behaviour again at subsequent crime scenes, they can be sure that they are dealing with the same offender.

While every crime has a *modus operandi*, not all crimes will have an obvious signature.

Example 9.1: *Modus operandi* and signature

A typical *modus operandi* for a vehicle hijacker might be to wait at a dark and isolated traffic light late at night, approach a car, smash the window, force the occupant out of the vehicle and then drive away with the vehicle. This is the suspect's *modus operandi*. However, there is nothing unique about this *modus operandi* and not necessarily anything to distinguish it from the *modi operandi* of many other hijackers.

On the other hand, if the suspect always wore a blue balaclava and surgical gloves, fired a warning shot when approaching the vehicle and left the victim tied up next to the road with cable ties, these behaviours would be unique enough to be considered as signature behaviours and will act as red flags to the investigator that the same suspect could be committing these crimes.

9.2.3 Practical examples of signature

Two types of signatures that play an important role in Criminal Investigative Analysis are *modus operandi*-based signatures and fantasy-based signatures.

Example 9.2: A *modus operandi*-based signature

A suspect breaks into apartments between 02:00 and 04:00 on a Sunday morning. He gains access to the flat by climbing up the drainpipe. He wears a blue balaclava and blue overalls. He only targets single women. The victims awaken with a large hunting knife pressed to their throat. The offender turns them over in their beds and ties their hands behind their back with a cable tie. He instructs them to count to 300 after he leaves before trying to free themselves.

Although individually these behaviours are not particularly unique, in combination any investigator reading the next victim's statement or attending such a scene of incident would automatically suspect that they are dealing with the same offender.

Example 9.3: A fantasy-based signature

During the abovementioned housebreaking the offender, after restraining the victim with the cable ties, turns the victim on her back, asks her what she likes to do with her boyfriend in bed sexually, and while raping her instructs her to say certain words or phrases to him, and to move her body as she would normally do while having consensual sex. After raping her vaginally he then rapes her anally and finally forces her to engage in oral sex with him. These behaviours reflect the offender's inner fantasy which he wants to act out.

Similar to *modus operandi* or signature, any investigator encountering these features again would realise that they are most likely dealing with the same offender.

9.2.4 Factors that may influence *modus operandi*

Various factors can influence or change an offender's *modus operandi.*

9.2.4.1 Criminal background of the offender

In the experience of the author the more criminally active an offender is, the more they will be able to learn new and more effective techniques for committing a crime and evading detection. Like the rest of us, offenders learn through experience and trial and error. Furthermore, criminals learn from being arrested, from television and often from being mentored by an experienced offender. In prison, offenders have many opportunities to learn from other offenders how to commit or not commit a crime, albeit from offenders who were themselves caught.

9.2.4.2 Media and literature

The media plays an important role when it comes to *modus operandi*. First, the news media reports on crimes and many offenders listen to, watch or read about their crimes or other crimes in these media. When offenders realise that their *modus operandi* has been made public, they would be inclined to alter their *modus operandi* so that they can commit more crimes successfully in the future.

Secondly, television programmes and films dealing with true or fictional crimes are popular and often reflect methods and techniques that are used by the police, albeit with a Hollywood flair. After watching such a programme, a criminal who may not have been aware of the existence of DNA typing may take steps to prevent leaving DNA at a future crime scene. Finally, literature, novels, magazines, the internet and textbooks are all open, available sources of police investigation techniques that an offender can access with little or no effort.

9.2.4.3 *Ad hoc* influences

During the crime itself things do not always go as planned, because any crime is an interaction between the offender, the victim and circumstances during the crime. Even with the best planning things can go wrong, forcing an offender to improvise to successfully carry out the crime. A victim may fight back, bystanders may intervene or the offender may get cold feet during the offence. All these circumstance may amount to *ad hoc* influences which may alter the offender's *modus operandi.*

9.2.5 Recording *modus operandi* information

Modus operandi information is often recorded in the investigation diary of an SAPS case file, or in the case docket. However, this information is frequently sketchy. If the investigator is doing an analysis of the offender's *modus operandi*, it is best to review the whole docket by studying the victim and witness statements, the post-mortem report (if relevant), medico-legal reports and any other forensic reports. If the investigator is assessing multiple cases, for example when confronted with a serial offender (whether it be a serial housebreaker, serial rapist or serial murderer) it is best to compile a table, or matrix, of each case with the relevant features, noting how often a particular feature occurs. An example of a matrix from a rape series is provided in Example 9.4.

Example 9.4: *Modus operandi* matrix

Count & Case number	37 Case number 676/11/08	30–36 Case number 1447/06/09	25–29 Case number 49/11/09	22– 24 Case number 764/2/10	18 –21 Case number 423/03/10
Approached 2 people	Yes				
Victim	White 11-year-old female	White 15-year-old female	White 12-year-old female	White 16-year-old female	White 16-year-old female
Modus operandi	Drove a white bakkie & kidnapped victim at gunpoint	Drove a white single cab bakkie & kidnapped victim at gunpoint	Drove single cab bakkie & kidnapped victim at gunpoint	Drove a single cab Bakkie & kidnapped victim at gunpoint	Drove a white single cab bakkie & kidnapped victim at gunpoint
Forced into vehicle on driver's side	Yes	Yes	Yes	Yes	Yes
Time & day of commission	Tuesday, 11/11/08 14:30	Monday, 22/06/09 12:15	Monday, 2/11/09 15:00	Sunday, 14/02/10 10:00	Sunday, 7/03/10 12:00
Location of crime scene(s)	Tried to kidnap victim in residential area	Kidnapped victim in residential area & took her to a secluded area	Kidnapped victim in residential area & took her to a secluded area	Kidnapped victim in residential area & took her to a secluded area	Kidnapped victim in residential area & took her to a secluded area
Motive for crime	Unsuccessful attempt	Sexual acts	Sexual acts	Sexual acts	Sexual acts
Sex acts	Unsuccessful attempt	Cunn; finger in vagina; penile rape	Fondled breasts; touched his penis	Fondled her breasts; penis in vagina	Blow job
Involve victim (sexually arouse victim, sexual questions, personal questions)	Unsuccessful attempt	Cunnilingus	No indication in statement		How many people has she slept with; tried to kiss

Modus operandi information of the suspect enables an expert to conduct a Criminal Investigative Analysis of the case under investigation.

9.3 CRIMINAL INVESTIGATIVE ANALYSIS

The starting point for discussing the field of Criminal Investigative Analysis (CIA) is offender profiling. Offender profiling as an investigative tool has been in use for a number of years throughout the world and in South Africa and is a familiar concept to many. However, there still seems to be confusion as to the exact meaning of the word 'profile' in this context as various agencies use the term to describe different activities. Furthermore, the popular media has created an image of a 'profiler' that has even influenced the academic understanding of profiling.

Originally the term 'offender profiling' involved solely the process of predicting offender characteristics based on crime scene information.[8] However, in recent years the term has been expanded to include a wide range of activities that behavioural science advisers, such as psychologists, psychiatrists, criminologists and specialist investigators, can contribute to investigations. All this is now grouped under the umbrella term Criminal Investigative Analysis. What was originally a specific activity (to develop an offender profile of an unknown offender) has become a term applied to a whole field. This has in essence led to much confusion in the profession.

As discussed below, David Canter, a well-known figure in the field, prefers to term the field 'Investigative Psychology' under which the activity of offender profiling is but one of the services provided. Similarly, Almond, Alison & Porter refer to 'Behavioural Investigative Advisers' who provide services that include offender profiling, risk assessments, DNA-intelligence-led screening, linkage analysis, psychological autopsies, equivocal death analyses and geographic profiling.[9]

This type of work was first consolidated into a field by the Federal Bureau of Investigation (FBI) in the late 1970s. The names of well-known authors such as Robert Ressler, Roy Hazelwood and John Douglas are associated with its early beginnings. Many of their early publications are still referred to today.

In this chapter the field will be referred to as Criminal Investigative Analysis, under which specific tasks such as offender profiling, geographic profiling, case linkage, psychological autopsies and equivocal death analysis reside.

9.3.1 Offender profiling

Various terms have been used to describe offender profiling. These include: criminal profiling, criminal personality profiling, crime scene profiling, behavioural profiling and psychological profiling, to name but a few. These terms have one thing in common: they attempt to use crime scene behaviour to devise an offender

8 Kocsis et al. (2002); Labuschagne (2003).
9 Almond et al. (2007).

profile, covering characteristics such as gender, age, race, intelligence, interpersonal relationships, employment, location of residence and other features of the unknown offender.[10] In other words, these terms attempt to describe the kind of person who committed the crime.

The person compiling the profile is usually referred to as the 'profiler'. However, it would be better to refer to these people as 'behavioural analysts', 'behavioural investigative advisers' or 'criminal investigative analysts' because *profiling* is usually just one service offered by people in such positions. Furthermore, the term 'profiler' has in many ways become associated with the Hollywood image of such persons, an unfortunate association which has led to many academics and law enforcement agencies being very sceptical of those offering these services.

9.3.1.1 Definition

The Investigative Psychology Section (IPS) of the South African Police Service (SAPS) defines offender profiling as:

> ... any activity specifically undertaken with the intent of assisting an investigator to determine the most likely type of individual to have committed a specific crime. The process would usually involve an assessment of the crime scene, attending the autopsy, examining all available docket material such as statements, photographs, forensic reports and investigative decisions. This information is then compared to any available research. Finally, hypotheses are formulated regarding the type of suspect who committed the crime. These hypotheses might be verbally communicated to the investigator but would normally also be formulated in a structured written report. The aim is to assist the investigator to focus his [or her] investigation on the most likely type of suspect.[11]

Most notable in the definition are the following:

- *The aim is to assist the investigating officer.* In other words, the person compiling the offender profile is not the person leading the investigation. A myth perpetuated by the media is that the 'profiler' is the one who leads or solves the case. Offender profiling is but one tool available to an investigator in an effort to help the investigator solve the case.
- *The offender profile is intended to indicate the type of person who could have committed such a crime.* In other words, the profile cannot be used to pinpoint a specific individual as a suspect. The profile is intended to be compared to possible suspects in an investigation. Those suspects who fit the characteristics indicated in the profile are prioritised above others who fit the profile to a lesser degree. Evidence is still needed to link a suspect to a crime

---

10 Gregory (2005); Woodhams & Labuschagne (2012).
11 Labuschagne (2003) 67.

and lead to a conviction. A profile has no probative, evidential value in court; it cannot be used to prove a specific person's guilt or innocence.

- *The process would usually involve assessing the crime scene, attending the post-mortem and examining all available docket material such as statements, photographs, forensic reports and investigative decisions.* This implies that the person compiling the offender profile must have access to confidential investigative information. The ideal is that this person should attend the crime scene and post-mortem in the case of a murder. If this is not possible, the person should revisit the crime scene and compare it to photographs of the crime scene and autopsy. Furthermore, the person should have access to reports relevant to the investigation, for example autopsy reports, ballistic reports and statements made by relevant witnesses. Frequently profiles are requested once a case has gone unsolved – this is often referred to as a 'cold case'. In this instance the offender profiler would be working primarily from the material available in the docket, supplemented by discussions with the investigating officer.
- *The information must be compared to available research.* With the popular media influencing the concept of offender profiling even in the minds of professionals, there are growing efforts to make the practice more scientific and evidence based. It is therefore essential that available and relevant research be used to support the statements made in any offender profile. This is not to say that the profiler's experience is ignored; experience is unrecorded research. Where available, research should be integrated into the offender profile.
- *Finally, hypotheses are made that can be communicated verbally, but these should be followed up in a structured, written report.* Investigations proceed rapidly and, as a result, information is often conveyed verbally as certain hypotheses are formulated by the person compiling the offender profile. Since a profile in a serial offence may be up to 20 pages or longer, it can take a long time to compile. During that time new information can come to the fore. To prevent misunderstandings, and to protect oneself in a legal environment, these hypotheses must be formulated into a structured written report that is an actual offender profile. This profile is then given to the investigator who requested it. Anyone who agrees to compile a profile but only gives verbal feedback and not a written report should be treated with circumspection.

9.3.1.2 Historical background

It is unlikely that we will ever know who penned the first profile of a suspect in a forensic investigation. Many have laid claim to having been the first. The concept of trying to understand the type of person who could have committed a certain crime is most likely as old as crime itself. It has been said that during the Jack the Ripper murders in London in 1888 a profile was compiled. Even the fictional character Sherlock Holmes makes deductions about the motives and personality of the criminals he seeks based on what he sees at a crime scene. One of the first incidences of offender profiling that came to the public's attention was James Brussel's 1956 profile of the 'Mad Bomber of New York' in the USA.[12]

The first law enforcement organisation to employ staff in this capacity was the FBI with the development of the Behavioral Science Unit where such well-known figures as John Douglas, Roy Hazelwood and Robert Ressler worked. Their initial work of interviewing imprisoned sexual murderers led to the development of the FBI's organised/disorganised typology, which became a prominent feature of profiling literature over the years. However, this typology has in recent years received much criticism for its lack of scientific rigour and lack of practical applicability. In South Africa this type of service has been offered since 1997 through the Investigative Psychology Unit (in 2011 renamed the Investigative Psychology Section (IPS)) of the SAPS, discussed in section 9.3.6.1 of this chapter. Prior to the establishment of the Investigative Psychology Unit in 1997, one person, Dr Micki Pistorius, was employed in the SAPS in this capacity, from 1994 until her resignation in 2000.

9.3.1.3 Offender profiling in court

Some say that since offender profiling does not stand up to admissibility standards for evidence in courtrooms, it is of no value. This is a misinformed point of view for two reasons: first, offender profiles were never intended to serve as evidential material in court and secondly, offender profiles were never intended to individualise a specific person. With regard to the first point, offender profiles are intended to help investigators focus on the most likely kind of person to have committed the crime in question. This is of great assistance when working with a large number of potential suspects in an investigation.

> **Example 9.5:** Using a profile as a starting point
>
> If investigators are looking for a suspect with a red sedan who committed a sexual murder in a particular area, they might obtain a list of all owners of red sedans in that town, and a list of all murder or rape parolees in the surrounding city blocks. This may generate a list of, for example, 50 possible suspects. Where does one begin? Here a profile can help to individualise and prioritise suspects with particular characteristics, for example age, race and occupation. The investigator then rank-orders the list of 50 possible suspects according to the profile.

As can be seen from this example, the profile indicates a type of person with certain characteristics. It can never be said that only the suspect possesses these

12 Gregory (2005).

characteristics or that only one person would have these characteristics. Therefore a profile can never individualise to the level of a fingerprint or DNA, but it was never intended to.

Using the standards for admissibility of evidence as a benchmark to judge profiling is unfair; it would be like judging the performance of a Ferrari on a 4x4 track. Profiling is an investigative aid and nothing more.

It must also be kept in mind that people use the term 'profile' in different senses. The author is often asked by prosecutors to compile a 'profile' of a suspect for sentencing. In actual fact what they are requesting is a *sentencing report* based on an assessment of the accused and his or her crime. It is therefore always important that the investigator clarifies exactly what the person is requesting and for what purpose the document is intended.

9.3.1.4 Process of offender profiling

Offender profiling involves analysing primarily crime scene information and interpreting that information to reach a meaningful conclusion. In a rape case the most important source of information is the victim's statement or an interview with the victim. The victim will be able to give the most valuable information about what happened, how it happened, when it happened and by whom the crime was committed. Other factors such as the location of the scene of incident and the time of day should also be considered. When one is dealing with a serial rapist, information about the various crimes is assessed individually and compared. When comparing crimes in a series, the profiler often looks for changes in behaviour across the series, such as an escalation of violence, which can be particularly revealing when predicting future behaviour of the yet to be arrested suspect.

When dealing with a murder or series of murders, the crime scene where the body was recovered and any other crime scene, such as the place where the suspect may have initially met the victim, become the primary source of information.

It is essential to understand that profiling is not guesswork, nor based on intuition or psychic abilities. One must understand the process of profiling, and also the crime which is being profiled. In other words, the profiler must be an expert on the crime they are profiling. A person may be an expert in profiling serial rapists, but that does not mean the same person will be able to profile arsonists. The profiler needs to be familiar with the typical features of the crime they are trying to profile. Without having a baseline knowledge of how these crimes are committed, the profiler will never be able to contextualise and understand the crime scene they are analysing.

Profiling is not something learnt from a book or in a classroom; it is learnt primarily through being mentored by an already experienced profiler, gaining experience in investigations in general, undergoing relevant training courses and being familiar with the relevant research. Ideally, accreditation with the International Criminal Investigative Analysis Fellowship (ICIAF) should be achieved. As the field grows, more and more research becomes available that can assist in providing evidence-based opinions about certain crime scene behaviours and features. In South Africa the only place where one can be trained as an offender profiler of criminal cases is in the Investigative Psychology Section (IPS) of the SAPS. This is due to the restrictions on private persons and unauthorised police officials regarding access to files, reports and crime scenes that are still under investigation.

9.3.2 Geographic profiling

People compiling offender profiles, specifically in serial cases, soon began to realise that offenders displayed certain geographical patterns of behaviour in terms of their crime scenes and that these could be of benefit when providing feedback to investigators. However, even before offender profilers came into the picture, crime scene geography was of interest to investigators. From the time of the Chicago School, which focused on human behaviour as determined by social structures and the physical environment rather than genetic and personal characteristics, geography has played a role in crime investigation. Many television programmes depict policemen standing around a map of a city with pins inserted into it, indicating areas where a series of crimes has occurred. Yet it is only recently that a more rigid scientific approach has been applied with the aid of computers to understand the geography of crime and other incidents.

The 1990s saw the re-emergence of a focus on the early works by Shaw & McKay,[13] originally published in 1942. This revival was referred to as the 'New Chicago School'. While adopting an ecological approach, it was also spawned by computerised mapping and spatial analysis techniques. Geographical Information Systems (GIS) allowed for the measurement of spatial aggregation and thereby opened up a host of possibilities with regard to the ecology of crime.[14]

Canter and Rossmo are two figures who stand out when it comes to geographic profiling.[15] Canter, for example, states that offenders rarely travel long distances to commit their crime(s) and are more likely to offend in a relatively small geographical area based around their homes. Similarly, Rossmo suggests that examining the exact location of a series of crimes can be helpful in identifying the most likely area in which an offender lives or works. Such input can be used to help prioritise suspects by address or area in which they live. This information

13 Shaw & McKay (1942).
14 Ainsworth (2002).
15 Canter (1994); Rossmo (1995); Rossmo (1997).

can also be used to increase visible policing patrols in that specific geographical area for crime prevention purposes.

One concern regarding geographic profiling is that the geographical profile can be skewed if inaccurate information is recorded or if information is missing, such as certain crimes not being included in the series because they were not reported, or if crimes not committed by the suspect are included. However, this criticism holds for any other form of profiling. So far this method has only been researched in Europe and the USA. As yet there has been little research in South Africa that puts these principles to the test. However, experience has shown that many of the features noted in overseas research have been observed in South Africa, such as the grouping of crime scenes close to each other and the proximity of the offender's residence to the crime scenes. While the generic suggestion, that offenders will offend in an area in which they feel comfortable, such as an area near their home or workplace, has been correct for some instances of serial offences in South Africa, there are also many examples where this has not been the case.

Example 9.6: Geographical patterns of some South African criminals

Samuel Sydino, the Capital Park serial murderer, murdered near his home, as did Sipho Twala, the Phoenix serial murderer; Kobus Geldenhuys, the Norwood serial rapist; and Cedric Maake, the Wemmerpan serial killer. Westonaria serial killer Jack Mogale lived close to his crime scenes. Moses Sithole, who operated in Atteridgeville, Boksburg and Cleveland, lived in Atteridgeville where he began his murders. He had previously been incarcerated in Boksburg prison but was obviously not living there when the Boksburg murders were committed.

In contrast, the Highwayman serial killer in Pretoria did not operate anywhere near his place of residence.

In other violent crimes, namely motor vehicle hijacking[16] and house robberies[17] studied in South Africa, it was found that the majority of the perpetrators committed their crimes within a certain radius of where they themselves lived or worked.

South Africa's socio-economic circumstances could be one reason why geographic profiling is not really useful in analysing serial crimes. A large portion of our population travels great distances to and from work and makes use of various forms of transport such as taxis. Also, due to the high rate of unemployment, people are often quite willing to go with a stranger if it may mean the promise of employment, thus victims are easily lured to out-of-the-way areas where the crime is then committed. In offender profiles compiled by the IPS, comments are always made regarding the geography and environment of the crime scenes.

16 Zinn (2004).
17 Zinn (2010).

9.3.3 Case linkage

Since the dawn of modern policing, investigators have been faced with the dilemma of having to assess which crimes had been committed by the same offender. Prior to the development of modern forensic techniques such as fingerprinting, tool-mark analysis and DNA, investigators had to rely on similarities between cases, ie *modus operandi*. There has been a renewed interest in studying and examining *modus operandi* because of an increased forensic awareness among offenders. Some attribute this to popular crime television series that portray forensic techniques.

Offender profilers are also faced with the question of which cases to include in an offender profile, in other words, which cases are part of a series and which are not. As mentioned above, if one includes cases that are not the work of the same offender then this could lead to inaccurate findings on the part of the profiler. This has led to the development of another tool known as 'linkage analysis'.

Case linkage analysis, sometimes referred to as comparative case analysis,[18] is useful during the further investigation phase. It can be used to help investigators decide which crimes to include and which to exclude from an investigation in the series, or how to focus their search for other similar crimes previously committed, or committed in neighbouring areas.[19] A linkage analysis can also be presented as evidence in court to convince the court that the same offender is responsible for a number of crimes. This is usually necessary when other forensic evidence may be lacking in certain of the crimes for which the offender has been charged.[20]

9.3.3.1 Understanding case linkage analysis

Well-known authors Hazelwood & Warren describe linkage analysis as a form of behavioural analysis used to determine the possibility that a series of crimes has been committed by one offender.[21] This is done by reviewing and assessing available information from various aspects of the crime pattern of the offender. This information includes the *modus operandi*, the ritual- or fantasy-based behaviours exhibited and the signature or unique combination of behaviours exhibited by the offender during the crimes.

However, Hazelwood & Warren do not specifically include another valuable feature of criminal behaviour that can be useful for linking cases, namely geographical behaviour,[22] as previously discussed. Authors such as Canter and Rossmo have written about the geographical behaviour of serial criminals, whether they

18 Bennel & Canter (2002); Merry (2000).
19 Santtila et al. (2005); Keppel (2000).
20 Labuschagne (2010).
21 Hazelwood & Warren (2003).
22 Hazelwood & Warren (2003).

be serial murderers, serial rapists or serial burglars.[23] Besides being useful in determining the offender's anchor point, such as a place of residence or employment, the proximity of crime scenes to one another can also be used in case linkage.[24] In the author's experience many of the assumptions about the geographical patterns of serial offenders hold true for the South African context. This point of view is also expressed by Hodgskiss in his research into South African serial murders.[25] A second valuable feature, which Hazelwood & Warren do not specifically mention, is the part that victimology plays in a linkage analysis.[26]

There are two important underlying assumptions regarding case linkage, namely consistency and variability.[27] Consistency relates to the belief that an offender will display some consistency in their behaviour across a series of offences;[28] variability relates to the belief that there is sufficient variation between different offenders, allowing them to be distinguished from one another in their criminal activities.[29]

Case linkage should not be confused with offender profiling. While it is not uncommon for an offender profiler to comment on case linkage aspects, it is not a requirement for a profiler to do so. The opposite is also true: a linkage analysis would usually not include offender profiling details as that is not the aim of a linkage analysis. This is especially so when a linkage analysis is to be used in court.[30]

9.3.3.2 Purpose of case linkage analysis

As mentioned briefly above, linkage analysis can have various uses depending on the stage of the criminal investigation in which it is used, and whether it is requested by an investigator or a prosecutor. At the start of an investigation it can be used to help investigators sift through cases to determine whether a serial pattern exists and which past and new cases should be included in the serial investigation. While the linkage analysis could be a stand-alone report, in South Africa it is often the first part of a broader offender profile.[31] Secondly, it can be used at the trial phase during the presentation of the prosecution's case to try to convince the court, along with other evidence, that the offender is responsible for all the crimes with which they have been charged. The linkage analysis may be useful if there are no eyewitnesses or forensic evidence to link the offender to the other cases for which they are on trial, but the way in which the crimes were committed (ie the *modus operandi*) is significantly similar and unique (remember the concepts of consistency and variability discussed above in section 9.3.3.1).

23 Canter (2003); Canter (2004); Rossmo (2000); Rossmo (1995); Rossmo (1997).
24 Keppel (1995).
25 Hodgskiss (2004).
26 Hazelwood & Warren (2003).
27 Santtila et al. (2005).
28 Woodhams & Labuschagne (2012).
29 Bateman & Salfati (2007); Woodhams & Grant (2006).
30 Labuschagne (2010).
31 Labuschagne (2003).

In South African courts the presiding officer (a judge or a magistrate) at a trial can decide, without expert evidence such as a linkage analysis being presented, that certain crimes are unique and similar enough in nature and circumstance to lead to the reasonable and logical finding that the same offender had committed the crimes. A linkage analysis is aimed at assisting the presiding officer to come to such a conclusion by providing the opinion of someone who is an expert in these types of crimes.[32]

9.3.3.3 Research base: a quest for scientific rigour

So far activities or techniques that fall within the realm of behavioural analysis or Criminal Investigative Analysis, such as offender profiling, have often lacked a solid research-based foundation to support the assumptions underlying these techniques. Linkage analysis, however, is one area that seems to have a slowly growing body of empirical support for its claims.[33]

A field that has proven to be meaningful when studying case linkage is that of personality psychology.[34] For many years the field of psychology has been studying, in non-forensic settings, how and why people do the same thing over and over in the same manner. This field acknowledges that while people are consistent because of their personality traits, the situation and circumstances in which people find themselves will also have an impact on their behaviour, and therefore on consistency. For example, in a life-or-death situation, such as a hostage-taking scenario, a person might behave very differently to the way they behave in their everyday life: a meek and mild person may become a pillar of strength and a leader to others.

(a) 'Evolution' in behaviour

To date much of the research relating to linkage analysis has focused on similarities in the different crimes in a series. This is based on the hypothesis from personality psychology that offenders are consistent in the way they behave across their criminal activities and that the behaviour of one offender during their crimes can be distinguished from the behaviour of another. While similarities are undoubtedly important and can perhaps be regarded as the 'heart and soul' of the linkage analysis assessment process, in the author's experience changes in offender behaviour across the series of crimes can be a very meaningful linkage factor.[35] This is echoed by Keppel & Birnes who describe behaviours such as 'increasing number of death-producing wounds from the first case to the last case' and 'decreasing number of defensive wounds from the first case to the last case'.[36] Grubin et al. also found that what they termed 'evolution' occurred across

32 Labuschagne (2010); Labuschagne (2006).
33 Labuschagne (2010); Santilla et al. (2005); Woodhams & Labuschagne (2012).
34 Woodhams et al. (2007).
35 Labuschagne (2010).
36 Keppel & Birnes (2009) 11.

a series, which can provide valuable information about whether an offender is in the early, middle or advanced stage of a series.[37] This was also noted by South African researcher Jackie de Wet when he analysed the sexual behaviour of South African serial rapists.[38] Similarly, Wentink, who analysed the first three offences of a sample of North American serial murderers, discovered that there was an evolution in that the offence behaviours became more thematically specific.[39]

(b) Serial murderers

Hodgskiss studied the offence behaviours of 13 convicted South African serial killers and found that offence behaviours evolved as the series progressed, with a clear *modus operandi* developing and becoming more thematically distinct.[40] This is often due to the progression of an offender's behaviour across a series of offences as more of the underlying fantasy gets enacted upon subsequent victims, or as the offender becomes more efficient in committing their crimes due to experience and confidence. It is incorrect to describe these purely as *changes* in behaviour in the sense that the offender is trying out new, previously unthought of actions.

It is perhaps better to describe these 'changes' as the acting out of more of the offender's original intention as the offender 'settles in' to their crime with each subsequent offence, in other words, more of the underlying fantasy is being acted out. Also, it is important to note that it is not in all aspects of the *modus operandi* that change occurs, for example victimology may remain the same, but specific behaviours may become more elaborate.

It is often these 'changes' that can be important linkage factors. These can be in the form of 'trial runs'.

Example 9.7: 'Trial runs' – Chané van Heerden and Maartens van der Merwe

In the Free State town of Welkom a young couple lured an unsuspecting victim to a local graveyard under the pretences of a 'blind date' between the female offender and the victim. Upon arrival the victim was stabbed to death and his body dismembered. Some body parts were taken home, among them the head of the victim, which the female offender then skinned the following day.

Prior to this incident, the offenders had killed and skinned a cat and had wanted to move on to something bigger such as a dog. Instead, they moved on to a human. The male offender had a fantasy of killing someone, while the female offender had a fantasy from a young age of skinning a human being.

37 Grubin et al. (2001).
38 De Wet (2008).
39 Wentink (2001).
40 Hodgskiss (2001).

Example 9.8: 'Trial runs' – Jose da Silva

Jose da Silva from Centurion in Pretoria eventually lured an interior decorator to his home whereupon he killed her with an axe and kept her body in a bath for a few days, before leaving her body along the N14 highway between Diepsloot and Muldersdrift.

He first began by making appointments with estate agents to view houses for sale but never committed any crime against them. He then escalated to inviting an interior decorator to his home, and the second interior decorator became the victim described above.

As Grubin et al. state, if behaviour is to provide a means for linking offences committed by one offender, it must be assumed that at least some behaviours remain consistent across the series of offences, or evolve in a predictable way.[41]

(c) Serial rapists

De Wet analysed the *modus operandi* of nine South African serial rapists who had a total of 75 victims.[42] His research revealed that offenders were consistent in their method of obtaining or luring their victims. For example, five offenders solely used a con-story such as offering employment when approaching their victims, and another two used a con-story in 94% and 89% of their incidents respectively. One offender used a surprise approach (such as approaching a victim by asking a question, then, once close, attacking her) in 75% of his cases, while only one offender had a mixture of methods of approach (con-story and surprise).

Regarding crime location, five of the nine offenders raped all their victims (in total 48) outside in an open space such as the veld. Three of the others were consistent in rape location in 90%, 86% and 75% of the incidents respectively. Five offenders were consistent in only attacking victims during the day, no offenders took precautions to hide their identity from the victims, and only one used a condom once during his series.

Woodhams & Labuschagne analysed solved and unsolved rape series in South Africa.[43] The purpose was to determine if solved series have higher similarities than series of rapes that are unsolved but linked by DNA. The reason for this research was to consider whether solved series might be more similar in nature, which led to their being identified as a series and subsequently solved, while unsolved series may be unsolved because of the lack of similarities across the series, which is the reason why they were unsolved. This research has helped

41 Grubin et al. (2001).

42 De Wet (2008).

43 Woodhams & Labuschagne (2012).

put this concern to rest. The research supported linkage issues and found that there was a significant degree of intra-series similarity among both solved and unsolved series.

9.3.3.4 Legal principles under which linkage evidence is admissible: similar fact evidence

Ormerod comments on the use of 'psychological profiling' as evidence in court. Some of the concerns expressed in this regard are also relevant to the use of linkage analysis in court.[44] He refers to the use of a psychological profile as an aid for the prosecutor to conduct a more effective cross-examination of the accused because a profile often highlights what the profiler thought was the motive and the fantasy underlying the crime. Should an offender take to the witness stand in their defence, these issues can be woven into the cross-examination of the accused in the hope that the offender will make certain admissions or statements under oath that will support the state's case.

In this case a psychological profile will not be playing an evidential role but rather a strategic one. A psychological profile may be used to highlight to the court how the accused fits the profile compiled during the investigation. However, the main problem is that the profile compiler, if they want to be honest, would have to concede that many people could 'fit' the characteristics described in the profile. It is therefore advisable to decline a prosecutor's request for the offender profile to be used as evidence, highlighting the problems mentioned above. It is also important to clarify what the prosecutor means when they request a profile because, as discussed earlier in this chapter, the prosecutor may be using the term 'profile' incorrectly to describe what they really need (eg a sentencing report).

One of the other difficulties of using an offender profile in a trial would be to overcome two laws of evidence: relevance and admissibility. While psychological or offender profiles may not stand up to cross-examination in court because of a lack of supporting research and their non-specificity (as discussed briefly above), it must be remembered that profiles are created primarily as an investigative tool and not as evidential material.[45] This is similar perhaps to the use of a polygraph during an investigation to help investigators decide on which possible suspects to focus or which ones to exclude, or a facial composite or 'Identikit' which may be placed in a newspaper by the police to help identify the suspect, but which will not be introduced as evidence in trial proceedings.

44 Ormerod (1999).

45 Gudjonsson & Haward (1999).

In South African courts, as is the case in courts in many other countries, an expert witness has primarily one role: to provide the court with expertise not typically within the knowledge framework of the court or jury (keeping in mind that in South Africa the jury system was abolished in 1969). For this to happen, a person must be qualified as an expert by the court, since as a general rule, opinion evidence is not admissible as evidence except when the witness is in a better position than the presiding officer or jury to form an opinion. What this means is that it is the court's (that is the judge or the magistrate's) responsibility to listen to the evidence and formulate an opinion about that evidence. A court cannot abdicate this task to a witness. As mentioned above, the exception is when the witness *is* in a better position to assess the evidence and formulate an opinion because of expert knowledge and experience that the court does not have.

The other important legal concept involved regarding the use of linkage analysis as evidence in court is that of 'similar fact' evidence. Generally the courts will not admit similar fact evidence because the evidence is irrelevant to the facts at hand and can be prejudicial to the accused person. This is why a person's previous convictions cannot be presented during the trial (only at sentencing) because such information might consciously or unconsciously sway the judge or magistrate to convict the accused of the crimes for which they are currently on trial, either because the person has convictions for similar crimes or to illustrate to the court that the accused is a 'bad' person because of their previous convictions (even if these may be for different crimes). Similar fact evidence is therefore regarded as irrelevant as it cannot prove or disprove the facts at hand in a current trial – the accused must be found guilty beyond a reasonable doubt.

The exception to the rule is if the evidence *can* contribute to the facts in issue. There must be a logical connection or nexus between the similar facts and the facts in issue. The greater the correspondence between similar fact evidence and the facts in issue in terms of time, place, manner and nature, the easier it is to conclude that the required nexus exists.[46] Similar fact evidence is often used when an accused stands charged of numerous crimes of a similar nature in one trial and the crimes are unique in their *modus operandi*, such as serial murder or serial rape, and where there is strong evidence linking the accused to at least some of the crimes, such as by means of DNA, fingerprints, witness evidence or an identity parade.[47] Based on the similarities of the *modi operandi* in the various cases, the court may conclude that the accused was also responsible for the other crimes. This can even be done without leading expert evidence regarding linkage during the trial, as per the case-law example discussed in Example 9.9.

46 Schwikkard (2002).
47 Petherick et al. (2005).

Example 9.9: Similar fact evidence

A case often cited regarding similar fact evidence is *S v D* (1991 2 SACR 543 (A)) where an accused person was found guilty of numerous crimes, including six counts of rape and one of robbery.

He appealed against one of the rape convictions and one of the robbery convictions, both against the same victim. The trial court had relied on circumstantial evidence to convict the accused on those counts. In a confession the accused admitted to committing the other crimes except the two mentioned above and he therefore wanted to appeal his conviction on those two counts (rape and robbery).

The Appeal Court held that the phrase 'sleep down', which was uttered during the incidents he admitted to committing and for which he had been found guilty, and which was also uttered in the incidents he denied committing, when taken into account with other similarities, did have sufficient weight to confirm identity.

These other similarities included the following: the rapes were committed in a particular area over a period of four months; the rapes were all committed during the morning or early afternoon; the offender would enter the house in a clandestine manner and confront the victim; he would first demand money then rape the victim. In almost every instance he removed or asked for the victim's watch. When these similarities were taken into account, along with the fact that the accused was found in possession of the victim's keys, the Appeal Court held that the accused had been correctly convicted.

Invariably, for someone to be indicted on a crime(s) they must have been linked to the crime(s) in some or other manner, such as by DNA, fingerprints or any of the other traditional means by which an offender is identified. In other words, something must have led the police to arrest that person. Without these links a prosecutor would most likely have declined to prosecute in the first place for lack of any evidence.

A linkage analysis is typically presented at the end of the state's case (in adversarial systems), once all the evidence is before the court. The relevance of similar fact evidence is therefore greatly determined by the strength of the other evidence available.[48] In this sense the linkage analysis presents the final, overarching piece of evidence, or the final 'layer' of evidence.

Due to their expertise in the psychological analysis of persons, the members of the Investigative Psychology Section of the SAPS are also called upon to perform other types of analyses, including a psychological analysis of the deceased, often referred to as a 'psychological autopsy'.

48 Schwikkard (2002).

9.3.4 Psychological autopsy

While an offender profile focuses on 'who', a psychological autopsy focuses on 'why' with reference to the victim of an incident. A psychological autopsy can best be described as an attempt to understand a person to whom the evaluator has no direct access and to explain why they behaved in a certain way. Usually this would be after an event such as a murder, suicide, disappearance or equivocal death scenario (see section 9.3.5) where the cause of death is not apparent from the scene itself.

A psychological autopsy would relate to an identified or known person. This differentiates it from an offender profile, which focuses on an unknown suspect who has committed an offence. The context of a psychological autopsy might not even be a crime, as in the case of an auto-erotic fatality. The profile is also different from the intelligence profile of a known person of interest who is still alive. Another way to describe a psychological autopsy would be to compare it to compiling a biography of a person who has already passed away by making use of various resources. Usually the main purpose of a psychological autopsy is to understand why a person behaved in a particular manner at a particular point in time.

> **Example 9.10:** Psychological autopsy
>
> An example of a psychological autopsy may be when a person dies shortly after committing a mass murder, and the authorities seek to understand what led to the crime being committed. Finding the answer may prevent future incidents.
>
> Another example may be when it is not clear if a person has committed suicide or died as a result of an accident, as in the case of an auto-erotic fatality. In that scenario an investigation into the person's state of mind would help to clarify if the person was displaying signs of depression prior to the incident – which might point more towards a suicide.

Psychological autopsies are often closely related to an equivocal death analysis, which is discussed in the next section.

9.3.5 Equivocal death analysis

An equivocal death analysis focuses primarily on assisting investigators with gaining clarity about an equivocal (undetermined) situation. It is therefore not necessarily as in-depth as a psychological autopsy and can sometimes be determined at the scene itself, without having to delve into the background of the deceased and recent events in their life. An equivocal death analysis usually relates to determining whether a death was the result of a murder, a suicide or an accident. As such it does not necessarily look into the 'psychology' of the deceased person.

Example 9.11: Equivocal death analysis

If what appears to investigators to be a suicide but to the trained eye has signs of an auto-erotic fatality, an investigation into the psychological state of the deceased might not be necessary.

For example, if there are indications of previous auto-erotic practices at the scene, a sexual theme to the scene, or a self-rescue mechanism present at the scene, these would be indicative of an auto-erotic fatality.

In other situations, the recovery of certain evidence may clarify if the situation was a murder, or an autopsy may reveal the cause of death. During such a process the analyst would also be on the lookout for indications of 'staging', ie where an offender tries to mislead the police into thinking the event had a different motive,[49] for example making a murder look like a suicide. One may also not know who the deceased is, in which case there will be no information as to the recent psychological state of the deceased. The purpose of an equivocal death analysis is to make a determination of murder, suicide or accident, thus making the situation unequivocal (completely clear; unambiguous).

To summarise: the difference between a psychological autopsy and an equivocal death analysis is that a psychological autopsy attempts to understand the person so as to determine why they behaved in a particular way, while an equivocal death analysis attempts to understand the incident so as to make it clear to the investigator what they are dealing with (a murder, a suicide or an accident).

9.3.6 Criminal Investigative Analysis in South Africa

Despite the image created in the media, not all law enforcement agencies have units similar to the FBI's original Behavioral Science Unit. Law enforcement agencies in some countries have formed their own investigation units that deal with investigative psychology or Criminal Investigative Analysis-related issues. In Europe some of the German states have Operational Case Analysis (OVA) units, and in the Netherlands National Police Agency there is a similar unit. The SAPS created the Investigative Psychology Section (IPS) in 1997 to fulfil this function for all SAPS investigations. Very often in other countries these services are fulfilled by non-law enforcement members such as academics, private practitioners or retired law enforcement officials.

9.3.6.1 Investigative Psychology Section (IPS) of the SAPS

The IPS has been in existence since 1997. It is a national section, which can be called upon to provide Criminal Investigative Analysis services throughout the country. The IPS has also assisted the neighbouring countries of Swaziland and

49 Keppel & Weis (2004).

Namibia with serial investigations and has cooperated with foreign law enforcement agencies such as Scotland Yard (on the 'Adam' torso murder, when the torso of a young Nigerian boy was discovered in the Thames River in England on 21 September 2001). The SAPS is one of the few police services in the world that has a full-time section devoted to providing this kind of support.

The IPS's mandate is to assist with any psychologically motivated crimes. These crimes include serial murders, serial rape, sexual murders, muti murders, infant rape, spree and mass murders, blackmail and death threats, and one-off murders with bizarre circumstances. Some of the well-known cases in which the IPS has assisted are: the Wemmerpan serial killer, the serial killer Moses Sithole, the rape of nine-month-old baby Tshepang in Upington, the 'Adam' torso murder in the Thames River (London), the Nasrec serial killer, the Capital Park serial killer Samuel Sydino, the Westonaria serial killer Jack Mogale, the Quarry serial murders, the Leigh Matthews murder, the 'Facebook' serial rapist and murderer Thabo Bester, and the Highwayman serial killer, to name a few. The IPS has a coordinator in each province to monitor and coordinate any investigations that would require its services. In 2013 the IPS decentralised and opened up satellite branches in all nine provinces. It employs experienced detectives with a background in violent or sexual crime investigations, clinical psychologists and researchers.

9.3.6.2 Roles of the IPS

The IPS has three overlapping roles within its mandate of providing support to investigating officers. These are investigative support, training of investigators, and research.

(a) Investigative support

The IPS provides Criminal Investigative Analysis support nationally to investigating officers by means of consultations, reports, crime scene analyses and offender profiles. It also provides 'witness-handling guidelines' for sensitive witnesses. The IPS's members are often called on to testify in court for cases in which they have assisted, very often for sentencing hearings. IPS members are all functional police officers and this unique position allows them access to crime scenes and autopsies. They are often involved in the interviewing of witnesses and suspects and in determining investigative strategies. They are literally involved from crime scene to courtroom. Many people doing similar work in foreign countries are appointed as civilian personnel and are therefore barred from such access.

After an investigation has taken place, IPS members can also be called upon to act as expert witnesses, should the need arise. This helps the prosecution by reducing the need to contact outside professionals who would require payment and who often lack the necessary specialised skills or insight into the specifics of the case at hand.

(b) Training

The IPS assists in the training of investigators, crime scene experts, prosecutors and other members of law enforcement and academia. An example of the specialised training offered by the IPS is the specialised three-week course known as the Psychologically Motivated Crimes Course. This course focuses on investigative issues unique to serial murder investigation, as well as issues related to serial rape, child molestation, sadism, sexual murders, muti murders and certain paraphilias. The focus is on the investigation of such crimes and the practical application of research and experience. The IPS has also presented training to neighbouring countries and other foreign law enforcement agencies such as Scotland Yard in England, the Los Angeles Sheriff's Department in California, the Monroe Sheriff's Department in Florida, the Australian Federal Police and the International Homicide Investigators Association.

(c) Research

Besides the investigative support and training roles, the IPS also has a research role. The research is aimed at supporting the section's investigative support and training functions by studying crimes from a local perspective and using local investigation techniques.

By providing an integrated service, the IPS has played a meaningful role in some of the most horrific and high-profile investigations the nation has seen in recent history.

9.4 SUMMARY

This chapter introduced the concepts of *modus operandi*, fantasy and signature. These three concepts often play a pivotal role as a starting point in what can broadly be described as Criminal Investigative Analysis. Within the broader spectrum of Criminal Investigative Analysis, offender profiling is an activity that has taken on a life of its own, partly due to the popular representation in the media of people providing this service. This perception is a powerful one which has influenced even the academic opinion of offender profiling, also in South Africa.

Besides discussing the various activities of a Criminal Investigative Analyst, this chapter has attempted to provide a South African definition of offender profiling as used by the Investigative Psychology Section (IPS) of the SAPS. It has also given brief definitions of the other uses of the word 'profiling' in the South African context, and focused on the concept of linkage analysis.

Mention was made of how a person providing a profiling service has a greater role to play in investigations. The IPS was used as an example of how such services can be provided.

REFERENCES

PB Ainsworth *Offender Profiling and Crime Analysis* (Willan Publishing 2002)

L Almond, L Alison & L Porter 'An evaluation and comparison of claims made in behavioural investigative advice reports compiled by the National Policing Improvements Agency in the United Kingdom' (2007) 4(2) *Journal of Investigative Psychology and Offender Profiling* 71–83

CR Bartol & AM Bartol *Criminal Behavior: A Psychosocial Approach* 7 ed (Prentice Hall 2005)

AL Bateman & CG Salfati 'An examination of behavioral consistency using individual behaviors of groups of behaviors in serial homicide' (2007) 25 *Behavioral Sciences and the Law* 527–544

C Bennel & DV Canter 'Linking commercial burglaries by modus operandi: Tests using regression and ROC analysis' (2002) 42 *Science and Justice* 1–12

D Canter *Criminal Shadows: Inside the Mind of the Serial Killer* (Harper Collins 1994)

D Canter *Mapping Murder: The Secrets of Geographical Profiling* (Virgin Publishing 2003)

D Canter 'Geographical profiling of criminals' (2004) 72(2) *Medico-Legal Journal* 53–66

J de Wet 'An exploratory analysis of serial rape in South Africa' (unpublished Doctoral thesis, University of Pretoria, 2008)

JE Douglas, AW Burgess, AG Burgess & RK Ressler *Crime Classification Manual: A Standard System for Investigating and Classifying Violent Crimes* (Jossey-Bass 1992)

JE Douglas & C Munn 'Violent crime scene analysis: Modus operandi, signature, and staging' (1992) 61(2) *FBI Law Enforcement Bulletin* 1–11.

N Gregory 'Offender profiling: A review of the literature' (2005) 7(3) *The British Journal of Forensic Practice* 29–34

D Grubin, P Kelly & C Brunsdon *Linking Serious Sexual Assaults Through Behaviour* (Home Office, London 2001)

GH Gudjonsson & LRC Haward *Forensic Psychology: A Guide to Practice* (Routledge 1999)

RR Hazelwood & JI Warren 'The relevance of fantasy in serial sexual crime investigations' in RR Hazelwood & AW Burgess (eds) *Practical Aspects of Rape Investigation: A Multidisciplinary Approach* 3 ed (CRC Press 2001) 83–95

RR Hazelwood & JI Warren 'Linkage analysis: Modus operandi, ritual, and signature in serial sexual crime' (2003) 8 *Aggression and Violent Behavior* 587–598

EW Hickey *Serial Murderers and Their Victims* 3 ed (Wadsworth/Thompson Learning 2002)

EW Hickey 'Paraphilia and signatures in crime scene investigation' in EW Hickey (ed) *Sex Crimes and Paraphilia* (Pearson Prentice Hall 2006) 95–107

B Hodgskiss 'A multivariate model of the offence behaviours of South African serial murderers' (unpublished Master's thesis, Rhodes University, 2001)

B Hodgskiss 'Lessons from serial murder in South Africa' (2004) 1(1) *Journal of Investigative Psychology and Offender Profiling* 67–94

RD Keppel 'Signature murders: A report of several related cases' (1995) 40(4) *Journal of Forensic Sciences* 670–674

RD Keppel 'Investigation of the serial offender: Linking cases through modus operandi and signature' in LB Schlesinger (ed) *Serial Offenders: Current Thoughts, Recent Findings* (CRC Press 2000) 121–133

RD Keppel & WJ Birnes *Serial Violence: Analysis of Modus Operandi and Signature Characteristics of Killers* (CRC Press 2009)

RD Keppel & JG Weis 'The rarity of "unusual" dispositions of victim bodies: Staging and posing' (2004) 49(6) *Journal of Forensic Science* 1–5

RN Kocsis, RW Cooksey & HJ Irwin 'Psychological profiling of offender characteristics from crime scene behaviors in serial rape offences' (2002) 46(2) *International Journal of Offender Therapy and Comparative Criminology* 144–169

GN Labuschagne 'Offender profiling in South Africa: Its definition and context' (2003) 16(4) *Acta Criminologica* 67–74

GN Labuschagne 'The use of a linkage analysis in the conviction of the Newcastle Serial Murderer, South Africa' (2006) 3 *Journal of Investigative Psychology and Offender Profiling* 183–191

GN Labuschagne 'The use of a linkage analysis as an investigative tool and evidential material in serial offences' in K Borgeson & K Kuehnle (eds) *Serial Offenders: Theory and Practice* (Jones & Bartlett Learning 2010) 187–215

S Merry 'Crime analysis: Principles for analysing everyday serial crime' in D Canter & L Alison (eds) *Profiling Property Crime* (Aldershot 2000) 297–318

D Ormerod 'Criminal profiling: Trial by judge and jury, not by criminal psychologist' in D Canter & L Alison (eds) *Profiling in Policy and Practice* (Ashgate Publishing 1999) 207–261

W Petherick, D Field, A Lowe & E Fry 'Criminal profiling as expert evidence' in W Patherick (ed) *Serial Crime: Theoretical and Practical Issues in Behavioral Profiling* (Elsevier 2005) 72–73

DK Rossmo *Geographic Profiling* (CRC Press 2000)

DK Rossmo 'Place, space and police investigation: Hunting serial violent criminals' in JE Eck & D Weisburd (eds) *Crime and Place: Crime Prevention Studies Volume 4* (Criminal Justice Press 1995) 217–235

DK Rossmo 'Geographic profiling' in JL Jackson & DA Bekerian (eds) *Offender Profiling* (Wiley 1997)

P Santtila, J Junkkila & NK Sandnabba 'Behavioural linking of stranger rapes' (2005) 2 *Journal of Investigative Psychology and Offender Profiling* 87–103

PJ Schwikkard 'Similar fact evidence' in PJ Schwikkard & SE van der Merwe (eds) *Principles of Evidence* (Juta 2002) 66–77

C Shaw & H McKay *Juvenile Delinquency and Urban Areas* (University of Chicago Press 1942)

BE Turvey *Criminal Profiling: An Introduction to Behavioral Evidence Analysis* 2 ed (Academic Press 2003)

N Wentink 'Serial sexual murder: Classification and development over a series of offences' (unpublished Master's thesis, University of Liverpool, 2001)

J Woodhams & T Grant 'Developing a categorization system for rapists' speech' (2006) 12(3) *Psychology, Crime & Law* 245–260.

J Woodhams, CR Hollin & R Bull 'The psychology of linking crimes: A review of the evidence' (2007) 12 *Legal and Criminological Psychology* 233–249.

J Woodhams & GN Labuschagne 'A test of case linkage principles with solved and unsolved serial rapes' (2012) 27 *Journal of Police and Criminal Psychology* 85–98, DOI 10.1007/s11896-011-9091-1

RJ Zinn 'Sentenced motor vehicle hijackers imprisoned in Gauteng as a source of crime intelligence' (MTech dissertation, Technikon SA, 2004).

RJ Zinn *Home Invasion: Robbers Disclose What You Should Know* (Tafelberg 2010)

FURTHER READING

PR Brooks, MJ Devine, TJ Green, BL Hart & MD Moore 'Serial murder: A criminal justice response' (1987) 54 (6) *Police Chief* 40–44

LH Hoffman & D Zeffert *The South African Law of Evidence* 4 ed (Butterworths 1988)

W Mischel 'Personality coherence and dispositions in a cognitive-affective personality system (CAPS) approach' in D Cervone & Y Shoda (eds) *The Coherence of Personality: Social-cognitive Bases of Consistency, Variability and Organisation* (Guilford Press 1999) 37–60

E van der Berg & SE van der Merwe 'Opinion evidence' in PJ Schwikkard & SE van der Merwe (eds) *Principles of Evidence* (Juta 2002) 79–99

J Woodhams & GN Labuschagne 'South African serial rapists: The offenders, their victims and their offences' (2011) 24(6) *Sexual Abuse: A Journal of Research and Treatment* 544–574, DOI: 10.1177/1079063212438921

Chapter 10

FORENSIC GEOGRAPHY

P M U Schmitz • A K Cooper

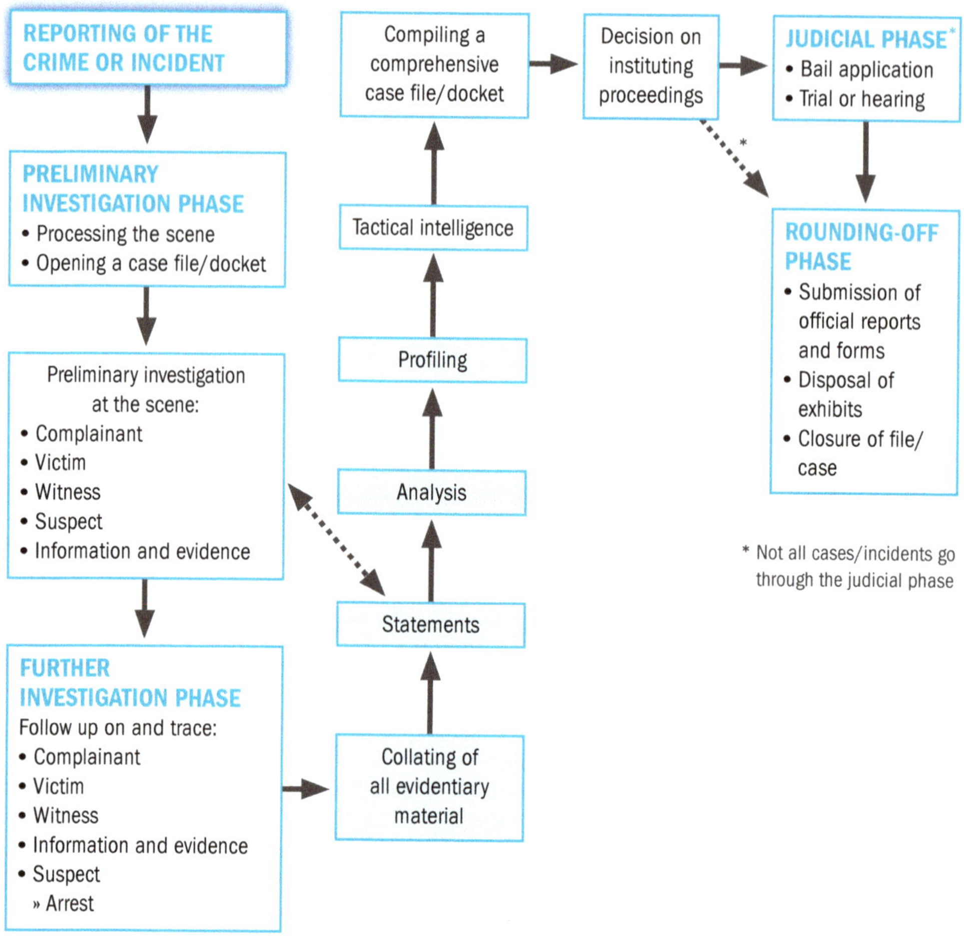

Figure 10.1: Areas of the crime investigation process covered in this chapter shown in shaded area

10.1 INTRODUCTION

In the 1970s forensic geography was seen as applied geography where the geographers acted as witnesses and consultants, and were compensated for carrying out their responsibilities.[1] Forensic geography is the discipline where the geographer does research and gives expert witness in a crime hearing, legal dispute or case where the spatial nature of the crime or dispute plays a pivotal role.[2] Forensic geography can be applied in both civil and criminal cases.[3] Some literature broadens this field into forensic geosciences or geoforensics, which includes pedology, mineralogy, petrology, geophysics, natural geography, remote

1 Lanegran (1978).
2 Brodsky (2003).
3 Morgan & Bull (2007); Mazhari (2010).

sensing, location data and Geographical Information Systems (GIS).[4] This chapter will concentrate on natural and human geography, remote sensing, location data and GIS, hence the title 'forensic geography'. Natural geography, also known as physical geography, looks at geomorphology, soils, sediments, climate, plants, etc, while human geography looks at the urban environment, population, economics, etc. Remote sensing encompasses both space and aerial platforms and includes satellite imagery, radar images, LIDAR images and aerial photography. Location data are points of interest to a case such as the location of a body, residences, shopping malls, where a crime was committed, the location of a cellphone tower, drug selling-points and banks, to name a few examples. GIS, in most instances, is the tool used to analyse and visualise the aforementioned.

According to Ruffell & McKinley[5] and Mazhari[6] geoforensics is at least over 200 years old and was used in India and China. Geoforensics was also used by the fictional character Sherlock Holmes where the fabled detective used soil and mud on shoes and clothes to determine the location of people.[7] This chapter will give an overview of forensic geography, listing South African examples as far as possible, followed by an in-depth discussion of geographic profiling and the use of cellphone data. The latter is an example of the use of location data and GIS.

10.2 OVERVIEW OF FORENSIC GEOSCIENCE AND FORENSIC GEOGRAPHY

Mazhari[8] indicated four main categories of forensic geosciences, namely:

- forensic pedology (soils), mineralogy and petrology
- forensic geophysics
- forensic natural and human geography and geomorphology
- forensic remote sensing, location data and GIS.

Morgan & Bull[9] used a twofold classification based on the scale at which the investigation is done, namely macro- and microscale. This is similar to Ruffell & McKinley's[10] large- and small-scale investigations. The Ruffell and McKinley[11] classification is problematic to geographers since they see large-scale as maps with a scale of 1:100 or 1:2 000 and small-scale as maps with a scale 1:250 000 and 1:1 000 000. To avoid this confusion, this chapter will use Morgan & Bull's[12] broad classification of macro- and microscale.

4 Morgan & Bull (2007); Mazhari (2010).
5 Ruffell & McKinley (2008).
6 Mazhari (2010).
7 Conan Doyle (1986); Ruffell & McKinley (2005).
8 Mazhari (2010).
9 Morgan & Bull (2007).
10 Ruffell & McKinley (2005).
11 Ruffell & McKinley (2005).
12 Morgan & Bull (2007).

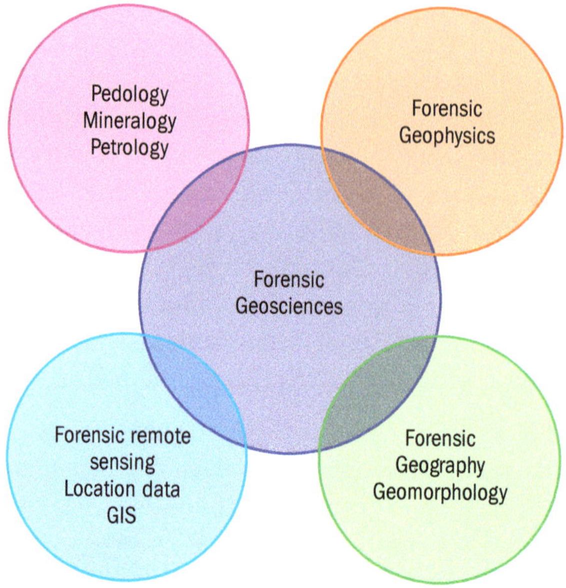

Figure 10.2: Mazhari's four categories of forensic geosciences

Table 10.1 and Figure 10.2 give the matrix of forensic geosciences based on the approaches of Mazhari and Morgan & Bull. The shaded area in the table indicates the domain of forensic geography.

Table 10.1: Morgan & Bull's classification of forensic geosciences

Scale	Macroscale	Microscale
Category		Pedology, mineralogy and petrology
	Forensic geophysics	
	Forensic natural and human geography and geomorphology	
	Forensic remote sensing, location data and GIS	

Examples of macroscale forensic geosciences would be forensic geomorphology, forensic remote sensing and aerial photography, location data and Geographic Information Systems (GIS). On the microscale it is the investigation of the physical, chemical and biological characteristics of the collected soil samples using microscopy, mineralogy, chemistry, DNA analysis and pollen analysis.[13] There is, however, the possibility of interplay between the two

13 Morgan & Bull (2007).

scales. For example, burial sites could be detected using ground-penetrating radar or through the use of landscape interpretation (macroscale),[14] but microscale investigation can be used to determine whether the bodies have been moved from one burial site to the next or where the people were executed and buried.[15] Another example of this interplay between macro- and microscale is the use of remote sensing and intelligence to determine illegal dumpsites and using X-ray diffraction of samples from the sites and suspects' clothes to link suspects to these sites.[16]

This chapter will give a few examples of forensic geoscience in general but will provide in-depth discussions on forensic geography. The myriad complexities associated with forensic geophysics is outside the scope of this book, hence the emphasis on forensic geography. The chapter focuses on techniques that will have wide application, namely the microscale identification of soils and rocks and forensic geography. The aim is to sensitise investigators to various forensic geoscience methodologies that are available to help them solve a crime.

10.2.1 Forensic pedology (soils), mineralogy and petrology (rocks)

This is the microscale application of forensic geosciences, studying soils, minerals and rocks using various techniques such as X-ray diffraction; X-ray powder diffraction; microscopy such as binocular microscopy, scanning electron microscopy and petrographic microscopy; spectrophotometry and laser granulometers.[17] In recent literature, forensic pedology, mineralogy and petrology are combined with biological analysis such as palynology (pollen analysis) and botanical analysis.[18]

X-ray diffraction and X-ray powder diffraction are used to identify minerals in soils, dust, rocks, building rubble and artificial materials such as glass, cosmetics, pharmaceuticals and plastic.[19] Microscopy is used to determine grain surface textures and granularities.[20] Spectrophotometry is used to analyse the colour of soils, sediments and rocks.[21] Laser granulometry is used to measure the particle sizes of soils, minerals and rocks.[22]

14 Morgan & Bull (2007).
15 Brown (2006).
16 Ruffell & Dawson (2009).
17 Ruffell & McKinley (2005); Morgan et al. (2006); Morgan & Bull (2007); Mazhari (2010); Morgan, Robertson et al. (2010); http://serc.carleton.edu/research_education/geochemsheets/techniques/SEM.html
18 Brown (2006); Morgan et al. (2006); Morgan & Bull (2007).
19 Ruffell & McKinley (2005).
20 Morgan et al. (2006); Morgan & Bull (2007).
21 Morgan & Bull (2007).
22 Morgan & Bull (2007).

Example 10.1: Microscale techniques to solve a crime

Here are some examples of microscale forensic pedology, mineralogy and petrology techniques that can be used to solve a crime:

- Concrete used to weigh down a body in a lake can be linked to a suspect's house using various particle sizes and thin-section analyses from disaggregated concrete from the victim and the suspect's respective houses.[23] Thin-section analysis is where the specimen, in this instance concrete, is cut into extremely thin slices for microscopic analysis.
- Spectrophotometry can be used to do a colour analysis of particles such as beach sand to determine the location of a suspect and a victim if sand was found on them (deceased) or on their clothing or other exhibits that belonged to them.[24]
- Areas of clothing that will gather silt, clay and pollen particles can be identified for use in forensic analysis.[25]
- Quartz grains can be used as a forensic reconstruction tool. Quartz grains are used to discriminate between different sites, for example where the murder occurred, where the body was buried and where the murderer established an alibi site to indicate that he or she was not at the location where the murder occurred and where the body was buried. The quartz grains recovered from the various sites and the clothes of the suspect are compared.[26]
- Mineralogy, grain size and surface texture of quartz grains and pollen analysis can be used to link suspects suspected of wildlife crime with crime scene locations or locations where wildlife occurs.[27] The methodology could be used to link recovered rhino horn to locations from where rhinos were poached and to link suspects to poaching sites.
- Mineralogy and pollen can be used to determine the removal of bodies from one mass grave to another in war crime investigations.[28]
- Laser granulometry is used to determine the distribution of particle sizes unique to a location. The particle sizes vary between 0,4 and 2 000 microns (a micron is one-thousandth of a millimetre). Each location has a unique distribution with regard to the number of particles in each size class. Lasers are used to determine the size and number of particles in each class from a sample[29]. Pye & Croft[30] recommend that this should be used in conjunction with other methods, such as those discussed previously.

The abovementioned examples show the application of pedology, mineralogy and petrology in forensics to help link suspects to a crime scene. The interested reader is referred to the textbook *Geoforensics* by Ruffell & McKinley.[31]

10.2.2 Forensic geophysics

Mazhari[32] indicates that forensic geophysics utilises methods developed for exploration purposes in geophysics. Examples are seismic methods where shock

23 Ruffell (2006).
24 Guedes et al. (2009).
25 Morgan, French et al. (2010).
26 Morgan et al. (2010).
27 Morgan, Robertson et al. (2006).
28 Brown (2006).
29 Pye & Croft (2004).
30 Pye & Croft (2004).
31 Ruffell & McKinley (2008).
32 Mazhari (2010).

waves are generated and recorded by geophones to analyse underlying rock strata for exploration and mining purposes; magnetic methods such as using ground-penetrating radar; resistivity methods, which look at the resistance of materials to electric currents; and electromagnetic surveying.[33] Ruffell & McKinley[34] discuss three examples of geophysical methods commonly used in forensic geophysics, namely:

- *Resistivity and electrical tomography*: Various types of materials, natural or anthropogenic, have various resistances to electrical currents. The differences are mapped and then used to determine the reasons for these changes. Depth resistivity is determined through the use of electrodes and the resultant depth map is known as a tomograph. This method is one of the methods used to detect burial sites.[35]
- *Electromagnetic surveys* look at the soil's ability to conduct an electric current. Anomalies in the survey could indicate the presence of a body in a shallow grave. Nobes[36] indicated that electromagnetic surveys combined with ground-penetrating radar could be used to find shallow graves for forensic purposes.
- *Ground-penetrating radar (GPR)* is one of the most commonly used methods to detect burial sites and non-metallic objects such as plastic land mines for forensic purposes.[37]

10.2.3 Forensic geography and forensic geomorphology

Geomorphology is part of natural geography. Natural geography is also known as physical geography. For the purpose of this chapter, we will use the term natural geography. As mentioned before, natural geography, apart from geomorphology, includes soil geography, plant geography and the oceans. Human geography looks as the interaction between humans and the landscape, such as urbanisation, land use and economic geography. Geomorphology is the study of surface phenomena such as erosion, sand dunes and rivers; and landforms such as hills and flood plains.[38]

Ruffell & McKinley[39] see forensic geomorphology as the forensic investigations of water issues such as water supply; pollution; accidental or wilful flooding, erosion or subsidence; and excessive deposition of materials. Trained geomorphologists can detect irregularities in the surface caused by subsidence which may indicate a grave or illegally buried waste.[40]

33 Ruffell & McKinley (2005); Ruffell (2006); Morgan & Bull (2007); Mazhari (2010).
34 Ruffell & McKinley (2005).
35 Morgan & Bull (2007).
36 Nobes (2000).
37 Ruffell & McKinley (2005); Ruffell (2006); Morgan & Bull (2007).
38 Mazhari (2010).
39 Ruffell & McKinley (2005).
40 Ruffell & McKinley (2005); Ruffell (2006).

Brodsky[41] gives an example of the use of economic geography (human geography) to determine an area of retail overlap. The results were used in a civil case dealing with breach of contract and damages between a manufacturer and a retailer. The retailer sued the manufacturer for damages owing to a competition, whose retail area overlapped with the retailer's exclusion zone. Brodsky[42] acted for the defence, namely the manufacturer, and used a retail gravity model and regional shift-share analysis from the economic geography discipline to prove that the complainant had sued excessively. The case was settled out of court based on the evidence brought by Brodsky.[43]

10.2.4 Forensic remote sensing, location data and GIS

10.2.4.1 Remote sensing

This section looks at the forensic use of remote sensing such as satellite imagery to detect environmental crime, for example the covert illegal release of waste into rivers or the atmosphere, or the extent of illegal turf mining in South Africa.[44] Remote sensing was also used to illustrate a land invasion in South Africa, which will be discussed in more detail in section 10.3.[45] Another example is the use of infrared and ultraviolet photography at crime scenes to detect disturbances such as changes in the vegetation and the presence of tyre tracks at the scene of incident.[46] In Figure 10.3 an example is given of a footprint in a house using ultraviolet photography. The investigator can then map the movements of the person through the house using the floor plan of the house.

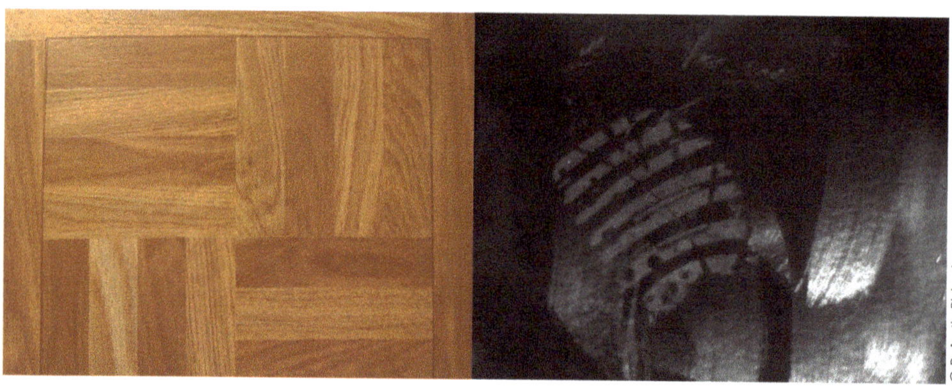

Figure 10.3: Athletic shoe impression on freshly waxed floor. Left - colour; right - near-UV[47]

41 Brodsky (2003).
42 Brodsky (2003).
43 Brodsky (2003).
44 Ruffell & McKinley (2005); Personal communication with C Eloff, Principal Researcher, CSIR Built Environment, Pretoria, South Africa on 14 September 2011.
45 Schmitz et al. (2002).
46 Ruffell & McKinley (2005); Ruffell (2006).
47 Richards (2010).

Gamma-ray spectrometry can detect radioactive material and is used to differentiate between buried weapons of mass destruction and nuclear waste.[48] The radioactive emission levels from nuclear waste are different to the radioactive emission levels from weapons of mass destruction. Aerial photography falls under the ambit of remote sensing.[49] Figure 10.4 shows the spectral gamma-ray map indicating uranium waste near a nuclear power station in Northern Ireland.

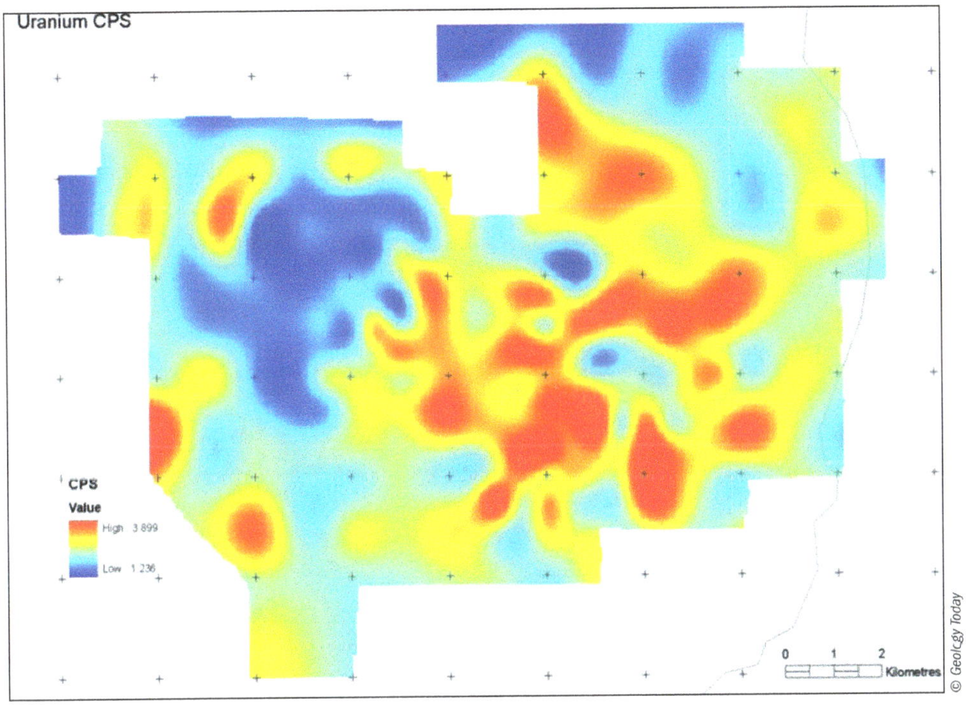

Figure 10.4: Spectral gamma-ray map showing concentrations of uranium waste[50]

10.2.4.2 Location data

Location data is usually gathered using a Global Positioning System (GPS). Global Navigation Satellite System (GNSS) is the generic term for global positioning. GPS is the US version of GNSS, GLONASS is the Russian version and Galileo the European version, to name a few examples. Many navigation systems can access several GNSS types. Cellphones and other navigation devices use data from cellphone base stations; this is known as assisted GPS.[51] GPS has become a colloquial term for any navigation system device.

48 Ruffell (2006).
49 Ruffell & McKinley (2005).
50 Figure 2 in Ruffell (2006).
51 Schmitz et al. (2009).

Examples of location data are body dump sites in a serial murder case; points of interest to a criminal investigation such as the location of the body, the position of a stationary vehicle based on tyre tracks or items that are linked to the scene of incident; illegal waste sites; and pollution point sources such as wastewater outlets into a river. Location data can also be used to reconcile crime scenes with those indicated by a suspect (as shown in Figure 10.5). Crime scenes such as burglaries, vehicle hijackings and robberies can be plotted to identify hotspots for these activities. These hotspots could then be used for intervention strategies, as illustrated in Figure 10.6.[52]

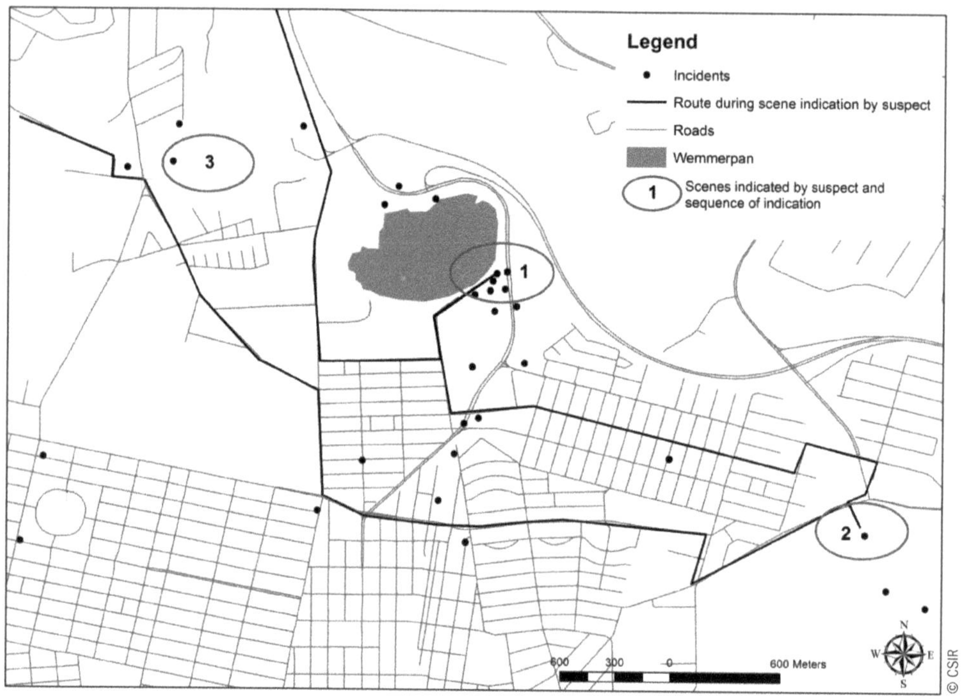

Figure 10.5: Reconciling crime scenes indicated by the suspect in the Wemmerpan serial killer investigations[53]

10.2.4.3 Geographic Information Systems (GIS)

Geographic Information Systems (GIS) is the tool that is used in most instances to visualise the aforementioned. GIS is also used in the spatial analysis of criminal behaviour to identify hotspots for a particular type of crime (see Figure 10.6); journey-to-crime; tracking of incidents across a neighbourhood; and geographic profiling of serial crimes such serial burglary, rape or murder.[54]

52 Cooper et al. (2000); Cooper et al. (2001); Schmitz (2004); Figure 2 in Schmitz & Cooper (2007a).
53 Map 3 in Cooper et al. (2000).
54 Rossmo (2000); Schmitz (2004); Morgan & Bull (2007).

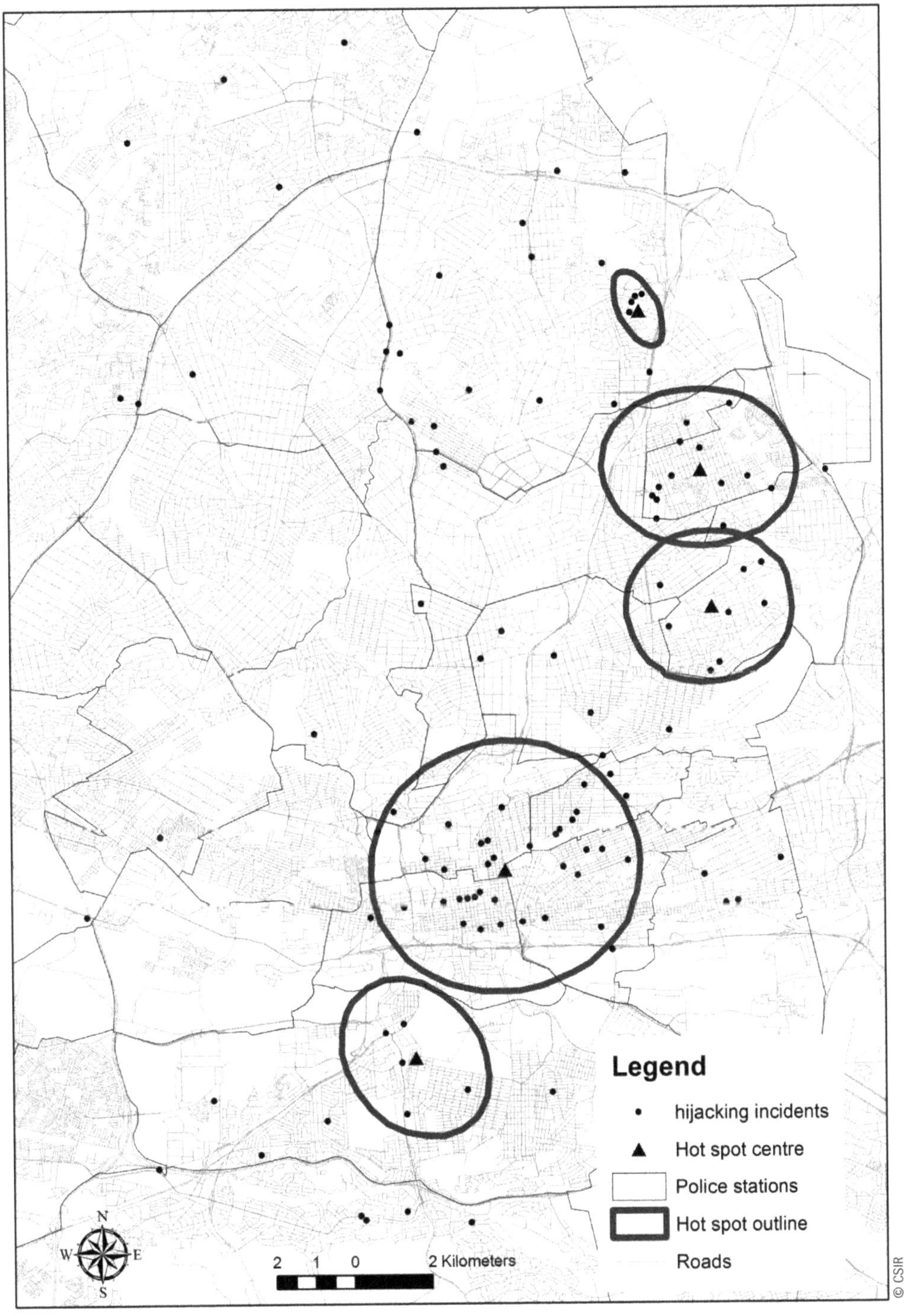

Figure 10.6: Hotspots for hijacking of vehicles in Johannesburg in 1998[55]

55 Slide 17 in Schmitz & Cooper (2007a).

10.3 EXAMPLES OF THE USE OF REMOTE SENSING IN SOUTH AFRICA

In section 10.2.4 forensic applications of remote sensing were discussed. In this section we focus on two South African examples of the use of forensic remote sensing. The first example is the Bredell land invasion, which was used by the state to evict informal settlers from the land they had invaded.[56] The second example illustrates the use of remote sensing to detect the extent of an environmental crime, namely illegal turf mining.[57]

10.3.1 The Bredell land invasion

Example 10.2: The Bredell land invasion

Owing to the housing shortage as well as the high influx of people from rural to urban areas in South Africa, people move into informal housing areas with the hope of finding a better life. On 27 June 2001 at Bredell, near Kempton Park in eastern Gauteng, several thousand people illegally invaded about 32 000 ha of land owned by the national government, the parastatals Transnet (railways) and Eskom (electricity supply), and two farmers. There, the land invaders set up an informal settlement. The land invasion had a political element, where the Pan Africanist Congress (PAC) charged money per plot from the informal settlers for any litigation processes they would have to oppose. Early in July 2001, the Pretoria High Court heard an application from the state and others to evict the squatters, which was granted. Forensic remote sensing played a critical part during the hearing and contributed to the granting of the eviction of the land invaders.[58]

Three SPOT panchromatic satellite images were used in the case, namely the images taken on 18 May, 24 June and 10 July 2001. The cadastre was overlaid on these images using GIS. These were used to show the increase in informal settlement activities over the period. The area under investigation changed from a mainly rough pasture as depicted on the image of 18 May 2001 (see Figure 10.7)[59] to an informal settlement as depicted on the image taken on 10 July 2001 (see Figure 10.8).

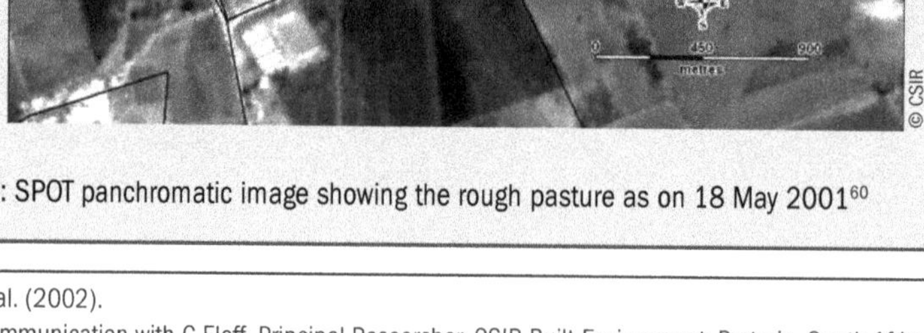

Figure 10.7: SPOT panchromatic image showing the rough pasture as on 18 May 2001[60]

→

56 Schmitz et al. (2002).

57 Personal communication with C Eloff, Principal Researcher, CSIR Built Environment, Pretoria, South Africa on 14 September 2011.

58 Schmitz et al. (2002).

59 Schmitz et al. (2002).

60 Figure 2 in Schmitz et al. (2002).

→

Figure 10.8 shows the land invasion as on 10 July 2001. The dashed line shows the area affected. This is an accurate reflection of the amount of detail that is visible on the image since the resolution of the satellite image was 10 m x 10 m. This illustrates why one needs a remote sensing specialist to assist in a case like this.

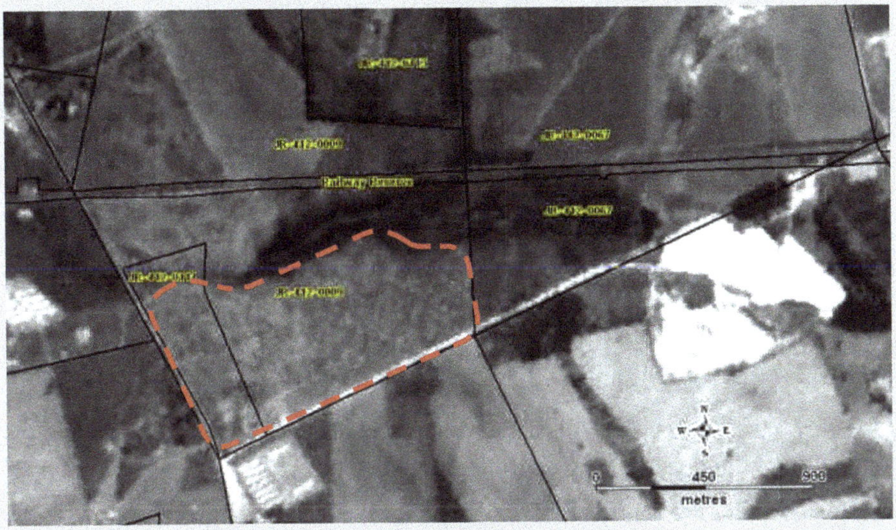

© CSIR

Figure 10.8: SPOT panchromatic image showing the invaded area as on 10 July 2001.[61]

The images were overlain with cadastral data and general reference data such as roads and rivers. Annotation was added to the images and the resultant maps were printed on A0 and A4 paper for presentation in court.[62]

61 Figure 3 in Schmitz et al. (2002).

62 Schmitz et al. (2002).

10.3.2 Illegal peat mining

Example 10.3: Illegal peat mining

Peat, as shown in Figure 10.9, can be defined as a highly organic material found in marshy or damp regions, composed of partially decayed vegetable matter. It is cut and dried for use as fuel or fertiliser. Peat in its natural form is mainly located in sensitive ecosystems such as wetland areas.

Figure 10.9: Peat

As a 'dry country', South Africa clearly has to protect its water resources and conserve sensitive ecosystems such as wetlands. The illegal mining of peat in South Africa is a problem and the environmental damage caused by these illegal actions is usually permanent. The use of bathometry measurements (sonar) and remote-sensing technologies enable the detection of change over time and the extent of the damage. Figure 10.10 shows the use of SPOT 5 satellite imagery to determine the extent of the environmental damage in a wetland in the North West province. Figure 10.10 shows the water-logged areas (light yellow and yellow areas) that were created through the illegal peat mining activities from 2006 to 2010.

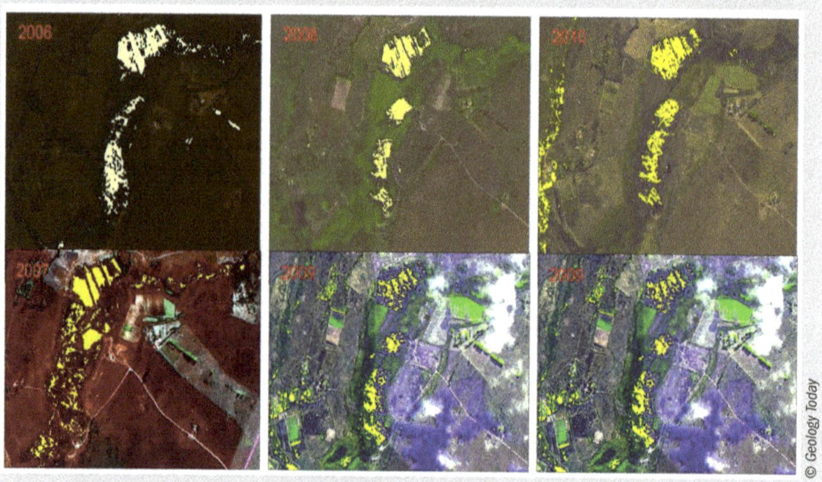

Figure 10.10: Environmental damage caused by illegal peat mining[63]

→

63 Eloff (2011).

→

Remotely sensed images can be supported by aerial photographs to show the environmental damage over a long period. This is clearly illustrated in Figure 10.11.

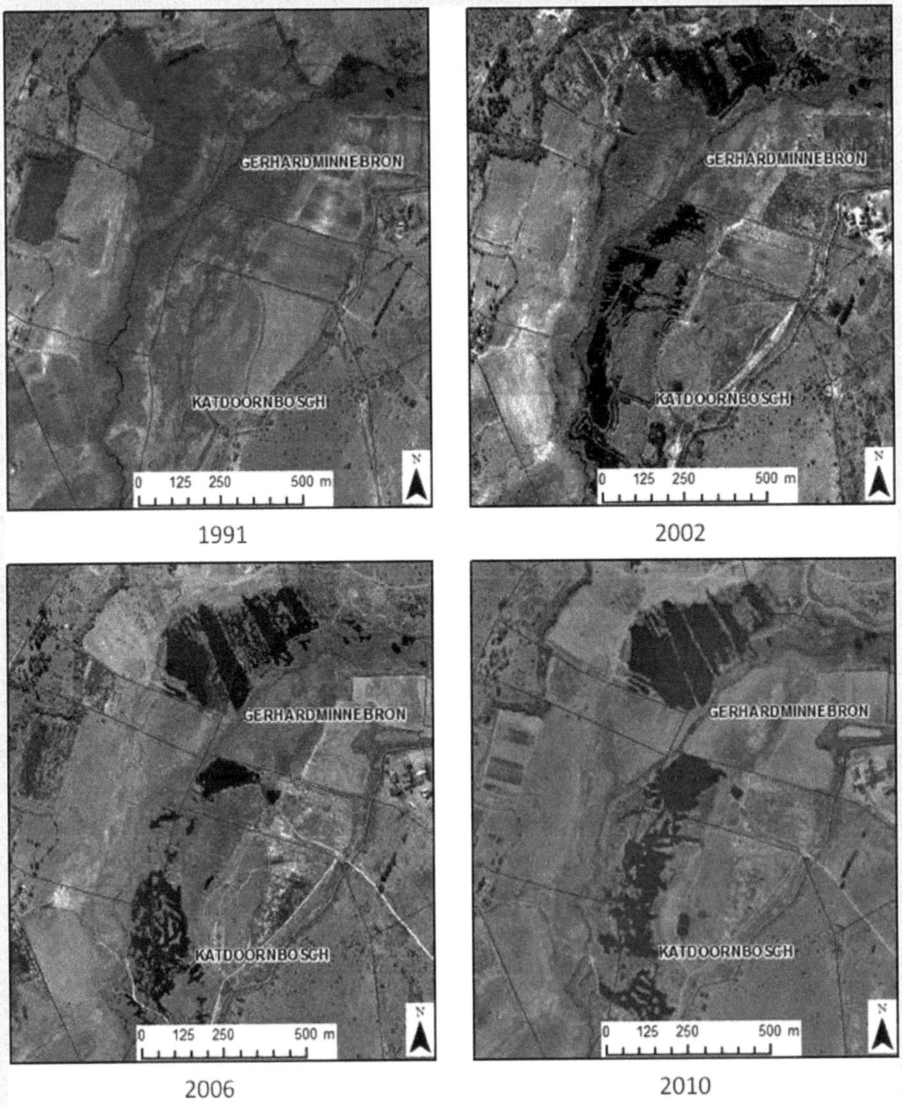

Figure 10.11: The extent of environmental damage caused by illegal mining activities in the North West province[64]

→

64 Eloff (2012).

→

A bathymetrical sensor can be used to detect the depth of the actual mining below the water surface. These values can be used to measure and model an accurate digital elevation model (DEM), which can be used to calculate the actual volume of material that was harvested from the specific area. The DEM is created using one-metre contour lines calculated from the bathometry values (see Figure 10.12). At the writing of this chapter the case is ongoing. These images and calculations are used as evidence to show the court the extent of environmental damage caused by this illegal mining activity at Katdoornbosch and Gerhard Minnebron in the North West province.

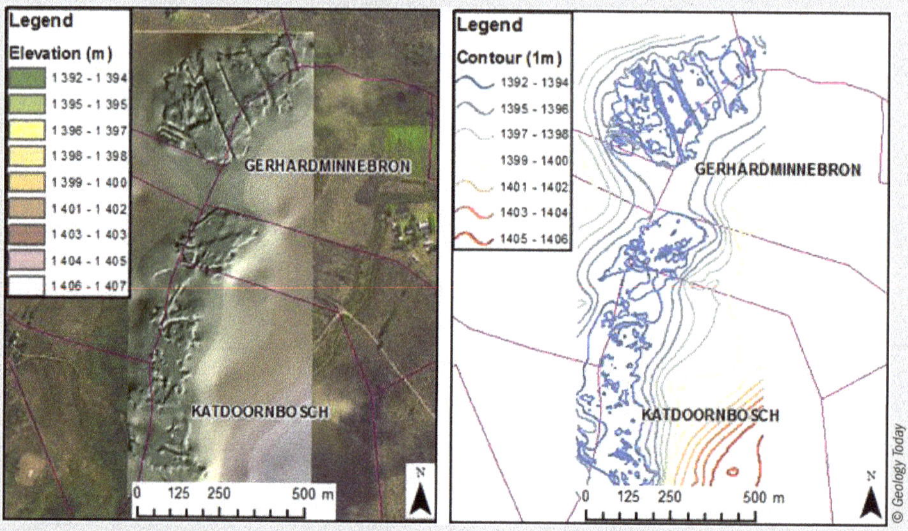

Digital elevation model

Bathometry values shows as 1 metre contour lines

Figure 10.12: Showing the bathometry that is used to calculate the extent of the environmental damage caused by illegal mining[65]

10.4 GEOGRAPHIC PROFILING

Geographic profiling is used to determine the anchor point or points from which a serial criminal operates. The anchor point is in most cases the residence but it could also be the workplace, a pub or other point of importance to the criminal. Geographic profiling takes into account the location of the incidents, such as burglaries or, in the event of serial murders or serial rapes, the encounter, attack, murder/rape and body dump/release sites. In most serial murder cases the body dump site is known to the investigators. In rape cases all sites are known since the victim is alive to indicate these sites.

65 Eloff (2012).

Geographic profiling uses an algorithm to determine the most probable area of a serial criminal's anchor point. The total area covered by the criminal based on incident locations is known as the hunting area. The geographic profile is based on the hunting area. The peak profile is that area of the geographic profile that shows the highest probability in which the criminal's anchor point could be located.[66]

10.4.1 Mental maps

An offender moves in time and space. This movement in time and space is determined by the offender's knowledge and mental map of the area. It is also governed by the least-effort principle. The mental map is a generalised map of the area which includes attractions as well as features such as roads, routes and landmarks to get to the attractions. Points-of-interest are locations that are of interest to a case, such as body dump sites, the locations of encounters, rape and release, as well other features such as lampposts, houses and roads. Attractions are special forms of points-of-interest that have an attraction for a serial offender to find suitable victims or a location to commit a crime. These could be shopping malls, the gym, nightclubs or candidate properties for burglaries, for example.

Mental maps are influenced by the person's geographic, social and economic (work) location as well as their access to different transport modes such as a car, taxi or train. In contrast to a person who owns their own motor vehicle, the mental map of a person who does not own a motor vehicle might consist of areas that can be reached and traversed on foot and areas restricted to taxi routes.[67]

Mental maps consist of the following elements:[68]

- *Paths*: routes of travel that tend to dominate most people's images of cities, for example freeways and railways
- *Edges*: boundaries or lines that help to organise cognitive maps, for example rivers, freeways and railways
- *Districts*: subareas with recognisable unifying characteristics consisting of well-established cores with fuzzy boundaries, for example business districts or poor, neglected areas
- *Nodes*: intense foci of activities, for example intersections, shopping malls or corner shops
- *Landmarks*: symbols used for orientation but which typically are not physically entered, for example high buildings, trees and structures like water towers, distinctive radio and cellphone towers or bridges.

66 Schmitz (2004).
67 Rossmo (2000).
68 Rossmo (2000).

Mental maps are created by the person's awareness space and activity space. Awareness space is the space of which a person has a general knowledge. The person's activity space is situated within this awareness space. The activity space is that area in which the person performs their daily activities, such as living, going to work, shopping, exercising and going to movies or restaurants. Some of these locations act as anchor points within the activity space and these are the locations of most importance to the person. Anchor points are typically the residence, pub or shebeen or other place of importance to the individual. The same accounts for offenders, who use these anchor points as the bases from which to commit their crimes.[69]

10.4.2 Journey-to-crime

The geography of crime looks at where and when a crime was committed. Criminals commit their crimes within their awareness space. The journey-to-crime is a method to describe the geography of crime. It determines that criminals in most instances will not travel far from their anchor point to commit a crime and that the number of incidents linked to a specific criminal will decrease in distance from the anchor point. Violent crimes tend to be committed closer to the anchor point than property crimes. High-crime neighbourhoods tend to influence the criminal's journey patterns.[70] Canter[71] indicated in his 1996 study that serial rapists in the United Kingdom travelled an average distance of approximately 2,5 km (1.53 miles) from their activity nodes to commit their crimes. Canter[72] further indicated that these serial rapists avoided any criminal activity within 1 km (0.61 miles) of their activity nodes. This is to minimise the risk of being detected by neighbours. House robbers and hijackers in South Africa usually commit their crimes in a radius of about 10 to 30 minutes' walking or driving distance from their activity nodes.[73]

The distance decay curve is used to model the decrease in criminal activity away from the anchor point. This curve is used in geographic profiling to determine the anchor point.[74] Rossmo[75] developed a methodology, namely the Criminal Geographic Targeting (CGT) algorithm, to determine the anchor point or points of a serial criminal. RIGEL is the proprietary software that uses the CGT algorithm. The next few examples illustrate the application of geographic profiling in South Africa using RIGEL. All the examples given are solved cases.[76]

69 Schmitz (2004).
70 Rossmo (2000).
71 Canter (1996).
72 Canter (1996).
73 Zinn (2003) 163; Zinn (2007) 154; Zinn (2010) 96.
74 Zinn (2010) 96.
75 Zinn (2010) 96.
76 Schmitz (2004).

10.4.3 Wemmerpan serial killer

Example 10.4: The Wemmerpan serial killer

The Wemmerpan serial killer started his series of murders in September 1995 in Johannesburg and was arrested in early 1998. The investigating officer, Brigadier Piet Byleveld, could link 86 cases in the series. What made this case interesting was that the investigating officers initially thought they had four independent series running simultaneously until the leading investigator made a breakthrough by linking the four series into one based on the offender's signature on an invoice.

As part of the Innovation Fund project in the late 1990s the CSIR got involved with the Wemmerpan serial killer case by mapping all the locations for court purposes and to demonstrate the use of GIS in investigation. As part of this demonstration the CSIR invited Dr Kim Rossmo to see whether his geographic profiling tool could be applied to South African conditions. The crime sites and the street network of Johannesburg were then emailed to Canada, where Rossmo and his team ran the geographic profile.

The results of the geographic profile are given in Figures 10.13 to 10.15. Figure 10.13 shows the geographic profile of the Wemmerpan serial killer.

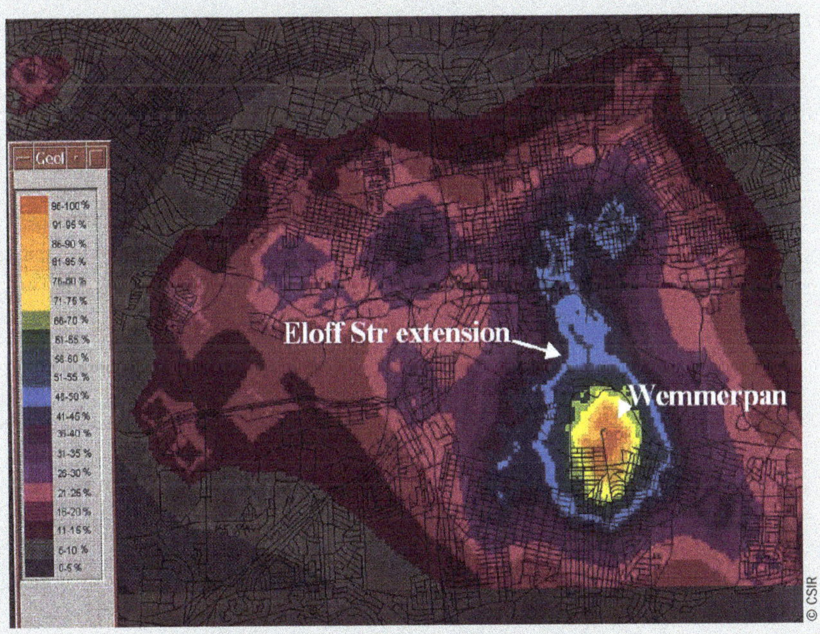

Figure 10.13: The Wemmerpan serial killer's geographic profile[77]

→

77 Figure 2 in Schmitz (2004).

→

Figure 10.14 shows the top 10% of the geographic profile, meaning the likelihood is 90% or more that the anchor point or anchor points of the serial killer will be found within the modelled area. Figure 10.15 shows a 'teardrop' pattern, indicating a primary and secondary anchor point.[78] The primary anchor point in this example indicates the serial killer's residence and the secondary anchor point was a place of work in downtown Johannesburg.[79] Figure 10.15 shows the top 1%, meaning there is a 99% likelihood of finding the anchor points in this area. The results showed that RIGEL could predict the residences of the serial killer in the top 1% of the hunting area. Upon arrest the suspect was staying in the second residence.[80]

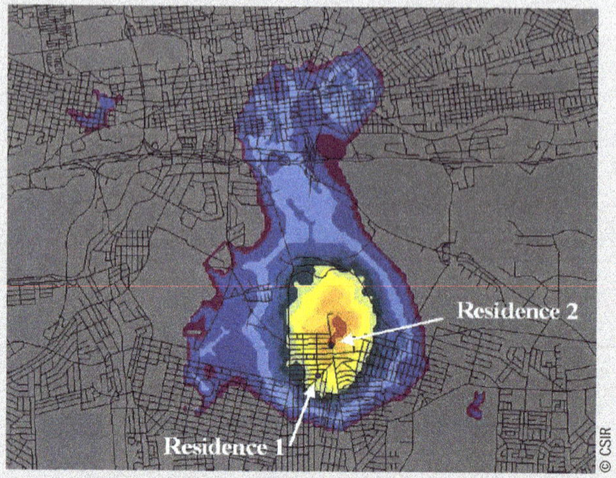

Figure 10.14: The top 10% of the geographic profile of the Wemmerpan serial killer[81]

Figure 10.15: The top 1% of the geographic profile of the Wemmerpan serial killer[82]

78 Rossmo (2000).
79 Figure 3 in Schmitz (2004).
80 Schmitz (2004).
81 Schmitz (2004).
82 Schmitz (2004).

10.4.4 Mine Dump serial killer

Example 10.5: The Mine Dump serial killer

The Mine Dump serial killer raped and murdered children in their teens, irrespective of their sex. He abducted the children and took them to secluded places among the mine dumps around Johannesburg to rape and murder them. He started his series in October 2002 and was arrested in December 2003. Fortunately, his last victim survived the attack and was able to lead the police to his 'home', which was a secluded place under a bridge of the M2 highway in Johannesburg.

He was one of many individuals who trawled areas with a trolley, picking up scrap metal and paper products for recycling to earn an income. This allowed him to scan his hunting area for suitable victims. The geographic profile, using the first five scenes out of 11, could predict the anchor point accurately. The reason for using only the first five scenes was to demonstrate that geographic profiling can be done early in the series to enable the investigating officers to search and arrest the serial killer as quickly as possible. Figure 10.16 shows the geographic profile of the serial killer and Figure 10.17 the top 3%, meaning a 97% probability of finding the serial killer at that location. The Mine Dump serial killer's geographic profile shows a 'bull's eye' pattern, indicating a single dominant anchor point.[83]

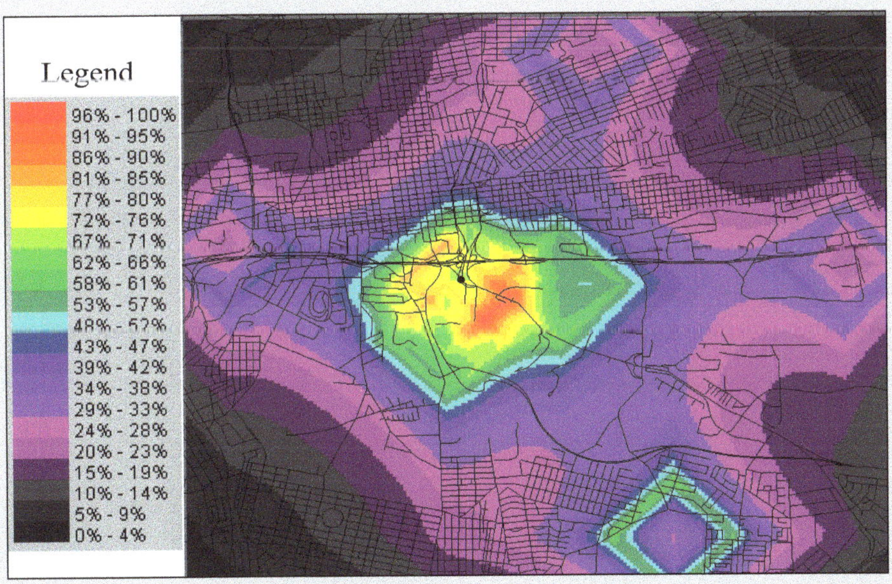

Figure 10.16: The geographic profile of the Mine Dump serial killer[84]

→

83 Rossmo (2000).

84 Figure 18 in Schmitz (2004).

→

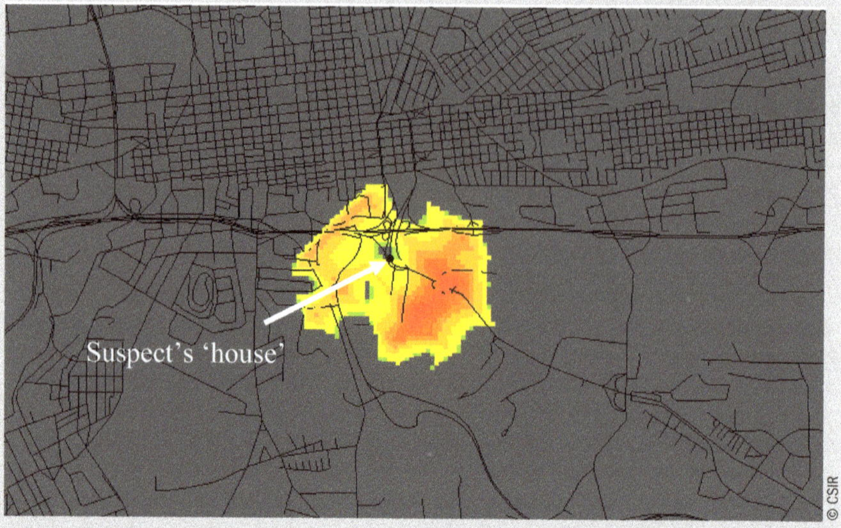

Figure 10.17: The top 3% of the geographic profile of the Mine Dump serial killer[85]

10.4.5 Norwood serial rapist

Example 10.6: The Norwood serial rapist

The Norwood serial rapist committed his first rape in May 1989 and his last one in August 1992. The serial rapist shows a distinct bi-modal pattern, indicating two anchor points of almost equal importance. The primary one of the two was the police quarters at the Norwood police station and the secondary one was his parents' home. The Norwood serial rapist was a police officer stationed at the Norwood police station who resided in the barracks behind the police station. He thus committed his crimes from where he was living or from his parents' home when he was visiting them when he was off duty and on his 'rest days'. Figure 10.18 shows the geographic profile of the Norwood serial rapist and Figure 10.19 the top 1% of the profile.

Figure 10.18: The Norwood serial rapist's geographic profile. Figure 10.16 shows the legend of the colour scheme.[86]

→

85 Figure 20 in Schmitz (2004).

86 Figure 26 in Schmitz (2004).

Figure 10.19: The top 1% of the geographic profile of the Norwood serial rapist.[87]

As the examples above illustrate, geographic profiling is a useful tool to assist investigators in finding a serial criminal. It reduces the search area for the suspect and allows for door-to-door searches and surveillance within the high-probability areas of the profile.

However, geographic profiling is not restricted to serial killing and rape. It can be applied to any crime series, such as serial arson, serial burglary, serial assault and serial armed robbery. The difficult part of geographic profiling is to establish whether the crime incidents belong to the same series. Once the series has been established based on *modus operandi* or other factors, such as fetishes left at the scene of incident, the neighbourhood, the target backcloth and the series location, coordinates can be used to establish the geographic profile.

10.5 ANALYSIS OF CELLPHONE DATA

Cellphone and/or landline telephone data has been used successfully to prosecute offenders in South Africa and elsewhere in the world. There are several tools available to extract and analyse cellphone data, such as XRY and Analyst Workstation.[88] XRY is used to extract information from a confiscated cellphone and Analyst Workstation to analyse links between various cellphone and landline numbers. This analysis places the offender in time and space using the information obtained from the detailed cellphone billing records.[89] Landline telephone data can also be used because landlines are linked to a physical address.

The data from cellular and landline telephones is used to determine the activity space in which the offender has committed the crime. The resultant map or maps created from this process can be used as evidence in court for prosecution purposes.

87 Figure 58 in Schmitz (2004).
88 Personal communication with C Linnen, Lt Col, detective in the Western Cape War Room, SAPS on 29 November 2011.
89 Cooper & Schmitz (2000); Schmitz et al. (2000); Schmitz & Cooper (2007b); Schmitz et al. (2009).

Cellphone and landline data is obtained by the investigating officer in terms of s 205 of the Criminal Procedure Act 51 of 1977. It is important to obtain the required permission to access private information; if the legal procedure is not followed, it will render the evidence useless.[90] This type of information will thus rarely, if ever, be at the disposal of private investigators. Point-of-interest data, for example the location of crime scenes, suspects' houses, the nightclub where gang members meet and the location where a hijacked vehicle was abandoned, is important to the case and is either captured by the investigating officer or by the forensic geographer using a Global Positioning System (GPS) device and other spatial datasets, as required.

10.5.1 Cellphone data

Detailed cellphone billing data is created when a subscriber uses the network by recording the transactions on the cellphone. These transactions consist of incoming and outgoing calls; short message service (SMS) and multimedia messaging service (MMS) transactions, and internet usage denoted on the billing record as General Packet Radio System (GPRS). The latter is linked to smartphones. Figure 10.20 gives an example of such a billing record in spreadsheet format. The data in Figure 10.20 has been made anonymous to protect the privacy of the subscriber and service provider.

KEY

The acronyms in the Call_Type column are:

- MOSMS: SMS originating, meaning outgoing SMS
- MTSMS: SMS terminating, meaning incoming SMS
- MTC: Mobile terminating call, meaning the cellphone has received a call (incoming call)
- CF: Call forward, meaning the cellphone was not available to receive the call and the call was forwarded to the messaging service of the service provider
- GPRS: Listed in the Call_Type column when the subscriber uses their cellphone to access the internet.

MSISDN	IMSI	IMEI	Call_Date	Call_Time	Call_Type	Call_Duration	Other_Party	Third_Party	Cell_Id	Cell_Name
2782123456x	6550154xx205880	352481x46119x1	24-Jun-11	13:10:00	MOSMS	0	2772541993x		210177	3G_Central_Park_NY_SGC
2782123456x	6550154xx205880	352481x46119x1	24-Jun-11	14:08:24	MTC	55	2779804841x		210172	3G_Central_Park_NY_SGC
2782123456x	6550154xx205880	352481x46119x1	24-Jun-11	14:30:38	MOSMS	0	2779804841x		210172	3G_Central_Park_NY_SGC
2782123456x	6550154xx205880	352481x46119x1	24-Jun-11	16:23:56	MOSMS	0	2779804841x		210172	3G_Central_Park_NY_SGC
2782123456x	6550154xx205880	352481x46119x1	24-Jun-11	16:24:03	MOSMS	0	2779804841x		210172	3G_Central_Park_NY_SGC
2782123456x	6550154xx205880	352481x46119x1	24-Jun-11	16:24:06	MOSMS	0	2779804841x		210172	3G_Central_Park_NY_SGC
2782123456x	6550154xx205880	352481x46119x1	24-Jun-11	16:24:11	MOSMS	0	2779804841x		210172	3G_Central_Park_NY_SGC
2782123456x	6550154xx205880	352481x46119x1	24-Jun-11	16:24:15	MOSMS	0	2779804841x		210172	3G_Central_Park_NY_SGC
2782123456x	6550154xx205880	352481x46119x1	24-Jun-11	16:24:21	MOSMS	0	2779804841x		210172	3G_Central_Park_NY_SGC
2782123456x	6550154xx205880	352481x46119x1	24-Jun-11	16:24:30	MOSMS	0	2779804841x		210172	3G_Central_Park_NY_SGC
2782123456x	6550154xx205880	352481x46119x1	24-Jun-11	16:24:34	MOSMS	0	2779804841x		210172	3G_Central_Park_NY_SGC
2782123456x	6550154xx205880	352481x46119x1	24-Jun-11	16:24:45	MOSMS	0	2779804841x		210172	3G_Central_Park_NY_SGC
2782123456x	6550154xx205880	352481x46119x1	24-Jun-11	16:38:48	CF	4	27821482123456x	2783730747x	210177	3G_Central_Park_NY_SGC
2782123456x	6550154xx205880	352481x46119x1	24-Jun-11	19:04:28	MTC	58	2782958488x		210177	3G_Central_Park_NY_SGC
2782123456x	6550154xx205880	352481x46119x1	24-Jun-11	19:52:38	MOSMS	0	2784439991x		210177	3G_Central_Park_NY_SGC
2782123456x	6550154xx205880	352481x46119x1	24-Jun-11	19:56:40	MTSMS	0			210177	3G_Central_Park_NY_SGC
2782123456x	6550154xx205880	352481x46119x1	25-Jun-11	7:40:38	MTC	27	2779811841x		210177	3G_Central_Park_NY_SGC
2782123456x	6550154xx205880	352481x46119x1	25-Jun-11	7:47:25	MTSMS	0			210177	3G_Central_Park_NY_SGC
2782123456x	6550154xx205880	352481x46119x1	25-Jun-11	8:27:05	MTSMS	0			210177	3G_Central_Park_NY_SGC
2782123456x	6550154xx205880	352481x46119x1	25-Jun-11	9:00:42	MTSMS	0			210177	3G_Central_Park_NY_SGC
2782123456x	6550154xx205880	352481x46119x1	25-Jun-11	9:03:12	MOSMS	0	2782978488x		210172	3G_Central_Park_NY_SGC

Figure 10.20: An example of detailed cellphone billing data

90 Lochner (2007).

10.5.2 Landline data

In South Africa the telephone lines are digital and Telkom is in a position to provide detailed transactional data on its subscribers, similar to those of cellphone service providers. Landlines are linked to a physical address, which enables the investigating officer to geocode the position of the telephone by means of an address spatial dataset.

10.5.3 Data on points of interest

All other data, except cellular and landline telephone data, falls into the category of data on points of interest. Points of interest include the scene of incident itself; locations of crime scenes identified by a suspect; places of interest in the case such as the residences, entertainment spots and recreational areas used by the suspect; cellphone base stations linked to the cellphone billing report; and GIS data such as roads, cadastre, suburbs, land use, land cover, geo-rectified digital aerial photography and satellite imagery. Figure 10.21 shows an example where the analysis of cellphone data was used to determine the activity space of a suspect combined with points-of-interest data related to the case. All the points of interest, with the exception of the burnt-out vehicle, are within the suspect's activity space.

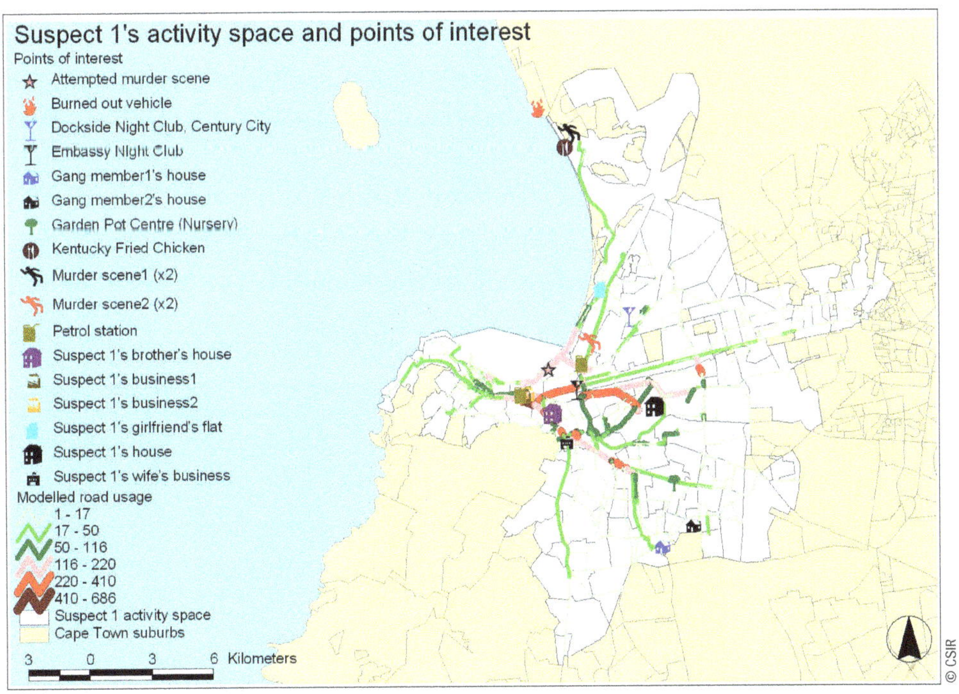

Figure 10.21: Activity space and points of interest of the suspect[91]

91 Slide 11 in Schmitz & Cooper (2007b).

10.5.4 Which data can be used?

From a forensic geography point of view the following elements of a detailed cellphone or landline billing record are useful:

- The cellphone and landline number(s) belonging to identified suspects and other persons of interest to the case.
- The cell triggered during the call. Cells are linked to a base station and cover a specific geographic area in which a cellphone transaction can be made. The cell's centroid or the base station coordinates are used to place the call geographically.
- The date and time stamp of the call type. This is linked to a location to determine the space-time behaviour of the suspect and to link the call with another suspect or person of interest to the case.

The time difference between calls can be used to approximate the travel speed of a suspect.[92] It can also be used to determine whether a distant base station that was triggered could have been reached by vehicle or not. If not, further investigation is required to determine why that base station was triggered and whether temperature inversions and humidity played a role. Temperature inversions can cause ducting, which can cause radio waves between 50 MHz and 1,2 GHz to be transported over large distances.[93] In South Africa the cellular frequencies are either in the 900 MHz or the 1,8 GHz range.[94] The 900 MHz range has a much wider reach than the 1,8 GHz range[95] and is thus prone to ducting when conditions are favourable.

Example 10.7: Ducting

In a murder case in Reservoir Hills, Durban, the cellphone data on the night of the murder indicated that a tower was triggered 8 km from the murder scene. However, the billing record indicated that just before that, a tower was triggered about 450 m from the scene. The time difference between these two cellphone transactions was one and a half minutes. If one takes the terrain and the road network into consideration, it was impossible for the person who used the cellphone to drive 8 km in one and a half minutes.

The only explanation was that ducting had occurred at that point. Using data from a weather balloon of the South African Weather Bureau it was clear that on the night of the murder there was a well-established temperature inversion layer. It was furthermore discovered that, if a person was standing at the back of the garden or house where the murder was committed, he would be in direct line of sight of the cellphone base station 8 km away. This combination of circumstances made it possible for the cellphone to use the signal from a cellphone tower 8 km away instead of a base station 450 m away because the signal from the latter was weakened by a row of very high eucalyptus trees. Figure 10.22 illustrates this concept. →

92 Lochner (2007).
93 Jones (2000).
94 Snyman (2007).
95 Snyman (2007).

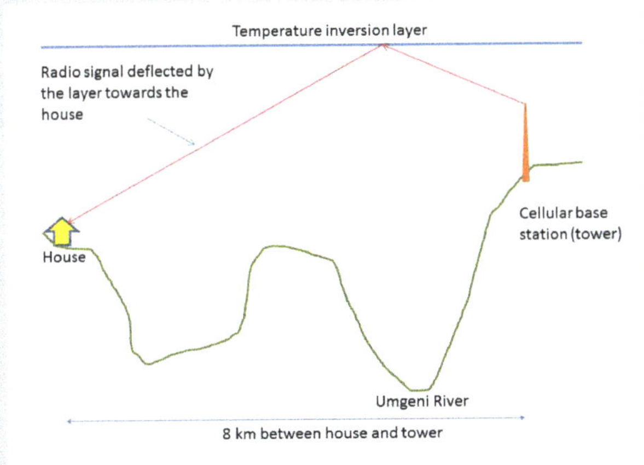

Figure 10.22: The effect of a temperature inversion layer on radio signals

Date, time and location can be used to create space-time prisms or graphs to indicate the suspect's location in time and space.[96] Figure 10.23 gives an example of a space-time graph based on cellphone base station coordinates and the time when these base stations were triggered in the Cape Town area by the cellphones the perpetrators were using before, during and after the murder of Taliep Petersen.[97] The black dotted line indicates the murder scene; the red line indicates the movements of Najwa Petersen, Taliep's wife; the blue line indicates the movements of Faheem Hendricks; the brown line those of Abdoer Raasiet Emjedi, and the green line those of Waheed Hassen through time and space to and from the crime scene. All the lines were plotted using the locations of the cellphone towers triggered.

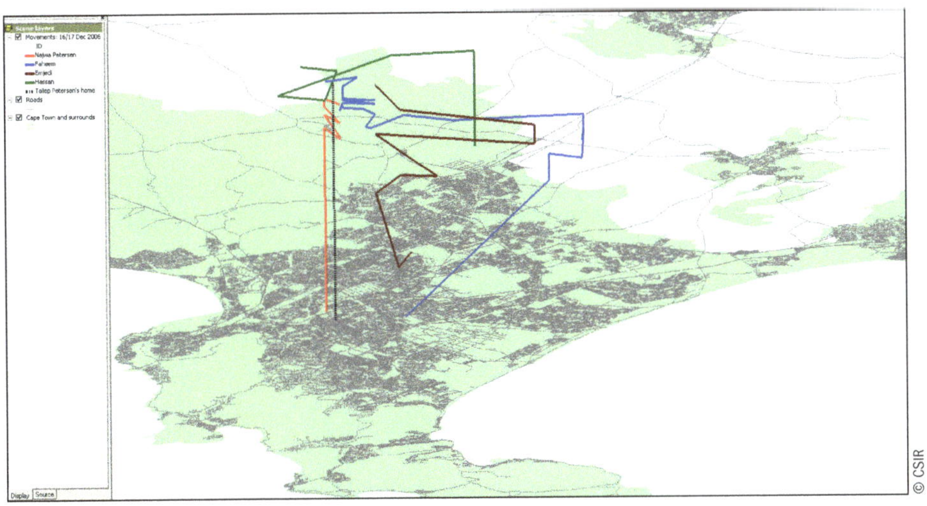

Figure 10.23: Space-time graph of the suspects' movements in the Taliep Petersen murder on 16/17 December 2006[98]

96 Elmes et al. (2007); Schmitz et al. (2009).

97 Schmitz et al. (2009).

98 Figure 5 in Schmitz et al. (2009).

10.5.5 Preliminary investigation of the data

Detailed billing records contain a huge amount of data, especially if the time period of the investigation covers several weeks and a large number of suspects and persons of interest to the case are involved. The investigating officer may only be interested in a few days in succession that are important to the case, as in the Taliep Petersen murder case. To extract the required data, the investigator can combine the detailed billing records from the various suspects and persons of interest on a single spreadsheet and arrange them chronologically using the date and time data of the transactions.

This exercise will give an overview of the geographic extent of the activity space, the distribution of usage in a day, the geographic mobility of the suspects and persons of interest, the chronological sequence, and the frequency of base station usage. This type of information can unravel the mystery of which suspects were involved and reveal their individual movements and cellphone usage during the crime, thus indicating each person's involvement in committing the crime.

10.6 METHODOLOGY USED TO ESTABLISH A FORENSIC MAP

The previous section gave an overview of the data required in the application of forensic geography. This section explains the methodology used to create a forensic map (geographic profile) based on the cellphone usage of suspects and persons of interest to the case. A state witness may be a person of interest.

10.6.1 Overview of Geographic Information Systems (GIS)

Geographic Information Systems (GIS) can be defined as follows:[99]

> A GIS is a computer-assisted system, combined with appropriate infrastructures, resources and management, that acquires, stores, retrieves, transforms, manipulates and displays geographical and related non-geographical data.

Spatial data express space in a GIS as the relationship between spatial features. Spatial features are expressed as objects that have a geographical component (latitude and longitude) as well as descriptive attributes, such as a road or a cellphone base station or a land parcel.[100] Spatial features such as cellphone base stations, erven (land parcels), farms, rivers, roads, crime scenes and mountains are derived from the real world and are represented in a GIS as a point, a line or a polygon.

Points describe objects such as the location of a body at a crime scene, points of interest to the case, as illustrated in Figure 10.21, as well as cellphone base stations. Rivers and roads are examples of a line feature, consisting of interconnected points with a start and end point and showing direction. Polygons are

99 Schmitz (2007).
100 Berhardsen (2002).

areas such as the cells of a cellphone service provider and suburbs, as shown in Figure 10.21. Points in lines and polygons are known as nodes and are joined by vertices (the lines between the nodes).[101] Figure 10.24 illustrates these concepts.

GIS has been used as the tool to analyse and map the spatial data related to the various examples given in this chapter.

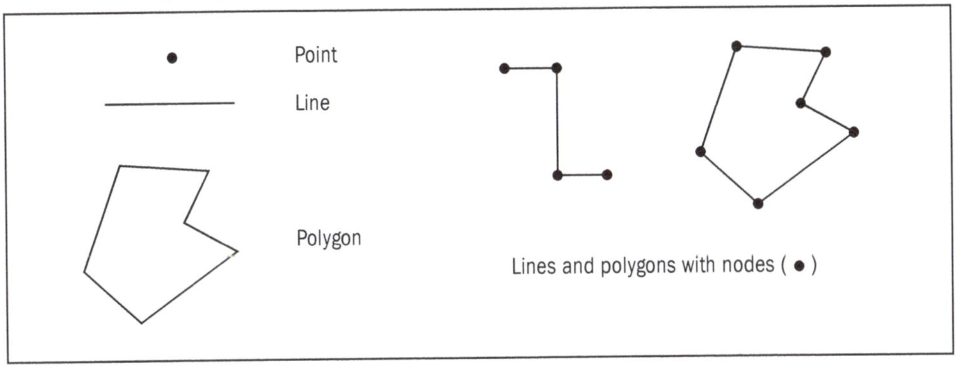

Figure 10.24: Points, lines and polygons

10.6.2 Overview of Global Positioning Systems (GPS)

A Global Positioning System (GPS), an example of a Global Navigation Satellite System (GNSS) (see section 10.2.4.2 of this chapter), consists of a constellation of satellites that transmits information and time to receivers on the ground.[102] Figure 10.25 shows such a constellation of GPS satellites.

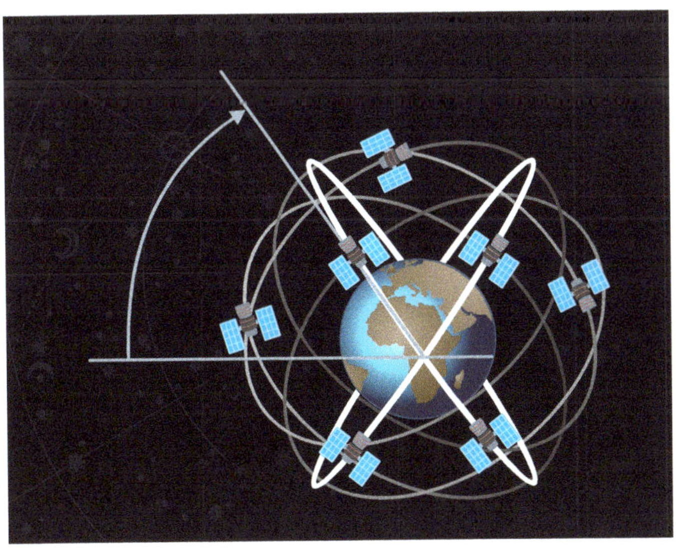

Figure 10.25: A constellation of GPS satellites[103]

101 Berhardsen (2002); Bolstad (2005).
102 Smithsonian Institute (2011).
103 Smithsonian Institute (2011).

A GPS receiver needs three or more satellites to determine its position. It uses the information of the satellite as well as the time the signal takes to travel to determine its position on the Earth's surface. Figure 10.26 illustrates the method to determine the location of a GPS receiver.

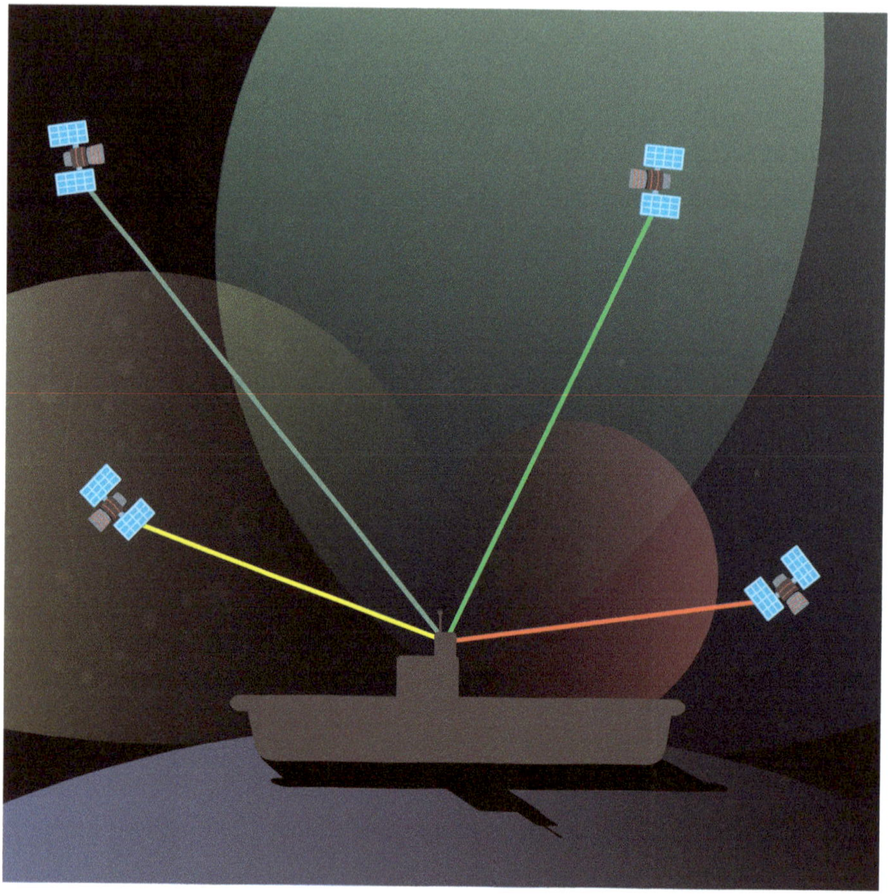

Figure 10.26: Determining the position of a GPS receiver[104]

Receivers require an unobstructed view of the sky, which may be difficult in urban areas or areas with dense vegetation. To overcome these problems, some GPS receivers have an assisted-GPS (aGPS) capability where GPS data is transmitted via ground stations or cellphone networks.[105] Figure 10.27 illustrates the concept of aGPS in a cellphone network.

104 Smithsonian Institute (2011).
105 Mobile Nation (2011).

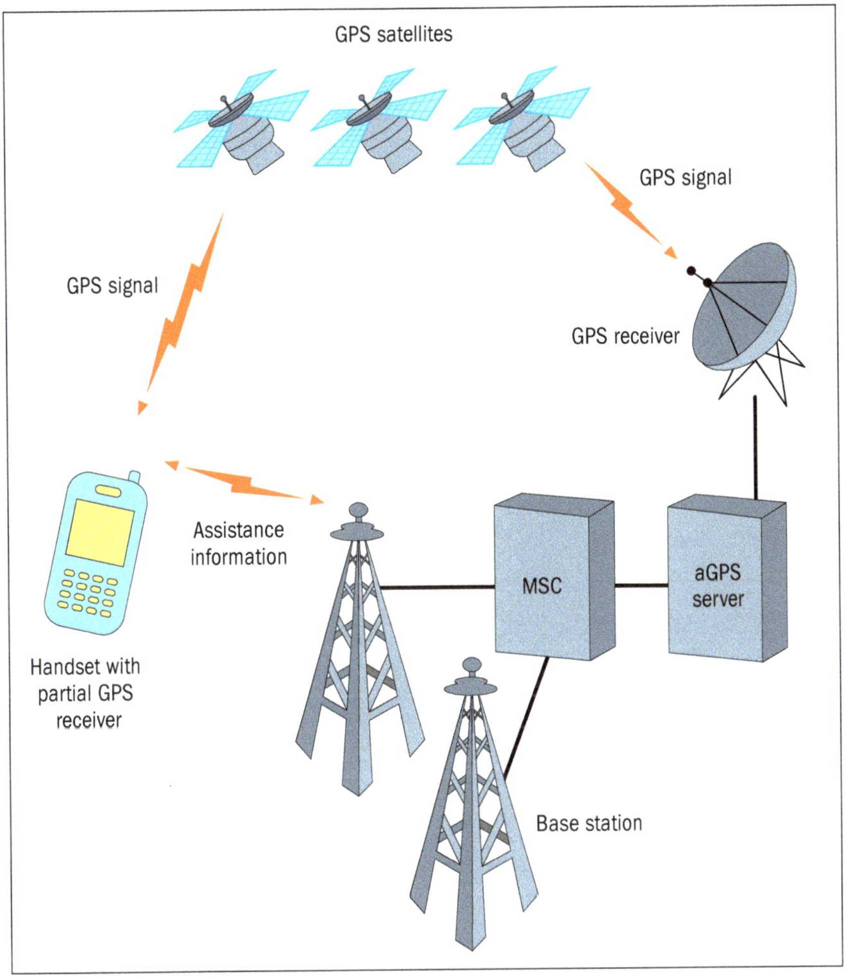

Figure 10.27: The aGPS concept[106]

GPS receivers are used to determine the geographical position of crime scenes, points of interest, routes taken by suspects and the position of cellphone base stations.

Figure 10.28 shows the crime scenes and scenes indicated by a suspect using a GPS. This example was used to illustrate the use of GPS as a tool to manage dockets in a serial murder case.

106 Mobile Nation (2011).

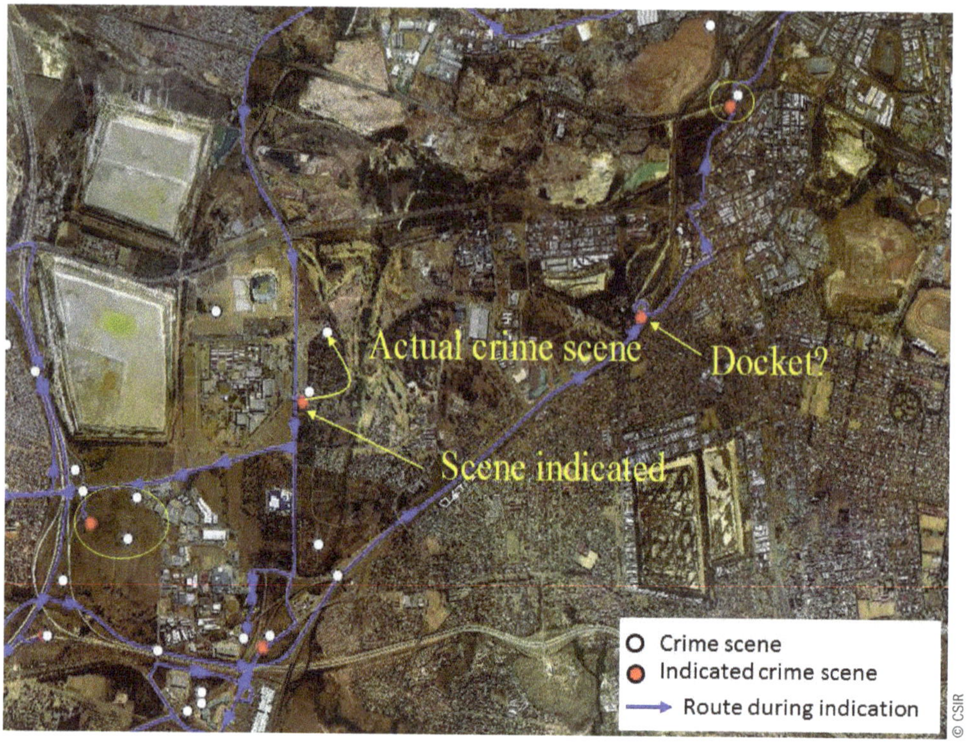

Figure 10.28: Locations of crime scenes and scenes indicated using a GPS[107]

10.6.3 Spreadsheets

As explained in section 10.5.1, the detailed cellphone billing records can be combined into a single spreadsheet for further analysis, and sorted chronologically.

KEY

The acronyms in the Call_Type column are:

MOSMS: SMS originating, meaning outgoing SMS

MTSMS: SMS terminating, meaning incoming SMS

MTC: Mobile terminating call, meaning the cellphone has received a call (incoming call)

CF: Call forward, meaning the cellphone was not available to receive the call and it was forwarded to the messaging service of the service provider

MOC: Mobile originating call, meaning the subscriber made a call on their cellphone (outgoing call)

GPRS: Listed in the Call_Type column when the subscriber uses their cellphone to access the internet.

107 Slide 29 in Schmitz & Cooper (2007a).

Example 10.8: Using a spreadsheet to link suspects and persons of interest

A truck was hijacked for its cargo in the Western Cape. The names of the suspects and persons of interest were added to the spreadsheet in Figure 10.29 to simplify the process of establishing a link between them.

ID	Number	Name	Date_Time	Call_Type	Call_Durat	Other_party	OP_Name	LinkID	Tower_ID	Cell_ID	Cell_Name	X_Coord	Y_Coord
332	2772X009Y33	Vernon	12/08/2003 08:42:40	MTC	16	27724XY6755	Selwyn	34	2122	21222	Dassenberg_2	18.51356	-33.49656
333	27724XY6755	Selwyn	12/08/2003 08:42:40	MOC	15	2772X009Y33	Vernon	34	2122	21222	Dassenberg_2	18.51356	-33.49656
210	27835X567Y1	Alec-Anna	12/08/2003 08:43:21	MOC	21	2772X6Y5712	Jan	35	1689	16892	Dassenberg	18.51356	-33.49661
334	2772X6Y5712	Jan	12/08/2003 08:43:22	MTC	21	27835X567Y1	Alec-Anna	35	2122	21222	Dassenberg_2	18.51356	-33.49656
335	2772X009Y33	Vernon	12/08/2003 08:47:53	MTC	33	27835X567Y1	Alec-Anna	36	2122	21222	Dassenberg_2	18.51356	-33.49656
412	27835X567Y1	Alec-Anna	12/08/2003 08:47:53	MOC	32	2772X009Y33	Vernon	36	2257	22571	RondebergVC	18.29639	-33.42003
471	27724XY6755	Selwyn	12/08/2003 08:49:42	MOC	45	27723X3Y856	Gary	37	2406	24062	Darling_2	18.3975	-33.42083
341	27723X3Y856	Gary	12/08/2003 08:49:42	MTC	45	27724XY6755	Selwyn	37	2123	21230	Rondeberg	18.29639	-33.42003
417	27835X567Y1	Alec-Anna	12/08/2003 08:54:15	MTC	10	27722XY2483	Zakkie	38	2257	22571	RondebergVC	18.29639	-33.42003
342	27722XY2483	Zakkie	12/08/2003 08:54:16	MOC	10	27835X567Y1	Alec-Anna	38	2123	21230	Rondeberg	18.29639	-33.42003
343	27722XY2483	Zakkie	12/08/2003 08:55:07	MTC	9	27835X567Y1	Alec-Anna	39	2123	21230	Rondeberg	18.29639	-33.42003
413	27835X567Y1	Alec-Anna	12/08/2003 08:55:07	MOC	7	27722XY2483	Zakkie	39	2257	22571	RondebergVC	18.29639	-33.42003

Figure 10.29: Determining the links between suspects and persons of interest

The methodology is to determine the call type of the first individual, namely Vernon Aspeling (top red arrow in Figure 10.29). The call type is 'MTC' (incoming call). The column 'Other_party' is the other party involved in the call, namely Alec Anna Mandoza. The next row shows Mandoza contacting Aspeling (second red arrow in Figure 10.29). The call type is 'MOC' (outgoing call) in Mandoza's row since he made the call to Aspeling. The date-time column and call duration values are used to establish the link. Once the link has been established, a link identification number is allocated in the 'LINK_ID' column. The link identification number in the example is 36. These two values must be identical between the two individuals. Using the same spreadsheet, the different cellphone base stations that transmitted the signals can be identified. This process is repeated until all the links have been established.

In some instances, especially between two different service providers, the time difference can be one or two seconds and the duration of the call may differ by a second or two, as illustrated in the rows where the LINK_ID is 38 and 39 in Figure 10.29.

10.6.4 Geographic positioning

In section 10.6.3, the different links between individuals and the cellphone base station used were identified, as shown below the yellow bar in Figure 10.30.

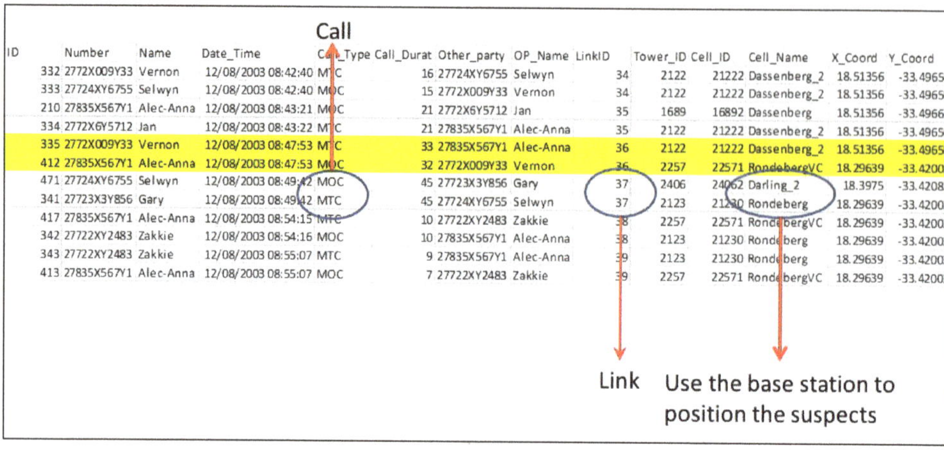

ID	Number	Name	Date_Time	Call_Type	Call_Durat	Other_party	OP_Name	LinkID	Tower_ID	Cell_ID	Cell_Name	X_Coord	Y_Coord
332	2772X009Y33	Vernon	12/08/2003 08:42:40	MTC	16	27724XY6755	Selwyn	34	2122	21222	Dassenberg_2	18.51356	-33.49656
333	27724XY6755	Selwyn	12/08/2003 08:42:40	MOC	15	2772X009Y33	Vernon	34	2122	21222	Dassenberg_2	18.51356	-33.49656
210	27835X567Y1	Alec-Anna	12/08/2003 08:43:21	MOC	21	2772X6Y5712	Jan	35	1689	16892	Dassenberg	18.51356	-33.49661
334	2772X6Y5712	Jan	12/08/2003 08:43:22	MTC	21	27835X567Y1	Alec-Anna	35	2122	21222	Dassenberg_2	18.51356	-33.49656
335	2772X009Y33	Vernon	12/08/2003 08:47:53	MTC	33	27835X567Y1	Alec-Anna	36	2122	21222	Dassenberg_2	18.51356	-33.49656
412	27835X567Y1	Alec-Anna	12/08/2003 08:47:53	MOC	32	2772X009Y33	Vernon	36	2257	22571	RondebergVC	18.29639	-33.42003
471	27724XY6755	Selwyn	12/08/2003 08:49:42	MOC	45	27723X3Y856	Gary	37	2406	24062	Darling_2	18.3975	-33.42083
341	27723X3Y856	Gary	12/08/2003 08:49:42	MTC	45	27724XY6755	Selwyn	37	2123	21230	Rondeberg	18.29639	-33.42003
417	27835X567Y1	Alec-Anna	12/08/2003 08:54:15	MTC	10	27722XY2483	Zakkie	38	2257	22571	RondebergVC	18.29639	-33.42003
342	27722XY2483	Zakkie	12/08/2003 08:54:16	MOC	10	27835X567Y1	Alec-Anna	38	2123	21230	Rondeberg	18.29639	-33.42003
343	27722XY2483	Zakkie	12/08/2003 08:55:07	MTC	9	27835X567Y1	Alec-Anna	39	2123	21230	Rondeberg	18.29639	-33.42003
413	27835X567Y1	Alec-Anna	12/08/2003 08:55:07	MOC	7	27722XY2483	Zakkie	39	2257	22571	RondebergVC	18.29639	-33.42003

Figure 10.30: Establishing the link to cellphone base stations

Each base station has a coordinate pair ('X-Coord' and 'Y-Coord') that is used to map the base station using a GIS, as shown in Figure 10.31. Figure 10.31 illustrates the actual mapping of the links. If the link spans between two different cellphone base stations it is shown as a line between the two base stations. If both individuals trigger the same base station the link is shown as a point, as illustrated in Figure 10.31.

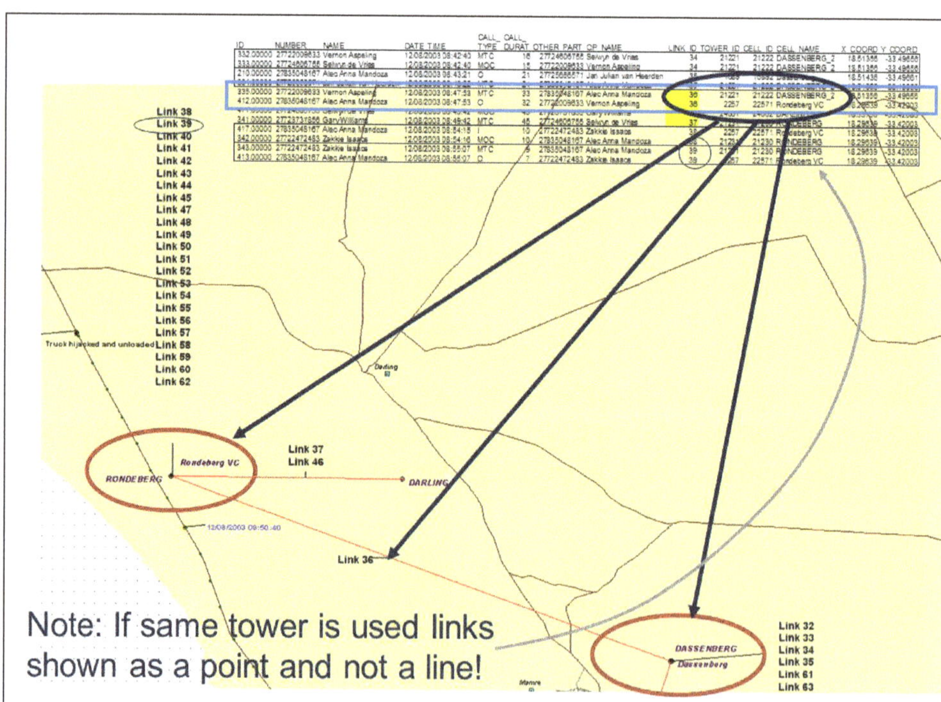

Figure 10.31: Mapping the links using the cellphone base stations as the geographic reference

In most instances, the geographic positions of the points of interest, as discussed in section 10.5.3, are determined using a GPS.

Example 10.9: Mapping the route of a hijacked truck

In this example the points of interest are the cellphone base stations, as illustrated above (Figure 10.31), and the route data as captured by the on-board GPS device of the truck that has been hijacked. The truck route is shown as points, as illustrated in Figure 10.32. Each point has a pair of coordinates and a date-time stamp (not shown in this example). The further apart these points are, the faster the truck was moving since these points are collected at specific time intervals. In this example the interval was five minutes.

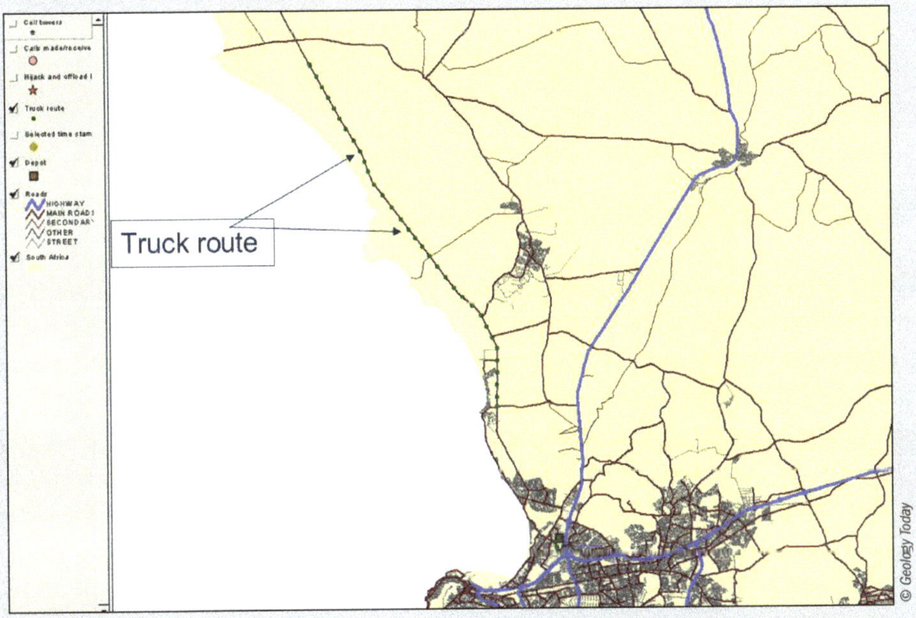

Figure 10.32: Mapping the truck's route

Other spatial data of interest to this example are roads and provinces.

10.6.5 Creating the final map

The links between the individuals are created as a single layer (map) using the GIS. The truck route, roads and provinces of South Africa are separate layers. The GIS has the ability to combine these layers into a single map. The attribute data such as the link numbers and names of the cellphone base stations are used to annotate the map. Figure 10.33 illustrates this.

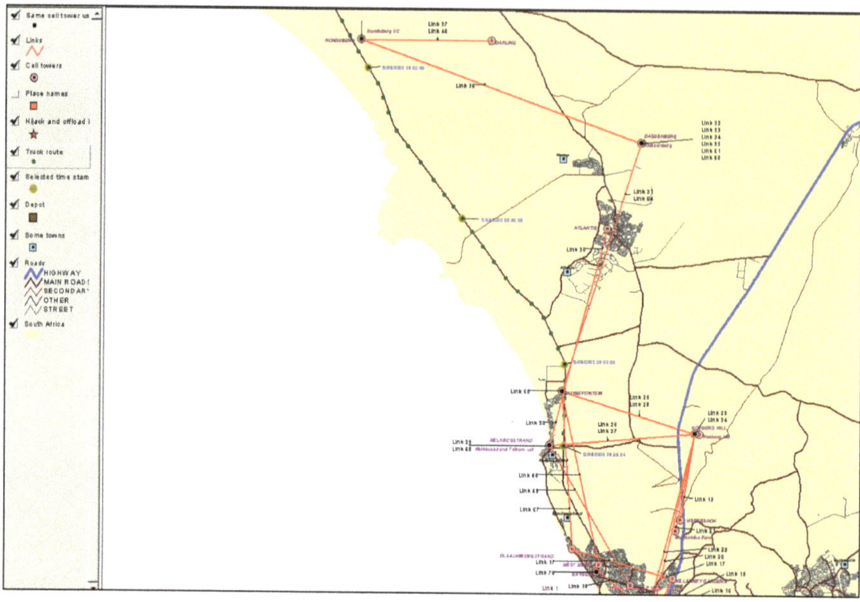

© Geology Today

Figure 10.33: Displaying all the relevant layers in a single map

These maps are created in cooperation with the investigator(s) and the prosecutor. Several iterations of the maps are necessary to ensure that the correct information will be displayed as evidence in court. The following can be learnt from maps like these:

- 'A picture paints a thousand words' – a complex sequence in a case can be shown in one picture. In Figure 10.33 the communication between the various suspects is shown relative to the position of the targeted truck in space and time.
- The map can be used to corroborate independently the evidence given by a state witness.
- The map can be used to break the alibi(s) given by the accused.
- The map can be used to place the accused in the immediate vicinity of the crime scene.
- The map can be used to show the conspiracy to commit a crime by showing the movements of the accused before, during and after the commission of the crime(s). The map can show that the accused made a reconnaissance trip to determine a suitable place to hijack the truck and to determine where the unmarked depot is located in order to follow the truck on the predetermined day. Another example is to use a 3D map to show the movement to and from a crime location, as illustrated in Figure 10.43.
- The map can show the secluded area where the cargo was offloaded. Another example is the location of bodies found in secluded areas. These can be enhanced by using aerial photographs as a backdrop, as in Figure 10.28. In

Figure 10.28 the accused committed the crimes a few metres from a road. The vegetation next to the road and the time of day, which was in the evening, offered enough protection to the accused to commit the crimes.

- The map can be used to show points of interest to the case relative to the crime incident locations in space and time, as illustrated in Figure 10.21.
- The map can be used to illustrate the sequence of crime scene indications (ie places where the murders took place) by an accused and corroborate it with the actual location of the crime scene that was captured by the investigating officer using a GPS, as illustrated in Figure 10.28.

10.7 CASE STUDIES

10.7.1 Introduction

In these case studies, forensic geography played a significant role in court proceedings and in most instances led to the conviction of the suspects. The following six case studies are examined:

1. The hijacking, rape and murder of a South African woman and the killing of her companion, an American male, in January 1998. Forensic geography was used to map the links between suspects using cellphones.
2. The Waterfront shooting incident. The victim was assassinated by a contract killer at the entrance to the V&A Waterfront in Cape Town.
3. The third example did not lead to a conviction of the suspect and the data was used after the court case for further research in forensic geography with the aim of establishing patterns for surveillance.
4. The hijacking of trucks for their cargo.
5. The murder of the famous South African musician, Taliep Petersen.
6. The establishment of geographic profiles of suspects who were arrested for stock theft in the Malmesbury area in the Western Cape province of South Africa.

10.7.2 Six case studies

Case study 10.1: Hijacking, rape and murder of a South African woman and murder of an American male in Cape Town

S v R Petersen and Others was the first case in South Africa where cellphone usage was mapped and used as forensic evidence in court. On 5 January 1998, just after midnight, a couple was hijacked on Signal Hill near Cape Town. The couple was held hostage while the gang drove them to a remote spot using the couple's car and their own vehicle. The man was murdered execution style at the first remote location and the woman was taken to another secluded spot where she was raped and murdered. Two of the four suspects were killed by the police at a roadblock when they resisted arrest. One of the two killed suspects was linked by DNA to raping the woman before she was murdered.[108] However, the police still had to prove the case against the two remaining suspects.

→

108 Schmitz et al. (2000).

→

The suspects used their own cellphone and that of one of the victims. The investigating officer obtained the detailed billing records of the cellphones. The CSIR was approached by the investigating officer and asked whether it was possible to map the identified calls. After consultation, the investigating officer obtained the geographic extent of the cells and locations of the base stations from the cellphone service providers. The centroid of the cell was used as the geographic reference, as illustrated in Figure 10.34.[109] Since the map shows all the calls made on 5 January 1998, only the time when a call was made was used to identify and number the link, as shown in Figure 10.34.

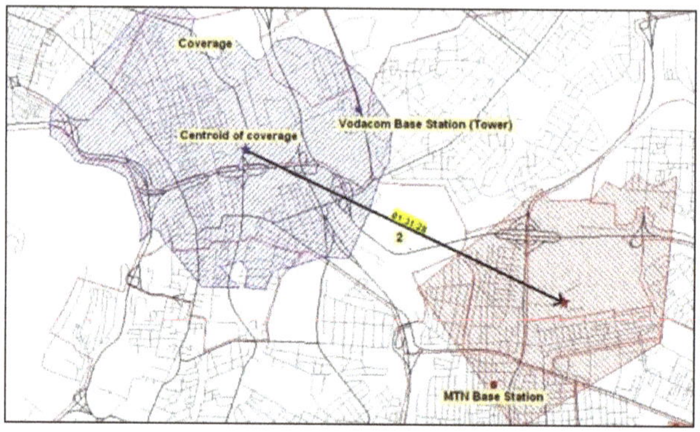

© Geology Today

Figure 10.34: Using the centroid of the cell as a geographic reference to map the links between suspects

The locations of the points of interest, given as places of interest in Figure 10.35, were mapped using the investigator's knowledge of the area. These points of interest, combined with the mapped cellphone usage, played a crucial role in court proceedings.[110] Figure 10.36 gives the final map that was used as evidence in court. The two suspects were convicted based on the mapped cellphone communications and points of interest and received life sentences for their part in the hijacking, hostage taking, rape of the woman and murder of both victims.

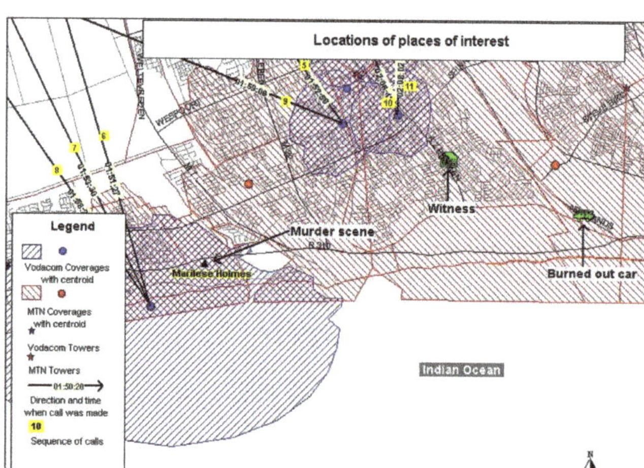

© Geology Today

Figure 10.35: Mapping of points of interest

→

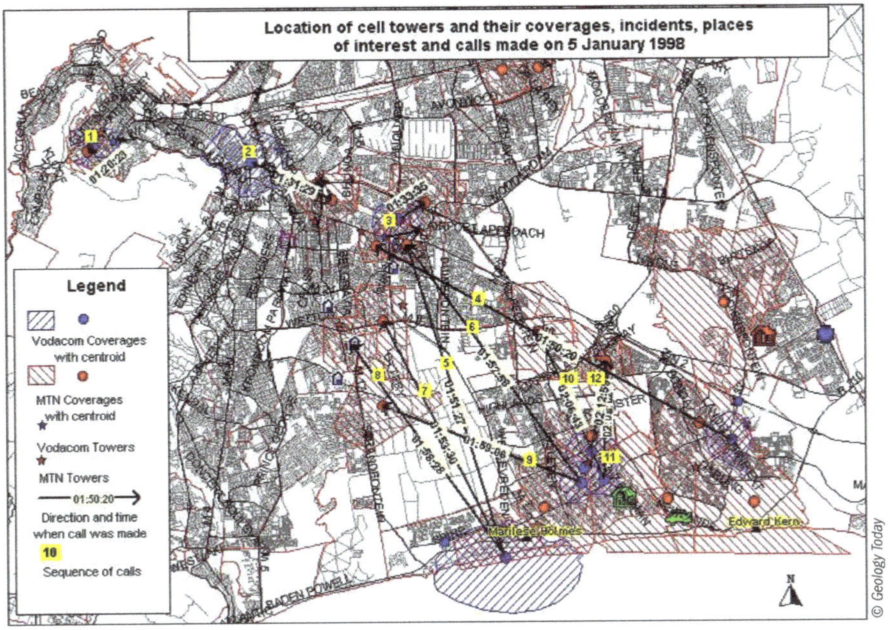

Figure 10.36: Final map that was used as evidence in court

The map that was produced was used as follows:[111]

- To show that the accused, being in possession of a cellphone, received a call from a public telephone, placing the accused in the immediate vicinity of where the victims' bodies were found. The accused insisted that he had been outside the area, thus the map broke the accused's alibi.
- To show how the two vehicles, the hijacked vehicle with the hostages and the gang's own vehicle, moved together away from the crime scene, got separated and through a quick succession of calls made a rendezvous.
- To corroborate the state witness's evidence that she had seen the hijacked vehicle as well as the victim's cellphone in their possession. The cellphone triggered the cell in which the state witness resided at the time of the accused's visit.

109 Schmitz et al. (2000).
110 Schmitz et al. (2000).
111 Schmitz et al. (2000).

Case study 10.2: Cape Town Waterfront shooting

The case of *S v D Osman* (CPV/98/0562H in the High Court of South Africa, Cape of Good Hope Provincial Division) followed shortly after the case discussed in Case study 10.1. The accused shot the victim at the entrance to the V&A Waterfront in Cape Town. From the cellphone records and other evidence gathered, the investigator and the prosecutor were of the opinion that it had been a contract murder.

The same procedure was followed to generate the map shown in Figure 10.37. The map shows the calls made and received by the accused. No links between the accused and the person who ordered the contract are shown since the prosecutor wanted to illustrate to the court that the accused had gone to the Waterfront, made the calls to positively identify the victim, committed the shooting and then immediately left the crime scene and returned home.

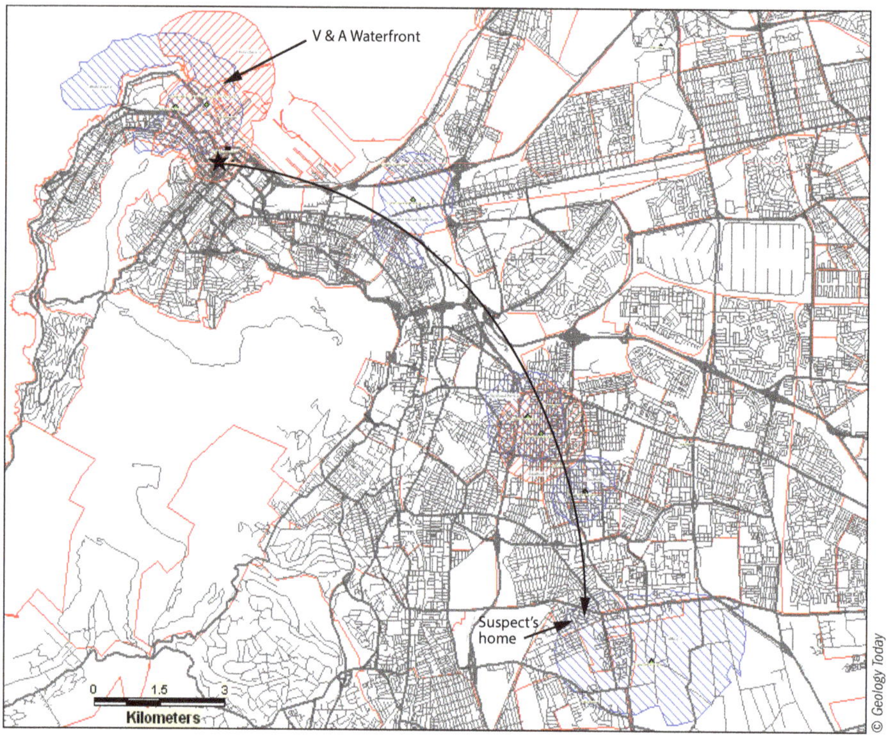

Figure 10.37: The communication just before and after the shooting incident

The data received from the cellphone service provider showed several overlaps. The subsequent cells are shown in different colours to illustrate the overlap and to indicate the geographical reach of each of these cells. In the overlapping regions the cellphone could have triggered one of the overlapping cells based on the signal strength of the cell at that particular location.

The map clearly shows the calls made and received at the V&A Waterfront entrance (the star in Figure 10.37) as well as the direction taken by the accused when leaving the crime scene after the shooting incident, as indicated by the long arrow. The accused's home was in the top left-hand corner of the bottom cell shown on the map.

Case study 10.3: The crime boss and the armourer

The case study of *S v Mr D* is based on several murders masterminded during 2002 by a person who at the time was believed to be a gang leader. This person is referred to as the 'crime boss' in this case study. The High Court judge ruled in favour of the defendant, who was released from custody. In order to protect the identity of the individuals in this case, they will be referred to as Mr D (the defendant), Suspect 1 (the crime boss) and Suspect 2 (the armourer).

The CSIR obtained permission to use the cellphone data for further research. The results shown in this case study can be used by investigating officers during their investigation of suspects. The initial work done by the CSIR was the mapping of links between Suspect 1 and several gang members during the commission of these murders.

First, cellphone data was used to determine the activity spaces of Suspect 1 and Suspect 2. Suspect 1 was from the Cape Flats and Suspect 2 was a drug addict and weapons aficionado from the affluent suburb of Plattekloof, Cape Town. The activity space of Suspect 1 and points of interest to this case are shown in Figure 10.21. Figure 10.38 shows the activity space of Suspect 2. The two activity spaces show a large overlap, although Suspect 1 avoided affluent suburbs such as Plattekloof, Constantia and Camps Bay, as illustrated in Figure 10.39.[112]

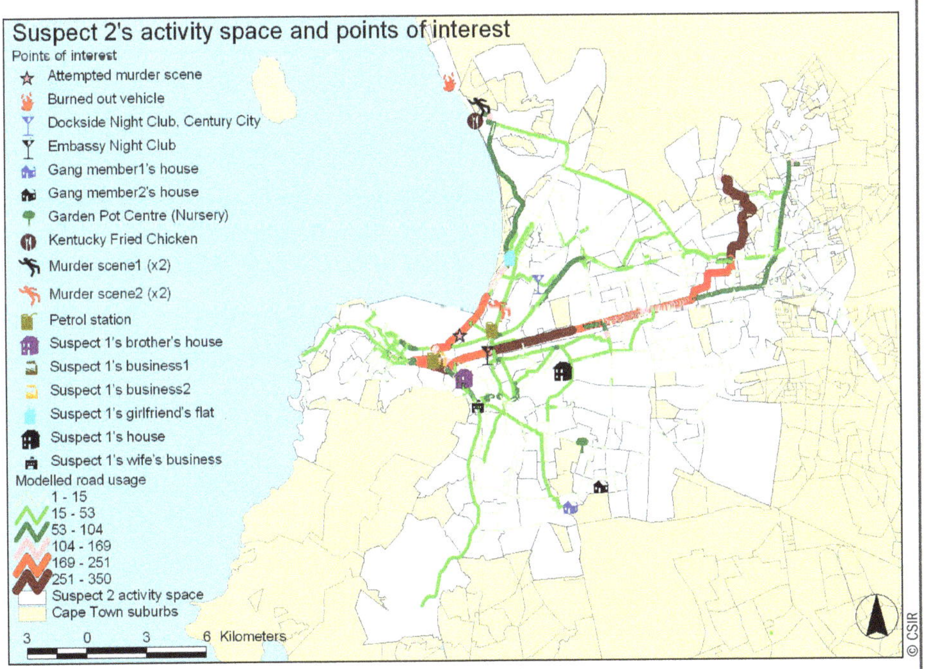

Figure 10.38: Suspect 2's activity space[113]

→

112 Schmitz & Cooper (2007b).

113 Slide 12 in Schmitz & Cooper (2007b).

→

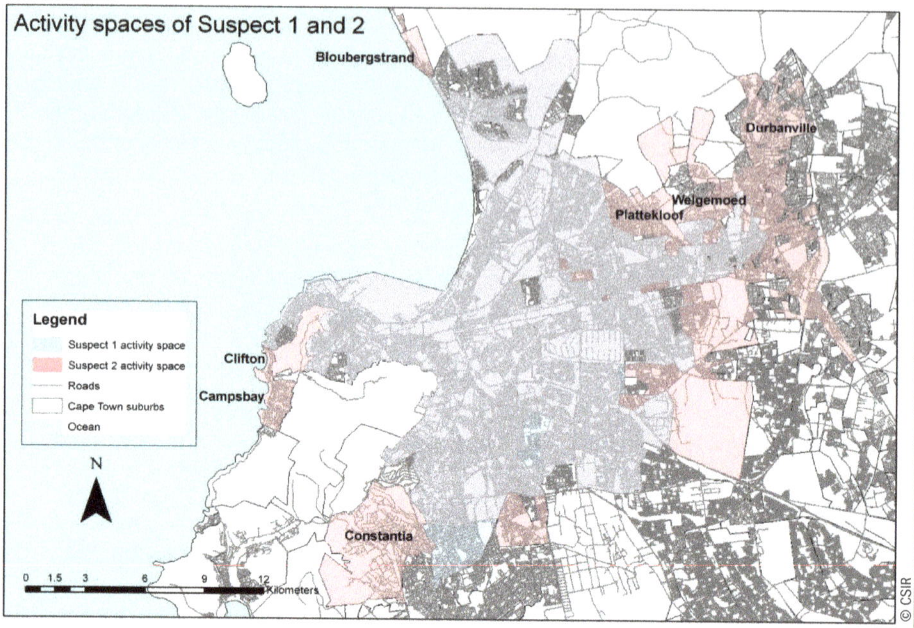

Figure 10.39: The overlapping activity spaces of Suspect 1 and Suspect 2[114]

Secondly, cellphone data was used to determine the possible routes preferred by the two suspects based on cellphone base station locations. Base stations were only selected when the next call triggered a different base station. These changes indicated movement. Flowmap, a software developed by the University of Utrecht in the Netherlands to model interactions and flows, was used to determine the possible route on the road network between the two base stations. The usage of base stations is superimposed on these routes. The larger the point on the map, the more frequently the base station was used. Suspect 1's routes and usage are given as an example. This is illustrated in Figures 10.40 and 10.41. Figure 10.40 shows Suspect 1's day pattern and Figure 10.41 shows his evening pattern. When comparing these patterns, there is a shift in anchor points from the Woodstock area in Cape Town during the day to the Brooklyn area close to the harbour during the evening.

These patterns indicate the anchor points of the suspects and the possible routes between them. The investigating officer could then investigate the area for possible attractions such as business premises fronting as a legal entity, nightclubs, residences and restaurants.[115] Investigators could also use this information to trace possible suspects, accomplices, suppliers of contraband, markets for stolen goods, etc and to refute a suspect's alibi.

→

114 Slide 13 in Schmitz & Cooper (2007b).
115 Schmitz & Cooper (2007b).

→

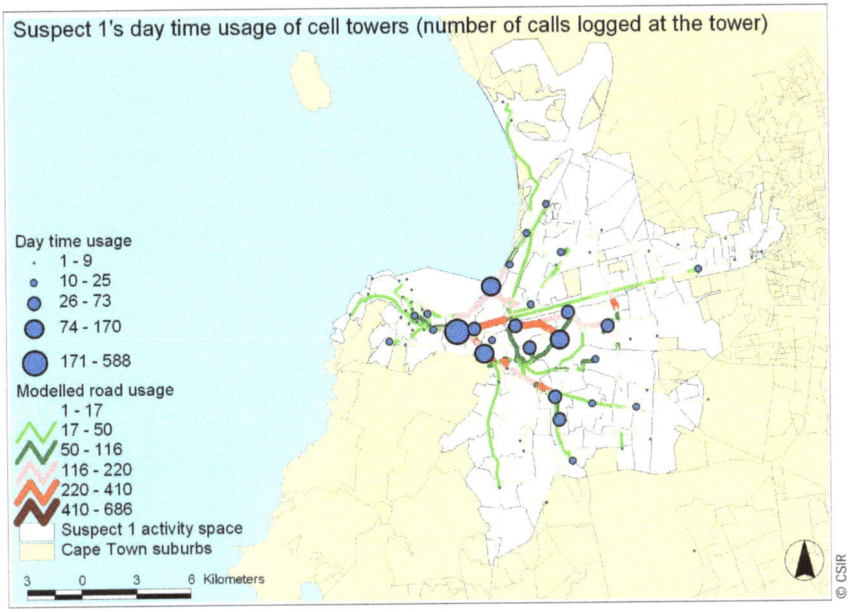

Figure 10.40: Suspect 1's routes and cellphone base station usage during the day[116]

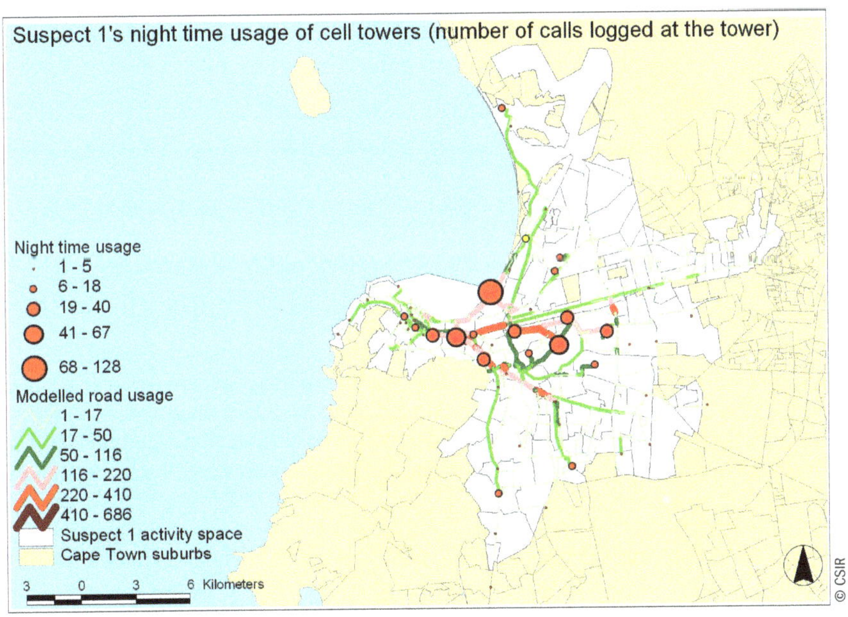

Figure 10.41: Suspect 1's routes and usage during the evening[117] →

116 Slide 14 in Schmitz & Cooper (2007b).
117 Slide 14 in Schmitz & Cooper (2007b).

→

Thirdly, cellphone data was used to show the daily usage pattern of the base stations that had the highest usage by Suspect 1. This shows which area in Cape Town he frequented the most at certain times within 24 hours. Figure 10.42 illustrates this concept. The first graph on the left-hand side of the figure shows that Suspect 1 was within the reception area of the base station in the morning and early afternoon, with a decrease in usage around midday and very low activity during the evening.

If the investigating officer identifies an attraction, the likelihood of encountering the suspect at the attraction would be around the times indicated by the two peaks in the graph.

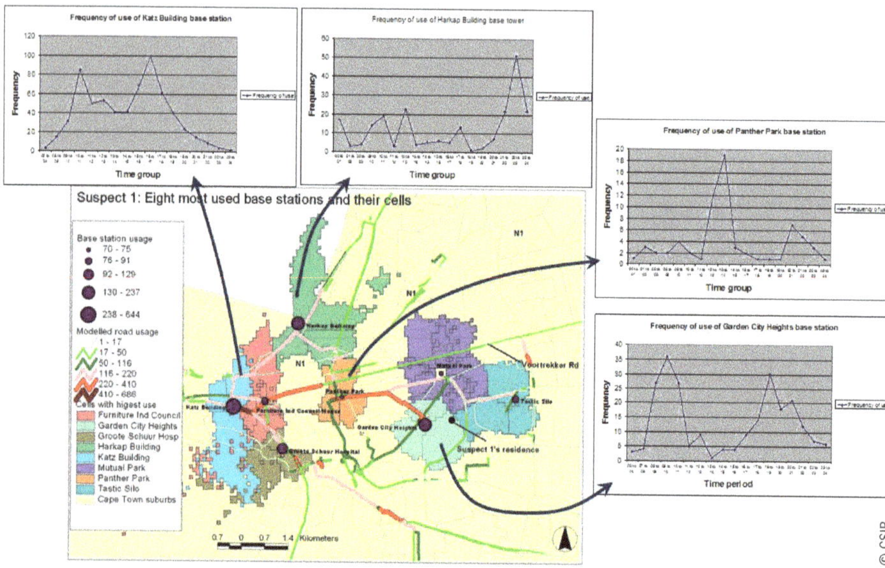

Figure 10.42: Usage patterns of four of the eight most frequently used cellphone base stations[118]

Going clockwise, the second graph indicates an anchor point in the evening. This could indicate a nightclub, a restaurant or a bar that the suspect frequented. The peak usage is between 22:00 and 23:00 in the evening. As it turned out, Suspect 1 used a nightclub within the reception area of the base station from which to conduct his drug-selling activities.[119] The third graph shows an interesting pattern: there is a peak around midday, which explains the trough around midday in the first graph. According to Capt Joe Dryden[120] the location of the base station indicated that Suspect 1 got his drugs from the 'wholesaler' during midday in the area covered by the base station, for distribution in the evening from the nightclub. The fourth and last graph shows the usage pattern at Suspect 1's residence. The peaks are in the early morning and late afternoon/early evening, indicating that he spent time at home before going to the area covered by the base station in the first graph in the morning and before leaving for the nightclub in the early evening. These patterns provide an insight into the suspect's daily movement patterns, which may guide the investigating officer's surveillance strategy.

118 Slide 17 in Schmitz & Cooper (2007b).

119 Personal communication with J Dryden, Detective Captain: Organised Crime Unit, South African Police Service, Western Cape province, South Africa in November 2006.

120 Personal communication with J Dryden, Detective Captain: Organised Crime Unit, South African Police Service, Western Cape province, South Africa in November 2006.

Case study 10.4: The hijacking of freight

The case of *S v De Vries and 10 others* (67/2005 in the High Court of South Africa, Cape of Good Hope Provincial Division) illustrates the use of forensic geography in establishing the movement of and communication between 11 suspects in three separate hijacking incidents. Trucks carrying a large quantity of cigarettes were targeted. Part of the hijacking gang resided in Johannesburg and the rest resided in Cape Town. The first incident occurred on 24 June 2003, the second on 12 August 2003 and the last on 2 October 2003. The calls from each suspect were extracted, linked and mapped for each of the incidents using the methodology described in section 10.6.

Figure 10.44 shows the hijacking incident on 24 June 2003. The *modus operandi* was to hold a fake roadblock using stolen police uniforms and stolen white vehicles with blue lights. The group assigned to the roadblock formation travelled ahead and stayed in communication with the group that was following the targeted vehicle carrying the cigarettes. The roadblock was set up at a predetermined location. The targeted vehicle was pulled over and the driver held hostage.

In Figure 10.44 the red lines indicate the communication between the suspects. The location of the cellphone towers triggered was used as the geographic reference. The blue dots show the truck's movement based on the data downloaded from the on-board GPS. The text in the figure indicates who was talking to whom and is linked to a specific red line.

On the day of the incident under discussion, the suspects followed the truck from Cape Town on the N1 towards Worcester. On the Worcester side of the Huguenot Tunnel, they set up the roadblock and hijacked the vehicle. Owing to the location, the suspects felt that they did not have a clear vision along the N1 to detect police and traffic police vehicles and were thus scared to transfer the load of cigarettes to their own truck. They decided to move to a second location. Still feeling vulnerable, they moved towards Rawsonville, completed their criminal activity and released the vehicle and the driver.

The three locations are indicated with a red star in Figure 10.44. Figure 10.43 shows the same map in three dimensions using Google Earth as backdrop. The flags indicate the hijacking, the location where they wanted to transfer the cigarettes, and the location where the transfer took place. The dots depict the base stations, the grey line shows the GPS-tracked route of the hijacked vehicle and the red lines indicate the communication between the suspects during the incident.

© Geology Today

Figure 10.43: The hijacking incident on 24 June 2003 shown in 3D

→

© Geology Today

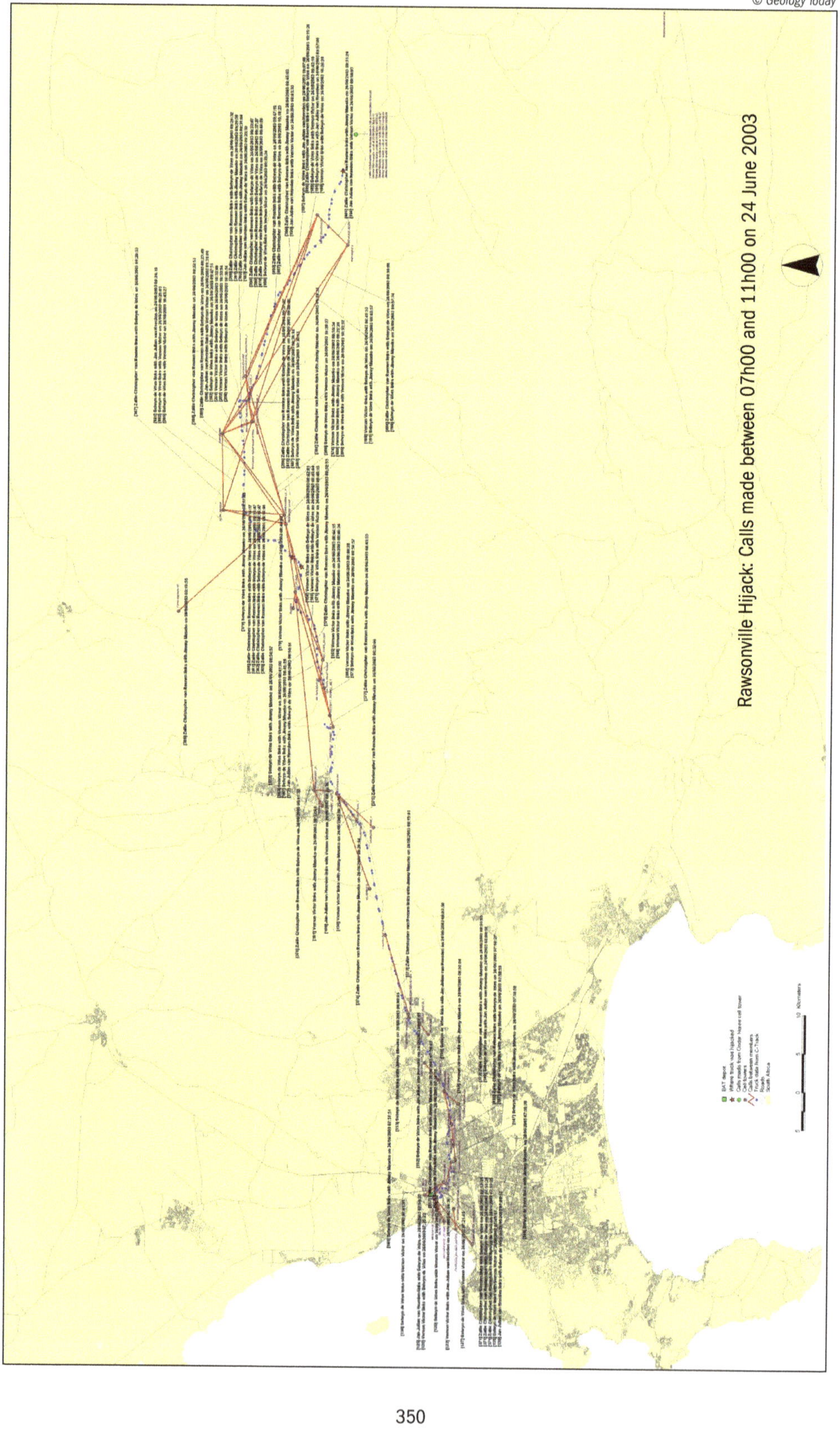

Figure 10.44: The hijacking incident on 24 June 2003 near Worcester and Rawsonville

Case study 10.5: The Taliep Petersen murder case

The case *S v N Petersen and 3 Others* (Case No 02/08 in the High Court of South Africa, Cape of Good Hope Provincial Division) was mentioned in section 10.5.4. On the night of 16 December 2006 Taliep Petersen, a famous South African musician and playwright, was murdered in his home in Athlone, Cape Town. Initially it looked like a house robbery that had gone wrong, but when the SAPS detectives started to investigate, it became clear that it had been premeditated murder. This was based on the fact that the crime scene did not reflect the *modus operandi* of a house robbery.[121]

The detectives obtained the data from records of the cellphone of Najwa Petersen, the deceased's wife, who was then identified as the prime suspect. From her cellphone's transactional content the detectives determined who she had contacted to arrange the murder. She had tried to delete his name and calls made to him from her cellphone. The detective tasked with retrieving the data from the cellphones did so using custom-made software that allows for the downloading of data from both the cellphone and the SIM card. From these downloads, the investigator was able to determine which name and calls had been removed from Najwa's cellphone. This person, Faheem Hendricks, turned state witness after intensive questioning by the detectives and identified three other persons, namely Abdoer Raasiet Emjedi, Waheed Hassen and Jefferson Snyders, who were also involved in the murder. The detectives then obtained the cellphone records of the state witness (Hendricks) and the other three suspects.[122]

The investigation revealed that the deceased was tied up and killed by a single shot to the head. However, the detectives never found the firearm and they could not determine from the suspects who had pulled the trigger for the fatal shot. The leading detective and the state prosecutor then asked the CSIR to analyse and map the movement of and communication between the suspects and the state witness using the cellphone records.[123]

The aim in using forensic geography in this case study had three objectives, namely:

- to illustrate that there had been collaboration between the accused and the state witness that the deceased should be killed
- to use the same maps to contradict the evidence (alibi) given by Najwa Petersen
- to create the maps in such a manner that they would be easily understood by the court.[124]

The methodology used to map the communications between and movement of the accused and the state witness through time and space for forensic purposes was as follows:

- The cellphone records of the accused and the state witness were separated, and the calls relevant to the case were separated from the other calls, using MS Excel.
- The isolated calls were sequenced to determine the chronological movement through time and space, using MS Excel. Communication between the suspects was colour-coded for ease of identification, for example the communication between Najwa Petersen and Faheem Hendricks was coded in red and the communication between Hendricks and Hassen in blue (see Figure 10.45).

→

121 Schmitz et al. (2009).
122 Schmitz et al. (2009).
123 Schmitz et al. (2009).
124 Schmitz et al. (2009).

→

- Based on the previous activity, a timeline was developed using MS Visio to illustrate the build-up of communication activities just before the murder on 16 December 2006, the lack of communication at the time when Taliep was being murdered, and the sharp drop in communication once the murder had been committed (see Figure 10.46).
- The cellphone base stations closest to the murder scene were determined, using ArcGIS.
- The various cells that could be triggered from the murder scene were illustrated, using MS PowerPoint, since the building plan of the house where the murder took place was available as a scanned image (see Figure 10.47).
- The various cellphone base stations that were triggered when the calls were made or received were determined using ArcGIS.
- Tables and maps were created for each day based on the timeline information, using MS Excel and ArcGIS respectively (see Figure 10.48 for the communication between the suspects and state witness on 16 December 2006), and a 3D map, showing the movements of the suspects during the night of 16/17 December 2006, was generated by ArcScene (see Figure 10.23).
- These tables, timelines and maps were presented to the High Court in a storyboard format on a poster and submitted as evidence in the court case.[125]

Sequence ID	Date	Time	Communication activity	Cells used Najwa	Faheem	Emjedi	Hassan
55	16/12/2006	10:16	Najwa P (082 566 7967) contacts Faheem (072 922 9617)	Kewtown 3	Sand Industria 1		
56		16:56	Emjedi (072 010 9819) contacts Hassan (078 169 8347)			Grassy Park 3	Symphony Secondary 3
57		16:58	Emjedi (072 010 9819) contacts Faheem (072 922 9617)		Mandalay 2	Retreat 1	
58		17:51	Emjedi (072 010 9819) contacts Hassan (078 169 8347)			Rylands 3	Symphony Secondary 3
59		20:11	Najwa P (082 566 7967) contacts Faheem (072 922 9617)	Kewtown 3	Westridge School 1		
60		20:15	Faheem (072 922 9617) contacts Emjedi (072 010 9819)		Westridge School 2	Ottery DCS 6	
61		20:19	Emjedi (072 010 9819) contacts Hassan (078 169 8347)			Neumans Farm 1	Symphony Secondary 3
62		20:20	Emjedi (072 010 9819) contacts Faheem (072 922 9617)		Rocklands 1	Neumans Farm 1	
63		21:20	Najwa P (082 566 7967) contacts Faheem (072 922 9617)	Kewtown 3	Mitchells Central 3		
64		21:23	Najwa P (082 566 7967) contacts Faheem (072 922 9617)	Crawford 1	Rocklands 1		
65		21:24	Emjedi (072 010 9819) contacts Hassan (078 169 8347)			Rylands 3	Symphony Secondary 3
66		21:25	Emjedi (072 010 9819) contacts Faheem (072 922 9617)		Mitchells Central 3	Rylands 3	
67		21:29	Najwa P (082 566 7967) contacts Faheem (072 922 9617)	Crawford 3	Mitchells Central 3		
68		22:06	Najwa P (082 566 7967) contacts Faheem (072 922 9617)	Kewtown 3	Mitchells Central 3		
69		22:20	Najwa P (082 566 7967) contacts Faheem (072 922 9617)	Crawford 3	Schaapskraal 1		
70		22:23	Faheem (072 922 9617) contacts Emjedi (072 010 9819)		Sand Industria 3	John Power Holiday Camp 3	
71		22:25	Emjedi (072 010 9819) contacts Hassan (078 169 8347)			John Power Holiday Camp 3	Symphony Secondary 3
72		22:26	Emjedi (072 010 9819) contacts Faheem (072 922 9617)		Lansdowne 1	John Power Holiday Camp 3	
73		22:27	Faheem (074 340 2038) contacts Hassan (078 169 8347)		Ellen Arthur Clothing		
74		22:36	Najwa P (082 566 7967) contacts Faheem (072 922 9617)	Kewtown 2	Rylands 1		
75		22:40	Faheem (074 340 2038) contacts Hassan (078 169 8347)		Rylands Primary School		Symphony Secondary 3
76		22:54	Faheem (074 340 2038) contacts Emjedi (072 010 9819)		Sunnyside Sportsfield	John Power Holiday Camp 3	
77		23:00	Hassan (078 169 8347) contacts Faheem (074 340 2038)		Sunnyside Sportsfield		Cravenby High School 3
78		23:03	Najwa P (082 566 7967) contacts Faheem (072 922 9617)	Kewtown 3	Crawford 1		
79		23:12	Faheem (074 340 2038) contacts Emjedi (072 010 9819)		Sunnyside Sportsfield	John Power Holiday Camp 3	
80		23:13	Emjedi (072 010 9819) contacts Faheem (072 922 9617)		Rylands 1	John Power Holiday Camp 3	
81		23:21	Faheem (074 340 2038) contacts Hassan (078 169 8347)		Sunnyside Sportsfield		Valkenberg Hospital
82		23:24	Hassan (078 169 8347) contacts Faheem (074 340 2038)		Sunnyside Sportsfield		Ledger House
83		23:26	Najwa P (082 566 7967) contacts Faheem (072 922 9617)	Crawford 1	Rylands 1		
84		23:27	Faheem (074 340 2038) contacts Hassan (078 169 8347)		Sunnyside Sportsfield		
85		23:27	Faheem (074 340 2038) contacts Hassan (078 169 8347)		Sunnyside Sportsfield		
86		23:31	Faheem (074 340 2038) contacts Emjedi (072 010 9819)		Sunnyside Sportsfield	John Power Holiday Camp 1	

Figure 10.45: The sequence of communication between the suspects and the state witness[126]

→

125 Schmitz et al. (2009).

126 Table 1 in Schmitz et al. (2009).

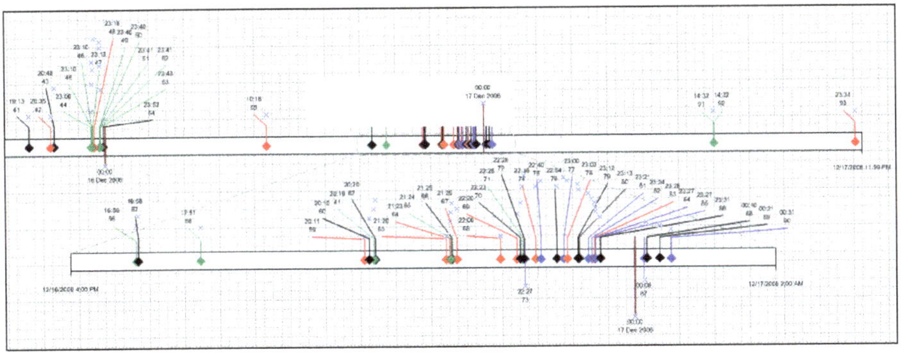

Figure 10.46: The timeline indicating the sequence of and communication between the suspects and the state witness[127]

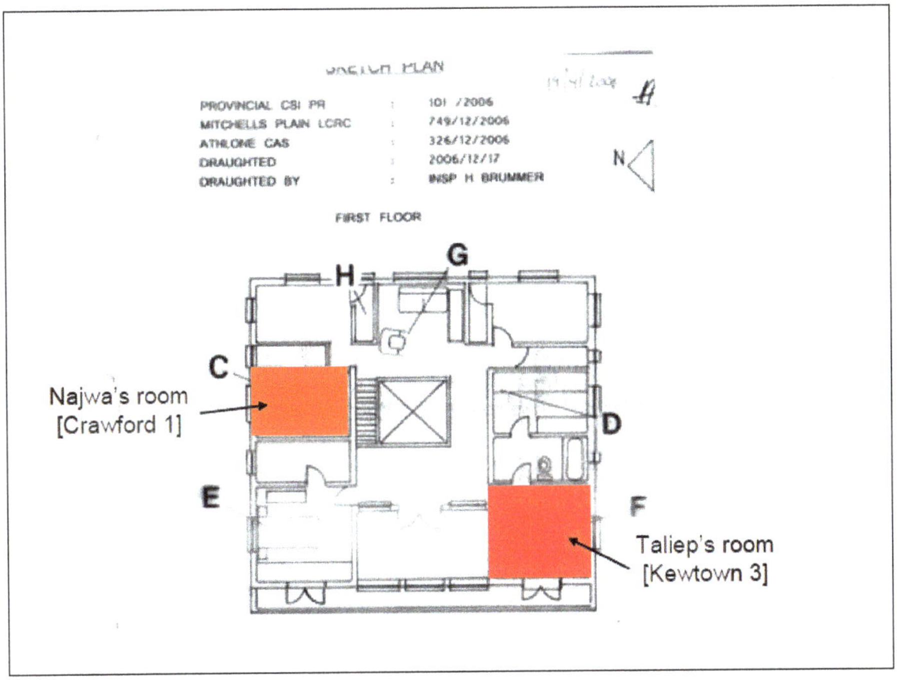

Figure 10.47: Various cellphone base stations triggered from different parts of the house where the murder took place[128]

127 Figure 1 in Schmitz et al. (2009).
128 Figure 3 in Schmitz et al. (2009).

→

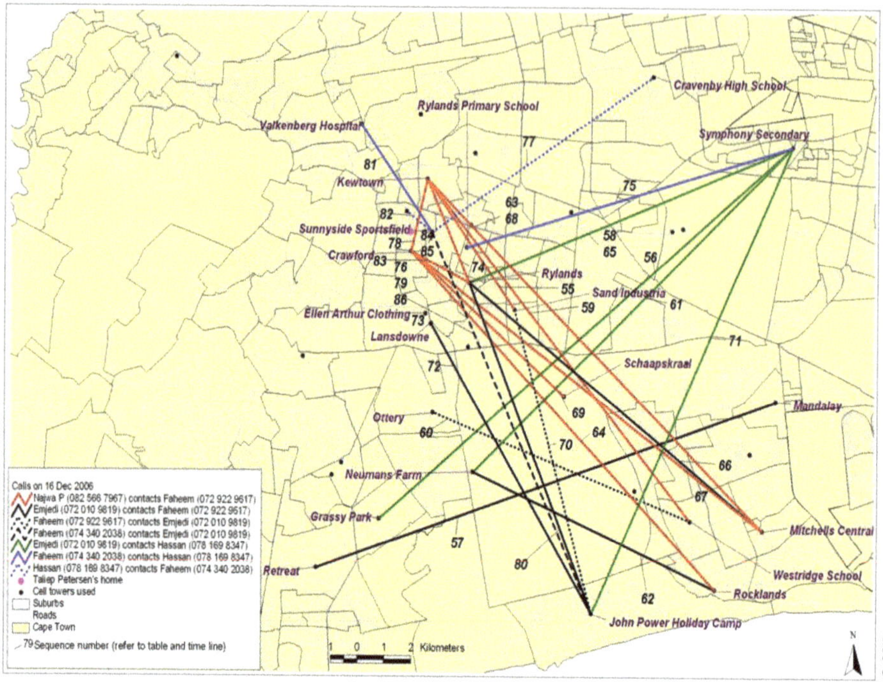

© CSIR

Figure 10.48: Sequence of and communication links between suspects and the state witness on 16 December 2006[129]

The maps revealed the following evidence:

- The timeline (Figure 10.46), tables (Figure 10.45 shows an example) and maps (Figures 10.48 and 10.23) clearly indicated that there had been collaboration between the accused and the state witness. The timeline showed the build-up to and the aftermath of the murder on 16 December. In the timeline the calls between the accused and the state witness increased in frequency up to the murder, no communication occurred during the commission of the murder and a few calls were made afterwards. The maps show the geographic distribution of the cellphone users and the 3D map (Figure 10.23) shows how the accused and state witness had congregated at the murder scene.
- The plan of the house indicating which cellphone towers are triggered from selected rooms in the house, as well as the maps, timeline and tables, were used to refute Najwa Petersen's alibi that she had been asleep in her room at the back of the house during the murder. The data clearly show her cellphone usage and also indicate that calls from her cellphone had triggered two cellphone base stations during the time period she alleged to have been asleep. This indicated that she had moved around the house when she made these calls.

129 Schmitz et al. (2009).

Case study 10.6: Stock theft

At the writing of this chapter, this case study is an ongoing court case. The dates of the incidents have been removed and the maps shown here are those that were presented as evidence in an open court at the Regional Court in Malmesbury and do not prejudice the court case. The suspects were caught red-handed with stock stolen from a farm in the Piketberg-Malmesbury area in the Western Cape. The investigating officer suspected the five people involved in three other stock thefts on the same farm and asked the CSIR if it could establish this using the detailed cellphone billing records of the suspects. Since the cells in rural areas are large – up to 72 km in diameter – it was decided to draw a geographic profile of the suspects on the evening of arrest and determine whether a similar geographic profile could be determined for the other three cases. The locations of the cellphone base stations were used as geographic references. The coverage area of selected base stations was used to illustrate the reach in rural areas and to indicate that the crime scene was within reach of a particular base station. Figure 10.49 shows the geographic profile of the suspects on the evening when they were arrested. Figure 10.50 shows a similar geographic profile for one of the other three stock-theft incidents.

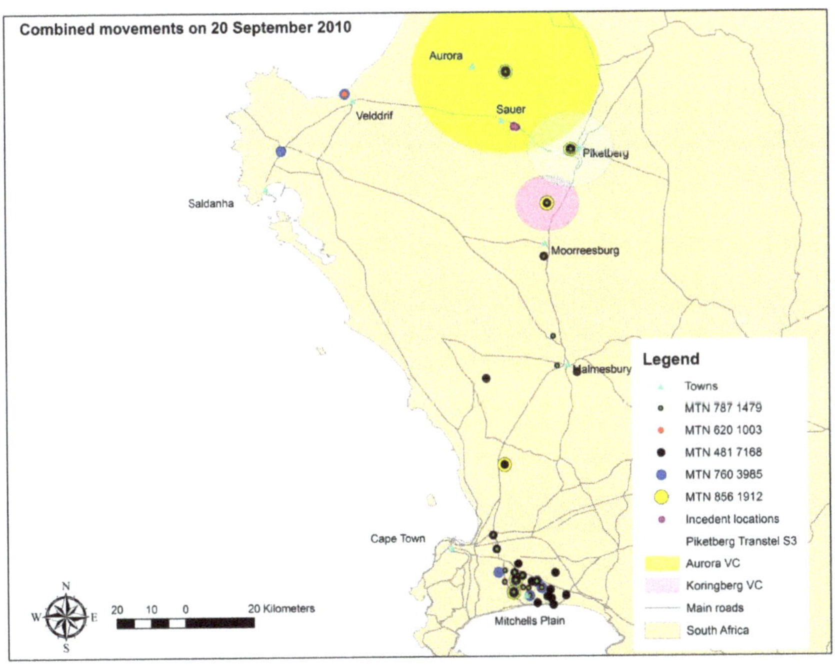

Figure 10.49: The geographic profile of the five suspects on the evening of their arrest

The map in Figure 10.49 shows the geographic profile of the accused on the night of the arrest. The accused stayed in Khayelitsha in Cape Town. On the night of their arrest they drove to the crime scene via Velddrif. While one of the accused herded the sheep into the kraal next to the road to Piketberg, the others drove around in the vicinity triggering various cellphone base stations. On their way back to Cape Town they were arrested near Velddrif. →

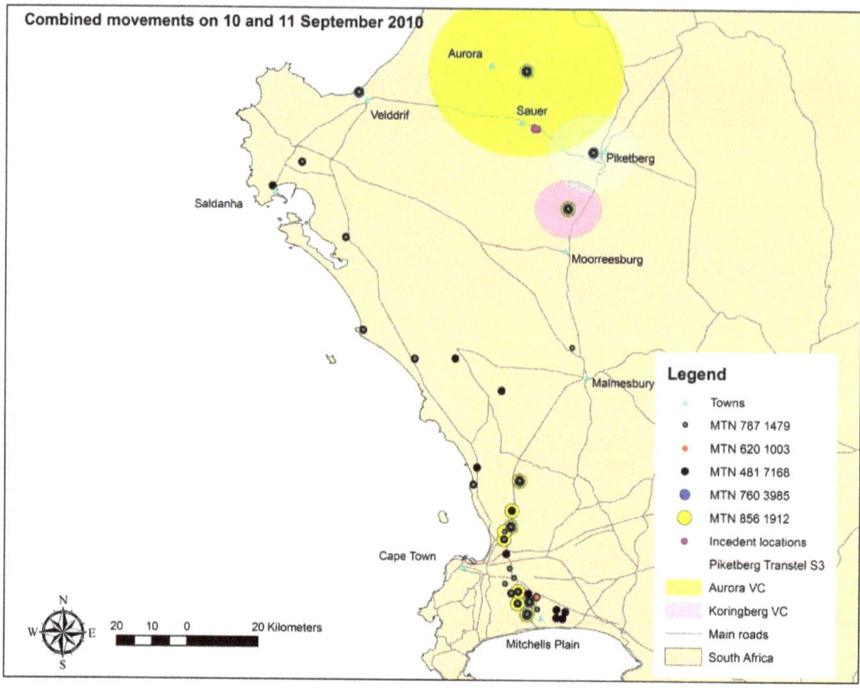

Figure 10.50: A similar geographic profile of one of the other stock-theft incidents

Figure 10.50 shows a similar pattern of cellphone base station usage as on the night of the accused's arrest. The other two maps not illustrated in this chapter also show a similar pattern. Thus it was possible to show via the maps that the accused had been involved in the other stock-theft incidents. Their cellphone data clearly indicated that on the other evenings between the incidents, the accused never left Cape Town.

10.8 SUMMARY

This chapter discussed the application of forensic geoscience and in particular forensic geography in the South African context. An overview of the various applications of forensic geoscience was given, ranging from the macro- to the micro-environment. The micro-environment looks at the use of microscopy, spectrometry and mineralogy as well as pollen analysis to link suspects to crime scenes or to establish where a victim was murdered and buried. The macroscale looks at the use of remote sensing and GIS for forensic purposes. A few South African examples were given to illustrate the use of these techniques in criminal investigations and proceedings. Several of the GIS examples given in section 10.7 have led to the successful conviction of suspects.

REFERENCES

T Berhardsen *Geographic Information Systems – An Introduction* 3 ed (John Wiley & Sons 2002)

P Bolstad *GIS Fundamentals – A First Text on Geographic Information Systems* 2 ed (Eider Press 2005)

H Brodsky 'Retail area overlap: A case in forensic geography' (2003) 55(2) *The Professional Geographer* 250–258

AG Brown 'The use of forensic botany and geology in war crimes investigations in NE Bosnia' (2006) 163 *Forensic Science International* 204–210

DV Canter 'The environmental range of serial rapists' (1996) *Psychology in Action* 217–230. Available at http://eprints.hud.ac.uk/9230/, accessed 4 December 2013

S Chainey & J Ratcliffe *GIS and Crime Mapping* (2005)

A Conan Doyle *Sherlock Holmes: The Complete Novels and Short Stories, Vol 1.* (Bantam Dell 1986)

AK Cooper, P Byleveld & PMU Schmitz *Using GIS to Reconcile Crime Scenes with Those Indicated by Serial Criminals* (2001) Paper presented at the Fifth Annual Crime Mapping Research Conference, Dallas, Texas (1–4 December 2001) Available on CSIR Researchspace at http://researchspace.csir.co.za/dspace/handle/10204/2779, accessed 2 July 2012

AK Cooper & PMU Schmitz *Mapping Crime Scenes and Cellphone Usage* (2000) Paper presented at the Fourth Annual International Crime Mapping Research Conference 'WHEREDUNIT? Investigating the Role of Place in Crime and Criminality' San Diego, California, USA (9–12 December 2000). Available on CSIR Researchspace at http://researchspace.csir.co.za/dspace/handle/10204/2788, accessed 2 July 2012

AK Cooper, PMU Schmitz, P Byleveld & DK Rossmo *Using GIS and Digital Aerial Photography to Assist in the Conviction of a Serial Killer* (2000) Paper presented at the Fourth Annual International Crime Mapping Research Conference 'WHEREDUNIT? Investigating the Role of Place in Crime and Criminality' San Diego, California, USA (9–12 December 2000). Available on CSIR Researchspace at http://researchspace.csir.co.za/dspace/handle/10204/2778, accessed 2 July 2012

G Elmes, C Titus, S Bergeron & J Rouse *'I Wasn't There': Space-Time Prisms for Criminal Investigation* (2007) Paper presented at the Ninth Crime Mapping Research Conference, Pittsburgh, PA, USA (28–30 March 2007)

C Eloff 'Dumping of chrome slag on the remainder of the farm Boschfontein No 268-JQ' (2012) Report submitted by the CSIR to the Department of Environmental Affairs (10 August 2012)

C Eloff *GIS & Remote Sensing Technological Tools for Spatial Intelligence* (2011) Presentation to UNISA Criminology students (11 July 2011)

A Guedes, H Ribeiro, B Valentim & F Noronha 'Quantitative colour analysis of beach and dune sediments for forensic applications: A Portuguese example' (2009) 190 *Forensic Science International* 42–51

EC Jones 'The basics of radio wave propagation' (2000) Available on the AE4TM Science and Photography website at http://ecjones.org/propag.html, accessed 3 December 2011

DA Lanegran 'The AAG at New Orleans' (1978) 10(4) *Area* 300–302

HT Lochner 'Kartering van selfoontegnologie' (unpublished MTech thesis, University of South Africa, 2007)

SA Mazhari 'An introduction to forensic geosciences and its potential for Iran' (2010) 2(1) *Journal of Geography and Geology* 77–82

Mobile Nation '*GPS vs aGPS: A Quick Tutorial*' (2011) Available at http://www.wpcentral.com/gps-vs-agps-quick-tutorial, accessed 2 December 2011

RM Morgan & PA Bull 'Forensic geoscience and crime detection: Identification, interpretation and presentation in forensic geoscience' (2007) 127(2) *Minerva Medicolegale* 73–89

RM Morgan, JC French, L O'Donnell & PA Bull 'The incorporation and distribution of trace geoforensic particulates on clothing: An introductory study' (2010) 50 *Science and Justice* 195–199

RM Morgan, J Robertson, C Lennard, K Hubbard & PA Bull 'Quartz grain surface textures of soils and sediments from Canberra, Australia: A forensic reconstruction tool' (2010a) 42(3) *Australian Journal of Forensic Sciences* 169–179

RM Morgan, P Wiltshire, A Parker & PA Bull 'The role of forensic geoscience in wildlife crime detection' (2006) 162 *Forensic Science International* 152–162

DC Nobes 'The search for "Yvonne": A case example of the delineation of a grave using near-surface geophysical methods' (2000) 45(3) *Journal of Forensic Science* 715–721

K Pye & DJ Croft 'Forensic geoscience: Introduction and overview' in K Pye & DJ Croft (eds) *Forensic Geoscience: Principles, Techniques and Applications* (Geological Society, London 2004) 1–5

A Richards 'Reflected ultraviolet imaging for forensics applications' (2010) Available at http://www.uvcorder.com/pdf/Reflected_UV_Imaging_for_Forensics_V2.pdf, accessed 2 July 2012

DK Rossmo *Geographic Profiling* (CRC Press 2000)

A Ruffell 'Forensic geoscience' (2006) 22(2) *Geology Today* 68–70

A Ruffell & L Dawson 'Forensic geology in environmental crime: Illegal waste movement and burial in Northern Ireland' (2009) 10 *Environmental Forensics* 208–213

A Ruffell & J McKinley 'Forensic geoscience: Applications of geology, geomorphology and geophysics to criminal investigations' (2005) 69 *Earth-Science Reviews* 115–122

A Ruffell & J McKinley *Geoforensics* (John Wiley & Sons 2008)

P Schmitz *Geographic Profiling* (2004)

PMU Schmitz 'The use of supply chains and supply chain management to improve the efficiency and effectiveness of GIS units' (unpublished PhD thesis, University of Johannesburg, 2007)

P Schmitz & A Cooper *Crime Mapping Research at the CSIR: 1997–2007* (2007a) Presentation by invitation to the Department of Geology and Geography, West Virginia University, Morgantown, WV, USA (23 March 2007)

P Schmitz & A Cooper *Using Mobile Phone Data Records to Determine Criminal Activity Space* (2007b) Presentation by invitation at the IQPC International GIS Crime Mapping Conference, Brussels, Belgium (25–26 September 2007) Available on CSIR Researchspace at http://researchspace.csir.co.za/dspace/handle/10204/1273 accessed 2 July 2012

P Schmitz, A Cooper & J Quick *Using Satellite Imagery for Crime Mapping in South Africa* (2002) Submission for the 6th Annual International Crime Mapping Research Conference, Denver, CO (December 2002) Available on CSIR Researchspace at http://researchspace.csir.co.za/dspace/handle/10204/2782, accessed 2 July 2012

P Schmitz, A Cooper, A Davidson & K Rossouw 'Breaking alibis through cell phone mapping' in *Crime Mapping Case Studies – Successes in the Field* (2000). Also available on CSIR Researchspace at http://researchspace.csir.co.za/dspace/handle/10204/2262, accessed 2 July 2012

PMU Schmitz, S Riley & J Dryden 'The use of mapping time and space as a forensic tool in a murder case in South Africa' (2009) in Conference proceedings for 24th International Cartographic Conference *'The World's Geo-Spatial Solutions'* (15 to 21 November 2009) Available on CSIR Researchspace at http://researchspace.csir.co.za/dspace/handle/10204/3869, accessed 2 July 2012

Smithsonian Institute *How Does GPS Work?* (National Air and Space Museum, Smithsonian Institute 2011) Available at http://www.nasm.si.edu/gps/work.html, accessed 2 December 2011

M Snyman *Cellular and Frequency and Radio Network Optimisation* (2007) Course offered at the University of Pretoria through Continuing Education

RJ Zinn 'Sentenced motor vehicle hijackers imprisoned in Gauteng as a source of crime intelligence' (unpublished MTech dissertation, Technikon SA, 2003)

RJ Zinn 'Incarcerated perpetrators of house robbery as a source of crime intelligence' (unpublished DLitt et Phil thesis, Unisa, 2007)

RJ Zinn *Home Invasions: Robbers Disclose What You Should Know* (Tafelberg 2010)

DIGITAL FORENSICS AND CYBERCRIME

11

Chapter

J Jordaan

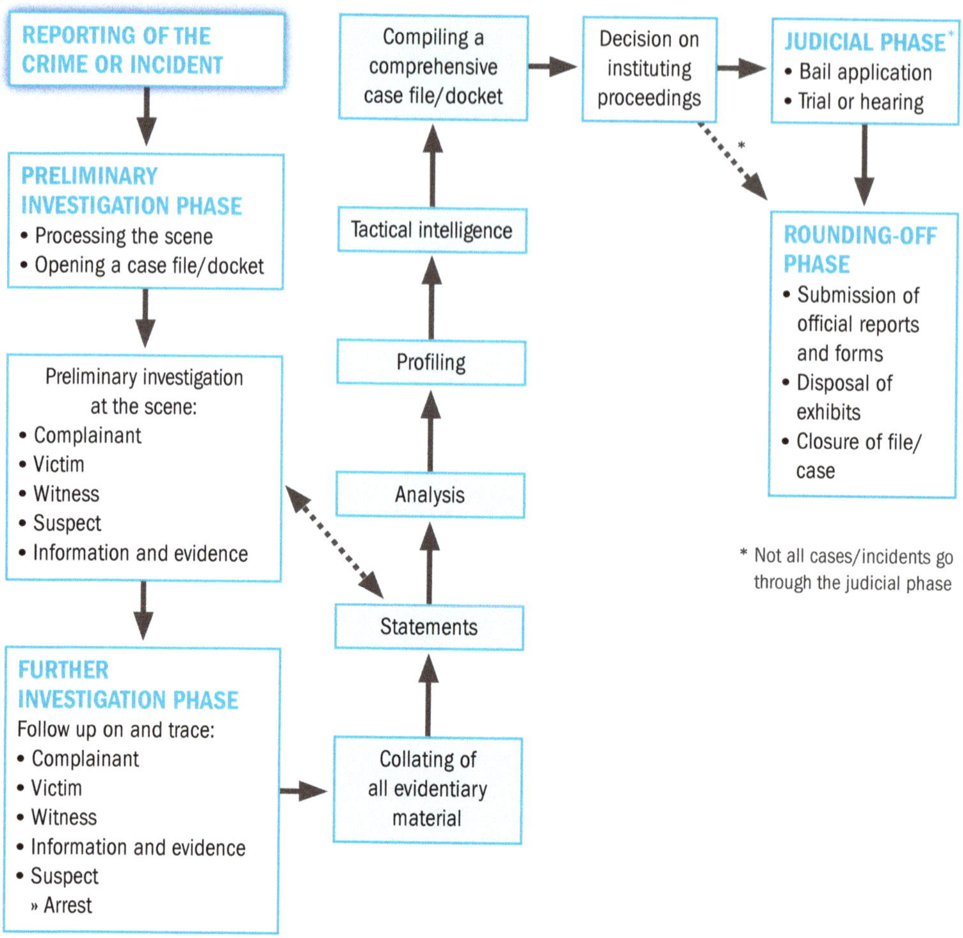

Figure 11.1: Areas of the crime investigation process covered in this chapter shown in shaded areas

11.1 INTRODUCTION

Computers, laptops, tablets, the internet and cellphones have fundamentally changed the way we interact and live our lives. Information technology has transformed human society by impacting on all aspects of humanity. Unfortunately, with criminality being intricately linked to humanity, information technology has influenced that as well.

Crime is a topic of much interest in contemporary society and there is a general sense in South Africa that crime is one of the biggest problems we face. The criminal justice system seeks to address crime through various processes, including investigation, and ultimately finding and prosecuting the offender in a court of law. A key requirement for proving a case in court is evidence; without evidence, no conviction is possible. As society has become more information-based, computers and digital devices have become a fundamental part of daily life. The role of these devices in crime and the digital information they contain have become part of the crime problem. Digital information, which exists in a binary state, can be used to store, transmit and process information in almost any other format such as letters, numbers, words, pictures, sound and video material.

Computers, information systems, communication devices and other digital devices are now used as tools to commit crimes, as the target of criminal activity and potentially to store digital evidence that can prove or disprove legal issues in dispute. As a result, the forensic investigation environment has changed fundamentally. These days any investigator must be comfortable with obtaining and collecting digital evidence, must understand how to make use of digital forensics, and be able to identify and investigate cybercrimes.

The digital forensics process can begin during the preliminary investigation phase (for example the identification and seizure of electronic devices at the primary crime scene) and continue into the further investigation phase (for example the identification and seizure of additional electronic devices as potential sources of evidence, and the forensic examination of these devices and the digital evidence they contain).

11.2 DIGITAL FORENSICS

Digital forensics began as a discipline in the mid-1980s as federal law enforcement agencies in the USA saw the increasing involvement of computers in crimes.[1] In the early 1990s the International Association of Computer Investigative Specialists created the first documented set of guidelines for digital forensics.[2] They were followed by the Association of Chief Police Officers, the International Organization on Digital Evidence, the Scientific Working Group on Digital Evidence, and the International Federation of Information Processing Working Group 11.9 on Digital Forensics.

Initial conceptual approaches to digital forensic practice were fragmented, which perpetuated the viewpoint that there was no standard approach to digital forensics. The development of common conceptual approaches was necessary for digital forensics to be considered a valid discipline of forensic science.[3] In 2003 digital forensics joined mainstream forensic science when the American Society of Crime Laboratory Directors/Laboratory Accreditation Board recognised digital forensics as a fully-fledged forensic science discipline.[4] Digital forensics has since been widely recognised as a valid forensic discipline.[5]

1 Jones & Valli (2009).
2 Pollitt (2008).
3 Rogers & Seigfried (2004).
4 Carrier (2005).
5 Britz (2009).

The practice of digital forensics did not start in a forensic laboratory. In the experience of the author, it developed as a result of police detectives and investigators around the globe, including South Africa, who realised in the early days of computing that computers may be the source of evidence. Digital forensics accordingly developed in an *ad hoc* manner rather than in a scientific one, but this has changed. Nowadays the development of digital forensics is increasingly scientific in nature.[6] Digital forensics is now a valid scientific discipline which is subject to the rigours and expectations of the greater field of forensic science.[7]

Digital forensics could be described as the application of scientific knowledge from the fields of computer science and information systems to a legal situation. These fields would include all the electronic or digital devices as well as the data they contain, as mentioned above.

In recent years, courts began to recognise digital forensics as a legitimate scientific method for discovering and proving facts that could be used to prove matters before a court of law, thereby endorsing the validity of digital forensics as a scientific discipline.[8]

11.2.1 Defining digital forensics

Digital forensics involves the preservation, identification, extraction and documentation of digital evidence stored as data or magnetically encoded information. In essence, digital forensics is about evidence from computers, digital media or digital devices that can stand up to scrutiny in court and convincingly serve as evidence. The objective of digital forensics is in essence quite simple: to recover, analyse and present digital evidence in such a way that it is usable as evidence in a court of law.[9]

One definition of digital forensics is that it is the science of acquiring, preserving, retrieving and presenting data that has been processed electronically and stored on computer media.[10] In another definition, digital forensics is the use of scientifically derived and proven methods towards the preservation, collection, validation, identification, analysis, interpretation, documentation and presentation of digital evidence derived from digital sources for the purpose of facilitating or furthering the reconstruction of events, or helping to anticipate unauthorised actions.[11] An example of reconstructing an event would be to determine exactly how a hacker gained unlawful access to a computer network, and what they did on that network.

---

6 Beckett & Slay (2007).
7 National Research Council (2009).
8 Volonino et al. (2007).
9 Vacca (2005).
10 Swanson et al. (2006).
11 McKemmish (2008).

A key element in the various definitions of digital forensics is the scientific nature of digital forensics. This is a strong indication that digital forensics is considered a scientific, or at the very least an applied scientific, discipline. Digital forensics could thus more appropriately be named digital forensic science.

A recent definition by Zatyko[12] of digital forensic science is that it is the application of computer science and investigative procedures for a legal purpose involving the analysis of digital evidence after proper search authority, chain of custody, validation with mathematics, use of validated tools, repeatability, reporting and possible expert presentation. Based on this definition, the scientific process of digital forensics consists of the following components:

- search authority
- chain of custody
- imaging/hashing function
- validated tools
- analysis
- repeatability (reproducibility) (quality assurance)
- reporting
- possible expert presentation.

11.2.2 Nature of digital forensics

The exchange principle of Edmond Locard, known as the Locard exchange principle (explained in chapter 2) forms the cornerstone of forensic science. This has evolved into two guiding principles and four processes, which can apply equally to digital and traditional physical evidence.[13] These principles and processes, and how they can relate to digital evidence, are reflected in Table 11.1.

Table 11.1: Principles and processes of forensic science applied to digital evidence

Principles of forensic science	Applicability to digital evidence
Transfer (Locard exchange principle) Whenever two items come into contact with each other, there is a reciprocal transfer of trace evidence or information from one to the other.	Digital evidence exhibits transference in its interactions.
The divisibility of matter The ability to impute characteristics to the whole from a separated piece.	Digital duplicates are representative of the original evidential items. →

12 Zatyko (2007).
13 Pollitt (2008).

→

Principles of forensic science	Applicability to digital evidence
Identification Identifies the nature of the evidence at a physical and structural level.	Description of the digital evidence in terms of: • physical structure (eg the number of cylinders, heads and sectors of a computer hard drive) • logical structure (an NTFS partition) • location (physically on the storage device, and the logical path) • content (eg an email or graphics file) • metadata.
Classification/Individualisation Classification is an attempt to determine a common origin, while individualisation uses a set of characteristics to uniquely identify a specimen.	File systems, partitions and individual file types have characteristics that allow for their classification, eg: • partition tables which define partitions • file allocation tables, master file tables, or inodes which define certain file systems • internal data structures of files which define what type of file they are. Individualisation can be achieved through the use of one-way mathematical hashing such as MD5 and SHA-1 to demonstrate the uniqueness of the data.
Association Association is an inference of contact between the source of the evidence and a target.	Association can be determined through interactions in the system, eg proving that a particular USB flash drive had been attached to a particular Windows computer through an analysis of the registry, and then showing that a particular file was copied to it through link files.
Reconstruction Reconstruction is the ordering of associations in time and space.	Dates and times relating to data, filing systems and network communications can be used to show sequences of events in computer systems.

To appreciate the value of digital forensic sciences, an investigator must understand the essential elements of forensic science. The essential elements of forensic science include the ability of the scientist to:[14]

- know the hypothesis or question to be tested
- establish that the items provided are suitable for the requirements of the case at hand
- confirm that the type of examination has been correctly selected
- confirm that the examination has been carried out competently
- summarise and collate the results of the examination
- interpret the results of the examination in accordance with established scientific principles
- consider any alternate hypotheses
- prepare a report or affidavit based on the findings of the examination
- present evidence in court
- ensure that all documentation used in the process is fit for the purpose for which it is intended.

A key factor in the forensic science process used in digital forensics is to ask one or more specific investigative or legal questions, which are ultimately translated into scientific questions.[15] These questions should be asked by the forensic scientist in response to questions posed by the investigator in the case, before any evidence is examined or analysed by the forensic scientist.

Other factors in the practice of forensic science include the concepts of repeatability (reproducibility), validation and verification.

- Repeatability is one of the primary means by which forensic scientists validate each other's results and thus combat the occurrence of scientific fraud. It can lead to the formalisation of scientific standards into commercial products.[16]
- Validation is defined as the confirmation by way of an examination and a demonstration of objective evidence that a particular forensic tool, forensic technique or forensic procedure functions correctly and as it was intended to function.[17]
- Verification is defined as the confirmation of a validation with forensic laboratory tools, techniques and procedures.[18]

In conducting the forensic science examination and analysis of evidence, a number of broad tests should be applied to the evidence so that forensic scientists can satisfy themselves and others that the results of their analysis are correct

14 Kershaw (2001).
15 Pollitt (2008).
16 Garfinkel et al. (2009).
17 Guo et al. (2009).
18 Guo et al. (2009).

in the context of the case at hand. Broad tests which should be applied to any forensic evidence include the following:[19]

- Is the evidence authentic? Does the evidence actually come from where it is said to have come from?
- Is the evidence reliable? Can the story that the evidence tells be believed, and is that story consistent? Are there any reasons to doubt that the computer on which digital evidence was found was working correctly?
- Is the evidence complete? Is the story that the evidence tells complete? Are there any other stories that the evidence may tell that may have a bearing on the case?
- Is the evidence free from interference and contamination?

To ensure that digital forensic evidence meets these tests, any approach to digital forensic science, by both investigators handling potential sources of digital evidence and digital forensic examiners, should encompass the following considerations and processes:

- Procedures that are well defined to address the various digital forensic tasks performed during the various phases of the digital forensic process (see section 11.9 of this chapter).
- Anticipation that the methodology used will be criticised by the opposition's legal practitioner in court on the grounds of failing to demonstrate authenticity, reliability and completeness, and that it has possibly been contaminated as a result of the forensic examination. To counter this, detailed documentation must be maintained for all processes and actions related to the evidence in question.
- The possibility that repeat tests will be carried out, possibly by forensic experts hired by the other side.
- The necessity of checklists to support each methodology used to ensure consistency.
- Anticipation of any problems relating to formal legal tests of admissibility by the opposition's legal practitioner in court. To counter this, all the relevant legal authorisations must be obtained prior to any examination and detailed documentation must be kept.
- The acceptance that any method used could almost certainly be subject to later modification or improvement because technology in the field of digital forensics changes so rapidly. This is especially relevant when cases take a long time to go to trial from the time that the digital forensic examination has been performed. In the time period leading up to the trial new methods, tools or techniques could have been developed that could give more accurate results.

---

19 Vacca (2005).

11.2.3 Stages in the digital scientific analysis method

At a fundamental level the principles and processes of forensic science as a discipline can be applied to the field of digital forensics. The application of the scientific method when digital data is being analysed is of critical importance for digital forensics to earn and maintain its place as a forensic science.

The scientific analysis method in digital forensic science involves four distinct stages:[20]

- Gathering information and making observations about the evidence. This phase involves verifying the integrity and authenticity of the evidence, reviewing the evidence, performing data carving and keyword searching. This phase is typically known as a digital forensic examination.
- Forming a hypothesis to explain the observations in the previous stage.
- Evaluating the hypothesis. This phase involves testing the hypothesis to determine if it is true, and if it is not, to revise the hypothesis and look at further tests.
- Drawing conclusions and communicating findings.

The scientific analysis method used in digital forensic science is illustrated in Figure 11.2 and may potentially require a digital forensic examiner to repeat these steps until a correct conclusion can be reached. For example, if tests and experiments disprove the hypothesis, a new one must be formed and subsequently evaluated.[21] In effect, experimentation is a natural part of the digital forensic process.

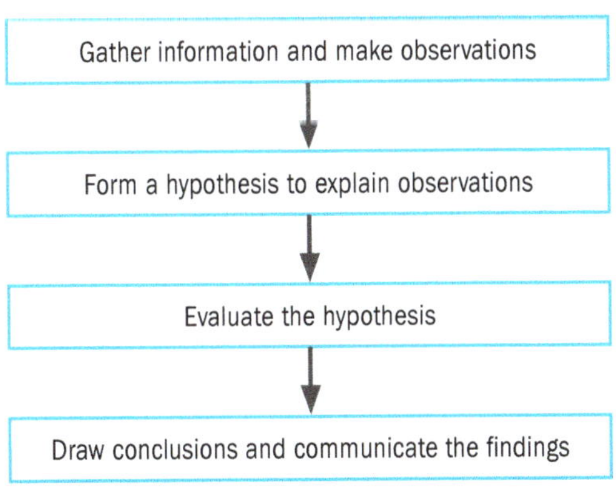

Figure 11.2: The scientific analysis method

The underlying fundamental process will remain the same for every digital forensic examination, even though the following aspects may differ:

- the data being examined

20 Casey & Rose (2010).
21 Casey & Rose (2010).

- the objectives of the investigation
- the resources available
- other factors such as the skills, knowledge and experience of the digital forensics practitioner applying the scientific analysis method.

A fundamental tenet of the digital scientific analysis method is the principle of repeatability (reproducibility),[22] which is a key requirement in forensics. The scientific analysis method also provides a safeguard against drawing incorrect conclusions because incomplete or inconsistent methods have been applied.[23]

In essence, the evidence from digital forensics is scientific evidence.

11.3 DIGITAL EVIDENCE

Evidence is the admissible information used by a court of law to reach a decision on any matter brought before it. Digital evidence is merely another type of evidence that a court can use to reach a decision in cases brought before it.

The internet and the proliferation of digital devices means that digital evidence can be present in virtually any case. It is not limited simply to so-called computer crimes but is relevant to the investigation of almost any crime.[24] Digital evidence is now a fundamental part of many investigations, for example SMS messages sent between two perpetrators while planning a crime, videos made using a cellphone to record an assault, or emails offering easy (but fraudulent) investment returns.

The increase in potential digital evidence in any matter under investigation means investigators need to understand the nature and value of digital evidence. In many instances this means they have to embrace a new approach to conducting investigations where traditional physical and witness-based evidence is being augmented with digital evidence.

Investigators will not usually themselves seize raw data at a scene of incident, as data is generally found on devices capable of being stored, such as computers, cellphones, etc. In many ways obtaining data is like obtaining a fingerprint: the investigator protects or secures the item containing the fingerprint but the fingerprint itself is lifted by a fingerprint expert. With digital evidence, the investigator often simply secures the storage device and the data is obtained by a digital forensic examiner.

A digital forensic examiner is a forensic scientist who specialises in the forensic examination of digital evidence and the devices containing digital evidence. Generally, digital forensic examiners have a degree in computer science or a similar

22 Beckett & Slay (2007).
23 Casey & Rose (2010).
24 Swanson et al. (2006) 548.

field, and often a postgraduate qualification in digital forensics. They also have extensive specialist training, not only in digital forensics but also in general information technology. Unlike forensic examiners who work in the more traditional branches of forensic science, digital forensic examiners must constantly undergo training to stay abreast of changes in technology. Often individuals who have only been trained in using digital forensic tools, such as EnCase or FTK, are considered to be qualified digital forensic examiners, but without the fundamental computer science and digital forensic science skills and knowledge, this is simply not the case. That would be like expecting a person who was trained in using a particular spreadsheet application like Excel to be a qualified accountant, simply by virtue of them being proficient in Excel.

11.3.1 Defining digital evidence

Evidence can be defined as anything that tends to logically prove or disprove a fact in issue in a judicial case.[25] In other words, it is anything that can help to establish the arrested person's guilt or innocence. Digital evidence is defined as information of a legal probative value that is either stored or transmitted in digital format.[26] It is any data stored on or transmitted by a computer that supports or refutes a hypothesis of how an offence occurred, or addresses a critical element of the offence, such as intention or an alibi. Digital evidence includes any computer hardware (containing data), software or data that can be used to prove who, what, when, where, why or how (the W×5; H principle explained in chapter 1) the incident being investigated occurred.[27]

Essentially digital evidence is any data stored or transmitted in some digital (binary) format that can be used in a criminal prosecution, civil litigation or disciplinary hearing, to either prove or disprove any aspect of the case. Examples of digital evidence include (but are not limited to):

- digital photographs
- digital videos (including CCTV footage)
- emails
- text messages (including SMS, MMS, BBM, WhatsApp, etc)
- websites and web pages
- documents
- spreadsheets.

11.3.2 Nature of digital evidence

Digital evidence is by its very nature fragile and can be easily altered, damaged or destroyed by improper handling or examination.[28] There are a number of

25 Swanson et al. (2006) 758.
26 Casey (2004) 12.
27 Solomon et al. (2005) 52.
28 Association of Chief Police Officers (2003) 6.

inherent challenges to its use in court, the most significant perhaps being the ease with which it can be manipulated or altered, either intentionally or accidentally, without leaving any obvious signs that this has been done.[29]

The simple act of an investigator switching on a computer to see what it contains alters hundreds of files without the investigator even realising it, thereby contaminating digital evidence. Opening a potentially suspicious file may alter the metadata associated with that file, thereby altering the file. Metadata is 'data about data', for example the date that a particular file was created is a form of metadata. Simply copying a suspicious file from a suspect's computer to another storage device such as a USB thumb drive alters the file. All these actions are the digital equivalent of trampling all over the evidence at a physical crime scene simply by walking around. Unfortunately these are all too common events, performed by investigators who do not understand the nature and fragility of digital evidence.

However, the very nature and features of digital evidence mitigate these risks:[30]

- Digital evidence can be duplicated exactly and a copy can be examined as if it were the original. Thus the copy can be examined without the need to examine the original data and potentially altering it.
- Using mathematical one-way hashing (see section 11.6 of this chapter) allows any alteration of digital evidence to be determined by comparing the hash values of the copies to the original.
- Digital evidence is difficult to destroy. Simply deleting the files and data does not actually remove them. Traces remain, which can be recovered using specific forensic procedures.
- When criminals try to destroy digital evidence, copies and associated latent evidence can still remain in places they are not aware of, due to the nature of how modern computer systems, servers and networks work.

Digital evidence is valuable evidence and should be treated no differently than traditional physical evidence, ie with respect and care. While the methods used to deal with digital evidence may seem complex and costly, when they are used correctly they produce evidence that is both compelling and cost effective. Like any other type of physical evidence, the improper handling or forensic processing of digital evidence can destroy its court value and make it inadmissible as evidence.[31]

From a digital forensics perspective the information created and stored on a computer or digital device can be seen as a double-edged sword. Not only can it provide compelling evidence in a variety of investigations; it can also introduce

29 Casey (2004) 12.
30 Casey (2004) 16.
31 Swanson et al. (2006) 548.

a level of complexity that can trip up even experienced digital forensic examiners.[32] The problem with digital forensic evidence is that it is often technically complex. The legal system's lack of technical awareness has led some presiding officers to make inappropriate assumptions because they are not always in the best position to evaluate the reliability of the digital evidence. The best way in which this can be addressed is to make use of experienced and well-trained digital forensic scientists who can interpret and explain the evidence to the court as expert witnesses.

11.4 USES OF DIGITAL EVIDENCE

Digital evidence can be used to answer certain fundamental questions relating to a case under investigation, including what happened when, who interacted with whom, where the evidence originated and who was responsible for creating the evidence.

While many people only consider digital evidence in a typical computer crime such as hacking or malware distribution, digital evidence is present in virtually every incident that is investigated. Digital evidence can be used to find answers to a number of questions.

Example 11.1: Digital evidence can answer various questions

- **When** did something happen in a time sequence or timeline? For example, when was a particular email sent or read, or when was a particular file printed? In a suicide investigation, the digital forensic investigator could establish that the suicide note was created on the victim's laptop several hours after their actual death. This could prove that it was not a suicide but possibly a murder.
- **Who** interacted with whom? For example, digital forensic evidence can be used to establish links between two parties, including which users were chatting in an internet chat room or had sent emails to each other, or establishing who a child pornographer had been talking to online or shared child pornography with.
- **What** was the origin of a particular digital evidence item? For example, on which particular computer did a particular document originate?
- **Which** user account was responsible for a particular transaction or event? For example, which user account was logged onto the computer when money was transferred from one bank account to another by means of internet banking?
- **How** did this particular offence take place? For example, reconstructing how a hacker managed to gain access to a secure computer network.

The complexity of digital information systems means that individual items of digital evidence may be interpreted in multiple ways, therefore corroborating information may be required to reach a factually correct conclusion.[33]

32 Casey & Rose (2010) 21.
33 Casey & Rose (2010) 21.

Case study 11.1: Uncovering the digital truth

Consider a case where a person is suspected of downloading child pornography from the internet. An examination of his computer finds pornographic pictures of children in the internet cache of the computer. This evidence may be interpreted that the user had visited a website and viewed child pornography. However, the web browser logs on the computer show that on the date that the websites were opened, the website from which the photos came was only accessed for a millisecond, as were a number of other pornographic websites in rapid succession. In other words, each website was opened for a split second, far faster than a person could do. A further examination reveals that the computer had been infected with a virus that had rapidly opened up random pornographic websites, including a site containing pornographic images of children, and that the user of the computer was not responsible at all.

If only the initial interpretation was considered, the digital forensic investigator would have reached an incorrect conclusion and an innocent person could have been prosecuted and/or punished.

While digital evidence can be used to answer a number of questions relevant to legal action, the one question that it cannot conclusively answer is who was physically using a particular device at any particular time. While it may be possible to make a circumstantial determination, it must always be kept in mind that digital evidence cannot physically link a suspect to an action. In other words, digital evidence is not physical evidence that can individualise a person, such as can be done with fingerprints or DNA, and thus cannot prove who was physically at the keyboard of a computer or using a cellphone when a particular file was created or a particular SMS sent. It can only link a device (a computer, cellphone, tablet) to a specific set of digital evidence created or stored on that device. However, this does not change the value that digital evidence brings to an investigation.

11.5 SOURCES OF DIGITAL EVIDENCE

Digital evidence can exist on any electronic device or storage media (such as optical, magnetic, or solid-state media) capable of processing or storing digital information. In our modern society our daily lives have become intertwined with technology. We store photographs, documents, videos, messages and so much more on electronic devices and use these devices to communicate. As technology develops, new devices are capable of storing digital information and new storage media may become commonplace. Investigators should try to stay up to date with technological developments to be aware of potential new sources of digital evidence. Take cellphones, for example. Cellphones have become commonplace. We use them not only to talk to each other but also to take photos or videos, send emails and access the internet. Nowadays every cellphone is a potential source of digital evidence and who is to say what new digital technology will be commonplace in the future? The digital information on a cellphone can actually help to create a profile of the user of the device through the usage patterns of specific applications and habits when the cellphone or applications are used. It becomes the electronic footprint of the owner of the device.

11.5.1 Common devices and media

Digital evidence can generally be considered to come from one of the following distinct categories of electronic devices or storage media. These devices have become the norm in our society and can be expected to be found in most organisations, many homes and certainly on many people. As illustrated below in Figures 11.3 to 11.11, these include:

- desktop computers
- portable computers (including laptops, netbooks and tablets)
- external and portable hard drives
- cellphones and smartphones
- portable media players
- USB thumb drives (memory sticks, flash drives)
- digital cameras
- flash memory cards
- CD or DVD disks.

Figure 11.3: Desktop computer

Figure 11.4: Portable computer

Figure 11.5: External and portable hard drive

Figure 11.6: Cellphones and smartphones

Figure 11.7: Portable media player

Figure 11.8: USB thumb drives (memory sticks, flash drives)

Figure 11.9: Digital camera

Figure 11.10: Flash memory cards

Figure 11.11: CD or DVD disks

11.5.2 Uncommon devices and media

Uncommon electronic devices and storage media are those that are not as commonly used in broader society, or those items that investigators generally do not associate with being a source of digital evidence in their investigations. As illustrated below in Figures 11.12 to 11.18, these include:

- server computers
- printers with an internal memory or a digital media storage capacity
- telephone answering machines or telephones with these capacities built in
- digital voice recorders
- GPS devices
- digital video recorders
- dedicated computer game consoles.

Figure 11.12: A server

Figure 11.13: Printer with an internal memory or a digital media storage capacity

Figure 11.14: Telephone with answering machine or telephone with these capacities built in

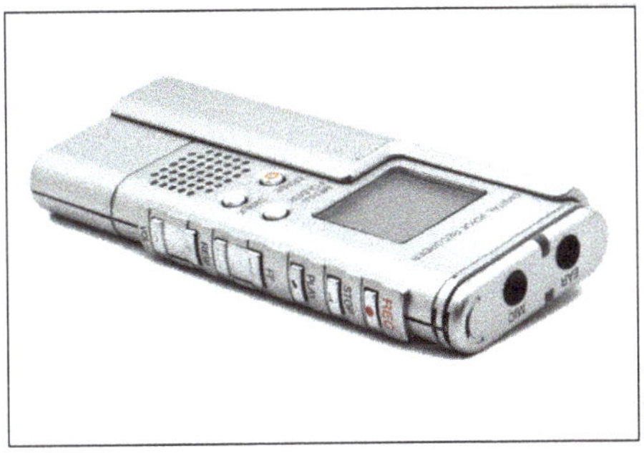

© iStock.com

Figure 11.15: Digital voice recorder

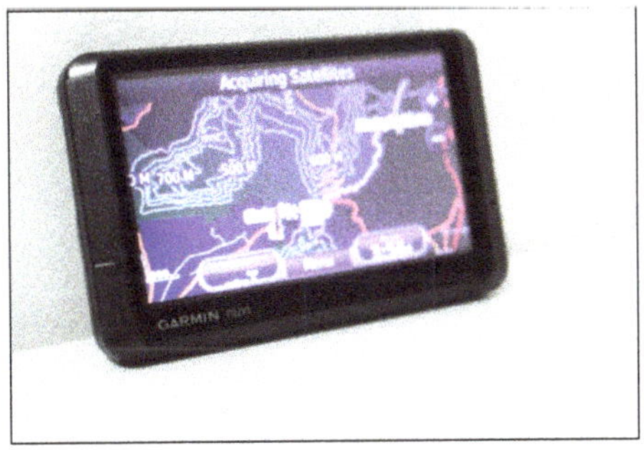

Figure 11.16: GPS device

Figure 11.17: Digital video recorder

Figure 11.18: Dedicated computer game console

The rapid development in technology and digital devices may lead to many devices that are currently considered uncommon becoming common and even outdated in only a few years. It is thus important that investigators constantly update their knowledge about new technology and digital devices that have come onto the market and the potential these devices may have for digital evidence.

11.5.3 Protected devices and media

Protected devices and media are those common and uncommon devices and media that are designed to prevent unauthorised access or usage through the use of some security mechanism. These can include biometric devices such as fingerprint readers or iris scanners, or devices that require a security access 'token' such as an encoded access card or a dongle.

11.5.4 Concealed devices and media

Electronic devices and storage media can be disguised, either commercially or through a process of 'moding', to look like something else. Forensic investigators should therefore be most vigilant, especially if the target of their investigation is very technologically aware or skilled. For example, in one case a USB thumb drive containing incriminating digital evidence was designed to look like a piece of sushi, and found stored in the suspect's refrigerator.

The use of wireless networking technology has also aided the concealment of certain electronic devices such as wireless routers and wireless network storage devices, and there have been examples of these devices hidden in ceilings or crawlspaces.

11.6 DIGITAL EVIDENCE IN RELATION TO THE ELECTRONIC COMMUNICATIONS AND TRANSACTIONS ACT

Prior to the Electronic Communications and Transactions Act 25 of 2002, the question of the admissibility of digital evidence in South Africa was a grey area. In general it was difficult to get digital evidence admitted as evidence in court.

The Act addresses the issue of digital evidence in South African law, and has allowed the use of digital evidence as evidence in legal proceedings. When assigning evidential weight to digital evidence, s 15(2) of the Electronic Communications and Transactions Act guides a court in how to evaluate the evidence.[34] A key factor to be considered in this regard is the reliability of the digital evidence and how its integrity was maintained.

In terms of current South African law, digital evidence and the concept of a data message as defined in terms of the Act are synonymous. Section 1 of the Electronic Communications and Transactions Act defines data as 'an electronic representation of information in any form', and a data message as 'any data that is generated, sent, received, or stored in electronic means'.

34 Van der Merwe et al. (2008) 115.

Section 15 of the same Act governs the admissibility and weight of data messages and, subsequently, digital evidence. Section 15(1) of the Act states that a data message (and thus digital evidence) cannot be ruled inadmissible simply by virtue of the evidence being in an intangible digital format, while s 15(2) goes on to state that information in a digital form must be given due evidential weight.

What is significant is s 15(3) of the Act, which sets out the guidelines for a South African court when assessing the evidential weight of digital evidence. This section requires a court to give due regard to:

- the reliability of the manner in which the data message (digital evidence) was generated, stored or communicated
- the reliability of the manner in which the integrity of the data message (digital evidence) was maintained
- the manner in which the originator of the data message (digital evidence) was established
- any other relevant factors.

These factors address at a fundamental level the need for establishing a proper chain of evidence and ensuring the reliability of the digital evidence by cryptographic means such as mathematical hashes.[35] Essentially, mathematical hashing is a digital forensic technique that creates a digital fingerprint of a single file or even of an entire digital storage medium. If even one bit of the data is changed, one will be able to determine that the data has been altered because the mathematical hash would no longer match the original one. While it is generally the responsibility of the digital forensic practitioner to analyse the hashing functions, investigators can still play a crucial role in ensuring that the courts would give due evidential weight to the digital evidence.

Investigators should never access any computers, cellphones or other electronic devices themselves to look for possible information of value, as they will very likely alter the evidence at a fundamental level. As stated above, this is the digital equivalent of trampling all over a physical scene of incident.

Example 11.2: Digital evidence is easily contaminated

In one investigation the investigators seized a USB thumb drive when they arrested a suspect, and later decided to plug it into a computer to view the files. They opened several files, found some that were relevant to their investigation and then handed the USB thumb drive to digital forensic practitioners to extract the evidence for court purposes. However, the forensic examination of the USB thumb drive showed that several of the files had been opened and inadvertently modified after the USB thumb drive had been taken into possession by the investigators. This created a problem with the integrity of the evidence as it could not be proven that the investigators had not somehow altered or manipulated the evidence to incriminate the suspects.

35 Van der Merwe et al. (2008) 115.

11.7 ADMISSIBILITY AND RELEVANCE OF DIGITAL EVIDENCE

For evidence to be usable in court proceedings, it must be both relevant and admissible. If evidence is not relevant or if it is not admissible, then it may not be considered in the case before court because it may unfairly prejudice or give an unfair advantage to one of the parties in the court case. For the purposes of this chapter, 'court' includes a formal court, such as a criminal court or a civil court, as well as any form of tribunal, such as a disciplinary hearing, that will be adjudicating on a matter requiring evidence where a legal decision will be made. In addition to the legal requirements and rules which govern the use of digital evidence in court, traditional concepts in the law of evidence nevertheless still apply.

Relevant evidence is evidence that can prove or disprove any of the facts in issue in the case.[36] When one looks at how individuals use their computers and other mobile devices, it is no understatement to say that traces of almost all aspects of our lives can be found on them. When one also considers the huge amount of data that can exist on a standard computer or smartphone, most of the data will not be relevant to a case under investigation. To illustrate this, a single Gigabyte of data (1 GB) is the equivalent of 212 000 A4 pages of information. It would be very easy for the investigator to be overwhelmed by the sheer volume of data that people can load onto their personal computers and smartphones, such as photos and videos of themselves and their friends. This could result in the investigator making the mistake of using digital evidence that is not really relevant. It is of the utmost importance that forensic investigators limit themselves to digital evidence that is relevant. 'Relevant' evidence is evidence that is relevant to the case under investigation. Relying on evidence that may ultimately be ruled irrelevant in legal proceedings could seriously undermine a case.

Evidence, including digital evidence, can be ruled either admissible or inadmissible. Admissible evidence is evidence that meets all regulatory and statutory requirements and that has been correctly obtained and handled.[37] Evidence that is deemed inadmissible in a legal proceeding cannot be considered by the court. The two most obvious mistakes an inexperienced investigator can make that will result in evidence not being admissible in court are to collect evidence in an illegal manner or to modify the evidence after it has come into the possession of the investigator/examiner. To ensure admissibility, it is critical that the legal requirements are complied with. These include the rules relating to search and seizure (see section 11.9.13 in chapter 11) the maintenance of a proper chain of custody (see section 6.7.3 in chapter 6) and ensuring that the digital evidence is not altered in any way.

36 Solomon et al. (2005) 66.

37 Solomon et al. (2005) 66.

The most common mistake leading to digital evidence being ruled inadmissible in court is that it was obtained without the correct legal authorisation. In a South African context this is an even more critical consideration as a result of s 86(1) of the Electronic Communications and Transactions Act 25 of 2002. At its most fundamental level, the practice of digital forensics involves accessing data stored on a device or medium, and examining and analysing that data. It is the digital forensic practitioner (ie a person specifically trained in digital forensic science rather than a general investigator) who will be accessing the data. The accessing of data is a fundamental part of the practice of digital forensics that is performed intentionally by the digital forensics practitioner. Data is accessed for the purposes of:

- imaging it for later forensic examination and analysis
- performing a live forensic examination or incident response process
- examining and analysing the contents of a forensic image made of the original data.

Section 86(1) of the Electronic Communications and Transactions Act states that any person who intentionally accesses or intercepts any data without authority is guilty of an offence. In terms of s 89(1), the maximum penalty for the contravention of s 86(1) is a fine or imprisonment for a period of no longer than 12 months. In the context of s 86(1) there is thus a legal onus on digital forensic practitioners to ensure that they have the appropriate authority to access the data in the first place to enable them to perform digital forensic acquisition, examination and analysis. In other words, unless a digital forensic practitioner has the necessary and relevant authority to image or examine and analyse digital data, any digital forensic process they apply in relation to that data would amount to a contravention of s 86(1) of the Electronic Communications and Transactions Act.

The necessary authority would be provided either by a relevant search warrant, the consent of the owner or custodian of the item, or a court order or subpoena. In an internal investigation, especially in an organisational environment, the owner or senior executive of the organisation who is considered the accountable person for all assets of the organisation may give permission. However, if the organisation does not have a policy in place that states that the organisation controls and has access to all data on any device owned by the organisation but used by its employees, employees could claim that they have the right to privacy with regard to their data, meaning that only they may give consent to access the data.

Other common mistakes by digital forensic examiners and investigators that can render digital evidence inadmissible include:[38]

- failure to create and maintain the proper documentation through all stages of the digital forensic process

38 Jones & Valli (2009) 10-11.

- the inadvertent modification of digital evidence
- failure to maintain the chain of custody
- failure by the digital forensic examiner or investigator to know when they have reached the limits of their knowledge and to ask for advice.

11.8 RELATIONSHIP BETWEEN DIGITAL EVIDENCE AND DIGITAL FORENSICS

Key factors in ensuring the admissibility, and in certain instances the relevance, of digital evidence involve processes based on the practices of criminalistics and forensic science. Digital forensics is a critical component in bringing digital evidence to court because it follows certain standard procedures. These procedures tend to persuade the court to admit digital evidence and give it due and proper evidential weight.[39] As digital forensics is a specialised field, the courts in South Africa have tended to treat evidence presented as a result of a digital forensics process as expert witness evidence, similar to that presented by a scientist.

Digital forensics provides for an expert witness to show the court that the digital evidence produced in court is exactly the same as when it was first seized. This is critical and a significant component of ensuring the admissibility of the evidence. It is for these reasons that various bodies have established universal standards and procedures for digital forensic experts to ensure that they provide guidance to courts on the admissibility of digital evidence.

11.8.1 Principles for handling computer-based digital evidence

The Association of Chief Police Officers[40] in the United Kingdom developed four basic principles for computer-based digital evidence to aid in the acceptance of digital evidence and the forensic examination thereof in a court of law. These principles have become widely accepted in the digital forensics discipline.

1. No action taken by an investigator or examiner should change data held on a computer or on storage media which may subsequently be relied upon in court.
2. In circumstances where an investigator or examiner must access original data held on a computer or on storage media, that person must be competent to do so and be able to give evidence explaining the relevance and the implications of their actions.
3. An audit trail or other record of all processes applied to computer-based digital evidence must be created and preserved, and it must be detailed enough to

39 Van der Merwe et al. (2008) 65.
40 Association of Chief Police Officers (2003) 4.

allow another independent digital forensic examiner to use these documents and achieve the same results by following the same processes.
4. The person in charge of an investigation has overall responsibility for ensuring that these principles are adhered to.

The principles established by the Association of Chief Police Officers in effect lay the fundamental ground rules for dealing with digital evidence and provide a mechanism to improve the admissibility of digital evidence in courts of law.

Physical evidence must also be collected by following rigorous and established procedures:

- to protect it from contamination or destruction
- to protect it from claims that it was tampered with or handled improperly
- to establish and preserve the chain of custody.

By following established forensic science practices, this fragile and easily altered form of evidence can be demonstrated to be authentic, whereas failure to do so could result in the digital evidence being excluded from a court of law, or at the very least being given limited evidential value. In many respects, digital evidence is simply another form of latent evidence that must be handled according to accepted forensic science principles within appropriate legal boundaries.

11.9 THE DIGITAL FORENSICS PROCESS

To make the most of digital evidence, investigators should make use of digital forensics. Digital forensic science as a process involves a number of distinct stages and it is crucial to understand digital forensics within that context. Both investigators and digital forensic examiners play different but complementary roles in this process.

The entire digital forensics process can be divided into three broad phases: a pre-examination phase, an examination phase, and a post-examination phase, running sequentially, as illustrated in Figure 11.19.

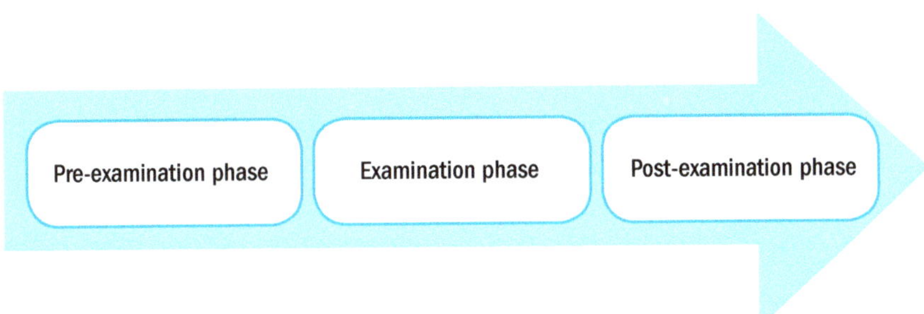

Figure 11.19: Phases of the digital forensics process

11.9.1 The pre-examination phase

The pre-examination phase in the digital forensic process consists of five specific processes that need to be completed before any digital evidence can be examined by a digital forensic examiner. These are:

- obtaining the legal authority or mandate to acquire and examine the digital evidence
- identifying all the legal elements of all allegations to be investigated in terms of the legal authority
- identifying all possible devices or media that may contain potentially relevant digital evidence, in terms of the legal authority
- seizing and transporting the evidence
- forensic acquisition of the digital evidence from the identified devices or media
- forensic authentication of the digital evidence acquired.

These processes run sequentially, as illustrated in Figure 11.20.

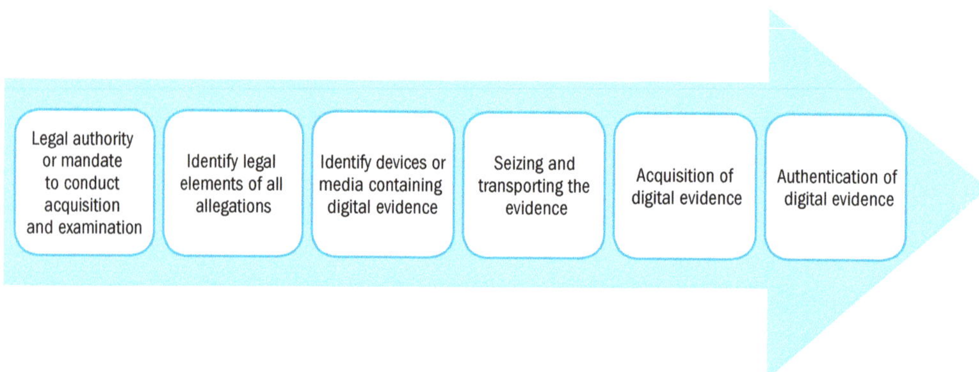

Figure 11.20: Processes in the pre-examination phase

11.9.1.1 Legal authority or mandate

The first step is to ensure that the digital forensic examiner has the correct legal authority to forensically acquire any digital evidence, and to subsequently examine and analyse such evidence. This step, ie obtaining the necessary legal authority, is traditionally performed by the investigator.

In the context of a digital forensic examination, appropriate authority includes:

- a search warrant or Anton Piller order (see section 7.7 in chapter 7)
- a subpoena or other court order
- consent from a person who can legally consent to the acquisition and examination of digital evidence.

The issue of consent as legal authority has potential challenges, especially in an organisational environment.

Example 11.3: Consent in an organisational environment

In a business, the accounting authority, who is accountable for all assets including computers, can consent to computers being examined by virtue of them belonging to the organisation. However, while the organisation may own the computers, they may not actually be in a position to consent to the examination of data, especially if the data on those computers is private data of the respective users of the computers. If the organisation does not have a policy in place that specifically states that all data on the organisation's computers can be accessed and examined by the organisation, users could claim that they have a constitutionally protected right to privacy.

In such an instance it is crucial that the investigator obtains a copy of the written policy, as well as either a copy of the suspect's employment contract in which they agree to abide by all policies, or a copy of a signed acknowledgement that they have read or received the policy.

11.9.1.2 Identifying the legal elements to be proved

The second step is for the investigator to identify all the legal elements of each allegation they are investigating and brief the digital forensic examiner, so that the digital forensic examiner has a good idea of what digital evidence may be legally relevant to the case at hand.

The legal authority not only authorises the acquisition and examination of the digital evidence, it also limits the scope of the potential digital evidence that may be used in subsequent legal proceedings. To ensure that only relevant digital evidence is ultimately presented in legal proceedings, investigators need to know the exact legal elements of each allegation they are investigating so that digital forensic examiners can be made aware of the types of digital evidence they should consider in their examinations.

11.9.1.3 Identifying the potential sources of digital evidence

With the legal authority in place and a clear understanding of the allegations being investigated, the third step requires investigators and digital forensic examiners to identify potential sources of digital evidence so that these can either be seized and forensically imaged and examined off-site, or forensically imaged on site. In other words, if conducting a search and seizure, investigators would have to identify electronic devices such as computers, cellphones and tablets that potentially contain the digital evidence they seek. Considering the number of potential sources of digital evidence, due diligence must be taken that all potentially relevant evidence is obtained. When one considers that a single 8 GB SD memory card, the size of a postage stamp, could potentially contain 1,6 million pages of information, and that it could be hidden virtually anywhere, searches must be especially thorough.

11.9.1.4 Seizing and transporting the evidence

Unless the physical devices and media containing the digital evidence are forensically imaged on site by a digital forensic examiner, it will be necessary for the investigator to seize these devices and take them to a digital forensic examiner for processing. It is essential that the investigator follows the correct procedure when carrying out such search-and-seize operations.

The most common types of storage devices were discussed in section 11.5. When encountered, these devices should be treated with as much care as any other physical item that is to be forensically examined. The following guidance deals with the majority of scenarios that may be encountered by an investigator, and the general principles, if adhered to, will ensure the best chance of evidence being recovered in an uncontaminated and therefore acceptable manner.

The majority of computers found during searches are desktop or laptop PCs. These machines usually consist of a screen, a keyboard and a main unit (with slots in the front for CDs and DVDs or other storage devices). Other devices are becoming more widespread, in particular tablet computers. These can hold large amounts of data, often in storage areas not immediately obvious to the investigator.

When considering the seizure of desktop or laptop computers, the approach taken to the actual seizure of the physical items will largely depend on whether or not the computers are powered on or off at the time of seizure. A key activity that an investigator must do, regardless of whether or not the computer is switched on or not, is to keep detailed notes of everything they do with regard to any computer evidence.

NOTE **Seizing computers that are NOT powered on**

If the computer is not powered on, the following steps should be taken when seizing the items:

- Secure the area in which the computer is found, and move any people on the scene away from the computer and any of its wires and cables, as well as from any power plugs.
- Check to ensure that the computer is actually off. The monitors may simply be switched off, or the computer may be in sleep mode.
- Label and photograph all the components of the computer, including the cables and the wall sockets and computer ports where they are plugged in, or at the very least draw a diagram, so that the computer set-up can be reconstructed in the digital forensic laboratory at a later date.
- Unplug the computer from the power socket. If the computer is a laptop, remove the battery as well.
- Seal all the components into properly labelled evidence bags.
- Search the area surrounding the computer for diaries, notebooks or even pieces of paper which may contain user names and passwords for the computer.
- If the owner of the computer is present, they should be interviewed to try and determine whether there are any passwords used on the computer, and if so, the investigator should try to obtain these.
- **Under no circumstances must the investigator switch the computer on.**

NOTE **Seizing computers that are powered ON**

If a computer is powered on and no digital forensic examiner is present, the following steps should be taken when seizing digital items:

- Secure the area in which the computer is found, and move any people on the scene away from the computer and any of its wires and cables, as well as from any power plugs.
- If the computer is connected to a network, whether via a cable or wireless connection, immediately contact a digital forensic examiner (it is advisable for the investigator to always have the telephone numbers of several digital forensic examiners on hand) for advice on how to proceed.
- If the computer screen is on, photograph the screen and its contents. If the screen is off, move the mouse or touch the touchpad (in the case of a laptop computer), to restore the screen, then photograph it.
- Label and photograph all the components of the computer, including the cables and the wall sockets and computer ports where they are plugged in, or at the very least draw a diagram, so that the computer set-up can be reconstructed in the digital forensic laboratory at a later date.
- Remove the power supply from the back of the computer **without closing down any programs or shutting down the computer.** This will prevent any changes from being made to any running programs or any other data on the computer.
- Unplug the computer from the power socket. If the computer is a laptop, remove the battery as well.
- Allow the equipment to first cool down before placing it into properly labelled evidence bags.
- Search the area surrounding the computer for diaries, notebooks or even pieces of paper which may contain user names and passwords for the computer.
- If the owner of the computer is present, they should be interviewed to try and determine whether there are any passwords used on the computer, and if so, the investigator should try to obtain these.
- Under no circumstances should the user or owner of the computer be allowed to access the computer while it is on, and the investigator should not act on any advice that they are given by bystanders or the suspect in relation to the computer.

Following the abovementioned process with regard to computers that are powered on will invariable result in the loss of some digital evidence. If the data on the computer is encrypted, it will most likely mean that the evidence will not be usable. It is therefore strongly advised when seizing computers to rather make use of a trained digital forensic examiner or an investigator who is specifically equipped and trained to seize digital evidence from powered-on computer systems.

If the computer to be seized is a server, it is advisable that it should only be done by a trained digital forensic examiner, as simply pulling the plug will cause considerable damage to the data and possibly the device.

NOTE **Seizing cellphones**

When seizing cellphones, investigators should follow these steps to ensure the integrity of the digital evidence contained on them:

- Handle the cellphone like any normal piece of physical evidence so as to preserve fingerprint and DNA evidence.
- **Under no circumstances should the cellphone be accessed by the investigator, as this will alter evidence on the phone.**
- If the cellphone is powered on, it must be placed in a Faraday bag or wrapped in several layers of aluminium kitchen foil. This will however increase the power consumption of the phone and drain the battery quickly, so it is vital that the phone be transported to the digital forensic laboratory for examination as quickly as possible. **If the phone is off, do not switch it on.**
- The power cables and connectors for the cellphone should be seized.
- Seal the cellphone and all its cables and power supply in an appropriate evidence bag.
- The owner or user of the cellphone should be interviewed to determine whether or not they use an access code to access the phone. If possible, the investigator should obtain this code.
- When transporting the items seized, it is crucial that they be secured and not placed near any strong magnetic sources such as car speakers. The items should also be protected from physical shocks. They should be kept clean of excessive dust and heat and should not be exposed to any liquids.

11.9.1.5 Forensic acquisition of digital evidence

Once the electronic devices containing potential digital evidence have been identified, a digital forensic examiner should make a forensic image of the data. In this step, a digital forensic examiner acquires one or more forensic images of the data contained on the electronic device using a variety of specialised digital forensic software and hardware. These can either be done on site, or off site, depending on the circumstances of the case. A forensic image is an exact duplicate of all the data contained on the electronic device. From a mathematical point of view the image is identical to the original. It is thus considered original evidence and not a copy. Forensic imaging should only be done by a qualified digital forensic examiner, or by an investigator who has received training in the forensic imaging of digital evidence and has the necessary tools to perform this function.

11.9.1.6 Authentication of forensic images

The final step of the pre-examination phase is to authenticate the forensic image of the digital evidence and mathematically verify that it is a mathematically identical duplicate of the source data (see section 11.6 for a discussion of mathematical hashing). If the forensic images are not authenticated, it could mean that all the digital evidence has not been correctly acquired. This process is performed by a digital forensic examiner. If it is not done, the digital evidence could be easily challenged in court.

11.9.2 The examination phase

The examination phase of the digital forensic process consists of five specific processes that need to be completed before a thorough digital forensic examination has been conducted. Unless all these steps are conducted, the evidential value of any digital evidence processed will be deficient. These steps are:

- confirming the legal parameters of the examination as established by the legal authority that was used to acquire the digital evidence
- authenticating the forensic images that were received for examination
- processing the forensic images using standardised digital forensic processes and methods
- examining and identifying the individual digital artefacts (individual files or part of a file that contains probative evidence) that were uncovered during the processing of the forensic image to determine and confirm their relevance to the case under investigation
- analysing and individualising the digital artefacts that were identified as relevant, and interpreting this evidence.

These processes run sequentially, as illustrated in Figure 11.21.

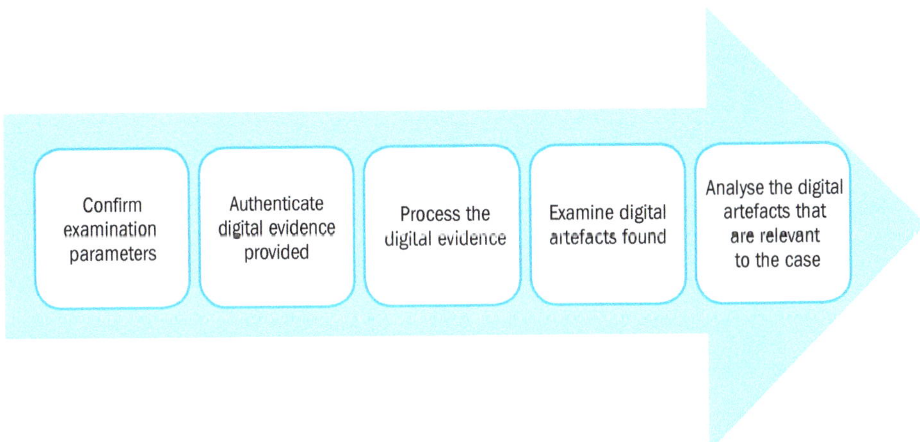

Figure 11.21: Processes in the examination phase

11.9.2.1 Confirming the examination parameters

The first step is to confirm the legal parameters of the examination to ensure that the correct legal authority is in place and that all the elements of the legal issues being investigated are understood. While this may seem to be a duplication of steps in the pre-examination phase, it quite often happens that the digital forensic examiner who examines the digital evidence is not the same person who acquired the digital evidence, therefore they need to confirm the legal authorisation and legal elements themselves before proceeding with the examination.

It is important that investigators work with digital forensic examiners to ensure that the digital forensic examiner who will be examining the digital evidence understands all the legal parameters of the investigation, and clearly understands the objectives of the examination for the case at hand.

11.9.2.2 Authenticating the digital evidence provided

The second step is to authenticate the forensic images received for examination and compare the mathematical hash of the forensic image when it was made to the mathematical hash of the forensic image received to ensure that they are the same. This will indicate that the digital evidence has not been altered from acquisition to examination.

11.9.2.3 Processing the digital evidence

Once the forensic images have been authenticated by the digital forensic examiner, the images will be processed using a number of digital forensic processes or methods to identify digital artefacts that may or may not be relevant to the investigation at hand. As each case is different, there is no single standardised set of processes that should be followed. Typical digital forensic processes that may be carried out during processing could include the following, among other things:

- reviewing the files in various user accounts so as to get an overview of the user's files and actions
- making a full text index of all textual data contained in the forensic images for the purpose of keyword searches – this allows the digital forensic examiner to rapidly find any files that contain a particular word or phrase that may be relevant to the investigation
- recovering and reconstructing deleted files – files that have been deleted can often be recovered using specific digital forensic processes
- reviewing graphic files to identify scanned documents or pictures of interest to the investigation – in the case of investigations involving sexual offences, a review of the graphic files is generally crucial
- identifying encrypted or password-protected files, and attempting to decrypt or otherwise access them
- reviewing log files and other system files so as to be able to reconstruct what has taken place.

11.9.2.4 Examining the digital artefacts

Once potentially relevant digital artefacts have been identified during the processing step, they are examined by the digital forensic examiner, often in conjunction with the investigator, to identify those data artefacts relevant to the investigation. Considering the amount of data that can potentially be identified during processing, this step is crucial to identify relevant evidence so that the court that will ultimately evaluate the evidence will not be inundated with irrelevant evidence. The examination phase essentially answers the 'what' question in the W×5; H principle.

11.9.2.5 Analysing relevant data artefacts

With relevant data artefacts identified, the digital forensic examiner needs to analyse these data artefacts to answer the 'who, what, when, where and how' questions, and to test this evidence in terms of the scientific method. It is during this step that the data artefacts are interpreted by the digital forensic examiner to explain their relevance to the case in question and highlight the relevant evidential value of each artefact.

11.9.3 The post-examination phase

The post-examination phase of the digital forensic process comprises five specific processes that need to be completed. These processes all ultimately lead to the presentation of the digital evidence in court. These steps are:

- a peer review of the results of the digital forensic examination process to ensure accuracy and the quality of the processes followed and the interpretations made
- documenting the entire examination in detail in an affidavit or report – this must be done by the digital forensic examiner
- reviewing the digital forensic examiner's affidavit or report for quality assurance purposes
- providing the finalised affidavit or report to the investigator who requested the digital forensic examination
- presenting the digital forensic examiner's evidence in court.

These processes run sequentially, as illustrated in Figure 11.22.

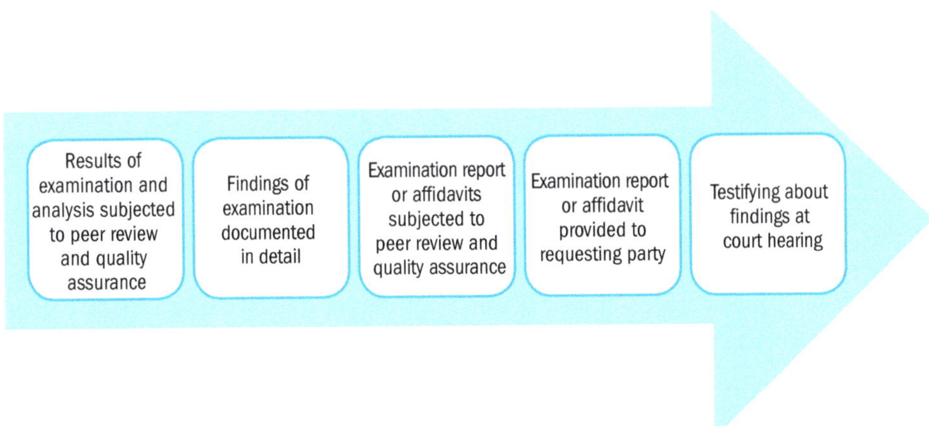

Figure 11.22: Processes in the post-examination phase

11.9.3.1 Examination and analysis peer review

Once the digital forensic examination phase has been completed, the work of the digital forensic examiner should be peer reviewed to check the accuracy of processes used and the correctness of interpretations made. This acts as a form of quality assurance to ensure that the court can rely on the digital evidence. If errors are identified, they can be corrected before the digital forensic examination is finalised.

11.9.3.2 Documenting the findings

With the peer review completed, the digital forensic examiner documents the entire digital forensic examination for court purposes. This record must be detailed enough so that another digital forensic examiner could follow the entire process and reach the same findings. It should also be written in such a way that it is easy to understand. This record usually includes various annexures, containing data artefacts and other digital evidence, which will be tabled as exhibits in court. The digital forensic examiner records the examination in the form of either an affidavit or a report. In general, affidavits, whether sworn or affirmed, are the preferred method of documentation.

11.9.3.3 Report/affidavit peer review

The digital forensic examiner's affidavit or report should then be reviewed for accuracy before it is released to the investigator who requested the digital forensic examination. At the very least it should be reviewed by another forensic examiner, but ideally it should be reviewed by a legal practitioner who understands digital forensics and digital evidence. This acts as a final quality assurance check before the digital forensic examiner's report or affidavit is released.

11.9.3.4 Testifying

The entire digital forensic process is concluded when the digital forensic examiner's evidence is presented and tested in court. A key factor for digital forensic examiners and investigators is that they need to properly brief the legal practitioner who will be calling them as witnesses so that the legal practitioner completely understands the evidence and the relevant technical complexities.

Due to the often complex technical nature of digital forensics evidence, it is important that the digital forensic examiner has the ability to translate these complex issues into easy-to-understand explanations so that the evidence can at least be understood in court and acted on accordingly.

11.10 CYBERCRIME

While digital evidence may be present in any crime, it is especially relevant to the area of cybercrime. However, many investigators regard cybercrime as too complex and are not sure how to handle it.

Computers, cellphones, the internet, social media and other information systems have become integrated components of human society and as such have created a whole new virtual environment – known as cyberspace – in which we live, work and play. Cyberspace has also become merely another place that criminals can use and exploit for their own purposes.

The computers and other devices that form part of cyberspace can play a number of roles in cybercrimes:[41]

- *As the target of a criminal act*: When computers or other devices are the target of a cybercrime, it is often the software that is attacked. For example, an individual's personal computer is infected with a malware program that enables the criminal to steal the user's internet banking username and password, so that money can be transferred out of the victim's bank account.
- *As the instrument with which a criminal act is committed*: When a computer or other device is the instrument with which a criminal act is committed, this device is often the point of origin of the criminal act. For example, a computer would be used to send emails containing the malware program. When this program is run by an unsuspecting user, it will steal their internet banking credentials and send them to the perpetrator.
- *As a repository of digital evidence of a criminal act that has been committed*: When a computer or other device is the repository of digital evidence of a criminal act that was committed, it contains some form of digital evidence of the criminal act. For example, a programmer used a computer to write malware, which he sold to criminals. They used the malware to commit a crime, but did not necessarily use the same computer to send out the emails. In effect, any computer or device that has been the target or instrument of a cybercrime should contain digital evidence of that crime and as such will also be considered a repository.

11.10.1 Myths about cybercrime

Cybercrime as a concept is often misunderstood and consequently does not often get the investigative attention it deserves. As a result it is often an underinvestigated crime. The three most common myths about cybercrime are:

- *Cybercrime is a new type of crime*: Cybercrime is not really a new type of crime, but simply creates new variations on already existing crimes. For

41 Cross (2008).

example, hacking into a computer system is fundamentally no different to housebreaking, except instead of breaking into a physical location to commit a criminal act such as theft, the criminal is breaking into a computer system to commit a criminal act such as theft. The inclusion of computers and information systems in crimes seems to have overcomplicated the situation: the focus often falls on the technology and not on the real underlying criminality, for example theft by electronically stealing money from a person's bank account.

- *Cybercrime is simply too complex*: Cybercrimes are certainly technical in nature, but to simply state that they are too complex does not address the fact that, like any crime, it is the responsibility of the investigator to study and understand the environment in which the crime takes place. Many crimes, such as fraud, are inherently complex, but that has not stopped investigators from investigating them. All that is required is that investigators do the necessary research.
- *Cybercrime is not a serious crime*: It has often been argued that cybercrimes are not serious crimes, but this is an erroneous assumption. When one looks at malware outbreaks, such as the 'I Love You' virus, the damage caused worldwide was in the hundreds of millions of dollars, and even organisations in South Africa were not spared. Similarly, phishing and internet banking fraud are responsible for huge losses around the world and organised crime is increasingly embracing cybercrime. Cybercrimes can result in a large number of victims and cause significant financial losses.

11.10.2 Defining cybercrime

Cybercrime is defined as the abuse and misuse of computers and information systems connected to the internet that result in either direct or indirect losses.[42] The key aspect of the definition is that the internet or other networked computer systems are the environment in which these crimes take place.

This clearly means that a vast number of potential crimes can be considered cybercrimes. However, when one looks at the evolution of information technology, networking and the internet, then hacking and activities that involve gaining unauthorised access to computer systems and the writing and dissemination of malicious software (malware) are considered 'traditional' cybercrimes. Other crimes, such as the dissemination of child pornography online and other criminal activities that are merely facilitated by the internet, are considered 'non-traditional' cybercrimes, but are cybercrimes nonetheless.

42 Britz (2009).

11.11 SUMMARY

Investigators can no longer conduct investigations without considering all the possible sources of digital evidence that may offer them clues or leads in their investigations, or even forensic proof. It is crucial that investigators understand digital evidence, where to find it, and how valuable it can be in their investigations. Overlooking or not even considering digital evidence means that potential evidence that could prove or disprove a case will not be taken into account.

Not only must investigators be familiar with digital forensics, they must understand the digital forensic science processes required to correctly collect, examine and analyse digital evidence. Understanding this means they will be able to collect evidence correctly and without potentially contaminating it, and will be able to effectively request a digital forensic examiner to scientifically examine the evidence.

This knowledge will enable investigators to deal with digital evidence confidently and thus make use of another type of evidence in their search for the truth.

REFERENCES

Association of Chief Police Officers *Good Practice Guide for Computer-Based Electronic Evidence* (2003) Association of Chief Police Officers, ACPO E-Crime Working Group. Available at http://www.7safe.com/electronic_evidence/ACPO_guidelines_computer_evidence.pdf or www.acpo.police.uk/policies.asp, accessed 22 November 2013.

J Beckett & J Slay '*Digital Forensics: Validation and Verification in a Dynamic Work Environment*' (2007) 40th Annual Hawaii International Conference on System Sciences 266–275

MT Britz *Computer Forensics and Cyber Crime: An Introduction* 2 ed (Prentice Hall 2009).

B Carrier *File System Forensic Analysis* (Addison-Wesley 2005)

E Casey *Digital Evidence and Computer Crime* 2 ed (Academic Press 2004)

E Casey & CW Rose 'Forensic analysis' in E Casey (ed) *Handbook of Digital Forensics and Investigation* (Academic Press 2010)

M Cross *Scene of the Cyber Crime* 2 ed (Syngress 2008)

S Garfinkel, P Farrell, V Roussev & G Dinolt 'Bringing science to digital forensics with standardized forensic corpa' (Elsevier 2009) *DFRWS 2009: The Proceedings of the Ninth Annual DFRWS Conference* S2–S11

Y Guo, J Slay & J Beckett 'Validation and verification of computer forensic software tools – search function' (Elsevier 2009) *DFRWS 2009: The Proceedings of the Ninth Annual DFRWS Conference* S12–S22

A Jones & C Valli *Building a Digital Forensic Laboratory* (Syngress 2009)

A Kershaw 'Expressing a standard' (2001) 41(3) *Science and Justice* 226–228

R McKemmish 'When is digital evidence forensically sound?' in I Ray & S Shenoi (eds) *Advances in Digital Forensics* (Springer 2008)

National Research Council *Strengthening Forensic Science in the United States: A Path Forward* (National Academic Press 2009)

M Pollitt 'Applying traditional forensic taxonomy to digital forensics' in I Ray & S Shenoi (eds) *Advances in Digital Forensics* (Springer 2008)

MK Rogers & K Seigfried 'The future of computer forensics: A needs analysis approach' (2004) 43(2) *Computers & Security* 12–16

MG Solomon, D Barrett & N Broom *Computer Forensics Jump Start* (Sybex 2005)

CR Swanson, NC Chamelin, L Territo & RW Taylor *Criminal Investigation* 9 ed (McGraw-Hill 2006)

JR Vacca *Computer Forensics: Computer Crime Scene Investigation* 2 ed (Thomson 2005)

D van der Merwe, A Roos, T Pistorius & S Eiselen *Information and Communications Technology Law* (LexisNexis 2008)

L Volonino, R Anzaldua & J Godwin *Computer Forensics Principles and Practices* (Prentice Hall 2007)

K Zatyko 'Defining digital forensics' (February/March 2007) *Forensic Magazine*. Available at http://www.forensicmag.com/articles/2007/01/commentary-defining-digital-forensics, accessed 22 November 2013.

FURTHER READING

The following publications are available on the internet and are valuable resources to investigators wishing to improve their knowledge and skills.

Investigations involving the internet and computer networks: http://nij.gov/nij/pubs-sum/210798.htm

Investigative uses of technology: devices, tools and techniques: http://nij.gov/nij/pubs-sum/213030.htm

Chapter

12 DEVELOPMENTS IN FORENSIC TECHNOLOGY

J H Smith • R J Zinn

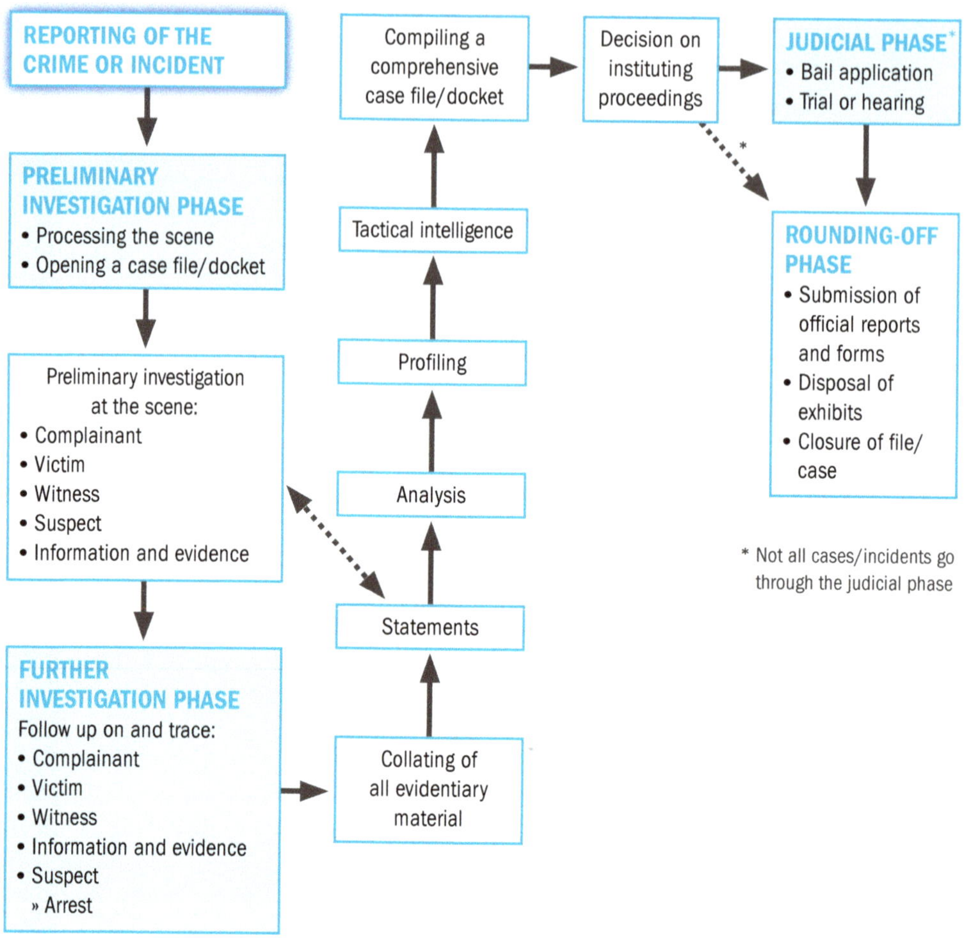

Figure 12.1: Areas of the crime investigation process covered in this chapter shown in shaded areas

12.1 INTRODUCTION

Recent advances in forensic technology are built on centuries of progress in the field of forensics. In recent years, however, forensic technology and its applications have been undergoing rapid advancement. This increased rate of development is, among other things, the result of the information era. The information era was brought about by the rapid developments in computers and the resultant sharing of information. The development in the ability and sophistication of computers and computer software also led to developments in instrumentation, machines and other equipment that are controlled by computer software. This increases the ability, accuracy and analytical scope of equipment used in forensic investigation.

The instrumentation used in forensic science is becoming more sensitive and fewer and fewer samples are required for scientific analysis. Chemical analyses and the identification of trace exhibits are becoming easier to perform and field applications are being developed that are used on site by the scene of incident examiner. What was previously not possible to perform in even the most advanced laboratories can nowadays be performed with portable equipment at the scene of incident. What was also previously unimaginable as far as science is concerned has, through the rapid development of computers, become possible.

One example that was brought about by the information era is the establishment of DNA markers. These DNA markers provide us with the ability to unlock human identification, such as genetic markers that provide information on what a person looks like or how they behave. Technologies already exist that can provide information about the eye colour of the donor of the DNA in a crime sample. In this developing field of science it will probably not be long before much more will be revealed about the donor of a sample than what can currently be established with DNA markers.

Other technological developments include the development of image enhancement technologies that enable investigators to trace and identify the characteristics of fingerprints, footprints and bite marks. These were previously untraceable without these technologies. With the advancement of information technology, the application of databases to collate and process large volumes of data in criminal investigation is also gaining momentum. The advantages of these new information technologies provide law enforcement agencies with valuable additional investigative tools to solve crimes and gain access to information that was previously not attainable.

Figure 12.1 illustrates which areas of the crime investigation process will be covered in this chapter.

12.2 NEW DEVELOPMENTS IN THE FORENSIC SCIENCE ENVIRONMENT

Forensic laboratories are increasingly employing automation to improve the number of samples they can analyse in a certain period of time. Thus the use of technology and chemistry improves the speed of analysis. The Forensic Science Laboratory of the South African Police Service (SAPS) is known for its leading role in this field. This laboratory introduced the Genetic Sample Processing System to analyse post-coital samples (vaginal samples collected from sexual assault victims) and the semi-automation of crime sample analysis (using liquid-handling stations to replace the manual pipetting or transfer of reagents to the samples) with a full laboratory sample and data management system. This is an electronic information system that keeps track of all analyses and the chain of custody of the samples. This laboratory was the first crime laboratory to perform the cell lysis step (breaking open of sperm cells to release the DNA) in the examination of post-coital samples on the deck of a robotic work station (a liquid-handling station that performs the transfer of reagents). This procedure is now being replicated in crime laboratories worldwide.

Forensic scientists are furthermore combining advances in miniaturisation and microchip technologies with well-established techniques of forensic DNA analysis. The fusion of these technologies (combining advances in instrumentation and chemistry technologies to allow DNA analysis to be performed away from laboratories) could revolutionise DNA typing and the speed at which results are made available in the field and applied at crime scenes. In other words, at some time in the future it may become possible to perform DNA analysis at the scene of incident in an instant.

Other interesting research conducted by forensic science laboratories includes the use of mass spectrometry (a method used to perform chemical analysis to determine the chemical composition of a sample) with a multi-tip pipetting robot. This will decrease the cost of analysis and increase the number of samples that can be analysed per day to several thousand. A further development is laser desorption mass spectrometry, another specialised chemical technique that can reduce analysis time to less than five minutes per sample compared to current conventional methods that take a few hours.

Furthermore, scientists from Erasmus MC University Centre in Rotterdam in the Netherlands[1] have successfully demonstrated that they can determine the age of an individual from blood stains. This will have direct application in cases where the age of the perpetrator who left a blood or saliva stain at the scene of incident may provide an important lead in the criminal investigation. It is now possible to also predict with 90% accuracy the natural colour of a person's hair from their DNA. It is thus expected that a validated test method for hair colour and an individual's age from blood and saliva stains should become available to forensic scientists within the next two to three years. If law enforcement agencies are permitted to use this technology, the investigator could obtain information about the perpetrator who left a blood or saliva stain that would provide a valuable lead in the investigation of the case.

12.3 OTHER DEVELOPING TECHNOLOGIES IN FORENSIC SCIENCE

Years ago, police depended on a brush to dust for fingerprints. Now they can use any of several hundred different chemicals and instrumental techniques to enhance fingerprints. Many forensic laboratories and investigators are also using

1 Zubakov et al. (2008).

advanced technology in instrumentation and illumination, such as a variety of light sources and lasers, to trace, enhance, view and record latent fingerprints. These include argon laser, X-ray detection and vacuum coating for the development of latent fingerprints on polythene. These modern techniques allow them to identify fingerprints that were difficult to recover several years ago.

A forensic light source comprises a powerful lamp containing the ultraviolet, visible and infrared components of light. It then filters down the light into individual colour bands (wavelengths) that enhance the visualisation of evidence by light interaction techniques. These techniques include fluorescence (the evidence glows), absorption (the evidence darkens), and oblique lighting (small-particle evidence is revealed). Different wavelengths are required for processing different types of surfaces. As a result, a forensic light source with tunable or multiple wavelengths is a coveted tool for any crime scene investigator. In many cases, the background surface will also glow under light-source illumination. In these cases it is necessary to tune to a wavelength of light that causes the fingerprint to glow, and not the background.[2]

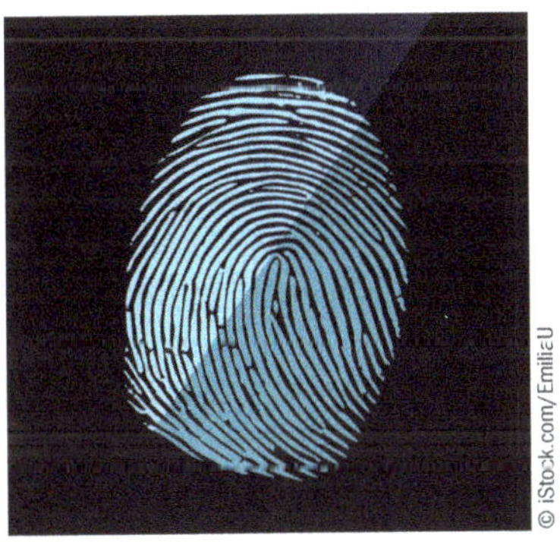

Figure 12.2: Fingerprints made visible by means of a light source[3]

Figure 12.3: Example of a forensic light source kit[4]

Forensic laboratories can process physical evidence using various methods, depending on the nature of the latent prints. In addition to dusting with powder, techniques include using chemicals such as iodine, ninhydrin reagents, silver nitrate and fluorescent reagents as well as cyanoacrylate (fast-acting adhesives such as superglue).

Another new developing field is the field of forensic photography. Colour enhancement and other technologies may be used to clarify an image when video tapes or photographs are scanned into a computer. This kind of image

2 Available at http://www.horiba.com/fileadmin/uploads/Scientific/Documents/Forensics/fls.pdf, accessed 31 March 2012.
3 Available at http://www.horiba.com/scientific/products/forensics/light-sources/forensic-light-source-applications, accessed 8 August 2013.
4 Available at http://store.sirchie.com/-Forensic-Light-Source-Kit-P941.aspx, accessed 30 March 2012.

enhancement may lead to the identification of a suspect that would otherwise not have been possible due to the poor quality of the original recorded image. Advances in image-enhancement technology are also helping police to visualise evidence, such as imprints (patterns left on hard surfaces) and impressions (three-dimensional patterns or indentations made in a softer medium such as mud, sand or snow) (see also section 2.5 in chapter 2).

A number of non-destructive photographic techniques have been developed to enhance imprints and impressions. These include the use of filters to vary contrast, and alternate lighting techniques such as oblique lighting, polarised light, ultraviolet light, infrared light and various wavelengths produced by alternate forensic light sources.

Images can also be enhanced with chemicals. The material picked up by a shoe to make an imprint could for example contain trace elements, minerals, blood and other compounds. These substances can be made more visible through enhancement using various chemicals.

It is now possible with a fingerprint-retrieving device using cyanoacrylate impregnated with an ultraviolet dye to detect latent fingerprints on all non-porous surfaces in about 20 seconds. Consequently a large house can be processed in less than two hours.

Technological advances to exploit ear biometrics as an identification tool are proving promising. The ear's structure remains stable with ageing and may be successfully used in conjunction with CCTV technology to identify individuals at entry points, such as border controls and airports.

Other innovative tools include a hand-held spectrometer for the on-site detection of explosives and illegal drug residues and a long-lasting fluorescent dye solution that allows a more detailed analysis of blood stains than can be done with conventional dyes.

12.4 ETHICAL DILEMMA

Although the development and benefits of new techniques in forensic science have significant scientific value, they also have consequences as far as legislation and ethics are concerned.

Presently the DNA technology applied in forensic science is regulated, inhibited or limited by the ethical and legislative limitations of each country's individual regime. There is thus no universal standardised norm and the absence of cooperation or information sharing is problematic for law enforcement purposes. The wide variety of intimate information that can be learnt from analysing the sample of a donor also requires continuous vigilance and often the promulgation of new legislation and ethical guidelines regarding human rights. These are thorny issues that sometimes require much debate. Legislative regimes and forensic laboratories have up to now largely steered clear of providing legislative guidelines on the use of forensic markers in the coding areas of the human genome or markers that rely on behaviour, medical conditions or physical conditions such as eye or hair colour or race.

If and what additional information should be included in a forensic DNA profile during a criminal investigation will be increasingly cause for debate. On the one hand there are advantages for law enforcement, and on the other hand the cost to an individual who gives up personal information. An individual's constitutional right to privacy will have to be considered, among other things.

Example 12.1: An ethical dilemma

The investigator has collected a sample from a suspect at the scene of incident and sends the sample for DNA analysis. In the process, it comes to light that the suspect is carrying a gene for a terminal disease.

The investigator now finds himself in an ethical dilemma.

Should he inform the suspect of this?

Would it be ethical to reveal this information during the trial?

Should he tell the suspect's spouse and/or family?

The ethical issue and its impact if personal information such as this should be revealed needs to be clarified before any such technologies can be employed at forensic laboratories. Thus, before forensic laboratories can consider implementing additional markers that carry personal information (for example eye or skin colour) into the forensic DNA profile, it will have to be acceptable to the public and approved by the legislative framework of the country.

There is also an ethical and legal debate on how long information on a suspect or convicted criminal should be stored on a database. Is it ethical to keep the personal details of a suspect, including fingerprints and DNA samples, on a database if that person has been exonerated, either during the investigation or by being acquitted in a trial, or should these details be removed? There is also the question of who should be allowed to have access to information on suspects and convicted criminals that is stored on a database. Should this information be shared in integrated databases with other law enforcement agencies or even public organisations involved in crime investigation or crime prevention activities? This is a complex debate that will require great wisdom and proper management so as not to infringe unduly on a person's rights and thereby undermine the integrity of forensic investigation as a science.

12.5 THE ADVANCEMENT OF INFORMATION TECHNOLOGY

The range of new information that can be obtained during a forensic investigation is increasing at a rapid rate. However, this brings about not only new investigative abilities but also a large volume of data. Collecting, storing, collating and analysing this data requires the use of computerised databases. These individual databases should ideally be integrated to allow access to all relevant information that can be used during an investigation.

At the same time the use of computers by criminals and other offenders automatically creates a computerised database that investigators can delve into to collect information and evidence. For example, law enforcement officials use digital forensic experts to mine the computer hard drives of narcotics dealers for records of their transactions or examine the email correspondence of murder victims to uncover motives and identify suspects.

Just as computer programmers develop computer software to make more applications available to the public, so computer programmers in the field of forensic investigation also develop software that can be applied in the solving of crimes (see chapter 11 for a detailed discussion of digital forensics). For example, existing software and hardware technologies enable digital forensic investigators to forensically examine the computer hard drive of a possible offender. Deleted files can be recreated, instant messaging chats can be recovered and all this data can be presented as evidence during a trial or hearing.

The disadvantage of the rapid changes in information technology is that criminals too are given tools which they can use to gain access to data or the private information of a person or company, which they then use to commit an offence. For example, through the internet criminals can gain access to a person or company's computers to obtain private information to perform identity theft or illegal banking transactions, or to change data that will negatively impact on a company's competitiveness or viability.

12.6 INDIVIDUAL INVESTIGATIVE DATABASES

National individual investigative databases to identify forensic investigative leads based on forensic DNA, ballistics, fingerprints and photographic/body images have become popular crime-fighting tools in the international forensic science arena. Other databases, such as databases on shoes, glass, gold, bank currency and fibres have also been developed to assist with the identification of particular substrates. Unique substrates or products can be traced back to a specific geographical region or manufacturer.

12.7 THE VALUE OF FORENSIC INVESTIGATIVE LEAD DATABASES

Forensic investigative lead databases can be used to link evidence found at a scene of incident to a suspect, or establish that the same perpetrator was involved in two or more crimes. This is done by comparing information on the characteristics of the evidence to the characteristics of evidence captured on the databases from previous scenes of incident.

Research has shown that many perpetrators, especially serious violent criminals in South Africa, are repeat offenders. It is therefore important that investigators obtain these forensic investigative leads as soon as possible.[5] Lives may even be saved if the investigator responds timeously. For example, if a serial offender is identified very early in his career as a murderer and the investigator follows up the leads provided to identify the perpetrator, the serial offender will be apprehended at the first possible opportunity and thereby be prevented from committing further murders.

It is best practice to share all corresponding references among investigators, such as forensic DNA investigative leads, Integrated Ballistic Identification System (IBIS) leads or Automated Fingerprint Identification System (AFIS) leads. The investigator should research which leads can link their cases to others on the various forensic lead databases, and discuss these with the investigators investigating those cases.

By combining the different forensic investigative leads, investigators can build a complete picture of the incident. This will help to focus the direction of the investigation. It may also provide a clear picture of the *modus operandi* of the perpetrator under investigation, or link new suspects who are associated with the perpetrator to the case.

12.8 FORENSIC DNA DATABASES

The use of a forensic DNA database is a powerful tool to provide investigative leads to identify suspects in cases where genetic material (DNA) has been left at the scene of incident.[6] A forensic DNA database is a collection of forensic DNA profiles obtained from crime scene samples, suspects and convicted offenders and used to perform comparative searches in order to establish an investigative lead. In other words, it is a collection of forensic DNA profiles from suspects and DNA evidence samples in various crime investigations over a number of years. These forensic DNA profiles are kept in a database for later comparison with DNA that may be discovered at a future scene of incident or obtained from a suspect who is arrested after a number of years.

5 Zinn (2010); Zinn (2003).

6 Smith (2000); Walsh et al. (2010); Hoyle (1998); Reilly (2001).

The real value of a forensic DNA database grows as the size of the database increases. The effectiveness of the forensic DNA database lies in the fact that the majority of crimes are committed by repeat offenders and previously recorded evidence can therefore be linked relatively quickly to the current suspect; various crimes can be shown to have been committed by the same offender, and the information can be used as evidence against the suspect. Studies in the UK (which launched its database in 1995) have shown that more than 60% of individuals sent to prison for violent offences and then released were rearrested for a similar offence (recidivism) in less than three years.[7] They can thus be easily identified should DNA be found at the crime scene and linked to DNA information stored on the DNA databases. Also, many 'cold cases' prior to the existence of forensic DNA databases can now potentially be linked to a suspect who has committed another crime. This is done by comparing the DNA found at the last scene of incident with the DNA results of historical cases loaded and kept on the databases to identify repeat offenders.

Initially it was believed that only forensic DNA profiles from convicted offenders in contact crimes such as sexual assault and murders should be loaded onto databases. This belief is changing, however. When the collection of DNA is expanded to include a larger variety of crimes, for example property crime, the database becomes a more effective investigative tool.[8]

Due to the decreasing cost of DNA analysis, forensic DNA databases are now including the forensic DNA profiles of all convicted (violent and non-violent) offenders and even of persons at arrest. In the USA, taking and analysing an inside cheek (buccal) swab of the arrestee's DNA is considered a legitimate police practice under the Fourth Amendment, similar to fingerprinting, photographing and the booking procedure of any person who is arrested.[9]

Researchers have found that many offenders do not limit their activities to crimes against property and may commit other offences, including violent crimes and drug-related offences. A Florida study revealed that 52% of that American state's DNA database 'hits' against murder and sexual assault cases matched individuals who were originally placed on the database for burglary convictions. In other words, a forensic DNA database will not only increase the likelihood of identifying known perpetrators, it will also increase the possibility of linking perpetrators to multiple scenes of incident or so-called crime series.

A forensic DNA investigated lead (sometimes referred to as a 'hit') occurs when a database search of a DNA profile obtained from biological evidence matches a profile already on the database, thus identifying or linking a suspect to a scene

7 A Matthe from UK Forensic Science Services. Presentation to SAPS Forensic Science Laboratory in 1998.
8 New York State Division of Criminal Justice Services (2003); Zedlewski & Murphy (2006).
9 Holland (2013).

of incident.[10] The UK has demonstrated that their database is much more useful and effective for investigating crimes such as burglaries and car theft than for violent crimes or sexual offences.[11] In a review performed during 2009 of five independent studies conducted in the USA, the evidence suggests that DNA testing has value when used to investigate a broad range of crime types.[12] As of August 2008, CODIS has produced more than 74 500 hits and assisted in more than 74 700 investigations in the USA.[13]

Although DNA evidence and forensic DNA databases are proving to play a significant role in solving crimes, the majority of crimes will not be solved through DNA evidence.[14] Many offences are reported that cannot be connected to an obvious crime scene. A case of cheque fraud would be a typical example. Furthermore, DNA will not be left at all crime scenes and not all exhibit material collected at the crime scene will yield a forensic DNA profile for comparison. Even where the discovery of DNA is possible and desirable, samples at the scene may be so partial or compromised by the presence of many people's DNA that they will be unusable.[15] It therefore needs to be noted that, as general practice, DNA is lifted from only a small proportion of scenes of incident and often only in certain types of offences.[16] In the UK the proportion of total crimes detected using DNA has been demonstrated to be low because crime-scene DNA profiles are loaded on the database for less than 1% of all recorded crimes.[17] In fact, the number of cases that can be solved using DNA analysis will always be limited by the number of scenes of incident from which DNA profiles can be collected and the need for corroborating evidence.

It is important not to overstate the value of DNA databases. These databases must be seen as another – albeit important – investigative tool available to law enforcement agencies to fight crime. Investigators must focus on collecting not only DNA evidence at crime scenes but also other forensic exhibit material and information. Many reported crimes are relatively minor and are solved because the victim and the perpetrator know each other, because the police may be on the scene of incident as the crime is taking place, or simply by normal policing or investigation. The investigator should therefore not substitute good investigation with an overreliance on DNA or technology to solve the crime. However, it remains crucial that investigators and scientists in the forensic industry keep developing and refining technology that can help them solve crimes.

10 Using DNA to solve Property crime. http://www.nij.gov/nij/topics/forensics/evidence/dna/property-crime/solving-crimes.htm, accessed 27 March.
11 GeneWatch (2006).
12 Wilson et al. (2010).
13 National Research Council (2009).
14 Briody & Prenzler (2005).
15 The National DNA Database - Home Affairs Committee (2009).
16 Wallace (2006).
17 The National DNA Database - Parliamentary Office of Science and Technology (2006).

12.8.1 The need for a more effective forensic DNA database

In this section, two examples illustrating the need for a more effective forensic DNA database in South Africa are discussed: the case of Moses Sithole, and 'Baby Tshepang'.

Example 12.2: The case of Moses Sithole

Moses Sithole is one of the most notorious serial offenders in the history of South Africa. Forensic DNA evidence played a significant role in the investigation and prosecution of his case.[18]

After Sithole's release from prison in 1994 for serving a sentence for rape, he started murdering his victims. He would entice his victims by pretending to be a businessman and offering them jobs. After gaining the victim's trust he would lure them to a field where he would rape and murder them. He went to tremendous lengths to leave almost no evidence behind and to remove the victims' belongings so as to delay their identification. Within a span of less than two years he had murdered more than 30 victims.

DNA evidence helped the investigators to link him to the offences and to identify him as the sole perpetrator. On 5 December 1997 Sithole was sentenced by Carstairs J to 50 years' imprisonment for each of the 38 murders, 12 years' imprisonment for each of the 40 rapes, and five years' imprisonment for each of the six robberies.

If the forensic DNA profile of Moses Sithole had been stored on a forensic DNA database after he had been arrested for his first offence, he could have been apprehended after being released from the correctional facility when his first victim was raped and murdered. This early identification could potentially have saved the lives of the 37 women who later became his victims.

Example 12.3: The case of 'Baby Tshepang'

In 2001 the vicious rape case of nine-month-old 'Baby Tshepang' was very prominent in the South African media. This case is known for the DNA evidence which exonerated six people and led to the conviction of the real perpetrator, David Potse.

Initially, due to the severity of the baby's injuries, it was believed that rape had been committed by several perpetrators. Six men were arrested shortly after the incident and detained for three months. However, forensic DNA testing exonerated them from the offence and prevented their further detention while the case was still under investigation.

If at the time an integrated DNA database had existed of all adult men or even of convicted offenders, it could have assisted in identifying the culprit in the 'Baby Tshepang' case from the outset (the National DNA Database currently consists only of DNA profiles collected from crime scenes (known as crime stains) and

18 Hancock (2011).

DNA samples of persons suspected of a crime/arrestees). This could have saved the six innocent men and their families the humiliation of arrest and disgrace in the eyes of the community in which they lived. They were detained for three months and all six lost their jobs.

Worldwide there has been advocacy to establish forensic DNA databases that are similar in composition to fingerprint databases. In many countries the fingerprint database consists of the fingerprint profiles of all persons who apply for an identification document and driver's licence. Presently advocates for a forensic DNA database are requesting that the database should contain profiles from crime samples, convicted offenders and charged persons in certain categories of crimes.

One such an example of advocates trying to bring about change in this regard in South Africa is the organisation called the 'DNA Project'. The DNA Project is endeavouring to advance justice through the expanded use of DNA evidence in conjunction with a national DNA criminal intelligence database, also known as a 'National DNA Database'. They state that they hope their efforts will translate into a change in legislation to allow for such a database. This would allow the comprehensive use of DNA analysis for crime detection and prevention in South Africa.[19]

12.8.2 Practical problems in developing a national integrated DNA database

The retention and use of, for example, both fingerprint profiles and forensic DNA profiles constitutes interference by the state in a person's right to privacy. There could be little, if anything, more private to individuals than the knowledge of their genetic make-up and subsequent information carried in the DNA reference sample which is used to obtain the forensic DNA profile. However, for practical reasons the forensic DNA profile, obtained by the SAPS Forensic Science Laboratory, does not contain any personal (except about the sex of the person) or medical information about the person.

The reason is that forensic DNA testing currently only targets areas of the genome that do not give any direct information of the person's predisposition. The laboratory only focuses on a small area of a person's DNA that does not contain genes or personal information. This is sometimes referred to as 'junk DNA'. This means the forensic profiles on the DNA database contain no personal information such as what the person looks like or how they behave. However, because the junk DNA differs from one person to the next, it is used in forensics to give a distinctive, individual DNA profile, which is used to identify a person. Thus forensic DNA testing only provides a person's identity through the alphanumeric string of characters.

19 DNA Project (2012).

The protection of personal data is of fundamental importance to a person's enjoyment of their right to a private and family life. Any infringements of an individual's rights must be balanced against the Constitution of the Republic of South Africa, 1996, which guarantees the right to privacy in s 14. This right includes the right not to have 'their person or home or property searched'. The mere fact that information about DNA characteristics is stored has privacy implications and is sufficient to warrant stricter accessing requirements.

These restrictions and legal limitations impact on the issue of when it would be justified to retain the information of a person on a DNA database. Would it be justified to do so merely because that person is a citizen of the country? Or because they were a suspect in a criminal investigation but never prosecuted? Or prosecuted and either acquitted or found guilty?

These restrictions and legal limitations also impact on the type of DNA coding that should be done during a criminal investigation, as explained above.

12.8.3 Legislative framework

At present there is no specific legislation in South Africa that specifically provides for the establishment and administration of a national forensic DNA database as a forensic investigative tool.

A need was expressed by the South African government to introduce legislation that would provide a specific framework for collecting and processing DNA samples and performing comparative searches on forensic DNA databases. To this end the Criminal Law (Forensic Procedures) Amendment Act 37 of 2013, commonly referred to as the 'DNA Act', was enacted on 27 January 2015. This Act is expected to become operational, with the exception of s 36D(1), before the end of 2014. This Act had not yet come into operation as at 1 July 2014; once in operation, it will amend the Criminal Procedure Act 51 of 1977 and the South African Police Service Act 68 of 1995. It will provide the legislative framework for the National Forensic DNA Database.

Section 37(1)*(c)* of the current Criminal Law (Forensic Procedures) Amendment Act 6 of 2010 provides that a police official may ascertain if the body of a person accused or convicted of a crime has any mark, characteristic or distinguishing feature or shows any particular condition or appearance. In other words, a police official may take reasonable steps to obtain any specimen or test results to explain the characteristics of a person's physical appearance or even the person's genetic make-up, which can be presented as evidence in court. Determining the blood group as well as the forensic DNA profile of a person is implicit in this specific paragraph. The Criminal Law (Forensic Procedures) Amendment Act 37 of 2013 now amends s 225 of the Criminal Procedure Act by inserting reference to bodily samples. The information derived from the bodily samples of an accused and corresponding information to another crime sample or bodily sample may be used in court proceedings. Section 37(2)*(a)* of the Act stipulates that a registered medical practitioner or a registered nurse is allowed to take the necessary steps, including taking a blood sample, to determine whether the body has any mark, characteristic or distinguishing feature. Furthermore, the court can order the taking of a blood sample as stipulated in s 37(3)*(b)* or as per s 36E(2) from persons not arrested, for investigative purposes or to exclude the person from the investigation. Thus buccal (inside cheek) samples may be taken at the request of the police official by order of the court. Other legislation such as s 113(2) of the Firearms Control Act 60 of 2000 and s 9(3) of the Explosives Act 15 of 2003 provides that bodily samples may be taken in offences punishable with a sentence of at least five years.

However, Regulation 944 (published in *Government Gazette* 9624 of 11 November 2011) in terms of the National Health Act 61 of 2003, has been published by the Minister of Health. This Regulation authorises a police official who has received the necessary authorised training by a medical practitioner to take non-intimate samples from individuals. Police officials who have been specifically trained in accordance with the National Health Act 61 of 2003 and the appropriate Regulations may collect a DNA reference (non-intimate) sample by means of taking a buccal (inside cheek) swab. Section 36D(1) and 36D(2) of the 'DNA Act' now aligns the Criminal Procedure Act to the National Health Act 61 of 2003 and provides that authorised persons from the South African Police Service and Independent Police Investigative Directorate take these DNA reference samples, in other words the buccal samples from certain categories of persons, in order to ascertain if the body of any person accused or convicted has a characteristic or distinguishing feature, namely the forensic DNA profile.[20] This is in line with international practice whereby law enforcement officers take non-intimate DNA reference samples of this nature.

During the deliberation of the legislation for the forensic DNA database, activists for the expansion of the DNA database were trying to persuade the government to make more amendments to the current legislation, such as retaining on the database the forensic DNA profiles of suspects who have been acquitted. These activists were calling for the implementation of a 'DNA Act' that would address gaps in South Africa's current legislation dealing with the collection, storage and use of DNA evidence and to provide for the expansion and administration of the National DNA Database.[21]

12.8.4 Constitutional and human rights issues

The genetic material known as DNA is the genetic blueprint of life and carries information that is expressed in the genetic attributes of each individual. Civil

20 Hartley (2012).
21 DNA Project (2012).

libertarians have expressed concern that the DNA of individuals can easily be abused for wrongful and unauthorised purposes. Furthermore, very private and medical information may be obtained from the DNA of an individual. A person's DNA may even be abused to stigmatise a person, for example to indicate that persons suffering from certain medical conditions may be more likely than any other person to commit a crime.

For these reasons the following fundamental human rights entrenched in the Bill of Rights in the South African Constitution need to be considered when taking DNA reference samples, performing DNA analysis, and managing and operating a forensic DNA database:

- **The right to human dignity (s 10):**
  Everyone has inherent dignity and the right to have their dignity respected and protected.

- **The right to privacy (s 14):**
  Everyone has the right to privacy, which includes the right not to have—
  (a) their person or home searched;
  (b) their property searched;
  (c) their possessions seized; or
  (d) the privacy of their communications infringed.

- **The right to equality (s 9):**
  (1) Everyone is equal before the law and has the right to equal protection and benefit of the law.
  (2) Equality includes the full and equal enjoyment of all rights and freedoms. To promote the achievement of equality, legislative and other measures designed to protect or advance persons, or categories of persons, disadvantaged by unfair discrimination may be taken.
  (3) The state may not unfairly discriminate directly or indirectly against anyone on one or more grounds, including race, gender, sex, pregnancy, marital status, ethnic or social origin, colour, sexual orientation, age, disability, religion, conscience, belief, culture, language and birth.
  (4) No person may unfairly discriminate directly or indirectly against anyone on one or more grounds in terms of subsection (3). National legislation must be enacted to prevent or prohibit unfair discrimination.
  (5) Discrimination on one or more of the grounds listed in subsection (3) is unfair unless it is established that the discrimination is fair.

- **The right to bodily and psychological integrity (s 12(2)(b))**
  (2) Everyone has the right to bodily and psychological integrity, which includes the right ...
  (b) to security in and control over their body.

- **The rights of arrested, detained and accused persons (s 35)**
  These rights include the presumption of innocence and not to be compelled to give self-incriminating evidence and the right to a fair trial.

- **Limitation of rights (s 36)**
  (1) The rights in the Bill of Rights may be limited only in terms of law of general application to the extent that the limitation is reasonable and justifiable in an open and democratic society based on human dignity, equality and freedom, taking into account all relevant factors, including:
  - *(a) the nature of the right;*
  - *(b) the importance of the purpose of the limitation;*
  - *(c) the nature and extent of the limitation;*
  - *(d) the relation between the limitation and its purpose; and*
  - *(e) less restrictive means to achieve the purpose.*

- **The rights of children (s 28)**
  (2) A child's best interests are of paramount importance in every matter concerning the child.
  This includes DNA taken for criminal investigative and retention purposes.

Canada has a similar Bill of Rights to South Africa. It is noteworthy that in a Canadian court case, namely *R v Briggs* ((2001) Canada (2001) 157 C.C.C. (3d) 38 (Ontario Court of Appeal)) the constitutionality of taking DNA samples from a person was challenged.

Case study 12.1: *R v Briggs*

In *R v Briggs* the court acknowledged that the taking of a DNA sample infringes bodily integrity and privacy rights; infringes privacy due to the information that is found in DNA; places the state's interests above those of an individual, and infringes the principle against self-incrimination. The court contended, however, that the limitation on rights created by the taking of DNA samples is justifiable for the following reasons:

- the limitation becomes relatively modest because after balancing the relevant interests a warrant is issued in terms of a court order
- taking a DNA sample is not physically invasive
- convicted persons lose the expectation that they may keep their identities secret from the state
- in terms of legislation, DNA samples are used only for the comparison of DNA profiles
- DNA is used as an investigating tool
- the interest of the state in fighting crime is for the public's benefit.

Many people oppose the expansion of the forensic DNA database and argue that the possible abuse or disadvantages of a database may outweigh its benefits. Innocent people may be stigmatised if their forensic DNA profile is on the database. It is thus argued that there should be certain limitations in setting up the database, specifically regarding the following:

- the people from which DNA reference samples are taken (for example, a sample must not be taken from minors or suspects or innocent people, but only from certain convicted felons)
- the storage of the DNA reference samples (the samples must be immediately destroyed after a forensic DNA profile is obtained because otherwise the samples might be used for all sorts of purposes, including research and cloning)
- the retention period of the forensic DNA profiles (finite periods must be defined for persons arrested or charged and for convicted felons – this must result in automatic expunging of the forensic DNA profile at the end of the defined period, which must be as short as possible)
- categories of offences (petty offences will add no value to the database, therefore the database must be limited to serious offences such as murder, sexual assault and property crimes)
- the information that is carried in the forensic DNA profile (the DNA profile must not contain personal genetic information)
- access and control (the database should be independent from law enforcement or the section responsible for casework analysis; there must be strict control as to who may gain access to the database; strict security measures must be in place)
- people who may practise forensic DNA and the operation of the forensic DNA database (the oversight to be conducted by the Portfolio Committee on Police should be legislated and an independent oversight board should be established to propose best practice and oversee the operations of forensic DNA analyses and the forensic DNA database).

However, a balance needs to be obtained between the rights of the individual and the right of society to fight and prevent crime. Section 36 of the Constitution ('Limitation of rights') provides for the limitation of individual rights if the limitation is reasonable and justifiable in an open and democratic society. Thus legislation and practice should afford appropriate safeguards to prevent any abuse of personal genetic information. It should also allow the state to keep forensic DNA profiles for comparison purposes, at least for persons charged with contact crimes such as murder and sexual assault, and also for property crime. The legislators have taken the concerns raised by human rights activists on board and the enacted 'DNA Act' clearly defines what a forensic DNA profile is and that it must not contain any personal information (except for the sex of the person) related to the person's medical, physical or psychological condition or characteristics. The forensic DNA profile, in other words the alphanumeric string of characters, is unique as far as the sequence of characters is concerned, but does indicate the sex of the person.

In the opinion of the authors there are too many ethical issues at stake to permit any other information in a forensic DNA profile, such as the person's predisposition to a specific disease or a certain type of behaviour. The definition in the 'DNA Act' is thus supported.

The need for safeguards is all the greater where personal data is processed automatically and when such data is used for police purposes. Section 15H to 15 M of the 'DNA Act' defines the limitations for storing forensic DNA profiles in the different Indices on the National Forensic DNA Database (NFDD). The forensic DNA profiles of persons under investigation, but not arrested or charged, are stored on the Investigative Index and must be removed within three months after an authorised officer is informed that the case is finalised. The forensic DNA profiles of persons that have been arrested and charged, but acquitted or the case withdrawn, must also be removed within three months after the authorised person is notified, but may not be stored on the NFDD for longer than three years. It further states that the forensic DNA profiles of minors arrested or charged may not be stored for longer than 12 months. It is advisable that the Regulations published by the Minister of Police and the SAPS National Instructions for the management of the forensic DNA database should ensure that such data is relevant and not excessive in relation to the purpose for which it is stored. The data should also be preserved in a form that permits identification of the data subjects, and for no longer than is required for the purpose for which that data is stored.

It is inappropriate and unlawful to keep a person's forensic DNA profile on the forensic DNA database for longer than the storage periods defined in the 'DNA Act' for comparison purposes.

Once a forensic DNA profile has been obtained, the actual DNA sample (non-intimate buccal swab) which contains all the genetic information of a person and which is potentially open for abuse, must be destroyed to respect the individual's right to privacy and restrict the possible infringement of using the sample to obtain personal genetic information, information on medical predispositions or physical information not relevant to the criminal proceedings.

12.8.5 Proposed safeguards for a DNA database from a practitioner's perspective

The following would be essential in operating a forensic DNA database to ensure that the purpose of the database is proportionate to the reason why the sample was obtained in the first place:

- The forensic DNA profile must be stored for the limited purpose of the detection and investigation of crime (or legally justifiable incident).
- Forensic DNA profiles are not of any use without a comparator forensic DNA profile from the crime scene/incident.

- The forensic DNA profiles are not to be made public.
- A code of conduct should be introduced to govern the conduct of the persons involved in collecting, collating and safeguarding the samples and information.

Regarding any bodily sample, crime scene sample or forensic DNA profile derived from such samples, s 15S of the 'DNA Act' states that any person who:

(a) uses or allows the use of those samples or forensic DNA profiles derived therefrom for any purpose other than those referred to in this Chapter; or
(b) tampers with or manipulates the process or the samples or forensic DNA profiles;
(c) falsely claims such samples or forensic DNA profiles derived therefrom to have been taken from a specific person whilst knowing them to have been taken from another person or source;
(d) discloses information in contravention of s 5N(2); or
(e) unlawfully loses, damages or destroys information on the NFDD, is guilty of an offence and liable in the case of a natural person, to imprisonment for a period not exceeding 15 years, and in the case of a juristic person, to a fine.

Section 15V provides for the establishment of a Forensic Oversight and Ethics Board that will oversee the compliance to the 'DNA Act' and forensic DNA practice. This Board will also receive and investigate complaints received from the public on alleged misuse of the sample or forensic DNA profile.

12.8.6 Retention and destruction of DNA samples

A distinction should be made between the DNA reference sample taken from a person and the forensic DNA profile derived from this sample. The DNA reference sample is the sample that contains the genetic information that may be potentially abused. Although forensic science laboratories do have the chemistry to analyse and store the samples, the sample can potentially be used by corrupt officials or non-ethical regimes for non-criminal purposes such as source material for medical research and cloning. It is for this reason that there is strong lobbying from libertarians for the destruction of DNA reference samples once the forensic DNA profile is obtained. The forensic DNA profile contains only an alphanumeric string of characters. This string contains no personal genetic, medical or physical information.

10 loci

D3S1358	vWA	FGA	AMEL	D8S1179	D21S11	D18S51	D5S818	D13S317	D7S820
16 1	14 1	20 1	X 1	10 1	28 1	13 1	12 1	11	8 1
17 1	17 1	21 1	Y 1	14 1	30 1	14 1		14	10 1

Figure 12.4: A typical forensic DNA profile with 10 loci

Even though the forensic DNA profile does not contain personal genetic information, there is a debate on how long this information should be stored in a database or whether it should be kept at all if a person is exonerated during the investigation.

Case study 12.2: Retention of forensic DNA profiles

The European Court of Human Rights made a finding in the *S and Marper v United Kingdom* case (European Court of Human Rights [2008] 2008 Application Nos 20562/04 and 30566/04), about the practice in the United Kingdom to retain all forensic DNA profiles for an indefinite period, even if someone had been exonerated in court or otherwise not prosecuted. The indefinite retention of samples and profiles provided by someone subsequently deemed not guilty or not prosecutable is the only issue that was addressed by this court. Furthermore, the United Kingdom is the only country in the world that systemically and indefinitely has retained profiles of people who were not ultimately convicted.

According to the finding of the court, where DNA samples are destroyed after obtaining a result and forensic DNA profiles expunged within a defined and limited period when a suspect's case is dropped or that person is found not guilty, there is no violation of human rights.

In South Africa the retention of forensic DNA data of persons suspected of an offence but subsequently cleared, persons charged but not prosecuted, and *accused* persons acquitted subsequent to a trial must also comply with the protection afforded in the Bill of Rights, especially in relation to the right to privacy, the right to human dignity and the right to equality. Any limitation of the constitutional rights of individuals and minors must also comply with the requirements contemplated in s 36 of the South African Constitution.

It is proposed by the authors that legislation should define that the forensic DNA profile of an innocent person should not be retained indefinitely. It may be argued that it is practical and justifiable to retain the forensic DNA profile on the law enforcement databases for two to three years. The forensic DNA profile of a convicted person may be retained for several years (for example five to 10 years) after the person has been released from prison or the sentence has been served. This will allow for recidivist offenders to be easily identified. These proposed time frames are in line with those of most other international jurisdictions and would most likely also be accepted by the Constitutional Court as a reasonable and fair balance between the rights of the individual and those of society should the retention periods ever be disputed by an aggrieved party.

It is noteworthy that during June 2012, the Portfolio Committee on Police discussed the first draft policy document which was compiled by the office of the Secretariat of Police.[22] The policy document on a DNA database formed the basis

22 Hartley (2012).

on which the Criminal Law (Forensic Procedure) Amendment Bill, B9D-2013, commonly known as the 'DNA Bill', was drafted for consideration by Parliament (see 12.8.3). The 'DNA Bill', which has since been passed by Parliament as the Criminal Law (Forensic Procedure) Amendment Act 37 of 2013 and is commonly referred to as the 'DNA Act', provides for different retention periods for different categories of persons and that innocent persons should have their forensic DNA profiles expunged within a reasonably short period. The 'DNA Act' defines specific limited retention periods for forensic DNA profiles derived from certain categories of persons or samples:

- crime samples (will most likely be retained for an indefinite period)
- convicted or sentenced offenders (will be retained for an indefinite period, unless a presidential pardon is granted)
- arrested or charged persons (must be expunged if a person is acquitted or the case is withdrawn)
- victims (will be expunged immediately when their case is finalised)
- volunteers such as parents of missing children or victims (will most likely be expunged within 30 days after the case is finalised)
- elimination samples derived from officials who come into contact with or process crime scenes or exhibits, and contractors and suppliers of DNA reagents, consumables and equipment (will be retained for an indefinite period, unless application to expunge is successful).

It is practice in South Africa that the DNA reference sample is destroyed once a forensic DNA profile is obtained. On taking the sample, the person is informed:

- why the sample is being taken
- that it will be loaded on the forensic DNA database for comparison purposes
- that it may also be used for law enforcement purposes (but nothing else)
- that the person may withdraw consent by informing the SAPS in writing.

If a person refuses consent, the courts are approached for a court order to take the sample, whereupon, if necessary, a sample may even be obtained by force.

12.8.7 Responsibilities of investigators

It is advisable that investigators should ensure that DNA reference samples are taken from persons charged in all contact crimes such as murder and sexual assault, and property crimes such as vehicle theft, robbery and theft from businesses and residences. The 'DNA Act' makes it obligatory for the SAPS to take a DNA reference sample in Schedule 8 offences, ie serious offences, property offences and offences against the state. Due to the nature of these crimes, it is expected that the perpetrator will leave DNA at the crime scene. This DNA can subsequently be lifted by the scene of incident examiner. Research has shown that many offenders in property crimes are repeat offenders and often graduate to more serious crimes such as contact crimes.[23] By obtaining a DNA reference sample from these offenders they can be easily detected and traced should they commit a crime again.

However, a database is only a useful tool if it is correctly managed. Investigators must take the necessary steps to manage the forensic DNA database so that it becomes an effective investigative tool by ensuring that:

- DNA reference samples (buccal samples) are taken from charged persons and individuals within the prescriptions of the legislative framework
- crime samples are lifted and submitted for forensic DNA analysis
- all prescribed procedures are followed by the investigator to ensure the integrity of the sample.

Suspects or charged persons in murder, sexual assault and property crimes must preferably be taken to a medical practitioner so that a DNA reference sample can be taken to compare their forensic DNA sample to the forensic DNA profile based on the DNA found at the scene of incident.

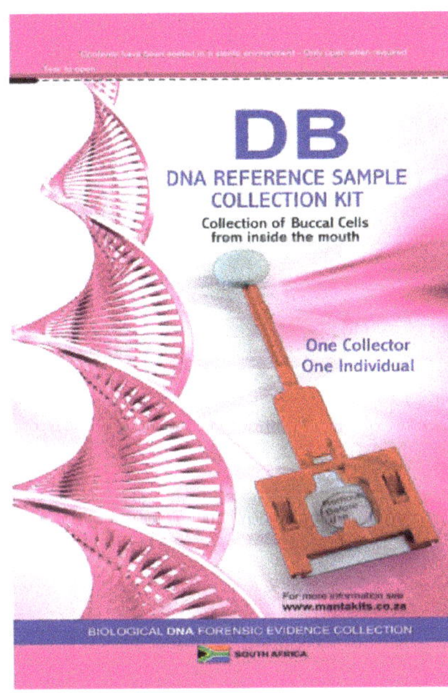

© Phillip Bekker, South African Police Service

Figure 12.5: Evidence collection kit to take the DNA reference sample

Even though an investigator might have been trained to obtain a buccal sample, it is advisable that investigators rather request another investigator who is not involved in investigating the case to take the samples. This is good practice and will also help to nullify arguments that the investigator had used some of the DNA from the suspect to plant evidence at the crime scene. The 'DNA Act' defines an authorised person who may take a DNA reference (buccal) sample and requires that a crime scene examiner may not take the sample from the person involved in the same case where he or she was the crime scene examiner. The DNA reference kits provided by the SAPS must be used to collect the samples.

23 Roman et al. (2008).

There are also other, more integrated databases that can assist during an investigation, which need continuous refinement and development. One such database is the Integrated Ballistic Identification (IBIS) system.

12.9 INTEGRATED BALLISTIC IDENTIFICATION SYSTEM (IBIS)

Ballistics is the science that deals with the motion of projectiles such as bullets, shells, rockets and aerial bombs (see section 5.8 in chapter 5). The Integrated Ballistic Identification System (IBIS) is another tool available to law enforcement officials that can be used to link different cases, persons or firearms to a crime. Unlike DNA, which directly links a person to a crime sample, only the owner of the firearm is implied as being involved because cartridges or bullets can be linked to the specific firearm. In practice, it must still be established who actually used the firearm at the scene of incident.

The Integrated Ballistic Identification System (IBIS) automatically processes the matching of one or many cartridges or bullets associated with an individual who has used the firearm, or a firearm previously used at a scene of incident. The characteristics of the exhibits (firearms, cartridges, bullets) initially discovered at the scene of incident are stored on IBIS. The system uses electronic and optical technology to digitally compare evidence stored in the database to existing and newly captured evidence in order to identify similar characteristics. The IBIS equipment photographs the surface of fired bullets and cartridges obtained from scenes of incident and SAPS laboratories. When a new image is entered on the database, the system searches for a match by using advanced mathematical algorithms to correlate the new image with images that have been previously stored.

If a match is found that links a case to other cases or associated firearm owners or users, the investigator will either be informed that there was a forensic lead or match, or that there is a match between the cartridge collected and an associated firearm user. In the first instance only two cases are linked; in the second instance a specific person may possibly be considered as the perpetrator. The investigating officer will be required to consider this new information along with other circumstantial evidence in the investigation of the case.

In addition to the forensic DNA database and IBIS, there is also a database containing the fingerprints of suspects and latent fingerprints that were collected at scenes of incident.

12.10 AUTOMATED FINGERPRINT IDENTIFICATION SYSTEM (AFIS)

The value of fingerprinting in forensic investigation was discussed in section 5.5 of chapter 5. When an individual is arrested and brought to the police station, their fingerprints are taken as part of the book-in process. Fingerprints are either taken by using the classical paper-and-inkpad method, or the fingers and palms are rolled on a glass plate located on the Live Scan Terminal. A scanner below the plate then reads the information from the prints. This information is electronically transmitted to a repository where a technician checks the prints for quality. After checking the prints, the technician transmits the information to the Automated Fingerprint Identification System (AFIS) for comparative searching. AFIS is an electronic database on which the fingerprint profiles from persons and fingerprints lifted from crime scenes (latent fingerprints) are loaded and stored for comparison.

AFIS is used to perform comparative searches whereby fingerprints from individuals are linked to a latent fingerprint lifted from a scene of incident, or where different scenes of incident are linked to one another by latent fingerprint matches. The *minutiae* (major features of fingerprints that can be used for comparative purposes) of latent (unknown) prints from scenes of incident are compared to those of the known fingerprints in the AFIS database.[24]

It is important that the fingerprints taken or lifted from a crime scene and submitted to AFIS are of good quality. Good quality fingerprint impressions will ensure that the ridge detail and pattern characteristics of an image created by AFIS are sufficient to search against the unsolved latent database, thus improving the likelihood of a positive match being made.

Within minutes after the quality-control technician at the police station has transmitted the information to AFIS, AFIS returns information on the three closest matches. A technician is then required to compare the (known) prints of the arrested person to the prints received from AFIS, and to determine whether the individual has a record of previous arrest or an active warrant outstanding for their arrest, or has provided false identifying information (if the official record on AFIS does not correspond to the name provided by the suspect).

The algorithm used for these comparative searches returns results to the technician with a numerical measure of the probability of a match (a 'score'). In the ten-print searching algorithm of fingerprints, it is unlikely that the system will report a possible match with a single candidate unless there are multiple records from the same candidate in the database.

---

24 Wikipedia online *'Minutiae'*. Available at http://en.wikipedia.org/wiki/Minutiae, accessed 28 May 2012.

Unfortunately the 'latent ten-print search' will frequently return many (often 50 or more) candidates because of limited and poor quality input data. Poor quality is due to the poor quality of the prints lifted at the crime scene, but often also to the poor quality of the prints obtained from the suspect at the police station. If a match is identified by the comparative search on AFIS and is confirmed by the examiner, the match between the latent print(s) and the known prints of an individual is communicated to the investigator.

12.11 INTEGRATED DATABASES WITHIN INCIDENCE INTELLIGENCE

The use of crime or incidence intelligence has become an integral part of the criminal investigation or crime prevention process.[25] The use of incidence intelligence has subsequently become part of the private or corporate forensic investigation process. This intelligence is derived from the analysis of all the information collated about crime, perpetrators, syndicates, organisations, markets for stolen goods, etc. However, intelligence is also collected about incidents or transgressions that are not necessarily criminal acts, such as transgressions in a corporate environment. In the rest of the chapter the word 'incidence' will be used in this context to refer to crimes and incidents that are not necessarily a crime.

Accurate incidence intelligence is dependent on valid and reliable information. Information is the life-blood of policing and investigation in general.[26] Information indicates the knowledge that has been observed, heard and experienced that can be of help to the investigator, policing authority or organisation concerned.[27] In scientific research methodology, textbook information is usually referred to as the data that is collected about a research problem. Scientific research and an investigation usually follow a similar process of collecting valid and reliable information about a problem to determine the truth.

Intelligence on a crime or an incident is the product of information that has been taken from its raw state and processed, refined, verified and evaluated.[28] Crime (incidence) intelligence, as defined by the US National Criminal Intelligence Sharing Plan (NCISP), is 'information that has been analyzed to determine its meaning and relevance'.[29] Furthermore, it is information that has been designed and formulated for action. Incidence intelligence can include such facts as who perpetrated what type of crime; why; when; where; syndicate activities; disposal of stolen property and other exhibits; markets for stolen goods;

25 Zinn (2010) 120.
26 Brown (1998) 54.
27 Marais (1992) 206.
28 Zinn (2010) 120.
29 US Department of Justice (2005).

telephone records; banking details, etc.[30] The more comprehensive and up-to-date the detail of the collected information, the better the resulting incidence intelligence will be.

Incidence intelligence has become a very valuable resource in combating crime and other transgressions and provides techniques for improving the basis of knowledge. However, it is merely a resource to help process information into an organised structure to assist an analyst in making the best deductions possible from the data.[31] These deductions enable decision makers and practitioners to take strategic and tactical, proactive, corrective and preventative steps in addressing an incidence problem. The utilisation of incidence intelligence forms an integral part of the proactive crime investigation cycle that is discussed in section 1.13 in chapter 1.

Modern developments have led to incidence intelligence becoming a science that includes analysing information obtained from as many sources as possible, including sources and databases from multiple agencies and departments; official and unofficial databases; national and international databases, and even multidisciplinary databases.[32] Although this obviously holds many benefits, it also gives rise to the practical problem of collating and processing a large volume of data.

Researchers concur that information on a transgression and the intelligence that is obtained from it have the most value if they are recorded in a database.[33] This view has been further highlighted in the statement by Jackson & Bekerian that offender profiling must be based on clinical experience, research and the statistical analysis of databases of offenders.[34]

The best value is obtained from integrated databases, which might even be maintained by different agencies, but have the ability to integrate or allow integrated searches of the data.

12.11.1 The value of an integrated computerised database for incidence intelligence

Since the public unrest in the USA in the 1960s, the Office of Law Enforcement Assistance (OLEA) has undertaken research on how to improve crime investigation through better crime-related data analysis techniques. The OLEA's research has found that the processing and analysis of crime information into crime intelligence by means of computers can have the following benefits:

- increasing the number of cases where arrests occur as a result of the correlation

30 Clarke et al. (2004) 218.
31 Johnson (2009) 267.
32 Johnson (2009) 263; Viotti et al. (2008) 69–70.
33 Ressler et al. (2004).
34 Jackson & Bekerian (1997).

of the *modus operandi* of the arrested suspects with information in other outstanding cases
- providing investigation leads to investigators by means of a list of possible suspects whose *modi operandi* is similar to those of previous crimes
- facilitating early and rapid identification of crime trends or patterns by means of *modus operandi* correlations
- increasing in the number of identifiable crime patterns discovered
- creating a means or an aid for measuring the results of crime-combating or crime-restricting programmes for specific crimes
- making available a greater number of bulletins based on crime patterns for use in patrolling and, in this way, raising not only the awareness of patrol officials about possible suspects but also the potential for early arrests
- creating hard evidence to raise the awareness of members of the public to pay attention to crimes that affect them directly and, in this way, obtaining their cooperation in crime-prevention programmes
- providing information linked to security considerations for the external design of new residential areas and commercial complexes
- obtaining information through which recommendations can be made to personnel (police) about possible programmes to solve crime problems
- serving as a resource in the coordination of special crime-restricting task team operations
- providing information on projected levels of offender activities and the identification of future (geographic) problem areas.[35]

By using standardised incidence report forms, the analyst can programme a computer to analyse the data using such criteria as time of day or type of victim or premises to help officers or investigators to predict future offences or transgressions within their jurisdiction or area of responsibility. The expert system concept, termed 'artificial intelligence', uses technology and police expertise to aid case solution by collecting, storing and analysing data that can match information taken from a scene of incident with information about potential suspects and their known *modus operandi*. Such systems depend on incidence information and integrated incidence intelligence databases.[36]

Furthermore, the New York City Police Department's Computer-Assisted Robbery System (CARS) can provide information on arrests for robbery made at a specific location, as well as the criminal history of the suspect arrested or questioned there.[37] This information is obtained from the analysis of integrated databases kept on crime incidents that occur within a specific area.

35 Osterburg & Ward (1997).
36 Gilbert (2010) 157.
37 Gilbert (2004).

However, Block & Weidman warn that the high expectations that have been linked to modern technology, inter alia for solving crimes and other incidents, must be balanced with realistic and practical considerations.[38] They also point out that statistical programs that attempt to identify geographic or *modus operandi* patterns on a large database are doomed to failure except when techniques are built into the program that search for out-of-the-ordinary patterns. They furthermore highlight the fact that the effectiveness of computers depends on the quality of the information that is captured (inputted), and that human experience plays an important role in the identification of extraordinary human behaviour.

The OLEA has also played another important role, namely that of laying down universal standards for all agencies. These include standards for the quality of data gathered and procedures for data collection in order to ensure the quality of the data. The value of interdepartmental cooperation and a multi-agency approach has been clearly discernible from the positive results achieved by the OLEA.[39]

All the knowledge of incidence patterns, information on the profiles of criminals and their *modus operandi*, and information from other sources must be collated in databases and processed into incidence intelligence. For practical purposes most of these databases are computerised. These databases are usually specific to particular law enforcement or other crime-combating agencies or entities, which unfortunately creates the situation that most of the databases are standalone sources of information. These databases could potentially be much more valuable if they were integrated or linked to provide more comprehensive and accurate crime information. Most policing agencies use their databases on crime information to extrapolate crime intelligence on the crime and criminals in their area of responsibility.

The most advanced countries in policing use this crime intelligence for intelligence-driven policing. In a number of these countries the police services have achieved notable success with an intelligence-driven style of policing, which comes down to proactive policing. The crime information they use is gathered by means of good investigation work and, with the cooperation of an experienced investigator, is processed into crime intelligence by means of a computer program. An example of an institution that is focused on converting crime information into crime intelligence is the Law Enforcement Intelligence Unit (LEIU) in the USA, an organisation comprising numerous police agencies, which evaluates and disseminates information on organised crime to member agencies.[40]

38 Block & Weidman (1976).
39 Tonry & Morris (1997).
40 Gilbert (2010) 439.

12.11.2 Examples of international best practice of intelligence-led policing based on integrated crime information databases

Example 12.4: HITS, Washington State, USA

The Washington State Homicide Investigation and Tracking System (HITS) is a database to which state agencies voluntarily submit information on murders, attempted murders, missing persons in whose case foul play is suspected, unidentified possible murder victims and predatory sex offences. The software program analyses the important characteristics of the reported crimes. Information is provided about cases with similar characteristics of the reported crimes and known suspects are identified.[41]

Data from more than 10 600 murder investigations and more than 8 200 sexual assaults have been collected through HITS and have been used to assist local law enforcement in the investigation of these crimes. The investigators who work with HITS also provide expertise to the local and national jurisdictions on murder and rape investigations.

HITS is based on developing and using computers in innovative ways to increasingly prevent and solve crimes.[42]

Example 12.5: ViCLAS, Canada

The Royal Canadian Mounted Police developed an integrated computer database called the Violent Crime Linkage System (ViCLAS) that has since been rolled out to a number of countries around the world. The database was first developed and tested in Canada. Since the implementation of ViCLAS across the country, the database continues to swell with cases. As of April 2007, there were approximately 300 000 cases on the system and over 3 200 linkages have been made thus far.

ViCLAS is a computer system that helps specially trained investigators to identify serial crimes and criminals by focusing on the linkages that exist among crimes committed by the same offender. When linkages are made between cases they are put into a 'series.' These 'series' can contain any number of linkages, depending on how many cases an offender has been involved in. There are currently more than 88 000 series on ViCLAS. These numbers confirm that there are a large number of serial offenders committing crimes on a regular basis in Canada. It is a well-known worldwide phenomenon that repeat offenders are responsible for committing a large portion of the crimes. Linkages are expected to increase dramatically as compliance rates increase and many provinces make reporting mandatory, as it is now in the provinces of Ontario and Quebec.[43] Compliance rates are based on the actual number of cases being put onto the system, as compared to mere reportable cases.

41 Gilbert (2010) 159.

42 HITS (2012).

43 Royal Canadian Mounted Police (2012).

Example 12.6: Compstat, NYPD, USA

The New York Police Department (NYPD) has achieved similar success through a combination of zero-tolerance policing, the 'broken-window' principle and the use of information technology known as 'Compstat', which analyses the crime statistics from crime databases on an ongoing basis. The crime intelligence obtained in this manner is then used as the foundation in the planning and formulation of crime-combating strategies. The successes of the NYPD measured, for example, from 1990 to 2006, include a decline of 73% in murders, 51% in rapes, 76% in robberies, 61% in felonious assaults and 81% in burglaries.[44]

Compstat meetings are held on a weekly basis with all NYPD precinct commanders in a policing district or area. During these meetings the updated information is shared and accessed through a central database. Joint plans and strategies are formulated at these meetings for the pre-emptive combating (proactive policing) of the various identified crimes and the policing of hotspots. The emphasis is placed on the immediate gathering and availability of crime information by means of an integrated database.

International integrated intelligence databases also focus on activities such as terrorism. The most important set of intelligence relations for the USA is the USA-UK collaboration agreement which also includes Canada, Australia and New Zealand. These five countries have virtually automatic electronic access to one another's interception facilities without the host nation necessarily knowing what the member is looking for. An added benefit for these countries is that the integrated databases also serve as a backup system for each individual country should their own intelligence system become inoperable. These systems also allow the member countries or organisation to get a second opinion on the available data to optimise their analysis of the data.[45]

Various integrated incidence intelligence databases have been established internationally, including centralised databases that are shared by policing agencies, departments and countries across international borders. These databases can be accessed by all member agencies. The latest developments in this field include the direct use of the database by means of technical aids in a police vehicle. This enables police officials to do a comparison of a suspect's fingerprints or photograph, taken by a digital camera in the vehicle, with the fingerprints or photographs of wanted persons on the database. All these cross-checks take only a few minutes and can be done before the person whose details are being investigated becomes impatient or is deprived of their freedom.[46]

44 Storch A (2006); New York Police Department (2007).
45 Viotti et al. (2008).
46 Zinn (2008).

Some of these databases are able to provide fast-time intelligence about serious and critical incidents on a national and international basis. The incidence intelligence is drawn from numerous intelligence databases, including those of INTERPOL and EUROPOL.[47] These and other initiatives are improving interagency data sharing and increasing the use of new technological aids. An added advantage of interagency sharing is the rapid bringing together of the previously fragmented databases of law enforcement agencies.

12.11.3 The value of intelligence-led policing, new technology, integrated databases and information sharing

The basic value of intelligence-led policing, new technology, integrated databases and information sharing, as far as the investigation of an incident is concerned, can be summarised as follows:

- Possible suspects in a geographic area can be identified on the basis that they fit the profile of persons committing the type of incident under investigation.
- Offenders on the database can be linked to the incident under investigation by means of identifying a similar *modus operandi*.
- Information (locally, nationally and internationally) on offenders, for example fingerprint records and photographs, can be made available to investigators.
- A better understanding of incidents and offenders can be achieved.
- Knowledge of the personality traits of the offenders under investigation can be used to identify the most effective interviewing techniques to be used.
- Information on the *modi operandi* of suspects who are under investigation can provide leads on where they might be found or the places they might frequent.
- Offences committed by the same suspect(s) can be linked.
- The associates of the suspect under investigation can be identified.
- Repeat offenders can be identified.
- It can be established whether the offender under investigation is part of a syndicate.
- The members of a syndicate and the masterminds of those syndicates can be identified.
- Possible transport routes used by the offenders under investigation can be identified.
- Places where the offender under investigation might commit the same offence again can be predicted.
- The location of the market for stolen goods where exhibits could be traced can be identified and those markets can be eliminated.

---

47 Specialist Crime Directorate (2006).

- Graphics showing links between accomplices or evidence linking the offender to the scene of incident can be provided.
- Inconsistencies in declarations can be spotted.
- Gaps in a chronological list of events can be identified.
- Incidence intelligence products can be developed through, for example, linkage analysis, incidence pattern and trend analysis, incidence threat analysis, incidence statistical analysis, geographic incidence analysis and profiling of the characteristics of the arrested offenders and incidents.[48]

12.12 OPEN AND RESTRICTED-ACCESS DATABASES

Thus far incidence intelligence has mainly been developed by using existing official databases or so-called closed (restricted access) databases. There are also other sources available that are not necessarily free-access or open-source, but are nevertheless accessible through the legal process. These are official South African databases such as the Population Register, the Border Movement Control System (BMC), the National Traffic Information System (NATIS) and the Home Affairs System and Government Network System (GOVNET). Other types of external semi-closed sources include information held by other government departments and/or institutes, organisations, non-government organisations (NGOs), municipalities, Civil Aviation, banks, the Registrar of Companies, hospitals, airports, ports of entry, security companies, the media, taxi forums, credit bureaux, insurance companies, business chambers, chambers of commerce and cellular network providers.[49] During a crime investigation, information can usually be obtained from these entities by submitting an application in terms of s 205 of the Criminal Procedure Act 51 of 1977. This section of the Act is used to obtain information pertaining to any alleged offence where the state has reason to believe that a certain individual has such information at their disposal, but is unwilling to disclose that information to the state (see the discussion of s 205 subpoenas in section 7.8.4 of chapter 7).[50]

There is also the reality of expanding the current official localised Automated Fingerprint Identification Systems (AFIS) in each country to a large integrated database on all convicted criminals internationally. This is theoretically possible, but the current technology still hampers the possibility of achieving the establishment of such an integrated system. Protocols will also have to be developed between countries to regulate the sharing of the information. However, recent international developments have already seen the expansion of databases

48 Zinn (2008).
49 Krause (2008).
50 Hiemstra (1987) 438.

that could previously handle only a few hundred thousand fingerprint records to databases being able to handle 22 million fingerprint records from various countries.[51] As technology develops further, we might see the establishment of even larger and better integrated databases at international level. This will also enable the expansion of existing AFIS databases to include more biometric data.

After their research in the USA in 2009 on identifying the needs of the forensic sciences community, the US Committee of the National Research Council found that there was a need to expand AFIS systems to improve feature identification and the reliability of latent print comparisons. There is also a need to make AFIS flexible enough to handle other kinds of biometric data in future (eg images, iris and palm scans and possibly genomic data).

Incidence analysts can also use a range of open-source databases. 'Open-source' refers to sources that are available and accessible to the general public and also to the police, such as printed and electronic media, literature sources and the internet. There are also open sources on the internet that can be used as incidence intelligence development tools. These internet sites, such as InfoMerger, provide access to software that can help communities to log crimes or suspicious incidents in their area, draw computerised graphs and reports from the data and organise community patrols. They enable communities and local police to manage crime prevention more effectively.[52]

Accessing these available data sources is at the moment still mostly restricted by the incompatibility of different computer programs and a resistance to sharing information. However, through innovative thinking, building of trust and the development of technology it is possible to use these sources in an integrated manner. In future these sources could, for example, include controlled access to records of vehicles driving through a tollroad access point; records of scanners that are used on throughways to scan the number plates of vehicles; records of tracking systems installed in vehicles; facial recognition of a person through CCTV cameras on streets, access points to neighbourhoods, banks and all other places where these cameras are installed; access control records kept by private and official entities including biometric authentication access control and systems; company records; medical treatment records, and every other digital records database imaginable. These databases will have to be linked through a platform and opened to searches with search engines similar to the search engines on the World Wide Web (www). It will enable the investigator of the future to trace a suspect or to have access to records that would provide a trail of a person's movements that could be traced back over years – for as long as these records are kept on a database. This would be an invaluable tool in combating crime.

---

51 National Research Council (2009) 271.

52 InfoMerger 'Merging Information Together'. Available at http://www.infomerger.co.za/cm/, accessed 30 May 2012.

12.13 DEALING WITH LARGE VOLUMES OF DATA DURING AN INVESTIGATION

These integrated international databases are potentially of great value to police services. However, researchers globally have found that the police infrequently use new technological aids and techniques.[53] They ascribe this, inter alia, to a closed police culture, an unwillingness to experiment, fixed ideas, short-term financial planning and, in some cases, a lack of vision and insight into the advantages associated with new technology.

The sheer volume of data nowadays at the disposal of the investigator may be one of the reasons why some investigators are intimidated by computerised technology and resources. However, there is a number of very good software packages available that an investigator can use to collate, process, compare and analyse the relevant data pertaining to a specific case. There are, for example, computer software products that can assist the investigator with the following:

- A comprehensive range of visualisation and analytical tools which enable the timely delivery of intelligence by quickly identifying connections, patterns and trends in complex data sets.

Example 12.7: Speeding up delivery of intelligence

During the investigation into the activities of a crime syndicate, telephone calls made between members of the syndicate were plotted to indicate when the telephone calls were made, from which numbers, to which numbers, how long the calls lasted, etc. These visualisation plots made it possible to identify the kingpin (who received and made the most calls) and the 'mastermind' who only received calls from the 'kingpin' after a 'job had been completed'.

- Flexible data acquisition and data models that allow for the rapid entry of information while supporting dynamic analytical thought processes.

Example 12.8: Ensuring rapid entry of information

The banking industry uses an intelligence product to which all the branches of a bank can upload on an ongoing basis data of incidents that have taken place. The software automatically identifies similar characteristics in the data such as the same *modus operandi* that might indicate that the same offender is targeting various branches of the bank.

- Simple communication of complex information with intuitive briefing charts that enable quick and accurate decision making.[54] Electronic maps can be used to depict crime 'hotspots' in a policing area.

53 Gay et al. (1984); Rheinier et al. (1979); Hough (1980); Ronczkowski (2004); Higgens (2004).
54 Analyst's Notebook (2012).

- Criminal intelligence platforms that are accessible to all the investigators in a country-wide organisation, giving them online accessibility to crime intelligence on the World Wide Web. In the example of the banking industry intelligence product mentioned above, the investigators would have controlled access to the central database via the internet.
- Law enforcement by efficiently predicting, preventing and responding to threats in real time.[55]

Example 12.9: Real-time response

In the case of abalone smuggling along the coastline of South Africa, police officers are able to detect emerging patterns, trends and 'hotspots' where the smugglers are currently active. This is based on an analysis of the reported cases registered on the Case Administration System (CAS) used by the SAPS. The CAS software analysis program is potentially able to determine crime trends, such as when and where the smugglers are harvesting the abalone, and can extrapolate when would be the most opportune time and place to catch them in the act.

- Automatically doing a search on a range of databases to, for example, instantly see an offender's criminal history, photographs, open warrants, gun permits and motor vehicle status.[56]
- The automation of time-proven analytical techniques such as association matrixes, link diagrams, time event charts, pattern analysis wheels and telephone toll charts.
- Automatic notification if a new person is entered or imported onto the database that is similar enough to an individual already on the database.[57]

12.14 SUMMARY

All these developments in the field of forensics are in one way or another linked to computer technology. Thus the forensic investigator not only has to be conversant with the use of a personal computer but must also know how to use these resources and technologies during a forensic investigation. The investigator has to be aware of the latest developments in the field and must be able to use the technology to collect information to solve a case.

It is unfortunately also true that 'nobody fully trusts new technology, especially not the courts'.[58] In general, courts have not embraced new technology and its demands on the justice system. The forensic investigator therefore needs to provide an expert witness in court to introduce and explain new methods and technology to the prosecutor and, if necessary, the court.

55 Pro Security Zone (2012).
56 GCN (2012).
57 Precision Computer Intelligence (2012).
58 Lessing (2007).

However, the new developments open up a new world of integrated databases, much more accurate data recording, the increase in the data footprint that an individual leaves behind as an electronic trail, and new possibilities of tracing suspects worldwide.

REFERENCES

Analyst's Notebook (Analyst Notebook Products 2012) Available at http://www.i2group.com/us/products/analysis-product-line/analysts-notebook, accessed 23 March 2012

PB Block & DR Weidman *Managing Criminal Investigation* (US Government Printing Office 1976)

M Briody & T Prenzler 'DNA databases and property crime: A false promise?' (2005) 37 *Australasian Journal of Forensic Sciences* 73–86

MF Brown *Criminal Investigation: Law and Practice* (Butterworth-Heinemann1998)

AV Clarke, JHW Cowley, M de Klerk, AJ Lamprecht, N Mendes, DC Myburg, AL van Schoor, M van Zyl & RJ Zinn *Investigation of Crime III: Study Guide 1 for OVM341S* (Technikon SA 2004)

'Developing fingerprints' from *What is Forensic Science?* Available at http://www.chm.bris.ac.uk/webprojects2002/thomson/what_is_forensic_science.htm and http://www.chm.bris.ac.uk/webprojects2002/thomson/fingerprints2.htm, accessed 27 November 2013

DNA Project 'Fighting crime through science' (2012) Available at http://dnaproject.co.za/about-us/what-we-do, accessed 22 March 2012

W Gay, TM Beall & W Bowers *A Four Site Assessment of the Integrated Criminal Apprehension Program* (University Science Center 1984)

GCN – The Online Authority for Goverment IT Professionals 'State taps BI software to share criminal info, link other agencies' (2012) Available at http://gcn.com/articles/2012/02/02/maryland-oracle-bi-software-criminal-justice.aspx, accessed 17 March 2012)

GeneWatch 'The DNA Expansion programme: Reporting real achievement?' (2006) GeneWatch UK Briefing February 2006. Available at http://www.genewatch.org/uploads/f03c6d66a9b354535738483c1c3d49e4/DNAexpansion_brief_final.pdf

JN Gilbert *Criminal Investigation* 6 ed (Pearson Prentice Hall 2004)

JN Gilbert *Criminal Investigation* 8 ed (Prentice Hall 2010)

C Hancock 'Misleading view of the database: Update' (2011) Available at http://dnaproject.co.za/blog/misleading-view-of-the-database-update

W Hartley 'Police back in Parliament to recommend DNA database' *Business Day* 19 June 2012. Available at http://www.businessday.co.za/articles/Content.aspx?id=174431 or http://dnaproject.co.za/new_dna/wp-content/uploads/2009/08/police-back-in-parliment-recommend-dna-database.pdf, accessed 19 June 2012

VG Hiemstra *Suid-Afrikaanse Strafproses* 4 ed (Butterworths 1987)

O Higgens 'Rising to the collection challenge' in JH Ratcliffe (ed) *Strategic Thinking in Criminal Intelligence* (Federation Press 2004)

J Holland 'Supreme Court says police can take DNA from those arrested' (3 June 2013) *Forensic Magazine*. Available at http://www.forensicmag.com/news/2013/06/supreme-court-says-police-can-take-dna-those-arrested, accessed 4 June 2013

JM Hough 'Managing with less technology' (1980) 20 *British Journal of Criminology* 344–357

R Hoyle 'The FBI's national DNA database' (1998) 16 *Nature Biotechnology* 987

JL Jackson & DA Bekerian (eds) *Offender Profiling Theory, Research and Practice* (Wiley Series in the Psychology of Crime, Policing and Law 1997)

TA Johnson *The War on Terrorism: A Collision of Values, Strategies, and Societies* (CRC Press 2009)

A Krause 'The Crime Threat Analysis Process' (unpublished Master's dissertation, University of South Africa, 2008)

M Lessing 'CSIR's Lessing aims to teach cyber criminals a lesson' (The Council for Scientific and Industrial Research (CSIR) 2007) Available at http://www.csir.co.za/researcher_profiles/Marthie_Lessing.html, accessed 27 March 2012

CW Marais *Physical Evidence in Crime Investigation* (Henmar Publications 1992)

National Research Council 'Strengthening Forensic Science in the United States: A Path Forward' (2009) Available at http://www.nap.edu/catalog/12589.html, accessed 30 March 2012

The National DNA Database – Home Affairs Committee (2009) Available at http://www.publications.parliament.uk/pa/cm200910/cmselect/cmhaff/222/222203.htm, accessed 12 March 2012

The National DNA Database – Parliamentary Office of Science and Technology (2006) Post note No 258

New York Police Department 'Compstat: Historical Perspective' (2007) Available at http://www.nyc.gov/html/nypd/pdf/chfdept/cscity.pdf.htm, accessed 15 August 2007

New York State Division of Criminal Justice Services. Final Report: New York Statewide Integrated DNA Program, National Institute of Justice DNA Laboratory Improvement Program (2003) Available at https://www.ncjrs.gov/pdffiles1/nij/grants/202732.pdf, accessed 22 March 2012

JW Osterburg & RH Ward *Criminal Investigation* 2 ed (Anderson 1997)

Precision Computer Intelligence 'CrimeLink Investigative Analysis Software' (2012) Available at http://www.pciusa.us/Crimelink.aspx, accessed 27 March 2012

Pro Security Zone 'Web-based criminal intelligence software for Pennsylvania Police' (2012) Available at http://www.prosecurityzone.com/News/Government_programmes/Law_enforcement_agencies/Web_based_criminal_intelligence_software_for_pennsylvania_police_8454.asp#axzz1qKoQR900, accessed 27 March 2012

P Reilly 'Legal and public policy issues in DNA forensics' (2001) 2(4) *Nature Reviews. Genetics* 313–317. Available at http://www.ncbi.nlm.nih.gov/pubmed/11283703, accessed 22 November 2013

RK Ressler, JE Douglas, AN Groth & AW Burgess 'Offender profilers: A multidisciplinary approach' in JH Campbell & D DeNevi (eds) *Profilers* (Promcthcus Books 2004)

B Rheinier, MR Greenless, MH Gibbens & SP Marshall *Law Enforcement Assistance Administration Report* (US Government Printing Office 1979)

JK Roman, S Reid, JA Reid, A Chalfin, WM Adams & C Knight 'The DNA field experiment: Cost effective analysis of the use of DNA in the investigation of high-volume crimes' Research Report: Uran Institute, Justice Policy Center (2008) Available at http://www.urban.org/UploadedPDF/411697 dna field experiment.pdf, accessed 22 November 2013

MR Ronczkowski *Terrorism and Organized Hate Crime* (CRC Press 2004)

Royal Canadian Mounted Police 'Violent Crime Linkage System (ViCLAS)' (2012) Available at http://www.rcmp-grc.gc.ca/tops-opst/bs-sc/viclas-salvac-eng.htm, accessed 23 March 2012

J Smith 'Establishing a DNA Criminal Intelligence Database in South Africa: An Investigative Study' Faculty of Economic Studies, Technikon Pretoria (2000)

Specialist Crime Directorate Metropolitan Police Service, London (2006) Available at http://www.met.police.uk/scd/units/intelligence.htm, accessed 1 November 2006

A Storch 'COMPSTAT – The Start of a Revolution in Policing' (2006) Available at http://www.worldwidelawenforcement.com/docs/COMPSTAT%20article.pdf, accessed 23 March 2012

M Tonry & MN Morris (eds) *Modern Policing* (University of Chicago Press 1997)

US Department of Justice 'National Criminal Intelligence Sharing Plan (NCISP)' (2005) Available at http://it.ojp.gov/documents/NCISP _Plan.pdf, accessed 30 October 2007

Using DNA to solve Property crime (n.d.) Available at http://www.nij.gov/nij/topics/forensics/evidence/dna/property-crime/solving-crimes.htm, accessed 27 March 2012

PR Viotti, MA Opheim & N Bowen *Terrorism and Homeland Security. Thinking Strategically About Policy* (CRC Press 2008)

H Wallace 'The UK National DNA Database: Balancing crime detection, human rights and privacy' (July 2006) The European Molecular Biology Organization Reports 26–30. Available at http://www.ncbi.nlm.nih.gov/pmc/articles/PMC1490298/, accessed 12 March 2012

SJ Walsh, JM Curran & JS Buckleton 'Modeling Forensic DNA Database Performance' (2010) 55 *Journal of Forensic Sciences* 1174–1183 DOI: 10.1111/j.1556-4029.2010.01426.x. Available at http://www.ncbi.nlm.nih.gov, accessed 30 March 2012

Washington State Office of the Attorney General 'Homicide Investigation Tracking System' (2012) Available at http://www.atg.wa.gov/HITS.aspx, accessed 22 March 2012

DB Wilson, D Weisburd & D McClure 'Does Forensic DNA Help to Solve Crime? The Benefit of Sophisticated Answers to Naive Questions' (2010) 26(4) *Journal of Contemporary Criminal Justice* 466-477. Available at http://intl-ccj.sagepub.com/content/26/4/458.full.pdf+html, accessed 26 January 2012

E Zedlewski & MB Murphy 'DNA analysis for "minor" crimes: A major benefit for law enforcement' (2006) 253 *National Institute of Justice Journal*. Available at http://www.nij.gov/journals/_253/dnaanalysis.html, accessed 30 March 2012

RJ Zinn 'Sentenced motor vehicle hijackers imprisoned in Gauteng as a source of crime intelligence' (2003) Available at http://www.unisa.ac.za/contents/docs/zinn.pdf, accessed 17 March 2012

RJ Zinn 'Incarcerated perpetrators of house robbery as a source of crime intelligence' (Unpublished doctoral thesis, University of South Africa, 2008)

RJ Zinn *Home Invasion: Robbers Disclose What You Should Know* (Tafelberg 2010)

D Zubakov, E Hanekamp, M Kokshoorn, W van Ijcken & M Kayser 'Stable RNA markers for identification of blood and saliva stains revealed from whole genome expression analysis of time-wise degraded samples' (2008) 122(2) *International Journal of Legal Medicine* 135–142

GLOSSARY

accused: A person or organisation that has been charged in a criminal court for the commission of a suspected crime.

acquired characteristics: Characteristics that have developed and formed over time.

activity space: A subset of the awareness space. This is the area in which a person moves about. Typical activity space is the space between home, work, recreation, shopping and school.

admissibility: A term used to describe whether or not a piece of evidence is going to be allowed to be used during the trial by one party. Usually the relevance of the evidence determines its admissibility.

admissibility requirements: Legislative instruments, such as the Criminal Procedure Act 51 of 1977 (CPA) and the Constitution, and legal procedures set certain requirements as to what evidence may be received and how it is to be used for the purpose of a criminal or civil trial, inquiries, inquests, etc. Evidence obtained or used in a manner that violates a person's constitutional rights will be found to be unconstitutional and inadmissible in a court of law.

admissible evidence: Any evidence that has been accepted by a court and forms part of the evidence considered in reaching a finding.

adversarial systems: Sometimes also referred to as an 'accusatorial' system. It has three features: (1) both parties are responsible for presenting evidence to support their cases; (2) the presiding officer (magistrate or judge) plays a passive role as the impartial umpire; (3) there is emphasis on oral evidence and the cross-examination of witnesses. This system is used in South Africa, the USA and the United Kingdom.

affidavit: A formal written statement of evidence by a person. This statement is either sworn under oath or affirmed by the person making it as being a true and accurate reflection of what is contained in the affidavit.

agent: Normally refers to a police officer who, for a period of time, assumes a made-up identity and infiltrates into a crime group or syndicate to obtain information and evidence about the activities of that group for court purposes.

aggravating circumstances: In relation to robbery or attempted robbery it means the wielding of a firearm or any other dangerous weapon; the infliction of grievous bodily harm; or a threat to inflict grievous bodily harm, by the offender or an accomplice on the occasion when the offence is committed, whether before, during or after the commission of the offence.

aliquot: A small, defined volume.

allele variations: One of two or more alternative forms of a gene, occupying the same position (locus) on paired chromosomes and controlling the same inherited characteristic.

alphanumerical indicator: A numbering convention used at a scene of incident when evidence is marked. It consists of both letters and numbers. For example, the bedroom in a robbery scene is marked 'B'. In the bedroom, two similar-looking 9 mm firearms are left behind by the suspects in two different locations, one on the bed and the other on the floor. 'B1' is allocated to the firearm on the bed while 'B2' is allocated to the firearm left on the floor.

anchor point: The most important location of a serial criminal from which they operate. In most instances it is the offender's residence.

ante-mortem: Preceding death; before death.

anterior cervical region: Front of the neck.

anthropogenic: An incident caused by humans. Generally used in an environmental sense such as 'anthropogenic global warming'.

anthropometry: A system of criminal identification developed by Alphonse Bertillon based on 11 measurements of the human frame.

Anton Piller order: A court order allowing the party to whom it has been granted to enter the premises designated in the order and to search, inspect and/or seize any items specified in the order. In effect it is the civil law equivalent of a criminal search warrant.

appeal: A request that a case be removed from a lower court to a higher court for the purpose of judicial review.

appellant: The person who lodges an appeal; *see also* appeal.

archaeologist: A person who performs the scientific study of material remains (as fossil relics, artefacts and monuments) of past human life and activities.

arches: A fingerprint pattern that has no deltas and no significant core. The ridges of the finger run continuously from one side of the finger to the other with no recurving.

area of interest: Any specific location at a scene of incident which may present relevant information or substantiating evidence of the incident under investigation.

associative evidence: Evidence that links two separate entities, whether they are people or objects, to a crime scene.

autoerotic fatality: A death resulting from risky sexual practices. Typically this refers to situations where the deceased was reducing the amount of oxygen to the brain while engaging in sexual behaviour such as masturbation. This type of death is accidental but is often mistaken for a suicide because a ligature around the neck is the most common means of reducing oxygen to the brain.

autosomal marker: Markers found on the non-sex-carrying chromosomes.

awareness space: A person's knowledge of an area, which includes places never visited.

balance of probabilities: The burden of proof used in civil courts to reach a finding. It is essentially a decision as to which party's version of the events is most probable based on the evidence presented.

ballistics: The study of bullets in motion or the study of firearm and ammunition technology. It consists of four branches of study, namely internal ballistics, external ballistics, intermediate ballistics and terminal ballistics.

ballistic evidence: Anything obtained from the study of firearm and ammunition technology that has relevance to an investigation and the proving or disproving of facts.

ballistic expert: An expert performing forensic examination of physical evidence such as firearms, ammunition, ammunition components, tool and tool marks submitted to the Forensic Laboratory for identification.

bathymetrical sensor: A sensor such as a sonar to determine the depth of the floor of a water body. The depth is measured from the surface to the floor of the water body. For example, if the swimming pool is 1,2 m deep, the depth is calculated from the surface of the water in the pool down to the floor of the pool.

beyond reasonable doubt: The standard of proof required in a criminal trial where the state must prove its case against the accused beyond any reasonable doubt.

binary state: The manner in which digital information exists, which is a number system consisting of ones and zeros. It is a base 2 number system. To illustrate this, the number 2 in the decimal system is 10 in the binary system; 3 in decimal is 11 in binary, and number 4 in decimal is 100 in binary.

binocular microscopy: A microscope with two eye pieces similar to binoculars.

biometric identification: Biometrics is the science of using one or more unique physical characteristics or behavioural traits to identify individuals. The best-known biometric identification method is fingerprinting. Other methods are based on facial, iris, voice, handwriting and signature recognition.

'broken-window' principle: Relates to small acts of deviance. For example, littering, graffiti and broken windows will, if ignored, escalate into more serious crime.

buccal swab: An inside cheek sample. *See also* non-intimate buccal samples.

bullet: A projectile propelled by a firearm, a sling or an airgun.

burden of proof: The duty of a party to the legal proceedings to prove the fact or facts in issue in those proceedings.

cadastre: A land parcel as registered at the Deeds Office.

cartridge: A cylindrical, usually metal casing containing an explosive charge and a bullet for rifles or other small arms.

case docket: *See* docket.

case file: The formal management structure and tool used by investigators external to the SAPS to facilitate and conduct inquiries and investigations. *See also* evidence file.

casualty log: A pro forma document used by first-responding personnel at a scene of incident to document the details of people injured and/or removed from the scene. It further allows for the recording of reference numbers, registration numbers of emergency vehicles, details of the medical facility where casualties are taken, personal particulars and contact details of emergency personnel and first responders.

Caucasian: Term used to denote the general physical type of some or all of the populations of Europe, North Africa, the Middle East, Central Asia and South Asia; also Caucasoid, Europid or Europoid.

CCTV footage: The use of closed-circuit television cameras to transmit a signal to a specific place, on a limited set of monitors, although it may employ point-to-point, point-to-multipoint, or mesh wireless links. CCTV is used for surveillance in areas that may need monitoring such as banks, casinos, airports, military installations and convenience stores.

cell: The area covered by a cellphone base station.

centroid: The centre of a polygon. It is a point and location given as coordinates.

chain of custody: The process put in place to maintain the integrity of physical evidence and to record its whereabouts and location during the investigation process; tracking and tracing the flow of exhibits from one point or person to the next point or person.

chromosomes: Organised compacted threadlike structures that carry hereditary information.

civil investigations: An investigation related to a civil matter. A civil matter is a court action (or pending court action) that is not criminal in nature. For example, an investigation related to the care of a child is a civil investigation if the opposing parent is trying to prove that their ex-spouse is not taking good care of the child. A civil investigation is any investigation that is not an investigation of a crime.

civil litigation: The process of resolving a legal dispute or other matter in a civil court of law, through the institution of legal proceedings by one party against another.

civil prosecution: The institution of a formal, non-criminal litigation process in a court of law to address a wrong.

civil remedy: *See* redress.

class characteristics: A feature of an item that is unique to a group of items or information in a non-individual context about some aspect of a crime scene; evidence that belongs to a class and that is not considered unique; intentional or recurring characteristics shared by one or more objects (eg size, pattern and brand) in that group. For example, a shoe print that was left by a male who wore a size 12 shoe, or a hair from a Caucasian female.

clinical pathology: The use of laboratory tests to evaluate changes in the body tissues and organs of a patient.

CODIS: The Combined DNA Index System provided by the FBI for law enforcement in the USA to store, maintain and search DNA profiles from crime scenes, offenders, arrested persons and missing persons.

comparative samples: Samples to which a forensic test is compared.

comparator forensic DNA profile: the forensic DNA profile that is used for comparison.

complainant: The person or organisation that makes a formal complaint that a crime has been committed.

conditional probabilities: The probability that an event will occur, when another event is known to occur or to have occurred.

confirmatory tests: A test performed to confirm the type of body fluid.

congenital characteristics: Characteristics inherited and determined by the genetics of the person.

consistency: The belief that an offender will display similar features in their behaviour across a series of offences.

con-story: A false story or ruse used to fool a victim into trusting the offender. For example, offering a potential rape victim employment so as to lure them to a secluded place where they are raped.

contaminants: Any material that is foreign and which is found at a location or in circumstances at a scene of incident where it should not be, or that is found in amounts greater than to be expected.

control sample ammunition: Ammunition fired by the forensic expert to test the firing mechanism of a disputed firearm. Also used to compare with ammunition found at the scene.

corporate investigator: A person who operates in a private capacity and for the benefit of another party, which may be a company, a private person, etc.

court: A formal body, established by law, for the administration of justice.

court order: An instruction given by a court to another party, which compels them to obey the instruction or find themselves in contempt of court.

crime: Unlawful and blameworthy conduct which is defined by law as a crime and for which punishment is prescribed.

crime intelligence: Information gathered, compiled, analysed, and/or disseminated to prevent and investigate criminal activity.

crime scene prints: Prints developed, identified and lifted from the scene of incident.

crime scene samples: Samples or exhibits found at the scene of incident of which the source, type and/or composition is unknown. Disputed samples are collected from the crime scene for processing and examination and compared to a reference sample in order to identify and individualise the sample.

criminal investigation: An official inquiry to uncover information about a crime that involves logic, objectivity and legal guidelines to identify, locate and prove the guilt of a criminal; an investigation into an act punishable by law in which evidence is gathered in terms of the CPA to solve the crime and prosecute the perpetrator in a court of law. An example would be if the police investigated a complaint of child abuse which resulted in the harm, or potential harm, of the child.

Criminal Investigative Analysis: The term used for the field which includes activities such as offender profiling, geographic profiling, equivocal death analysis and linkage analysis.

criminal prosecution: The prosecution of a perpetrator in a court of law for an unlawful act they have committed.

criminalistics: Another term for forensic science, most often associated with crime scene investigation.

cross-examination: The phase during the testifying process in court where the legal practitioner who is opposing the legal practitioner who has called a person to testify, may question the person.

culpability: Responsibility for a fault or a wrong.

cynoacrylate fuming (superglue) method: A method using chemical vapours to visualise fingerprints on objects. The cynoacrylate is warmed to produce fumes that react with the invisible fingerprint residues and atmospheric moisture to form a white polymer on the fingerprint ridges. The ridges can then be recorded.

data carving: A process of recovering data from digital storage media, which can identify structured data, such as a particular type of graphic file, from unstructured data.

death interval: The time that elapses after death has occurred.

defence witness: A witness who has been called by the defence to testify on its behalf in legal proceedings.

deltas: The point on a fingerprint ridge at or in front of the point where the 'type lines' separate or diverge.

denominator: Bottom part of a fraction.

dental stone: A calcined gypsum derivative similar to plaster of Paris but stronger, used for making dental cases and dies. It is also called artificial stone. It is nowadays the preferred material used for the removal of impression evidence from soil by creating a three-dimensional physical copy of a footprint or tyre impression.

detective: Synonym for 'investigator'.

digital artefact: A file or fragment of a file in a digital format, which is used as digital evidence.

digital evidence: Any evidence that can be obtained in digital form, eg evidence from computer systems, cellular telephones, digital photos or fax machines.

digital information: Any information that is stored or transmitted in a digital format.

diploid genome: Having a pair of each type of chromosome, so that the basic chromosome number is doubled.

disputed cast: An unknown imprint (of a shoe or tyre) that was collected at a scene of incident by means of dental stone. The disputed cast is then compared with a known cast for identification purposes.

disputed documents: The documents being disputed in a court of law; documents whose origin or authenticity is unknown or uncertain.

disputed firearm: A firearm gathered as evidence and allegedly used in the commission of crime and submitted to a forensic laboratory for examination.

disputed samples: *See* crime scene samples.

distance decay curve: The number of crime incidents caused by a criminal reduces drastically the further they move away from the anchor point. This can be expressed as a mathematical function.

DNA reference samples: Reference samples such as blood or buccal samples taken from a subject to compare if he or she has the same or a different forensic profile to the disputed or crime sample.

docket: The formal management structure and tool (file) used by the SAPS to facilitate and conduct the investigation process. It is captured in an officially numbered file and consists of six pages.

dongle: A device that must be plugged into a computer to enable a program linked to it to run. Think of it as being similar to a key for a car.

due diligence: The process of being very thorough in your actions to ensure that you do not miss something of material significance.

electronic dental record systems: Software applications that have been specifically developed to help capture dental observations of patients and victims that could prove useful for comparative dental analysis.

epithelial cells: Skin cells.

equivocal death analysis: A criminal investigative analysis tool that attempts to determine if a death occurred as a result of a murder, suicide or accident.

evidence: The admissible information used by a court of law to reach a decision on any matter brought before the court for adjudication.

evidence file: A file used by investigators in the workplace or corporate environment for the secure filing and organisation of evidential documents relevant to an investigation. The evidence file serves the same purpose as a case docket in police investigations.

evidence impression marks: Class and individual characteristics of physical evidence examined by a ballistic expert during the identification process.

evidence in chief: The evidence provided by a person during the examination-in-chief phase of testifying in court.

evidential material: The matter or material that may be lawfully placed before the tribunal in order to prove the facts in issue. It may include admissible oral statements, documents in writing, material objects or exhibits such as a gun, a knife, fingerprints, footprints, admissions by parties, legitimate inferences from facts and circumstances and also presumptions of law. In short, any matter legitimately usable, which tends to establish the truth or falsity of a fact in issue.

evidential value: Exhibits which may contribute to making a forensic finding.

examination: A detailed inspection or investigation.

exclusion probability: An estimate of the proportion of the population that has a genotype composed of at least one allele not observed in the mixed profile.

exhibit: Evidence in physical form brought before the court.

exhibit control room: In the corporate environment the exhibit control room serves the same purpose as the SAPS 13 storage facility used by the SAPS.

exhibit log: A pro forma document used by members assigned to the collection of evidence at a scene of incident. The exhibit log allows for comprehensive recording of all information relevant to the collection, management and safekeeping of exhibits at a scene of incident. Information recorded on the exhibit log includes the address of the scene of incident; personal particulars of the exhibits official and of any official who handles exhibits; complete case reference and forensic seal, kit and bag numbers; and description of items and where they were found.

expert witness: A person who, by virtue of a specialised skill, knowledge or experience, testifies in court about their area of expertise to help the court interpret specific evidence.

expunge: To remove a forensic DNA profile or fingerprint profile from the database.

extended writing: An attempt to write exactly like someone else does; copying someone's handwriting.

extractor: A small part of a firearm, sometimes resembling a hook, that is used to remove a cartridge or cartridge cases from the chamber of a firearm.

fantasy: The underlying blueprint for many psychologically motivated crimes. A fantasy may develop over many years and eventually the offender acts it out when they commit the crime.

Faraday bag: A container that blocks all radio waves from entering or leaving the container. It is most commonly used to prevent mobile phones from communicating with the cellular network, or with any other wireless network.

fixed points: A permanent or other structure used as a known starting point for measurements depicting the size, distance and relational aspects to reconstruct scenes of incident.

forensic DNA profile: The results obtained from forensic DNA analysis of bodily samples taken from a person or from a crime scene, providing a unique string of alphanumeric characters for identity reference. These results may not contain any information on the health, medical condition, mental characteristics or predisposition or physical information of the person other than the gender.

forensic image: A specific type of data file containing an exact duplicate of all the data from a data source, which is mathematically identical to the original. It can also contain metadata in relation to the imaging process.

forensic investigation: The practice of lawfully establishing evidence and facts that are to be presented in a court of law or at another form of hearing or tribunal.

forensic odontology: The application of dentistry for legal purposes to identify the source of bite marks or to identify a dead person.

forensic pathology: A medical examination that concentrates closely on the types and causation of injuries, and the causes of sudden and unnatural death.

forensic photography: Also called forensic imaging or crime scene photography. The art of producing an accurate reproduction of a crime scene or accident scene using photography for the benefit of a court or to help in an investigation.

forensic remote sensing: The use of sensors that are either attached to an aircraft or satellite that returns an image of the Earth's surface. Sensors include cameras; hyperspectral sensors, which include infrared sensors that measure the sun's reflections from the Earth; radar and lidar. The first two are seen as passive sensors that use reflected sunlight, whereas the latter two are active sensors, ie they send a radar signal or laser beam to Earth and receive the reflected signal. The reflected signal is used to create an image of the area of interest. Lidar is an acronym for Light Detection and Ranging.

forensic serology: The study of blood, saliva, semen and other bodily fluids in criminal casework and other legal matters to determine the type and characteristics of blood, test body fluids, examine blood stains and prepare a testimony or presentation for a trial, among other things.

friction ridges: The ridges present on the skin of the fingers, toes, palms and soles of the feet which make contact with the surface under normal touch. In humans and some primates this skin forms ridges and valleys. Friction ridge skin forms classifiable patterns on the end joints of the fingers.

genes: The working subunit of heredity of an organism or person.

genome: Entirety of an organism's hereditary information contained in the DNA.

genotypes: Genetic makeup of an organism or group of organisms with reference to a single trait, set of traits, or an entire complex of traits.

Geographic Information Systems (GIS): A computer-assisted system, combined with appropriate infrastructures, resources and management, that acquires, stores, retrieves, transforms, manipulates and displays geographical and related non-geographical data.

geographic profiling: A criminal investigative analysis tool that attempts to use crime scene locations to predict the home location of the offender as well as future crime scene locations.

geomorphology: The study of the nature and history of landforms created through the process of weathering, erosion and deposition. The forensic geomorphologist is able to detect small changes in the landscape that could indicate the location of shallow graves and disturbances caused by small-scale illegal mining such as panning activities.

grooves: Spiral rifling cut or formed inside the barrel of a firearm.

hacking: The process of gaining unlawful access to a computer system or computer network, often via the internet.

haploid: A cell containing only one set of the chromosomes.

haplotype: A group of alleles that may occur at a given locus of different genes on a single chromosome that are closely enough linked to be inherited, usually as a unit.

Hardy–Weinberg principle: This principle states that the different occurring frequencies with respect to the forms of a gene and the genetic makeup of an organism or group of organisms in a population remain constant from generation to generation unless specific disturbing influences are introduced.

human genome: *See* genome

human geography: Human geography looks at the world created by humans. It studies the cultural or built environment such as cities, the cultural distributions and communities. It studies specifically the geographic distribution of these as well as the interactions between them in space and time.

hunting area: Known area to the serial criminal where suitable victims can be found.

hypostasis: When the normal blood circulation ceases, the cellular portion of the blood gravitates to the lowest-lying parts of the body, causing colour change; commonly called 'death-staining'.

identification: The classification process by which an entity is placed in a predefined, limited or restricted class.

identification parade: The placing of a suspect with a group of other people of similar characteristics (such as build, race, hair colour, type and weight) so that a witness or victim of a crime has the opportunity to identify the perpetrator of the crime.

identification subject: A person who is required to be identified.

identity theft: The criminal act of assuming another's identity for some type of gain, normally financial.

imprint evidence: Marks or indentations caused by pressure when making contact with any surface under normal touching.

***in situ*:** A Latin term meaning 'in the original position'. When an exhibit is documented *in situ* it means that it has not been moved or tampered with.

inadmissible evidence: Any evidence that the court has rejected or that is not presented because it does not meet the requirements of admissibility stipulated by law.

incidence intelligence: Crime intelligence as well as intelligence about other forms of transgressions, for example the transgression of a company's internal policies.

incident: An event or happening. In the context of this book the investigation of crime is meant to include the investigation of a crime, a transgression or an incident. 'Incident' may also include a crime or a transgression.

incident report forms: The form used to capture crime scene particulars and information such as the name of the police station, the name of the complainant, the case number and a full description of exhibits; reports generated on the occurrence of different offences or transgressions in a given period for a given area of responsibility.

indented writing: An imprint that appears on the page or surface underneath the original page that contains the actual writing.

individual characteristics: Unintentional, random and unique features (eg scratches, cuts, tears and abrasions) of the object that distinguish it from other objects with the same class characteristics.

individualisation: To establish the uniqueness of an item through examination and experimentation; to show that no other item is exactly like the one in question.

information: Data or knowledge about a subject.

informer: A person who provides information, usually for remuneration, to the police or other organisations, about the illegal activities of a person or group.

inode: Also called an 'index node'. An inode is a data structure found on various operating systems that use UNIX as a base, which stores information about file system objects.

inquiry: The formal search for information in relation to a specific task.

intelligence: Processed information that may indirectly assist investigations.

intelligence on the crime or incident: The product of information that has been taken from its raw state and processed, refined, verified and evaluated.

internet cache: A storage location used by many internet browsers to store the contents of web pages viewed, to improve viewing of these pages at a later stage if the contents of the source website has not changed.

intimate samples: Pubic hair or a sample taken from the genitals or anal orifice or a sample of blood, but excluding buccal samples.

invariability: Never changing.

investigation: The act or process of investigating a crime or incident to search out and examine the particulars of that event in order to learn the facts about something hidden, unique or complex, and especially to find a motive, cause or culprit for the crime or incident.

Investigative Psychology Section: The section in the SAPS that is responsible for providing Criminal Investigative Analysis services for investigations.

investigator: A person who investigates crimes and who searches for the truth. 'Investigator' can describe a rank or job in the SAPS (detective), and also refer to a statutory or corporate/private investigator or a civilian who is called a private detective.

jointly and severally liable: A situation where all members of a group can be held liable for their own actions and the actions of one or more members of the group.

journey-to-crime: The trip a criminal makes between their residence and the location where they commit a crime. This is expressed in either distance or time travelled.

juristic person: An organisation or entity that has been given certain legal rights in terms of the law.

known impression markings: Marks made by the object suspected of causing the imprint or impression. These marks are compared to marks identified by an expert in the forensic laboratory.

laser granulometers: A laser used to determine the particle sizes of a sample. The result is known as particle size distribution (PSD). The PSD is one of the techniques used to link a sample to a specific location for forensic purposes.

latent fingerprints: Fingerprints left at the crime scene which are not immediately visible to the naked eye.

least-effort principle: A principle that is adopted by criminals to commit crimes closest to their anchor points. For example, if there are several places to burgle (houses with flatscreen TVs) at various distances from the criminal's residence, the nearest place will most likely be chosen.

legal practitioner: An attorney or advocate admitted to practise as such in a court of law.

liability: The amount owed by a party, or the legal duty or obligation of a party in court proceedings.

lifter report form: *See* incident report form.

ligatures: Any type of material in the form or a rope or string and may include electric flex, nylon, clothing, bed sheets, chains, dog leads, washing lines, luggage straps or various other objects used to tie, bind, restrain, strangle or hang victims.

linkage analysis: A criminal investigative analysis tool that attempts to determine which cases can be linked to one offender by analysing the crime scene behaviour of the offender.

Locard exchange principle: According to Edmond Locard, when two objects come into contact, materials are transferred from one object to the other; the basis for proving contact by the analysis of microscopic evidence.

location data: Data about a specific location. Attribute data is used to describe the entity at the specified location and coordinates are used to place the entity on a map. Coordinates are generally obtained using a GPS.

locus: The position of a gene on a chromosome.

loops: A fingerprint pattern with ridges entering on one side of the print, forming a wave, and flowing out on the same side.

magnetic media: Storage media used to store digital information on a magnetic medium such as a hard drive platter or a magnetic tape.

malleable: When it is said that a person's *modus operandi* is 'malleable' it means that it can be influenced or changed.

malware: Malicious software, which includes computer viruses.

mandate: A commission or contract by which one person authorises, instructs or delegates another person to act on their behalf.

mandibular teeth: Lower teeth, in the lower jaw (mandible).

markers: The genetic locations or systems used in the DNA test chemistry.

mathematical one-way hashing: A process whereby data is processed by a hashing algorithm (commonly MD5 or SHA1) to produce a unique fixed-length hexadecimal number, which is essentially a 'digital fingerprint' for that data.

matrix: A table or chart used to highlight similarities in a series of crimes.

maxillary teeth: Upper teeth, in the upper jaw (maxilla).

Mendelian: Mendelian inheritance (or Mendelian genetics or Mendelism) is a scientific description of how hereditary characteristics are passed from parent organisms to their offspring.

metadata: Data about data. Metadata describes certain characteristics of other data. The date and time that a computer file was last modified is an example of metadata.

microdotting: A microparticle with a diameter smaller than 1,8 mm, which bears a unique optically readable microdot identifier of which the content and structure complies with Microdot Standard SANS 534-1. It is legible with equipment that magnifies the text 60 times.

minutiae: In biometrics and forensic science, minutiae are major features of a fingerprint. These features can be used to compare one print to another.

mitochondrial DNA: The double-stranded DNA found exclusively in mitochondria (which is outside the nucleus of the cell). This is inherited from the mother.

***modus operandi* (MO):** The manner in which a crime has been committed; an offender's pattern of operation (method of preparing for and committing crime). When collected, stored and classified, MO information can help to identify and apprehend a perpetrator. It can also be useful in developing strategies for deterring crime.

Mongoloid: Constituting or characteristic of a race of humankind native to Asia and classified according to physical features.

mutation: A relatively permanent change in hereditary material involving either a physical change in chromosome relations or a biochemical change in the makeup of genes.

muti murder: The practice of targeting another human being for the purpose of removing body parts to use as ingredients in a traditional potion. Victims usually die as a result of the attack. Typically breasts or genitals are removed for these purposes.

natural geography: Also known as physical geography, it looks at the natural environment such as the atmosphere, hydrosphere (water), biosphere (plants and animals) and geosphere (the Earth). The latter includes geomorphology that looks at the Earth's surface and the processes involved such as erosion that formed the Earth's surface.

natural person: A physical living human being.

Negroid: A term used to refer to individuals and populations that share certain morphological and skeletal traits that are generally associated with Black African ancestry.

ninhydrin reagents: A chemical used to detect latent fingerprints. It reacts with the amino acids in the fingerprint, giving a visible deposit.

non-coding DNA: The areas of the DNA that do not encode proteins and do not contain information on a person's predisposition to medical conditions.

non-intimate buccal samples: A reference sample taken from the inside cheek of the mouth of a person.

non-random mating: Selective breeding.

NTFS partition: NTFS stands for 'new technology file system'. An NTFS partition is a method used to structure the storage area of digital media commonly used by various Microsoft operating systems, such as Windows 7 and Windows 8.

nucleotides: In DNA they are the four chemical structures, namely guanine (G), adenine (A), thymine (T) and cytosine (C).

numerator: Top part of a fraction.

obligate paternal allele: Whatever allele the mother does not have is the obligate paternal allele. In other words, the obligate paternal alleles in the child all have corresponding alleles in the alleged father.

offender profiling: A criminal investigative analysis tool that attempts to describe the characteristics of the offender who committed the crime under review.

optical media: Storage media used to store digital information that uses lasers to read the stored data of the media; it includes CDs, DVDs and Blu-ray.

organised crime: All crimes as defined in terms of the Prevention of Organised Crime Act 121 of 1998.

origin identification: The analysis of organic and inorganic solids and fluids to determine whether the disputed sample and the example have a common origin.

palynology: The study of dust, spores, pollen and other fine particulates.

paraphilias: An umbrella term for abnormal sexual disorders as classified by the Diagnostic and Statistical Manual of the American Psychiatric Association. This includes such paraphilias as paedophilia, exhibitionism (flashing) and voyeurism (Peeping Tom).

pathologist: A physician who specialises in the diagnosis of disease by examining cells, body fluids and tissues.

peak profile: The part of the profile with the highest probability of finding the anchor point of a serial criminal. This is used to narrow down the search area to find the serial criminal.

pedigree relationships: Depicting relationships in a diagram of family relationships using symbols to represent people and lines to represent genetic relationships.

perjury: The criminal offence of lying under oath or affirmation.

perpetrator: The person or organisation that commits a crime.

person of interest: A person who may be linked to a crime scene, but is not at that point in time considered to be the suspect.

petrographic microscopy: A field of microscopy that uses a specialised microscope that polarises light to identify minerals and rocks. Light waves are in two planes at a 90-degree angle from one another and the polariser eliminates one of these planes.

phenotypes: Physical characteristics such as the colour of the eyes.

phishing: A form of fraud, facilitated by means of email and the internet, whereby the victim receives an email which appears to be from a legitimate source, requesting the victim to act in a certain way, such as updating their banking details, and directing them to a website that looks legitimate, where they either are targeted by malware or their usernames and passwords are stolen.

physical evidence: Evidence of a tangible nature that may be of importance during an investigation or a subsequent judicial proceeding; any object that can help to clarify an event under investigation.

plaintiff: The party that brings a legal action against another party in civil litigation.

police: The term 'police' is used as a noun to indicate an official organisation whose job is to make sure that people obey the law, to catch criminals, and to protect people and their property.

policing: Policing is a direct result of the fact that society is not able to police itself and requires an external mechanism for social control.

polygraph: A machine that charts how respiration and other bodily functions change when the person being tested is asked specific questions.

polymorphism: When two or more phenotypes (clearly different observable characteristics or traits such as the colour of eyes) exist in the same population of a species.

post-coital: After sexual intercourse.

post-mortem: The internal and external examination of a body after death has occurred.

prescription: The period within which a plaintiff must institute civil action against a defendant once they become aware of the potential claim against the defendant.

presiding officer: A magistrate or a judge who presides over court proceedings, hears and evaluates all admissible and relevant evidence brought before them, and gives judgment in the case at hand.

presumptive testing: A test performed to indicate the possible type of body fluid, for example if it is semen, blood or saliva.

primer residue: Particles that remain after firing a firearm, mainly composed of burnt and unburnt particles from the explosive primer, the propellant, as well as components from the bullet, the cartridge case and the firearm used. These particles are deposited onto any nearby surface such as the hands and clothes of the shooter, the clothes of a bystander, etc.

private investigator: A person who, in a private capacity and for the benefit of a third party, investigates the identity, actions, character, background or property of another person, without the consent of that person.

probative value: Something of probative value is something that can prove or disprove a matter in court.

prosecution: The process of instituting criminal proceedings against a person or organisation in a criminal court for the alleged violation of a criminal, common or statutory law.

psychological autopsy: A criminal investigative analysis tool that attempts to understand why a person behaved in a particular manner at a certain point in time.

psychologically motivated crimes: Crimes that have an inner, psychological motive, as opposed to non-psychologically motivated crimes which are often inspired by a profit or gain motive. Examples include crimes such as serial murder, child molestation and rape.

putrefaction: The decomposition process of organic matter, especially protein and body organs, by the action of micro-organisms, which results in a bad smell.

pyrotechnician: A chemical analysis expert dealing with fires and their causes.

quantum: The amount of money awarded for damages in civil court trials.

quasi-judicial procedures: A hearing that does not take place in a court of law. During the hearing formal proceedings are used to hear evidence from both parties involved and for a person to reach a finding based on this evidence.

rapid-fire questions: Questions asked in rapid succession without allowing time to answer properly between questions.

reagent: A substance or mixture added to a system in order to bring about a chemical reaction.

recidivism: A person's relapse into criminal behaviour.

redress: Any method available in law for the enforcement, protection or recovery of rights.

reference samples: Physical evidence whose origin is known, such as blood or hair from a suspect, that can be compared to crime scene evidence. Also called control samples, controls, known samples or knowns, reference samples are used to make a comparison with the disputed or crime sample in order to make a forensic finding. They are samples of a similar matrix or that contain similar characteristics, features or chemicals to the disputed or crime sample. Reference samples may also be used to assure that analyses have been properly performed and that results are reliable and accurate. Reference samples are obtained from the victim, family members, any paramedics/police officers who may have been at the crime scene, suspects and other known sources. Examples include known combustible substances used for arson cases, known drug samples for suspected illegal drug samples, known blood types in violent crime investigations, known DNA types for trace evidence cases and handwriting samples.

relevance: A legal term relating to admissibility. Evidence must be related to the facts which a court is considering. For evidence to be relevant, it must be possible to use the evidence to prove or disprove something that a court must decide upon.

repository: A receptacle in which something else is stored.

reproducibility: To produce a copy or representation of.

respondent: The party in civil litigation against whom a case has been instituted.

restorative justice: An approach to justice that focuses on repairing the harm caused by crime while holding offenders responsible for their actions, by providing an opportunity for the parties directly affected by the crime – victims(s), offender(s) and community – to identify and address their needs in the aftermath of the crime, and seek a resolution that affords healing, reparation and reintegration, and prevents further harm.

rigor mortis: The process of body muscles and joints stiffening after death.

SAPS: The South African Police Service as constitutionally mandated in terms of s 205 of the Constitution as the only national police service responsible for upholding and enforcing the law.

SAPS 13 storage facilities: The SAPS 13 storage facility usually comprises a walk-in safe for the safekeeping of exhibits and a variety of evidential material at police stations, units and laboratories. A register (SAPS 13) is used to record each exhibit in the storage facility. An SAPS 13 register number is allocated to each exhibit, which is clearly described in the register with complete details of the member who registered the exhibit and the circumstances and place where it was found or seized.

scanning electron microscopy: A microscope that creates an image of the object by scanning the object with a focused beam of electrons.

scene of incident: This includes a crime scene and the scene where the incident (which does not necessarily constitute a criminal act) took place. It may include any location, visible or implicit, which may contain information and/or physical or non-physical, direct or indirect evidence that suggests, directly or indirectly, that a crime, civil delict or corporate irregularity was committed.

scientific method: A fundamental aspect of science whereby a hypothesis is developed based on observations, and then tested through experimentation or other structured and impartial methods to confirm or refute the hypothesis.

sentencing report: A report compiled for the purpose of assisting the presiding officer (magistrate or judge) in deciding an appropriate sentence for a person who has been convicted. Various types of professionals, such as psychologists, criminologists or social workers, can compile such reports.

serial murder: A psychologically motivated crime when an offender commits a second, separate murder and the motive is an inner psychological desire to murder.

sexual harassment: Unwanted conduct of a sexual nature, which is unwelcome, unsolicited and unreciprocated. Sexual attention becomes sexual harassment if the behaviour is persisted in, although a single incident of harassment can constitute sexual harassment; and/or the recipient has made it clear that the behaviour is considered offensive; and/or the perpetrator should have known that the behaviour is regarded as unacceptable.

sexual murder: A murder that has a sexual theme to it. This theme can be evidenced by any of the following: rape of the victim, nakedness of the victim, pornography at the crime scene, mutilation of the sexual organs and a sexual positioning of the victim even if clothed.

shoulders (in fingerprints): Points at which the recurving ridge definitely turns inwards or curves.

signature: The offender's 'calling card'; crime scene behaviour that would allow an investigator to know that a crime is that of a specific offender.

silver nitrate: A chemical used to detect latent fingerprints on paper. Silver nitrate is sprayed onto the fingerprint where it reacts with the chlorides, to give the insoluble silver salt, silver chloride.

single-source DNA: A forensic DNA profile originating from only one person.

SMS message: SMS stands for 'short message service'; a text message that can be sent between cellphones.

solid-state media: Storage media made up of solid-state memory chips that are used to store the data.

spatial aggregation: Grouping together of geographical locations.

speaker recognition: *See* voice biometrics.

spectrophotometry: Measures the number of waves reflected back from an object. The waves range from near-ultraviolet to near-infrared wavelengths. The visible spectrum lies between these wavelengths.

SPOT: A French satellite that remotely senses the Earth's surface. Several versions of the satellite have been built. The first was launched in 1986 and the newest to be launched soon is SPOT 7.

statute of limitations: The maximum amount of time from when a crime has been committed within which the state may institute criminal prosecution against the perpetrator.

statutory investigator: An investigator who has been formally appointed in terms of a specific law or statute to investigate specific matters spelled out in that law or statute.

submental area: Area under the chin.

substance: A particular kind of matter with uniform properties, such as an intoxicating, stimulating or narcotic chemical or drug, especially an illegal one.

suspect: A person or organisation that is suspected of having committed a crime.

tactical intelligence: An intelligence product that supports investigations and operational policing activities to achieve law enforcement objectives.

tamper-evident seal: Used in a large variety of products to secure the product by preventing unwanted access. Tamper-evident seals on forensic bags and containers used for the collection of exhibits usually consist of an adhesive strip. If the seal was tampered with, it becomes immediately evident. Also called tamper-evident mechanisms.

target backcloth: The spatial distribution of suitable victims for the serial criminal. If a serial rapist prefers school girls between the ages of 13 and 16, then the various high schools in an area form the target backcloth.

tattooing: Marks on the bullet wound or clothing of the victim, a muzzle impression on the skin or powder fragments in the entrance area or around the wound.

ten-print searching algorithm: The code definition to perform a comparative search on ten defined attributes.

tomography: The cross-section image of an object using a penetrating wave such as an X-ray.

tonal and spatial recognition: The most accurate representation of trace evidence through high-resolution capturing to provide a true reflection of trace evidence characteristics and accurate colour reproduction.

touch-DNA: DNA in skin cells left behind by touching an object with the hands or lips.

transgression: An infringement or violation of a law, command or duty. In the context of this book the investigation of crime is meant to include 'the investigation of a crime, a transgression or an incident' and when we refer to an incident it may also include a crime or a transgression.

tribunals: Courts of justice.

ulna: The bone in the forearm that runs on the little finger side of the wrist.

USB thumb drive: USB stands for 'universal serial bus'. A USB thumb drive is a small digital storage device, usually about the size of one's thumb (or smaller), that uses a USB connection to connect to an electronic device.

variability: The belief that there are sufficient differences between the behaviour of different offenders to distinguish them from one another with reference to their criminal activities.

victimology: The type of victim that an offender targets. In a series there are often similarities between the victims targeted by the offender.

voice biometrics: Specialised technology based on the fact that each individual's voice is unique and different and verifies the identity of the speaker based on numerous vocal tract characteristics as well as style of speech.

voice prints: A method of speaker identification in which the pitch, rate of speech and articulation are evaluated, as well as certain anatomical factors not under the speaker's conscious control; also known as sound spectrographs.

wads: In a shotgun cartridge a plastic or felt plug which separates the propellant from the shot. The wad prevents the gas from blowing through the shot.

white-collar crime: Financially motivated and non-violent crimes committed for illegal monetary gain.

whorls: Ridge patterns that form concentric circles in the centre of the finger pad. Whorls contain patterns with two or more deltas and a recurve precedes each delta.

wireless router: A network device which allows computers and other electronic devices to connect to it and, by extension, to other devices connected to it and to the internet, via radio signals and not physical cables.

witness identification: Relates to the linking of the perpetrator to the crime by means of accounts of events from the statements of witnesses and complainants.

witness log: A pro forma document used by members at a scene of incident to record the details of witnesses and possible sources of information. Information recorded on the witness log includes complete case reference numbers, personal particulars and the contact details of witnesses.

X-ray diffraction: Used to determine the mineral composition of rock or sand samples. Each mineral has its own unique characteristics when X-rayed and the resultant X-ray diffraction 'picture' is used to identify the minerals.

ANNEXURE 1: EXAMPLE OF A SECTION 212 STATEMENT (DRUGS)

LAB NO 1234/12
SOPHIATOWN CAS 3241/01/2012

AFFIRMATION IN TERMS OF SECTION 212 OF THE CRIMINAL PROCEDURE ACT 51 OF 1977:

ALBERT ACKERMAN affirms, in accordance with s 212 sub-s (4)*(a)* of the Criminal Procedure Act 51 of 1977 as follows:

1.

I am a warrant officer in the South African Police Service, with service number 0434123-1, attached to the Chemistry Section of the Forensic Science Laboratory as a forensic analyst, and am in the service of the State.

2.

I have a National Diploma in Analytical Chemistry from Tshwane University of Technology. I have 15 years' practical experience in chemical analysis.

3.

I, during the performance of my official duties, on 2012-01-28 received one sealed evidence bag, with unique number AB 200056439T, from the Drug Analysis Sub-section Administration. The seal was intact. The bag was opened by me. The evidence bag was marked inter alia '**Sophiatown SAP 13/5697/2012 CAS 3241/01/2012**' and contained the following:

3.1 four plastic sachets containing traces of powder.
3.2 two glass pipes containing residue.
3.3 glass pieces containing residue.

4.

I was requested to examine the exhibit material in order to determine whether it contains any substances as listed in the Schedule of the Medicines and Related Substances Control Act 101 of 1965 and/or the Drugs and Drug Trafficking Act 140 of 1992.

5.

I, during the performance of my official duties, analysed the exhibit material with a process requiring skill in chemistry by making use of the technique of gas chromatography coupled to mass spectrometry (GC-MS). GC-MS is an internationally accepted comparative analytical technique where compounds are characteristically separated in the gas phase and characteristic patterns (mass spectra) of the separated compounds are obtained. The identity of unknown compounds was thus established by comparing their separation characteristics (retention time) and characteristic patterns (mass spectra) with those of known reference material collected on the same instrument under the same conditions. Prior to use, the gas chromatograph (GC) was evaluated and the mass spectrometer (MS) was internally calibrated. The GC and MS were deemed suitable for use.

1/2

LAB NO 1234/12
SOPHIATOWN CAS 3241/01/2012

6.

6.1 I analysed the exhibit material as mentioned in paragraph 3.1 by comparison with reference material using the abovementioned technique and determined that it contains methcathinone. Methcathinone is listed in Part III of Schedule 2 of the Drugs and Drug Trafficking Act 140 of 1992.

6.2 I analysed the exhibit material as mentioned in paras 3.2 and 3.3 using the abovementioned technique but did not detect any substance as listed in the Schedules of the Medicines and Related Substances Control Act 101 of 1965 and/or the Drug and Drug Trafficking Act 140 of 1992.

7.

I, during the performance of my official duties, kept the exhibit material exclusively under my safekeeping for purposes of analysis thereof, by placing it behind lock and key from 2012-1-28 to 2012-02-24, after which it was placed and sealed in an evidence bag with the unique number JA72002198563T.

8.

I know and understand the contents of this declaration.

I confirm that the contents of this affirmation are true.

0434123-1

....

WARRANT OFFICER A ACKERMAN

I certify that the deponent has acknowledged that he knows and understands the contents of this declaration which was confirmed before me, and the deponent's signature was placed thereon in my presence at PRETORIA on 2012-02-24 at 09:25.

012345657

....

CAPTAIN MB MPANZA
COMMISSIONER OF OATHS
Forensic Science Laboratory
270 Pretoria Road
Silverton
CAPTAIN: SOUTH AFRICAN POLICE SERVICE

2/2

ANNEXURE 2: EXAMPLE OF A SECTION 212 STATEMENT (BALLISTICS)

LAB 710918
SOPHIATOWN CAS 2134/01/2012

AFFIDAVIT

GIDEON MAFFA declares under oath and in terms of section 212(4)*(a)* and 212(8)*(a)* of Act 51 of 1977 as amended by section 6 of Act 34 of 1998 that:—

1.

I am a lieutenant colonel in the South African Police with Persal number 0920798-6, and in service of the state. I am attached to the Ballistics Unit of the Forensic Science Laboratory, Silverton, Pretoria.

2.

I have been attached to the Ballistics Unit since 1994 as an examiner of Forensic Ballistic cases. I have to date examined the amount of 2 300 cases.

2.1 **I have inter alia received in-service training in the following aspects of Forensic Ballistics Science:**

- 2.1.1 Identification of ammunition, fired bullets and fired cartridge cases.
- 2.1.2 The use of microscopic equipment.
- 2.1.3 Microscopic individualisation of ammunition.
- 2.1.4 Microscopic individualisation of fired bullets and fired cartridge cases.
- 2.1.5 Microscopic individualisation of firearms.
- 2.1.6 Identification of firearms.
- 2.1.7 The examination of firearm mechanics.
- 2.1.8 The examination of homemade devices.
- 2.1.9 Restoration of obliterated marks on metals.

2.2 **I obtained the following tertiary qualifications:**

- 2.2.1 National Technical certificates 2, 3, 4 (PE Technical College)
- 2.2.2 T1 Mechanical (PE Technicon)
- 2.2.3 Qualified diesel mechanic with full apprenticeship at PE Municipality
- 2.2.4 Advanced Programme in Forensic Criminology (UNISA) majoring in Ballistics

2.3 **I have visited the following firearm/ammunition factories:**

- 2.3.1 Somchem
- 2.3.2 Swartklip Products
- 2.3.3 Vector

3.

On 2012-01-15 during the performance of my official duties I received a sealed plastic bag, marked inter alia 'SOPHIATOWN CAS 2134/01/2012', sealed with seal number FSC-720302, from Case Administration of the Forensic Science Laboratory, containing the following exhibits:

3.1 One (1) x (7,62 x 25 mm) calibre Norinco, model 54 semi-automatic pistol, number filed off, and marked by me 710918/12.
One (1) x magazine.

3.2 Three (3) x (7,62 x 25 mm) cartridge cases marked by me 710918/12 A, B and C.

1/2

LAB 710918
SOPHIATOWN CAS 2134/01/2012

4.

4.1. I examined the firearm mentioned in 3.1 and found it to be:

4.1.1 a semi-automatic firearm due to it being self-loading, capable of discharging three shots with a single depression of the trigger.

4.1.2 The device was designed to discharge centre-fire ammunition.

4.2 I examined the firearm mentioned in 3.1, tested it, and found it to be in working order. I fired cartridges marked 123T1-T3 respectively for test purposes.

5.

I compared the tests mentioned in paragraph 4.3 with the fired jackets and cartridge cases (A, B and C) mentioned in paragraph 3.2 using a comparison microscope and found:

5.1 It can be stated that the cartridge cases mentioned in paragraph 3.2 were fired from the firearm mentioned in paragraph 3.1.

6.

6.1 After applying the electro-magnetic process I determined that the serial number of the firearm mentioned in 3.1 is 20030728.

7.

The abovementioned conclusions were arrived at by means that require a knowledge and skill in certain branches of physics and ballistics.

8.

During the performance of my official duties the exhibits mentioned were, for the purpose of their examination, kept in my custody under lock and key, from 2012-01-15 until 2012-01-17.

I KNOW AND UNDERSTAND THE CONTENT OF THIS DECLARATION.

I HAVE NO OBJECTION TO TAKING THE PRESCRIBED OATH.

I CONSIDER THE PRESCRIBED OATH TO BE BINDING ON MY CONSCIENCE.

________________________ 00207086

G MAFFA LIEUTENANT COLONEL

I certify that the deponent has acknowledged that he knows and understands the contents of this declaration which was sworn to before me and the deponent's signature was placed thereon, in my presence at Silverton on 2012-01-18 at 10:15.

____

COMMISSIONER OF OATHS
HENNIE LOCHNER
FORENSIC BALLISTICS UNIT
SILVERLAKE STREET
SILVERTON
COLONEL: SA POLICE SERVICE

2/2

ANNEXURE 3: EXAMPLE OF THE STRUCTURE OF A STATEMENT

PREAMBLE

Identification of deponent

David Mario van der Watt, 36 years of age, identity number 6107295997089, residing at 27 Thabo Street, Florida and employed as an electrician, at Nolight Industries, 78 Dykor Street, Pretoria, with telephone number (w) 012 123 4567, (h) 011 098 7654. My cellphone number is 0732281551.

I declare under oath in English:

BODY

1

When — Where — Property What — Crime

On Monday, 30 April 2011 at approximately 13:00, I left the electrical workshop at Nolight and went for lunch. I left my Acer laptop with serial number 0722381441 on my desk. I did lock my office.

2

When — Crime element — Crime How

At approximately 13:10 on the same day, I arrived back at the electrical workshop and immediately found that the door was not locked. I also found that my Acer laptop was no longer on my desk. I searched the entire workshop but could not find any trace of the laptop. When I returned to my office I noticed that one of the laptop's power cables that normally leads to the laptop was still plugged into the wall. It appeared as if it had been ripped out of the laptop, because the opposite end of the cable was damaged and three multicoloured wires were hanging from the plastic casing.

3

Who

I do not suspect any person of the theft. However, from the time and attendance records it is clear that only Mr Moses Naido had been in the electrical workshop between 10:00 and 13:00 on the day in question.

____

Signature of deponent

1/2

Paragraph number

4

The replacement value of the laptop and all its components amounts to R12 987.00. On the back of the laptop my initials were engraved (DMvdW) as well as my employee number 3456789. I am not insured against theft. I would be able to identify my laptop should it be found, because of my name and employee number being engraved on the back of the laptop.

CONCLUSION

5

At 13:35 I reported the incident to the security officer on duty, Rudolph Berning. I requested him to investigate the matter and to prosecute the offender, if possible. I gave nobody permission to enter my office and to take my laptop.

Crime element

ADMINISTERING OF THE OATH/AFFIRMATION

6

I know and understand the contents of this declaration.

I have no objection to taking the prescribed oath.

Oath

I consider the prescribed oath to be binding on my conscience.

____

Signature of complainant

I certify that the statement was taken down by me and that the deponent has no objection to taking the prescribed oath and that he acknowledged that he knows and understands the content of this statement. This statement was sworn before me and the deponent's signature was placed thereon in my presence in Pretoria on 30 April 2011 at 16:45.

Certificate

____

Signature of person taking the statement

Commissioner of Oaths: Full names and surname

Address: 20 Towers Street, Pretoria West

Rank:

____

Signature of deponent

2/2

ANNEXURE 4: EXAMPLE OF A DETAILED STATEMENT WITH ANNEXURES

XXX, declares under oath in English:

1

I am an adult female, identity number 731203 0072 088, currently employed at the Xxxx Municipality, xxx, telephone number xxx and fax number xxx as Senior Committee Clerk.

2

I was approached by the Special Investigating Unit on behalf of the Provincial Government of the Western Cape, to give an affidavit concerning irregularities that are taking place at the Xxxx Municipality.

3

I am responsible for the following:

The full secretariat functions of the Council consisting of:

a) Logistic arrangements, compiling agendas, writing minutes and voice-recording of full Council meetings, management meetings (not voice recorded), meetings of Portfolio Committee Corporate Services and Finances as well as meetings of ad hoc committees.
b) Proofreading and final processing of agendas and minutes compiled by my assistant, Ms xxx, for Portfolio Committee Technical Services, Portfolio Committee Community Services and Executive Mayoral Committee.
c) Liaising with councillors.
d) Travel arrangements for councillors.
e) Accommodation arrangements for councillors.
f) Press releases as instructed by the Municipal Manager.
g) Arrangements for and recording of Strategic Planning Sessions by Council.
h) Compiling Annual Reports with information received from the Municipal Manager and departmental heads.

I received training in:

a) The Local Government: Municipal Finance Management Act 56 of 2003
b) Various courses in Local Government systems and legislation.

The process regarding different committees can be described as follows (see Annexure CT 1: Rules of order for Council meetings held by the Xxxx Municipality):

1) Portfolio Committees do not have any delegated powers; they review departmental reports and make recommendations to the Executive Mayoral Committee. These meetings are scheduled once a month, on the second Tuesday of the month.
2) The Executive Mayor makes resolutions in accordance with his delegated powers (see Annexure CT 2: Schedule of Delegations as approved on 27 October 2004 at the General Council meeting of the Xxxx Municipality) or alternatively makes recommendations to Council. These meetings are scheduled once a month.
3) At General Council meetings, reports and minutes of Executive Mayoral Committee meetings are tabled:
   i. Resolutions for information (little or no discussion allowed)
   ii. Recommendations for resolution

1/9

These meetings are scheduled to take place once every three months.

It often occurs that the Executive Mayor makes decisions regarding urgent issues. As no formal meeting took place in this regard, the secretariat either receives an instruction to compile 'minutes' after the meeting has taken place, although no member of the secretariat was present; or the Executive Mayor reports on these matters verbally, during the Council meeting. There is a standing agenda item for this purpose.

4

The following information came to my attention in my capacity as Senior Committee Clerk. On 26 April 2005 the Xxxx Municipality's full Council was informed by the Executive Mayor that the committee will be going overseas (see Annexure CT 3: Minutes of Council meeting dated 26 April 2005). The announcement was made by xxx, the Executive Mayor. The overseas visit was not a point of discussion on the agenda and no formal itinerary or breakdown of expenditure was presented. A previous resolution was passed on 26 November 2003 relating to international relations. The Municipal Manager, Mr xxx, was given instructions to investigate potential local governments in the world with whom international relations could be established (see Annexure CT 4: Resolution – International Relations dated 26 November 2003).

5

On Friday 6 May 2005, I received an instruction from the Municipal Manager, Mr xxx, to assist him with the arrangements for the Executive Mayoral Committee's visit abroad. I finalised all arrangements with regard to the visit abroad as per instructions received.

6

In May 2005 the Municipal Manager, Mr xxx, signed a Standard Credit Card Charge Form in favour of Penciltravel at Tyger Valley (see Annexures CT 5.1 and CT 5.2: Standard Credit Card Charge Forms), that covers the flight ticket of Mrs xxx, the wife of Mr xxx, the Executive Mayor, to the value of R8 950.00 (see Annexures CT 6.1 and 6.2: Flight tickets, as well as Annexure CT 7: Signed flight itinerary by Mr xxx, Municipal Manager) and accommodation to the value of R9 505.00 (see Annexure CT 8: Standard Credit Card Charge Form in favour of Penciltravel for the total accommodation expenses, including the accommodation of Mrs xxx for accommodation as listed in Annexure CT 9: Itinerary, signed by Mr xxx, Municipal Manager).

A Standard Credit Card Charge Form in favour of Simpson Tours to the amount of R11 850, which served as payment for the accommodation of the whole delegation, including Mrs xxx, for the Hotel Lagos Inn in Lyon, France was signed by the Municipal Manager, Mr xxx (see Annexure CT 10: Standard Credit Card Charge Form in favour of Simpson Tours; Annexure CT 11: Signed accommodation itinerary signed by Mr xxx, Director: Corporate Services, and Annexure CT 12: Fax dated 23 May 2005 from Penciltravel referring to a confirmation voucher from Simpson Tours, that accommodation for Mrs xxx's stay in Lyon was included in the Credit Card Charge Form referred to in Annexure CT 10: Standard Credit Card Charge Form in favour of Simpson Tours).

The service charges, invoice No. LS/84484, regarding Mrs xxx's expenses was confirmed via an email to myself, dated 26 May 2005, by xxx of Penciltravel (see Annexure CT 13: Email from Penciltravel to xxx dated 26 May 2005). Mr xxx paid Mrs xxx's visa application (see Annexure CT 14: Visa payment) personally but claimed the expense back. The only reason why the Municipal Manager, Mr xxx, paid with his personal cash for the visa applications was the fact that he had forgotten the Council's credit card at the office and that the French Consulate only accepts cash or postal orders. He paid for Council expenses out of his own pocket and requested me to provide him with the receipts in order to claim the expenses back from the Council.

2/9

7

On 19 May 2005 a delegation of the Xxxx Municipality, comprising the following people, left for overseas to promote foreign relations (see Annexure CT 3: Minutes of Council meeting dated 26 April 2005):
Councillor xxx (Executive Mayor) and Mrs xxxx (spouse)
Councillor xxx (Executive Deputy Mayor)
Councillor xxx (Speaker)
Councillor xxx (Chairperson of Portfolio Committee: Finance)
Councillor xxx (Chairperson of Portfolio Committee: Community Services)
Councillor xxx (Chairperson of Portfolio Committee: Technical Services)
(The above persons serve on the Executive Mayoral Committee.)
Mr xxx (Municipal Manager)
Mr xxx (Director: Finance)

8

On the xxx 2005 an article appeared in the xxx newspaper (see Annexure CT 15: Article xxx dated xxx 2005). On 26 May 2005, Mr xxx of the DA indicated that the Mayor had paid for his wife's expenses. In a follow-up article in the xxx newspaper dated xxx 2005 (see Annexure CT 16: Article in the xxx newspaper dated xxx 2005) 'xxxx', it was stated that the Executive Mayor, Mr xxx, had paid the total costs relating to the expenses of his wife, Mrs xxx, for the trip abroad. The Assistant Director: Finance, Mr xxx, indicated on 23 May 2005, that there had been a budget for the trip abroad. He indicated that the amount of R364 800.00 had been budgeted in vote 11002036 (see Annexure CT 17: Extract from 2004/2005 budget). This budget vote represents the total subsistence and travelling costs for the full Council for the entire financial year. On a question from myself as to why I was instructed to pay all expenses relating to the trip from vote 11002299 (Council Expenses: Sundries), the Assistant Director: Finance, Mr xxx, indicated that all expenses would be reconciled to the proper budget vote once the Director: Finance, Mr xxx, returned and all expenses were known.

9

At the time this affidavit was drafted, the total expenditure with regard to the trip abroad was not known, as expenses for travelling/transport between destinations (excluding air transport), meals and other expenses were settled abroad. A summary of costs incurred is attached (see Annexure CT 18 and CT 19: Summary of cost). It is not at this stage known to what extent Mrs xxx, the Mayor's wife, benefited from payments made abroad. The Assistant Director: Finance, Mr xxx, verbally indicated on 3 March 2005, that an amount of R20 000.00 was deposited by Mrs xxx, the Mayor's wife, in favour of the Municipality and in lieu of her expenses. This was verified in the form of a deposit slip, receipt number 182000 dated 27 May 2005 (see Annexure CT 20: Receipt from Xxxx Municipality). I was also subsequently advised that a further R6 000.00 was deposited on 1 June 2005 on behalf of Mrs xxx. As of the date of this affidavit, I was unable to verify this.

10

At a special Council meeting dated 26 April 2005, the draft budget for the financial year 2005–2006 was tabled by the Executive Mayor, Mr xxx. Reference was made to a meeting held on 4 February 2005, when the draft budget was presented to the full council in adherence to s 16(2) of the Local Government: Municipal Finance Management Act 56 of 2003 (see Annexure CT 21.1 & CT 21.2: Minutes of a Special meeting of the Xxxx Municipality dated 26 April 2005, as well as the Annexure to the Minutes of the Special Council meeting dated 26 April 2005, page 4, last paragraph of the Executive Mayor's Budget Speech). A contravention of the Local Government: Municipal Finance Management Act 56 of 2003 took place as the criteria of s 16(2) of the Local Government: Municipal Finance Management Act 56 of 2003 were not

3/9

adhered to. It is my respectful submission that no such meeting took place on 4 February 2005, as reported by the Executive Mayor, Mr xxx, as no record (formal notification, agenda, minutes or attendance register) of such meeting of the full Council exists. The minutes of the meeting held on 4 February 2005, if a such meeting took place, should have been tabled at the Council meeting held on 26 April 2005, but it was not on the agenda. The meeting of 4 February 2005 was only mentioned in the Mayor's Budget Speech. As previously stated, I am responsible to take the minutes at all Council meetings. Neither myself nor Ms xxx, my assistant, was present at a meeting on 4 February 2005 nor did we give notice of such a meeting.

11

While I was in the process of compiling the agenda for the Council meeting scheduled to take place on 26 April 2005, the Municipal Manager, Mr xxx, requested the minutes of the meeting held on 4 February 2005. I told him that there were no minutes and he wanted to know why not. I told him I was not aware that a Council meeting had taken place on 4 February 2005 and had not sent out such notices. He informed me that a meeting did take place and blamed the Director: Corporate Services, Mr xxx, and the Director: Finance, Mr xxx, for the fact that no record of the meeting existed.

12

Council meetings are scheduled to take place once in three months (quarterly). If a meeting was scheduled/planned, notice of a Special Council meeting should have been given – which to my knowledge was not done. The date of 4 February 2005 was not approved as part of the scheduled General Council meetings for the year 2005 – thus confirming that a Special Council meeting should have been called.

13

The 2005–2006 budget should not have been approved by the Council as misleading information regarding compliance to s 16(2) of the Local Government: Municipal Management Finance Act 56 of 2003 was given during the meeting by the Executive Mayor, Mr xxx, and no proof was provided confirming adherence to s 17(3)*(a)* to *(m)* of the Local Government: Municipal Finance Management Act 56 of 2003.

14

It is therefore not possible to prove that the requirements as set out in s 16(2) of the Local Government: Municipal Finance Management Act 56 of 2003 have been met. The draft budget was however presented to the Executive Mayoral Committee and the Portfolio Committee: Finance. There is also no proof that s 17(3)*(a)* to *(m)* of the Local Government: Municipal Finance Management Act 56 of 2003 has been adhered to.

15

A further irregularity that has occurred is that performance bonuses have been paid and backdated in the absence of a performance agreement to the following persons:
Mr xxx (Municipal Manager): three years' bonuses retrospectively
Mr xxx (Director: Finance): two years' bonuses retrospectively
Mr xxx (Director: Community Services): one year's bonus retrospectively
Mr xxx (Director: Corporate Services): one year's bonus retrospectively

16

It is a requirement of s 57 of the Local Government: Municipal Systems Act 32 of 2000 that performance agreements must be concluded with all Section 57 appointments. The performance agreement sets the targets and time frames for such procedures to evaluate performance and the intervals for evaluating such performances. The objectives and performances must be practical and measurable and based on key performance indicators as set out in the municipality's integrated performance plan.

4/9

The performance agreement must be signed within a reasonable time after appointment and within one month after the beginning of each financial year.

17

The former Executive Mayor was responsible for drawing up a performance agreement with Mr xxx, the Municipal Manager. As Municipal Manager, Mr xxx should have drawn up performance agreements with the other managers.

No such agreements were concluded with any of the people receiving performance bonuses. The result was that no performance indicators existed, and no assessment of performance was therefore possible. The bonuses should correlate with the performance measured.

18

The bonuses were further authorised by a Mayoral Committee that was not in power during the financial year during which the bonuses were granted. It is general accepted accounting practice that after a financial year has lapsed no payment can be made out of that particular year's budget.

19

The absence of performance agreements were clearly noted during several meetings. The minutes of the General meeting of the Xxxx Municipality held on 29 October 2004 (see Annexure CT 22.1: Minutes of the General meeting of the Xxxx Municipality held on 29 October 2004 – Item /04/10/27/6.4.18), refers to minutes of the Mayoral Committee meeting held on 15 October 2004, where the report of the Portfolio Committee: Corporate Services was tabled before the Executive Mayor, Mr xxx. The minutes of the Portfolio Committee: Corporate Services meeting held on 14 September 2004 clearly state that for the previous financial years no performance indicators were accepted and that there were no measurements to determine whether or not the Council and officials had met their targets.

The decision taken on 27 October 2004 by the Xxxx Municipality General meeting indicates that no performance measurement system or key performance indicators existed for the current and previous financial years. The agenda for the Mayoral Committee meeting scheduled for 30 March 2005 (see Annexure CT 23: Agenda for the Mayoral Committee meeting scheduled for 30 March 2005) refers to the xxx Report as well as comments on the xxx Report given to the Mayoral Committee on 9 November 2004 (see Annexure CT 24: Letter dated 7 November 2004) and on 5 March 2005 (see Annexure CT 25: Letter dated 5 March 2005).

The xxx Report dated 4 November 2004 (see Annexure CT 26: xxx Report) for the year ending 30 June 2004, was accompanied by a letter dated 9 November 2004, forwarded by Mr xxx to the Executive Mayor, Mr xxx (see Annexure CT 24: Letter dated 9 November 2004).

The report clearly states that performance measuring is the responsibility of the accounting officer and also indicates that a performance management system was not in place at the time the auditing took place.

20

In accordance with s 46(1)*(a)* of the Local Government: Municipal Systems Act 32 of 2000, a municipality is compelled to include a performance report in its annual report for the period being audited 1 July 2003 to 30 June 2004. No performance report existed and no annual report was tabled.

During a Council meeting on 27 October 2004 it was resolved that the IDP manager should compile a process plan for the handling of Key Performance Indicators to present to the Mayor (see Annexure CT 22.1: Minutes of the General meeting of the Xxxx Municipality held

5/9

on 27 October 2004 – Item /04/10/27/6.4.18). A further resolution was passed regarding draft Key Performance Indicators for the xxxx Region as well as a plan of action regarding final approval of Key Performance Indicators (see Annexure CT 22.2: Minutes of the General meeting of the Xxxx Municipality held on 27 October 2004 – Item /04/10/27/6.4.38 – Action plan and Resolution).

The letter to the Executive Mayor from Mr xxx, dated 8 March 2005, refers to the Auditor General's report and indicates the following (see Annexure CT 25: Letter dated 8 March 2005):

1. A process was in place to finalise the performance and that it would be implemented from July 2005.
2. Performance indicators, although developed, must still be accepted.
3. Performance targets, based on the new Key Performance Indicators (KPIs), could not be finalised before the budget was finalised.

The performance management system with Key Performance Indicators was only approved on 26 April 2005 and implemented on a trial basis.

21

The In-Committee General meeting minutes dated 27 October 2004 (see Annexure CT 27: In-Committee General meeting minutes dated 27 October 2004), refers to the minutes of an In-Committee meeting of the Executive Mayoral Committee held on 18 October 2004. The subject was the payment of performance bonuses. It is noted that no performance contracts for the Municipal Manager, Mr xxx, and other Section 57 appointments exist, and that no performance indicators were agreed to. The opinion of SALGA Western Cape, previously WEGLOGO, was that the Municipal Manager, Mr xxx, must give guidance regarding the performances of Section 57 appointments.

Upon a report tabled at the said meeting, it was agreed that the performance bonuses should be approved in principle.

The minutes of the Mayoral Committee meeting held on 14 November 2004 (see Annexure CT 28: Minutes of the Mayoral Committee meeting held on 14 November 2004) indicates that the performance bonuses of 15% were approved in the absence of performance indicators on the grounds of good services rendered.

There were no criteria in the minutes for performance bonuses. The fact that reports of departmental heads existed on which grounds the bonuses were paid out, was first mentioned in the Portfolio Committee: Finance meeting held on 8 March 2005 (see Annexure CT 29: Minutes of the Portfolio Committee: Finance meeting held on 8 March 2005). No mention of these reports was made at the meeting that took place on 15 November 2005.

22

During the said Executive Mayoral Committee meeting, held on 15 November 2005, the whole Mayoral Committee as well as the following officials was present:

- Mr xxx (Municipal Manager)
- Mr xxx (Director: Finance)
- Mr xxx (Director: Community Services, Social and Economic Development)
- Mr xxx (Divisional Head: Roads)
- Mr xxx (Assistant Director: Water Provisioning)

No member of the secretariat was present. The minutes were compiled after the meeting by the Committee clerk. Ms xxx was merely given an instruction to draft the minutes of the said meeting that had taken place on 15 November 2004. No detailed discussion was dictated to be minuted as background to the resolutions with regard to the performance bonuses.

6/9

23

During the discussion and resolution of minute items BM 04/11/15/1.1.2–1.4.1 (see Annexure CT 28: Minutes of the Mayoral Committee meeting held on 14 November 2004) all of the above officials remained present and did not excuse themselves while their performance bonuses were discussed. The minutes of the Executive Mayoral Committee meeting dated 14 November 2004 was approved during an Executive Mayoral Committee meeting held on 26 November 2004 (see Annexure CT 30: Minutes of the Executive Mayoral Committee meeting held on 26 November 2004), without any amendments, thus confirming the presence of the said officials during the approval of the performance bonuses. The minutes of the Executive Mayoral Committee meeting dated 14 November 2004, was noted by Council on 26 January 2005.

24

The Executive Mayor, Mr xxx, has the power to award performance bonuses. Thus the correct procedure was followed with regard to the approval of the minutes of 14 November 2004 at the Executive Mayoral meeting of 26 November 2004. All Executive Mayoral decisions should however be reported to Council, thus both minutes of 14 and 26 November were tabled at the General Council meeting on 26 January 2005 (see Annexure CT 31: Minutes of the General Council meeting on 26 January 2005) for information.

The exact amounts to be paid out as performance bonuses were never confirmed in any official council document or minutes (as required by normal procedures). The Director of Finance, Mr xxx, to my knowledge ordered the Senior Accountant – Salaries, Mrs xxx, to pay certain amounts to himself, Mr xxx, Mr xxx and Mr xxx. The only reference to specific amounts was brought to my attention while compiling an agenda item for the Portfolio Committee: Corporate Services, that was supposed to be tabled at a meeting, scheduled for 12 October 2004. This agenda item was however retracted before the agenda was finalised (see Annexure CT 32: Retracted agenda item of the Portfolio Committee: Corporate Services meeting held on 12 October 2004).

25

The minutes of the meeting of the Portfolio Committee: Finance held on 8 March 2005 (see Annexure CT 29: Minutes of the Portfolio Committee: Finance meeting held on 8 March 2005) indicates that the following issues were raised:

Councillor xxx wanted to know whether the financial report for the year ending 31 January 2005 reflected the performance bonuses or if they were incorporated in the December 2004 report. He also wanted to know which criteria had been used to determine the amounts paid. The Director: Finance, Mr xxx, confirmed that a resolution in this regard was made during an In-Committee meeting of the Executive Mayoral Committee.

The Municipal Manager, Mr xxx, mentioned that the performance bonuses were paid out in accordance with the criteria according to Key Performance Indicators as set out in the National Regulations and that they were based on reports by the departmental heads to the Executive Mayoral Committee.

Councillor xxx stated that the Council must have a performance management system with performance indicators according to which performance is measured and bonuses are paid. He mentioned that bonuses must correlate with performance measurements. Councillor xxx wanted to know from the Municipal Manager, Mr xxx, if the officials had adhered to the requirements.

The Chairman, Dr xxx, confirmed that payments were made based on the reports of the departmental heads. Councillor xxx indicated that the report was measured by the Mayoral Committee, based on their capabilities and insight in the department heads' work field.

7/9

The Chairperson, Dr xxx, ruled that the matter was closed for discussion and did not answer questions whether the departmental heads had been measured according to their performance contracts and Key Performance Indicators. His question as to which extent the Integrated Development Plan was used was also not answered.

26

I thought about these matters over a period of time, and given the inconsistencies that I have mentioned herein, and given my duty to reveal maladministration, I approached my colleague, Mr xxx, in his capacity as the Legal Official of the Council. Mr xxx suggested to me that we compile a report and record the alleged maladministration. The annexures to the said report are contained in the annexures to this affidavit (see Annexure CT 33: Report – xxx).

27

I know and understand the contents of this affidavit.

I do not have any objection to take the prescribed oath.

I consider the oath to be binding on my conscience.

....

SENIOR COMMITTEE CLERK

I certify that the deponent has acknowledged that she knows and understands the contents of this affidavit, which was signed and sworn to before me at Cape Town on this .... day of .... 20XX at ....

....

COMMISSIONER OF OATHS

FULL NAME: xxx

ADDRESS: SIU

xxx

xxx

CAPACITY: FORENSIC INVESTIGATOR

8/9

ANNEXURES
CT 1: Rules of order for Council meetings held by the Xxxx Municipality
CT 2: Schedule of Delegations as approved on 27 October 2004 at the General Council meeting of the Xxxx Municipality
CT 3: Minutes of Council meeting dated 26 April 2005
CT 4: Resolution: International Relations dated 26 November 2003
CT 5.1 and CT 5.2: Standard Credit Card Charge Forms
CT 6.1 and 6.2: Flight tickets
CT 7: Signed flight itinerary by Mr xxx, Municipal Manager
CT 8: Standard Credit Card Charge Form in favour of Penciltravel for the total accommodation expenses
CT 9: Itinerary, signed by Mr xxx, Municipal Manager
CT 10: Standard Credit Card Charge Form in favour of Simpson Tours
CT 11: Signed accommodation itinerary
CT 12: Fax dated 23 May 2005 from Penciltravel refering to a confirmation voucher from Simpson Tours
CT 13: Email from Penciltravel to xxx dated 26 May 2005
CT 14: Visa payment
CT 15: Article in the xxx newspaper dated 22 May 2005
CT 16: Article in the xxx newspaper dated 29 May 2005
CT 17: Extract from 2004/2005 budget
CT 18 and CT 19: Summary of cost
CT 20: Receipt from Xxxx Municipality
CT 21.1: Minutes of a Special meeting of the Xxxx Municipality dated 26 April 2005
CT 21.2: Annexure to the Minutes of the Special Council meeting dated 26 April 2005, page 4 last paragraph of Executive Mayor's Budget Speech
CT 22.1: Minutes of the General meeting of the Xxxx Municipality held on 27 October 2004 – Item /04/10/27/6.4.18
CT22.2: Minutes of the General meeting of the Xxxx Municipality held on 27 October 2004, Item/04/10/27/6.4.38 – Action plan and Resolution
CT 23: Agenda for the Mayoral Committee meeting scheduled for 30 March 2005
CT 24: Letter dated 9 November 2004
CT 25: Letter dated 8 March 2005
CT 26: Auditor General Report
CT 27: In-Committee General meeting minutes dated 27 of October 2004
CT 28: Minutes of the Mayoral Committee meeting held on the 15 of November 2004
CT 29: Minutes of the Portfolio Committee: Finance meeting held on 8 March 2005
CT 30: Minutes of the Executive Mayoral Committee meeting held on 24 November 2004
CT 31: Minutes of the General Council meeting on 26 January 2005
CT 32: Retracted agenda item of the Portfolio Committee: Corporate Services meeting held on 12 October 2004
CT 33: Report – xxx

9/9

INDEX

D

E

Q

R

W

X

Y

Z

Annette Giani: p 125 (top right); Anita Kleinsmidt: p 125; Austin Richards: p 312; CSIR: pp 314, 315, 316, 317, 318 (top), 323, 324, 325, 326, 327, 329, 331, 336, 345, 346, 347, 348, 352, 353, 354; Geology Today: 313, 318, 319, 320, 328, 337, 338, 339, 340, 342, 343, 344, 349, 350, 355, 356; Lochner & Zinn Crime Scene Investigation: p 88; iStock.com/EmiliaU: p 401; iStock.com/RichLegg: p 58; iStock.com/Sproetniek: p 130; iStock.com/Suljo: p 104; iStock.com: pp 128 (far right), 377 (middle left); Joe Giacalone: p 153; Lara Monday: pp 57, 375, 376, 377; Louwra Marais: pp 11, 21, 22, 25, 37, 44, 59 (right), 62, 63, 68, 76, 96, 110, 112, 122, 135, 136, 137, 139, 140, 145, 149, 151, 152, 160, 191, 192, 193, 210, 211, 250, 276, 306, 308, 333, 334, 335, 362, 369, 383, 384, 389, 391, 398; Marlene Rose: pp 226, 229; Marwaan Manuel: p 59 (left); Sarooben Chetty: pp 198 (bottom left and right), 376 (bottom); Phillip Bekker: pp 166, 185, 198 (top right), 419; Tasneem Davids: p53; Tiro Ramatlhatse: p 177; William McGear: p 198 (top and bottom); Yobe Mvula: p 125 (top left); Yogi Naidoo: p 61

www.ingramcontent.com/pod-product-compliance
Lightning Source LLC
LaVergne TN
LVHW070828220926
848486LV00029B/151
9780702186479